UNCERTAINTY in ECONOMICS

This is a volume in
ECONOMIC THEORY, ECONOMETRICS,
AND MATHEMATICAL ECONOMICS

A Series of Monographs and Textbooks

Consulting Editor: KARL SHELL, *Cornell University*

A list of recent titles in this series appears at the end of this volume.

UNCERTAINTY in ECONOMICS

Readings and Exercises

Revised Edition

Edited by

PETER DIAMOND

Department of Economics
Massachusetts Institute of Technology
Cambridge, Massachusetts

MICHAEL ROTHSCHILD

Department of Economics
University of California, San Diego
La Jolla, California

ACADEMIC PRESS, INC.
(Harcourt Brace Jovanovich, Publishers)
San Diego New York Berkeley Boston
London Sydney Tokyo Toronto

Academic Press, Inc.
San Diego, California 92101

United Kingdom Edition published by
Academic Press Limited
24–28 Oval Road, London NW1 7DX

Library of Congress Cataloging-in-Publication Data

Uncertainty in economics : readings and exercises / edited by Peter Diamond, Michael Rothschild. -- Rev. ed.
p. cm. -- (Economic theory, econometrics, and mathematical economics)
Includes index.
ISBN 0-12-214851-7 (alk. paper)
1. Uncertainty. 2. Risk. I. Diamond, Peter A. II. Rothschild, Michael, Date. III. Series.
HB615.U55 1989
330--dc20 89-14847
CIP

Printed in the United States of America
89 90 91 92 9 8 7 6 5 4 3 2 1

To Our Parents

Contents

Preface

For a number of years we have been teaching courses on the economics of uncertainty. Since no textbook presented the material we wanted to cover, we relied on published and unpublished articles for the reading material. These articles make up the selections of this book. We think this book can serve several purposes. For students in places without courses in uncertainty, it provides a guide to what at least two economists think most interesting in the literature. Being in the habit of commenting on, as well as presenting, the materials we lecture on, it was natural to include some commentary. Feeling that mastery of theory comes as much from doing theory as from reading it, we have included a fair number of problems. These come from several sources and vary greatly in difficulty. In some papers we have eliminated the examples and replaced them with problems. Some comments we might have made seemed better made by problems. Some problems were designed to try to develop simple computational skills. Others require some development of techniques of proof. A few move into the area of design of models in which to prove results. These are the hardest, and may well be too difficult to include in a volume that comes without answers. Some of the problems have been found very difficult by our students; none of them seems worth spending a lifetime on, or even more than a weekend.

We have not attempted complete coverage of the economics of uncertainty. The readings are based on what we like to teach and what we feel is necessary to cover to reach what we like to teach. We are most fascinated by the ways in which markets function (and malfunction) when market participants have incomplete information. To understand this, one must study how uncertainty affects both individual behavior and standard equilibrium theory. We have no doubt left out many areas of real significance, many items other people like to teach, and quite possibly some things we would like to teach.

We must express our debt to our students who have made the development of this material worthwhile for us. In addition we would like to thank the many people with whom we have discussed uncertainty over the years. We are particularly indebted to Dennis Carlton, Oliver Hart, Steven Shavell, and Charles Wilson for reading, commenting on, and correcting a draft of this manuscript, and to Barbara Feldstein for flawless typing and retyping.

Neither of us teaches uncertainty courses at present. We have not attempted a thorough revision of this book but have limited ourselves to updating references, changing a few discussions and one article, and adding material on search theory, a relatively new topic at the time of the first edition.

I. Individual Choice in a Static Setting

The papers in this first section examine individual choice under uncertainty where the individual is making a single decision. The first three papers discuss the relevance of expected utility maximization for positive and normative theories of individual choice. (We have not included anything on stochastic, as opposed to determinate, choice.) We then turn to the comparative statics of behavior of individuals who are expected utility maximizers. This is the most commonly used assumption in economic analyses, and so one should understand it without losing sight of the criticisms that have been made of it or of the availability of alternatives. Most of the selections in Parts II and III model individual behavior as expected utility maximization.

1

J. S. Tamerin and H. L. P. Resnik, Risk taking by individual option – Case study – Cigarette smoking, *in* "Perspectives on Benefit Risk Decision Making," pp. 73–84. Washington, D.C.: National Academy of Engineering, 1972

In this paper, two psychiatrists discuss the possibility that some of the people, some of the time, are not trying to make rational decisions, whatever they may be. This very real possibility is relevant both for considering how to do welfare analysis for individuals behaving in this mode and for examining markets where suppliers are dealing with several types of demanders. A recurring question in normative analysis is how much respect is to be given consumer sovereignty? The answer invariably involves balancing the desire to help individuals to make better choices against the danger of forcing them to do what they do not really want to do and the unpleasantness of using force per se. An issue in positive analysis is how markets with imperfect information work when some of the consumers live by the rules set down by theorists and others do not. Does one group ruin the market for the other, or improve it for the other, or are there niches for suppliers who will choose to specialize in one group or the other? The analysis of markets with imperfect information is the subject of Parts II and III.

John S. Tamerin and Harvey L. P. Resnik

Risk Taking by Individual Option—Case Study:
Cigarette Smoking

How does an individual decide to expose himself to risk? Since risk is defined as a chance of injury, damage, or loss,[1] an individual in taking a risk must, presumably, have some notion of benefit or gain. The benefits are obvious in some types of risk taking. These vary from the potential monetary rewards associated with entreprenurial activity in business, to the satisfactions of professional recognition[2] and societal improvement for the innovative scientist.

Risk taking of this kind may be constructive, creative, and healthy. It frequently yields positive results for the individual and society.[3] Constructive risk taking, in addition to the obvious benefits, can be distinguished from other kinds of risk taking by certain characteristic features:

1. Conscious deliberation. In healthy risk taking, the individual takes a calculated risk. He carefully weighs benefits against costs, and makes a deliberate choice.[4,5,6]

2. Adequate preparation. Healthy risk taking is not impulsive or haphazard. Individuals carefully plan and train for such activities (whether they are in industry or in space).[7,8]

3. Positive rather than negative aims. Healthy risk taking arises out of a desire to grow, to achieve, to test oneself, to master and control the environment.[9] It does not originate from the need to diminish or deny basic feelings of worthlessness or inadequacy. It does not come from an ingrained wish for self-destruction. Such acts are, characteristically, undertaken to heighten awareness or for self-actualization,[10] and not to reduce tension or psychic pain. In fact, self-discipline, self-confidence, security, and high self-esteem may be necessary for healthy, constructive risk taking.[11,12] The individual must trust his abilities and his environment. He must feel secure in his capacity to cope.[13] Such risk takers choose oc-

cupations where boldness and independence are necessary factors in success. In fact, in creative and competitive occupations, those who achieve prominence are likely to be greater risk takers than are their less productive peers.[14]

4. Personal responsibility for outcome. In healthy risk taking the individual takes chances in which he can, to a considerable extent, have the responsibility for the outcome. He avoids risks in which outcome is left entirely to chance or is otherwise completely beyond his control, because such activities give him no sense of personal achievement.[15]

In contrast to constructive risk taking, there are other areas of human behavior where the benefits seem less apparent and the risks more obvious. In these situations, the actions are characteristically taken with little deliberation, incomplete planning (or no planning at all), for negative reasons, and without responsibility for outcome. This kind of risk taking is generally associated with individual psychopathology and may thus come to the attention of the psychotherapist. Such acts are usually impulsive or compulsive. They have a driven quality and the inner pressure is often described as irresistible. The act may vary from compulsive gambling to kleptomania, from drug abuse to skyjacking, from wrist slashing to automobile recklessness. In all instances, an absence of rational decision making is apparent. The individuals involved typically respond in a patterned, repetitive, and maladaptive manner. Furthermore, they are unable to stop this repetitive behavior of their own accord, nor can they be distracted by substitute gratifications or dissuaded by rewards or punishments. The capacity to adapt behavior to reality considerations has been lost. These people are not free to act by individual option. Whether symptomatically an alcoholic or a compulsive gambler, these individuals appear to be driven by inflexible, irrational forces beyond their conscious control.

It is characteristic of this type of neurotic risk taking that the reality risk far outweighs the reality benefits. In fact, although the risks are clear and apparent, the reality benefits are uncertain or questionable. This is evident in such acts as kleptomania, particularly when practiced by the affluent. In these instances, the gain is clearly more symbolic than real. When kleptomaniacs are studied psychologically, it becomes evident that the real aim of their behavior is something quite different from obtaining the stolen object for its monetary value. Fenichel[16] illustrated this point in describing the case of a middle-aged woman driven to petty thievery. During the psychiatric evaluation of this patient, the real benefit of her stealing became obvious. Although invariably frigid during sexual intercourse, she consistently experienced sexual excitement at the moment of theft. The gain in stealing was, therefore, more sexual (i.e., a symbolic representation of doing the forbidden) than monetary.

Neurotic risk taking is motivated primarily by negative aims rather than by the achievement of any positive goals. Such acts are carried out to rid the individual of tension and to diminish subjective feelings of distress. The kinds of behavior used to decrease feelings of discomfort vary widely—compulsive gambling, kleptomania, narcotic abuse, alcohol abuse, and many others. Often, the individual who takes neurotic risks will choose several of these patterns almost indiscriminately, to relieve feelings of psychic pain. It is well known that a drug user frequently abuses a variety of addicting and habituating substances. A considerable number of heroin addicts began as alcoholics.[17] Conversely, the heroin addict who is thought to be stabilized on methadone will often turn to abuse of alcohol or other drugs. Sometimes the individual hopes to remove negative feelings by a single act. Hence, he may impulsively, in a single dramatic act such as a highly lethal suicide attempt, or skyjacking, or even a political assassination, attempt to rapidly and magically solve chronic feelings of despair, hopelessness, and low self-esteem.

Finally, in neurotic risk taking the outcome is invariably left to chance. The successful solution rests not on personal competence or mastery, but on magic or powerful forces external to the individual. Nowhere is this more clearly demonstrated than in the compulsive gambler. Gamblers characteristically believe in the magical significance of numbers and make important monetary decisions based on hunches about them. Psychoanalytic studies[18, 19] have revealed that gambling represents an attempt to conquer and compel fate in a magical way to protect and reward the individual. Quite literally the gambler is constantly looking to be smiled on and taken care of by Lady Luck. The gamble with death is a well-recognized aspect of repetitive suicidal behaviors.[20]

How prevalent is neurotic risk taking? We know that most of the conditions described as manifestations of neurotic risk taking are encountered in a relatively small segment of the population. Even alcoholism, clearly the most prevalent of the risk-taking behaviors cited, is estimated to be present in only about 7 percent of the adult drinking population, or 4 percent of the total adult population.[21]

A less obvious form of individual risk taking, but one which must now be considered in that category, is cigarette smoking. In 1970, 36 percent of the adult population in the United States (or 44.5 million adults) smoked cigarettes.[22] This grim figure raises the question of whether neurotic risk taking is primarily the province of a relatively small group of extremely disturbed individuals, or whether it may be the national pasttime.

To consider this question, the first issue is whether or not continued cigarette smoking, in the year 1971, represents a neurotic risk-taking behavior. As we have indicated, a neurotic act is characterized by its maladaptive qualities, its repetitiveness, and by an inflexibility in the face of reality considerations. Stated in terms of a rational decision-making process, the risk in a neurotic act far exceeds the reality benefits. Is this true of cigarette smoking? What are the risks? What are the benefits?

Among the major risks of cigarette smoking in terms of disability, morbidity, and mortality, are the following:

1. *As a cause of excess disability.* Whether measured by working days lost, days spent in bed, or days of restricted activity due to illness or injury, the rates are higher for smokers. Each year, 77 million working days are lost, 88 million days are spent ill in bed, and 306 million days are spent in restricted activity as a result of smoking.[23] Heavy smokers between the ages of 40 and 69 are hospitalized 50 percent more frequently than nonsmokers.[24]

2. *As a cause of excess morbidity.* In all countries for which reliable statistics are available, there has been a striking increase in lung cancer in recent decades—paralleling the rapid rise in cigarette smoking.[23] More than 30 retrospective studies in 10 countries have shown that the risk of lung cancer is 15 to 30 times greater for smokers than for nonsmokers.[23]

Though the risk of disease attributable to smoking is most dramatically seen in lung cancer, this is but one of many risked by the smoker. Heart disease, bronchitis, emphysema, peptic ulcer, sinusitis and other chronic illnesses are found much more frequently among smokers than nonsmokers.

3. *As a cause of excess mortality.* Repeatedly, studies have shown that the greatest risk the smoker takes is that of shortening his life span. The life expectancy of a man 25 years of age is reduced by 4.6 years if he smokes less than half a pack a day; by 5.5 years if he smokes half a pack to 1 pack a day; by 6.2 years if he smokes 1 to 2 packs; and by 8.3 years if he smokes 2 or more packs a day. Since 8.3 years is equivalent to 4.4 million minutes, this amounts to a loss of almost 6 minutes for each cigarette smoked. In effect, a minute of life is forfeited for each minute of smoking.[24]

Another way of looking at this risk is in terms of percentages. The chances of a man of 25 dying before he becomes 65 (i.e., during his peak years of family and professional responsibilities) are 50 percent greater if he smokes less than half a pack of cigarettes a day than if he is a nonsmoker; 70 percent greater if he smokes half a pack to 1 pack a day; 77 percent greater if he smokes 1 to 2 packs a day; and 109 percent greater (more than twice as great) if he smokes 2 or more packs a day.[24] The decrease in life expectancy of the 2-pack-a-day smoker is almost equal to the increase in life expectancy that medical science has made possible over the past 50 years. In effect, the cigarette smoker is sacrificing all of the health gains that have been made in the last half-century. In 1965, it was estimated by the Surgeon General that 240,000 men would die prematurely from cigarette-associated diseases. By 1967, the estimate was up to more than 300,000. Translated into daily averages, these figures mean an estimate of about 800 premature deaths a day attributable to cigarette smoking.[24]

The very personal risk of cigarette smoking is clear. Why, then, do people continue to smoke cigarettes? What are the personal benefits of smoking? These may be roughly divided into pharmacological and psychological benefits.

PHARMACOLOGICAL BENEFITS

The nicotine in cigarettes has been considered by many investigators to be the most important element in smoking. In fact, Lewin commented in 1931, "The decisive factor in the effect of tobacco is nicotine and it matters little whether it passes directly into the organism or whether it is smoked."[25] This was further highlighted by Johnston's research.[26] He gave nicotine hypodermically to 35 volunteers, comparing its effects, and particularly its psychic effects, to those of tobacco smoking. It was found that all of the volunteers who were smokers reported a pleasant sensation and, when given an adequate dose of nicotine, were disinclined to smoke for some time thereafter.

Nicotine acts on the central nervous system, exerting an interesting biphasic effect that is unique among the pleasure poisons. This was observed over two centuries ago by the pipe-smoking country people who remarked:

> Tobacco reek, tobacco reek,
> It makes me hale when I am sick.
> Tobacco reek, tobacco reek,
> When I am hale, it makes me sick.[25]

More recently, this important biphasic action has been concisely described by Johns[25]: "We use tobacco because when the nervous system is stimulated, nicotine sedates; and when it is depressed, nicotine stimulates." Although the biphasic response can be observed in the individual smoker, it has been found clinically that in a total population of smokers, some are predominantly stimulated whereas others are predominantly relaxed by smoking. Factor analytic studies[27] have distinguished the individual who smokes to enhance pleasure and stimulation from the smoker who smokes to reduce tension, or for purposes of sedation. In the latter group, the tranquilizing effect is so pronounced that a number of investigators[25] have suggested considering tobacco as a tranquilizing drug. Such a concept has received further experimental support from studies of the localized effect of nicotine on specific areas of the brain. These studies have revealed that nicotine accumulates in the hippocampus, one of the major components of the limbic system, which is that portion of the brain known to play a central role in the experiencing of emotion. After large doses of nicotine, the electroencephalographic recordings from the hippocampus show the same changes observed following the administration of certain tranquilizers.[28]

PSYCHOLOGICAL BENEFITS

The psychological benefits of cigarette smoking are multiple and complex. Cigarette smoking is often initiated during adolescence with a feeling of defiance for authority. By this act, the individual fantasizes being at least as strong or as powerful as the adults who have made the rules. The rebellion against authority that is symbolized by smoking, combined with a fantasy of strong individuality and manliness,[29] has been picked up by the advertising industry and linked to various brands of cigarettes. This fantasy of individuality and manliness is personified by the Marlboro man, and the defiance and rebellion have been cast either in strident sexual terms, as with Virginia Slims or Silva Thins, or in a more humorous, light-hearted manner, as with Benson and Hedges 100's. Obviously, the success of these brands reflects the fact that important psychological needs are being addressed by the advertising images–images the individual smoker unconsciously identifies with through the act of smoking.

Another obvious psychological benefit of smoking that has been dealt with extensively in the psychoanalytic literature is oral gratification. As early as 1922, commenting on the role of orality in smoking, Brill said that "As the receptor of nourishment, the mouth zone seems to require almost constant stimulation, especially when the individual is laboring under difficulties."[30]

In the child, oral activity increases in the face of stress or frustration. The adult smoker similarly increases his smoking in response to stress. When the smoker is compelled to give up this gratification, reversion to another form of orality such as nail-biting, compulsive eating, drinking, or gum chewing, is almost invariably noted. The capacity of cigarettes to serve as pacifiers for human tension had, in fact, been recognized long before psychiatry emerged as a separate medical discipline. Jean Nicot, who introduced tobacco into France, reported to his Queen, Catherine de Medici, that smoking led to "a quiet tranquility and great submissiveness of disposition, so that through general use of tobacco, Her Majesty's subjects would become easy to govern."[25]

In addition to reducing tension, cigarettes have the positive capacity of inducing feelings of pleasure and well-being. This is recognized in the well-established customs of cigarette breaks, the cigarette with a cup of coffee at the end of a meal, and the cigarette with a drink in a convivial social setting. This linkage of cigarettes with pleasure has been further intensified by the advertising industry, which has coupled smoking with the moment of relaxation–"The late nights, and skipping lunch, and now the job is done and it's the L & M moment"; or with the return of pleasurable memories from the past (Winston) "That down home taste"; or to a bucolic retreat from urban pressures "Never hot, never dry, always Kool" or "You can't take the country out of Salem"

But nowhere has the pleasure of tobacco been more joyfully expressed than in the jingle:

> Tobacco is a dirty weed. I like it.
> It satisfies no normal need. I like it.
> It makes you thin, it makes you lean.
> It takes the hair right off your bean.
> It's the worst darn stuff I've ever seen.
> I like it.[31]

It might be added that all of the pleasures and tranquilization resulting from smoking cigarettes occur in the absence of the intellectual disorganization or the social disinhibition (i.e., loss of control) that accompanies the use of a majority of abusable drugs, including alcohol. It is not surprising, then, that in a recent psychoanalytic study of smoking, Marcovitz commented:[32]

> If there ever comes a time when cigarette smoking can be really detoxified, I believe there will be very few people who will not smoke. One can readily suppose that were it not for the identification of smoking with dirt, disease, and depravity, it would be a universal indulgence. . . . Smoking can be used in the service of the id, the ego, or the superego, or any of these together. . . . In brief, smoking is one of the lasting pleasures in life.

This represents a summary of the benefit–risk relationship facing the cigarette smoker whenever he lights up. What makes his decision particularly difficult is that he must weigh immediate pharmacological and psychological benefits against long-term statistical risks. However, in many ways such a conflict represents a prototype of the reality principle in which an individual must sacrifice immediate pleasure, either for pleasure at some distant period or to achieve a long-range reality goal. If a neurotic act is one that follows the pleasure principle (i.e., the need for immediate gratification) in an impulsive or compulsive way, while denying or disregarding long-range reality considerations, then cigarette smoking must be considered a neurotic act. Furthermore, cigarette smoking shares all of the four features of neurotic risk-taking behavior:

1. *Absence of conscious deliberation.* Until recently, and even now, in many instances, there has been little weighing by smokers of the benefit–risk relationship of their behavior.

2. *Lack of adequate preparation.* Cigarette smoking has often been characterized by a driven need. If planning has played any part in the process, its primary purpose, as in alcoholism, has been to never run out of the addictive substance so that the individual will never be forced to experience the deprivation he so greatly fears.

3. *Negative rather than positive aims.* People generally smoke in order to feel more comfortable. Furthermore, like drug abuse, smoking may increase during times of psychic stress. In fact, many smokers report smoking only during periods of stress at work. National surveys have revealed that the hard-core smokers

who have been most resistant to change have been the people who smoke essentially to reduce tension, rather than those who smoke to increase pleasure.[33] Furthermore, studies have revealed that those who continue to smoke have a higher level of neuroticism[34] and anxiety[35,36] than those who are able to quit. Specifically, regarding other risk-taking behaviors, it has been shown that there is a higher prevalence of cigarette smoking among drivers who are involved in automobile accidents than among a control group of non-accident drivers.[35]

4. *Abnegation of personal responsibility for outcome.* Consequences are left to chance. It is characteristic of smokers to play the numbers game, almost like gamblers. The gambler expects to be selected as the winner from among many; the smoker anticipates that he will not be among the losers punished by premature death for continued smoking. The smoker prefers taking his statistical chance to accepting the personal responsibility of quitting. "I am going to die of something. Why not lung cancer?"

If cigarette smoking represents a national neurosis or a national form of neurotic risk-taking, what can be done about it?

1. The reality risk must be brought into sharper focus for the individual smoker. Newspapers and magazines extensively publicized the Surgeon General's Report of 1964 that warned of the health consequences of smoking. Since then, other research has been presented that describes scientifically and statistically the risks involved in smoking. However, through broad public education and through the media, the risks must be publicized and dramatized in personally meaningful ways with which the individual smoker can identify. The majority of the smoking public has gradually come to accept the general significance and validity of the Surgeon General's findings. Even in 1966, in a comprehensive survey, Horn[33] found that of 3,000 individuals with histories of cigarette smoking, 91 percent indicated an awareness of the threat that cigarette smoking poses to health. Unfortunately, there has been a much more gradual acceptance of the personal implications of these findings. In effect, what we are witnessing on a massive scale is a conscious intellectual acceptance of the health findings, but an unconscious emotional denial of the personal message. Smokers are accepting the words, but resisting the meaning. The reasons for this denial are similar to those seen in any other form of neurotic risk taking.

By the defense of denial, the individual seeks to perpetuate a long-established form of instinctual gratification. Furthermore, the denial represents an unconscious homeostatic mechanism in which the individual attempts to avoid both the pain of losing a meaninful object and constant companion (the cigarette), and the very specific and well-recognized pain of a withdrawal syndrome, which, in some instances, can last for weeks or months.

However, until the individual smoker personalizes the message, he will not move beyond the impulsiveness and nondeliberation characteristic of neurotic risk taking. He must first believe that the risk can, indeed, happen to him before he will stop, wait, and examine carefully and meaningfully the benefit–risk relationship.

2. Smoking must be seen as a symptom and a maladaptive defense against negative affect. It is essential that we recognize that continued cigarette smoking may be only the symptom of an underlying problem. Like other symptomatic acts, such as drug abuse, suicide attempts, sexual promiscuity, or juvenile delinquency, it represents an unsuccessful attempt to cope with and master painful feelings and may result in an illness more severe and painful than the problem the individual was trying to solve. Since smoking represents an attempt to diminish painful feelings, one approach to reducing the need for smoking on a superficial level has been to provide tangible substitutes. Among those that have been devised are the nicotine substitutes, such as lobeline, either in the form of tablets, commercially marketed as Nikoban or Bantron, or in lozenges and chewing gum, and an ersatz cigarette of plastic with menthol flavor inside instead of tobacco. A more realistic approach lies in helping the individual to face and withstand the pain, anxiety, and feelings of loss that may follow cessation of smoking. The courage to cope with these affects can sometimes be enhanced by the support of sympathetic and empathic groups, patterned on the Alcoholics Anonymous model. Furthermore, nonsmokers in the environment have to be educated to comprehend the tremendous pharmacological and psychological importance of cigarettes to the smoker. The inevitability of certain transient personality disorganization associated with cessation (i.e., restlessness and irritability) must be understood and accepted in order for the family and others to be maximally supportive to the smoker during this difficult phase.

It is essential to promote the message of self-mastery as part of this process. The individual smoker must come to believe that maturity and courage lie in the ability to give up smoking, rather than in the fantasized identification with the rugged individuals portrayed as smokers by the advertising industry.

Ego defenses will always be necessary to protect individuals from their internal drives and from the pressures of reality. However, the difference between psychological health and sickness lies in the choice of defenses and the degree to which they are utilized by the individual. In dealing with the day-to-day pressures of life, millions of individuals have chosen the defense of smoking to cope with and minimize painful feelings throughout the day. Through intensive education, including the use of antismoking messages, the smoker must come to feel that the defense of smoking is a particularly self-destructive one, as is the defense of excessive drinking or narcotics abuse. The smoker must then struggle to develop alternative mechanisms that are less destructive. Just as the ex-alcoholic must learn that he can successfully get through the day without a drink, the ex-smoker must discover that he can exist without a cigarette.

It is of interest that the most effective predictor of whether an individual will or will not relinquish the defensive use of smoking is whether he knows someone whose health has been adversely affected by smoking. Eisinger[37] found that individuals who had such an acquaintance were almost three times as likely to give up smoking. In the same context, a recent study has revealed that among the medical specialties, the most successful in quitting smoking are internists and radiologists, who have repeated contact with the disease consequences of smoking,[38] and those with poor records are psychiatrists who have the least direct contact with the sequellae.[39] The explanation may be that through the process of identification the smoker becomes sufficiently fearful to be willing finally to tolerate the discomfort involved in giving up smoking.

3. The smoker must accept responsibility for his act within his sociofamilial setting. The adult cigarette smoker must be motivated to accept personal responsibility for the consequences of his smoking. The defense of comfortably leaving the outcome in the lap of the gods must be confronted. This approach has, in fact, become one of the most important and effective thrusts of the antismoking campaign (e.g., in films, in TV messages, on posters). These have forced the smoker to take a hard look at the fact that through premature death resulting from an unwillingness to stop smoking he is losing–and abandoning–the family he loves. Furthermore, as part of the parent's responsibility, the exemplar role has been stressed (i.e., the message "Like father, like son"). Many ex-smokers report that this family-oriented approach has finally motivated them to quit.

Neurotic risk-taking behavior is not simple to treat even on a one-to-one basis. When 45 million people opt to take this type of risk, the problem becomes infinitely more complex. This is particularly true when the behavior is well entrenched and amply reinforced by a $9 billion industry that spends over $300 million a year to convey the message to smokers that cigarette smoking means pleasure, relaxation, romance, maturity, sophistication, and sexuality–to mention a few of the fantasized rewards.

However, a massive antismoking campaign has been going on to curb this national neurosis. Within the last four years, 10 million adults have quit. This is an extraordinary experiment in psychosocial engineering because, unlike Prohibition, the thrust is designed to influence the individual's option–his free choice. However, before an individual can opt to "join the unhooked generation" he must be brough to an emotional conviction of the serious risk to himself of continued smoking. He must be willing to tolerate and work through the almost inevitable period of discomfort as he develops new defenses, and he must accept personal responsibility for his behavior. Only then can he meaningfully examine the benefit-risk relationship and make a rational decision.

REFERENCES

1. *Webster's New World Dictionary,* The World Publishing Co., Cleveland, 1966.
2. T. Parsons, *Essays in Sociological Theory: Pure and Applied,* Free Press, Glencoe, III., 1949, pp. 34–49; 50–68.
3. D. C. McClelland, *The Achieving Society,* Van Nostrand, Princeton, N. J. 1961.
4. D. C. McClelland, "The Calculated Risk: An Aspect of Scientific Performance," in *The 1955 University of Utah Research Conference on the Indentification of Creative Scientific Performance.* C. W. Taylor, ed. University of Utah Press, Salt Lake City, 1956, p. 96.
5. D. C. McClelland, "Business Drive and National Achievement," *Harvard Bus. Rev.,* July-August: 99–112, 1962.
6. R. Radloff and R. Helmrich, "Under the Sea," *Psychol. Today,* Sept. 1969.
7. Living Dangerously, *Wall Street Journal,* Mar. 4; 10; 17; 26; Apr. 1; 1971.
8. S. Z. Klausner, *Why Man Takes Chances,* Anchor Books, Garden City, N. Y., 1968.
9. R. W. White, "Motivation Reconsidered: The Concept of Competence," *Psychol. Rev. 66*:297–335, 1959.
10. K. Goldstein, *Human Nature in the Light of Psychopathology,* Harvard University Press, Cambridge, 1940.
11. R. L. Taylor and F. T. Melges, "Games People (including Patients) Play," *Med. Opin. Rev.,* Feb.: 30–39, 1971.
12. A. H. Maslow, *Toward a Psychology of Being,* Van Nostrand, Princeton, N. J., 1962.
13. R. de Charms, *Personal Causation,* Academic Press, New York, 1968.
14. D. W. MacKinnon, *The Creative Person,* University of California Press, Berkeley, 1961.
15. J. W. Atkinson, "Motivational Determinants of Risk-Taking Behavior," *Psychol. Rev. 64*:359–372, 1957.
16. O. Fenichel, *The Psychoanalytic Theory of Neurosis.* W. W. Norton, New York, 1945.
17. A. Toll, "Case Study on the Attitudes of Drug Addicts to Treatment," *Brit. J. Addict. 65*:139–158, 1970.
18. R. R. Greenson, "On Gambling," *American Imago 4*:61–77, 1946.
19. E. Bergler, The Psychology of Gambling, Hill & Wang, New York, 1957.
20. J. M. A. Weiss, "The Gamble with Death in Attempted Suicide," *Psychiatry* 20:17–25, 1957.
21. F. C. Redlich and D. X. Freedman, *The Theory and Practice of Psychiatry,* Basic Books, New York, 1966, p. 753.
22. *New York Times.* April 7, 1971.
23. C. M. Fletcher and D. Horn, "Smoking and Health," WHO *Chron.* 24:345–370, 1970.
24. H. S. Diehl, *Tobacco and Your Health,* McGraw-Hill, New York, 1969.
25. P. S. Larson, H. B. Haag, and H. Silvette, *Tobacco: Experimental and Clinical Studies,* Williams & Wilkins, Baltimore, 1961.
26. L. Johnston, "Tobacco Smoking and Nicotine," *Lancet 243*:742, 1942.
27. F. F. Ikard, D. E. Green, and D. Horn, A Scale to Differentiate between Types of Smoking as Related to the Management of Affect. *Internat. J. Addict. 4*:649–659, 1969.
28. M. Jarvik, "How Smoking Affects the Brain," *The Sciences* 6:1–4, 1966.
29. J. T. Fodor, L. H. Glass, and J. M. Weiner, "Smoking Behavior, Cognitive Skills, and Educational Implications," *J. of School Health 36*:94–98, 1968.
30. A. A. Brill, "Tobacco and the Individual," *Internat. J. Psychoanal. 3*:430–444, 1922.

31. G. L. Hemminger, in *Familiar Quotations,* 11th ed., J. Bartlett, ed., Little , Brown & Co., Boston, 1937, p. 943.
32. E. Marcovitz, "On the Nature of Addiction to Cigarettes." *J. Am. Psychoanal. Assn. 17*: 1074–1096, 1969.
33. D. Horn, and S. Waingrow, "Smoking Behavior Change," in *Studies and Issues in Smoking Behavior.* S. Z. Zagona, ed., University of Arizona Press, Tucson, 1967.
34. B. H. Burns, "Chronic Chest Disease, Personality and Success in Stopping Cigarette Smoking," *Brit. J. Prevent. Soc. Med. 23*:23–27, 1969.
35. J. D. Matarazzo, and G. Saslow, "Psychological and Related Characteristics of Smokers and Nonsmokers," *Psychol. Bull. 57*:493–513, 1960.
36. J. L. Schwartz, and M. Dubitzky, "Maximizing Success in Smoking Cessation Methods," *Amer. J. Public Health 59*:1392–1399, 1969.
37. R. Eisinger, Psychosocial Predictors of Smoking Behavior Change. Soc. Sci. Med. (in press) 1971.
38. J. S. Tamerin, and R. Eisinger, Cigarette Smoking and the Psychiatrist, Amer. J. Psychiat. 128:10, April 1972.
39. J. S. Tamerin and H. L. P. Resnick, "Psychiatrists Shrink From Giving Up Cigarettes," Journal of the American Medical Association, Volume 219, February 14, 1972, pp. 823–828.

2
A. Tversky and D. Kahneman, Judgment under uncertainty: Heuristics and biases, *Science* **185** (1974), 1124–1131

Here two psychologists examine the mistakes people commonly make in thinking about uncertainty. (For further examples of this literature, see Kahneman *et al.* (1982) and Nisbet and Ross (1980). Even if people are trying to be rational, their understanding of the stochastic nature of the universe, not to mention automobiles, may make them less than fully successful. This fact has implications for welfare analysis and market behavior. In a 1979 paper, the same authors offer an alternative to expected utility maximization that, they feel, describes individual behavior better (at least some of the time). For one survey of the successes and failures of expected utility to explain individual behavior, see Slovic and Lichtenstein (1971). For an interesting example of testing of expected utility, see Binswanger (1980, 1981) and Quizon *et al.* (1984).

In an interesting examination of individual behavior in a market setting, an interdisciplinary group led by Kunreuther (1976, 1978) has examined individual response to the availability of flood and earthquake insurance. This research has examined how much individuals know about insurance availability (whether it exists, how much it costs, what appears in the fine print), what elements correlate with purchase of insurance (neighbors with insurance, exposure to past floods or earthquakes, perceived exposure to future ones), and what degree of risk aversion (if any) would justify individual decisions either to have or not to have insurance, given reported estimates of damage probability and potential for damage. Not surprisingly, some people are doing things that do not seem to make sense. Others seem to have very little information about relevant opportunities. These conclusions, again, seem important for understanding how markets might work and how one might make welfare judgments. They also suggest the importance of selling efforts for market efficiency.

In a context of more mundane commodities, Brown and Oxenfeldt (1972) have examined the abilities of consumers to distinguish high-price from low-price supermarkets. Their findings are supportive of the hypothesis that some people are more responsive to their own theories of the determinants of prices than they are to moderate differences in actual prices.

References

H. Binswanger, Attitudes toward risk: experimental measurement in rural India, *Amer. J. Agricultural Econ.* **62** (1980), 395–407.

H. Binswanger, Attitudes toward risk: theoretical implications of an experiment in rural India, *Econ. J.* **91** (1981), 867–890.

F. E. Brown and A. R. Oxenfeldt, "Misperceptions of Economic Phenomena." New York: Speir and Douth, 1972.

D. Kahneman and A. Tversky, Prospect theory: An analysis of decisions under risk, *Econometrica* **47** (1979), 263–291.

D. Kahneman, P. Slovic, and A. Tversky, "Judgment Under Uncertainty: Heuristics and Biases," Cambridge: Cambridge University Press, 1982.

H. Kunreuther, Limited knowledge and insurance protection, *Public Policy* **24** (1976), 227–261.

H. Kunreuther *et al.*, "Disaster Insurance Protection." New York: Wiley, 1978.

R. Nisbet and L. Ross, "Human Inference: Strategies and Shortcomings of Social Judgment," Englewood Cliffs, New Jersey: Prentice-Hall, Inc., 1980.

J. Quizon, H. Binswanger, and M. Machina, Attitudes toward risk: further remarks, *Econ. J.* **94** (1984), 144–148.

P. Slovic and S. Lichtenstein, Comparison of Bayesian and regression approaches to the study of information processing in judgment, *Organizational Behavior and Human Performance* **6** (1971), 649–744.

Judgment under Uncertainty: Heuristics and Biases

Biases in judgments reveal some heuristics of thinking under uncertainty.

Amos Tversky and Daniel Kahneman

Many decisions are based on beliefs concerning the likelihood of uncertain events such as the outcome of an election, the guilt of a defendant, or the future value of the dollar. These beliefs are usually expressed in statements such as "I think that . . . ," "chances are . . . ," "it is unlikely that . . . ," and so forth. Occasionally, beliefs concerning uncertain events are expressed in numerical form as odds or subjective probabilities. What determines such beliefs? How do people assess the probability of an uncertain event or the value of an uncertain quantity? This article shows that people rely on a limited number of heuristic principles which reduce the complex tasks of assessing probabilities and predicting values to simpler judgmental operations. In general, these heuristics are quite useful, but sometimes they lead to severe and systematic errors.

The authors are members of the department of psychology at the Hebrew University, Jerusalem, Israel.

The subjective assessment of probability resembles the subjective assessment of physical quantities such as distance or size. These judgments are all based on data of limited validity, which are processed according to heuristic rules. For example, the apparent distance of an object is determined in part by its clarity. The more sharply the object is seen, the closer it appears to be. This rule has some validity, because in any given scene the more distant objects are seen less sharply than nearer objects. However, the reliance on this rule leads to systematic errors in the estimation of distance. Specifically, distances are often overestimated when visibility is poor because the contours of objects are blurred. On the other hand, distances are often underestimated when visibility is good because the objects are seen sharply. Thus, the reliance on clarity as an indication of distance leads to common biases. Such biases are also found in the intuitive judgment of probability. This article describes three heuristics that are employed to assess probabilities and to predict values. Biases to which these heuristics lead are enumerated, and the applied and theoretical implications of these observations are discussed.

Representativeness

Many of the probabilistic questions with which people are concerned belong to one of the following types: What is the probability that object A belongs to class B? What is the probability that event A originates from process B? What is the probability that process B will generate event A? In answering such questions, people typically rely on the representativeness heuristic, in which probabilities are evaluated by the degree to which A is representative of B, that is, by the degree to which A resembles B. For example, when A is highly representative of B, the probability that A originates from B is judged to be high. On the other hand, if A is not similar to B, the probability that A originates from B is judged to be low.

For an illustration of judgment by representativeness, consider an individual who has been described by a former neighbor as follows: "Steve is very shy and withdrawn, invariably helpful, but with little interest in people, or in the world of reality. A meek and tidy soul, he has a need for order and structure, and a passion for detail." How do people assess the probability that Steve is engaged in a particular occupation from a list of possibilities (for example, farmer, salesman, airline pilot, librarian, or physician)? How do people order these occupations from most to least likely? In the representativeness heuristic, the probability that Steve is a librarian, for example, is assessed by the degree to which he is representative of, or similar to, the stereotype of a librarian. Indeed, research with problems of this type has shown that people order the occupations by probability and by similarity in exactly the same way (*1*). This approach to the judgment of probability leads to serious errors, because similarity, or representativeness, is not influenced by several factors that should affect judgments of probability.

Insensitivity to prior probability of outcomes. One of the factors that have no effect on representativeness but should have a major effect on probability is the prior probability, or base-rate frequency, of the outcomes. In the case of Steve, for example, the fact that there are many more farmers than librarians in the population should enter into any reasonable estimate of the probability that Steve is a librarian rather than a farmer. Considerations of base-rate frequency, however, do not affect the similarity of Steve to the stereotypes of librarians and farmers. If people evaluate probability by representativeness, therefore, prior probabilities will be neglected. This hypothesis was tested in an experiment where prior probabilities were manipulated (*1*). Subjects were shown brief personality descriptions of several individuals, allegedly sampled at random from a group of 100 professionals—engineers and lawyers. The subjects were asked to assess, for each description, the probability that it belonged to an engineer rather than to a lawyer. In one experimental condition, subjects were told that the group from which the descriptions had been drawn consisted of 70 engineers and 30 lawyers. In another condition, subjects were told that the group consisted of 30 engineers and 70 lawyers. The odds that any particular description belongs to an engineer rather than to a lawyer should be higher in the first condition, where there is a majority of engineers, than in the second condition, where there is a majority of lawyers. Specifically, it can be shown by applying Bayes' rule that the ratio of these odds should be $(.7/.3)^2$, or 5.44, for each description. In a sharp violation of Bayes' rule, the subjects in the two conditions produced essentially the same probability judgments. Apparently, subjects evaluated the likelihood that a particular description belonged to an engineer rather than to a lawyer by the degree to which this description was representative of the two stereotypes, with little or no regard for the prior probabilities of the categories.

The subjects used prior probabilities correctly when they had no other information. In the absence of a personality sketch, they judged the probability that an unknown individual is an engineer to be .7 and .3, respectively, in the two base-rate conditions. However, prior probabilities were effectively ignored when a description was introduced, even when this description was totally uninformative. The responses to the following description illustrate this phenomenon:

Dick is a 30 year old man. He is married with no children. A man of high ability and high motivation, he promises to be quite successful in his field. He is well liked by his colleagues.

This description was intended to convey no information relevant to the question of whether Dick is an engineer or a lawyer. Consequently, the probability that Dick is an engineer should equal the proportion of engineers in the group, as if no description had been given. The subjects, however, judged the probability of Dick being an engineer to be .5 regardless of whether the stated proportion of engineers in the group was .7 or .3. Evidently, people respond differently when given no evidence and when given worthless evidence. When no specific evidence is given, prior probabilities are properly utilized; when worthless evidence is given, prior probabilities are ignored (*1*).

Insensitivity to sample size. To evaluate the probability of obtaining a particular result in a sample drawn from a specified population, people typically apply the representativeness heuristic. That is, they assess the likelihood of a sample result, for example, that the average height in a random sample of ten men will be 6 feet (180 centimeters), by the similarity of this result to the corresponding parameter (that is, to the average height in the population of men). The similarity of a sample statistic to a population parameter does not depend on the size of the sample. Consequently, if probabilities are assessed by representativeness, then the judged probability of a sample statistic will be essentially independent of sample size. Indeed, when subjects assessed the distributions of average height for samples of various sizes, they produced identical distributions.

For example, the probability of obtaining an average height greater than 6 feet was assigned the same value for samples of 1000, 100, and 10 men (*2*). Moreover, subjects failed to appreciate the role of sample size even when it was emphasized in the formulation of the problem. Consider the following question:

A certain town is served by two hospitals. In the larger hospital about 45 babies are born each day, and in the smaller hospital about 15 babies are born each day. As you know, about 50 percent of all babies are boys. However, the exact percentage varies from day to day. Sometimes it may be higher than 50 percent, sometimes lower.

For a period of 1 year, each hospital recorded the days on which more than 60 percent of the babies born were boys. Which hospital do you think recorded more such days?

- ► The larger hospital (21)
- ► The smaller hospital (21)
- ► About the same (that is, within 5 percent of each other) (53)

The values in parentheses are the number of undergraduate students who chose each answer.

Most subjects judged the probability of obtaining more than 60 percent boys to be the same in the small and in the large hospital, presumably because these events are described by the same statistic and are therefore equally representative of the general population. In contrast, sampling theory entails that the expected number of days on which more than 60 percent of the babies are boys is much greater in the small hospital than in the large one, because a large sample is less likely to stray from 50 percent. This fundamental notion of statistics is evidently not part of people's repertoire of intuitions.

A similar insensitivity to sample size has been reported in judgments of posterior probability, that is, of the probability that a sample has been drawn from one population rather than from another. Consider the following example:

Imagine an urn filled with balls, of which ⅔ are of one color and ⅓ of another. One individual has drawn 5 balls from the urn, and found that 4 were red and 1 was white Another individual has drawn 20 balls and found that 12 were red and 8 were white. Which of the two individuals should feel more confident that the urn contains ⅔ red balls and ⅓ white balls, rather than the opposite? What odds should each individual give?

In this problem, the correct posterior odds are 8 to 1 for the 4 : 1 sample and 16 to 1 for the 12 : 8 sample, assuming equal prior probabilities. However, most people feel that the first sample provides much stronger evidence for the hypothesis that the urn is predominantly red, because the proportion of red balls is larger in the first than in the second sample. Here again, intuitive judgments are dominated by the sample proportion and are essentially unaffected by the size of the sample, which plays a crucial role in the determination of the actual posterior odds (*2*). In addition, intuitive estimates of posterior odds are far less extreme than the correct values. The underestimation of the impact of evidence has been observed repeatedly in problems of this type (*3*, *4*). It has been labeled "conservatism."

Misconceptions of chance. People expect that a sequence of events generated by a random process will represent the essential characteristics of that process even when the sequence is short. In considering tosses of a coin for heads or tails, for example, people regard the sequence H-T-H-T-T-H to be more likely than the sequence H-H-H-T-T-T, which does not appear random, and also more likely than the sequence H-H-H-H-T-H, which does not represent the fairness of the coin (2). Thus, people expect that the essential characteristics of the process will be represented, not only globally in the entire sequence, but also locally in each of its parts. A locally representative sequence, however, deviates systematically from chance expectation: it contains too many alternations and too few runs. Another consequence of the belief in local representativeness is the well-known gambler's fallacy. After observing a long run of red on the roulette wheel. for example, most people erroneously believe that black is now due, presumably because the occurrence of black will result in a more representative sequence than the occurrence of an additional red. Chance is commonly viewed as a self-correcting process in which a deviation in one direction induces a deviation in the opposite direction to restore the equilibrium. In fact, deviations are not "corrected" as a chance process unfolds, they are merely diluted.

Misconceptions of chance are not limited to naive subjects. A study of the statistical intuitions of experienced research psychologists (5) revealed a lingering belief in what may be called the "law of small numbers," according to which even small samples are highly representative of the populations from which they are drawn. The responses of these investigators reflected the expectation that a valid hypothesis about a population will be represented by a statistically significant result in a sample—with little regard for its size. As a consequence, the researchers put too much faith in the results of small samples and grossly overestimated the replicability of such results. In the actual conduct of research, this bias leads to the selection of samples of inadequate size and to overinterpretation of findings.

Insensitivity to predictability. People are sometimes called upon to make such numerical predictions as the future value of a stock, the demand for a commodity, or the outcome of a football game. Such predictions are often made by representativeness. For example, suppose one is given a description of a company and is asked to predict its future profit. If the description of the company is very favorable, a very high profit will appear most representative of that description; if the description is mediocre, a mediocre performance will appear most representative. The degree to which the description is favorable is unaffected by the reliability of that description or by the degree to which it permits accurate prediction. Hence, if people predict solely in terms of the favorableness of the description, their predictions will be insensitive to the reliability of the evidence and to the expected accuracy of the prediction.

This mode of judgment violates the normative statistical theory in which the extremeness and the range of predictions are controlled by considerations of predictability. When predictability is nil, the same prediction should be made in all cases. For example, if the descriptions of companies provide no information relevant to profit, then the same value (such as average profit) should be predicted for all companies.

If predictability is perfect, of course, the values predicted will match the actual values and the range of predictions will equal the range of outcomes. In general, the higher the predictability, the wider the range of predicted values.

Several studies of numerical prediction have demonstrated that intuitive predictions violate this rule, and that subjects show little or no regard for considerations of predictability (*1*). In one of these studies, subjects were presented with several paragraphs, each describing the performance of a student teacher during a particular practice lesson. Some subjects were asked to *evaluate* the quality of the lesson described in the paragraph in percentile scores, relative to a specified population. Other subjects were asked to *predict*, also in percentile scores, the standing of each student teacher 5 years after the practice lesson. The judgments made under the two conditions were identical. That is, the prediction of a remote criterion (success of a teacher after 5 years) was identical to the evaluation of the information on which the prediction was based (the quality of the practice lesson). The students who made these predictions were undoubtedly aware of the limited predictability of teaching competence on the basis of a single trial lesson 5 years earlier; nevertheless, their predictions were as extreme as their evaluations.

The illusion of validity. As we have seen, people often predict by selecting the outcome (for example, an occupation) that is most representative of the input (for example, the description of a person). The confidence they have in their prediction depends primarily on the degree of representativeness (that is, on the quality of the match between the selected outcome and the input) with little or no regard for the factors that limit predictive accuracy. Thus, people express great confidence in the prediction that a person is a librarian when given a description of his personality which matches the stereotype of librarians, even if the description is scanty, unreliable, or outdated. The unwarranted confidence which is produced by a good fit between the predicted outcome and the input information may be called the illusion of validity. This illusion persists even when the judge is aware of the factors that limit the accuracy of his predictions. It is a common observation that psychologists who conduct selection interviews often experience considerable confidence in their predictions, even when they know of the vast literature that shows selection interviews to be highly fallible. The continued reliance on the clinical interview for selection, despite repeated demonstrations of its inadequacy, amply attests to the strength of this effect.

The internal consistency of a pattern of inputs is a major determinant of one's confidence in predictions based on these inputs. For example, people express more confidence in predicting the final grade-point average of a student whose first-year record consists entirely of B's than in predicting the grade-point average of a student whose first-year record includes many A's and C's. Highly consistent patterns are most often observed when the input variables are highly redundant or correlated. Hence, people tend to have great confidence in predictions based on redundant input variables. However, an elementary result in the statistics of correlation asserts that, given input variables of stated validity, a prediction based on several such inputs can achieve higher accuracy when they are independent of each other than when they are redundant or correlated. Thus, redundancy among inputs decreases accuracy even as it increases confidence, and people are often confident in predictions that are quite likely to be off the mark (*1*).

Misconceptions of regression. Suppose a large group of children has been examined on two equivalent versions of an aptitude test. If one selects ten children from among those who did best on one of the two versions, he will usually find their performance on the second version to be somewhat disappointing. Conversely, if one selects ten children from among those who did worst on one version, they will be found, on the average, to do somewhat better on the other version. More generally, consider two variables X and Y which have the same distribution. If one selects individuals whose average X score deviates from the mean of X by k units, then the average of their Y scores will usually deviate from the mean of Y by less than k units. These observations illustrate a general phenomenon known as regression toward the mean, which was first documented by Galton more than 100 years ago.

In the normal course of life, one encounters many instances of regression toward the mean, in the comparison of the height of fathers and sons, of the intelligence of husbands and wives, or of the performance of individuals on consecutive examinations. Nevertheless, people do not develop correct intuitions about this phenomenon. First, they do not expect regression in many contexts where it is bound to occur. Second, when they recognize the occurrence of regression, they often invent spurious causal explanations for it (*1*). We suggest that the phenomenon of regression remains elusive because it is incompatible with the belief that the predicted outcome should be maximally representative of the input, and, hence, that the value of the outcome variable should be as extreme as the value of the input variable.

The failure to recognize the import of regression can have pernicious consequences, as illustrated by the following observation (*1*). In a discussion of flight training, experienced instructors noted that praise for an exceptionally smooth landing is typically followed by a poorer landing on the next try, while harsh criticism after a rough landing is usually followed by an improvement on the next try. The instructors concluded that verbal rewards are detrimental to learning, while verbal punishments are beneficial, contrary to accepted psychological doctrine. This conclusion is unwarranted because of the presence of regression toward the mean. As in other cases of repeated examination, an improvement will usually follow a poor performance and a deterioration will usually follow an outstanding performance, even if the instructor does not respond to the trainee's achievement on the first attempt. Because the instructors had praised their trainees after good landings and admonished them after poor ones, they reached the erroneous and potentially harmful conclusion that punishment is more effective than reward.

Thus, the failure to understand the effect of regression leads one to overestimate the effectiveness of punishment and to underestimate the effectiveness of reward. In social interaction, as well as in training, rewards are typically administered when performance is good, and punishments are typically administered when performance is poor. By regression alone, therefore, behavior is most likely to improve after punishment and most likely to deteriorate after reward. Consequently, the human condition is such that, by chance alone, one is most often rewarded for punishing others and most often punished for rewarding them. People are generally not aware of this contingency. In fact, the elusive role of regression in determining the apparent consequences of reward and punishment seems to have escaped the notice of students of this area.

Availability

There are situations in which people assess the frequency of a class or the probability of an event by the ease with which instances or occurrences can be brought to mind. For example, one may assess the risk of heart attack among middle-aged people by recalling such occurrences among one's acquaintances. Similarly, one may evaluate the probability that a given business venture will fail by imagining various difficulties it could encounter. This judgmental heuristic is called availability. Availability is a useful clue for assessing frequency or probability, because instances of large classes are usually recalled better and faster than instances of less frequent classes. However, availability is affected by factors other than frequency and probability. Consequently, the reliance on availability leads to predictable biases, some of which are illustrated below.

Biases due to the retrievability of instances. When the size of a class is judged by the availability of its instances, a class whose instances are easily retrieved will appear more numerous than a class of equal frequency whose instances are less retrievable. In an elementary demonstration of this effect, subjects heard a list of well-known personalities of both sexes and were subsequently asked to judge whether the list contained more names of men than of women. Different lists were presented to different groups of subjects. In some of the lists the men were relatively more famous than the women, and in others the women were relatively more famous than the men. In each of the lists, the subjects erroneously judged that the class (sex) that had the more famous personalities was the more numerous (*6*).

In addition to familiarity, there are other factors, such as salience, which affect the retrievability of instances. For example, the impact of seeing a house burning on the subjective probability of such accidents is probably greater than the impact of reading about a fire in the local paper. Furthermore, recent occurrences are likely to be relatively more available than earlier occurrences. It is a common experience that the subjective probability of traffic accidents rises temporarily when one sees a car overturned by the side of the road.

Biases due to the effectiveness of a search set. Suppose one samples a word (of three letters or more) at random from an English text. Is it more likely that the word starts with r or that r is the third letter? People approach this problem by recalling words that begin with r (road) and words that have r in the third position (car) and assess the relative frequency by the ease with which words of the two types come to mind. Because it is much easier to search for words by their first letter than by their third letter, most people judge words that begin with a given consonant to be more numerous than words in which the same consonant appears in the third position. They do so even for consonants, such as r or k, that are more frequent in the third position than in the first (*6*).

Different tasks elicit different search sets. For example, suppose you are asked to rate the frequency with which abstract words (thought, love) and concrete words (door, water) appear in written English. A natural way to answer this question is to search for contexts in which the word could appear. It seems easier to think of contexts in which an abstract concept is mentioned (love in love stories) than to think of contexts in which a concrete word (such as door) is mentioned. If the frequency of words is judged by the availability of the contexts in which they appear, abstract words will be judged as relatively more numerous than concrete words. This bias has been observed in a recent study (*7*) which showed that the judged frequency of occurrence of abstract words was much higher than that of concrete words, equated in objective frequency. Abstract words were also judged to appear in a much greater variety of contexts than concrete words.

Biases of imaginability. Sometimes one has to assess the frequency of a class whose instances are not stored in memory but can be generated according to a given rule. In such situations, one typically generates several instances and evaluates frequency or probability by the ease with which the relevant instances can be constructed. However, the ease of constructing instances does not always reflect their actual frequency, and this mode of evaluation is prone to biases. To illustrate, consider a group of 10 people who form committees of k members, $2 \leqslant k \leqslant 8$. How many different committees of k members can be formed? The correct answer to this problem is given by the binomial coefficient $\binom{10}{k}$ which reaches a maximum of 252 for $k = 5$. Clearly, the number of committees of k members equals the number of committees of $(10 - k)$ members, because any committee of k members defines a unique group of $(10 - k)$ nonmembers.

One way to answer this question without computation is to mentally construct committees of k members and to evaluate their number by the ease with which they come to mind. Committees of few members, say 2, are more available than committees of many members, say 8. The simplest scheme for the construction of committees is a partition of the group into disjoint sets. One readily sees that it is easy to construct five disjoint committees of 2 members, while it is impossible to generate even two disjoint committees of 8 members. Consequently, if frequency is assessed by imaginability, or by availability for construction, the small committees will appear more numerous than larger committees, in contrast to the correct bell-shaped function. Indeed, when naive subjects were asked to estimate the number of distinct committees of various sizes, their estimates were a decreasing monotonic function of committee size (*6*). For example, the median estimate of the number of committees of 2 members was 70, while the estimate for committees of 8 members was 20 (the correct answer is 45 in both cases).

Imaginability plays an important role in the evaluation of probabilities in real-life situations. The risk involved in an adventurous expedition, for example, is evaluated by imagining contingencies with which the expedition is not equipped to cope. If many such difficulties are vividly portrayed, the expedition can be made to appear exceedingly dangerous, although the ease with which disasters are imagined need not reflect their actual likelihood. Conversely, the risk involved in an undertaking may be grossly underestimated if some possible dangers are either difficult to conceive of, or simply do not come to mind.

Illusory correlation. Chapman and Chapman (*8*) have described an interesting bias in the judgment of the frequency with which two events co-occur. They presented naive judges with information concerning several hypothetical mental patients. The data for each patient consisted of a clinical diagnosis and a drawing of a person made by the patient. Later the judges estimated the frequency with which each diagnosis (such as paranoia or suspiciousness) had been accompanied by various features of the drawing (such as peculiar eyes). The subjects markedly overestimated the frequency of co-occurrence of natural associates, such as suspiciousness and peculiar eyes. This effect was labeled illusory correlation. In their erroneous judgments of the data to which they had been exposed, naive subjects "rediscovered" much of the common, but unfounded, clinical lore concerning the interpretation of the draw-a-person test. The illusory correlation effect was extremely resistant to contradictory data. It persisted even when the correlation between symptom and diagnosis was actually negative, and it prevented the judges from detecting relationships that were in fact present.

Availability provides a natural account for the illusory-correlation effect. The judgment of how frequently two events co-occur could be based on the strength of the associative bond between them. When the association is strong, one is likely to conclude that the events have been frequently paired. Consequently, strong associates will be judged to have occurred together frequently. According to this view, the illusory correlation between suspiciousness and peculiar drawing of the eyes, for example, is due to the fact that suspiciousness is more readily associated with the eyes than with any other part of the body.

Lifelong experience has taught us that, in general, instances of large classes are recalled better and faster than instances of less frequent classes; that likely occurrences are easier to imagine than unlikely ones; and that the associative connections between events are strengthened when the events frequently co-occur. As a result, man has at his disposal a procedure (the availability heuristic) for estimating the numerosity of a class, the likelihood of an event, or the frequency of co-occurrences, by the ease with which the relevant mental operations of retrieval, construction, or association can be performed. However, as the preceding examples have demonstrated, this valuable estimation procedure results in systematic errors.

Adjustment and Anchoring

In many situations, people make estimates by starting from an initial value that is adjusted to yield the final answer. The initial value, or starting point, may be suggested by the formulation of the problem, or it may be the result of a partial computation. In either case, adjustments are typically insufficient (*4*). That is, different starting points yield different estimates, which are biased toward the initial values. We call this phenomenon anchoring.

Insufficient adjustment. In a demonstration of the anchoring effect, subjects were asked to estimate various quantities, stated in percentages (for example, the percentage of African countries in the United Nations). For each quantity, a number between 0 and 100 was determined by spinning a wheel of fortune in the subjects' presence. The subjects were instructed to indicate first whether that number was higher or lower than the value of the quantity, and then to estimate the value of the quantity by moving upward or downward from the given number. Different groups were given different numbers for each quantity, and these arbitrary numbers had a marked effect on estimates. For example, the median estimates of the percentage of African countries in the United Nations were 25 and 45 for groups that received 10 and 65, respectively, as starting points. Payoffs for accuracy did not reduce the anchoring effect.

Anchoring occurs not only when the starting point is given to the subject, but also when the subject bases his estimate on the result of some incomplete computation. A study of intuitive numerical estimation illustrates this effect. Two groups of high school students estimated, within 5 seconds, a numerical expression that was written on the blackboard. One group estimated the product

$$8 \times 7 \times 6 \times 5 \times 4 \times 3 \times 2 \times 1$$

while another group estimated the product

$$1 \times 2 \times 3 \times 4 \times 5 \times 6 \times 7 \times 8$$

To rapidly answer such questions, people may perform a few steps of computation and estimate the product by extrapolation or adjustment. Because adjustments are typically insufficient, this procedure should lead to underestimation. Furthermore, because the result of the first few steps of multiplication (performed from left to right) is higher in the descending sequence than in the ascending sequence, the former expression should be judged larger than the latter. Both predictions were confirmed. The median estimate for the ascending sequence was 512, while the median estimate for the descending sequence was 2,250. The correct answer is 40,320.

Biases in the evaluation of conjunctive and disjunctive events. In a recent study by Bar-Hillel (*9*) subjects were given the opportunity to bet on one of two events. Three types of events were used: (i) simple events, such as drawing a red marble from a bag containing 50 percent red marbles and 50 percent white marbles; (ii) conjunctive events, such as drawing a red marble seven times in succession, with replacement, from a bag containing 90 percent red marbles and 10 percent white marbles; and (iii) disjunctive events, such as drawing a red marble at least once in seven successive tries, with replacement, from a bag containing 10 percent red marbles and 90 percent white marbles. In this problem, a significant majority of subjects preferred to bet on the conjunctive event (the probability of which is .48) rather than on the simple event (the probability of which is .50). Subjects also preferred to bet on the simple event rather than on the disjunctive event, which has a probability of .52. Thus, most subjects bet on the less likely event in both comparisons. This pattern of choices illustrates a general finding. Studies of choice among gambles and of judgments of probability indicate that people tend to overestimate the probability of conjunctive events (*10*) and to underestimate the probability of disjunctive events. These biases are readily explained as effects of anchoring. The stated probability of the elementary event (success at any one stage) provides a natural starting point for the estimation of the probabilities of both conjunctive and disjunctive events. Since adjustment from the starting point is typically insufficient, the final estimates remain too close to the probabilities of the elementary events in both cases. Note that the overall probability of a conjunctive event is lower than the probability of each elementary event, whereas the overall probability of a disjunctive event is higher than the probability of each elementary event. As a consequence of anchoring, the overall probability will be overestimated in conjunctive problems and underestimated in disjunctive problems.

Biases in the evaluation of compound events are particularly significant in the context of planning. The successful completion of an undertaking, such as the development of a new product, typically has a conjunctive character: for the undertaking to succeed, each of a series of events must occur. Even when each of these events is very likely, the overall probability of success can be quite low if the number of events is large. The general tendency to overestimate the probability of conjunctive events leads to unwarranted optimism in the evaluation of the likelihood that a plan will succeed or that a project will be completed on time. Conversely, disjunctive structures are typically encountered in the evaluation of risks. A complex system, such as a nuclear reactor or a human body, will malfunction if any of its essential components fails. Even when the likelihood of failure in each component is slight, the probability of an overall failure can be high if many components are involved. Because of anchoring, people will tend to underestimate the probabilities of failure in complex systems. Thus, the direction of the anchoring bias can sometimes be inferred from the structure of the event. The chain-like structure of conjunctions leads to overestimation, the funnel-like structure of disjunctions leads to underestimation.

Anchoring in the assessment of subjective probability distributions. In decision analysis, experts are often required to express their beliefs about a quantity, such as the value of the Dow-Jones average on a particular day, in the form of a probability distribution. Such a distribution is usually constructed by asking the person to select values of the quantity that correspond to specified percentiles of his subjective probability distribution. For example, the judge may be asked to select a number, X_{90}, such that his subjective probability that this number will be higher than the value of the Dow-Jones average is .90. That is, he should select the value X_{90} so that he is just willing to accept 9 to 1 odds that the Dow-Jones average will not exceed it. A subjective probability distribution for the value of the Dow-Jones average can be constructed from several such judgments corresponding to different percentiles.

By collecting subjective probability distributions for many different quantities, it is possible to test the judge for proper calibration. A judge is properly (or externally) calibrated in a set of problems if exactly Π percent of the true values of the assessed quantities falls below his stated values of X_{Π}. For example, the true values should fall below X_{01} for 1 percent of the quantities and above X_{99} for 1 percent of the quantities. Thus, the true values should fall in the confidence interval between X_{01} and X_{99} on 98 percent of the problems.

Several investigators (*11*) have obtained probability distributions for many quantities from a large number of judges. These distributions indicated large and systematic departures from proper calibration. In most studies, the actual values of the assessed quantities are either smaller than X_{01} or greater than X_{99} for about 30 percent of the problems. That is, the subjects state overly narrow confidence intervals which reflect more certainty than is justified by their knowledge about the assessed quantities. This bias is common to naive and to sophisticated subjects, and it is not eliminated by introducing proper scoring rules, which provide incentives for external calibration. This effect is attributable, in part at least, to anchoring.

To select X_{90} for the value of the Dow-Jones average, for example, it is natural to begin by thinking about one's best estimate of the Dow-Jones and to adjust this value upward. If this adjustment—like most others—is insufficient, then X_{90} will not be sufficiently extreme. A similar anchoring effect will occur in the selection of X_{10}, which is presumably obtained by adjusting one's best estimate downward. Consequently, the confidence interval between X_{10} and X_{90} will be too narrow, and the assessed probability distribution will be too tight. In support of this interpretation it can be shown that subjective probabilities are systematically altered by a procedure in which one's best estimate does not serve as an anchor.

Subjective probability distributions for a given quantity (the Dow-Jones average) can be obtained in two different ways: (i) by asking the subject to select values of the Dow-Jones that correspond to specified percentiles of his probability distribution and (ii) by asking the subject to assess the probabilities that the true value of the Dow-Jones will exceed some specified values. The two procedures are formally equivalent and should yield identical distributions. However, they suggest different modes of adjustment from different anchors. In procedure (i), the natural starting point is one's best estimate of the quantity. In procedure (ii), on the other hand, the subject may be anchored on the value stated in the question. Alternatively, he may be anchored on even odds, or 50-50 chances, which is a natural starting point in the estimation of likelihood. In either case, procedure (ii) should yield less extreme odds than procedure (i).

To contrast the two procedures, a set of 24 quantities (such as the air distance from New Delhi to Peking) was presented to a group of subjects who assessed either X_{10} or X_{90} for each problem. Another group of subjects received the median judgment of the first group for each of the 24 quantities. They were asked to assess the odds that each of the given values exceeded the true value of the relevant quantity. In the absence of any bias, the second group should retrieve the odds specified to the first group, that is, 9 : 1. However, if even odds or the stated value serve as anchors, the odds of the second group should be less extreme, that is, closer to 1 : 1. Indeed, the median odds stated by this group, across all problems, were 3 : 1. When the judgments of the two groups were tested for external calibration, it was found that subjects in the first group were too extreme, in accord with earlier studies. The events that they defined as having a probability of .10 actually obtained in 24 percent of the cases. In contrast, subjects in the second group were too conservative. Events to which they assigned an average probability of .34 actually obtained in 26 percent of the cases. These results illustrate the manner in which the degree of calibration depends on the procedure of elicitation.

Discussion

This article has been concerned with cognitive biases that stem from the reliance on judgmental heuristics. These biases are not attributable to motivational effects such as wishful thinking or the distortion of judgments by payoffs and penalties. Indeed, several of the severe errors of judgment reported earlier occurred despite the fact that subjects were encouraged to be accurate and were rewarded for the correct answers (*2, 6*).

The reliance on heuristics and the prevalence of biases are not restricted to laymen. Experienced researchers are also prone to the same biases—when they think intuitively. For example, the tendency to predict the outcome that best represents the data, with insufficient regard for prior probability, has been observed in the intuitive judgments of individuals who have had extensive training in statistics (*1, 5*). Although the statistically sophisticated avoid elementary errors, such as the gambler's fallacy, their intuitive judgments are liable to similar fallacies in more intricate and less transparent problems.

It is not surprising that useful heuristics such as representativeness and availability are retained, even though they occasionally lead to errors in prediction or estimation. What is perhaps surprising is the failure of people to infer from lifelong experience such fundamental statistical rules as regression toward the mean, or the effect of sample size on sampling variability. Although everyone is exposed, in the normal course of life, to numerous examples from which these rules could have been induced, very few people discover the principles of sampling and regression on their own. Statistical principles are not learned from everyday experience because the relevant instances are not coded appropriately. For example, people do not discover that successive lines in a text differ more in average word length than do successive pages, because they simply do not attend to the average word length of individual lines or pages. Thus, people do not learn the relation between sample size and sampling variability, although the data for such learning are abundant.

The lack of an appropriate code also explains why people usually do not detect the biases in their judgments of probability. A person could conceivably learn whether his judgments are externally calibrated by keeping a tally of the proportion of events that actually occur among those to which he assigns the same probability. However, it is not natural to group events by their judged probability. In the absence of such grouping it is impossible for an individual to discover, for example, that only 50 percent of the predictions to which he has assigned a probability of .9 or higher actually came true.

The empirical analysis of cognitive biases has implications for the theoretical and applied role of judged probabilities. Modern decision theory (*12, 13*) regards subjective probability as the quantified opinion of an idealized person. Specifically, the subjective probability of a given event is defined by the set of bets about this event that such a person is willing to accept. An internally consistent, or coherent, subjective probability measure can be derived for an individual if his choices among bets satisfy certain principles, that is, the axioms of the theory. The derived probability is subjective in the sense that different individuals are allowed to have different probabilities for the same event. The major contribution of this approach is that it provides a rigorous subjective interpretation of probability that is applicable to unique events and is embedded in a general theory of rational decision.

It should perhaps be noted that, while subjective probabilities can sometimes be inferred from preferences among bets, they are normally not formed in this fashion. A person bets on team A rather than on team B because he believes that team A is more likely to win; he does not infer this belief from his betting preferences. Thus, in reality, subjective probabilities determine preferences among bets and are not derived from them, as in the axiomatic theory of rational decision (*12*).

The inherently subjective nature of probability has led many students to the belief that coherence, or internal consistency, is the only valid criterion by which judged probabilities should be evaluated. From the standpoint of the formal theory of subjective probability, any set of internally consistent probability judgments is as good as any other. This criterion is not entirely satisfactory, because an internally consistent set of subjective probabilities can be incompatible with other beliefs held by the individual. Consider a person whose subjective probabilities for all possible outcomes of a coin-tossing game reflect the gambler's fallacy. That is, his estimate of the probability of tails on a particular toss increases with the number of consecutive heads that preceded that toss. The judgments of such a person could be internally consistent and therefore acceptable as adequate subjective probabilities according to the criterion of the formal theory. These probabilities, however, are incompatible with the generally held belief that a coin has no memory and is therefore incapable of generating sequential dependencies. For judged probabilities to be considered adequate, or rational, internal consistency is not enough. The judgments must be compatible with the entire web of beliefs held by the individual. Unfortunately, there can be no simple formal procedure for assessing the compatibility of a set of probability judgments with the judge's total system of beliefs. The rational judge will nevertheless strive for compatibility, even though internal consistency is more easily achieved and assessed. In particular, he will attempt to make his probability judgments compatible with his knowledge about the subject matter, the laws of probability, and his own judgmental heuristics and biases.

Summary

This article described three heuristics that are employed in making judgments under uncertainty: (i) representativeness, which is usually employed when people are asked to judge the probability that an object or event A belongs to class or process B; (ii) availability of instances or scenarios, which is often employed when people are asked to assess the frequency of a class or the plausibility of a particular development; and (iii) adjustment from an anchor, which is usually employed in numerical prediction when a relevant value is available. These heuristics are highly economical and usually effective, but they lead to systematic and predictable errors. A better understanding of these heuristics and of the biases to which they lead could improve judgments and decisions in situations of uncertainty.

References and Notes

1. D. Kahneman and A. Tversky, *Psychol. Rev.* **80**, 237 (1973).
2. ———, *Cognitive Psychol.* **3**, 430 (1972).
3. W. Edwards, in *Formal Representation of Human Judgment*, B. Kleinmuntz, Ed. (Wiley, New York, 1968), pp. 17–52.
4. P. Slovic and S. Lichtenstein, *Organ. Behav. Hum. Performance* **6**, 649 (1971).
5. A. Tversky and D. Kahneman, *Psychol. Bull.* **76**, 105 (1971).
6. ———, *Cognitive Psychol.* **5**, 207 (1973).
7. R. C. Galbraith and B. J. Underwood, *Mem. Cognition* **1**, 56 (1973).
8. L. J. Chapman and J. P. Chapman, *J. Abnorm. Psychol.* **73**, 193 (1967); *ibid.*, **74**, 271 (1969).
9. M. Bar-Hillel, *Organ. Behav. Hum. Performance* **9**, 396 (1973).
10. J. Cohen, E. I. Chesnick, D. Haran, *Br. J. Psychol.* **63**, 41 (1972).
11. M. Alpert and H. Raiffa, unpublished manuscript; C. A. S. von Holstein, *Acta Psychol.* **35**, 478 (1971); R. L. Winkler, *J. Am. Stat. Assoc.* **62**, 776 (1967).
12. L. J. Savage, *The Foundations of Statistics* (Wiley, New York, 1954).
13. B. De Finetti, in *International Encyclopedia of the Social Sciences*, D. E. Sills, Ed. (Macmillan, New York, 1968), vol. 12, pp. 496–504.
14. This research was supported by the Advanced Research Projects Agency of the Department of Defense and was monitored by the Office of Naval Research under contract N00014-73-C-0438 to the Oregon Research Institute, Eugene. Additional support for this research was provided by the Research and Development Authority of the Hebrew University, Jerusalem, Israel.

3

J. H. Drèze, Axiomatic theories of choice, cardinal utility, and subjective probability: A review, *in* "Allocation under Uncertainty: Equilibrium and Optimality" (J. Drèze, ed.), pp. 3–23. New York and Toronto: Wiley, 1974.

There are many presentations of the different axiom sets from which it is possible to infer expected utility maximization. We have selected a recent one that discusses the axioms in depth, rather than concentrating on the details of a proof of the expected utility theorem. For a leisurely and lucid presentation of the theory of choice under uncertainty, the reader should consult Raiffa (1968).

Recent theoretical work has explored weakening the axioms described here to have a generalization of expected utility theory. For a detailed presentation see Machina (1982). For a survey of extensions of the expected utility axioms, see Machina (1983). A comprehensive revision of this piece is forthcoming from Cambridge University Press.

References

M. Machina, Expected utility theory without the independence axiom, *Econometrica* **50** (1982), 277–323.

M. Machina, "The economic theory of individual behavior toward risk; theory, evidence, and new directions," IMSSS Technical Report 433, Stanford University, 1983.

H. Raiffa, "Decision Analysis, Introductory Lectures on Choices under Uncertainty," Reading, Massachusetts: Addison-Wesley, 1968.

1 Axiomatic Theories of Choice, Cardinal Utility and Subjective Probability: a review

Jacques H. Drèze[1]
CORE, LOUVAIN

Most of the papers collected in this volume rely, explicitly or implicitly, upon (i) a formal description of uncertainty situations in terms of the concepts of events, acts and consequences; and (ii) an axiomatic theory of individual choices, which justifies the representation of preferences among acts by their expected utility.

The purpose of this introductory essay is to review these concepts and axioms against the background of their economic applications. The essay is not a systematic exposition of the theory (results will be stated without proofs); neither is it a survey of contributions to the theory (only a few key references will be used). Rather, it is a *review* of the main properties of the concepts and of the axiomatic theory, with a discussion of their usefulness and limitations in economic applications.[2]

Section I provides an element of historical perspective. Section II reviews the concepts of events, acts and consequences. Section III reviews the axioms of a normative theory of individual choice under uncertainty and their main implication (the moral expectation theorem). Section IV reviews some objections that have been raised against the normative appeal of the axioms. Section V is devoted to a general discussion of the usefulness and limitations of the theory. Section VI relates the concepts of the general theory to those underlying economic applications presented elsewhere in this volume.

I. HISTORICAL PERSPECTIVE

On 13 May 1952, the participants in a symposium on 'Foundations and Applications of the Theory of Risk-Bearing' [11] held in Paris

[1] I am grateful to Louis-André Gérard Varet, Louis Gevers, Roger Guesnerie, Agnar Sandmo and Dieter Sondermann for their comments on a first draft of this paper.

[2] Participants in the conference had been urged to become acquainted beforehand with the theory of individual choice under uncertainty, as exposed for instance by Savage [29] or Arrow [4]; and with the model of allocation of resources under uncertainty introduced by Arrow [3] and Debreu [5].

heard successively L. J. Savage present 'An Axiomatisation of Reasonable Behavior in the Face of Uncertainty' [31] and K. Arrow analyse 'The Role of Securities in the Optimal Allocation of Risk-Bearing' [3]. These two papers have influenced deeply the development of the theory of resource allocation under uncertainty. In order to appreciate the significance of these two papers, one must look back at the state of the theory of risk-bearing prior to the 1952 symposium in Paris.

Those who have the privilege of youth and who received their training in this field after these two papers were published,[1] can still get a picture of the previous state of affairs from the survey paper published by Arrow in 1951 [2]. Actually, that paper presents, in an orderly manner, a spectrum of approaches and results that could, at that time, be grasped only by those who had fully mastered a highly diversified literature.

Arrow surveys the status of theories 'explaining how individuals choose among alternate courses of actions when the consequences of their actions are incompletely known to them' ([2], p. 1). It is noteworthy that he proceeds from the following premise ([2], p. 9): 'It is understood that in economic situations the consequences about which uncertainty exists are commodity bundles or money payments over future dates.' His survey deals successively with two topics: the description of uncertain consequences, and the ordering of courses of actions (whose uncertain consequences have been described in some way).

With reference to the *description of the consequences* resulting from a given course of action, the major distinction is between 'those [descriptions] which use exclusively the language of probability distributions and those which call for some other principle, either to replace or to supplement' ([2], p. 8). The first category is further subdivided according to the chosen interpretation of probability (see Savage [29], p. 3, for a concise description of alternative approaches). The second category reflects the views of scholars of no lesser standing than the economists Keynes, Knight and Shackle, the statisticians Neyman, Pearson and Wald.

With reference to the *ordering of courses of action*, sharper issues arise when the problem has been recognised as that of ordering probability distributions of consequences. In the 1930s and early 1940s, economists like Hicks [18], Marschak [23] and Tintner [34]

[1] The proceedings of the Conference appeared (in French) in November 1953; Savage's contribution was fully developed in his book, *The Foundations of Statistics* [29] which appeared in 1954; Arrow's paper did not become available in English until 1963, but the material in his paper is covered and extended by Debreu in chapter 7 of the *Theory of Value* [5], which appeared in 1959.

were debating whether the ordering of such distributions could be based on their means and standard deviations alone (as in [18]), or on these two and other parameters as well (as in [23]), or should more generally be represented by a 'risk preference functional' (as in [34]).

An axiomatic approach to the ordering of probability distributions, recognising explicitly the 'mutually exclusive' nature of alternative consequences, had been introduced by Ramsey [28]. This approach was revived in successively clearer and simpler terms by von Neumann and Morgenstern [25] and Marschak [24], gaining increasing recognition for the existence of a utility function which permits the representation of an ordering among probability distributions of consequences by the mathematical expectation of the utility of these consequences.

Still, by 1951, this approach was far from being generally accepted (see, for instance, the various papers by Allais in [11] and elsewhere); and its applicability was limited to those situations where the probability distribution of consequences was somehow given. The main suggestions contained in Arrow's survey, insofar as other situations are concerned, came from the minimax school of Wald [35] (extended to 'minimax regret' by Savage [30]) and from the specific theory of Shackle [33]. The shortcomings of these approaches are exposed by Arrow.[1]

The defects of this state of affairs were numerous. The lack of agreement among specialists was rather confusing for the beginning student. There was no general conceptual framework, within which one could identify the difficulties specific to certain classes of problems, and assess the significance of specific results.

The most useful theoretical contribution seemed to be that of von Neumann and Morgenstern – yet it was still surrounded by rather obscure discussions. Its applicability seemed restricted to situations where probabilities reflecting the beliefs of the decision-maker could be objectively defined; its relation to the neo-classical theories of consumer choice and of the firm had not been spelled out; and its exposition in terms of 'consequences' identified with wealth was a continuous source of misunderstandings.[2] The need for a more general theory was thus acute.

[1] Arrow's survey devotes a few pages to the work of de Finetti, Ramsey, Rubin and Chernoff on axiomatic theories of '*a priori* probabilities'. However, little emphasis is placed on these developments, the significance of which was by no means evident at that time.

[2] This is perhaps best evidenced by the famous article of Friedman and Savage [12], where a single function is assumed to describe satisfactorily the utility of wealth to both a consumer and his heirs; and by the attention paid to the reinterpretation by Markowitz [22] of the Friedman-Savage analysis.

II. THE CONCEPTUAL FRAMEWORK

It is by now standard practice to describe a problem of individual decision under uncertainty (or a 'game against nature') in terms of a matrix where:

(i) the rows correspond to alternative, mutually exclusive courses of action open to the decision-maker;
(ii) the columns correspond to alternative, mutually exclusive courses of future events;
(iii) the entries of the matrix correspond to the consequences for the decision-maker resulting from a given course of action under a specific course of events.

Such a description aims at starting from primitive concepts, endowed with an operational meaning in terms of observable phenomena. Thus, the uncertainty is traced back to its source (the future course of events), instead of being described in derived terms – a probability distribution, for instance. And the consequences need not be commodity bundles or money payments; their description may encompass any relevant consideration – from which, possibly, a consumption vector or budget constraint may eventually result.

The trilogy of rows, columns and entries of the matrix, corresponding to 'what the decision-maker does, what nature does, what happens to the decision-maker' admits of a natural abstract representation in terms of two sets. Denoting a course of action by a, a course of future events by s, one then considers the set A of elements $a, a', \ldots$ and the set S of elements $s, s', \ldots$;[1] every entry of the matrix may then be denoted by an ordered pair (a, s). This formal structure is fully adequate as a starting point of the theory. In the same way as 'the currently prevalent axiomatic treatment of probability as a branch of measure theory seems designed to keep the technical development of the theory from being bogged down in the difficulties of the 'foundations' ([2] p. 406) so the exclusive reliance upon the sets A, S and their cartesian product $A \times S$ makes it possible to develop the theory of choice under uncertainty without facing explicitly any difficulties of interpretation.

Expositors of the theory discuss concisely the interpretation of the basic concepts. Thus, Savage ([29], p. 9) proposes 'the following nomenclature . . . as brief, suggestive, and in reasonable harmony with the usages of statistics and ordinary discourse:

[1] The words 'course of action', 'action' and 'act' are here treated as synonyms; the same remark applies to 'course of future events', 'state of the world' and 'state'.

the *world*: the object about which the person is concerned;
a *state* (of the world): a description of the world, leaving no relevant aspect undescribed;
the *true* state (of the world): the state that does in fact obtain, i.e. the true description of the world.'

He then completes his set of definitions as follows:

an *event*: a set of states;
a *consequence*: anything that may happen to the person;
an *act*: a function attaching a consequence to each state of the world.[1]

The primitive concepts are thus states and consequences. The formal theory is based upon a set of states S, a set of events (to be denoted $E, E', \ldots$) given by the σ-algebra of S, a set of consequences C and a set of acts given by the mappings of S into C. To consider every such mapping as an act means, of course, to consider hypothetical acts, which do not correspond to courses of action effectively open to the decision-maker.[2]

Some of these hypothetical acts (e.g. constant acts) are needed in the construction of the theory.

The cardinality of the sets S and C has important technical implications. S must be at least denumerably infinite. On the other hand, the theory is easier to develop for acts with only a finite number of distinct consequences.

Before turning to the axioms, three properties of the concepts of events, acts and consequences should be stressed. These properties define the class of decision situations which the theory aims at encompassing; the reasonableness of the axioms should be appraised with reference to those situations only.

(1) *About Events*

Events must be defined with *interpersonal objectivity* and their occurrence must lie *beyond the control of the decision-maker*. These two aspects are covered by the interpretation of events as circumstances upon which bets can be placed, since the very idea of a bet[3] presupposes that (i) it can be ascertained with interpersonal objectivity who has won the bet, and (ii) neither party to the bet can unilaterally enforce his winning.

[1] This definition is motivated as follows: 'If two different acts had the same consequences in every state of the world, there would from the present point of view be no point in considering them two different acts at all. An act may therefore be identified with its possible consequences' ([29], p. 14).

[2] For instance, many consumers could buy a lottery ticket giving them a very small chance of winning a million dollars, but very few have access to a course of action giving them the certainty of winning that amount.

[3] As distinct from a 'challenge'.

The relevance of these remarks for economic applications is the following: (i) uncertainty of the decision-maker about his own tastes at a future date cannot be described through distinct events corresponding to distinct preference structures, since this would violate the condition of interpersonal objectivity;[1] (ii) 'moral hazards', that is, uncertainties that lie (at least in part) under the control of the decision-maker, cannot be described through events either.[2]

(2) *About Consequences*

'In the description of a consequence is included all that the agent values' ([4], p. 45); accordingly, commodity bundles will generally prove inadequate to define consequences. To quote Savage:

> Before going on a picnic with friends, a person decides to buy a bathing suit or a tennis racket. . . . The possession of the tennis racket and the possession of the bathing suit are to be regarded as acts, not consequences. . . . The consequences relevant to the decision are such as these: a refreshing swim with friends, sitting on a shadeless beach twiddling a brand new tennis racket while one's friends swim, etc. . . .([29], p. 25).

Even in those cases where commodity bundles prove adequate to define consequences, a careful definition of commodities may be required. Thus, a person buying 6 eggs, some of which may conceivably be bad, is in fact buying x good eggs and $6-x$ bad eggs, where x is an *unknown* integer, $0 \leq x \leq 6$. This purchase may be described by a point in the two-dimensional space of 'good' and 'bad' eggs, the location of the point being a function of the state of the world (x).[3]

(3) *About Constant Acts*

The assumption that every consequence can be attained in any state (which implies the existence of constant acts) precludes the explicit consideration of events that are of significant value to the decision-maker; thus, a person's death is clearly a circumstance on which bets can be placed (e.g. through a life-insurance contract), but it is also a

[1] With reference to the economics of insurance, a contract specifying that 'I shall receive a certain capital if I develop a taste for Bourbon whisky' would be viewed by the company as equivalent to a sure promise of that capital, since the event mentioned in the contract is not amenable to their verification.

[2] With reference to the economics of insurance again, 'moral hazards' (e.g. arson) occur when the person's actions (as opposed to his tastes) escape verification.

[3] Whereas '6 good eggs' is arithmetically equal to two times '3 good eggs' the same property of addition does not hold for '6 eggs, some of which are good', unless specific assumptions about the determinants of the quality of the eggs are added.

'vital' element in the description of consequences. In defining constant acts, a consequence like 'being alive, poor and healthy' should be attainable in the event that the decision-maker dies – which stretches the imagination of mere mortals a bit too far, in my opinion. It thus seems best to exclude such circumstances from explicit consideration.[1]

These properties being understood, it should be clear that the basic concepts offer a medium for the description of problems of decision under uncertainty, which is far more general and flexible than previously available alternatives. To some extent, the gain in clarity and generality is comparable to that achieved by relying upon the formal concept of probability space as the starting point of probability theory. The general conceptual framework can always be particularised to handle specific problems – but the nature of the particular assumptions is then easily assessed.

III. AXIOMS OF A NORMATIVE THEORY

Consistency of preferences is traditionally identified with the existence of a simple ordering among the objects of choice; that is, of preferences which are complete and transitive. The preference relation itself is a primitive concept.

To assume that a preference relation is a simple ordering is to assume that the decision-maker behaves neither like Buridan's ass, who died of starvation half-way between a bale of hay and a pail of water, because he could not decide which, his hunger or his thirst, he should satisfy first; nor like Grimm's Hans in Glück, who received a precious gift, then made a series of exchanges, each of which looked favourable to him, and eventually reverted to his initial position.

In the theory of choice under uncertainty reviewed here, the assumption that there exists a simple ordering is successively applied to

(i) acts;
(ii) acts, conditionally on events;
(iii) consequences;
(iv) events.

Using the symbol $\gtrsim$ to mean 'preferred or indifferent', the first assumption reads:
For all $a, a', a'' \in A$:

(i) either $a \gtrsim a'$ or $a' \gtrsim a$;
(ii) $a \gtrsim a'$ and $a' \gtrsim a'' \Rightarrow a \gtrsim a''$.

[1] See, however, page 19 (note 1).

Some definitions are needed to state the other three assumptions. It will be said that 'a' is not preferred to a, given E (or conditionally on E)' if and only if $b \gtrsim b'$ whenever:

$$\left.\begin{array}{l} c(a, s) = c(b, s) \\ c(a', s) = c(b', s) \end{array}\right\} \forall s \in E; \quad c(b, s) = c(b', s) \;\forall s \in \tilde{E}.$$ [1]

To assume that conditional preference, given an arbitrary event E, is well defined (is a simple ordering) is to say that the consequences $c(b, s) = c(b', s)$, $s \in \tilde{E}$, are irrelevant to the choice between b and b': if two acts have identical consequences under a certain event ($\tilde{E}$), then the choice between them should proceed as if that event did not exist as a possibility; that is, the choice should not depend in any way upon the nature of these identical consequences. The justification for this assumption (sometimes called 'Sure Thing Principle', as in [29], and sometimes called 'Strong Independence Axiom', as in [24]) is that an event E and its complement $\tilde{E}$ are mutually exclusive, so that the attractiveness of the consequences associated with E should be assessed independently of those consequences associated with $\tilde{E}$. The logic of this reasoning seems compelling, even though the implications of the assumption are very strong, as one may realise with the help of an example introduced in the next section.

With conditional preferences well defined, one may define the 'nullity' (subjective impossibility) of an event E either by the condition '$a \gtrsim a'$ given E for all $a, a' \in A$' or by the condition '$a \gtrsim a'$ given $\tilde{E}$ if, and only if, $a \gtrsim a'$'. A preference relation among consequences is then easily defined as follows: $\bar{c} \gtrsim \bar{c}'$ if, and only if, $a \gtrsim a'$ given E whenever $c(a, s) = \bar{c}$, $c(a', s) = \bar{c}'$ for all $s \in E$, E being non-null (but otherwise arbitary). To assume that this relation is well defined (is a simple ordering) is to assume that consequences are so defined that preferences among them are never modified by knowledge of the event that obtains.

Finally, if $\bar{c}$ and $\bar{c}'$ are two consequences such that $\bar{c} \gtrsim \bar{c}'$, the event E is said to be 'revealed at least as likely' as the event E' if, and only if,

$a \gtrsim a'$ whenever:
$c(a, s) = \bar{c}$, $s \in E$; $\quad c(a, s) = \bar{c}'$, $s \in \tilde{E}$;
$c(a', s) = \bar{c}$, $s \in E'$; $\quad c(a', s) = \bar{c}'$, $s \in \tilde{E}'$.

This definition states that if a person prefers to stake a prize on E rather than on E', then we may infer that the person regards the occurrence of E as more likely than the occurrence of E'. To assume that this relation is well defined (is a simple ordering among events) is to assume that which one of two events a person prefers to stake a

[1] $\tilde{E}$ denotes the complement of E (in S).

prize on, does not depend upon the nature of the prize.[1] Within the conceptual framework of the theory, it seems hard to object to this assumption, even though the implications of the assumption are very strong, as one may realise with the help of an example introduced in the next section.

The four assumptions just reviewed may be summarised by saying that a consistent decision-maker is assumed always to be able to compare (transitively) the attractiveness of acts, of hypothetical acts and of consequences as well as the likelihood of events. These requirements are minimal, in the sense that no consistency of behaviour may be expected if any one of them is violated; but they are very strong, in the sense that all kinds of comparisons are assumed possible, many of which may be quite remote from the range of experience of the decision-maker. This is also the reason why the axioms have more normative appeal than descriptive realism; few people would insist on maintaining, consciously, choices that violate them, but their spontaneous behaviour may frequently fail to display such rigorous consistency.

In order to avoid the trivial case of generalised indifference, it is further assumed that one does not have $c \gtrsim c'$ for all c, c'.

In the theory of consumer choice under certainty, one typically starts with an assumption of simple ordering among commodity bundles.[2] Specific theorems in economics rely upon assumptions about preferences that have no counterpart in the general theory reviewed here; such is the case for the assumptions of desirability and convexity frequently made about preferences among vectors in Euclidian space. There is, however, another assumption which plays an important role in many economic models, and which has a counterpart in the theory of decision under uncertainty; namely, the assumption of continuity. The intuitive concept of continuity of preference is that consequences which are 'close' to each other in some real (physical) sense must also be 'close' to each other in terms of preferences: $c \not\precsim \bar{c}$ implies $c' \not\precsim \bar{c}$ for all c' sufficiently close to c (in terms of Euclidian distance).

Continuity of preferences is necessary (and almost sufficient) for the representation of preferences by a continuous real-valued function.

Continuity is frequently described as a 'technical' assumption, to distinguish its nature from the 'logical' assumption of consistency

[1] Remember that a 'prize' is a consequence, and consequences are defined so comprehensively that preferences among them are never modified by knowledge of the event that obtains.

[2] Some results of economic interest do not require the assumption of complete preferences; see, e.g. [32].

(identified with the existence of a simple ordering). A certain structure must be placed on the objects of choice in order for the technical assumption of continuity to be meaningful. In general, no particular structure applies to the sets A, C or S. But a rich structure can be created by assuming that non-null events can be partitioned at will into other non-null events (for instance, by means of such random mechanisms as dice or coins). This possibility is introduced by means of the assumption of *atomlessness* (if E is non-null, E contains E' less likely than E and non-null). Sequences of non-null events, each of which is contained in, and is less likely than, the preceding one (i.e. monotonic decreasing sequences) are then used to introduce a *continuity* assumption which has the desired implications for representation of preferences by real-valued functions.[1] Atomlessness and continuity are 'technical' assumptions, that bear upon the structure of events as well as upon preferences; and insofar as they bear upon preferences, they reflect 'convenience' rather than logical necessity. Thus, Arrow [4] refers to a simple ordering among objects of choice as being 'the hallmark of rationality' (p. 47), and to the axiom of continuity as being 'the harmless simplification almost inevitable in the formalisation of any real-life problem' (p. 48).

From the assumptions reviewed so far, one deduces the celebrated 'moral expectation theorem' for acts with finitely many distinct consequences,[2] namely:

- there exists a (countably-additive) probability measure P,
- there exists a real-valued function of consequences U, defined up to a linear transformation,

such that

$$\text{if } c(a, s) = c_i \text{ for all } s \in E_i,\ c(a', s) = c_i' \text{ for all } s \in E_i',$$
$$a \lesssim a' \text{ if, and only if, } \sum_i P(E_i)U(c_i) \leq \sum_i P(E_i')U(c_i').$$

The theorem states that the orderings of consequences and events are representable, respectively, by a cardinal utility function and by a probability measure, in such a way that the ordering among acts is representable by their expected utility. In particular, the ordering among acts can be constructed by first constructing independently P and U, and then computing expected utilities.[3]

[1] For precise statements of these assumptions, see [4], pp. 48 and 77.

[2] An additional assumption of 'dominance', namely: '$a \lesssim c(a', s)$ given E for every $s \in E$ implies $a \lesssim a'$ given E', is required to extend the theorem to acts with infinitely many distinct consequences.

[3] An example of these constructions, which may serve as a useful revision of the theory, is given in [26].

By way of concluding this section, I will illustrate by a simple example how the utility of *information about events* can be inferred from the expected utility of acts. Consider the events E and E', with $P(E)=\frac{1}{2}$, $P(E')=\frac{1}{4}$, $P(E\cap E')=\frac{1}{8}$. Let the act a have two possible consequences, c and c', with

$U(c)=1$, $U(c')=-1$ and
$c(a, s)=c$ for all $s\in E\cap \tilde{E}'$ and for all $s\in \tilde{E}\cap E'$
$c(a, s)=c'$ otherwise.

Clearly, the expected utility of a is zero, with conditional expectations of $\frac{1}{2}$ given E and $-\frac{1}{2}$ given $\tilde{E}$. Let, finally, the act a' be such that $c(a', s)=c$ for all s such that $c(a, s)=c'$, $c(a', s)=c'$ for all s such that $c(a, s)=c$. Again, the expected utility of a' is equal to 0, with conditional expectations of $-\frac{1}{2}$ given E and $\frac{1}{2}$ given $\tilde{E}$.

If the decision-maker is offered the choice between a and a', he will be indifferent between these two acts, and his expected utility will be equal to 0. Should he know whether E is true or not, he could choose a if E is true, a' if E is not true, with an expected utility of $\frac{1}{2}$ in either case. Hence, information about E would have a utility value of $\frac{1}{2}$.

IV. OBJECTIONS TO THE NORMATIVE APPEAL OF THE AXIOMS

Although objections to the descriptive realism of the theory have been numerous, objections to its normative appeal have been addressed almost exclusively to the assumption regarding conditional preference. The objections have been sustained by examples of simple choice situations, where violations of the axioms of conditional preference are frequently observed among rankings of acts elicited through casual or systematic questionnaires. Two clever examples, due respectively to Maurice Allais and Daniel Ellsberg, will be reproduced here.

The example of Allais consists of four acts, the consequences of which depend upon the drawing of a ball from an urn containing 100 numbered balls. These consequences consist of prizes, expressed say in thousands of dollars, and described in Table 1.1.

TABLE 1.1

NUMBER ON BALL DRAWN AT RANDOM

Acts	*0*	*1–10*	*11–99*
a	50	50	50
a'	0	250	50
b	50	50	0
b'	0	250	0

Many people report the ranking $a \not\precsim a' \not\precsim b' \not\precsim b$: the certainty of 50 thousand dollars is preferred to a lottery offering 89 chances in a hundred of 50 thousand and 10 chances in a hundred of 250 thousand; but a lottery offering 10 chances in a hundred of 250 thousand is preferred to a lottery offering 11 chances in a hundred of 50. On the other hand, the axiom of conditional preference requires: $a \not\precsim a'$ if, and only if, $b \not\precsim b'$, since the identical consequences associated, by either a and a' or b and b', with the event '11–99' should not affect the rankings within these two pairs of acts.

The example of Ellsberg consists of four acts, the consequences of which depend upon the drawing of a ball from an urn containing 90 coloured balls. It is specified that 30 balls are red, the other 60 being either black or white; the number of black (white) balls is *not* specified. Accordingly only the events 'red' and 'black *or* white' have objectively defined numerical probabilities. The Acts are described in Table 1.2.

TABLE 1.2

COLOUR OF BALL DRAWN AT RANDOM

Acts	*Red*	*Black*	*White*
a	50	0	0
a'	0	50	0
b	50	0	50
b'	0	50	50

Many people report the ranking $b' \not\precsim b \not\precsim a \not\precsim a'$, which violates the axiom of conditional preference. Reportedly, a is better than a' because a entails an 'objective' probability of $\frac{1}{3}$ of winning the prize, whereas no 'objective' probability of gain is offered by a'. A similar argument applies to $b' \not\precsim b$.

These two examples rely upon an illusory complementarity operating across mutually exclusive events. In the example of Allais, the consequence associated with the event '11–99' looks 'complementary' to the other consequences in the case of act a, but not in the case of act b. The illusory nature of this 'complementarity' is perhaps best evidenced by the fact that a person insisting on the preferences '$a \not\precsim a'$, $a' \not\precsim a$ given 0–11' would prefer to a an act a^0 whereby the person would first be informed whether the event '11–99' obtains; if it obtains, the person receives 50; otherwise, the person may choose between a and a' (and would choose a'). The ranking would then be $a^0 \not\precsim a \not\precsim a'$ – but a^0 (with the assumed strategy) is *identical* to a'!

In the example of Ellsberg, the event 'white' looks complementary to the event 'black' in the case of act b', but not in the case of act a'. To bring out the illusory nature of that complementarity, it is helpful to consider also an act a^0 promising 50 if the ball is *white*, zero otherwise. One then typically finds that persons preferring a to a' are indifferent between a' and a^0. It may then be remarked that a 50–50 chance of either a' or a^0 entails an objective probability of $\frac{1}{3}$ of winning the prize, *irrespective* of the number of black (white) balls, and should be indifferent to a; thus (in an obvious notation): $a \not\lesssim a' \sim a^0 \sim (a', a^0; \frac{1}{2}; \frac{1}{2}) \sim a$, which brings out the contradiction quite explicitly.

In both examples, the root of the difficulty is that a decision-maker must decide upon his preferences between a and a' conditionally on a certain event (0–11 in Table 1.1, red or black in Table 1.2); once that ranking is ascertained, consistent choices follow. The temptation to avoid facing squarely the issue of conditional preference is cleverly exploited in constructing the examples. I feel strongly that they belong to the family of 'optical illusions', their main purpose being to remind us of the strength of the assumptions of consistency and of the usefulness of decomposing logically complex choice situations into their elementary components.

Finally, I would like to mention another example, which was constructed during the Bergen Conference. Four acts are involved, with consequences depending upon the toss of a coin. Some consequences are monetary prizes ($\lesseqgtr 0$), others are tickets for a concert (the person is assumed to be fond of classical music, and equally eager to attend either one of two concerts planned for the same evening). Several participants at the conference mentioned the ranking $a' \not\lesssim a \not\lesssim b \not\lesssim b'$.

TABLE 1.3

OUTCOME OF COIN TOSS

Acts	*Heads*	*Tails*
a	\$1,000	hear Beethoven's Ninth Symphony (concert A)
a'	\$1,000	hear Mozart's *Requiem* (concert B)
b	\$ – 1,000	Concert A
b'	\$ – 1,000	Concert B

One may try to reconcile this understandable ranking with the axiom of conditional preference by claiming that 'concert A' or 'concert B' are not consequences, whereas 'attending concert · in an elated mood', and 'attending concert · in a depressed mood' are consequences. This reinterpretation raises, however, a subtle issue of dependence of the consequences upon the *acts*. Alternatively (or consequently?) one may recognise this type of situation as a limitation to the realm of applicability of the theory – a limitation, however, that may be regarded as innocuous from the viewpoint of economics.

V. MERITS AND LIMITATIONS OF THE THEORY

In this section, I will propose an evaluation of the merits and limitations of the theory under review from the successive viewpoints of its relevance, usefulness, generality and integration with other theories. In each case, merits and limitations will be mentioned successively, in that order. I will then conclude with an overall evaluation.

(1) *Relevance*

(i) *The theory has strong normative appeal.* The normative appeal of a theory may be measured by the acceptability of its premises and the strength of the conclusions derived from them. As indicated in section IV, I personally regard the axioms of the theory under review as perfectly acceptable. It seems generally agreed that the moral expectation theorem is a strong conclusion based upon these premises. Yet, my interest in the theory derives, in large part, from a slightly different consideration.

Scientists should not attempt, in a professional capacity, to prescribe values or norms of behaviour; but they should explain how, and under what conditions, scientific methods can be brought to bear upon realistic problems. If we accept the view that the values and judgements of a person are eminently relevant to his own decisions, then it seems clear that a consistent assessment of these values and judgements is a necessary condition for scientific reasoning to be brought to bear on his decision problems; and the theory under review has the great merit of telling us that the condition is also sufficient.

To be more specific: whether a person wants to accept a bet involving one chance in eleven of losing 50 thousand dollars, and ten chances in eleven of winning 200 thousand dollars, seems to be for that person to decide; but if a scientist is to use that person's choice in this simple situation to prescribe solutions in more complex situations, then it is a minimal requirement that the choice be unambiguous; (unstable or) intransitive preferences do not meet that minimal requirement; consequently, persons with (unstable or) intransitive preferences not only risk having unfair bets placed against them, they also deprive themselves of the potential assistance of scientists in solving decision problems.

In other words, a person who does not accept the axioms of simple ordering for conditional acts, consequences and events, should not expect any assistance from scientific methods in handling decision problems.

(ii) *The theory has doubtful descriptive realism.* Three remarks will be made in this respect:

(i) casual empiricism suggests that spontaneous behaviour of reasonable persons may fail to satisfy the axioms of the theory;
(ii) the formalisation of even the simplest decision problems proves amazingly intricate, and this casts doubts upon the possibility of using the theory as a model within which future choices could be predicted on the basis of past observations;
(iii) it may still be true (but remains to be demonstrated?) that economic theories based upon the behavioural assumption of expected utility maximisation will have implications that are borne out by empirical tests, and have predictive power.

(2) *Usefulness*

(i) *The theory is of substantial theoretical usefulness.* A normative theory of decision can be helpful in two ways:

(i) in resolving logical difficulties connected with the statement of problems and criteria for solving them;
(ii) in bringing powerful scientific methods to bear upon the solution of decision problems.

On both counts, the theory under review is extremely helpful.

(i) The description of decision problems in terms of acts, events and consequences, is 'far more general and flexible than previously available alternatives' (*supra*, p. 9). The maximisation of expected utility is a generally applicable decision criterion, which resolves logical difficulties previously regarded as serious.
(ii) The theory brings the powerful mathematical theory of probability to bear upon decision problems. Since a decision-maker's judgements about the likelihood of events are summarised in a probability measure, the rules of conditional probability and Bayes' theorem can be used to incorporate new information.[1]

(ii) *The theory is of limited practical usefulness.* The practical usefulness of the theory is subject to limitations stemming from three problems, which the theory, as such, leaves entirely open, namely:

(i) the calibration of probabilities;
(ii) the calibration of utilities;
(iii) the discovery of an optimal act from a given set.

[1] Arrow remarks ([4], p. 46): 'The influence of experience on beliefs is of the utmost importance for a rational theory of behaviour under uncertainty, and failure to account for it must be taken as a strong objection to theories such as Shackle's [33]'.

Experiments dealing with individual ability to make realistic probability assessments point strongly towards systematic biases [27]. This is not surprising, since hardly anybody has ever been trained in assessing probabilities; and it is by no means clear how such training could be effective. As for individual ability to calibrate utilities, very little is known on that score.

The third problem is the subject-matter of optimisation theory, operations research and statistical decision theory. The class of decision problems under uncertainty which can be handled formally is still very limited, and problems of sequential decision raise very serious difficulties.[1]

(3) *Generality*

(i) *The theory has almost complete formal and logical generality.* The formal generality of the theory derives from its ability to encompass situations that were previously distinguished as calling for distinct formalisms – for instance, situations of 'risk' where the relative frequencies in repeated observations invited the formalism of probability, as opposed to situations of 'uncertainty' where the absence of such observations precluded the use of that formalism.

The logical generality of the theory derives from its main conclusion, which justifies the use of expected utility as a single decision criterion. This result provides a single answer to a variety of questions with which economists and statisticians were concerned, and to which they were tempted to offer distinct answers (ranging from 'risk preference functional' to minimax solutions).

Although this view is not generally accepted, I personally understand the expected utility criterion to be applicable to (non-cooperative) games of strategy as well. If the pure strategies of the opponent(s) are treated as events and if the pay-off of the game is understood to be expressed in utility terms, then one may regard the specific object of the theory of games as being the assessment of the probabilities of events, the ultimate decision criterion being the maximisation of expected utility (under due recognition for the influence of strategy choices on the probabilities of the events).

(ii) *The applicability of the theory is limited by its conceptual structure.* It was emphasised in section II that events and consequences had to be defined in such a way that:

(i) every consequence can be attained in any state;
(ii) the occurrence of any event can be verified with interpersonal objectivity and lies beyond the control of the decision-maker.

As was noted there, these conditions preclude explicit consideration of events which are themselves of value to the decision-maker

[1] On this topic, see the last section of [9].

(e.g. his own death), or which have a dimension of 'moral hazard'. This is a serious limitation for economic applications.[1]

(4) *Integration with Other Theories*

(i) *Economics, statistics and decision theory.* A major merit of the theory under review lies in the provision of an integrated framework within which the disciplines of economics, statistics and decision theory can be developed jointly. Uncertainty in economics can best be described through events and consequences. Utility analysis is only natural for economists. The existence of a probability measure on events provides the bridge with statistical theory, whereby empirical information can be used to revise previous judgements. A systematic development of statistical procedures, designed to facilitate such revisions, is currently under way, and goes under the name of 'Bayesian statistics'.[2]

(ii) *Individual versus group decisions.* The theory under review is presented with reference to a single decision-maker. Yet it must be recognised that many, if not most, decision problems of interest to social scientists call for group decisions. In economics, the abstract 'consumer' is typically a family, and most families consist of more than a single person; the abstract 'producer' is typically a firm, grouping many individuals; and problems of 'social choice' arise specifically from the presence of several decision-makers, with distinct values and judgements, and typically with conflicting interests. Savage ([29], p. 154) also advances the view that '. . . *statistics proper* can perhaps be defined as the art of dealing with vagueness and *with interpersonal difference* in decision situation'. One is thus naturally led to wonder about the integration of the theory with other work dealing explicitly with group decisions.

The most important theorem on group decisions in economics is Arrow's impossibility theorem [1], which has drawn attention to the difficulties inherent in group decisions based on ordinal preferences (rankings) of the members. Cardinal preferences (a utility function defined up to a linear transformation) open a natural avenue to overcome these difficulties. When there is unanimous agreement about the probabilities, reasonable axioms proposed by Harsanyi [17] lead to a group utility function, which is a weighted average of individual utility functions. In the absence of agreement about the

[1] I have shown elsewhere [7] that such situations could be encompassed in a generalised theory, at the cost of considerable formal complexity, and within the limitations of a serious identification problem.

[2] An additional axiom is required to validate these procedures, namely an axiom which states that the probability of any event E, *after* making an observation x, is equal to the prior probability of E conditionally on x (that is the probability of E given x *before* making the observation).

probabilities, a group probability measure may be defined as a weighted average of the individual measures, but Madansky [21] has shown that the weights must be revised in the light of new information. And Zeckhauser has proved another important impossibility theorem: there does not exist, in general, a group utility function which aggregates individual utilities, and a group probability measure which aggregates individual probability measures, in such a way that admissible group decisions maximise the expectation of the group utility (in terms of the group probabilities). Further results on this problem have been established by Wilson [36].[1]

(5) *Overall Evaluation*

If one refers to the earlier situation, as outlined in section I, the merits of the theory under review are substantial, and generally outweigh its limitations. In my opinion, the theory provides a starting point for research on the economics of uncertainty that is both natural and satisfactory. Specific applications may call for further specifications or for specific extensions; and one should remain conscious of the doubtful descriptive realism of the theory. But that being understood, it seems fruitful to investigate economic models relying, explicitly or implicitly, upon the axioms or conclusions of the theory.

VI. LINK WITH ECONOMIC APPLICATIONS

Several chapters of this book [15, 16, 14, 10] proceed from a description of uncertainty in terms of events and states of the world. In these models, decisions about production and allocation of commodities are evaluated from the viewpoint of consumer preferences. Given a list of commodities and a list of possible states, a consumption plan for a consumer is a vector specifying his consumption of every commodity in every state. Such a consumption plan corresponds to an act in the terminology used here. Thus, acts are functions from the state of the world to the commodity space. Does it follow that points in the commodity space define consequences? It was noted on p. 8 above that 'commodity bundles will generally prove inadequate to

[1] When the group decisions concern the production and allocations of commodities, Pareto-optimal decisions can be sustained by a price system for contingent claims to commodities (see [15] below). These prices admit of an expected utility interpretation: under appropriate normalisation, undiscounted prices for a numeraire commodity have all the properties of a probability measure on the events; prices for other commodities, expressed in terms of the numeraire conditionally on any given event, measure the utility of these commodities (see [15] and [8]). In this sense, efficient group decisions sustained by a price system admit of an expected utility interpretation.

define consequences'. This is also the reason why it is *not* assumed in these papers that preferences among consumption vectors are independent of the state that obtains. It is thus natural to think about consequences as being elements of the Cartesian product of the state space and the commodity space.[1]

These papers rely upon the assumption of a simple ordering among acts. Typically, assumptions of continuity and convexity are made about this ordering. As was explained in section III, continuity of preferences among acts with values in a Euclidian space is a rather different assumption from the monotone continuity axiom of the theory of subjective probability, and convexity assumptions have no place in the general theory.

Under continuity, the simple ordering of acts is representable by a continuous real-valued function, defined up to a *monotonic* transformation. Values of that function correspond to expected utilities of the acts in the general theory. Under the assumption of conditional preference, the simple ordering of acts with finitely many consequences is representable by an *additive* function, that is by a sum, over the states, of continuous real-valued functions of the consumption in those states. (Of course, the additive property is not preserved by non-linear transformations.) Each such function then corresponds to the product of the probability of the state by the utility of the consequences attained in that state. The assumption of conditional preference, which is equally justified in these models as in the general theory, is not introduced explicitly so long as it is not required to establish general results.

A discussion of the convexity assumption, and of its relation to risk aversion when points in the commodity space define consequences, is given by Arrow in section IV of [3].

Delbaen's chapter on stochastic preferences [6] deserves a special mention. At first sight, it might appear that stochastic preferences among the objects of choice are the very negation of consistent preferences, i.e. of a simple ordering of the objects of choice. Earlier work on this subject (by Georgescu–Roegen [13] or Luce [20] for instance) seemed to proceed in that spirit. But the same remark does not apply to the approach introduced by Hildenbrand [19] and followed by Delbaen. Indeed, the work of these authors seems better described in terms of consequences belonging to the Cartesian product of a state-space and a commodity-space – a formal structure already discussed above. The new element seems to be that the relevant state-space is specific to each consumer, so that states are implicitly defined by uncertainty about consumer tastes. Given the state, commodity vectors are ordered consistently.

[1] That is also the approach followed in [7].

REFERENCES

[1] K. J. Arrow, *Social Choice and Individual Values* (New York: Wiley, 1951).

[2] K. J. Arrow, 'Alternative Approaches to the Theory of Choice in Risk-Taking Situations', *Econometrica*, vol. XIX (1951), pp. 404–37.

[3] K. J. Arrow, 'Le rôle des valeurs boursières pour la répartition la meilleure des risques', pp. 41–7 in [11], translated as 'The Role of Securities in the Optimal Allocation of Risk-Bearing', *Review of Economic Studies*, vol. XXXI (1964), pp. 91–6.

[4] K. J. Arrow, 'Exposition of the Theory of Choice under Uncertainty', pp. 44–89 in *Essays in the Theory of Risk-Bearing*, by K. J. Arrow (Amsterdam: North-Holland, 1970).

[5] G. Debreu, *Theory of Value* (New York: Wiley, 1959).

[6] F. Delbaen, 'Stochastic Preferences and General Equilibrium Theory', chapter 7 *infra*.

[7] J. H. Drèze, 'Fondements logiques de la probabilité subjective et de l'utilité', in *La Décision* (Paris: CRNS, 1961), pp. 73–87.

[8] J. H. Drèze, 'Market Allocation under Uncertainty', *European Economic Review*, vol. II (1971), pp. 133–65.

[9] J. H. Drèze, 'Econometrics and Decision Theory', *Econometrica*, vol. XL (1972), pp. 1–17.

[10] J. H. Drèze, 'Investment under Private Ownership: Optimality, Equilibrium and Stability', chapter 9 *infra*.

[11] *Econométrie*, Colloque International XL (Paris: CRNS, 1953).

[12] M. Friedman, and L. J. Savage, 'The Utility Analysis of Choices Involving Risk', *Journal of Political Economy*, vol. LVI (1948), pp. 279–304.

[13] N. Georgescu-Roegen, 'Threshold in Choice and the Theory of Demand', *Econometrica*, vol. XXVI (1958), pp. 157–68.

[14] L. Gevers, 'Competitive Equilibrium of the Stock Exchange and Pareto Efficiency', chapter 10 *infra*.

[15] R. Guesnerie, and T. de Montbrial, 'Allocation under Uncertainty: a survey', chapter 4 *infra*.

[16] R. Guesnerie, and J. Y. Jaffray, 'Optimality of Equilibrium of Plans, Prices and Price Expectations', chapter 5 *infra*.

[17] J. Harsanyi, 'Cardinal Welfare, Individualistic Ethics and Interpersonal Comparisons of Utility', *Journal of Political Economy*, vol. LXIII (1955), pp. 309–21.

[18] J. R. Hicks, 'The Theory of Uncertainty and Profit', *Economica*, vol. XI (1931), pp. 170–89.

[19] W. Hildenbrand, 'Random Preferences and Equilibrium Analysis', *Journal of Economic Theory*, vol. III (1971), pp. 414–29.

[20] R. D. Luce, *Individual Choice Behavior* (New York: Wiley, 1959).

[21] A. Madansky, 'Externally Bayesian Groups', Memorandum RM–4141–PR, The Rand Corporation, November 1964.

[22] M. Markowitz, 'The Utility of Wealth', *Journal of Political Economy*, vol. LX (1952), pp. 151–8.

[23] J. Marschak, 'Money and the Theory of Assets', *Econometrica*, vol. VI (1938), pp. 311–25.

[24] J. Marschak, 'Rational Behaviour, Uncertain Prospects, and Measurable Utility', *Econometrica*, vol. XVIII (1950), pp. 111–41.

[25] J. von Neumann, and O. Morgenstern, *Theory of Games and Economic Behavior* (Princeton: Princeton University Press, 1953).

[26] J. Pratt, H. Raiffa and R. Schlaifer, 'The Foundations of Decision under

Uncertainty: An Elementary Exposition', *Journal of the American Statistical Association*, vol. LIX (1964), pp. 353–75.

[27] H. Raiffa, 'Assessments of Probabilities', mimeographed, 1969.

[28] F. P. Ramsey, 'Truth and Probability', in *The Foundations of Mathematics and Other Logical Essays* (London: Routledge and Kegan Paul, 1931), pp. 156–98.

[29] L. J. Savage, *The Foundations of Statistics* (New York: Wiley, 1954).

[30] L. J. Savage, 'The Theory of Statistical Decision', *Journal of the American Statistical Association*, vol. XLVI (1951), pp. 55–67.

[31] L. J. Savage, 'Une axiomatisation du comportement raisonnable face à l'incertitude', pp. 29–34 in [13].

[32] D. Schmeidler, 'Competitive Equilibria in Markets with a Continuum of Traders and Incomplete Preferences', *Econometrica*, vol. XXXVII (1969), pp. 578–85.

[33] G. L. S. Shackle, *Expectation in Economics* (Cambridge: Cambridge University Press, 1952).

[34] G. Tintner, 'The Theory of Choice under Subjective Risk and Uncertainty', *Econometrica*, vol. IX (1941), pp. 298–304.

[35] A. Wald, *Statistical Decision Functions* (New York: Wiley, 1950). (2nd ed., Bronx, N.Y., Chelsea, Publ. Co., 1971.)

[36] R. Wilson, 'On the Theory of Syndicates', *Econometrica*, vol. XXXVI (1968), pp. 119–32.

4
J. W. Pratt, Risk aversion in the small and in the large, *Econometrica* 32 (1964), 122–136

In conventional consumer theory, we divide an individual's response to a price change into income and substitution terms. By and large we feel we have a fairly good idea about the empirical nature of income effects for different goods. In addition we have some theorems on the substitution effects (properties of the Slutsky matrix) that hold for well-behaved choice problems. Together with these general properties, a number of specific functional forms for utility functions (or some dual function) have been explored to derive the implications for demand behavior as a consequence of the particular restrictions of functional form. In particular, separability has received considerable attention. When we turn to uncertainty theory, we can parallel these efforts, as well as examining new questions that were not available without uncertainty. One example of a new question is the response of security purchases to the change in riskiness of the security. This question will be explored below. Closer to the traditional framework, one can construct an analog to the Slutsky equation (see, e.g., Fischer, 1972).

In a sense to be made clearer in Chapter 5, we can take the expected utility hypothesis to represent a particular restriction on the functional form of the utility function. It is natural to ask what demand properties can be deduced as a consequence of this restriction. In addition, comparative static statements can be expressed in terms of simple properties of the utility function and of the probability distribution. In this paper, a number of different demand properties are all related to indices of risk aversion. Thus, behavior in different areas can all be related to the same parameter (and thus to each other). In addition this approach can be used to make statements about systematic differences in behavior across individuals. In reprinting this paper, the author has corrected some typographical errors and has made the following Addendum to foonote 2:

In retrospect, I wish footnote 2 had made clear that Robert Schlaifer's contribution included formulating originally the concept of decreasing risk aversion in terms of the probability premium and proving that it implies $r(x)$ is decreasing, i.e., that (c′) implies (a′) in Theorem 2.

For some additional measures of risk aversion and their uses, see Ross (1981) and Machina (1982).

References

S. Fischer, Assets, contingent commodities, and the Slutsky equations, *Econometrica* **40** (1972), 371–386.

M. Machina, A stronger characterization of declining risk aversion, *Econometrica* **50** (1982), 1069–1079.

S. Ross, Some stronger measures of risk-aversion in the small and in the large, *Econometrica* **49** (1981), 621–638.

Econometrica, Vol. 32, No. 1–2 (January–April, 1964)

RISK AVERSION IN THE SMALL AND IN THE LARGE[1]

BY JOHN W. PRATT

This paper concerns utility functions for money. A measure of risk aversion in the small, the risk premium or insurance premium for an arbitrary risk, and a natural concept of decreasing risk aversion are discussed and related to one another. Risks are also considered as a proportion of total assets.

1. SUMMARY AND INTRODUCTION

LET $u(x)$ BE a utility function for money. The function $r(x) = -u''(x)/u'(x)$ will be interpreted in various ways as a measure of local risk aversion (risk aversion in the small); neither $u''(x)$ nor the curvature of the graph of u is an appropriate measure. No simple measure of risk aversion in the large will be introduced. Global risks will, however, be considered, and it will be shown that one decision maker has greater local risk aversion $r(x)$ than another at all x if and only if he is globally more risk-averse in the sense that, for every risk, his cash equivalent (the amount for which he would exchange the risk) is smaller than for the other decision maker. Equivalently, his risk premium (expected monetary value minus cash equivalent) is always larger, and he would be willing to pay more for insurance in any situation. From this it will be shown that a decision maker's local risk aversion $r(x)$ is a decreasing function of x if and only if, for every risk, his cash equivalent is larger the larger his assets, and his risk premium and what he would be willing to pay for insurance are smaller. This condition, which many decision makers would subscribe to, involves the third derivative of u, as $r' \leqq 0$ is equivalent to $u'''u' \geqq u''^2$. It is not satisfied by quadratic utilities in any region. All this means that some natural ways of thinking casually about utility functions may be misleading. Except for one family, convenient utility functions for which $r(x)$ is decreasing are not so very easy to find. Help in this regard is given by some theorems showing that certain combinations of utility functions, in particular linear combinations with positive weights, have decreasing $r(x)$ if all the functions in the combination have decreasing $r(x)$.

The related function $r^*(x) = xr(x)$ will be interpreted as a local measure of aversion to risks measured as a proportion of assets, and monotonicity of $r^*(x)$ will be proved to be equivalent to monotonicity of every risk's cash equivalent measured as a proportion of assets, and similarly for the risk premium and insurance.

These results have both descriptive and normative implications. Utility functions for which $r(x)$ is decreasing are logical candidates to use when trying to describe the behavior of people who, one feels, might generally pay less for insurance against

[1] This research was supported by the National Science Foundation (grant NSF-G24035).

a given risk the greater their assets. And consideration of the yield and riskiness per investment dollar of investors' portfolios may suggest, at least in some contexts, description by utility functions for which $r^*(x)$ is first decreasing and then increasing.

Normatively, it seems likely that many decision makers would feel they ought to pay less for insurance against a given risk the greater their assets. Such a decision maker will want to choose a utility function for which $r(x)$ is decreasing, adding this condition to the others he must already consider (consistency and probably concavity) in forging a satisfactory utility from more or less malleable preliminary preferences. He may wish to add a further condition on $r^*(x)$.

We do not assume or assert that utility may not change with time. Strictly speaking, we are concerned with utility at a specified time (when a decision must be made) for money at a (possibly later) specified time. Of course, our results pertain also to behavior at different times if utility does not change with time. For instance, a decision maker whose utility for total assets is unchanging and whose assets are increasing would be willing to pay less and less for insurance against a given risk as time progresses if his $r(x)$ is a decreasing function of x. Notice that his actual expenditure for insurance might nevertheless increase if his risks are increasing along with his assets.

The risk premium, cash equivalent, and insurance premium are defined and related to one another in Section 2. The local risk aversion function $r(x)$ is introduced and interpreted in Sections 3 and 4. In Section 5, inequalities concerning global risks are obtained from inequalities between local risk aversion functions. Section 6 deals with constant risk aversion, and Section 7 demonstrates the equivalence of local and global definitions of decreasing (and increasing) risk aversion. Section 8 shows that certain operations preserve the property of decreasing risk aversion. Some examples are given in Section 9. Aversion to proportional risk is discussed in Sections 10 to 12. Section 13 concerns some related work of Kenneth J. Arrow.[2]

Throughout this paper, the utility $u(x)$ is regarded as a function of total assets rather than of changes which may result from a certain decision, so that $x=0$ is equivalent to ruin, or perhaps to loss of all readily disposable assets. (This is essential only in connection with proportional risk aversion.) The symbol $\sim$ indicates that two functions are equivalent as utilities, that is, $u_1(x) \sim u_2(x)$ means there exist constants a and b (with $b>0$) such that $u_1(x)=a+bu_2(x)$ for all x. The utility functions discussed may, but need not, be bounded. It is assumed, however, that they are sufficiently regular to justify the proofs; generally it is enough that they be twice continuously differentiable with positive first derivative, which is already re-

[2] The importance of the function $r(x)$ was discovered independently by Kenneth J. Arrow and by Robert Schlaifer, in different contexts. The work presented here was, unfortunately, essentially completed before I learned of Arrow's related work. It is, however, a pleasure to acknowledge Schlaifer's stimulation and participation throughout, as well as that of John Bishop at certain points.

quired for $r(x)$ to be defined and continuous. A variable with a tilde over it, such as $\tilde{z}$, is a random variable. The risks $\tilde{z}$ considered may, but need not, have "objective" probability distributions. In formal statements, $\tilde{z}$ refers only to risks which are not degenerate, that is, not constant with probability one, and interval refers only to an interval with more than one point. Also, increasing and decreasing mean nondecreasing and nonincreasing respectively; if we mean strictly increasing or decreasing we will say so.

2. THE RISK PREMIUM

Consider a decision maker with assets x and utility function u. We shall be interested in the *risk premium* π such that he would be indifferent between receiving a risk $\tilde{z}$ and receiving the non-random amount $E(\tilde{z})-\pi$, that is, π less than the actuarial value $E(\tilde{z})$. If u is concave, then $\pi \geqq 0$, but we don't require this. The risk premium depends on x and on the distribution of $\tilde{z}$, and will be denoted $\pi(x,\tilde{z})$. (It is not, as this notation might suggest, a function $\pi(x,z)$ evaluated at a randomly selected value of z, which would be random.) By the properties of utility,

$$u(x+E(\tilde{z})-\pi(x,\tilde{z}))=E\{u(x+\tilde{z})\}\,. \tag{1}$$

We shall consider only situations where $E\{u(x+\tilde{z})\}$ exists and is finite. Then $\pi(x,\tilde{z})$ exists and is uniquely defined by (1), since $u(x+E(\tilde{z})-\pi)$ is a strictly decreasing, continuous function of π ranging over all possible values of u. It follows immediately from (1) that, for any constant μ,

$$\pi(x,\tilde{z})=\pi(x+\mu,\,\tilde{z}-\mu)\,. \tag{2}$$

By choosing $\mu=E(\tilde{z})$ (assuming it exists and is finite), we may thus reduce consideration to a risk $\tilde{z}-\mu$ which is actuarially neutral, that is, $E(\tilde{z}-\mu)=0$.

Since the decision maker is indifferent between receiving the risk $\tilde{z}$ and receiving for sure the amount $\pi_a(x,\tilde{z})=E(\tilde{z})-\pi(x,\tilde{z})$, this amount is sometimes called the cash equivalent or value of $\tilde{z}$. It is also the asking price for $\tilde{z}$, the smallest amount for which the decision maker would willingly sell $\tilde{z}$ if he had it. It is given by

$$u(x+\pi_a(x,\tilde{z}))=E\{u(x+\tilde{z})\}\,. \tag{3a}$$

It is to be distinguished from the bid price $\pi_b(x,\tilde{z})$, the largest amount the decision maker would willingly pay to obtain $\tilde{z}$, which is given by

$$u(x)=E\{u(x+\tilde{z}-\pi_b(x,\tilde{z}))\}\,. \tag{3b}$$

For an unfavorable risk $\tilde{z}$, it is natural to consider the insurance premium $\pi_I(x,\tilde{z})$ such that the decision maker is indifferent between facing the risk $\tilde{z}$ and paying the non-random amount $\pi_I(x,\tilde{z})$. Since paying π_I is equivalent to receiving $-\pi_I$, we have

$$\pi_I(x,\tilde{z})=-\pi_a(x,\tilde{z})=\pi(x,\tilde{z})-E(\tilde{z})\,. \tag{3c}$$

If $\tilde{z}$ is actuarially neutral, the risk premium and insurance premium coincide.

The results of this paper will be stated in terms of the risk premium π, but could equally easily and meaningfully be stated in terms of the cash equivalent or insurance premium.

3. LOCAL RISK AVERSION

To measure a decision maker's local aversion to risk, it is natural to consider his risk premium for a small, actuarially neutral risk $\tilde{z}$. We therefore consider $\pi(x,\tilde{z})$ for a risk $\tilde{z}$ with $E(\tilde{z})=0$ and small variance σ_z^2; that is, we consider the behavior of $\pi(x,\tilde{z})$ as $\sigma_z^2 \to 0$. We assume the third absolute central moment of $\tilde{z}$ is of smaller order than σ_z^2. (Ordinarily it is of order σ_z^3.) Expanding u around x on both sides of (1), we obtain under suitable regularity conditions[3]

$$u(x-\pi)=u(x)-\pi u'(x)+O(\pi^2)\,, \tag{4a}$$

$$\begin{aligned} E\{u(x+\tilde{z})\} &= E\{u(x)+\tilde{z}u'(x)+\tfrac{1}{2}\tilde{z}^2u''(x)+O(\tilde{z}^3)\} \\ &= u(x)+\tfrac{1}{2}\sigma_z^2 u''(x)+o(\sigma_z^2)\,. \end{aligned} \tag{4b}$$

Setting these expressions equal, as required by (1), then gives

$$\pi(x,\tilde{z})=\tfrac{1}{2}\sigma_z^2\, r(x)+o(\sigma_z^2)\,, \tag{5}$$

where

$$r(x) = -\frac{u''(x)}{u'(x)} = -\frac{d}{dx}\log u'(x)\,. \tag{6}$$

Thus the decision maker's risk premium for a small, actuarially neutral risk $\tilde{z}$ is approximately $r(x)$ times half the variance of $\tilde{z}$; that is, $r(x)$ is twice the risk premium per unit of variance for infinitesimal risks. A sufficient regularity condition for (5) is that u have a third derivative which is continuous and bounded over the range of all $\tilde{z}$ under discussion. The theorems to follow will not actually depend on (5), however.

If $\tilde{z}$ is not actuarially neutral, we have by (2), with $\mu=E(\tilde{z})$, and (5):

$$\pi(x,\tilde{z})=\tfrac{1}{2}\sigma_z^2\, r(x+E(\tilde{z}))+o(\sigma_z^2)\,. \tag{7}$$

Thus the risk premium for a risk $\tilde{z}$ with arbitrary mean $E(\tilde{z})$ but small variance is approximately $r(x+E(\tilde{z}))$ times half the variance of $\tilde{z}$. It follows also that the risk premium will just equal and hence offset the actuarial value $E(\tilde{z})$ of a small risk $(\tilde{z})$, that is, the decision maker will be indifferent between having $\tilde{z}$ and not having it when the actuarial value is approximately r(x) times half the variance of $\tilde{z}$. Thus $r(x)$

[3] In expansions, $O(\ )$ means "terms of order at most" and $o(\ )$ means "terms of smaller order than."

may also be interpreted as twice the actuarial value the decision maker requires per unit of variance for infinitesimal risks.

Notice that it is the variance, not the standard deviation, that enters these formulas. To first order any (differentiable) utility is linear in small gambles. In this sense, these are second order formulas.

Still another interpretation of $r(x)$ arises in the special case $\tilde{z}=\pm h$, that is, where the risk is to gain or lose a fixed amount $h>0$. Such a risk is actuarially neutral if $+h$ and $-h$ are equally probable, so $P(\tilde{z}=h)-P(\tilde{z}=-h)$ measures the *probability premium* of $\tilde{z}$. Let $p(x,h)$ be the probability premium such that the decision maker is indifferent between the status quo and a risk $\tilde{z}=\pm h$ with

$$(8) \qquad P(\tilde{z}=h)-P(\tilde{z}=-h)=p(x,h)\,.$$

Then $P(\tilde{z}=h)=\frac{1}{2}[1+p(x,h)]$, $P(\tilde{z}=-h)=\frac{1}{2}[1-p(x,h)]$, and $p(x,h)$ is defined by

$$(9) \qquad u(x)=E\{u(x+\tilde{z})\}=\tfrac{1}{2}[1+p(x,h)]u(x+h)+\tfrac{1}{2}[1-p(x,h)]u(x-h)\,.$$

When u is expanded around x as before, (9) becomes

$$(10) \qquad u(x)=u(x)+hp(x,h)u'(x)+\tfrac{1}{2}h^2u''(x)+O(h^3)\,.$$

Solving for $p(x,h)$, we find

$$(11) \qquad p(x,h)=\tfrac{1}{2}hr(x)+O(h^2)\,.$$

Thus for small h the decision maker is indifferent between the status quo and a risk of $\pm h$ with a probability premium of $r(x)$ times $\frac{1}{2}h$; that is, $r(x)$ is twice the probability premium he requires per unit risked for small risks.

In these ways we may interpret $r(x)$ as a measure of the *local risk aversion* or *local propensity to insure* at the point x under the utility function u; $-r(x)$ would measure locally liking for risk or propensity to gamble. Notice that we have not introduced any measure of risk aversion in the large. Aversion to ordinary (as opposed to infinitesimal) risks might be considered measured by $\pi(x,\tilde{z})$, but π is a much more complicated function than r. Despite the absence of any simple measure of risk aversion in the large, we shall see that comparisons of aversion to risk can be made simply in the large as well as in the small.

By (6), integrating $-r(x)$ gives $\log u'(x)+c$; exponentiating and integrating again then gives $e^c u(x)+d$. The constants of integration are immaterial because $e^c u(x)+d\sim u(x)$. (Note $e^c>0$.) Thus we may write

$$(12) \qquad u\sim\int e^{-\int r}\,,$$

and we observe that the local risk aversion function r associated with any utility function u contains all essential information about u while eliminating everything arbitrary about u. However, decisions about ordinary (as opposed to "small") risks are determined by r only through u as given by (12), so it is not convenient entirely to eliminate u from consideration in favor of r.

4. CONCAVITY

The aversion to risk implied by a utility function u seems to be a form of concavity, and one might set out to measure concavity as representing aversion to risk. It is clear from the foregoing that for this purpose $r(x)=-u''(x)/u'(x)$ can be considered a measure of the concavity of u at the point x. A case might perhaps be made for using instead some one-to-one function of $r(x)$, but it should be noted that $u''(x)$ or $-u''(x)$ is not in itself a meaningful measure of concavity in utility theory, nor is the curvature (reciprocal of the signed radius of the tangent circle) $u''(x)(1+[u'(x)]^2)^{-3/2}$. Multiplying u by a positive constant, for example, does not alter behavior but does alter u'' and the curvature.

A more striking and instructive example is provided by the function $u(x)=-e^{-x}$. As x increases, this function approaches the asymptote $u=0$ and looks graphically less and less concave and more and more like a horizontal straight line, in accordance with the fact that $u'(x)=e^{-x}$ and $u''(x)=-e^{-x}$ both approach 0. As a utility function, however, it does not change at all with the level of assets x, that is, the behavior implied by $u(x)$ is the same for all x, since $u(k+x)=-e^{-k-x}\sim u(x)$. In particular, the risk premium $\pi(x,\tilde{z})$ for any risk $\tilde{z}$ and the probability premium $p(x,h)$ for any h remain absolutely constant as x varies. Thus, regardless of the appearance of its graph, $u(x)=-e^{-x}$ is just as far from implying linear behavior at $x=\infty$ as at $x=0$ or $x=-\infty$. All this is duly reflected in $r(x)$, which is constant: $r(x)=-u''(x)/u'(x)=1$ for all x.

One feature of $u''(x)$ does have a meaning, namely its sign, which equals that of $-r(x)$. A negative (positive) sign at x implies unwillingness (willingness) to accept small, actuarially neutral risks with assets x. Furthermore, a negative (positive) sign for all x implies strict concavity (convexity) and hence unwillingness (willingness) to accept any actuarially neutral risk with any assets. The absolute magnitude of $u''(x)$ does not in itself have any meaning in utility theory, however.

5. COMPARATIVE RISK AVERSION

Let u_1 and u_2 be utility functions with local risk aversion functions r_1 and r_2, respectively. If, at a point x, $r_1(x)>r_2(x)$, then u_1 is locally more risk-averse than u_2 at the point x; that is, the corresponding risk premiums satisfy $\pi_1(x,\tilde{z})>\pi_2(x,\tilde{z})$ for sufficiently small risks $\tilde{z}$, and the corresponding probability premiums satisfy $p_1(x,h)>p_2(x,h)$ for sufficiently small $h>0$. The main point of the theorem we are about to prove is that the corresponding global properties also hold. For instance, if $r_1(x)>r_2(x)$ for all x, that is, u_1 has greater local risk aversion than u_2 everywhere, then $\pi_1(x,\tilde{z})>\pi_2(x,\tilde{z})$ for every risk $\tilde{z}$, so that u_1 is also globally more risk-averse in a natural sense.

It is to be understood in this section that the probability distribution of $\tilde{z}$, which determines $\pi_1(x,\tilde{z})$ and $\pi_2(x,\tilde{z})$, is the same in each. We are comparing the risk premiums for the same probability distribution of risk but for two different utilities. This does not mean that when Theorem 1 is applied to two decision makers, they must have the same personal probability distributions, but only that the notation is imprecise. The theorem could be stated in terms of $\pi_1(x,\tilde{z}_1)$ and $\pi_2(x,\tilde{z}_2)$ where the distribution assigned to $\tilde{z}_1$ by the first decision maker is the same as that assigned to $\tilde{z}_2$ by the second decision maker. This would be less misleading, but also less convenient and less suggestive, especially for later use. More precise notation would be, for instance, $\pi_1(x,F)$ and $\pi_2(x,F)$, where F is a cumulative distribution function.

THEOREM 1: *Let $r_i(x)$, $\pi_i(x,\tilde{z})$, and $p_i(x)$ be the local risk aversion, risk premium, and probability premium corresponding to the utility function u_i, $i=1,2$. Then the following conditions are equivalent, in either the strong form (indicated in brackets), or the weak form (with the bracketed material omitted).*

(a) $r_1(x) \geqq r_2(x)$ *for all* x [*and* $>$ *for at least one* x *in every interval*].

(b) $\pi_1(x,\tilde{z}) \geqq [>] \pi_2(x,\tilde{z})$ *for all* x *and* $\tilde{z}$.

(c) $p_1(x,h) \geqq [>] p_2(x,h)$ *for all* x *and all* $h>0$.

(d) $u_1(u_2^{-1}(t))$ *is a* [*strictly*] *concave function of* t.

(e) $\dfrac{u_1(y)-u_1(x)}{u_1(w)-u_1(v)} \leqq [<] \dfrac{u_2(y)-u_2(x)}{u_2(w)-u_2(v)}$ *for all* v, w, x, y *with* $v<w\leqq x<y$.

The same equivalences hold if attention is restricted throughout to an interval, that is, if the requirement is added that $x, x+\tilde{z}, x+h, x-h, u_2^{-1}(t), v, w$, and y, all lie in a specified interval.

PROOF: We shall prove things in an order indicating somewhat how one might discover that (a) implies (b) and (c).

To show that (b) follows from (d), solve (1) to obtain

$$\pi_i(x,\tilde{z}) = x + E(\tilde{z}) - u_i^{-1}(E\{u_i(x+\tilde{z})\}) . \tag{13}$$

Then

$$\begin{aligned} \pi_1(x,\tilde{z}) - \pi_2(x,\tilde{z}) &= u_2^{-1}(E\{u_2(x+\tilde{z})\}) - u_1^{-1}(E\{u_1(x+\tilde{z})\}) \\ &= u_2^{-1}(E\{\tilde{t}\}) - u_1^{-1}(E\{u_1(u_2^{-1}(\tilde{t}))\}) , \end{aligned} \tag{14}$$

where $\tilde{t} = u_2(x+\tilde{z})$. If $u_1(u_2^{-1}(t))$ is [strictly] concave, then (by Jensen's inequality)

$$E\{u_1(u_2^{-1}(\tilde{t}))\} \leqq [<]\, u_1(u_2^{-1}(E\{\tilde{t}\})) . \tag{15}$$

Substituting (15) in (14), we obtain (b).

To show that (a) implies (d), note that

$$(16)\qquad \frac{d}{dt}u_1(u_2^{-1}(t)) = \frac{u_1'(u_2^{-1}(t))}{u_2'(u_2^{-1}(t))},$$

which is [strictly] decreasing if (and only if) $\log u_1'(x)/u_2'(x)$ is. The latter follows from (a) and

$$(17)\qquad \frac{d}{dx}\log\frac{u_1'(x)}{u_2'(x)} = r_2(x)-r_1(x)\,.$$

That (c) is implied by (e) follows immediately upon writing (9) in the form

$$(18)\qquad \frac{1-p_i(x,h)}{1+p_i(x,h)} = \frac{u_i(x+h)-u_i(x)}{u_i(x)-u_i(x-h)}\,.$$

To show that (a) implies (e), integrate (a) from w to x, obtaining

$$(19)\qquad -\log\frac{u_1'(x)}{u_1'(w)} \geqq [>] -\log\frac{u_2'(x)}{u_2'(w)} \quad \text{for}\quad w<x\,,$$

which is equivalent to

$$(20)\qquad \frac{u_1'(x)}{u_1'(w)} \leqq [<] \frac{u_2'(x)}{u_2'(w)} \quad \text{for}\quad w<x\,.$$

This implies

$$(21)\qquad \frac{u_1(y)-u_1(x)}{u_1'(w)} \leqq [<] \frac{u_2(y)-u_2(x)}{u_2'(w)} \quad \text{for}\quad w\leqq x<y\,,$$

as may be seen by applying the Mean Value Theorem of differential calculus to the difference of the two sides of (21) regarded as a function of y. Condition (e) follows from (21) upon application of the Mean Value Theorem to the difference of the reciprocals of the two sides of (e) regarded as a function of w.

We have now proved that (a) implies (d) implies (b), and (a) implies (e) implies (c). The equivalence of (a)–(e) will follow if we can prove that (b) implies (a), and (c) implies (a), or equivalently that not (a) implies not (b) and not (c). But this follows from what has already been proved, for if the weak [strong] form of (a) does not hold, then the strong [weak] form of (a) holds on some interval with u_1 and u_2 interchanged. Then the strong [weak] forms of (b) and (c) also hold on this interval with u_1 and u_2 interchanged, so the weak [strong] forms of (b) and (c) do not hold. This completes the proof.

We observe that (e) is equivalent to (20), (21), and

$$(22)\qquad \frac{u_1(w)-u_1(v)}{u_1'(x)} \geqq [>] \frac{u_2(w)-u_2(v)}{u_2'(x)} \quad \text{for}\quad v<w\leqq x\,.$$

6. CONSTANT RISK AVERSION

If the local risk aversion function is constant, say $r(x)=c$, then by (12):

(23) $u(x)\sim x$ if $r(x)=0$;

(24) $u(x)\sim -e^{-cx}$ if $r(x)=c>0$;

(25) $u(x)\sim e^{-cx}$ if $r(x)=c<0$.

These utilities are, respectively, linear, strictly concave, and strictly convex.

If the risk aversion is constant locally, then it is also constant globally, that is, a change in assets makes no change in preference among risks. In fact, for any k, $u(k+x)\sim u(x)$ in each of the cases above, as is easily verified. Therefore it makes sense to speak of "constant risk aversion" without the qualification "local" or "global."

Similar remarks apply to constant risk aversion on an interval, except that global consideration must be restricted to assets x and risks $\tilde{z}$ such that $x+\tilde{z}$ is certain to stay within the interval.

7. INCREASING AND DECREASING RISK AVERSION

Consider a decision maker who (i) attaches a positive risk premium to any risk, but (ii) attaches a smaller risk premium to any given risk the greater his assets x. Formally this means

(i) $\pi(x,\tilde{z})>0$ for all x and $\tilde{z}$;
(ii) $\pi(x,\tilde{z})$ is a strictly decreasing function of x for all $\tilde{z}$.

Restricting $\tilde{z}$ to be actuarially neutral would not affect (i) or (ii), by (2) with $\mu=E(\tilde{z})$.

We shall call a utility function (or a decision maker possessing it) *risk-averse* if the weak form of (i) holds, that is, if $\pi(x,\tilde{z})\geqq 0$ for all x and $\tilde{z}$; it is well known that this is equivalent to concavity of u, and hence to $u''\leqq 0$ and to $r\geqq 0$. A utility function is *strictly risk-averse* if (i) holds as stated; this is equivalent to strict concavity of u and hence to the existence in every interval of at least one point where $u''<0, r>0$.

We turn now to (ii). Notice that it amounts to a definition of strictly decreasing risk aversion in a global (as opposed to local) sense. On would hope that decreasing global risk aversion would be equivalent to decreasing local risk aversion $r(x)$. The following theorem asserts that this is indeed so. Therefore it makes sense to speak of "decreasing risk aversion" without the qualification "local" or "global." What is nontrivial is that $r(x)$ decreasing implies $\pi(x,\tilde{z})$ decreasing, inasmuch as $r(x)$ pertains directly only to infinitesimal gambles. Similar considerations apply to the probability premium $p(x,h)$.

THEOREM 2: *The following conditions are equivalent.*
(a′) *The local risk aversion function* $r(x)$ *is* [*strictly*] *decreasing.*

(b′) *The risk premium* $\pi(x,\tilde{z})$ *is a [strictly] decreasing function of* x *for all* $\tilde{z}$.

(c′) *The probability premium* $p(x,h)$ *is a [strictly] decreasing function of* x *for all* $h>0$.

The same equivalences hold if "increasing" is substituted for "decreasing" throughout and/or attention is restricted throughout to an interval, that is, the requirement is added that x, $x+\tilde{z}$, $x+h$, *and* $x-h$ *all lie in a specified interval.*

PROOF: This theorem follows upon application of Theorem 1 to $u_1(x)=u(x)$ and $u_2(x)=u(x+k)$ for arbitrary x and k.

It is easily verified that (a′) and hence also (b′) and (c′) are equivalent to

(d′) $u'(u^{-1}(t))$ is a [strictly] convex function of t.

This corresponds to (d) of Theorem 1. Corresponding to (e) of Theorem 1 and (20)–(22) is

(e′) $u'(x)u'''(x) \geqq (u''(x))^2$ [and $>$ for at least one x in every interval].

The equivalence of this to (a′)–(c′) follows from the fact that the sign of $r'(x)$ is the same as that of $(u''(x))^2 - u'(x)u'''(x)$. Theorem 2 can be and originally was proved by way of (d′) and (e′), essentially as Theorem 1 is proved in the present paper.

8. OPERATIONS WHICH PRESERVE DECREASING RISK AVERSION

We have just seen that a utility function evinces decreasing risk aversion in a global sense if an only if its local risk aversion function $r(x)$ is decreasing. Such a utility function seems of interest mainly if it is also risk-averse (concave, $r \geqq 0$). Accordingly, we shall now formally define a utility function to be [*strictly*] *decreasingly risk-averse* if its local risk aversion function r is [strictly] decreasing and nonnegative. Then by Theorem 2, conditions (i) and (ii) of Section 7 are equivalent to the utility's being strictly decreasingly risk-averse.

In this section we shall show that certain operations yield decreasingly risk-averse utility functions if applied to such functions. This facilitates proving that functions are decreasingly risk-averse and finding functions which have this property and also have reasonably simple formulas. In the proofs, $r(x)$, $r_1(x)$, etc., are the local risk aversion functions belonging to $u(x)$, $u_1(x)$, etc.

THEOREM 3: *Suppose* $a>0$: $u_1(x)=u(ax+b)$ *is [strictly] decreasingly risk-averse for* $x_0 \leqq x \leqq x_1$ *if and only if* $u(x)$ *is [strictly] decreasingly risk-averse for* $ax_0+b \leqq x \leqq ax_1+b$.

PROOF: This follows directly from the easily verified formula:

$$r_1(x) = ar(ax+b)\,. \tag{26}$$

THEOREM 4: *If* $u_1(x)$ *is decreasingly risk-averse for* $x_0 \leqq x \leqq x_1$, *and* $u_2(x)$ *is decreasingly risk-averse for* $u_1(x_0) \leqq x \leqq u_1(x_1)$, *then* $u(x)=u_2(u_1(x))$ *is decreasingly* *risk-averse for $x_0 \leqq x \leqq x_1$, and strictly so unless one of u_1 and u_2 is linear from some x on and the other has constant risk aversion in some interval.*

PROOF: We have $\log u'(x) = \log u_2'(u_1'(x)) + \log u_1'(x)$, and therefore

$$r(x) = r_2(u_1(x))u_1'(x) + r_1(x) . \tag{27}$$

The functions $r_2(u_1(x))$, $u_1'(x)$, and $r_1(x)$ are $\geqq 0$ and decreasing, and therefore so is $r(x)$. Furthermore, $u_1'(x)$ is strictly decreasing as long as $r_1(x) > 0$, so $r(x)$ is strictly decreasing as long as $r_1(x)$ and $r_2(u_1(x))$ are both >0. If one of them is 0 for some x, then it is 0 for all larger x, but if the other is strictly decreasing, then so is r.

THEOREM 5: *If $u_1, \ldots, u_n$ are decreasingly risk-averse on an interval $[x_0, x_1]$, and $c_1, \ldots, c_n$ are positive constants, then $u = \Sigma_1^n c_i u_i$ is decreasingly risk-averse on $[x_0, x_1]$, and strictly so except on subintervals (if any) where all u_i have equal and constant risk aversion.*

PROOF: The general statement follows from the case $u = u_1 + u_2$. For this case

$$r = -\frac{u_1'' + u_2''}{u_1' + u_2'} = \frac{u_1'}{u_1' + u_2'} r_1 + \frac{u_2'}{u_1' + u_2'} r_2 ; \tag{28}$$

$$r' = \frac{u_1'}{u_1' + u_2'} r_1' + \frac{u_2'}{u_1' + u_2'} r_2' + \frac{u_1'' u_2' - u_1' u_2''}{(u_1' + u_2')^2} (r_1 - r_2) \tag{29}$$

$$= \frac{u_1' r_1' + u_2' r_2'}{u_1' + u_2'} - \frac{u_1' u_2'}{(u_1' + u_2')^2} (r_1 - r_2)^2 .$$

We have $u_1' > 0$, $u_2' > 0$, $r_1' \leqq 0$, and $r_2' \leqq 0$. Therefore $r' \leqq 0$, and $r' < 0$ unless $r_1 = r_2$ and $r_1' = r_2' = 0$. The conclusion follows.

9. EXAMPLES

9.1. *Example 1.* The utility $u(x) = -(b-x)^c$ for $x \leqq b$ and $c > 1$ is strictly increasing and strictly concave, but it also has strictly *increasing* risk aversion: $r(x) = (c-1)/(b-x)$. Notice that the most general concave quadratic utility $u(x) = \alpha + \beta x - \gamma x^2$, $\beta > 0$, $\gamma > 0$, is equivalent as a utility to $-(b-x)^c$ with $c = 2$ and $b = \frac{1}{2}\beta/\gamma$. Therefore a quadratic utility cannot be decreasingly risk-averse on any interval whatever. This severely limits the usefulness of quadratic utility, however nice it would be to have expected utility depend only on the mean and variance of the probability distribution. Arguing "in the small" is no help: decreasing risk aversion is a local property as well as a global one.

9.2. *Example 2.* If

$$(30)\qquad u'(x)=(x^a+b)^{-c} \quad \text{with} \quad a>0, c>0\,,$$

then $u(x)$ is strictly decreasingly risk-averse in the region

$$(31)\qquad x>[\max\{0, -b, b(a-1)\}]^{1/a}\,.$$

To prove this, note

$$(32)\qquad r(x)= -\frac{d}{dx}\log u'(x) = \frac{ac}{x+bx^{1-a}}\,,$$

which is $\geqq 0$ and strictly decreasing in the region where the denominator $x+bx^{1-a}$ is $\geqq 0$ and strictly increasing, which is the region (30). (The condition $x\geqq 0$ is included to insure that x^a is defined; for $a\geqq 1$ it follows from the other conditions.)

By Theorem 3, one can obtain a utility function that is strictly decreasingly risk-averse for $x>0$ by substituting $x+d$ for x above, where d is at least the right-hand side of (31). Multiplying x by a positive factor, as in Theorem 3, is equivalent to multiplying b by a positive factor.

Given below are all the strictly decreasingly risk-averse utility functions $u(x)$ on $x>0$ which can be obtained by applying Theorem 3 to (30) with the indicated choices of the parameters a and c:

$$(33)\qquad a=1, 0<c<1:\quad u(x)\sim(x+d)^q \quad \text{with} \quad d\geqq 0, 0<q<1\;;$$

$$(34)\qquad a=1, c=1:\quad u(x)\sim\log(x+d) \quad \text{with} \quad d\geqq 0\;;$$

$$(35)\qquad a=1, c>1:\quad u(x)\sim-(x+d)^{-q} \quad \text{with} \quad d\geqq 0, q>0\;;$$

$$(36)\qquad a=2, c=.5:\quad u(x)\sim\log(x+d+[(x+d)^2+b]) \quad \text{with} \quad d\geqq|b|^{\frac{1}{2}}\;;$$

$$(37)\qquad a=2, c=1:\quad u(x)\sim\arctan(\alpha x+\beta) \text{ or } \log(1-(\alpha x+\beta)^{-1}) \quad \text{with} \quad \alpha>0, \beta\geqq 1\;;$$

$$(38)\qquad a=2, c=1.5:\quad u(x)\sim[1+(\alpha x+\beta)^{-2}]^{-\frac{1}{2}} \text{ or } -[1-(\alpha x+\beta)^{-2}]^{-\frac{1}{2}} \quad \text{with} \quad \alpha>0, \beta\geqq 1\,.$$

9.3. *Example 3.* Applying Theorems 4 and 5 to the utilities of Example 2 and Section 6 gives a very wide class of utilities which are strictly decreasingly risk-averse for $x>0$, such as

$$(39)\qquad u(x)\sim-c_1e^{-cx}-c_2e^{-dx} \quad \text{with} \quad c_1>0, c_2>0, c>0, d>0\,.$$

$$(40)\qquad u(x)\sim\log(d_1+\log(x+d_2)) \quad \text{with} \quad d_1\geqq 0, d_2\geqq 0, d_1+\log d_2\geqq 0\,.$$

10. PROPORTIONAL RISK AVERSION

So far we have been concerned with risks that remained fixed while assets varied. Let us now view everything as a proportion of assets. Specifically, let $\pi^*(x,\tilde{z})$ be the *proportional risk premium* corresponding to a proportional risk $\tilde{z}$; that is, a decision maker with assets x and utility function u would be indifferent between receiving a risk $x\tilde{z}$ and receiving the non-random amount $E(x\tilde{z})-x\pi^*(x,\tilde{z})$. Then $x\pi^*(x,\tilde{z})$ equals the risk premium $\pi(x,x\tilde{z})$, so

$$\pi^*(x,\tilde{z}) = \frac{1}{x}\,\pi(x,x\tilde{z})\;. \tag{41}$$

For a small, actuarially neutral, proportional risk $\tilde{z}$ we have, by (5),

$$\pi^*(x,\tilde{z})=\tfrac{1}{2}\sigma_z^2 r^*(x)+o(\sigma_z^2)\,, \tag{42}$$

where

$$r^*(x)=xr(x)\;. \tag{43}$$

If $\tilde{z}$ is not actuarially neutral, we have, by (7),

$$\pi^*(x,\tilde{z})=\tfrac{1}{2}\sigma_z^2 r^*(x+xE(\tilde{z}))+o(\sigma_z^2)\;. \tag{44}$$

We will call r^* the *local proportional risk aversion* at the point x under the utility function u. Its interpretation by (42) and (44) is like that of r by (5) and (7).

Similarly, we may define the *proportional probability premium* $p^*(x,h)$, corresponding to a risk of gaining or losing a proportional amount h, namely

$$p^*(x,h)=p(x,xh)\;. \tag{45}$$

Then another interpretation of $r^*(x)$ is provided by

$$p^*(x,h)=\tfrac{1}{2}hr^*(x)+O(h^2)\,, \tag{46}$$

which follows from (45) and (11).

11. CONSTANT PROPORTIONAL RISK AVERSION

If the local proportional risk aversion function is constant, say $r^*(x)=c$, then $r(x)=c/x$, so the utility is strictly decreasingly risk-averse for $c>0$ and has negative, strictly increasing risk aversion for $c<0$. By (12), the possibilities are:

$$u(x)\sim x^{1-c} \quad \text{if} \quad r^*(x)=c<1\,, \tag{47}$$

$$u(x)\sim \log x \quad \text{if} \quad r^*(x)=1\,, \tag{48}$$

$$u(x)\sim -x^{-(c-1)} \quad \text{if} \quad r^*(x)=c>1\;. \tag{49}$$

If the proportional risk aversion is constant locally, then it is constant globally, that is, a change in assets makes no change in preferences among proportional risks. This follows immediately from the fact that $u(kx)\sim u(x)$ in each of the cases above. Therefore it makes sense to speak of "constant proportional risk aversion" without the qualification "local" or "global." Similar remarks apply to constant proportional risk aversion on an interval.

12. INCREASING AND DECREASING PROPORTIONAL RISK AVERSION

We will call a utility function [strictly] increasingly or decreasingly proportionally risk-averse if it has a [strictly] increasing or decreasing local proportional risk aversion function. Again the corresponding local and global properties are equivalent, as the next theorem states.

THEOREM 6: *The following conditions are equivalent.*

(a″) *The local proportional risk aversion function $r^*(x)$ is [strictly] decreasing.*

(b″) *The proportional risk premium $\pi^*(x,\tilde{z})$ is a [strictly] decreasing function of x for all $\tilde{z}$.*

(c″) *The proportional probability premium $p^*(x,h)$ is a [strictly] decreasing function of x for all $h>0$.*

The same equivalences hold if "increasing" is substituted for "decreasing" throughout and/or attention is restricted throughout to an interval, that is, if the requirement is added that x, $x+x\tilde{z}$, $x+xh$, and $x-xh$ all lie in a specified interval.

PROOF: This theorem follows upon application of Theorem 1 to $u_1(x)=u(x)$ and $u_2(x)=u(kx)$ for arbitrary x and k.

A decreasingly risk-averse utility function may be increasingly or decreasingly proportionally risk-averse or neither. For instance, $u(x)\sim -\exp[-q^{-1}(x+b)^q]$, with $b\geqq 0$, $q<1$, $q\neq 0$, is strictly decreasingly risk-averse for $x>0$ while its local proportional risk aversion function $r^*(x)=x(x+b)^{-1}[(x+b)^q+1-q]$ is strictly increasing if $0<q<1$, strictly decreasing if $q<0$ and $b=0$, and neither if $q<0$ and $b>0$.

13. RELATED WORK OF ARROW

Arrow[4] has discussed the optimum amount to invest when part of the assets x are to be held as cash and the rest invested in a specified, actuarially favorable risk. If $\tilde{\imath}$ is the return per unit invested, then investing the amount a will result in assets $x+a\tilde{\imath}$. Suppose $a(x, \tilde{\imath})$ is the optimum amount to invest, that is $a(x, \tilde{\imath})$ maximizes $E\{u(x+a\tilde{\imath})\}$. Arrow proves that if $r(x)$ is [strictly] decreasing, increasing, or constant for all x, then $a(x, \tilde{\imath})$ is [strictly] increasing, decreasing, or constant, respectively, except that $a(x, \tilde{\imath})=x$ for all x below a certain value (depending on $\tilde{\imath}$). He also proves a theorem about the asset elasticity of the demand for cash which is equivalent to the statement that if $r^*(x)$ is [strictly] decreasing, increasing, or constant for all x, then the optimum proportional investment $a^*(x, \tilde{\imath})=a(x, \tilde{\imath})/x$ is [strictly] increasing, decreasing, or constant, respectively, except that $a^*(x, \tilde{\imath})=1$ for all x below a certain value. In the present framework it is natural to deduce these re-

[4] Kenneth J. Arrow, "Liquidity Preference," Lecture VI in "Lecture Notes for Economics 285, The Economics of Uncertainty," pp. 33-53, undated, Stanford University.

sults from the following theorem, whose proof bears essentially the same relation to Arrow's proofs as the proof of Theorem 1 to direct proofs of Theorems 2 and 6. For convenience we assume that $a_1(x, \tilde{\imath})$ and $a_2(x, \tilde{\imath})$ are unique.

THEOREM 7: *Condition* (a) *of Theorem* 1 *is equivalent to*
(f) $a_1(x,\tilde{\imath}) \leqq a_2(x,\tilde{\imath})$ *for all* x *and* $\tilde{\imath}$ [*and* $<$ *if* $0 < a_1(x,\tilde{\imath}) < x$].
The same equivalence holds if attention is restricted throughout to an interval, that is, if the requirement is added that x *and* $x+\tilde{\imath}x$ *lie in a specified interval.*

PROOF: To show that (a) implies (f), note that $a_j(x,\tilde{\imath})$ maximizes

$$v_j(a) = \frac{1}{u_j'(x)} E\{u_j(x+a\tilde{\imath})\}, \qquad j=1,2. \tag{50}$$

Therefore (f) follows from

$$\frac{d}{da}\{v_1(a)-v_2(a)\} = E\left\{\tilde{\imath}\left(\frac{u_1'(x+a\tilde{\imath})}{u_1'(x)} - \frac{u_2'(x+a\tilde{\imath})}{u_2'(x)}\right)\right\} \leqq [<] 0, \tag{51}$$

which follows from (a) by (20).

If, conversely, the weak [strong] form of (a) does not hold, then its strong [weak] form holds on some interval with u_1 and u_2 interchanged, in which case the weak [strong] form of (f) cannot hold, so (f) implies (a). (The fact must be used that the strong form of (f) is actually stronger than the weak form, even when x and $x+\tilde{\imath}x$ are restricted to a specified interval. This is easily shown.)

Assuming u is bounded, Arrow proves that (i) it is impossible that $r^*(x) \leqq 1$ for all $x > x_0$, and he implies that (ii) $r^*(0) \leqq 1$. It follows, as he points out, that if u is bounded and r^* is monotonic, then r^* is increasing. (i) and (ii) can be deduced naturally from the following theorem, which is an immediate consequence of Theorem 1 (a) and (e).

THEOREM 8: *If* $r_1(x) \geqq r_2(x)$ *for all* $x > x_0$ *and* $u_1(\infty)=\infty$, *then* $u_2(\infty)=\infty$. *If* $r_1(x) \geqq r_2(x)$ *for all* $x<\varepsilon$, $\varepsilon>0$, *and* $u_2(0)=-\infty$, *then* $u_1(0)=-\infty$.

This gives (i) when $r_1(x)=1/x$, $r_2(x)=r(x)$, $u_1(x)=\log x$, $u_2(x)=u(x)$. It gives (ii) when $r_1(x)=r(x)$, $r_2(x)=c/x$, $c>1$, $u_1(x)=u(x)$, $u_2(x)=-x^{1-c}$.

This section is not intended to summarize Arrow's work,[4] but only to indicate its relation to the present paper. The main points of overlap are that Arrow introduces essentially the functions r and r^* (actually their negatives) and uses them in significant ways, in particular those mentioned already, and that he introduces essentially $p^*(x,h)$, proves an equation like (46) in order to interpret decreasing r^*, and mentions the possibility of a similar analysis for r.

Harvard University

Exercise on demand for insurance

To get some further feeling for the properties of expected utility maximization, we now analyze the demand for insurance when the cost of insurance exceeds the expected value of benefits (as will generally be the case because insurance companies have administrative costs). We consider two separate problems. First, we analyze what leads an individual to prefer full insurance to no insurance. Then, we consider the design of a policy that is optimal for a single individual. Here we abstract from the problems of adverse selection and moral hazard, which will play a significant role in the readings in Part II. [We also ignore the issues that arise when the events that generate losses also alter the utility function so that the consumer is maximizing the expectation of a utility function that is different in different states of nature. For a discussion of state-dependent utility functions, see Shavell (1977).] This exercise is based on the analysis of Arrow (1963), several comments on that article, and a paper by Shavell (1977).

Consider a risk-averse consumer maximizing the expectation of a smooth utility function U, who has wealth W and faces a financial loss X ($X < W$) with a (known) probability p.

1 What is the equation for the maximal amount the consumer would be willing to pay for insurance that would give him back the amount X in the event of loss?

Let $\Pi(p, X)$ be the excess of the amount defined in answer to question 1 over the expected value of loss.

2 Show that Π has the following properties:

a. $\Pi(0, X) = \Pi(1, X) = \Pi(p, 0) = 0$.

b. Π is continuous.

c. For $X > 0$, Π is concave in p.

d. For $1 > p > 0$, Π increases with X.

Assume that insurance is available at its expected cost to the insuring firm. The costs of insurance companies are the losses of the insured, a constant k_1 per policy written, a constant k_2 per claim paid, and a constant k_3 per dollar of claim paid. We now consider whether an individual prefers full insurance or no insurance.

3 For $k_1 > 0$, $k_2 = k_3 = 0$, show that there exist functions $X^*(p)$, $p^*(X)$, and $p^{**}(X)$ such that insurance is purchased for $X > X^*(p)$ and for p satisfying $p^*(X) < p < p^{**}(X)$ and not otherwise.

4 For $k_2 > 0, k_1 = k_3 = 0$, show that there exists a function $p^{***}(X)$ such that insurance is bought for $p < p^{***}(X)$ and not otherwise.
5 For $k_3 > 0, k_1 = k_2 = 0$, and pX constant at value V, show that there exists a function $X^{**}(V)$ such that insurance is purchased for $X > X^{**}(V)$ when p is correspondingly small (i.e., satisfies $pX = V$).
[*Hint:* Use concavity of U to sign the appropriate derivative. $X^{**}(V)$ might be infinite.]
6 For $k_3 > 0, k_1 = k_2 = 0$, and a given p, show that there is a utility function such that for three values of loss X_1, X_2, X_3, with $X_1 < X_2 < X_3$, insurance is purchased for loss X_1 or X_3 but not for loss X_2.
[*Hint*: Try a utility function with three separate segments that have differing degrees of risk aversion.]

We now turn to the question of the design of an optimal policy assuming that some insurance is always better than none. For this part of the exercise we assume that there are two possible losses X_1 and X_2 (with $X_1 < X_2$) and the probabilities of a loss of X_1 is p_1, of a loss of X_2 is p_2, and of no loss is $1 - p_1 - p_2$. We continue to assume that insurance is available at expected cost. (We ignore the possibility of insuring the loss X_i only some of the time.)

7 Assuming no administrative costs, show that the consumer maximizes expected utility by purchase of complete insurance (that is, a policy that pays X_1 if the loss is X_1 and X_2 if the loss is X_2).
8 If the only administrative costs are fixed costs per policy written, $k_1 > 0$, $k_2 = k_3 = 0$ (and assuming it is worthwhile to purchase insurance), show that the optimal policy is full insurance.

The following propositions are proved in the sources cited above. The reader might try to prove them for himself.

9 If the only administrative costs are per claim made ($k_2 > 0, k_1 = k_3 = 0$) then the optimal policy is either full insurance or a policy that pays nothing in the event of one loss and a positive amount in the event of the other. Show that it might pay to insure just X_1 or just X_2. Can you derive the formula for the optimal benefit if just X_2 is insured?
[*Hint.* Show that if $X_1 = X_2$ it might pay to insure X_1 and not X_2.]
10 If the only administrative costs are per dollar of claim paid ($k_3 > 0$, $k_1 = k_2 = 0$) then the optimal policy pays all the losses above a deductible amount d (d might be larger or smaller than X_1). Can you derive a formula for the optimal d?

References

K. Arrow, Appendix to uncertainty and the welfare economics of medical care, *Am. Econ. Rev.* 53 (1963), 969–973.

V. F. Boland, Comment, *Am. Econ. Rev.* **55** (1965), 1172-1173.
D. S. Lees and R. G. Rice, Comment, *Am. Econ. Rev.* **55** (1965), 140-154.
S. Shavell, Theoretical issues in medical malpractice, *in* "The Economics of Medical Malpractice" (R. Helms, ed.), Washington, D.C.: American Enterprise Institute, 1977.

5

M. E. Yaari, Some remarks on measures of risk aversion and their uses, *Journal of Economic Theory* 1 (1969), 315–329

To gain some feeling for the importance of the assumption of expected utility maximization for the analysis of risk aversion, we turn now to an article that explores the same issues, using the state preference approach but not the hypothesis of expected utility maximization.[1] Here, consumption in each different state of nature is simply treated as an alternative commodity. As in standard consumer theory, indifference curves in commodity space completely describe the structure of preferences. If the individual's preferences are compatible with the expected utility hypothesis we have the result that one can construct the entire preference map from knowledge of the amount of utility received whenever the individual consumes the same amount independent of the outcome of the random variable and knowledge of the probabilities of the different states of nature. This result allows the inference of general properties of the utility function from the willlingness to take small bets at different levels of wealth. Without the expected utility hypothesis, information about willingness to take large bets does not follow from willingness to take small bets at a safe initial wealth. It is a valuable exercise to develop two different ways of thinking about the same problem, since each approach handles some issues better than the other. The exercise in Chapter 8 asks the reader to convert the analysis of that chapter into this setting. Below we shall use the state preference approach repeatedly.

The proof of Remark 7 given in the text is not correct. The remark, however, is correct. It is a good exercise for the reader to seek the error in the remark. It is a much harder exercise to try to construct an alternative proof. One has been provided by Mayshar (1975), who also points out that Yaari's generalization of Remark 7 to many goods does not go through as described.

For further results using this approach see the comments to the next reading and the exercises in Chapter 8.

Reference

J. Mayshar, Further remarks on measures of risk aversion and their uses, *J. Econ. Theory* **10** (1975), 100–109.

[1] For additional discussion of the state preference approach see Chapter 11.

JOURNAL OF ECONOMIC THEORY **1**, 315–329 (1969)

Some Remarks on Measures of Risk Aversion and on Their Uses

MENAHEM E. YAARI*

The Hebrew University of Jerusalem

In this essay, measures of risk aversion are looked upon from the point of view of the "states of nature" approach to decision making under uncertainty. This point of view turns out to be quite useful in the formulation of axioms concerning the change in risk aversion as certain environmental parameters (e.g., wealth) vary. A simple portfolio selection problem (with one risky security) is used as a setting for the discussion.

I

Consider a random event E, and let $\sim E$ denote its complement. (The term "random event" is taken here in the colloquial sense of "something that could happen" rather than in the formal sense of a measurable subset of a sample space on which there is defined a probability measure.) We may define a *gamble* on the event E and its complement as a real valued function on the set $\{E, \sim E\}$. In other words, a gamble on E and its complement is an ordered pair of real numbers, say $\langle x_1, x_2 \rangle$, where x_1 is the number of dollars to be received if E occurs, and x_2 is the number of dollars to be received if E fails to occur. Thus, for example, the pair $\langle -2, 1 \rangle$ is the gamble whose holder pays two dollars if E occurs and receives one dollar if E fails to occur. Let $\succsim$ be a decision maker's preference ordering of the set of all such money gambles on E and its complement. Assume that the relation $\succsim$ satisfies the following standard axioms:

I. $\succsim$ *is a complete weak ordering.*

II. $\succsim$ *is monotone, in the sense that if* $x \gg y$, *then* $x \succ y$.[1]

III. $\succsim$ *is continuous. In other words, for all gambles* y, *the sets* $\{x | x \succsim y\}$ *and* $\{x | y \succsim x\}$ *are closed.*

IV. $\succsim$ *is convex. That is, the set* $\{x | x \succsim y\}$ *is convex for every gamble* y.

In the present context, Axiom IV goes by the name of *risk aversion.*

* In am indebted to Peter A. Diamond and David Levhari for their comments, and to the Maurice Falk Institute for Economic Research in Israel for research support.

[1] Let $x = \langle x_1, x_2 \rangle$ and $y = \langle y_1, y_2 \rangle$. Then, $x \gg y$ means $x_1 > y_1$ and $x_2 > y_2$. $x \succ y$ means $x \succsim y$ but not $y \succsim x$.

In standard consumer theory, we require all commodity bundles to be nonnegative. Here, commodity bundles are gambles, and the latter must be allowed to have negative components. However, nonnegativity is replaced by boundedness from below. Specifically, if we let W be the decision maker's current wealth, then the only gambles which he can consider are ones where possible losses do not exceed W. In other words, the set of all admissible gambles is given by

$$\{\langle x_1, x_2\rangle | x_1 \geqq -W \quad \text{and} \quad x_2 \geqq -W\}.$$

The preference ordering $\succsim$ is assumed to be defined on this set.

Let the symbol $\hat{0}$ be used to denote the origin, $\langle 0, 0\rangle$. The decision maker will *accept* a gamble x if, and only if, $x \succsim \hat{0}$. Therefore, let us refer to the set $\{x | x \succsim \hat{0}\}$ as the decision maker's *acceptance set*. Our axioms tell us that the acceptance set is convex, and that it is bounded below by the graph of a continuous, nonincreasing function, passing through the origin. We shall refer to this function as the decision maker's *acceptance frontier*.

Now consider two decision makers, Mr. A and Mr. B, and let their acceptance sets be denoted S_A and S_B, respectively. Mr. A and Mr. B could, of course, be the same individual, observed at different wealth levels, at different levels of information, etc. It seems quite natural to say that Mr. A is *more risk averse* than Mr. B if S_A is a subset of S_B, i.e., if every gamble which is acceptable to A is also acceptable to B.[2] The relation "is more risk averse than . . ." is a partial ordering of the set of decision makers. It is a global concept. The corresponding local concept may be defined as follows: We say that Mr. A is *locally more risk averse* than Mr. B if there exists an open disc D, centered at the origin, such that $D \cap S_A$ is a subset of $D \cap S_B$. In other words, A is locally more risk averse than B if all sufficiently small gambles which are acceptable to A are also acceptable to B. The relation "is locally more risk averse than . . ." is also a partial ordering of decision makers, and it obviously contains the relation "is more risk averse than . . .". Given that we are dealing with a partial ordering, it might be of interest to see under what conditions two decision makers are comparable in this ordering.

Let f be a decision maker's acceptance frontier. For convenience, assume that f is differentiable at the origin. Then, the quantity p, defined by

$$p = \frac{f'(0)}{f'(0) - 1}$$

[2] It would be more accurate, but also more cumbersome, to say in this case that Mr. A is *at least as risk averse as* Mr. B.

is referred to as the decision maker's *subjective probability* for the event E. This definition follows the Ramsey–Savage notion of deriving the subjective probability of the event E from the odds at which the decision maker is willing to make small bets on E.[3] It is, of course, possible to define subjective probability in an analogous fashion also in the case where the acceptance frontier is not differentiable at the origin. Note, however, that in the absence of differentiability, subjective probability is no longer unique.

Remark 1. In order for Mr. A and Mr. B to be comparable in the partial ordering "is locally more risk averse than . . ." it is necessary that the set of subjective probabilities for E of one of them be contained in the set of subjective probabilities for E of the other. In particular, if acceptance frontiers are differentiable at the origin, then a necessary condition for Mr. A and Mr. B to be comparable in the ordering is that their subjective probabilities coincide. In other words, A and B can only be comparable in the ordering if their acceptance frontiers are tangent (to each other) at the origin.

The proof of this remark is straightforward.

Suppose that Mr. A and Mr. B are, in fact, comparable in the ordering "is locally more risk averse than . . .". Then, clearly, the *second* derivative of the acceptance frontier (if it exists) will provide us with criteria for determining who, among these two men, is higher on the ordering. Specifically, we have:

Remark 2. Let all acceptance frontiers be twice differentiable at 0, and assume that Mr. A and Mr. B are comparable in the ordering "is locally more risk averse than . . .". Let the acceptance frontiers of Mr. A and Mr. B be denoted f_A and f_B, respectively. Then, a necessary condition for Mr. A to be locally more risk averse than Mr. B is given by the inequality

$$f_A''(0) \geqq f_B''(0),$$

and a sufficient condition for Mr. A to be locally more risk averse than Mr. B is given by the inequality

$$f_A''(0) > f_B''(0).$$

The proof, once again, is straightforward.

This last remark clearly suggests the use of the second derivative of the acceptance frontier, evaluated at the origin, as a measure of local

[3] The decision maker's *subjective odds* for the event E are given by the quantity $-f'(0)$.

risk aversion. Note that, by the term "measure of local risk aversion," we do not mean to imply that the second derivative of the acceptance frontier at the origin is a numerical representation of the ordering "is locally more risk averse than . . .". In fact, Mr. A could be strictly more risk averse (locally as well as globally) than Mr. B, whole $f_A''(0) = f_B''(0)$. This is simply a re-statement of the fact that it is not possible, in general, to deduce the behavior of a function in an interval from information about its derivatives at a point in the interval.

The decision maker need not be a maximizer of expected utility for our measure of local risk aversion to be applicable. However, if it happens that the decision maker *is* a maximizer of expected utility, then this measure leads immediately to the Arrow–Pratt [*1*, *2*] measure of risk aversion. For suppose that a decision maker, faced with the possibility of betting on an event E, decides which bets to take on the basis of expected utility. Let his utility function be denoted u, and let his current wealth be denoted W. Finally, let his acceptance frontier be denoted f_W, to indicate that at different wealth levels the decision maker will, in general, have different acceptance frontiers. Then, the acceptance frontier f_W is given by the equation

$$pu(W+t)+(1-p)u(W+f_W(t)) = u(W),$$

where p is the probability which the decision maker assigns to the event E. We shall assume that u is twice differentiable, which implies that f_W is also twice differentiable. Upon differentiating once, we find, as indeed we should, that

$$p = \frac{f_W'(0)}{f_W'(0)-1};^4$$

and upon differentiating again, we obtain

$$f_W''(0) = \frac{p}{(1-p)^2}\left[-\frac{u''(W)}{u'(W)}\right].$$

The quantity in brackets is precisely the Arrow–Pratt index of risk aversion. In other words, the risk aversion measure $f_W''(0)$ is *proportional* to the Arrow–Pratt measure, since the probability p cannot depend upon W. (Indeed, we know that the probability p is common to all the decision makers who are comparable in the ordering "is locally more averse than . . .".)

We see from this last equation that the Arrow–Pratt index of local risk aversion has the same shortcoming that $f_W''(0)$ has: It could happen that the Arrow–Pratt index is equal at two wealth levels, and yet the

[4] To get this result, one needs to have $u'(W) > 0$. But this follows from our strong monotonicity axiom.

decision maker could be strictly more risk averse (in terms of accepted gambles) at one of these wealth levels than at the other.

Now, what about the Arrow–Pratt measure of *relative* risk aversion? Can it be constructed in a similar fashion? The answer is in the affirmative. Let the pair of real numbers $\langle r_1, r_2 \rangle$ stand for the following gamble: "You will receive an amount equal to $100r_1$ percent of your wealth if E occurs, and you will receive an amount equal to $100r_2$ percent of your wealth if E fails to occur." Thus, for example, the pair $\langle -1/2, 1/2 \rangle$ will now stand for the contract under which the decision maker undertakes to pay one half of his wealth if E occurs, in return for which he is to receive one half again on his wealth if E fails to occur. Let us refer to such contracts as *relative gambles.* The decision maker's preference ordering over regular gambles induces a preference ordering over relative gambles, in the following obvious manner: A relative gamble $\langle r_1, r_2 \rangle$ is preferred or equivalent to a relative gamble $\langle r_1', r_2' \rangle$ if, and only if, the regular gamble $\langle Wr_1, Wr_2 \rangle$ is preferred or equivalent to the regular gamble $\langle Wr_1', Wr_2' \rangle$, where W denotes current wealth. The set of all relative gambles preferred or equivalent to the origin is, as before, the decision maker's acceptance set (for relative gambles) and it is bounded below by the graph of a function, say g_W, where, once again, we use W to denote current wealth. If f_W is the decision maker's acceptance frontier for regular gambles, then the relationship between g_W and f_W is given by

$$g_W(t) = \frac{1}{W} f_W(Wt),$$

for all t. This follows immediately from the relationship between the decision maker's preference ordering for regular gambles and his preference ordering for relative gambles.

By differentiating this last equation twice, we find that

$$g_W''(0) = W f_W''(0).$$

Now, the quantity $g_W''(0)$ may be regarded as a natural measure of the decision maker's *aversion to relative risk.* The argument which leads to this observation is completely analogous to our previous argument, where $f_W''(0)$ was proposed as a natural measure of aversion to absolute (i.e., non-relative) risk. And if the decision maker happens to be a maximizer of expected utility, then we can substitute for $f_W''(0)$ in the foregoing equation, and obtain

$$g_W''(0) = \frac{p}{(1-p)^2}\left[-\frac{Wu''(W)}{u'(W)}\right].$$

The expression in brackets is, of course, the Arrow–Pratt index of relative risk aversion.

II

Measures of risk aversion have one major use: They facilitate the formulation of certain axioms on decision making under uncertainty, and these axioms may, in turn, lead to empirically meaningful conclusions. Here, for example, are three fairly reasonable axioms which make use of the notion of "measuring" risk aversion: (1) Greater wealth can never lead to greater risk aversion. (2) Greater information (about the physical nature of the various random events) can never lead to greater risk aversion. (3) Greater family size can never lead to lower risk aversion. These axioms (and others like them) have obvious uses in predicting the behavior of decision makers. However, a great deal depends on exactly how each axiom is stated. Indeed, each of the three statements above is not really an axiom, but a heading for a whole class of possible axioms which, while similar in spirit, may differ greatly. In order to explore this issue a little bit further, let us turn to the following "classical" query in the economics of uncertainty: How will variations in wealth affect a decision maker's portfolio of risky and non-risky securities? The answer, as everyone knows, depends on the way in which variations in wealth affect risk aversion. Consider the simplest possible portfolio selection problem: A decision maker is presented with a security which bears a net rate of return of α per dollar if the event E occurs, and β per dollar if E fails to occur. To get a nontrivial case, we shall assume that of the two numbers, α and β, one is positive and the other is negative; say $\alpha > 0$, $\beta < 0$. Assume also that the decision maker can buy this security or sell short in any amount, provided he has adequate resources to cover his losses. Let W be the decision maker's wealth, and let A be the amount of the security purchased. Then, A is restricted by the inequalities $-W/\alpha \leqq A \leqq -W/\beta$, where a negative value of A indicates selling short. (If selling short is not permitted, then A is restricted by the inequalities $0 \leqq A \leqq -W/\beta$.) Now, the purchase of an amount A of securities is clearly equivalent to engaging in the gamble $\langle \alpha A, \beta A \rangle$. Thus, the decision maker's *opportunity locus* is given by the set

$$\left\{ \langle \alpha A, \beta A \rangle \,\middle|\, -\frac{W}{\alpha} \leqq A \leqq -\frac{W}{\beta} \right\}.$$

This is a downward sloping line segment, which passes through the origin. Its slope is given by the ratio β/α. The negative of this ratio, $-\beta/\alpha$, will be referred to as the *market odds* on the event E. We may also refer to the quantities $-\beta/(\alpha-\beta)$ and $\alpha/(\alpha-\beta)$ as the *market probabilities* of E and $\sim E$, respectively. The decision maker will invest in the risky security in such a way as to maximize his preferences. In other words, he will choose A^* in such a way that, among all admissible points of the form

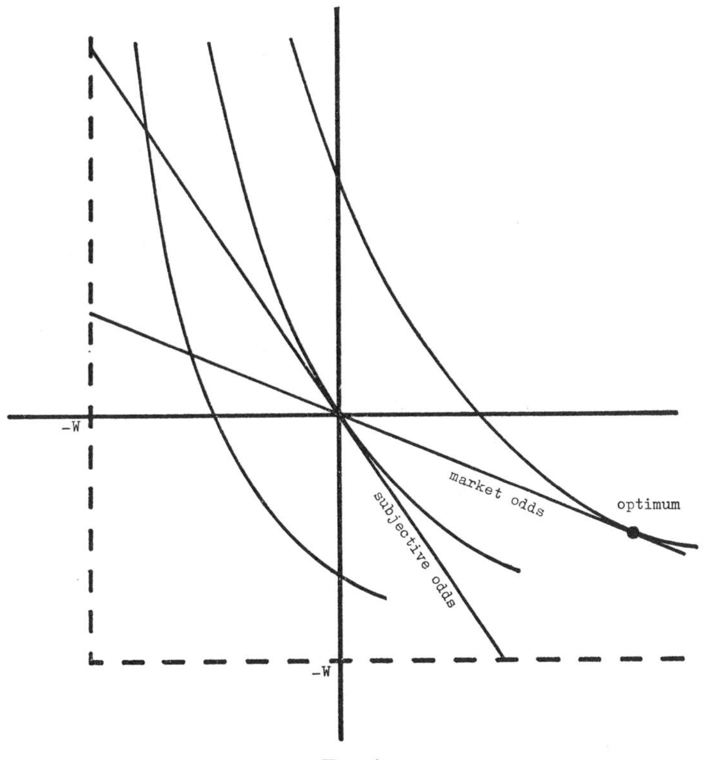

FIG. 1.

$\langle \alpha A, \beta A \rangle$, the point $\langle \alpha A^*, \beta A^* \rangle$ will be on the highest indifference curve. (See Fig. 1.)

It is obvious, from Fig. 1, that the decision maker will buy, sell short, or stay put according to whether or not there is a divergence between his subjective probability and the market probability for the event E. Specifically, we have:

Remark 3. Refraining from both purchasing and selling short is optimal if, and only if, the market probability for E coincides with a subjective probability for E.[5] If all the subjective probabilities for E exceed the market probability for E, then purchasing is optimal. Finally, if all the subjective probabilities for E fall short of the market probability for E, then selling short is optimal. In the case where the subjective probability for E is unique and where the decision maker's preferences are strictly convex (so that the optimal action is also unique) the foregoing assertion

[5] Recall that, in the non-differentiable case, subjective probability is not unique.

reduces to the following: Purchasing is optimal if, and only if, the decision maker's subjective probability for E exceeds the market probability, and selling short is optimal if, and only if, the market probability for E exceeds the decision maker's subjective probability.

It is possible also to state the assertions in Remark 3 in terms of the expected rate of return of the risky security. For example, in the case of a unique subjective probability and strictly convex preferences, we have the following: The decision maker will buy or sell short if, and only if, the expected rate of return from the risky security, reckoned with respect to his subjective probability distribution, is different from 0. He will buy if (and only if) the expected rate of return is positive, and he will sell short if (and only if) the expected rate of return is negative. And if selling short is not permitted, then it is still true that the decision maker will buy if, and only if, the expected return from the risky security is positive. This observation should be compared with Arrow's result in [*1*], where he gets the same condition for a decision maker who maximizes expected utility.

Let us return, however, to our attempt at determining how variations in wealth affect investment in the risky security, whether in purchases or in short sales. We are looking for a proposition to the effect that if risk aversion is nonincreasing with wealth, then investment in the risky security (whether via purchases or via short sales) is nondecreasing with wealth. To this end, we must state exactly in what sense we mean risk aversion to be nonincreasing with wealth. The following axiom seems reasonable:

AXIOM V. *For every pair of wealth levels, W and W', satisfying $W' \geqq W$, and for every gamble x, if x is accepted at the wealth level W, then it is also accepted at the wealth level W'.*

If Axiom V holds, then we shall say that the decision maker exhibits *nonincreasing global risk aversion.*

It seems natural at this point to examine the following assertion: If the decision maker satisfies Axioms I–V, then his investment in the risky security (whether in purchases or in short sales) is nondecreasing in wealth.

Unfortunately, this assertion is false. A counterexample is contained in Fig. 2. The preference ordering depicted in Fig. 2 satisfies Axioms I–V, and yet, with market odds as depicted in the figure, we find investment in the risky security decreasing as wealth increases. Indeed, at low wealth levels, investment in the risky security decreases (as wealth increases) by more than the increase in wealth. In other words, Axiom V is not even

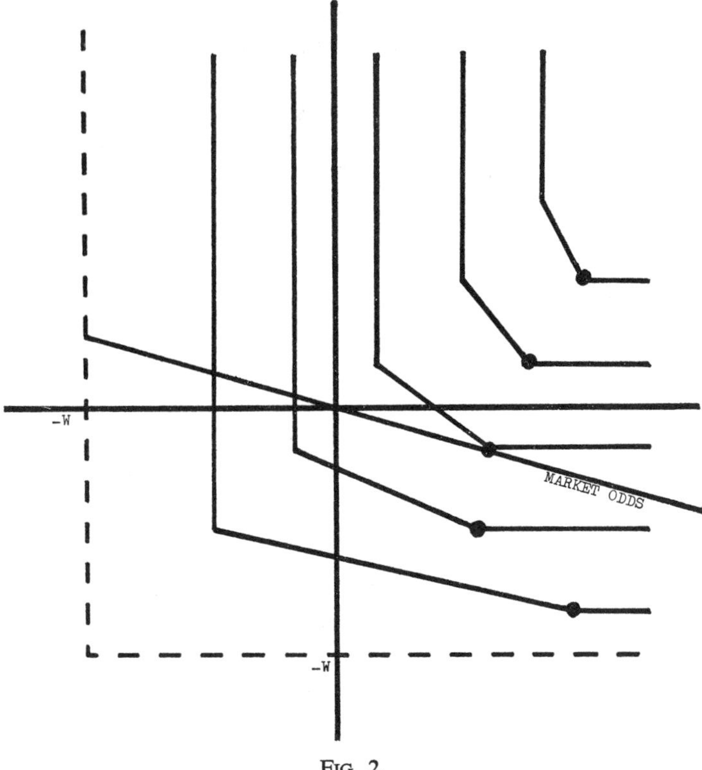

FIG. 2.

strong enough to rule out inferiority of the conditional commodities on which the preference ordering is based.[6]

Axiom V does lead to the following results:

Remark 4. If the decision maker's preferences satisfy nonincreasing global risk aversion, then there exists a real number p, such that p is a subjective probability for E at all wealth levels.

Proof. By Remark 1, the set of subjective probabilities shrinks as wealth increases. In other words, if W and W' are two wealth levels satisfying $W \geqq W'$, and if p is a subjective probability at W', then p is also a subjective probability at W. Now, it is easy to establish that, at

[6] Fig. 2 shows also that there is no hope of getting a *local* theorem to the effect that, say, if local risk aversion is decreasing locally, then small changes in wealth will always lead to changes in the same direction in the decision maker's investment in the risky security.

each wealth level, the set of subjective probabilities is compact. Therefore, there exists a subjective probability common to all wealth levels.

Remark 5. If the decision maker's preferences satisfy nonincreasing global risk aversion, and if purchasing is optimal at one wealth level, while selling short is optimal at another (or the same) wealth level, then staying put (i.e., neither purchasing nor selling short) is optimal at both wealth levels.

Proof. This follows from Remarks 3 and 4.

This last remark says that, under nonincreasing global risk aversion, if the decision maker engages in purchases of the risky security at one wealth level, then there is no reason for him to switch to selling short at another wealth level, and vice versa. Let us now proceed to motivate the axiom from which it follows that the *amount* of the risky security purchased (or sold short) is nondecreasing with wealth.

Consider a decision maker, and assume that this decision maker has already contracted a gamble $x = \langle x_1, x_2 \rangle$, either because he had chosen to do so, or because he had been made to do so. In other words, the decision maker is already under an obligation which will bring him x_1 dollars if E occurs, and x_2 dollars if E fails to occur. Now suppose that a further gamble, say $y = \langle y_1, y_2 \rangle$, is offered to him. Let us examine whether it is reasonable to postulate the following: If the decision maker accepts the gamble y (on top of x) at his present wealth level, then he will also accept y (on top of x) at all higher wealth levels. At first blush, this postulate may not seem unreasonable. However, on second thought, we see that it is, in fact, much too strong. The decision maker's willingness to engage in the gamble y may stem from a desire to *hedge* against his existing bet, x. Now, the desire to hedge against a given gamble may very well be greater at low wealth levels than at high ones. The above-mentioned postulate precludes this possibility. To get around this problem, it is necessary to introduce an explicit distinction between bets on E and bets on $\sim E$: Let $z = \langle z_1, z_2 \rangle$ be a gamble. If $z_1 \geqq z_2$, then we shall say that z is a *bet on* E; and if $z_2 \geqq z_1$, then we shall say that z is a *bet on* $\sim E$. Assume, once again, that the decision maker has already contracted a gamble x, and that he is now being offered a gamble y, on top of x. Clearly, the gamble y can be considered a hedge against the gamble x only if x and y are bets on opposite events, that is, only if x is a bet on E and y is a bet on $\sim E$, or if x is a bet on $\sim E$ and y is a bet on E. The axiom which we shall now state refers only to the case in which hedging considerations do not arise, namely to the case where x and y are bets on the same event. If x is, say, a bet on E and y is also a bet on E, then it seems entirely reasonable to postulate that if the decision maker accepts y (on top of x) at a low wealth level, then he also accepts y (on top of x) at higher wealth levels. In other words, if the decision maker is willing to go farther out on a limb at a given wealth level, then there is no reason why he should not be willing to do the same thing at higher wealth levels. This is, in fact, the axiom which we are looking for.

AXIOM V′. *Let x and y be gambles, and let w be a nonnegative real number. If x and y are bets on the same event and $x+y \succsim x$, then $x+y+\hat{w} \succsim x+\hat{w}$, where $\hat{w}$ is defined by $\hat{w} = \langle w, w \rangle$.*

We shall refer to Axiom V′, for want of a better name, as the axiom of *nonincreasing total risk aversion.* Nonincreasing total risk aversion implies nonincreasing global risk aversion, but not conversely.

Remark 6. Assume that Axioms I–IV and V′ are satisfied, and let W and W' be two levels of wealth, satisfying $W' \geqq W$. Suppose that, at the level W, investing an amount A in the risky security is optimal. If $A \geqq 0$, then there exists an A', satisfying $A' \geqq A$, such that investing A' is optimal at the level W'. And if $A \leqq 0$, then there exists an A', satisfying $A' \leqq A$, such that investing A' is optimal at W'.

Proof. Assume, without loss of generality, that the ordering $\succsim$ describes the decision maker's preferences when his wealth level is W. Consider the case where $A \geqq 0$, and define $x = \langle \alpha A, \beta A \rangle$. x is a bet on the event E. Now let A^* be an optimal amount of investment at the wealth level W'. If $A^* \geqq A$, there is nothing more to prove. Assume, therefore, that $A^* < A$. By Remark 5, we may assume also that $A^* \geqq 0$. Define a real number w and a gamble x' by

$$w = W' - W,$$
$$x' = \langle w + \alpha A^*, w + \beta A^* \rangle.$$

The x' is a gamble which represents optimal investment at the wealth level W', when viewed from the wealth level W. Since $A^* \geqq 0$, x' is a bet on the event E. Writing $\hat{w} = \langle w, w \rangle$, we obtain

$$x = x' - \hat{w} + y,$$

where $y = \langle \alpha(A - A^*), \beta(A - A^*) \rangle$. Since $A^* < A$, we have that y, like x and x', is a bet on the event E. And since x is optimal at the wealth level W, and $x' - \hat{w}$ is feasible at the same wealth level, we have

$$x' - \hat{w} + y \succsim x' - \hat{w}.$$

22

From Axiom V′, it now follows, since $x' - \hat{w}$ and y are bets on the same event, that

$$x' + y \gtrsim x'.$$

Now, $x' + y = x + \hat{w}$. Hence, we have

$$x + \hat{w} \gtrsim x'.$$

But x' is optimal at the wealth level W', and $x + \hat{w}$ is feasible at the same wealth level. Therefore, the foregoing assertion tells us that $x + \hat{w}$ must also be optimal at W'. And since $x + \hat{w}$ is the gamble which represents an investment of A at the wealth level W', we have the desired result. The proof for the case where $A \leqq 0$ is analogous.

If the decision maker's preferences are strictly convex, then the optimal amount of investment in the risky security is unique, and then Remark 6 reduces to the assertion that investment in the risky security is nondecreasing in absolute value with wealth.

Axiom V′ is, in fact, the weakest assumption which implies that investment in any arbitrary risky security is nondecreasing with wealth. Specifically, we have:

Remark 7. Given Axioms I–IV, if the conclusion in Remark 6 holds for all possible market odds, then Axiom V′ is satisfied.

Proof. Assume that x and y are bets on E, such that $x + y \gtrsim x$, while $x + \hat{w} \succ x + y + \hat{w}$, where $\hat{w} = \langle w, w \rangle$ and $w > 0$. Let the components of y be denoted y_1 and y_2. We know, since y is a bet on E, that $y_1 \geqq y_2$. However, since $x + y \gtrsim x$ and $x + \hat{w} \succ x + y + \hat{w}$, we have, by monotonicity of preferences, that $y_1 > 0$ and $y_2 < 0$. Hence, the straight line, call it L, which passes through both x and $x + y$, is negatively sloped. We may look upon an appropriate segment[7] of the line L as the opportunity locus for investment in a risky security at some wealth level. Let this wealth level be denoted W. Similarly, let the straight line which passes through both $x + \hat{w}$ and $x + y + \hat{w}$ be denoted L'. Then, an appropriate segment of L' can be looked upon as the opportunity locus for investments in the *same* risky security, but at a higher wealth level, namely at the level $W' = W + w$. By continuity of preferences, both of these opportunity loci possess optimal points. Furthermore, the assertion $x + y \gtrsim x$, in conjunction with convexity of preferences, implies that the set of optimal points on L either has the point x at its extreme or lies entirely to the southeast of x. On the other hand, the assertion that $x + \hat{w} \succ x + y + \hat{w}$,

[7] Namely, the segment of gambles which do not involve losses that are greater than the decision maker's wealth.

again in conjunction with the convexity of preferences, implies that the set of optimal points on L' lies strictly to the northwest of the point $x+\hat{w}$. This contradicts the conclusion of Remark 6.

We may summarize Remarks 6 and 7, for the case where the decision maker's preference ordering is strictly convex, as follows: The assertion that investment in a risky security is nondecreasing with wealth is equivalent to nonincreasing total risk aversion.

The response of investment in a risky security to variations in wealth was investigated, for the case where the decision maker is a maximizer of expected utility, by Arrow [*1*]. In order to obtain that investment in a risky security is nondecreasing with wealth, Arrow assumes that the Arrow–Pratt measure of local risk aversion is nonincreasing everywhere, as wealth increases. Our Remark 7 above tells us that, in the presence of the dominance axiom, i.e., the axiom needed to obtain the expected utility hypothesis, Arrow's assumption is actually strong enough to imply nonincreasing total risk aversion. It is simple to verify that the converse of this assertion is also true: In the presence of the dominance axiom, nonincreasing total risk aversion implies that the Arrow–Pratt measure of local risk aversion is globally nonincreasing. Thus, for an expected utility maximizer, investment in a risky security increases with wealth, for all securities and at all wealth levels, if and only if the Arrow–Pratt measure of risk aversion is decreasing with wealth everywhere. Note that the corresponding local assertion (locally decreasing risk aversion implies locally increasing investment in a risky security) is not true.

III

A brief comment may be in order, concerning what happens if, instead of just two events, E and $\sim E$, we have a family $\{E_1, E_2, \ldots, E_n\}$ of n mutually exclusive and exhaustive events—or states of nature, as they are often called. In this case, a gamble is given by an n-tuple of real numbers, say $\langle x_1, x_2, \ldots, x_n \rangle$, where x_i is the amount of money to be received if the event E_i occurs. Axioms I–IV do not have to be changed at all to accomodate this new situation. Given that Axioms I–IV hold, one can define the decision maker's subjective probability distribution (at a given wealth level) as an n-tuple $\langle p_1, p_2, \ldots, p_n \rangle$ which determines a supporting hyperplane to the set of accepted gambles at the origin, appropriately normalized. (The monotonicity axiom, Axiom II, guarantees that the numbers $p_1, p_2, \ldots, p_n$ will all be nonnegative.)

The axiom of nonincreasing global risk aversion is the same in the case of n events as in the case of two. However, in order to write down the axion of nonincreasing total risk aversion, we must first give a definition of what we mean by two gambles being bets on the same event. Let $x = \langle x_1, \ldots, x_n \rangle$ and $y = \langle y_1, \ldots, y_n \rangle$ be gambles. We say that x and y are bets on the same (composite) event if the inequality $(x_i - x_j)(y_i - y_j) \geqq 0$ holds for all i and j. With this definition, we may interpret the axiom of nonincreasing total risk aversion as an axiom for the n-event case.

A risky security in the n-event case is characterized by an n-tuple of real numbers, $\langle \alpha_1, \ldots, \alpha_n \rangle$, where α_i is the rate of return per dollar invested, if the event E_i occurs. Define $\alpha^* = \max \alpha_i$ and $\alpha_* = \min \alpha_i$. We know that $\alpha^* > 0$ and $\alpha_* < 0$, or else we get a trivial portfolio problem. Let A be the amount invested in the risky security, and let W be the decision maker's current wealth. Then, the opportunity locus for investments is given, if selling short is permitted, by

$$\left\{ \langle \alpha_1 A, \ldots, \alpha_n A \rangle \,\middle|\, -\frac{W}{\alpha^*} \leqq A \leqq -\frac{W}{\alpha_*} \right\},$$

and, if selling short is not permitted, by

$$\left\{ \langle \alpha_1 A, \ldots, \alpha_n A \rangle \,\middle|\, 0 \leqq A \leqq -\frac{W}{\alpha_*} \right\}.$$

Note that these opportunity loci are *line segments* in n-space (and not sections of hyperplanes, as is the case in standard consumer theory).

Remarks 1 and 3–7 are all valid in this new setting, and Remark 2 is valid after an appropriate modification. All the proofs remain virtually unchanged.

IV

It is, perhaps, worthwhile to point out, in conclusion, that the intuitive appeal of the axioms which were discussed above depends rather crucially on the nature of the random events being considered. Specifically, if the occurrence or non-occurrence of a certain random event is, in and of itself, a matter relevant to the decision maker's well-being, then Axioms V and V′ lose much of their appeal. For example, if we let E and $\sim E$ stand for the decision maker's health and ill-health, respectively, then it is no longer reasonable to assert that all the gambles which are accepted at a given wealth level will also be accepted at higher wealth levels. Furthermore, the very notion of defining subjective probabilities from the odds at which one is willing to bet loses its appeal when random events are, in and of themselves, relevant to the decision maker's preferences. This is why Ramsey [3] chose to work with what he called *ethically neutral* events (or ethically neutral propositions), i.e., with events that are *not* directly relevant to the decision maker's preferences.

Only in one case is the lack of "ethical neutrality" easily overcome. If the occurrence of a random event is equivalent, from the decision maker's point of view, to a monetary gain (or loss) of fixed magnitude, then all that is required to make Axioms V and V′ sound perfectly reasonable is a suitable prior translation of the coordinate system. The theorems which follow from these transcribed axioms are themselves transcribed versions of the theorems which hold under ethical neutrality. If the occurrence of a random event is directly relevant to the decision maker's preferences but is *not* equivalent to a fixed monetary gain (or loss), then there no longer exists a straightforward way to alter the axioms so as to restore their appeal.

REFERENCES

1. Arrow, K. J., "Aspects of the Theory of Risk-Bearing." Helsinki (1965).

2. Pratt, J. W., Risk aversion in the small and in the large, *Econometrica* **32** (1964), 1–2.

3. Ramsey, F. P., Truth and probability, "The Foundations of Mathematics and Other Essays." New York (1950).

6

M. Rothschild and J. Stiglitz, Increasing risk I: A definition, *Journal of Economic Theory* 2 (1970), 225–243

This paper considers the problem of defining an increase in risk in a way that can be used for economic purposes. The authors find a set of equivalent formulations that are intuitive and well defined. This definition, in turn, is used in the next chapter, together with assumptions on the utility function, to sign the response of an expected utility maximizer to an increase in risk.

JOURNAL OF ECONOMIC THEORY 2, 225–243 (1970)

Increasing Risk: I. A Definition*

MICHAEL ROTHSCHILD

Harvard University, Cambridge, Massachusetts 02138

AND

JOSEPH E. STIGLITZ

Cowles Foundation, Yale University, New Haven, Connecticut 06520 and Gonville and Caius College, Cambridge, England

I. INTRODUCTION

This paper attempts to answer the question: When is a random variable Y "more variable" than another random variable X?

Intuition and tradition suggest at least four plausible—and apparently different—answers to this question. These are:

1. *Y is Equal to X Plus Noise*

If we simply add some uncorrelated noise to a random variable, (r.v.), the new r.v. should be riskier[1] than the original. More formally, suppose Y and X are related as follows:

$$Y \underset{d}{=} X + Z, \tag{1.i}$$

where "$\underset{d}{=}$" means "has the same distribution as" and Z is a r.v. with the property that

$$E(Z \mid X) = 0 \qquad \text{for all } X.^{2} \tag{1.ii}$$

* The research described in this paper was carried out under grants from the National Science Foundation and the Ford Foundation.

[1] Throughout this paper we shall use the terms more variable, riskier, and more uncertain synonomously.

[2] David Wallace suggested that we investigate this concept of greater riskiness. Arthur Goldberger has pointed out to us that (1.ii) is stronger than lack of correlation as earlier versions of this paper stated.

That is, Y is equal to X plus a disturbance term (noise.) If X and Y are discrete r.v.'s, condition (1) has another natural interpretation. Suppose X is a lottery ticket which pays off a_i with probability p_i ; $\Sigma p_i = 1$. Then, Y is a lottery ticket which pays b_i with probability p_i where b_i is either a payoff of a_i or a lottery ticket whose expected value is a_i. Note that condition (1) implies that X and Y have the same mean.

2. *Every Risk Averter Prefers X to Y*

In the theory of expected utility maximization, a risk averter is defined as a person with a concave utility function. If X and Y have the same mean, but every risk averter prefers X to Y, i.e., if

$$EU(X) \geqslant EU(Y) \qquad \text{for all concave } U \tag{2}$$

then surely it is reasonable to say that X is less risky than Y.[3]

3. *Y Has More Weight in the Tails Than X*

If X and Y have density functions f and g, and if g was obtained from f by taking some of the probability weight from the center of f and adding it to each tail of f in such a way as to leave the mean unchanged, then it seems reasonable to say that Y is more uncertain than X.

4. *Y Has a Greater Variance Than X*

Comparisons of riskiness or uncertainty are commonly restricted to comparisons of variance, largely because of the long history of the use of the variance as a measure of dispersion in statistical theory.

The major result of this paper is that the first three approaches lead to a single definition of greater riskiness, different from that of the fourth approach. We shall demonstrate the equivalence as follows. In Section II, it is shown that the third approach leads to a characterization of increasing uncertainty in terms of the indefinite integrals of differences of cumulative distribution functions (c.d.f.'s). In Section III it is shown that this indefinite integral induces a partial ordering on the set of distribution functions which is equivalent to the partial ordering induced by the first two approaches.

In Section IV we show that this concept of increasing risk is not equivalent to that implied by equating the risk of X with the variance of X. This suggests to us that our concepts lead to a better definition of increasing risk than the standard one.

It is of course impossible to prove that one definition is better than

[3] It might be argued that we should limit our discussion to increasing concave functions. Imposing this restriction would gain nothing and would destroy the symmetry of some of the results. For example, since $U(X) = X$ and $U(X) = -X$ are both concave functions, condition (2) implies that X and Y have the same mean.

another. This fact is not a license for agnosticism or the suspension of judgment. Although there seems to us no question but that our definition is more consistent with the natural meaning of increasing risk than the variance definition, definitions are chosen for their usefulness as well as their consistency. As Tobin has argued, critics of the mean variance approach "owe us more than demonstrations that it rests on restrictive assumptions. They need to show us how a more general and less vulnerable approach will yield the kind of comparative static results that economists are interested in [8]." In the sequel to this paper we show how our definition may be applied to economic and statistical problems.

Before we begin it will be well to establish certain notational conventions. Throughout this paper X and Y will be r.v.'s with c.d.f.'s, F and G, respectively. When they exist, we shall write the density functions of F and G as f and g. In general we shall adhere to the convention that F is less risky than G.

At present our results apply only to c.d.f.'s whose points of increase lie in a bounded interval, and we shall for convenience take that interval to be [0, 1], that is $F(0) = G(0) = 0$ and $F(1) = G(1) = 1$. The extension (and modification) of the results to c.d.f.'s defined on the whole real line is an open question whose resolution requires the solution of a host of delicate convergence problems of little economic interest. $H(x, z)$ is the joint distribution function of the r.v.'s X and Z defined on $[0, 1] \times [-1, 1]$, the cartesian product of [0, 1] and [−1, 1]. We shall use S to refer to the difference of G and F and let T be its indefinite integral, that is, $S(x) = G(x) - F(x)$ and $T(y) = \int_0^y S(x)\,dx$.

II. The Integral Conditions

In this section we give a geometrically motivated definition of what it means for one r.v. to have more weight in the tails than another (Subsections 1 and 2). A definition of "greater risk" should be transitive. An examination of the consequence of this requirement leads to a more general definition which, although less intuitive, is analytically more convenient (Subsections 3 and 4).

1. *Mean Preserving Spreads: Densities*

Let $s(x)$ be a step function defined by

$$s(x) = \begin{cases} \alpha \geqslant 0 & \text{for } a < x < a + t \\ -\alpha \leqslant 0 & \text{for } a + d < x < a + d + t \\ -\beta \leqslant 0 & \text{for } b < x < b + t \\ \beta \geqslant 0 & \text{for } b + e < x < b + e + t \\ 0 & \text{otherwise,} \end{cases} \tag{3.i}$$

642/2/3-2

where

$$0 \leqslant a \leqslant a + t \leqslant a + d \leqslant a + d + t$$
$$\leqslant b \leqslant b + t \leqslant b + e \leqslant b + e + t \leqslant 1 \tag{3.ii}$$

and

$$\beta e = \alpha d. \tag{3.iii}$$

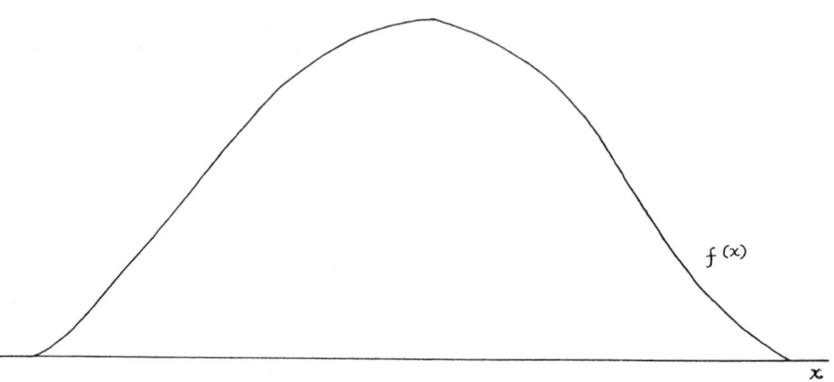

FIGURE 1

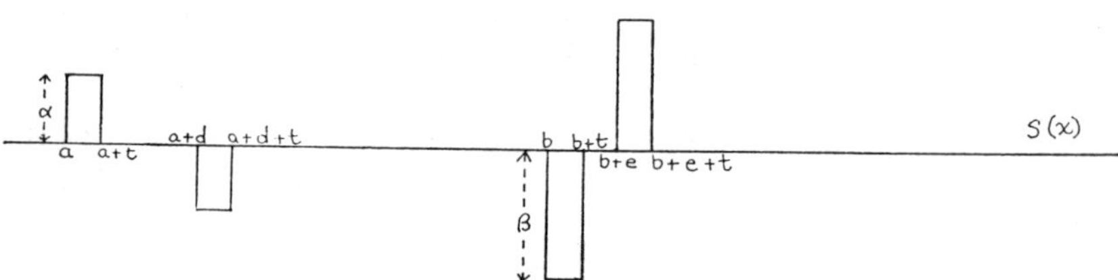

FIGURE 2

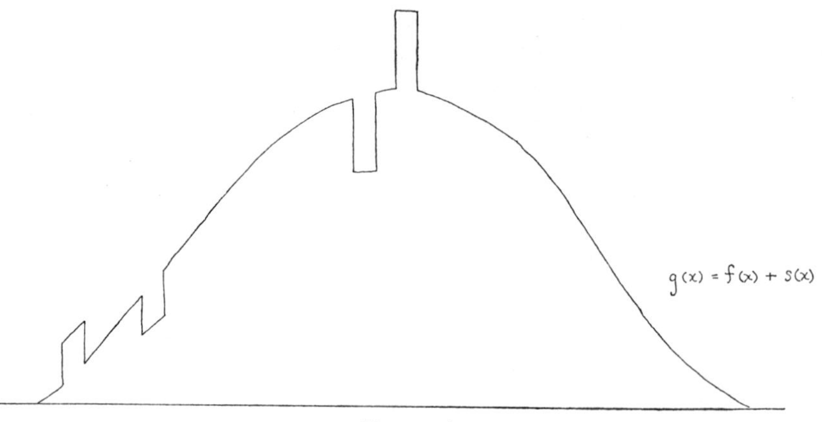

FIGURE 3

Such a function is pictured in Fig. 2. It is easy to verify that $\int_0^1 s(x)\,dx = \int_0^1 xs(x)\,dx = 0$. Thus if f is a density function and if $g = f + s$, then $\int_0^1 g(x)\,dx = \int_0^1 f(x)\,dx + \int_0^1 s(x)\,dx = 1$ and $\int_0^1 xg(x)\,dx = \int_0^1 x(f(x) + s(x))\,dx = \int_0^1 xf(x)\,dx$. It follows then that if $g(x) \geqslant 0$ for all x, g is a density function[4] with the same mean as f. Adding a function like s to f shifts probability weight from the center to the tails. See Figs. 1 and 3. We shall call a function which satisfies conditions (3) a mean preserving spread (MPS) and if f and g are densities and $g - f$ is a MPS we shall say that g differs from f by a single MPS.

2. *Mean Preserving Spreads: Discrete Distributions*

We may define a similar concept for the difference between discrete distributions. Let F and G be the c.d.f.'s of the discrete r.v.'s X and Y. We can describe X and Y completely as follows:

$$\Pr(X = \hat{a}_i) = \hat{f}_i \qquad \text{and} \qquad \Pr(Y = \hat{a}_i) = \hat{g}_i ,$$

where $\sum_i \hat{f}_i = \sum_i \hat{g}_i = 1$, and $\{\hat{a}_i\}$ is an increasing sequence of real numbers bounded by 0 and 1. Suppose $\hat{f}_i = \hat{g}_i$ for all but four i, say i_1, i_2, i_3, and i_4 where $i_k < i_{k+1}$. To avoid double subscripts let $a_k = \hat{a}_{i_k}$, $f_k = \hat{f}_{i_k}$, and $g_k = \hat{g}_{i_k}$, and define

$$\gamma_k = g_k - f_k$$

Then if

$$\gamma_1 = -\gamma_2 \geqslant 0 \qquad \text{and} \qquad \gamma_4 = -\gamma_3 \geqslant 0, \tag{4.i}$$

Y has more weight in the tails than X and if

$$\sum_{k=1}^{4} a_k \gamma_k = 0, \tag{4.ii}$$

the means of X and Y will be the same. See Fig. 4. If two discrete r.v.'s X and Y attribute the same weight to all but four points and if their differences satisfy conditions (4) we shall say that Y differs from X by a single MPS.

3. *The Integral Conditions*

If two densities g and f differ by a single MPS, s, the difference of the corresponding c.d.f.'s G and F will be the indefinite integral of s. That is,

[4] That is, if $f(x) \geqslant \alpha$ for $a + d < x < a + d + t$ and $f(x) \geqslant \beta$ for $b < x < b + t$.

$s = g - f$ implies $S = G - F$ where $S(x) = \int_0^x s(u)\, du$. S, which is drawn in Fig. 5, has several interesting properties. The last two of these ((6) and (7) below) will play a crucial role in this paper, and we will refer to them as the integral conditions. First $S(0) = S(1) = 0$. Second, there is a z such that

$$S(x) \geqslant 0 \quad \text{if} \quad x \leqslant z \qquad \text{and} \qquad S(x) \leqslant 0 \quad \text{if} \quad x > z. \tag{5}$$

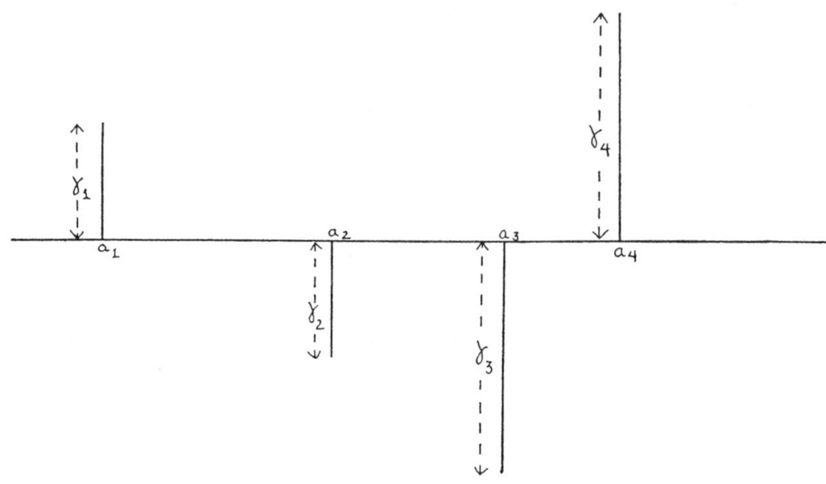

FIGURE 4

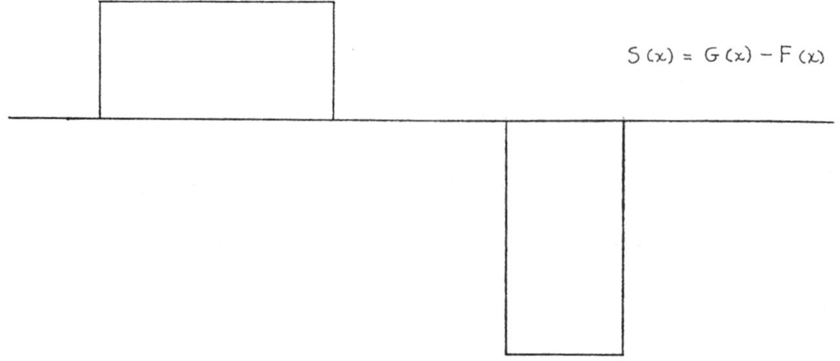

FIGURE 5

Thirdly, if $T(y) = \int_0^y S(x)\, dx$ then

$$T(1) = 0 \tag{6}$$

since $T(1) = \int_0^1 S(x)\, dx = xS(x)]_0^1 - \int_0^1 xs(x)\, dx = 0$.

Finally, conditions (5) and (6) together imply that

$$T(y) \geqslant 0, \qquad 0 \leqslant y < 1. \tag{7}$$

If G and F are discrete distributions differing by a single MPS and if $S = G - F$ then S satisfies (5), (6), and (7). See Fig. 6.

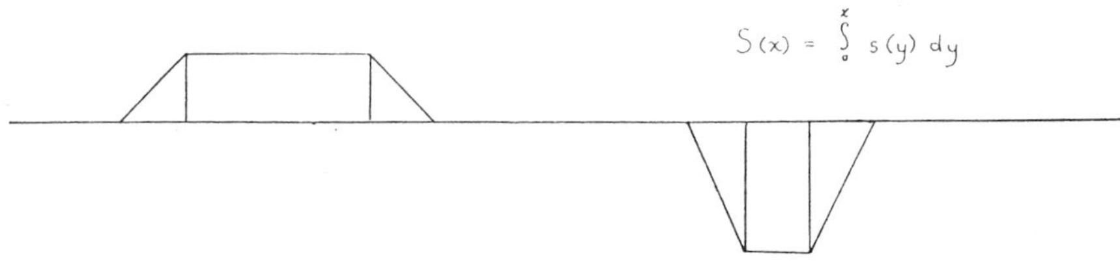

FIGURE 6

4. *Implications of Transitivity*

The concept of a MPS is the beginning, but only the beginning, of a definition of greater variability. To complete it we need to explore the implications of transitivity. That is, for our definition to be reasonable it should be the case that if X_1 is riskier than X_2 which is in turn riskier than X_3, then X_1 is riskier than X_3. Thus, if X and Y are the r.v.'s with c.d.f.'s F and G, we need to find a criterion for deciding whether G could have been obtained from F by a sequence of MPS's. We demonstrate in this section that the criterion is contained in conditions (6) and (7) above.[5]

We will proceed by first stating precisely in Theorem 1(a) the obvious fact that if G is obtained from F by a sequence of MPS's, then $G - F$ satisfies the integral conditions ((6) and (7)). Theorem 1(b) is roughly the converse of that statement: That is, we show that if $G - F$ satisfies the integral conditions, G could have been obtained from F to any desired degree of approximation by a sequence of MPS's.

THEOREM 1(a). *If* (a) *there is a sequence of c.d.f.'s* $\{F_n\}$ *converging (weakly) to* G, (*written* $F_n \to G$)[6] *and* (b) F_n *differs from* F_{n-1} *by a single* MPS, (*which implies* $F_n = F_{n-1} + S_n = F_0 + \sum_{i=1}^{n} S_i$, *where* $F_0 \equiv F$, *and where each* S_i *satisfies* (6) *and* (7)), *then* $G = F + \sum_{i=1}^{\infty} S_i = F + S$ *and* S *satisfies* (6) *and* (7).

The proof, which is obvious, is omitted.

[5] Condition (5) could not be part of such a criterion for it is easy to construct examples of c.d.f's which differ by two MPS's such that their difference does not satisfy (5).

[6] Let $E(u) = \int_0^1 u(x)\, dG(x)$ and $E_n(u) = \int_0^1 u(x)\, dF_n(x)$. Then $F_n \to G$ if and only if $E_n(u) \to E(u)$ for all continuous u on [0, 1]. See [3, p. 243].

THEOREM 1(b). *If $G - F$ satisfies the integral conditions* (6) *and* (7), *then there exist sequences F_n and G_n, $F_n \to F$, $G_n \to G$, such that for each n, G_n could have been obtained from F_n by a finite number of MPS's.*

The proof is an immediate consequence of the following two lemmas: the first proves the theorem for step functions with a finite number of steps; and the second states that F and G may be approximated arbitrarily closely by step functions which satisfy the integral conditions.

LEMMA 1. *If X and Y are discrete r.v.'s whose c.d.f.'s F and G have a finite number of points of increase, and if $S = G - F$ satisfies* (6) *and* (7), *then there exist c.d.f.'s, $F_0, \ldots, F_n$ such that $F_0 = F$, $F_n = G$, and F_i differs from F_{i-1} by a single MPS.*

Proof. S is a step function with a finite number of steps. Let $I_1 = (a_1, a_2)$ be the first positive step of S. If I_1 does not exist, $S(x) \equiv 0$ implying that $F = G$ and the lemma is trivally true. Let $I_2 = (a_3, a_4)$ be the first negative step of $S(x)$. By (7), $a_2 < a_3$. Let γ_1 be the value of $S(x)$ on I_1 and $-\gamma_2$ be the value of $S(x)$ on I_2.

Either

$$\gamma_1(a_2 - a_1) \geqslant \gamma_2(a_4 - a_3) \tag{8}$$

or

$$\gamma_1(a_2 - a_1) < \gamma_2(a_4 - a_3). \tag{9}$$

If (8) holds, let $\hat{a}_4 = a_4$. There is an $\hat{a}_2$ satisfying $a_1 < \hat{a}_2 \leqslant a_2$ such that

$$\gamma_1(\hat{a}_2 - a_1) = \gamma_2(\hat{a}_4 - a_3). \tag{10}$$

If (9) holds, let $\hat{a}_2 = a_2$; then there is an $\hat{a}_4$ satisfying $a_3 < \hat{a}_4 < a_4$ such that (10) holds. Define $S_1(x)$ by

$$S_1(x) = \begin{cases} \gamma_1 & \text{for } a_1 < x < \hat{a}_2 \\ -\gamma_2 & \text{for } a_3 < x < \hat{a}_4 \\ 0 & \text{otherwise.} \end{cases}$$

Then if $F_1 = F_0 + S_1$, F_1 differs from F by a single MPS and $S^{(1)} = G - F_1$ satisfies (6) and (7).

We use this technique to construct S_2 from $S^{(1)}$ and define F_2 by $F_2 = F_1 + S_2$. Because S is a step function with a finite number of steps, the process terminates after a finite number of iterations.

LEMMA 2. *Let F and G be c.d.f.'s defined on* [0, 1]. *Let $T(y) = \int_0^y (G(x) - F(x))\, dx$. If*

$$T(y) \geqslant 0, \qquad 0 \leqslant y \leqslant 1, \tag{6}$$

and

$$T(1) = 0 \tag{7}$$

then, for each n, there exists F_n *and* G_n, *c.d.f.'s of discrete r.v.'s with a finite number of points of increase, such that if*

$$\| F_n - F \| = \int_0^1 | F_n(x) - F(x)| \, dx$$

and

$$\| G_n - G \| = \int_0^1 | G_n(x) - G(x)| \, dx,$$

then[7]

$$\| F_n - F \| + \| G_n - G \| \leqslant \frac{4}{n} \tag{11}$$

and if $T_n(y) = \int_0^y (G_n(x) - F_n(x)) \, dx$ *then*

$$T_n(y) \geqslant 0 \tag{12}$$

and

$$T_n(1) = 0. \tag{13}$$

Proof. We prove this by constructing F_n and G_n for fixed n. For $i = 1, \ldots, n$ let $I_i = ((i-1)/n, i/n)$. Let $\bar{f}_i = F(i/n)$ and define $\bar{F}_n$ by $\bar{F}_n(x) = \bar{f}_i$ for $x \in I_i$ (see Fig. 7). Since F is monotonic $\bar{F}_n(x) \geqslant F(x)$. It follows also from monotonicity that $\| F_n - F \| \leqslant 1/n$. If $\hat{F}_n(x)$ is any step function constant on each I_i such that $\hat{F}_n(x) \in F(I_i)$ for $x \in I_i$ then $\| \hat{F}_n - \bar{F}_n \| \leqslant 1/n$ and

$$\| \hat{F}_n - F \| \leqslant \| \hat{F}_n - \bar{F}^n \| + \| \bar{F}_n - F \| \leqslant \frac{2}{n}.$$

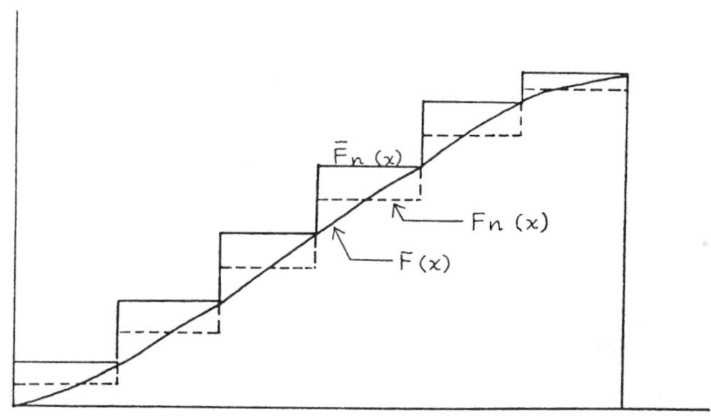

FIGURE 7

[7] Condition (11) implies weak convergence. See [3, p. 243].

Similarly if $\hat{G}_n(x)$ is a step function such that $x \in I_i$ implies $\hat{G}_n(x) \in G(I_i)$ then $\| \hat{G}_n - G \| \leqslant 2/n$.

For every i there exist $f_i \in F(I_i)$ and $g_i \in G(I_i)$ such that $(g_i - f_i)/n = \int_{I_i} (G(x) - F(x))\, dx$. Let $\hat{F}_n(x) = f_i$ and $\hat{G}_n(x) = g_i$, $x \in I_i$. We now show that $\hat{F}_n$ and $\hat{G}_n$ satisfy (11), (12), and (13). We have already shown that (11) is satisfied. Observe that

$$\begin{aligned}\hat{T}_n(1) &= \int_0^1 (\hat{G}_n(x) - \hat{F}_n(x))\, dx \\ &= \sum_{i=1}^{n} \int_{I_i} (\hat{G}_n(x) - \hat{F}_n(x))\, dx \\ &= \sum_{i=1}^{n} \frac{g_i - f_i}{n} = \sum_{i=1}^{n} \int_{I_i} (G(x) - F(x))\, dx \\ &= \int_0^1 (G(x) - F(x))\, dx = T(1) = 0,\end{aligned}$$

so that (13) is satisfied. It remains to show that $\hat{T}_n(y) \geqslant 0$. If $y = j/n$ for $j = 0, 1,\ldots, n$, then $\hat{T}_n(y) = T(j/n) \geqslant 0$ so we need only examine the case where $y = j/n + \alpha, 0 < \alpha < 1/n$. Then, $\hat{T}_n(x) = T(j/n) + \alpha(g_j - f_j)$. If $g_j > f_j$ both terms of the sum are positive. If $g_j < f_j$ then

$$T\left(\frac{j}{n}\right) + \alpha(g_j - f_j) > T\left(\frac{j}{n}\right) + \frac{1}{n}(g_j - f_j) = T\left(\frac{j+1}{n}\right) \geqslant 0.$$

This completes the proof except for a technical detail. Neither $\hat{F}_n$ nor $\hat{G}_n$ are necessarily c.d.f.'s. We remedy this by defining $F_n(x) = \hat{F}_n(x)$ for $x \in (0, 1)$ and $F_n(0) = 0$ and $F_n(1) = 1$. G_n is defined similarly and if $\hat{F}_n$ and $\hat{G}_n$ satisfy (11), (12), and (13) so do F_n and G_n.

III. Partial Orderings of Distribution Functions

A definition of greater uncertainty is, or should be, a definition of a partial ordering on a set of distribution functions. In this section we formally define the three partial orderings corresponding to the first three concepts of increasing risk set out in Section I and prove their equivalence.

1. *Partial Orderings*

A partial ordering $\leqslant_p$ on a set is a binary, transitive, reflexive and antisymmetric[8] relation. The set over which our partial orderings are defined is the set of distribution functions on [0, 1]. We shall use $F \leqslant_p G$

[8] A relation $\leqslant_p$ is antisymmetric if $A \leqslant_p B$ and $B \leqslant_p A$ implies $A = B$.

interchangeably with $X \leqslant_p Y$ where F and G are the c.d.f.'s of the r.v.'s X and Y.

2. *Definition of* $\leqslant_I$

Following the discussion of the last section we define a partial ordering $\leqslant_I$ as follows: $F \leqslant_I G$ if and only if $G - F$ satisfies the integral conditions (6) and (7).

LEMMA 3. *$\leqslant_I$ is a partial ordering.*

Proof. It is immediate that $\leqslant_I$ is transitive and reflexive. We need only demonstrate antisymmetry. Assume $F \leqslant_I G$ and $G \leqslant_I F$. Define S_1 and S_2 as follows:

$$S_1 = G - F \qquad \text{and} \qquad S_2 = F - G.$$

Thus $S_1 + S_2 = 0$. Furthermore, if $T_i(y) = \int_0^y S_i(x)\,dx$, then $T_i(y) \geqslant 0$, since $F \leqslant_I G$ and $G \leqslant_I F$. Since $0 = \int_0^y (S_1(x) + S_2(x))\,dx = T_1(y) + T_2(y) = 0$ and $T_i(y) \geqslant 0$, $T_i(y) = 0$. We shall prove this implies that $S_1(x) = 0$ a.e. (almost everywhere), or $F(x) = G(x)$ a.e. This will prove the lemma.[9]

Since $S_1(x)$ is of bounded variation (it is the difference of two monotonic functions) its discontinuities form a set of measure zero. Let us call this set N. Define

$$\hat{S}_1(x) = \begin{cases} 0 & \text{for} \quad x \in N \\ S_1(x) & \quad \text{otherwise.} \end{cases}$$

Then $\int_0^y S_1(x)\,dx = \int_0^y \hat{S}_1(x)\,dx = T_1(y)$. Suppose there is an $\hat{x}$ such that $\hat{S}_1(\hat{x}) \neq 0$, say $\hat{S}_1(\hat{x}) > 0$. Then $\hat{S}_1(x) > 0$ for $x \in (\hat{x} - \epsilon, \hat{x} + \epsilon)$ for some $\epsilon > 0$ (since $\hat{S}_1(x)$ is continuous at $\hat{x}$). Then, $T_1(x - \epsilon) < T_1(x + \epsilon)$. This contradiction completes the proof.

3. *Definition of* $\leqslant_u$

We define the partial ordering $\leqslant_u$ corresponding to the idea that X is less risky than Y if every risk averter prefers X to Y as follows. $F \leqslant_u G$ if and only if for every bounded concave function U, $\int_0^1 U(x)\,dF(x) \geqslant \int_0^1 U(x)\,dG(x)$. It is immediate that $\leqslant_u$ is transitive and reflexive. That $\leqslant_u$ is antisymmetric is an immediate consequence of Theorem 2 below.

4. *Definition of* $\leqslant_a$

Corresponding to the notion that X is less risky than Y if Y has the same distribution as X plus some noise is the partial ordering $\leqslant_a$ which

[9] We shall follow the convention of considering two distribution functions to be equal if they differ only on a set of measure zero.

we now define. $F \leqslant_a G$ if and only if there exists a joint distribution function $H(x, z)$ of the r.v.'s X and Z defined on $[0, 1] \times [-1, 1]$ such that if

$$J(y) = \Pr(X + Z \leqslant y),$$

then

$$F(x) = H(x, 1), \qquad 0 \leqslant x \leqslant 1,$$
$$G(y) = J(y), \qquad 0 \leqslant y \leqslant 1,$$

and

$$E(Z \mid X = x) = 0 \qquad \text{for all } x. \tag{14}$$

The equivalent definition in terms of r.v.'s follows: $X \leqslant_a Y$ if there exists an r.v. Z satisfying (14) such that

$$Y \underset{d}{=} X + Z. \tag{15}$$

It is important to realize that (15) does *not* mean that $Y = X + Z$.

For the special case where X and Y are discrete distributions concentrated at a finite number of points, the relation $\leqslant_a$ can be given a useful and tractable characterization. Without loss of generality assume that X and Y are concentrated at the points $a_1, a_2, ..., a_n$. Then the c.d.f.'s of X and Y are determined by the numbers

$$f_i = \Pr(X = a_i)$$

and

$$g_i = \Pr(Y = a_i).$$

Then $X \leqslant_a Y$ if and only if there exist n^2 numbers $c_{ij} \geqslant 0$ such that

$$\sum_j c_{ij} = 1, \qquad i = 1, ..., n, \tag{16}$$

$$\sum_j c_{ij}(a_j - a_i) = 0, \qquad i = 1, ..., n, \tag{14'}$$

and

$$g_j = \sum_i f_i c_{ij}, \qquad j = 1, ..., n. \tag{15'}$$

To see that this is so, define an r.v. Z conditional on X as follows,

$$c_{ij} = \Pr(Z = a_j - a_i \mid X = a_i).$$

Then (16) states that this equation in fact defines a r.v. while (14′) and (15′)

are the analoges of (14) and (15). These conditions can be written in matrix form:

$$Ca = a, \tag{14''}$$

$$g = fC, \tag{15''}$$

$$Ce = e, \tag{16''}$$

where $e = (1,..., 1)$ is the vector composed entirely of 1's. If f^1, f^2, and f^3 are vectors defining the c.d.f.'s of the discrete r.v.'s X^1, X^2, and X^3, $(f_i^k = \Pr(X^k = a_i))$, and if $X^1 \leqslant_a X^2$ and $X^2 \leqslant_a X^3$ then there exist matrices C^1 and C^2 such that $C^1a = C^2a = a$; $C^1e = C^2e = e$, while $f^2 = f^1C^1$ and $f^3 = f^2C^2$. Let $C^* = C^1C^2$. Then $f^3 = f^1C^*$ and $C^*a = C^1C^2a = C^1a = a$ and similarly $C^*e = e$. We have proved

LEMMA 4. *If X^1, X^2, and X^3 are concentrated at a finite number of points, then $X^1 \leqslant_a X^2 \leqslant_a X^3$ implies $X^1 \leqslant_a X^3$.*

5. *Equivalence of $\leqslant_I$, $\leqslant_a$, $\leqslant_u$*

We now state and prove the major result of this paper.

THEOREM 2. *The following statements are equivalent:*

(A) $F \leqslant_u G$;

(B) $F \leqslant_I G$;

(C) $F \leqslant_a G$.

Proof. The proof consists of demonstrating the chain of implications (C) ⇒ (A) ⇒ (B) ⇒ (C). Throughout the proof we adhere to the notational conventions introduced at the end of Section I.

(a) $X \leqslant_a Y \Rightarrow X \leqslant_u Y$.

By hypothesis there is an r.v. Z such that $Y \underset{a}{=} X + Z$ and $E(Z \mid X) = 0$. For every fixed X and concave U we have, upon taking expectations with respect to Z, by Jensen's inequality

$$E_X U(X + Z) \leqslant U(E(X + Z)) = U(X).$$

Taking expectations with respect to X,

$$EE_X U(X + Z) \leqslant EU(X)$$

or

$$EU(Y) \leqslant EU(X).$$

(b) $F \leqslant_u G \Rightarrow F \leqslant_I G.$[10]

If $S = G - F$ then $F \leqslant_u G$ implies $\int_0^1 U(x)\, dS(X) \leqslant 0$ for all concave U. Since the identity function and its negative are both concave we have that $\int_0^1 x\, dS(x) \leqslant 0$ and $\int_0^1 (-x)\, dS(x) \leqslant 0$ so that $\int_0^1 x\, dS(x) = 0$. Integrating by parts we find that $T(1) = 0$. It remains to show that $T(y) \geqslant 0$ for all $y \in [0, 1]$. For fixed y, let $b_y(x) = \text{Max}(y - x, 0)$. Then $-b_y(x)$ is concave and $0 \leqslant \int_0^1 b_y(x)\, dS(x) = \int_0^y (y - x)\, dS(x) = yS(y) - \int_0^y x\, dS(x)$. Integrating the last term by parts we find that

$$\begin{aligned} -\int_0^y x\, dS(x) &= -xS(x)\Big]_0^y + \int_0^y S(x)\, dx \\ &= -yS(y) + T(y). \end{aligned}$$

Thus, $T(y) = \int_0^1 b_y(x)\, dS(x) \geqslant 0$.

(c) $F \leqslant_I G \Rightarrow F \leqslant_a G$.

We prove this implication first for the case where F and G are discrete r.v.'s which differ by a single MPS. Using the notation of Section II.2, let F and G attribute the same probability weight to all but four points $a_1 < a_2 < a_3 < a_4$. Let $\Pr(X = a_k) = f_k$ and $\Pr(Y = a_k) = g_k$. If $\gamma_k = g_k - f_k$, then

$$\gamma_1 = -\gamma_2 \geqslant 0, \qquad \gamma_4 = -\gamma_3 \geqslant 0 \tag{4.i}$$

and

$$\sum_{k=1}^{4} \gamma_k a_k = 0 \tag{4.ii}$$

are the conditions that G differs from F by a single MPS. To prove that $F \leqslant_a G$ we need only show the existence of $c_{ij} \geqslant 0$ $(i, j = 1, 2, 3, 4)$ satisfying (14′), (15′), and (16). Consider,

$$\{c_{ij}\} = \begin{pmatrix} 1 & 0 & 0 & 0 \\ \dfrac{\gamma_1(a_4 - a_2)}{f_2(a_4 - a_1)} & \dfrac{g_2}{f_2} & 0 & \dfrac{\gamma_1(a_2 - a_1)}{f_2(a_4 - a_1)} \\ \dfrac{\gamma_4(a_4 - a_3)}{f_3(a_4 - a_1)} & 0 & \dfrac{g_3}{f_3} & \dfrac{\gamma_4(a_3 - a_1)}{f_3(a_4 - a_1)} \\ 0 & 0 & 0 & 1 \end{pmatrix} \tag{17}$$

[10] We are indebted to David Wallace for the present simplified form of the proof. For continuously differentiable U, the reverse implication may be proved simply by integration by parts.

It is easy to verify that the c_{ij} defined by (17) do satisfy (16) and (14′). Thus if we define Z, as before, by

$$c_{ij} = \Pr(Z = a_j - a_i \mid X = a_i)$$

then Z is a random variable, conditional on X, satisfying $E(Z \mid X) = 0$. It remains to establish (15′) or that $Y \underset{d}{=} X + Z$. Consider $Y^1 = X + Z$. Y^1 is a discrete r.v. which, since $E(Z) = 0$, has the same mean as Y. It can differ from Y only if it attributes different probability weight to the points a_1, a_2, a_3, a_4. But,

$$\begin{aligned}\Pr(Y^1 = a_2) &= \Pr(X = a_2) \cdot \Pr(Z = 0 \mid X = a_2)\\ &= f_2 \cdot \frac{g_2}{f_2} = g_2 = \Pr(Y = a_2).\end{aligned}$$

Similarly, $\Pr(Y^1 = a_3) = \Pr(Y = a_3)$. Then Y and Y^1 can differ in the assignment of probability weight in at most two points. But $\Pr(Y = a_1) > \Pr(Y^1 = a_1)$ implies $\Pr(Y^1 = a_4) > \Pr(Y = a_4)$ which in turn implies that $E(Y^1) > E(Y)$, a contradiction. Thus, $Y \underset{d}{=} Y^1 \underset{d}{=} X + Z$.

Lemmas 1 and 4 allow us to extend this result to all discrete distributions with a finite number of points of increase. We use Theorem 1(b) to extend it to all c.d.f.'s. If $F \leqslant_I G$, there exists sequences $\{F_n\}$ and $\{G_n\}$ of discrete distributions with a finite number of points of increase such that $F_n \to F$ and $G_n \to G$ and $F_n \leqslant_I G_n$. We have just shown $F_n \leqslant_a G_n$. Let X_n and Y_n be the r.v.'s with distributions F_n and G_n. There is for each n an $H_n(x, z)$, the joint distribution function of the r.v.'s X_n and Z_n, such that if $J_n(y) = \Pr(X_n + Z_n \leqslant y)$, then

$$J_n(y) = G_n(y), \tag{18}$$

$$F_n(x) = H_n(x, 1), \tag{19}$$

and

$$E(X_n \mid Z_n) = 0. \tag{20}$$

Since H_n is a discrete distribution function Eq. (20) can be phrased as

$$\int_0^1 \int_{-1}^1 u(x) z \, dH_n(x, z) = 0 \tag{21}$$

for all continuous functions u defined on [0, 1]. Since H_n is stochastically bounded, the sequence $\{H_n\}$ has a subsequence $\{H_{n'}\}$ which converges to a distribution function[11] $H(x, z)$ of the r.v.'s X and Z. Since $H_{n'}(x, 1) = F_{n'}(x) \to F$, $H_{n'}(x, 1) \to F$. Similarly, $J_{n'} \to G$. Let

$$M_{n'} = \int_0^1 \int_{-1}^1 u(x) z \, dH_{n'}(x, z).$$

[11] See [3, pp. 247, 261].

By the definition of weak convergence $M_{n'} \to \int_0^1 \int_{-1}^1 u(x)z\, dH(x, z)$. But $\{M_{n'}\}$ is a sequence all of whose terms are 0 and it must therefore converge to 0. Therefore $\int_0^1 \int_{-1}^1 u(x)z\, dH(x, z) = 0$, which implies $E(Z \mid X) = 0$. This completes the proof.

6. *Further Remarks*

We conclude this section with two remarks about these orderings.

A. *Partial versus Complete Orderings.* In the previous subsection, we established that $\geqslant_a$, $\geqslant_I$, and $\geqslant_u$ define equivalent partial orderings over distributions with the same mean. It should be emphasized that these orderings are only partial, that is, if F and G have the same mean but $\int_0^1 (F(x) - G(x))\, dx = T(y)$ changes sign, F and G cannot be ordered. But this means in turn that there always exist two concave functions, U_1 and U_2, such that $\int_0^1 U_1\, dF(x) > \int_0^1 dG(x)$ while $\int_0^1 U_2\, dF(x) < \int_0^1 U_2\, dG(x)$; that is, there is some risk averse individual who prefers F to G and another who prefers G to F. On the other hand, the ordering $\geqslant_V$ associated with the mean-variance analysis ($X \leqslant_V Y$ if $EX = EY$ and $EX^2 \leqslant EY^2$) is a complete ordering, i.e., if X and Y have the same mean, either $X \leqslant_V Y$ or $X \geqslant_V X$.[12]

B. *Concavity.* We have already noted that if U is concave, $X \leqslant_I Y$ implies $EU(X) \leqslant EU(Y)$. Similarly, given any differentiable function U which over the interval [0, 1] is neither concave nor convex, then there exist distribution functions F, G, and H, $F \geqslant_I G \geqslant_I H$, such that $\int_0^1 U(x)\, dF \leqslant \int_0^1 U(x)\, dG$, but $\int_0^1 U(x)\, dG \geqslant \int_0^1 U(x)\, dH$.

In short, $\geqslant_I$ defines the set of all concave functions: A function U is concave if and only if $X \leqslant_I Y$ implies $EU(X) \leqslant EU(Y)$.

[12] Another way of making this point is to observe that $\geqslant_V$ is stronger than $\geqslant_I$ because many distributions which can be ordered with respect to $\geqslant_V$ cannot be ordered with respect to $\geqslant_I$. Clearly there exist weaker as well as stronger orderings than $\geqslant_I$. One such weaker ordering, to which we drew attention in earlier versions of this paper, is the following. A r.v. X which is a mixture between a r.v. Y and a sure thing with the same mean—a random variable concentrated at the point $E(Y)$—is surely less risky than Y itself. We could use this notion to define a partial ordering $\geqslant_M$. It is obvious that $\geqslant_M$ implies $\geqslant_I$ since the difference between X and Y satisfies the integral conditions. It is also clear that $\geqslant_M$ is a very weak ordering in the sense that very few r.v.'s can be ordered by $\geqslant_M$. In fact if $\bar{Y}$ is the sure thing concentrated at $E(Y)$ than it can be shown that $Y \geqslant_M X$ iff $X \underset{d}{=} aY + (1 - a)\bar{Y}$ for $0 \leqslant a \leqslant 1$. This indicates that $\geqslant_M$ is not a particularly interesting partial ordering. We are indebted to an anonymous referee for pointing out the deficiencies of $\geqslant_M$.

IV. Mean-Variance Analysis

The method most frequently used for comparing uncertain prospects has been mean-variance analysis. It is easy to show that such comparisons may lead to unjustified conclusions. For instance, if X and Y have the same mean, X may have a lower variance and yet Y will be preferred to X by some risk averse individuals. To see this, all we need observe is that, although $F \leqslant_u G \Rightarrow F \geqslant_V G$ (since variance is a convex function), $F \geqslant_V G$ does not imply $F \geqslant_u G$. Indeed by arguments closely analogous to those used earlier, it can be shown that a function U is quadratic if and only if $X \geqslant_V Y$ implies $EU(X) \geqslant EU(Y)$. An immediate consequence of this is that if $U(x)$ is any nonquadratic concave function, then there exists random variables X_i, $i = 1, 2, 3$, all with the same mean such that $EX_1^2 < EX_2^2$ but $EX_2^2 > EX_3^2$ while $EU(X_1) < EU(X_2) < EU(X_3)$, i.e., the ranking by variance and the ranking by expected utility are different.

Tobin has conjectured that mean-variance analysis may be appropriate if the class of distributions—and thus the class of changes in distributions—is restricted. This is true but the restrictions required are, as far as is presently known, very severe. Tobin's proof is—as he implicitly recognizes (in [7, pp. 20–21])—valid only for distributions which differ only by "location parameters." (See [3, p. 144] for a discussion of this classical concept.) That is, Tobin is only willing to consider changes in distributions from F to G if there exist a and b ($a > 0$) such that $F(x) = G(ax + b)$. Such changes amount only to a change in the centering of the distribution and a uniform shrinking or stretching of the distribution—equivalent to a change in units.

There has been some needless confusion along these lines about the concept of a two parameter family of distribution functions. It is undeniable that all distributions which differ only by location parameters form a two parameter family. In general, what is meant by a "two parameter family"? To us a two parameter family of distributions would seem to be any set of distributions such that one member of the set would be picked out be selecting two parameters. As Tobin has put it, it is "one such that it is necessary to know just two numbers in order to describe the whole distribution." Technically that is, a two parameter family is a mapping from E^2 into the space of distribution functions.[13] It is clear that for this broad definition of two parameter family, Tobin's conjecture cannot possibly hold, for nothing restricts the range of this mapping.

Other definitions of two parameter family are of course possible. They involve essentially restrictions to "nice" mappings from E^2 to the space of

[13] Or some subset of E^2; we might restrict one or both of our parameters to be nonnegative.

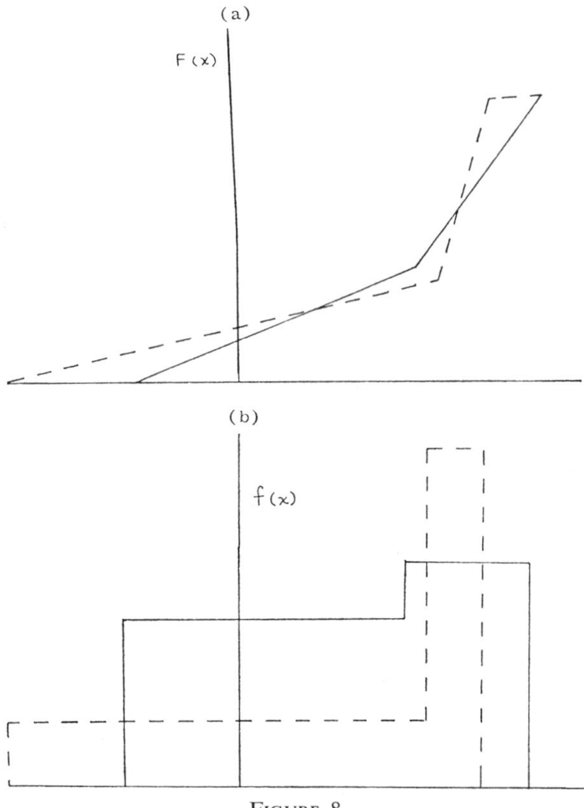

FIGURE 8

distribution functions, e.g., a family of distributions with an explicit algebraic form containing only two parameters which can vary. It is easy, however, to construct examples where if the variance, σ^2, changes with the mean, μ, held constant, $\partial T(y)/\partial\sigma^2$ changes sign, where $T(y, \sigma^2, \mu) = \int_0^y F(x, \sigma^2, \mu)$; that is, there exist individuals with concave utility functions who are better off with an increase in variance.[14]

[14] Consider, for instance, the family of distributions defined as follows: $(a, c > 0)$. (In this example, for expositional clarity we have abandoned our usual convention of defining distributions over [0, 1])

$$F(x; a, c) = \begin{cases} 0 & \text{for } x \leqslant 1 - 0.25/a \\ ax + 0.25 - a & \text{for } 1 - 0.25/a \leqslant x \leqslant 1 + (2c - 0.5)/c - a) \\ cx + 0.75 - 3c & \text{for } 1 + (2c - 0.5)/(c - a) \leqslant x \leqslant 3 + 0.25/c \\ 1 & \text{for } x > 3 + 0.25/c \end{cases}$$

Two members of the family with the same mean but different variances are depicted in Fig. 8(a). They clearly do not satisfy condition (7). The density functions are illustrated in Fig. 8(b).

ACKNOWLEDGMENTS

This is a revised version of papers presented at the Cowles Symposium on Capital Theory and Uncertainty (November, 1968), and at the Chicago Growth Symposium (November, 1967).

The authors are deeply indebted to the participants in the symposiums and to David Ragozin, Peter Diamond, David Wallace, and David Grether.

Our problem is not a new one, nor is our approach completely novel; our result is, we think, new. Our interest in this topic was whetted by Peter Diamond [2]. Robert Solow used a device similar to our Mean Preserving Spread (Section II, above) to compare lag structures in [6]. The problem of "stochastic dominance" is a standard one in the (statistics) operations research literature. For other approaches to the problem, see, for instance, [1]. [4, 5] have recently provided an alternative proof to our Theorem 2(b) and its converse (p. 238).

REFERENCES

1. S. A. BESSLER AND A. F. VEINOTT, JR., Optimal policy for a dynamic multi-echelon inventory model, *Naval Research Logistics Quarterly* **13** (1966), 355–387.
2. P. A. DIAMOND, Savings decisions under uncertainty, Working paper no. 71, Institute of Business Economic Research, University of California, Berkeley, June 1965.
3. W. FELLER, "An Introduction to Probability Theory and Its Applications," Vol. II, Wiley, New York, 1966.
4. J. HADER AND W. RUSSELL, Rules for ordering uncertain prospects, *Amer. Econ. Rev.* **59** (1969), 25–34.
5. G. HANOCH AND C. LEVY, Efficiency Analysis of Choices Involving risk, *Review of Economic Studies* **36** (1969).
6. R. M. SOLOW, A note on dynamic multipliers, *Econometrica* **19** (1951), 306–316.
7. J. TOBIN, The theory of portfolio selection, *in* F. Hahn and F. Brechling, "The Theory of Interest Rates," MacMillan, London, 1965.
8. J. TOBIN, Comment on Borch and Feldstein, *Rev. Econ. Studies* **36** (1969), 13–14.

642/2/3-3

Comment

The major result of this paper (Theorem 2) was discovered long ago. A proof of the equivalence of the partial orderings $\leqslant_I$ and $\leqslant_u$ can be found in the classic treatise *Inequalities* (Hardy *et al.*, 1953). The equivalence between $\leqslant_a$ and $\leqslant_u$ is the basic result of a branch of statistical decision theory known as the comparison of experiments.[1] Kolm (1969) who, unlike Rothschild and Stiglitz, was well aware of their origins, seems to have been the first to apply these results to economic problems. Most of his work is in French, although some of it is in English. Two examples are given in the references below. Kolm (1969) and Atkinson (1970) observed that the principles used in describing an individual's evaluations of the random distribution of monetary rewards could be used to describe the social evaluation of the distributions of monetary income among individuals. The reader of Chapter 5 will have observed that the additive structure of preferences that the expected utility theorem assumes is not essential for this analysis. For further results without the assumption of additivity, see Dasgupta *et al.*, (1973) and Rothschild and Stiglitz (1973).

These definitions of increased risk have proved quite useful in comparative static analysis of a variety of economic problems. In a companion piece to this article, Rothschild and Stiglitz (1971) gave several examples of how this approach could be used to derive comparative static results. Some of those results are contained in the exercises in the next chapter. There you are asked to use the partial ordering $\leqslant_u$ (and a variant discussed in Chapter 7) to investigate the effects of increased uncertainty. The following brief selection from the second Rothschild-Stiglitz article shows how the partial ordering $\leqslant_a$ may be used for the same purpose.

A. Diversification Theorem

Assume an individual can purchase shares of two securities whose value next period (per dollar invested) is described by identical but independent distribu-

[1] The equivalence between $\leqslant_a$ and $\leqslant_u$ holds in much more general settings. A relatively elementary discussion and proof for vector-valued discrete random variables can be found in the last chapter of Blackwell and Girschick (1954). For a more advanced treatment, see Mayer (1966) or Strassen (1965). We know of no definition of $\leqslant_I$ that holds for these more general cases.

tions. How should he allocate his given initial wealth, i.e., how should he choose b to maximize

$$EU(W) = EU((be_1 + (1 - b)e_2)W_0)$$

where U is a concave function? We prove that, independent of the utility function, b should be set at $\frac{1}{2}$. We can write

$$y_b = (be_1 + (1 - b)e_2)W_0 = y_{1/2} - (b - \tfrac{1}{2})(e_1 - e_2)W_0$$

Note that

$$E(e_1 - e_2 | y_{1/2}) = 0$$

i.e., the expected value of the difference between two identically distributed independent random variables, given only that their sum be a particular number, is zero. Since y_b has the same distribution as $y_{1/2}$ plus a random variable whose expectation conditional on $y_{1/2}$ is zero, by Theorem 2 of this reading, y_b is more variable than $y_{1/2}$ for all $b \neq \frac{1}{2}$, i.e., $y_{1/2}$ is preferred to y_b by all individuals with concave utility functions.

Exercise Extend this argument to the following two cases:

(a) The assets are symmetrically but not independently distributed, that is, $F(e_1, e_2) = F(e_2, e_1)$ for all e_1 and e_2.
[*Hint:* $e_1 - e_2 = \frac{1}{2}[(e_1 - e_2) - (e_2 - e_1)]$.]

(b) There are n independent identically distributed assets.

References

A. Atkinson, On the measurement of inequality, *J. Econ. Theory* **2** (1970), 244–263.

D. Blackwell and M. A. Girschick, "Theory of Games and Statistical Decisions." New York: Wiley, 1954.

P. Dasgupta, A. Sen, and D. Starrett, Notes on the measurement of inequality, *J. Econ. Theory* **6** (1973), 180–187.

G. H. Hardy, J. E. Littlewood, and G. Polya, "Inequalities," 2nd ed. London: Cambridge Univ. Press, 1953 (1st ed., 1934).

S. C. Kolm, "Le Choix Financiers et Monetaires." Paris: Dunod, 1966.

S. C. Kolm, The optimal production of social justice, *in* "Public Economics" (J. Margolis and H. Guitton, eds.). New York: Macmillan, 1969.

P. A. Mayer, "Probabilities and Potentials." New York: Blaisdell, 1966.

M. Rothschild and J. Stiglitz, Increasing risk II: Its economic consequences, *J. Econ. Theory* **3** (1971), 66–84.

M. Rothschild and J. Stiglitz, Some further results on the measurement of inequality, *J. Econ. Theory* **6** (1973), 188–204.

V. Strassen, The existence of probability measures with given marginals, *Ann. Math. Statist.* **36** (1965), 423–439.

7
Notes and exercises on increasing risk[1]

Before considering the use of the definition in Chapter 6 to analyze the effects of an increase in risk, we shall state formally a mathematical structure that can be used to answer these questions. In addition we shall state a companion definition and show how the alternative definition can also be used for comparative static results.

For a random variable θ lying between 0 and 1, let us consider a family of distributions $F(\theta, r)$ with densities $f(\theta, r)$. Increases in the family index r represent mean preserving increases in risk if they satisfy the two constraints

$$\int_0^1 F_r(\theta, r)\, d\theta = 0 \tag{1}$$

$$\int_0^y F_r(\theta, r)\, d\theta \geqslant 0 \qquad \text{for} \quad 0 \leqslant y \leqslant 1 \tag{2}$$

These two conditions correspond to the integral conditions in the previous chapter.

Now consider a consumer choice problem where ex post utility is increasing in the random variable θ:

$$\alpha^*(r) \quad \text{maximizes} \quad \int U(\theta, \alpha)\, dF(\theta, r) \tag{3}$$

(We assume that U is concave in α.)

The optimal level of α satisfies the first-order condition

$$\int U_\alpha(\theta, \alpha)\, dF(\theta, r) = 0 \tag{4}$$

To examine how the choice of α varies with the riskiness of the distribution of θ, we can implicitly differentiate the first-order condition (4):

$$\frac{d\alpha^*}{dr} = -\frac{\int U_\alpha(\theta, \alpha)\, dF_r(\theta, r)}{\int U_{\alpha\alpha}(\theta, \alpha)\, dF(\theta, r)} \tag{5}$$

[1]This material is drawn from Diamond and Stiglitz (1974).

Applying integration by parts to the numerator twice, we have

$$\begin{aligned} \int U_\alpha(\theta,\alpha)\,dF_r(\theta,r) &= \int U_\alpha(\theta,\alpha) f_r(\theta,r)\,d\theta \\ &= -\int U_{\alpha\theta}(\theta,\alpha)F_r(\theta,r)\,d\theta \\ &= \int U_{\alpha\theta\theta}(\theta,\alpha)\Big[\int_0^\theta F_r(s,r)\,ds\Big]\,d\theta \end{aligned} \tag{6}$$

By (2), the term in brackets is positive. Therefore, the entire integral is positive if $U_{\alpha\theta\theta}$ is everywhere positive, i.e., if U_α is a convex function of θ. Thus we can conclude that α^* increases with a mean preserving increase in risk when this condition holds.

Frequently in economics we examine the effects of changes in parameters where the changes are accompanied by compensation to preserve the level of utility. We can analogously examine an increase in risk that preserves expected utility. Paralleling (1) and (2) we define a mean utility-preserving increase in risk as one that satisfies the two constraints

$$\int_0^1 U_\theta(\theta,\alpha)F_r(\theta,r)\,d\theta = 0 \tag{7}$$

$$\int_0^y U_\theta(\theta,\alpha)F_r(\theta,r)\,d\theta \geqslant 0 \qquad \text{for} \quad 0 \leqslant y \leqslant 1 \tag{8}$$

While these conditions could be examined at any value of α, it is natural to examine them at the optimal level $\alpha^*(r)$. Paralleling the discussion above we can conclude that α^* increases with a mean utility-preserving increase in risk if $U_\theta U_{\alpha\theta\theta} - U_{\alpha\theta}U_{\theta\theta}$ is everywhere positive.

To see the workings of these two results, we now consider two different choice problems as an exercise:

Consider a saver with a single investment opportunity having a risky rate of return i. Assume he selects consumption c to maximize expected utility with the utility function $u = B_1(c) + B_2[(w - c)(1 + i)]$. (Assume that the constraint $0 \leqslant c \leqslant w$ is not binding at the optimal level of consumption.)

1 Show that a mean utility-preserving increase in the riskiness of the distribution of the rate of return increases (decreases) savings as relative risk aversion in period 2, $-xB_2'(x)/B_2''(x)$, is decreasing (increasing) with consumption.

2 Show that a mean preserving increase in the riskiness of the distribution of the rate of return increases (decreases) savings as relative risk aversion in period 2 is decreasing (increasing) with consumption and greater (less) than unity.

Consider a division of initial wealth w between safe and risky assets having rates of return m and i, respectively. Let the level of holdings of the risky asset s be chosen to maximize expected utility, which can be written $\int B[w(1 + m) + s(i - m)]\,dF(i)$. (Assume that the constraint $0 \leqslant s \leqslant w$ is not binding.)

3 Show that the optimal level of risky asset holdings decreases with a mean utility-preserving increase in risk when the utility function B has decreasing absolute risk aversion and increasing relative risk aversion.

4 Show that the optimal level of risky asset holdings decreases with a mean preserving increase in risk when the utility function B has decreasing absolute risk aversion and increasing relative risk aversion that is less than or equal to unity.

For further analyses along these lines see Meyer (1977).

References

P. Diamond and J. Stiglitz, Increases in risk and in risk aversion. *J. Econ. Theory* 8 (1974), 337–360.

J. Meyer, Choice among distributions, *J. Econ. Theory* **14** (1977), 326–336.

8

H. E. Leland, Savings and uncertainty: The precautionary demand for saving, *Quarterly Journal of Economics* 82 (1968), 465–473

This paper considers sufficient conditions on the utility function to sign the response of savings to a small introduction of risk of noninterest income, starting from a position of no risk. Since it does only local analysis, the considerations are slightly different from those in the two previous chapters.

In the exercise that follows this reading, we consider analysis of the same proposition in the setting used by Yaari in Chapter 5.

SAVING AND UNCERTAINTY: THE PRECAUTIONARY DEMAND FOR SAVING *

HAYNE E. LELAND

I. INTRODUCTION

The "precautionary" demand for saving usually is described as the extra saving caused by future income being random rather than determinate. While often rendered lip service by economists, the effect of uncertainty on saving seldom has been graced by formal analysis. When rigor is absent, economists have tended to equate the precautionary demand for saving with the concept of risk avoidance. In the few attempts at rigor, the effect of uncertainty on saving becomes obfuscated by generality.

We shall consider a two period model of consumption. Income in the first period is known. A subjective probability distribution for income in the second period also is known. The consumer must determine his consumption (and therefore his saving or dissaving) for the first period before he knows the actual value of his second period income.

In particular, we are interested in the level of saving as future income becomes more uncertain about a given expected value. It will be shown that risk aversion alone is insufficient to guarantee a positive precautionary demand for saving. But additional assumptions on certain risk properties of utility functions, assumptions which would seem to have considerable intuitive and empirical support, will be introduced to guarantee the positive effect of uncertainty on saving.

Finally, a section will be devoted to the important implications the theoretical results may have on the theory and estimation of the consumption function. No empirical work, however, has been undertaken for this paper.

* The author wishes to thank Professor F. Modigliani for his comments, and particularly Professor A. R. Dobell and a referee for their comments and suggestions.

Quarterly Journal of Economics **82**, 465–473.

II. A Two Period Model of Consumption

In this section we develop a two period model of consumption similar to that of Dreze.[1] We shall not, however, consider the rate of interest paid on saving in the first period to be a random variable. This simplifies the analysis; further, it would seem that many of the usual outlets for consumer saving, including saving deposits and government bonds, offer a fixed monetary rate of return.

We assume the consumer attempts to maximize the expected value of utility for the two periods. He will make his saving (or dissaving) decision in conjunction with his known first period income. His second period consumption will, of course, be a random variable, dependent on the actual value of second period income. Mathematically, we may formulate the problem:

(1) Maximize $E[U(C_1, C_2)]$

subject to

(2) $C_1 = (1 - k)I_1$

(3) $C_2 = I_2 + (1 + r)kI_1$

(4) $E(I_2) = I_2^*$

(5) $E(I_2 - I_2^*)^2 = \sigma^2.$

$U(C_1, C_2)$ relates consumption in periods 1 and 2 to utility. It is a cardinal utility function, for maximizing an expected value necessitates the weighted summation of different levels of U. I_1 is the (fixed) income in period 1, and I_2 is the random income in period 2. The first two moments of the distribution of I_2 are given by (4) and (5). The control variable is k, which measures the saving rate. Clearly k must have an upper limit of 1. An exact lower limit to k is impossible to define; we shall simply assume that C_2 will always be nonnegative.

Problem (1) is a simple calculus problem. Setting the derivative of $E[U(C_1, C_2)]$ with respect to the control k equal to zero yields the first order condition

(6) $E(U_1) = (1 + r)E(U_2),$

where $U_1 = \partial U/\partial C_1$, etc. If I_2 is known to equal its expected value, then (6) reduces to the familiar condition

(7) $U_1 = (1 + r)U_2 .$

From the definition of $E(U_1)$ and $E(U_2)$, condition (6) may be rewritten as

(8) $\int_{I_2} U_1 (C_1, C_2)f(I_2)\,dI_2 = (1 + r) \int_{I_2} U_2 (C_1, C_2)f(I_2)\,dI_2 .$

1. J. Dreze, "Epargne et Consommation en Avenir Aleatoire," Discussion Paper No. 6601, Center for Operations Research and Econometrics, Universite Catholique de Louvain.

That is, for $E[U(C_1, C_2)]$ to be maximized, k must be chosen to satisfy condition (8).

III. The Effect of Uncertainty on Saving

Let us assume an optimal saving rate k^o has been determined for the situation in which I_2 is known to equal its expected value I_2^*. From (2) and (3), this k^o will determine a (C_1^o, C_2^o) such that condition (7) is satisfied:

(9) $U_1^o = (1 + r)U_2^o,$

where the superscript indicates the appropriate partials are evaluated at (C_1^o, C_2^o). Will this k^o also satisfy the necessary condition (8) when uncertainty about I_2 increases? We may expand $E(U_1)$ in a Taylor series about (C_1^o, C_2^o). As only C_2 is random for fixed k, we need expand $E(U_1)$ as a function of C_2 alone:

(10) $$E(U_1)^o = \int_{I_2} [U_1^o + U_{12}^o (C_2 - C_2^o) + (1/2)U_{122}^o (C_2 - C_2^o)^2 + \ldots]f(I_2)\,dI_2,$$

where $E(U_1)^o = E(U_1)$ when $k = k_0$.

From condition (3), we see that for fixed k, $(C_2 - C_2^o) = (I_2 - I_2^*)$. Substituting this for each $(C_2 - C_2^o)$ and integrating term by term yields

(11) $E(U_1)^o = U_1^o + (1/2)U_{122}^o \sigma^2 +$ (higher order terms).

If higher order moments are finite, we may generally assume they are of $o(\sigma^2)$.[2] Thus for small σ^2 we have the local result

(12) $E(U_1)^o = U_1^o + (1/2)U_{122}^o \sigma^2 + o(\sigma^2).$

Similarly, expanding $E(U_2)^o$ about (C_1^o, C_2^o) yields

(13) $(1 + r)E(U_2)^o = (1 + r)\ [U_2^o + (1/2)U_{222}^o \sigma^2 + o(\sigma^2)].$

Utilizing (9), we see the sign of $[E(U_1)^o - (1 + r)E(U_2)^o]$ depends upon the sign of

(14) $[U_{122}^o - (1 + r)U_{222}^o] \cdot \sigma^2,$

or, substituting for $(1 + r)$ from (9),

(15) $[U_{122}^o - (U_1^o/U_2^o)U_{222}^o] \cdot \sigma^2.$

If this term is zero (and higher order terms are zero as well), then $E(U_1)^o = (1 + r)E(U_2)^o$, and k^o is optimal for the uncertain as well as the certain case. If $U(C_1, C_2)$ is quadratic, all third (and higher) derivatives will be zero; in this case, optimal saving would not be affected by the degree of uncertainty. *We must reject the association of precautionary demand for saving with simple risk avoidance*:

2. See, for example, J. W. Pratt, "Risk Aversion in the Small and in the Large," *Econometrica*, Vol. 32 (Jan. 1964), pp. 122–36.

clearly a quadratic utility function can reflect risk avoidance, but it does not imply a positive precautionary demand for saving.

The assumption that k^o yields a regular maximum to the utility function under certainty implies

$$(16) \qquad \frac{d^2U^o}{dk^2} = \frac{d[(1+r)U_2{}^o - U_1{}^o]}{dk} < 0\,.$$

It may easily be shown that $d^2[E(U)^o]/dk^2 = d^2U^o/dk^2 + O(\sigma^2)$. Thus for small σ^2,

$$(17) \qquad \frac{d^2[E(U)^o]}{dk^2} = \frac{d[(1+r)E(U_2)^o - E(U_1)^o]}{dk} < 0\,.$$

If (15) is negative, $(1+r)E(U_2)^o > E(U_1)^o$. (17) implies this inequality will be lessened by increasing k above the initial value k^o. Under reasonable regularity assumptions we may say that the optimal k will be larger than k^o when uncertainty is present, and the more uncertainty, the greater will be the optimal k. Thus if we can guarantee (15) is negative, we can prove that, for small risks, the precautionary demand for saving is positive.

IV. Decreasing Risk Aversion and Precautionary Saving

Economists are wont to assume first partials of utility functions positive, and second partials negative. Rarely are they interested in higher order derivatives. We shall show, however, that a simple and intuitively appealing extension of risk tendencies from one to two variable utility functions will guarantee the negativity of (15).

Pratt has defined a measure of risk aversion for a single argument utility function: $r(I) = -U''(I)/U'(I)$, where I is income.[3] He shows that the risk premium P (the amount one would pay for surety instead of facing an actuarially neutral gamble) is proportional to $r(I)$ when the variance of I is small. Intuition and fact lead both Pratt and Arrow [4] to assume that risky investment is not an inferior good — that is, $r(I)$ decreases as I increases.

Intuitively, the above condition implies a person would be happier taking a 55/45 bet on +\$10,000/−\$10,000 when he earns one million dollars per year than when he earns ten thousand dollars per year. Mathematically, this may be expressed

$$(18) \qquad \frac{d(-U_{11}/U_1)}{dI} < 0, \text{ or}$$

3. *Ibid.*
4. K. J. Arrow, "Comment" in *Review of Economics and Statistics*, XLV (Supplement: Feb. 1963), 24–27.

$$(19) \qquad \frac{U_1(U_{111}) - U_{11}^2}{U_1^2} > 0.$$

Note that as U_1 is always assumed to be positive, U_{111} must be positive to satisfy condition (19). A simple behavioral concept thus fixes the sign of a third derivative. It might also be noted that if $U(C_1, C_2)$ is additive, all cross partial derivatives will be zero. The Pratt assumption assures U_{222} is positive, which in turn assures that (15) is negative. The Pratt assumption combined with additive utility generates a positive precautionary demand for saving. If we do not assume additive utility, an extension of the Pratt assumption must be made to guarantee a positive precautionary demand for saving.

An intuitively appealing extension of Pratt's assumption to utility functions of more than one variable would be that, along an indifference curve, aversion towards an actuarially neutral bet on one variable decreases as that variable increases. In a simple example, this implies the following: say a person were indifferent between the following consumption situations:

	C_1	C_2
Situation I	30	10
Situation II	10	30

where the consumptions are known with certainty, and are not transferable between time periods. Now let us say C_2 becomes uncertain, with expected value 10 in the first situation, expected value 30 in the second. In each case, the *same variance* is associated with the risk. In the new (risky) situation, our assumption is that Situation II will now be preferred to Situation I, as risk occurs in a variable which is larger in Situation II than in Situation I. That is, although the consumer was indifferent between the situations under certainty, the second will be preferred to the first when uncertainty in C_2 is present. Let us term this principle decreasing risk aversion to concentration: we become less averse to risk in a variable as that variable becomes increasingly predominant in a constant utility bundle. To see the mathematical implications of this assumption, consider two bundles (C_1^o, C_2^o) and (C_1^1, C_2^1) such that

$$(20) \qquad U(C_1^o, C_2^o) = U(C_1^1, C_2^1), \text{ and } C_2^1 > C_2^o.$$

Let C_2 now become a random variable in both time periods, with expected values equal to the quantities in (20), and common variance σ^2. Using a Taylor Series expansion and neglecting terms of $o(\sigma^2)$ gives

$$(21) \qquad E[U(C_1^0, c_2^0)] = U(C_1^0, C_2^0) + (1/2)U_{22}^0\sigma^2$$

(22) $E[U(C_1^1, c_2^1)] = U(C_1^1, C_2^1) + (1/2)U_{22}^1\sigma^2$

where $U_{22}^o = \partial^2 U/\partial C_2^2$ evaluated at (C_1^o, C_2^o), etc., and lower case c's indicate random variables.

Our assumption of decreasing risk aversion to concentration implies

(23) $E[U(C_1^1, c_2^1)] > E[U(C_1^o, c_2^o)]$,

which with (20), (21), and (22) implies

(24) $U_{22}^1 > U_{22}^o$.

Generalizing this relationship to hold for any two constant utility bundles yields

(25) $$\left.\frac{d(U_{22})}{dC_2}\right|_{U \text{ constant}} > 0, \text{ or (expanding)}$$

$$[U_{222} - (U_2/U_1)U_{122}] > 0.$$

Multiplying (25) by $(-U_1/U_2)$, a negative number, implies (15) is negative, which we required for a positive precautionary demand for saving. A simple behavioral assumption, decreasing risk aversion to concentration, has therefore fixed the sign of (15), a term involving third partial derivatives. If this assumption is accepted, the precautionary demand for saving will be positive.

V. Speculations on the Consumption Function

A positive precautionary demand for saving would have important potential effects on both the theory and the estimation of the consumption function. If y represents current income, Y discounted expected future income, A assets, r a vector of relevant interest rates, and σ^2 a measure of the subjective variability of Y, we could write the consumption function

(26) $C = f(y, Y, A, r, \sigma^2)$

with $\partial f/\partial\sigma^2$ negative, rather than the usual $C = f(y, Y)$ or $C = f(y, Y, A, r)$.

Because theory leads us to expect σ^2 to be a significant variable in (26), any cross-section attempt to relate C to y, Y, and A alone could lead to serious specification error. Let b_1 be the least squares estimate of the coefficients of the independent variables when C is regressed on y, Y, and A alone. If β_2 is the true coefficient of σ^2 in the additive form of (26), then

(27) $E(b_1) = \beta_1 + (X_1'X_1)^{-1}(X_1'X_2)\beta_2$,

where β_1 is the vector of true coefficients of y, Y, and A; X_1 is the matrix of observations on these three variables, and X_2 the observations on σ^2. Note that the term $(X_1'X_1)^{-1}(X_1'X_2)$ is nothing more than the vector of least squares coefficients when σ^2 is regressed on y, Y, and A. We would generally expect these coefficients to be positive: σ^2 would be likely to increase as y, Y, and A (which might be large because of σ^2 being large) increase. From the previous theoretical analysis, we know β_2 is negative. Thus from (27) we surmise that when a measure of σ^2 is omitted from the consumption function,

(28) $\quad E(b_1) < \beta_1;$

that is, the least squares estimate of the coefficients of y, Y, and A are all *downward biased.*

This bias would be larger, the larger is σ^2. It is not surprising that Liviatan, in a cross-section analysis comparing savings of self-employed with salaried personnel having the same expected income, finds Friedman's "errors in variables" hypothesis unable to explain all the discrepancy between the two groups.[5] Indeed, on the basis of the above results, we would expect the self-employed to save more, as their incomes are more variable.

The existence of a precautionary demand for saving could also be used to explain the discrepancy between long-run time series estimates, and cross-section estimates of the propensity to consume. As is well known, cross-section estimates imply percentage saving increases as income increases, while time series imply this percentage remains nearly constant.

The discrepancy could be explained by our analysis if we make several broad assumptions. First, it is assumed that in cross-section data, higher incomes have higher variability. This variability, considerably more than proportional to the level of income, results from the more speculative nature of most high incomes. If, therefore, shapes of utility functions are not too different about expected values, one would surmise that persons with higher incomes have a larger precautionary demand for saving, in percentage as well as in absolute terms.

In the long run, however, one would not expect variability to rise with income as rapidly as it does in the cross section. In 1900 an annual expected income of \$8,000 was high, and probably quite variable about that level. An expected annual income of \$8,000 today is not exceptional for regular salaried personnel, and is undoubtedly less variable than its equivalent in 1900. Thus the same

5. N. Liviatan, "Tests of the Permanent-Income Hypothesis," in C. Christ (ed.), *Measurement in Economics* (Stanford, Calif.: Stanford University Press, 1963).

person today would save less than he did in 1900, although he had the same expected income in both periods. Precautionary demand, therefore, would lead to a smaller estimate of the propensity to consume using cross-section data, and would be a reasonable explanation of the divergences between long-run and cross-section estimates of the marginal propensity to consume. Of course, detailed empirical work would be necessary to isolate the effect of the precautionary demand for saving.

VI. Conclusion

A simple two period model has been developed to analyze rigorously the precautionary demand for saving, that demand which results solely from the uncertainty of future income. Two possible sets of assumptions were shown to assure the precautionary demand is a positive function of uncertainty. The first set is that the utility function be additive in C_1 and C_2, and reflect Pratt's principle of decreasing absolute risk aversion. If we do not wish to restrict our consideration to additive utility functions, a further assumption, termed the principle of decreasing risk aversion to concentration, is sufficient to obtain a positive sign on the precautionary demand for saving.

With the conclusion that saving will be a positive function of uncertainty, it was shown that least squares estimates of coefficients of short period and permanent income, as well as of assets, would be downward biased in estimating a consumption function, when a measure of income variability is not included in the regression. Finally, it was shown that differences in cross-section and time series income variability could provide a reasonable explanation of the difference between cross-section and time series estimates of the marginal propensity to consume.

The simplest possible model has been developed to analyze the precautionary demand for saving. Clearly it would be desirable to extend the model to the saving decision over more than two time periods. One cannot simply set up a multiperiod model similar to that above and use the calculus to derive results. Such a model would unrealistically imply that all future saving is determined in the current or first time period. The actual nature of saving is sequential: it need only be determined for the current period. The calculus of variations or dynamic programming would be suitable tools for analysis. In general, however, these models are mathematically formidable when uncertainty is introduced; they also assume additive utility functions, which might be considered a limitation.

A multiperiod model would be necessary to explore fully the effect of assets on the precautionary demand for saving. Until further progress is made with the more powerful intertemporal models of optimization under uncertainty, we must accept the two period model and its conclusion that, under reasonable assumptions, there does exist a positive precautionary demand for saving.

HARVARD UNIVERSITY AND STANFORD UNIVERSITY

Exercise on savings under uncertainty[1]

The Leland article considers savings in the context of a continuous random variable (of noninterest income) and expected utility maximization. To relate the different approaches to consumer choice, it is instructive to examine the same problem in a contingent commodity setting, like the one used above by Yaari. The student who wants to test his ability to formulate models in this area can see the exercise as proving the Leland theorem in the setting of the Yaari article, and stop reading at this point (but return after completion, to questions 7–9). The student wanting a little guidance to this development can work through the exercise step by step.

1 To set up the simplest intertemporal choice problem with a safe present and uncertain future, what three commodities should we define?

2 Paralleling Yaari (Chapter 6), what axioms of choice in this three-dimensional space will give us well-defined preferences and well-defined subjective probabilities?

3 What is the initial endowment point for a consumer with certain present income and uncertain future income? certain present and certain future income?

4 What shifts in the initial endowment point correspond to an increase in risk, expected future income held constant? What shifts correspond to an increase in risk, utility held constant?

5 In a similar fashion to Yaari's axiom V, (p. 90), state an axiom that expresses the Leland condition that "along an indifference curve, aversion towards an actuarily neutral bet on one variable decreases as that variable increases" (p. 133).

6 In this contingent commodity setting, prove the Leland theorem that a consumer, satisfying the axiom you defined in answer to question 5, increases his savings in response to a small increase in risk of his future noninvestment income, if his future investment income is safe.

7 In a similar fashion to Yaari's axiom V′ (p. 93), state a global extension of the axiom stated in answer to question 5 that does not require a certain initial position.

8 Using the axiom stated in answer to question 7, prove a global extension of the theorem proved in answer to question 6.

[1]This exercise is based on unpublished work by P. Diamond and M. E. Yaari. We are grateful to Professor Yaari for permitting its inclusion here.

9 Do you find the Leland axiom plausible? Would you find it more or less plausible if we were dealing with two specific commodities rather than present income and future income? (Before answering the latter question you might want to consider particular pairs of commodities with simple utility structures like scotch and gin or left shoes and right shoes.)

9
Three omitted topics: Mean-variance analysis, the expected value of information, and auctions

A large literature analyzes both individual behavior and market equilibrium under the assumption that individuals care only about the mean and variance of the consumption they receive. See Markowitz (1959) for individual behavior and Jensen (1972) for (stock) market equilibrium. Many writers have criticized the mean-variance approach because the conditions under which it is strictly appropriate (given the assumption of expected utility maximization) are extremely limited. Strong assumptions about utility functions or about the distribution of random prospects must be made. If no assumptions are made about the random variables being compared, then mean-variance analysis is appropriate if and only if the decision-maker's preferences are quadratic (Machina and Rothschild 1987). However, the quadratic utility function has empirically implausible properties (eventually negative marginal utility, absolute risk aversion increasing with income). Mean-variance analysis is most often used to analyze portfolio choice. It is well known that if asset returns are normally distributed, then portfolios (which are linear combinations of individual assets) are also normally distributed. Since normal distributions are characterized by their first two moments, mean-variance analysis is appropriate here. Chamberlain (1983) completely characterized the class of distributions for which mean-variance analysis is appropriate. While restrictive, that class—the spherically symmetric distributions—is much broader than the normal distribution. See also the related work by Ross (1978) on two fund separability. This remains a useful, easily manageable example and one that has received considerable attention. Since the analysis we wish to examine does not rely on mean-variance analysis, we do not dip into this large literature.

Consider an individual selecting a control variable before he knows the outcome of a random variable. Compare the expected utility he can achieve with that he could achieve if he knew the outcome of the random variable before choosing the control variable (and given the same distribution of the random variable). The difference between these two is the utility value of perfect information about the random variable. (We could alternatively define the amount he would be willing to pay in consumption units so that his utility with perfect knowledge had the same expectation as his utility given his subjective probabilities.) This concept has received some attention and is relevant for the analysis of information. Nelson and Winter (1964) have related the value of information from weather forecasting to the nature of the production decision to be made.

Gould (1974) has considered the proposition of whether when the world becomes riskier the expected value of perfect information increases. For several different definitions of increased risk he shows that this need not be the case. Given some assumptions on utility functions, it is possible to show that increasing risk increases the value of information (see Laffont, 1976). This interesting area has not had much interaction with equilibrium analysis.

There is now a large literature on auctions. For a recent survey, see McAfee and McMillan (1987). For important originating articles, see Vickrey (1961), Wilson (1977), and Milgrom and Weber (1982).

References

G. Chamberlain, A characterization of the distributions that imply mean-variance utility functions, *J. Econ. Theory* **29** (1983), 185–201.

J. P. Gould, Risk, stochastic preference, and the value of information, *J. Econ. Theory* **8** (1974), 64–84.

M. C. Jensen, Capital markets: Theory and evidence, *Bell J. Econ.* **3** (1972), 357–398.

J. J. Laffont, Risk, stochastic preference, and the value of information: A comment, *J. Econ. Theory* **12** (1976), 483–487.

M. Machina and M. Rothschild, Risk, in J. Eatwell, M. Milgate, and P. Newman (eds.), "The New Palgrave: A Dictionary of Economics," London: MacMillan Press, 1987.

H. Markowitz, "Portfolio Selection," New York: Wiley, 1959.

R. P. McAfee and J. McMillan, Auctions and bidding, *J. Econ. Literature* **25** (1987), 699–738.

P. Milgrom and R. Weber, A theory of auctions and competitive bidding, *Econometrica* **50** (1982), 1089–1122.

R. Nelson and S. Winter, A case study in the economics of information and coordination: The weather forecasting system, *Quart. J. Econ.* **78** (1964), 420–441.

S. Ross, Mutual fund separation in financial theory—the separating distributions, *J. Econ. Theory* **17** (1978), 254–286.

W. Vickrey, Counterspeculation, auctions, and competitive sealed tenders, *J. Finance* **16** (1961), 8–37.

R. Wilson, A bidding model of "perfect" competition, *Rev. Econ. Studies* **44** (1977), 511–518.

10

T. Rothenberg and K. Smith, The effect of uncertainty on resource allocation, *Quarterly Journal of Economics* **85** (1971),440–453 (part of the article is omitted)

We have considered several individual choice problems and commented on the comparison of demand and expected utility at different parameter values. It is unfortunately very tempting to go from discussion of a single individual to conclusions about equilibrium that may not be valid. For example, the profits of a firm are convex in the wage it has to pay. This implies that the firm is a risk lover. Can one conclude from this that firms, or society, are better off in a random rather than certain environment? While we know that a firm would prefer a random wage to the certainty of facing the expected value of that random wage, the introduction of uncertainty will not generally preserve the mean. Thus the analysis of equilibrium will differ from the analysis of the isolated individual. There is a fairly sizable literature on stabilization and speculation. We have selected this article for the simplicity of the argument that it makes. The article contains references for readers seeking to go further into this subject. For a sample of other work see the exchange between Samuelson (1972) and Waugh (1944) and the as yet unpublished paper by Hanoch (1974). For partial equilibrium analyses of demand uncertainty see the recent papers of Carlton (1977) and Sheshinski and Drèze (1976).

References

D. Carlton, Uncertainty, production lags and pricing, *Am. Econ. Rev. Pap. Proc.* 67 (1977), 244–249.

G. Hanoch, Desirability of price stabilization or destabilization, Harvard Institute of Economic Research Paper #35, 1974.

P. Samuelson, The consumer does benefit from feasible price stability, *Quart. J. Econ.* 86 (1972), 476–493.

E. Sheshinski and J. Drèze, Demand fluctuations, capacity utilitzation, and costs, *Am. Econ. Rev.* **66** (1976), 731–742.

F. V. Waugh, Does the consumer benefit from price instability? *Quart. J. Econ.* 58 (1944), 602–614.

THE EFFECT OF UNCERTAINTY ON RESOURCE ALLOCATION IN A GENERAL EQUILIBRIUM MODEL *

THOMAS J. ROTHENBERG
KENNETH R. SMITH

I. INTRODUCTION

Previous research on the effects of uncertainty on resource allocation can be classified into two groups. On the one hand, there are the general equilibrium models that introduce uncertainty by considering markets for contingent claims. The work of K. J. Arrow, G. Debreu, P. A. Diamond, and R. Radner is typical of this group.[1] These general equilibrium studies have concentrated almost entirely on questions of welfare economics. Using a very general framework, they have examined the conditions under which a competitive equilibrium with futures markets will in some sense be optimal. They have not examined the comparative static questions concerning how changes in the amount of uncertainty affect the equilibrium prices and quantities traded. On the other hand, there are the partial equilibrium models that concentrate on the individual firm or the individual consumer who is assumed to optimize facing given prices. The stochastic inventory and Markovitz-type portfolio analyses belong to this group. More examples may be found in recent articles on the theory of the firm under uncertainty (e.g., J. H. Drèze and J. J. Gabszewicz, W. Y. Oi, M. Rothschild, and

* The research reported here was begun while the authors were visitors at the Center for Operations Research and Econometrics, Catholic University of Louvain (Belgium). Additional financial support was provided by the Center for Research in Management Science, University of California, Berkeley, and the Research Committee of the Graduate School, University of Wisconsin. An earlier version of this paper was presented at the Winter Meetings of the Econometric Society, December 1969. We wish to acknowledge the helpful comments of the discussant Professor Yoram Barzel and the referee of this journal.

1. K. J. Arrow, "The Role of Securities in the Optimal Allocation of Risk-bearing," *Review of Economic Studies*, XXXI (1964), 91–96. G. Debreu, *Theory of Value: An Axiomatic Analysis of Economic Equilibrium* (New York: J. Wiley and Sons, 1959). P. A. Diamond, "The Role of a Stock Market in a General Equilibrium Model with Technological Uncertainty," *American Economic Review*, LVII, 4 (1967), 759–76. R. Radner, "Competitive Equilibrium Under Uncertainty," *Econometrica*, XXXVI, 1 (1968), 31–58.

K. R. Smith).[2] These partial equilibrium models have yielded a number of interesting results regarding the effect of uncertainty on profitability and factor utilization. The problem with these results, as we shall show below, is that they are not necessarily valid in a general equilibrium model where the feedback from other sectors is allowed for. Our purpose, therefore, is to investigate some comparative static questions regarding the impact of uncertainty in a less partial setting.

In this paper we examine the effects of uncertainty on welfare, resource allocation, and income distribution within the context of a simple competitive general equilibrium model. Specifically, we investigate the traditional static two-factor–two-good model in the presence of uncertainty in the production process. We assume that, in the short run, the allocation of capital between the two industries is fixed and that economic agents make their decisions with respect to production and labor input under certainty. Capital decisions, however, must be made in advance before some of the relevant short-run exogenous variables are known. Firms are assumed to possess probability distributions over these variables and choose capital to maximize expected profit.

We study the effects of uncertainty under two alternative assumptions about the technology. In the first model, it is assumed that the basic random variable is the total supply of labor services. The supply may be random as a result of the variability in the number of workers in the labor force or, more plausibly, as a result of the variability in the efficiency of a fixed labor force. In the short run (with capital fixed) firms choose labor to maximize profit; the wage rate is determined to clear the market given a specific supply of labor. In the long run firms choose capital to maximize expected profits given the probability distribution on the wage rate. That distribution is, of course, induced by the probability distribution on the total supply of labor services. In the second model, the labor supply is nonrandom, but the production function in one industry contains a random parameter. Again the firms choose capital to maximize expected profits given the induced probability distribution

2. J. H. Drèze and J. J. Gabszewicz, "Demand Fluctuations, Capacity Utilization and Prices," *Operations Research Verfahren*, III (1967), 119–41. Walter Y. Oi, "The Desirability of Price Instability Under Perfect Competition," *Econometrica*, XXIX, 1 (1961), 58–64. M. Rothschild, "Changing Demand: Its Costs and Consequences," paper presented at the December 1968 meetings of the Econometric Society. K. R. Smith, "Risk and Optimal Utilization of Capital," *Review of Economic Studies*, XXXVII (1970), 253–59, and "The Effect of Uncertainty on Monopoly Price, Capital Stock and Utilization of Capital," *Journal of Economic Theory*, I, 1 (1969), 48–59.

on wages. However, the firm with the random production function must also consider the direct effect of the random parameter on its short-run decisions. In both models we concentrate on the production sector and assume that output is sold at fixed prices to an outside world.

II. Some Partial Equilibrium Results

Before continuing with our models it is useful to look at some partial equilibrium results under similar assumptions. Consider a competitive firm that produces according to a production function

$$A = F(K,L) \tag{2.1}$$

where A represents the amount of output produced, K represents the amount of fixed input (capital), and L represents the amount of variable input (labor). Suppose that the quantity of fixed input cannot be easily changed in the short run, but that the (nonstorable) output and variable input can be readily bought and sold at prices p and w, respectively. For given K the firm maximizes profits by hiring enough labor so that the marginal value product of labor equals the wage rate:

$$pF_L = w. \tag{2.2}$$

Solving (2.1) and (2.2), one may write the optimal amount of labor input as

$$L^* = L^*(p,w,K)$$

and the short-run profit (or quasi-rent) attained as

$$\begin{aligned} \Pi^* &= \max_L \,[pF(K,L) - wL] \\ &= pF[K,L^*\,(p,w,K)] - wL^*\,(p,w,K) = \Pi^*\,(p,w,K). \end{aligned} \tag{2.3}$$

Although the prices p and w are known to the firm in the short run when it is time to make decisions concerning the variable input, they are not necessarily known to the firm when it must make long-run decisions concerning the fixed factors. Suppose that p is known with certainty, but that w is viewed as a random variable possessing a subjective probability distribution. If capital decisions are based on expected profits, the firm will examine

$$E[\Pi^*\,(p,w,K)]$$

where the expectation is with respect to the probability function on w. The natural question arises: if, for fixed p and K, the mean of w is held constant at $E[w]$, does expected profit rise or fall with increased variability?[3] The answer depends on the convexity of the Π^* function with respect to w. Differentiating (2.3) yields

$$\frac{\partial \Pi^*}{\partial w} = -L^* \qquad \frac{\partial^2 \Pi^*}{\partial w^2} = \frac{-1}{pF_{LL}} \tag{2.4}$$

where F_{LL} is the second partial derivative of F with respect to L. With diminishing returns, F_{LL} is negative and the function (2.3) has the shape drawn in Figure I. The average value of the profit

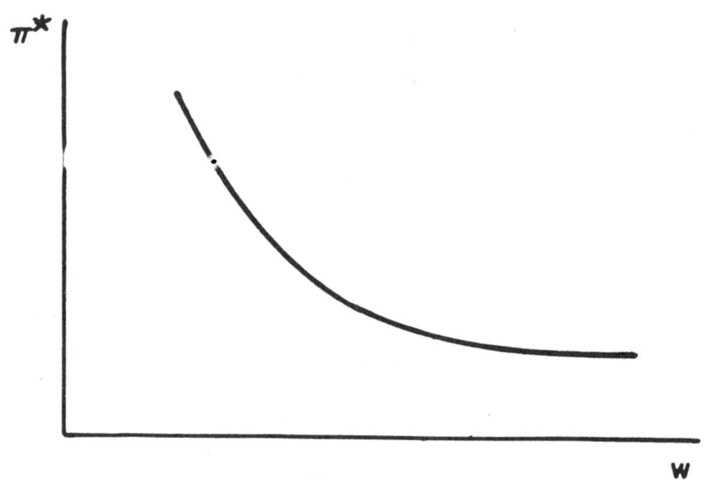

FIGURE I

function is higher than the function evaluated at the average w. Thus we have the surprising result that expected profit will be greater under uncertainty than under certainty.[4] Furthermore, if firms are trying to maximize expected profits, we would expect capital to flow toward firms that face a highly uncertain wage rate.

There are two problems with the above analysis. First, the issue of why the price of labor is random is not raised. Presumably

3. Traditionally, the variance has been taken as a measure of variability. It is more convenient, however, to define an increase in variability (or uncertainty) in terms of a "mean preserving spread." A probability distribution is said to undergo a mean preserving spread if some mass is moved away from the mean in such a way that the resulting distribution has the same mean as the original. Under this definition we have the following result: For any convex function $f(x)$, the expected value $E[f(x)]$ rises when variability increases. See, for example, M. Rothschild and J. E. Stiglitz, "Increasing Risk: A Definition and Its Economic Consequences," Cowles Foundation Discussion Paper 275, 1969.

4. That result was apparently first stated by Walter Oi, *op. cit.*, for a firm facing a variable output price. It may be noted in passing that a probability distribution at one point of time is mathematically equivalent to variability over time; thus, our results on the effects of uncertainty can also be interpreted as the effects of time variability.

the wage rate is random because of unpredictable movements in tastes, factor supplies, technical change, etc. If the random wage is a result of more basic random variables, it is important to examine a model where these basic variables enter the analysis explicitly. Second, the above analysis ignores the interaction of various firms in the economy. If all firms face a random wage and attempt to expand, prices of scare resources will have to rise. This feedback could reverse, at least for some firms, the result that expected profits rise with uncertainty.

III. Model One: Random Labor Supply

1. The Model

We consider an economy consisting of two industries. The first industry produces good A and is referred to as industry A. The second industry produces good B and is referred to as industry B. Each industry has a production function that describes the relationship between the flow of output and the flow of factor inputs.[5] We assume there are only two inputs, labor services and capital services, and that the production functions exhibit constant returns to scale and diminishing returns to individual factors. There is a given quantity K of capital services that must be allocated between the two industries. The allocation must be made once and for all before the labor input decisions need be made. When firms are making labor-hiring decisions, there is a known fixed amount L of labor services available. However, when capital decisions must be made, this quantity is not yet known and is considered to be a random variable. The price of A in terms of B is assumed to be exogenous and known to equal p. Further, it is assumed that each firm is a price taker and, for fixed K, attempts to maximize short-run profits. In the long run capital is allocated so that expected profit rates are the same in each industry.

In the short run where K_A, K_B, and L are given, the solution of this competitive general equilibrium problem must satisfy

$$\begin{aligned} (3.1) \qquad A &= F(K_A,L_A) \\ B &= G(K_B,L_B) \\ K &= K_A + K_B \\ L &= L_A + L_B \\ pF_L &= w = G_L \end{aligned}$$

5. We shall follow the convention of using the symbols A and B to represent not only the names of the commodities but also the number of units produced. This should cause no confusion.

where F and G are production functions that we assume possess derivatives up to the third order. These equations yield the equilibrium values [6]

$$(3.2)\qquad \begin{aligned} A &= A(K_A,L)\\ B &= B(K_A,L)\\ L_A &= L_A(K_A,L)\\ L_B &= L_B(K_A,L)\\ w &= w(K_A,L). \end{aligned}$$

Although the parameter L is fixed in the short run when labor decisions have to be made, it is a random variable possessing a probability distribution at the time capital decisions must be made. Hence, the short-run equilibrium values must also be treated as random variables. If we assume that capital is allocated in the long run so that expected profit rates are equalized, we have the additional equilibrium condition

$$(3.3)\qquad E\left[\frac{pA - wL_A}{K_A}\right] = E\left[\frac{B - wL_B}{K_B}\right].$$

The expectation is with respect to the joint probability distribution on A, B, L_A, L_B, and w that is induced through (3.2) by the basic distribution on L.

Before asking comparative static questions regarding the effect on equilibrium prices and quantities of increasing uncertainty, it is useful to examine the short-run equations (3.2). Differentiating the condition $pF_L = G_L = w$, we find

$$(3.4)\qquad \begin{aligned} \frac{\partial L_A}{\partial L} &= \frac{G_{LL}}{pF_{LL} + G_{LL}} > 0\\ \frac{\partial L_B}{\partial L} &= \frac{pF_{LL}}{pF_{LL} + G_{LL}} > 0\\ \frac{\partial w}{\partial L} \equiv w'(L) &= \frac{pF_{LL}G_{LL}}{pF_{LL} + G_{LL}} < 0. \end{aligned}$$

Under diminishing returns F_{LL} and G_{LL} are both negative, implying that in years where L is greater than average both firms will use more labor than average and the wage rate will be lower than average.

2. *Welfare*

In a model of production without a demand sector, the sim-

6. Since by definition $K_A + K_B = K$ and K is assumed fixed, we delete K_B as an independent variable in (3.2). Also, for typographical convenience, we will not use an asterisk to denote the optimal short-run decision variables.

plest measure of welfare is national income. Since A and B are random we have a random national income

$$(3.5)\qquad Y = pA(K_A,L) + B(K_A,L) = pF[K_A,L_A,(K_A,L)] + G[K - K_A,L_B(K_A,L)].$$

Expected national income $E[Y]$ is a function of K_A and the parameters of the probability distribution on L. Letting V be a measure of variability such that an increase in V implies a mean preserving spread, we can answer our question — how does uncertainty affect expected income — by investigating the sign of

$$(3.6)\qquad \frac{dE[Y]}{dV} = \frac{\partial E[Y]}{\partial V} + \frac{\partial E[Y]}{\partial K_A}\frac{dK_A}{dV}.$$

Using the result that the derivative of an expected value equals the expected value of the derivative, we have from (3.5)

$$(3.7)\qquad \frac{\partial E[Y]}{\partial K_A} = E[(pF_L - G_L)\frac{dL_A}{dK_A} + pF_K - G_K] = E[pF_K - G_K]$$

since short-run equilibrium requires $pF_L = G_L$. But, under constant returns to scale, we have

$$pF_K - G_K = \frac{\Pi_A}{K_A} - \frac{\Pi_B}{K_B}$$

and (3.7) is simply the difference in expected profit rates. Thus, when evaluated at the long-run competitive equilibrium, the partial derivative (3.7) equals zero and we have

$$\frac{dE[Y]}{dV} = \frac{\partial E[Y]}{\partial V}.$$

That is, the effect of uncertainty on expected national income can be obtained by examining the relationship between Y and L for fixed K_A and K_B. Expected national income will rise or fall with uncertainty according to whether Y is a convex or concave function of L. Holding the allocation of capital constant, we find from (3.5)

$$(3.8)\qquad \frac{\partial Y}{\partial L} = pF_L\frac{dL_A}{dL} + G_L\frac{dL_B}{dL} = w\left(\frac{dL_A}{dL} + \frac{dL_B}{dL}\right) = w.$$

But, from (3.3), the derivative of w with respect to L is negative. Thus, Y is concave in L and expected national income under uncertainty is less than the national income that would obtain if L were known to equal $E[L]$ with certainty. We may summarize this result as follows: *For an economy in long-run equilibrium an increase in uncertainty lowers expected national income.*

3. Resource Allocation

In this section we examine the effect of uncertainty on the equilibrium allocation of the fixed stock of capital. Since we have assumed that capital moves to equate the expected profit rates in the two industries, we begin by looking at the short-run profit functions. The individual firms maximize short-run profits in competitive output and labor markets. Hence, we have for industry A

$$\Pi_A = \max_{L_A} [pF(K_A,L_A) - wL_A].$$

A similar equation holds for industry B. But the wage rate w is a function of the total supply of labor L. For fixed p and K_A we have

$$\Pi_A = \max_{L_A} [pF(K_A,L_A) - w(L)L_A] = \Pi_A[w(L)]. \tag{3.9}$$

That is, profit is a function of the wage rate, which in turn is a function of the basic random variable, the supply of labor. In order to see how uncertainty affects profits (for given capital allocation), we examine the convexity of Π_A with respect to L. Differentiating (3.9), we obtain

$$\frac{d^2\Pi_A}{dL^2} = w'' \frac{d\Pi_A}{dw} + (w')^2 \frac{d^2\Pi_A}{dw^2} \tag{3.10}$$

where w' and w'' are the first two derivatives of the function relating the wage rate to the supply of labor.

It is informative to compare (3.10) with the partial equilibrium result (2.4). If we ignore L and assume that w is the basic random variable, we are led to examine $(d^2\Pi_A/dw^2)$ and to conclude that uncertainty raises expected profits. However, if L is the basic random variable, we must consider not only the effect on profits of random w, but also the feedback effect on w. The partial equilibrium analysis considered the case where the variability of w increases but $E[w]$ remains constant. By considering the basic random variable L in a general equilibrium system, it can be seen that (as long as w'' is not zero) the average wage rate must necessarily change when we increase uncertainty. Thus the first term in (3.10) represents this effect of the changing mean of w, while the second term represents the effect of the changing variability. If the first term is positive (or only slightly negative), then expected profits, for fixed K_A, will increase with uncertainty as in the partial equilibrium model. However, if this "mean effect" is large in absolute value and negative, the result may be reversed.

We have already seen in (2.4) that $d\Pi_A/dw$ is negative. Now we must examine w''. Differentiating the function $w'(L)$ given in (3.4), we obtain

$$(3.11) \qquad w''(L) = \frac{p[p^2 F_{LL}{}^3 G_{LLL} + G_{LL}{}^3 F_{LLL}]}{(pF_{LL} + G_{LLL})^3}$$

which will be positive if the third derivatives F_{LLL} and G_{LLL} are positive and will be negative if the third derivatives are negative. Thus we have the common problem in the theory of uncertainty: the answer depends crucially on third derivatives, about which economists have traditionally had little to say. It is possible to exhibit reasonable production functions with either positive or negative third derivatives. However, for the classes of production functions often used in aggregate empirical research, third derivatives are almost always positive. For example, in the class of constant elasticity of substitution production functions, F_{LLL} will be positive as long as the elasticity of substitution is greater than one-half.[7] It would appear that, with a reasonable degree of substitutability between the two factors in production, w'' will be greater than zero and uncertainty will raise expected wages. The "mean effect" will, therefore, typically have the opposite sign from the "variability effect" and the partial equilibrium result need not hold.

Without specifying the exact form for the production functions F and G, we cannot say whether (3.10) will be positive or negative. However, (3.10) can be rewritten in order to see more clearly the types of circumstances under which uncertainty raises expected profits. It will be more convenient to examine profit per unit of capital rather than total profit.

Substituting from (2.4) and dividing by K_A, we write the second derivative of the profit rate as

7. Consider a production function $F(K,L)$ with constant returns to scale and a constant elasticity of substitution σ. For such a function we have the identities

$$\sigma = \frac{F_L F_K}{F F_{LK}} \text{ and } LF_{LL} + KF_{LK} = 0$$

holding for all values of K and L. Thus, we write F_{LL} as

$$F_{LL} = -\frac{F_L F_K}{\sigma F}\frac{K}{L}.$$

Differentiating, we obtain

$$F_{LLL} = \frac{F_{LL}}{L\sigma}[(2-\sigma)\alpha - (1+\sigma)]$$

where $\alpha = LF_L/F$ is the elasticity of output with respect to labor. Since α must be between zero and one, we can conclude that F_{LLL} is positive as long as σ is greater than one-half. If σ is less than one-half the sign of F_{LLL} depends on the value of α (which in turn depends on K and L). If α remains near two-thirds for all plausible K and L, F_{LLL} is positive as long as σ is greater than one-fifth.

$$(3.12)\qquad \frac{\partial^2\left(\frac{\Pi_A}{K_A}\right)}{\partial L^2} = \frac{1}{K_A}\frac{\partial^2 \Pi_A}{\partial L^2} = -\,w''\frac{L_A}{K_A} + (w')^2\frac{1}{pK_A|F_{LL}|}$$

where the absolute value of the reciprocal of F_{LL} is a measure of the short-run flexibility of the firm. The more flexible the firm in the short run, the more likely the positive effect of wage variation on average profit will outweigh the negative effect of higher average wages, and the firm will benefit from uncertainty. Further, rewriting (3.12) in terms of the elasticity of substitution σ_A and the elasticity of output with respect to labor $\alpha = F_L L_A/F$, we have

$$(3.13)\qquad \frac{1}{K_A}\frac{\partial^2 \Pi_A}{\partial L^2} = -w''\frac{L_A}{K_A} + \frac{(w')^2}{w}\frac{\sigma_A}{1-\alpha}\frac{L_A}{K_A} = w''\frac{L_A}{K_A}\left[\frac{\phi\sigma_A}{1-\alpha} - 1\right]$$

where

$$(3.14)\qquad \phi = \frac{(w')^2}{ww''} > 0$$

is a weighting factor measuring (inversely) the strength of the feedback of the random labor supply on the average wage rate. Under the assumption that w'' is positive, ϕ will also be positive.

If L equals $E[L]$ with certainty, we have the long-run equilibrium condition

$$\frac{r}{w} = \frac{F_K}{F_L} \equiv \frac{L_A}{K_A}\frac{1-\alpha}{\alpha}$$

where r is the profit rate. Thus, when evaluated at the certainty equilibrium, (3.13) can be written as

$$(3.15)\qquad \frac{1}{K_A}\frac{\partial^2 \Pi_A}{\partial L^2} = w''\frac{r}{w}\frac{\alpha}{1-\alpha}\left[\frac{\phi\sigma_A}{1-\alpha} - 1\right].$$

For fixed K_A, the effect of uncertainty on the expected profit rate depends on whether the profit rate function is convex or concave in L. If (3.15) is positive, then this function is convex in a neighborhood of the certainty labor supply, $E[L]$, and the introduction of a small amount of uncertainty must raise the expected profit rate. If (3.15) is negative, the opposite result holds. With positive w'' (3.15) has the same sign as the term in square brackets. This term will be positive if the elasticity of substitution σ_A, the general equilibrium weight ϕ, and the output elasticity of labor α are all large.[8] In general, the second derivative of the profit rate is a mono-

8. Of course, σ_A, ϕ, and α are not necessarily constants but, in general, depend on L. Our analysis refers to these functions when evaluated as $E[L]$.

tonically increasing function of σ_A and ϕ; however, α (a measure of the labor intensity of the industry) enters in a more complicated way. The problem seems to be that α appears in the second derivative function for two reasons. A high value of α implies a high use of labor and hence a large negative "mean effect" resulting from the higher average wage rate. But a high value of α implies (for any given σ_A) a high degree of short-run flexibility and hence a large positive "variability effect" resulting from the random wage rate.

All of the above has concerned the profit rate of just industry A. The allocation of capital depends on the difference in profit rates:

$$\Delta(L) = \frac{\Pi_A}{K_A} - \frac{\Pi_B}{K_B}.$$

If, for fixed K_A and K_B, Δ is convex in a neighborhood of $E[L]$, then the expected profit rate differential rises with the introduction of a small amount of uncertainty, making industry A more attractive. Conversely, if Δ is concave in L, uncertainty makes B relatively more attractive. Thus, the effect of uncertainty on capital allocation depends on the second derivative of the function $\Delta(L)$. Using our previous results, we have

$$\text{(3.16)} \quad \Delta'' = w''\left[\frac{L_B}{K_B} - \frac{L_A}{K_A}\right] + (w')^2\left[\frac{1}{pK_A|F_{LL}|} - \frac{1}{K_B|G_{LL}|}\right]$$

which, when evaluated at the zero variance long-run equilibrium, can be written as

$$\text{(3.17)} \quad \Delta'' = \frac{w''r}{w}\left[\frac{\beta}{1-\beta} - \frac{\alpha}{1-\alpha} + \phi\left(\frac{\sigma_A\alpha}{(1-\alpha)^2} - \frac{\sigma_B\beta}{(1-\beta)^2}\right)\right]$$

where $\alpha = L_AF_L/F$, $\beta = L_BG_L/G$, and $r = pF_K = G_K$.

Examining (3.17), we see that the industry with the higher elasticity of substitution tends to gain from uncertainty. The effect of labor intensity is less clear. If industry A is more labor-intensive than industry B (i.e., $\alpha > \beta$), then the mean effect favors industry A, but the variability effect favors industry B. If α and β are near one, the latter effect dominates because of the squared terms. If α and β are near zero, the mean effect will dominate as long as ϕ is sufficiently small. We show in the Appendix that this is indeed the case at least for production functions with constant elasticities of substitution. Suppose $\sigma_A = \sigma_B$ and the common value is a constant lying between one-half and one. Then we have the following result: *If α and β are both near zero, uncertainty causes capital to flow away from the labor-intensive industry; if α and β are both near unity, uncertainty causes capital to flow toward the labor-intensive* *industry*. For α and β in an intermediate range or for one small and the other large, the answer depends on the initial allocation of labor or, what amounts to the same thing, the relative output price p. These general statements are demonstrated in the Appendix.

For the case of two Cobb-Douglas production functions ($\sigma_A = \sigma_B = 1$), we can obtain a more precise answer. The effect of uncertainty on capital allocation depends only on the two (constant) labor elasticities α and β and on the certainty equilibrium labor allocation $l = L_A/L_B$. We have

$$\phi = (1 - \alpha)(1 - \beta)\frac{(1 - \alpha) + l(1 - \beta)}{(2 - \beta)(1 - \alpha)^2 + l(2 - \alpha)(1 - \beta)^2} \tag{3.18}$$

and

$$\Delta'' = \frac{w''r}{w}(\beta - \alpha)\frac{(1 - 2\alpha) + l(1 - 2\beta)}{(2 - \beta)(1 - \alpha)^2 + l(2 - \alpha)(1 - \beta)}. \tag{3.19}$$

These expressions are most easily understood in a graph. In Figure II the cross-hatched regions indicate combinations of α and β for which Δ'' is positive and hence uncertainty causes the movement of capital into industry A. The white regions indicate combinations

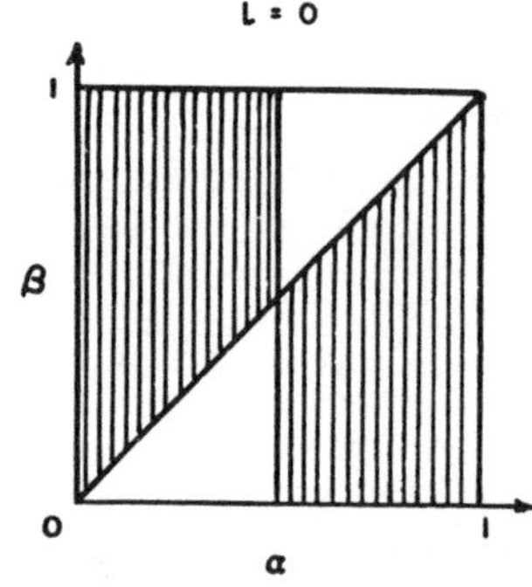

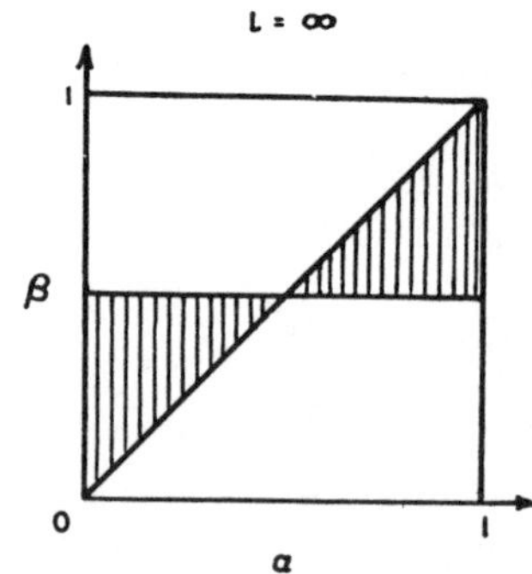

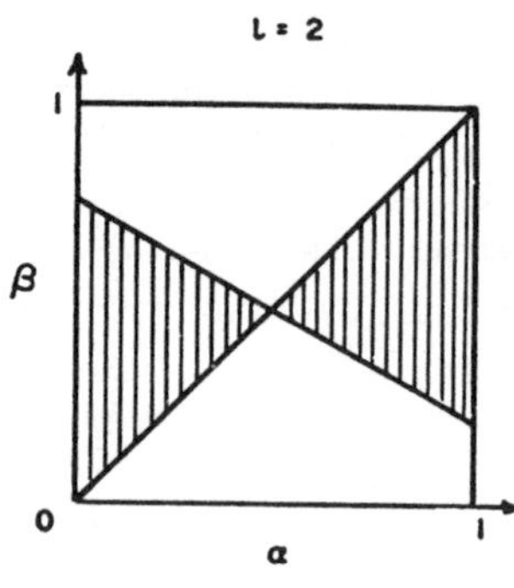

FIGURE II

of α and β for which Δ'' is negative. These figures can be summarized as follows: If $\alpha < \beta < 1/2$ or if $\alpha > \beta > 1/2$, then capital flows to industry A as a result of uncertainty. If $\beta < \alpha < 1/2$ or $\beta > \alpha > 1/2$, then capital flows to industry B. For all other combinations the result depends on the certainty allocation of labor. In general, the less labor an industry has initially, the more likely the introduction of uncertainty will result in that industry's attracting capital.

4. Average Wage Rate

In this section we examine what happens to the expected wage rate when uncertainty is introduced into our general equilibrium model. From (3.1) we have

$$(3.20)\qquad E[w] = E\{G_L[K - K_A, L_B(K_A, L)]\}$$

which depends on K_A and the parameters of the probability distribution of L. Again with V as a measure of variability, the effect of a mean preserving spread is given by

$$(3.21)\qquad \frac{dE[w]}{dV} = \frac{\partial E[w]}{\partial V} + \frac{\partial E[w]}{\partial K_A}\frac{dK_A}{dV}.$$

The first term considers the effect of uncertainty on the expected wage rate for fixed K_A, whereas the second term accounts for the fact that uncertainty also changes the allocation of capital between the two industries. Since $w(L)$ is a convex function under our assumption that w'' is positive, we know that the first term is positive. Now

$$(3.22)\qquad \frac{\partial E[w]}{\partial K_A} = -E[G_{LK} + G_{LL}\frac{\partial L_A}{\partial K_A}]$$
$$= -E\left[\frac{pF_{LK}G_{LK}(K_B/L_B - K_A/L_A)}{pF_{LL} + G_{LL}}\right]$$

which has the sign of $K_B/L_B - K_A/L_A$. Thus, (3.22) is positive if industry A is more labor-intensive than industry B and is negative if industry A is less labor-intensive. Our conclusions concerning the effect of variability on the allocation of capital were given in the previous section. Combining these results, we have the following conclusion: *If α and β are both large and if the common elasticity of substitution lies between one-half and one, then the average wage rate is higher under uncertainty.* For other combinations of α and β the result is not easily given since the two terms in (3.21) will have different signs.

This analysis does not in itself say anything about the distribution of income between labor and capital since a rise in the expected wage rate $E[w]$ does not necessarily imply a rise in the expected wage bill $E[wL]$. There is, however, an interesting implication of our result. Consider a situation where there are two groups making up the random labor supply. One group supplies a fixed quantity of labor services, whereas the second group supplies a variable quantity (thus, causing the randomness). Under these conditions, if the labor elasticities are large, the group providing the fixed quantity of labor services gains on average from the uncertainty introduced by the second group.

Appendix

The general equilibrium weight that arises in Model One can be written as

$$\phi = \frac{(w')^2}{ww''} = \frac{pF_{LL}{}^2G_{LL}{}^2(pF_{LL} + G_{LL})}{w(p^2F_{LL}{}^3G_{LLL} + G_{LL}{}^3F_{LLL})}.$$

For production functions with constant elasticities of substitution, this may be rewritten as

$$\phi = \frac{(1-a)^2(1-\beta)\sigma_B + (1-\beta)^2(1-a)\sigma_A l}{(1-a)^2\psi_B\sigma_B + (1-\beta)^2\psi_A\sigma_A l}$$

where

$$l = \frac{L_A}{L_B}$$

$$\psi_A = 1 + \sigma_A - a(2 - \sigma_A)$$

$$\psi_B = 1 + \sigma_B - \beta(2 - \sigma_B).$$

If σ_A and σ_B are greater than one-half, both ψ_A and ψ_B are necessarily positive.

The second derivative of the difference in profit rates (3.17) may be written as

$$\Delta'' = \frac{w''r}{w}\left[\frac{\sigma_A a}{(1-a)^2} - \frac{\sigma_B\beta}{(1-\beta)^2}\right](\phi - \chi)$$

where

$$= \frac{a(1-a)(1-\beta)^2 - \beta(1-\beta)(1-a)^2}{\sigma_A a(1-\beta)^2 - \sigma_B\beta(1-a)^2}.$$

Setting $\sigma_A = \sigma_B = \sigma$ and $\beta = \lambda a$, we have

$$\lim_{a\to 0}\,[\phi(a) - \chi(a)] = \frac{-1}{\sigma(1+\sigma)}.$$

Therefore, for small a and β and for all $\sigma > 1/2$, we have

$$\Delta'' \approx \frac{w''r\sigma}{w}\left[\frac{\beta}{(1-\beta)^2} - \frac{a}{(1-a)^2}\right]\frac{1}{\sigma(1+\sigma)}$$

and we conclude that Δ'' is greater than zero (and hence, K_A increases with uncertainty) if $\beta > \alpha$. Conversely, Δ'' is less than zero (and K_B increases) if $\alpha > \beta$.

In similar fashion, setting $\sigma_A = \sigma_B = \sigma$ and $(1 - \beta) = \lambda(1 - \alpha)$, we have

$$\lim_{\alpha \to 1} [\phi(\alpha) - \chi(\alpha)] = 0$$

$$\lim_{\alpha \to 1} \frac{\phi(\alpha) - \chi(\alpha)}{1 - \alpha} = \frac{\lambda(1 + \lambda l)}{(2\sigma - 1)(1 + \lambda^2 l)} - \frac{\lambda}{\sigma(\lambda + 1)},$$

the last expression being positive as long as σ lies between one-half and one. Therefore, for large α and β and for $1/2 < \sigma < 1$, we have

$$\Delta'' \approx \frac{w'' r \sigma}{w} \left[\frac{\alpha}{(1 - \alpha)^2} - \frac{\beta}{(1 - \beta)^2} \right] \left[\frac{\lambda(1 + \lambda l)}{(2\sigma - 1)(1 + \lambda^2 l)} - \frac{\lambda}{\sigma(\lambda + 1)} \right] (1 - \alpha)$$

and we conclude that Δ'' is greater than zero if $\alpha > \beta$ and Δ'' is less than zero if $\beta > \alpha$.

University of California, Berkeley
University of Wisconsin, Madison

II. General Equilibrium in a Static Setting

We considered individual choice in Part I. Now we turn to models of market equilibrium. In Part III we consider the individual problem of sequential choice and equilibria, which are built around the notion of sequential choice. In this part we consider models that, like the certainty general equilibrium model, are built around a single choice. Of course, choice of a strategy is a single choice, and so this distinction is not clear, but merely suggestive. This part starts with a chapter from G. Debreu's *Theory of Value.* Debreu extends the conventional treatment of competitive general equilibrium to the uncertainty setting by identifying commodities delivered in different states of nature as different commodities, assuming that there are separate markets for these different commodities. This model provides a framework for examining the operation of markets under uncertainty even though actual economies do not have complete contingent commodity markets. The next paper explores the limitations on equilibrium that occur when different individuals have different amounts of information and trading is restricted to states of nature that an individual is capable of identifying. The following paper considers the effect of restricting trade in contingent commodities to those trades that can be effected through the stock and bond markets.

Another way of considering the problem of incomplete markets is to note that information difficulties can create problems in the definition of a commodity. This occurs in two different ways. Using the terminology of insurance theory, these are adverse selection and moral hazard. The former occurs when there is a set of commodities that are different from the point of view of the purchaser, but are treated as identical by the market. We shall first consider an exercise and a reading to show one element of inefficiency in simple competitive models. We shall then look at insurance markets where the attempt to separate high-risk from low-risk purchasers of insurance creates difficulty for the existence of equilibrium as well as possible inefficiences in the market. Then we will turn to signaling equilibria, where individuals try to distinguish themselves from others who might otherwise appear the same to potential traders.

Moral hazard arises when individual behavior that is not easily observed by a supplier affects the cost of supplying to the particular demander. We have two readings analyzing possible responses to this situation. We then turn to two articles describing actual market responses to the presence of these complications, Arrow on medical care and Cheung on crop sharing. An analysis of public investment in the face of uncertainty completes this part.

11
G. Debreu, "Theory of Value," Chapter 7, pp. 98–102. New York: Wiley, 1959

In "Theory of Value," G. Debreu lays out the basic theory of competitive general equilibrium in a lucid and elegant fashion. In this chapter he shows how the basic ideas can be extended to include uncertainty in the economy. An important point to notice is that firms do not need to evaluate random or uncertain outcomes. They choose a production plan (which *is* a random variable) in order to maximize profits (which are *not* random). The profits from different random production plans are determined by the tastes and judgments of individual consumers. In this structure there is no need for a theory of how firms value random outcomes that differs from that of certainty theory. As we note in the comment following Chapter 13, the structure of the theory can change considerably when firms cannot use complete markets to value their production plans.

CHAPTER 7

UNCERTAINTY

7.1. INTRODUCTION

The analysis is extended in this chapter to the case where uncertain events determine the consumption sets, the production sets, and the resources of the economy. A contract for the transfer of a commodity now specifies, in addition to its physical properties, its location and its date, an event on the occurrence of which the transfer is conditional. This new definition of a commodity allows one to obtain a theory of uncertainty free from any probability concept and formally identical with the theory of certainty developed in the preceding chapters.

7.2. EVENTS

An economy whose activity extends over T elementary time-intervals, or dates, will be studied. It is assumed that the uncertainty of the environment during that period originates in the choice that Nature makes among a finite number of alternatives. These alternatives will be called *events at T* and indicated by an index e_T running from 1_T to k_T. Once e_T is given, atmospheric conditions, natural disasters, technical possibilities, . . . are determined for the entire period.

At the beginning of date t, the agents of the economy have some information about the event at T which will obtain. This information can be formally presented as follows. The set of events at T is partitioned into non-empty subsets called *events at t* and indicated by an index e_t running from 1_t to k_t. At the beginning of date t, every agent knows to what event at t the event at T which will obtain belongs. At the beginning of date $t + 1$, further information is available, i.e., the partition which defines the events at $t + 1$ is derived by partitioning the events at t. The events at $t = 1, \cdots, T$ can be conveniently represented by the vertices of a tree with the vertex 1_0 corresponding to the absence of information prevailing initially. In fig. 1 such an event tree is drawn for the particular case where $T = 3$.

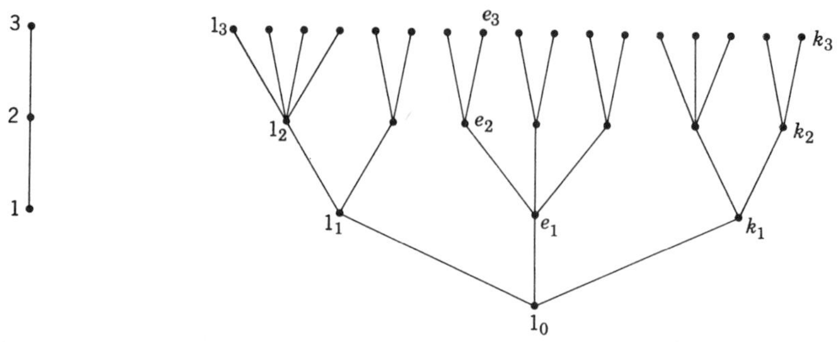

Fig. 1

7.3. Commodities and Prices

Wheat with specified physical characteristics available at location s, at date t will play entirely different economic roles according to the event at t which obtains (in particular, according to precipitation during the growing season). One is thus led to define a *commodity* in this new context by its physical characteristics, its location, and its event (or vertex of the event tree; this vertex defining implicitly the date of the commodity). A contract for delivery of wheat between two agents takes, for example, the form: the first agent shall deliver to the second agent, who shall accept delivery, five thousand bushels of wheat of a specified type at location s, at event e_t. If e_t does not obtain, no delivery takes place. It was remarked in Chapter 2 that the definition of a certain commodity might require several dates (and several locations). Therefore the definition of an uncertain commodity may require here several events (and several locations). Summing up, the concept of uncertain commodity is derived from the concept of certain commodity by substituting the tree structure of events for the line structure of dates and replacing everywhere "date" by "event."

It is assumed that there is only a finite number l of commodities; these are indicated by an index h running from 1 to l. It is also assumed that the quantity of any one of them can be any real number. Given a sign convention for the inputs and the outputs of an *agent*, a complete plan of action, or more briefly an *action*, for him is represented by a point a of the *commodity space* R^l. The plan of action a made initially for the whole future specifies for each good and service the quantity that he will make available, or that will be made available to him, at each location, at each date, and at each event.

The *price* p_h of the hth commodity is a real number interpreted as the amount paid (in the sense of 2.1) initially by (resp. to) the agent who commits himself to accept (resp. to make) delivery of one unit of that commodity. Payment is irrevocably made although delivery does not take place if specified events do not obtain. An agent who buys a bushel of No. 2 Red Winter Wheat available in Chicago at date *t in any event* buys in fact as many commodities as there are events at t. The usual futures "price" thus corresponds to a *sum* of prices of uncertain commodities. The *price system* is the l-tuple $p = (p_1, \cdots, p_h, \cdots, p_l)$. The *value* of an action a relative to the price system p is the inner product $p \cdot a$.

7.4. Producers

An action y_j of the jth *producer* is called a *production* (inputs are negative and outputs positive). Let $y_j(e_T)$ denote the vector of the components of y_j associated with the unicursal path from the vertex 1_0 of the event tree to the vertex e_T, and let $Y_j[e_T]$ be the certain production set associated with the same path. The production y_j is possible if and only if $y_j(e_T)$ belongs to $Y_j[e_T]$ for every event e_T at T. The set of productions y_j possible for the jth producer is a subset of the commodity space R^l denoted Y_j and called the *production set* of the jth producer.

It is easy to interpret the assumptions of 3.3 on production sets in this new context, and to relate them to the corresponding assumptions in the case of certainty. For example, if $Y_j[e_T]$ is convex for every event e_T at T, then Y_j is clearly convex.

Given a price system p and a production y_j, the *profit* of the jth producer is $p \cdot y_j$. Considering the price system as a datum, the jth producer tries to maximize his profit in his production set. For this he needs neither an appraisal (conscious or unconscious) of the likelihoods of the various events, nor an attitude toward risk. His behavior amounts to maximizing the value of the stock outstanding of the jth corporation. In other words, the jth corporation announces a production plan y_j; as a result, its share has a determined value on the stock market; it chooses its plan so as to maximize the value of its share.

7.5. Consumers

An action x_i of the ith *consumer* is called a *consumption* (inputs are positive and outputs negative). Exactly as for a producer, one defines the *consumption set* X_i of the ith consumer. It is assumed that the set X_i is completely preordered by the preferences $\underset{i}{\precsim}$ of the ith consumer. This *preference preordering* reflects the tastes of the consumer for goods and services (including, in particular, their spatial and temporal specifications), his personal appraisal of the likelihoods of the various events, and his attitude toward risk.

The assumptions of 4.3 on consumption sets, and of 4.5–4.7 on preference preorderings are again easily interpreted in this context of uncertainty and related to the corresponding assumptions in the case of certainty. Most interesting are the three convexity assumptions on preferences of 4.7. Attention will be focused on:

(a) If $x_i^2 \underset{i}{\succsim} x_i^1$, then $tx_i^2 + (1 - t)x_i^1 \underset{i}{\succsim} x_i^1$,

which is the weakest (when preferences satisfy the continuity assumption (a) of 4.6). This axiom for uncertain consumptions implies an attitude of risk-aversion for the ith consumer. To see this, consider the case of one date and two events which are the outcomes *Head* and *Tail* of the tossing of a coin. Let b and c be two certain consumptions, and denote by (b, c) the uncertain consumption which associates b with event *Head* and c with event *Tail*, by (c, b) the uncertain consumption which makes the reverse association. Assume moreover that (b, b) is not indifferent to (c, c), i.e., that the certain consumptions b and c are not indifferent. If (b, c) is indifferent to (c, b), i.e., if the ith consumer appraises *Head* and *Tail* as being equally likely, (a) asserts that $((b + c)/2, (c + b)/2)$, i.e., the certainty of consuming $(b + c)/2$, is at least as desired as the uncertain consumption (b, c) or (c, b).

Given a price system p and his *wealth* w_i, the ith consumer tries to satisfy his preferences $\underset{i}{\precsim}$ in the subset of X_i defined by the wealth constraint $p \cdot x_i \leqq w_i$.

7.6. Equilibrium

Finally the *total resources* are a given vector ω of R^l such that, for every event e_T at T, the vector $\omega(e_T)$ of the components of ω associated with the unicursal path from the vertex 1_0 of the event tree to the vertex e_T coincides with the certain total resources associated with that path. The formal description of an *economy* $E = ((X_i, \underset{i}{\precsim}), (Y_j), \omega)$ is thus identical with that given in 5.3. In particular, an *attainable state* of E is an $(m + n)$-tuple $((x_i), (y_j))$ of actions such that

$$x_i \in X_i \text{ for every } i,\ y_j \in Y_j \text{ for every } j,\ \sum_{i=1}^{m} x_i - \sum_{j=1}^{n} y_j = \omega.$$

The equality expresses that the actions of the agents are compatible with the total resources, i.e., for every event e_T at T,

$$\sum_i x_i(e_T) - \sum_j y_j(e_T) = \omega(e_T).$$

A *private ownership economy* $\mathscr{E}$ is described by an economy $((X_i, \underset{i}{\precsim}), (Y_j), \omega)$, the *resources* (ω_i) of the consumers and their *shares* (θ_{ij}). The ω_i are points of R^l satisfying $\sum_{i=1}^{m} \omega_i = \omega$, and the θ_{ij} are non-negative real numbers satisfying $\sum_{i=1}^{m} \theta_{ij} = 1$ for every j. Given a price system p and productions (y_j) for the n producers the wealth of the ith consumer is $w_i = p \cdot \omega_i + \sum_{j=1}^{n} \theta_{ij} p \cdot y_j$.

The formal identity of this theory of uncertainty with the theory of certainty developed earlier allows one to apply here all the results established in the preceding chapters. In particular, sufficient conditions for the existence of an equilibrium for the private ownership economy $\mathscr{E}$ are given by theorem (1) of 5.7.

7.7. Optimum

In the same fashion, theorems (1) of 6.3 and (1) of 6.4 applied to the economy E yield sufficient conditions for an equilibrium relative to a price system to be an optimum, and for an optimum to be an equilibrium relative to a price system.

Notes

1. This chapter is based on the mimeographed paper, "Une économie de l'incertain," written by the author at Electricité de France in the summer of 1953. The analysis of the theory of value under uncertainty in terms of choices of Nature originated in K. J. Arrow [2], where the risk-aversion implication of weak-convexity of preferences is established. The definition of the preference preordering in 7.5 has been suggested by the work of L. J. Savage [1].

A similar approach has been taken by E. Baudier [1]. A different attack has been tried by M. Allais [2].

2. The assumption that markets exist for all the uncertain commodities introduced in 7.3 is a natural extension of the usual assumption that markets exist for all the certain commodities of Chapter 2 (see in particular 2.6).

References

The references in the notes at the end of this section are

M. Allais, "Généralisation des théories de l'équilibre économique général et du rendement social au cas du risque," pp. 81–120. Econométrie, Paris: Centre National de la Recherche Scientifique, 1953.

K. J. Arrow, "Le rôle des valeurs boursières pour la répartition la meilleure des risques," pp. 41–48. Econométrie, Paris: Centre National de la Recherche Scientifique, 1953 [translated as The role of securities in the optimal allocation of risk, *Rev. Econ. Stud.* **31** (1964), 91–96].

E. Baudier, L'introduction du temps dans la théorie de l'équilibre général, *Les cahiers économique* (1954), 9–16.

L. J. Savage, "The Foundations of Statistics." New York: Wiley, 1954.

Exercise on equilibrium prices and consumption[1]

Consider an exchange economy with a continuum of states of nature and a single consumer good.

Let $p(\theta)$ be the price of a unit of consumption for delivery if state of nature θ occurs. Let $c_i(\theta)$ and $h_i(\theta)$ be the consumption and subjective probabilities of individual i in this economy. Assume that man i maximizes expected utility with a strictly concave utility function $u_i(c_i)$ and an income I_i.

1 Set up the consumer choice problem and determine the first-order condition for expected utility maximization.
2 Show that two individuals with the same subjective probabilities have consumption patterns the relative variation in which depends on the indexes of risk aversion (see Chapter 4):

$$\text{If} \quad h_1(\theta) = h_2(\theta) \qquad \text{then} \quad \frac{dc_1/d\theta}{dc_2/d\theta} = \frac{u_2''/u_2'}{u_1''/u_1'}$$

[*Hint:* Try logarithmic differentiation of the first-order condition.]
3 Show that for two people with the same subjective probabilities, $c_1(\theta_1) = c_1(\theta_2)$ implies $c_2(\theta_1) = c_2(\theta_2)$.
4 Assuming everyone in the economy has the same subjective probabilities, derive an equation relating the percentage price change across states of nature to output variation and the indexes of risk aversion of consumers.

[1]This exercise is based on the Appendix to Chapter 13.

Comment

Risks in an economy may occur in such a form that the law of large numbers helps to determine the structure of equilibrium prices. When this is so, the theory is considerably simplified. Consider, for example, an exchange economy with a large number of identical individuals, each of whom has a random endowment. These random endowments are identically and independently distributed. If individuals are risk averse, then in equilibrium aggregate net demand will be approximately the same in most realizations of the economy. Thus, the distribution of prices that might occur in the economy has little variation. If, in addition, there is insurance for individuals of the risk associated with their individual endowments, then each person can consume approximately the mean of his endowment. For presentation and extensions of this argument, see the work of Hildenbrand (1971) and Malinvaud (1972).

There is an additional sizable literature that does not fit into the scheme of this book—that of temporary equilibrium. In this literature, markets exist for present commodities and for a limited number of future commodities (basically bonds). Individuals form expectations about the future, and equilibrium in the present is dependent on expectations about the future. Since markets reopen in the future, expectations are not necessarily correct. Equilibria in temporary equilibrium models do not have the strong optimality properties that equilibria in models with complete Arrow-Debreu securities have. For a discussion on this issue see Svensson (1976). For a survey of this literature see Grandmont (1977).

We also do not consider the literature that examines the development of a stochastic economy over time and analyzes the asymptotic distribution of the equilibrium. There are a number of analyses of this type. For examples, see Green and Majumdar (1975), Lucas (1978), and Mirman (1973). Lucas's work has given rise to considerable recent activity. See, for example, Kydland and Prescott (1982).

References

J. M. Grandmont, Temporal general equilibrium theory, *Econometrica* **45** (1977), 535–572.

J. Green and M. Majumdar, The nature of stochastic equilibria, *Econometrica* **43** (1975), 647–660.

W. Hildenbrand, Random preferences and equilibrium analysis, *J. Econ. Theory* **3** (1971), 414–429.

F. Kydland and E. Prescott, Time-to-build and aggregate fluctuations, *Econometrica* **50** (1982), 1345–1370.

R. E. Lucas, Jr., Asset prices in an exchange economy, *Econometrica* **46** (1978), 1429–1445.

E. Malinvaud, The allocation of individual risks in large markets, *J. Econ. Theory* 5 (1972), 312–328.

L. J. Mirman, The steady state behavior of a class of one sector growth models with uncertain technology, *J. Econ. Theory* 6 (1973), 219–242.

L. E. O. Svensson, Sequences of temporary equilibria, stationary point expectations and Pareto efficiency, *J. Econ. Theory* 9 (1976), 169–183.

12

R. Radner, Competitive equilibrium under uncertainty, *Econometrica* **36** (1968), 31–58

This paper extends the general equilibrium analysis of the previous reading by examining the states of nature that particular individuals are capable of distinguishing. Equilibrium is examined under the condition that individuals engage in no trades that would involve delivery or receipt of goods based on distinctions that the individual is unable to make. The alternative extreme would permit two persons to trade provided one of them is able to distinguish states of nature. This would entail a great degree of trust and would ignore the communication costs when one party has to inform the other that his actions are now expected. In practice some institutions do rely on trust (together with some policing of honesty). One thinks of public accountants scrutinizing the records of corporations as a check that the managers do provide to owners the correct portion of profits. Many circumstances involve agency relations where an individual hires another to make decisions for him. These too rely on trust, which is not included in the model. Thus the model represents one extreme of possible extensions of the model from Chapter 11.

Econometrica, Vol. 36, No. 1 (January, 1968)

COMPETITIVE EQUILIBRIUM UNDER UNCERTAINTY[1]

BY ROY RADNER

This paper explores how far one can go in applying the modern theory of competitive equilibrium to the case of uncertainty. In the first part, the analyses of Arrow and Debreu are extended to the case in which different economic agents may have different information about the environment. The second part deals with the limitations of the Arrow-Debreu type of model, and discusses the difficulties associated with nonconvexities in the production of information, with information generated by spot markets, and with limitations on the computational capacities of economic agents. It is argued that the demand for liquidity arises from, among other things, the last two phenomena, and thus does not appear to be amenable to analysis by means of the "neoclassical" theory of competitive equilibrium

1. INTRODUCTION[2]

THE PURPOSE of this paper is to explore how far one can go in applying the modern theory of competitive equilibrium (as exemplified, say, by Debreu's *Theory of Value*)[3] to the case of uncertainty. In Sections 2–9, I extend the analysis of Arrow [**1**] and Debreu [**2**] to the case in which different economic agents may have different information about the environment. The treatment of information used here derives from statistical decision theory generally (e.g., Savage [**7**]), and more particularly from the theory of teams (Marschak and Radner [**4**], Radner [**5**]).

I conclude that if economic decision makers have unlimited computational capacity for choice among strategies, then even if there is uncertainty about the environment, and different agents have different information and different beliefs about the environment, then one can apply the standard theorems on the existence and optimality of competitive equilibrium. In such a theory there is no role for money and liquidity. All contracts are negotiated at the beginning of the history of the economy, and from then on all actions are determined by already chosen strategies. Such strategies may, of course, take account of new information as it becomes available.

On the other hand, I argue that a demand for liquidity arises from *computational limitations*, and would be present even in a world of certainty about the environment if that world were sufficiently complicated. I suggest further that there is a basic difficulty in incorporating computational limitations in a "classical" equilibrium theory based on optimizing behavior, and that this presents an obstacle to

[1] This research was supported in part by the Office of Naval Research under Contract ONR 222(77) with the University of California. Reproduction in whole or in part is permitted for any purpose of the United States Government.

[2] I am grateful to G. Debreu and K. J. Arrow for helpful comments on an earlier draft of this paper. In particular, I feel they helped to clarify my thoughts on the material of Sections 10 and 11, although they might well disagree after reading this material.

[3] See Debreu [**2**] in the list of references at the end of the paper.

an extension of the classical theorems of welfare economics to cover the case of a monetary economy.

I also argue that if decision makers receive information about each other's behavior as well as about the environment, then this introduces a type of externality (interdependence) among their decision rules. This type of externality has the result that decision makers must take account of uncertainty about each other's behavior as well as about the environment. It, too, may give rise to a demand for liquidity. In particular, the introduction of "spot" markets as well as futures markets results in this type of externality, and thus does not appear to be amenable to analysis by means of the "classical" theory of competitive equilibrium.

The distinction between (1) uncertainty and information about the environment, and (2) uncertainty and information about others' behavior or the outcome of as yet unperformed computations appears to be fundamental. The analyses of Arrow [**1**] and Debreu [**2**] deal with uncertainty about the environment.[4] The "world" is divided into two sets of variables: decision variables, which are controlled by economic agents, and environmental variables, which are not controlled by any economic agent. Following the terminology of statistical decision theory, I shall call a complete specification of the environment a "state of nature." A state of nature is a complete description of the environment from the beginning to the end of the economic system in question. In Sections 2–8 of this paper I assume that each economic agent (consumer or producer) obtains or has information about the environment at every date, and that he knows in advance what kind of information he will have (even though he typically doesn't know in advance exactly what that information will be). At the beginning of time each agent chooses a strategy, subject to some constraints; this strategy determines his receipts and deliveries of goods and services at all dates. The actual receipts and deliveries at a given date will depend upon the information that the agent has at that date. This information, in turn, depends upon the state of nature, so that, in effect, a strategy determines how receipts and deliveries at each date will depend upon the state of nature. Different agents may, of course, have different information.

Since receipts and deliveries at each date depend, directly or indirectly, on the state of nature, it is natural to assume that a market exists for delivery of each commodity at each date conditional on each state of nature, at least in principle. I hasten to add that this assumption is natural only if each agent has unlimited computational ability. (As a matter of fact, depending upon the structure of information available to the various agents, some of these markets may be unnecessary or inactive; this topic is discussed in Section 8.) I assume, therefore, that there is a price for delivery of each commodity at each date conditional on each state of nature. With such a system of prices there is no uncertainty about the cost or value of a given strategy. This last point may at first surprise the reader, and needs some

[4] In general, so does statistical decision theory; see Savage [**7**].

emphasis. Since the consequences of any strategy are completely described by specifying the receipts or deliveries of each commodity at each date in each state, and each such receipt or delivery can be valued according to its corresponding (conditional) price, the cost of any strategy is simply the sum of products of such conditional prices times the quantities. Note that the "price" of *unconditional* delivery of a given commodity at a given date is the sum, over all states of nature, of the corresponding conditional prices.

In outlining the assumptions about the behavior of producers and consumers, I shall first limit myself to the case of a fixed structure of information for each economic agent in the economy. For certain purposes it is useful to make a distinction between a *strategy* and an *act*. A *strategy* determines inputs and outputs at each date as a function of incoming information. The incoming information is determined by some information process (e.g., observation) as a function of the state of nature. Combining an information process with a strategy yields an *act*, namely a function that determines inputs and outputs at each date as a function of the state of nature. (The distinction between strategies and acts is of importance in the case of communication among decision makers; see discussion below, and Sections 10 and 11.)

Each producer is characterized by a *production possibility set*, i.e., a set of feasible production acts. This set expresses all of the constraints on his production, including the constraints imposed on his acts by the structure of information available to him at each date. Any one act of a producer determines his inputs and/or outputs of each commodity at each date in each state of nature. For a given set of prices, the *profit* corresponding to a production act is the net value of the act, computed in the manner described above.

A consumer is characterized by a consumption possibility set, preferences, resources, and shares in productive enterprises. His *consumption possibility* set is a set of feasible consumption acts, expressing, among other things, the constraints imposed by the structure of his information. His *preferences* among acts reflect his tastes for consumption, his beliefs about the relative likelihood of the several states of nature, and his attitude towards risk. Following Debreu, I do not find it necessary to assume that a consumer's preferences are sufficiently regular so as to permit scaling in terms of subjective probabilities and von Neumann-Morgenstern utilities. I do assume, however, that consumers are risk-averse or risk-neutral (convexity of preferences). The *resources* of each consumer consist of specified quantities (possibly zero) of each commodity at each date in each state of nature. His *shares* consist of some fraction (possibly zero) of the profit of each producer (not necessarily the same fraction for each). For given prices, his *wealth* is the sum of the value of his resources and his profit shares.

An *equilibrium* is a set of prices, together with acts of consumers and producers, such that (a) each consumer maximizes his preferences within his consumption possibility set, subject to his wealth constraint; (b) each producer maximizes profits within his production possibility set; and (c) total demand equals total supply, at every date and in every state of nature. Note that it is assumed that producers and consumers are "price-takers." Note, too, that in maximizing profits the beliefs concerning likelihoods of states and the attitudes towards risk of the producers are irrelevant and play no role in their behavior, since for given prices there is no uncertainty about the value of a production act. On the other hand, beliefs and attitudes towards risk do play a role in consumer behavior, although for given prices and given production plans there is no uncertainty about a consumer's wealth.

In such an economy, which I might call the "Arrow-Debreu world,"[5] all contracts are negotiated at the beginning of the history of the economy, as I mentioned above, and from then on all actions are determined by the already chosen acts. There is no need to revise any strategies, because the choice of a strategy has already taken account of the structure of information in the future, i.e., what information will be available at each date. Since (1) all accounts are settled at the beginning, (2) there is no revision of strategies, and (3) the present value of each producer and each consumer is known with certainty at the beginning, it follows that there is no need for money or liquidity and no incentive to trade shares. Using the techniques of Debreu [**2**, **3**], one can demonstrate, under "classical conditions" (convexity and continuity of production and consumption sets, and of preferences, etc.), the existence of an equilibrium, the Pareto optimality of an equilibrium, and that, roughly speaking, every Pareto-optimal configuration of strategies is an equilibrium relative to some price system for some distribution of resources (Sections 5 and 6).

The Arrow-Debreu world has been criticized as a model of reality, or even as a normative model of planning, for requiring the existence of too many markets. The limits on the information available to the agents, however, and in particular the differences among the information structures of the several agents, will typically have the effect of drastically reducing the number of required markets (Section 8). First, there is no need for contracts that depend upon information that is not available in the economy. Second, the net trade between any group of agents and the group of all other agents in the economy can at most depend upon information that is common to both groups; "common to both groups" means here that at least one agent in each group must have the information in question. These considerations somewhat diminish the force of the above criticism, but are far from eliminating it altogether.

Up to this point, I have assumed that the structure of information available to each agent at each date is fixed in advance. The choice of information structure can be included in the model simply by taking account of the real costs of obtaining information in the formal description of the consumption and production possibil-

[5] The model just described, with the exception of the possibility of different agents having different information, is due to Debreu [**2**, Ch. 7], and represents an extension and generalization of Arrow [**1**].

ity sets. With this formulation, however, the convexity assumption may be seriously criticized. This problem, with an example, is discussed in Section 9.

In the Arrow-Debreu world a competitive equilibrium achieves a Pareto-optimum relative to a given structure of information by making available to all agents in the economy some additional information, namely the equilibrium prices. As I have already emphasized, these are prices in a futures market; all strategies are determined at the beginning and no revision of strategies is contemplated. Suppose, however, that new markets were introduced at later dates; would there be any incentive to trade in these new markets? In general there would, because the equilibrium prices in such markets would convey additional information beyond that contemplated in the original structure of information. These prices would depend, at a given date, on the evolution of the economy up to that date, including the evolution of the environment, both through direct observations of the environment made by economic agents, and indirectly through the decisions made up to that date, which determine the stocks at the beginning of that date. Unfortunately, in order correctly to infer something about the state of nature from the value of the new prices, an agent must in principle know the strategies used by other agents up to that date.

An agent may choose a strategy determining how his inputs and outputs will depend upon his information, including the "spot" prices in the later markets, but such a strategy will not independently determine an act! The acts of all the agents will be determined jointly by their choice of strategies. In this sense, the introduction of spot markets introduces "external effects" among the acts of the several agents in the economy. Thus, although the introduction of spot markets makes available to the economy acts that were not available with the initial structure of information, it also destroys one of the important conditions for the "classical" analysis of competitive equilibrium. In particular, an agent will no longer be able to assign a definite value to a strategy for given prices in the futures market. There would typically arise a demand for liquidity, but unless agents could correctly predict the strategies of others, and calculate the consequences, he could not determine his optimal demand for liquidity!

The structure of information generated by spot markets is a special case of what has elsewhere been called *network information* (Marschak and Radner, [**4**]). The model of network information is described in Section 10, with a discussion of the resulting externalities, and the particular case of market information is discussed in Section 11.

The Arrow-Debreu world is strained to the limit by the problem of choice of information. It breaks down completely in the face of limits on the ability of agents to compute optimal strategies. I have already hinted at the nature of the difficulty at the beginning of this introduction. This problem is explored a little in Section 12. The discussion there points to a model in which there is a succession of temporary equilibria, with the existence at each date of a limited number of markets for current and future delivery. In such a model each agent faces not only uncertainty about the environment, but also about the outcome of his own future computations, about future prices (as distinct from "futures prices") and about the existence of various markets in the future. This additional type of uncertainty leads to the constant revision of strategies, and therefore to trading at every date (not just in the beginning of time, as in the Arrow-Debreu world), to the importance of probability judgments and risk-taking by producers, to the demand for money and liquidity, and to the trading of shares, to mention only a few additional phenomena. This computational uncertainty also seems to be an obstacle to the definition of concepts of individual and social optimum, except possibly in a long-run statistical sense.

I conclude this Introduction with some suggestions on strategies for reading this paper. The reader armed only with arithmetic and a little algebra, and without much patience for abstract formulation and symbolism, should proceed immediately to Section 7, in which I present an extended example, and then read the example of Section 9, and Sections 10 through 13. The rest of the paper, with the exception of Theorems 1 and 2 of Section 5 on the existence of equilibrium, is abstract but mathematically elementary. The new techniques of Debreu [**3**] are helpful in analyzing the question of existence of equilibrium, as is shown in Theorems 1 and 2 of Section 5. Here the difficulty is that, because of the limits on information, each agent's set of feasible strategies lies in a linear subspace of the space of all possible strategies, and these subspaces are typically different for different agents. Thus, for example, the assumption of "free disposal" is not appropriate here.

2. STATES AND ACTS

Consider an economy with T dates (elementary time periods), and C different "commodities" at each date, where "commodities" are to be interpreted broadly, including goods and services, distinguished possibly according to age, location, etc.

Let S denote a finite set, to be interpreted as the set of alternative "states of nature." The states in S are mutually exclusive, and the set S is exhaustive. Each state in S determines the entire history of all aspects of the economy that are beyond the control of any of the agents. (See Savage [**7**, Chapter 2] for a detailed discussion of this concept.)

An *act* of an economic agent (producer or consumer) is a T-tuple $\alpha = (\alpha_1, \alpha_2, \ldots, \alpha_T)$, where for each t, α_t is a function from S to the C-dimensional Euclidean vector space R^C. For a producer, the cth coordinate of $\alpha_t(s)$ is to be interpreted as his output of commodity c at date t, if s is the true state of nature ("outputs" are positive, "inputs" are negative). For a consumer the cth coordinate of $\alpha_t(s)$ is his input of commodity c at date t, if s is the true state (but here "inputs" (consumption) are positive, "outputs" are negative).[6]

A *price system* is a nonzero T-tuple $p=(p_1, \ldots, p_T)$, where for each t, p_t is a function from S to R^C. The cth coordinate of $p_t(s)$ is to be interpreted as the price of commodity c at date t if state s obtains.

For two vectors, $u=(u^c)$ and $v=(v^c)$, in R^C denote by $u \cdot v$ the inner product $u \cdot v \equiv \Sigma_c u^v v^c$. The same "dot product" notation will be used to denote the *value*, $p \cdot \alpha$, *of an act* α *relative to a price system* p: $p \cdot \alpha \equiv \Sigma_s \Sigma_t p_t(s) \cdot \alpha_t(s)$.

If S has $|S|$ elements (finite), then every act and every price system may be regarded as a point in a Euclidean space of $T \cdot C \cdot |S|$ dimensions. This space will be denoted by A.

3. FIXED INFORMATION ABOUT THE ENVIRONMENTS; STRATEGIES

In Sections 4–9 of this paper the information on which a given economic agent bases his decisions at a given date t will be characterized by a partition, say $\mathscr{S}_t$, of the set S of states. The T-tuple $\mathscr{S}=(\mathscr{S}_1, \ldots, \mathscr{S}_T)$ of these partitions will be called the *information structure* for the agent in question. The information structure $\mathscr{S}$ is assumed to constrain the acts of the agent as follows: for every t, every set M in $\mathscr{S}_t$,

(3.1) if s and s' are both in M, then $\alpha_t(s) = \alpha_t(s')$.

To say that M is a set in $\mathscr{S}_t$ expresses the idea that if the true state is in M, then the agent's information at date t enables him to determine that the true state is in M, but not to determine which of the states in M is the true state. (See Savage [7, Ch. 6].) If the agent cannot distinguish, at date t, between the different states in M, then he cannot make his decision at t depend upon s within M; hence the constraint (3.1).

For any information structure $\mathscr{S}$ let $\mathscr{A}(\mathscr{S})$ denote the set of all acts that are compatible with $\mathscr{S}$, i.e., satisfy (3.1). The set $\mathscr{A}(\mathscr{S})$ is a linear subspace of A, the linear space of all acts, with the usual definitions of addition and scalar multiplication of functions.[7]

Relative to the given set of states, at a given date, the partition in which every set consists of a single state represents "complete information;" whereas, the partition consisting of the set S alone represents "no information."

For two partitions, $\mathscr{U}$ and $\mathscr{V}$, of S, I shall say that $\mathscr{U}$ *is as fine as* $\mathscr{V}$ if for every $U \in \mathscr{U}$ and $V \in \mathscr{V}$ either $U \subseteq V$ or $U \cap V = \varnothing$.

[6] I have followed closely the terminology of Debreu [2]. However, Debreu calls an "action" what I have called an "act"; the latter term is used in Savage [7].

[7] For each t let $\mathscr{S}_t^*$ be the smallest algebra of sets containing the partition $\mathscr{S}_t$. Then condition (3.1) is equivalent to the requirement that α_t be $\mathscr{S}_t^*$-measurable. In any extension of this treatment to infinite sets of states, it would be natural to describe information in terms of σ-algebras $\mathscr{S}_t^*$, and acts α such that α_t is $\mathscr{S}_t^*$-measurable. In the finite case, $\mathscr{S}_t^*$ is the family of all unions of sets in $\mathscr{S}_t$.

If an agent did not forget any information from one date to the next, then one would represent this by a structure of information $\mathscr{S}$ in which each partition $\mathscr{S}_t$ was at least as fine as the preceding one; one might call this an *expanding* information structure. Debreu [**2**, Ch. 7] treats the case in which all the economic agents have the same expanding information structure. Arrow [**1**] does not consider dated information and action; he also assumes implicitly that all agents have the same information.

It may help the reader to relate the present abstract representation of information about the environment to an equivalent one that is perhaps more familiar. One may think of the information about the environment as deriving from an observation, expressed in the form of some measurement, signal, etc. For a given economic agent at a given date t, let the set of possible alternative observations be denoted by $\tilde{B}_t$. A decision rule at that date would assign to every possible observation $\tilde{b}_t$ in $\tilde{B}_t$ a vector of inputs and outputs, i.e., a point in the commodity space, R^C. A T-tuple of such rules will be called a *strategy*. Thus a strategy is a T-tuple $\beta = (\beta_1, \ldots, \beta_T)$ such that for each t, β_t is a function from $\tilde{B}_t$ to R^C.

The particular method of observation used will determine a relation between the state of nature and the observation. Assuming that the state of nature includes a description of all environmental factors relevant to the method of observation (including disturbances, defects of the observational instruments, "noise," etc.), the method of observation will be characterized by a function from S to $\tilde{B}_t$, say $\tilde{\beta}_t$. Every such function $\tilde{\beta}$ determines a partition $\mathscr{S}_t$ of S, as follows: a set is in $\mathscr{S}_t$ if and only if it is the set of all states mapped into a given observation in $\tilde{\beta}_t$. Conversely, every partition $\mathscr{S}_t$ of S may be represented as a "method of observation" by taking $\tilde{B}_t$ to be identical with $\mathscr{S}_t$, and $\tilde{\beta}_t$ to be the function that assigns to every state in S the set in $\mathscr{S}_t$ that contains it. Of course, more than one "method of observation" may lead to the same partition, but (aside from the question of cost) they will be equivalent from the point of view of the decision maker.

If a method of observation $(\tilde{B}_t, \tilde{\beta}_t)$ is followed by the use of a decision rule β_t, the result will be a component of an act, namely $\alpha_t(s) = \beta_t[\tilde{\beta}_t(s)]$. Indeed, given a T-tuple of methods of observation, with corresponding information structure $\mathscr{S} = (\mathscr{S}_1, \ldots, \mathscr{S}_T)$, the set of acts generated by the set of all possible strategies is exactly the set $\mathscr{A}(\mathscr{S})$ of all acts that are compatible with $\mathscr{S}$.

4. CONSUMERS AND PRODUCERS

Following Debreu [**2**], the agents of an economy are divided into *consumers* and *producers*. Consumer i is characterized by:

(a) an information structure $\mathscr{S}_i = (\mathscr{S}_{i1}, \ldots, \mathscr{S}_{iT})$;

(b) a consumption set, X_i, assumed to be a subset of $\mathscr{A}(\mathscr{S}_i)$, representing the set of feasible acts for i;

(c) a complete preordering, $\lesssim_i$, on X_i, describing the preferences of i;

(d) a T-tuple, $\omega_i = (\omega_{i1}, \ldots, \omega_{iT})$, in $\mathscr{A}(\mathscr{S}_i)$, representing the resources of i (thus $\omega_{it}(s)$ represents the vector of quantities of commodities available to consumer i at date t if s is the true state, not as a consequence of any economic action; for example, these might include stocks inherited from the past at the first date, and hours of available labor at future dates);

(e) a set of nonnegative numbers θ_{ij}, where j runs over the set of producers; the number θ_{ij} represents the share in producer j held by consumer i. The numbers θ_{ij} must satisfy, of course, the accounting constraint $\Sigma_i \theta_{ij} = 1$, each j.

Producer j is characterized by:

(a′) an information structure $\mathscr{T}_j = (\mathscr{T}_{j1}, \ldots, \mathscr{T}_{jT})$;

(b′) a production set Y_j, assumed to be a subset of $\mathscr{A}(\mathscr{T}_j)$, representing the set of feasible acts for j.

Given a price system p, the *profit* for producer j is the value of his act, i.e., $p \cdot y_j$. The *wealth* of consumer i is the sum of the value of his resources plus his share of the profits of the producers, i.e., $w_i = p \cdot \omega_i + \Sigma_j \theta_{ij} p \cdot y_j$.

In the descriptions of consumers and producers just given, the information structures are behind the scenes to the extent that every agent's acts are constrained to be compatible with his information structure; recall that $X_i \subseteq \mathscr{A}(\mathscr{S}_i)$ and $Y_j \subseteq \mathscr{A}(\mathscr{T}_j)$. One may bring these constraints more clearly to the fore by supposing that for each agent there is a basic set of "potentially feasible" acts, and that his actual feasible set consists of all potentially feasible acts that are compatible with a given information structure.

In the case of a consumer with a given sequence ω_i of resources, it is not meaningful to consider an information structure $\mathscr{S}_i$ that is so "coarse" that $\omega_i \notin \mathscr{A}(\mathscr{S}_i)$. Since producers are not assumed to have any initial resources, no such limitation need be placed on their information structures.

For each consumer i let X_i^1 denote his set of potentially feasible acts, and let Y_j^1 denote the corresponding set for producer j. Further, for each consumer i let ω_i denote his (given) resources.

For two information structures $\mathscr{S} = (\mathscr{S}_t)$, $\mathscr{S}' = (\mathscr{S}'_t)$ I shall say that $\mathscr{S}$ is *as fine as* $\mathscr{S}'$ if, for every t, $\mathscr{S}_t$ is as fine a partition as $\mathscr{S}'_t$ (see Section 3). For each consumer i let $\mathscr{S}_i^0$ denote the least fine information structure with which ω_i is compatible.

By an *information structure for the economy* I shall mean an $(m+n)$-tuple $\mathscr{I} = ((\mathscr{S}_i), (\mathscr{T}_j))$ of information structures, with $\mathscr{S}_i$ and $\mathscr{T}_j$ corresponding to consumer i and producer j, respectively. $\mathscr{I}$ is *admissible* if, for every consumer i, $\mathscr{S}_i$ is as fine as $\mathscr{S}_i^0$. As noted above, for any given resources of consumers, it makes sense to consider only admissible information structures for the economy. The minimal admissible information structure, $\mathscr{I}^0$, is defined by

$$\mathscr{S}_i = \mathscr{S}_i^0 \qquad (i = 1, \ldots, m),$$

$$\mathscr{T}_{jt} = \{R^C\} \equiv \mathscr{T}_{jt}^0 \qquad (j = 1, \ldots, n;\ t = 1, \ldots, T).$$

The maximal information structure, $\mathscr{I}^1$, is characterized by taking every $\mathscr{S}_{it}$ and every $\mathscr{T}_{jt}$ to be the partition of S into one-element sets (i.e., complete information; see Section 3).

For any admissible information structure $\mathscr{I} = ((\mathscr{S}_i), (\mathscr{T}_j))$ for the economy, define

$$X_i(\mathscr{I}) = X_i^1 \cap \mathscr{A}(\mathscr{S}_i),$$

$$Y_j(\mathscr{I}) = Y_j^1 \cap \mathscr{A}(\mathscr{T}_j).$$

An economy is generated by an information structure $\mathscr{I}$ by taking $X_i(\mathscr{I})$ to be the consumption set for consumer i, with resources ω_i, and with the restriction to $X_i(\mathscr{I})$ of the original preference preordering $\lesssim_i$ on X_i^1; and by taking $Y_j(\mathscr{I})$ to be the production set for producer j.

As pointed out in Section 3, for any information structure $\mathscr{S}$ for an agent, $\mathscr{A}(\mathscr{S})$ is a linear subspace of the set A of all possible acts. If consumer i has information structure $\mathscr{S}_i$, then his set X_i of consumption acts is obtained from the potentially feasible set, X_i^1, by adding a number of linear constraints, namely the constraints (3.1). A corresponding remark applies to producers.

Economic agents may come to the market with prior information about the environment. Prior information enters the model in two ways: (i) if an agent knows at the beginning that the state s is in a certain state E (i.e., that the event E has occurred), then his information structure at each date should reflect the fact that at each date he will know whether or not the true state is in E; (ii) a consumer who knows that s is in E will reflect this fact in his preference ordering; thus for him the marginal utility of consumption contingent on any state not in E will be zero; if his preferences are representable in terms of expected utility, then his personal prior probability of E will be unity.[8] Some comments are perhaps called for here. Although formally every agent is assumed to plan what he would do in each state, it would not in fact be necessary for a consumer to plan what he would consume in states he considers impossible *a priori*. Presumably he would plan to consume nothing in such states, or at least he would not pay anything for consumption in such states. If an agent knew that an event E obtained, but not all agents knew this, the agent in question might find himself in a position in which he could sell, at a positive price, a contract for delivery contingent on an event that he already knew could not occur. *Caveat emptor*! Whether or not this raises any moral questions, it does raise the question of whether or not an agent's information includes knowledge of other agents' information structures. In the real world of contracts between individuals this question does arise. For example, it is not considered correct to make a bet on the outcome of a race whose results you already know.

[8] More generally, his prior information will be summarized in his own personal probability distribution.

But in the Arrow-Debreu world, individuals make contracts with an impersonal "market," so this issue does not arise, and individuals are free to make such contracts.

For each fixed information structure, each consumer is required only to have a preference preordering on the set of acts available to him, where this set already reflects his information structure. On the other hand, if we wish to consider the whole range of economies generated by varying the information structures, then we must assume that each consumer's preferences are defined on the entire set of his potentially feasible acts.

In the case of a fixed information structure, a consumer can, in his preferences, "aggregate" events that his information will not permit him to distinguish. This is brought out clearly in the case in which his preferences are representable by an expected utility function.

In a "static" situation, let $x(s)$ denote his consumption in state s, $P(s)$ his personal prior probability of state s, and $u(c)$ his utility for the sure consumption c. His expected utility of a consumption plan $x(\cdot)$ is $\Sigma_s P(s)u[x(s)]$. If $E_1, \ldots, E_K$ is a partition of S, and $x(s)$ is constant on each event E_k, say equal to $x(E_k)$, then the expected utility of $x(\cdot)$ is

$$\sum_k \left[\sum_{s \in E_k} P(s) \right] u[x(E_k)] = \sum_k \operatorname{Prob}(E_k) u[x(E_k)] .$$

Thus the individual need only make precise his personal probabilities of the events E_k. Warning: this does not imply that if he were to make precise the individual probabilities $P(s)$ they then would be equal for all states in a given event E_k.

5. EQUILIBRIUM

An equilibrium is a price system together with acts of consumers and producers such that, for the given price system, (a) each consumer maximizes his preferences subject to his wealth constraint, (b) each producer maximizes his profits, and (c) total demand equals total supply. Formally, if there are m consumers and n producers, an equilibrium is an $(m+n+1)$-tuple $(x_1^*, \ldots, x_m^*, y_1^*, \ldots, y_n^*, p^*)$ such that p^* is a price system and such that

(a.1) for every i, $x_i^* \in X_i$ and $p^* \cdot x_i^* \leqslant w_i^* \equiv p^* \cdot \omega_i + \Sigma_j \theta_{ij} p^* \cdot y_j^*$;
(a.2) for every i, if $x_i \in X_i$ and if $p^* \cdot x_i \leqslant w_i^*$, then $x_i \precsim_i x_i^*$;
(b) for every j, $y_j^* \in Y_j$, and if $y_j \in Y_j$ then $p^* \cdot y_j \leqslant p^* \cdot y_j^*$;
(c) $\Sigma_i (x_i^* - \omega_i) = \Sigma_j y_j^*$.

In this section I shall first give sufficient conditions for the existence of an equilibrium for a given structure of information in the economy. I shall then give sufficient conditions on the potentially feasible sets for there to exist an equilibrium for any structure of information in the economy that is compatible with the resources of consumers.[9]

First, then, I consider the case of a given structure of information for each agent in the economy, as described in the previous sections. The main difficulty that arises here in the question of existence of equilibrium is that, with the restrictions imposed on acts by a given information structure, the simpler theorems on existence will typically not be applicable. For example, the assumption of free disposal is inappropriate here, at least in its usual form; even though a given act α is compatible with an information structure $\mathscr{S}$, the set of acts $\leqslant \alpha$ (in the vector sense) will typically contain acts that are not compatible with $\mathscr{S}$. However, the analysis of Debreu [3] does provide appropriate conditions. Before stating his result, I need to introduce some additional notation. An $(m+n)$-tuple $((x_i), (y_j))$ of acts is attainable if (a) for each i, $x_i \in X_i$; (b) for each j, $y_j \in Y_j$; and (c) $\Sigma_i(x_i - \omega_i) = \Sigma_j y_j$. An act x_i is attainable for consumer i if it is part of some attainable $(m+n)$-tuple of acts. Let $\hat{X}_i$ denote the set of attainable acts for consumer i. Define $x_i >_i \hat{X}_i$ to mean $x_i >_i x_i'$ for all $x_i' \in \hat{X}_i$. Further define:

$$D_i \equiv \{x_i : x_i \in X_i \cdot x_i >_i \hat{X}_i\},$$

$$D' \equiv \Sigma_i(D_i - \{\omega_i\}),$$

and define D as the smallest cone with vertex at 0 that contains D'. The set $D_i - \{\omega_i\}$ may be interpreted as the set of net trades by consumer i that would make him better off than in any attainable state of the economy.

Also define $X \equiv \Sigma_i X_i$, $Y \equiv \Sigma_j Y_j$, and $\omega \equiv \Sigma_i \omega_i$. Finally, for any set W, its *asymptotic cone*[10] will be denoted by $\underset{\sim}{A}W$.

The following theorem on the existence of an equilibrium is drawn from Debreu [3, pp. 259–260, 269–270].

THEOREM 1: *An equilibrium exists if*:

(a.1) $\underset{\sim}{A}X \cap (-\underset{\sim}{A}X) = \{0\}$;

for every i;

(a.2) X_i *is closed and convex*;

(b.1) (*nonsatiation in attainable set*) *for every* x_i *in* $\hat{X}_i$ *there is an* x_i' *in* X_i *such that* $x_i' >_i x_i$;

(b.2) (*continuity of preference*) *for every* x_i' *in* X_i *the sets* $\{x_i : x_i \in X_i \cdot x_i >_i x_i'\}$ *and* $\{x_i : x_i \in X_i \cdot x_i \lesssim_i x_i'\}$ *are closed*;

(b.3) (*convexity of preference*) *for every* x_i' *in* X_i *the set* $\{x_i : x_i \in X_i \cdot x_i \gtrsim_i x_i'\}$ *is convex*;

[9] This section is substantially more technical than the rest of the paper. The reader may skip here to the next section without loss of continuity.

[10] Given W, for any number $k \geqslant 0$ let W_k denote the smallest closed cone with vertex 0 containing all points in W with norm (length) at least k; then $\underset{\sim}{A}W \equiv \cap_{k \geqslant 0} W_k$. See Debreu [2, pp. 22, 23].

(c.1) *Y is closed and convex and the relative interiors*[11] *of* $(X-\{\omega\})$ *and of* Y *have a nonempty intersection;*

(c.2) *for every* i, $[\underset{\sim}{A}Y-Int_C D]\cap[X_i-\{\omega_i\}]\neq\varnothing$, *where*[12] $C\equiv\Sigma_i\mathscr{A}(\mathscr{S}_i)$;

(d.1) 0 *is in* Y_j, *for every* j; *and*

(d.2) $(\underset{\sim}{A}X)\cap(\underset{\sim}{A}Y)=\{0\}$.

PROOF:[13] By the theorem and footnote 7 of Debreu [3, p. 259], there exists a quasi-equilibrium, say $((x_i^*), (y_j^*), p^*)$, such that[14] $p^*\cdot(\underset{\sim}{A}Y-D)\leqslant 0$, and hence $p^*\cdot D\geqslant 0$ and $p^*\cdot\underset{\sim}{A}Y\leqslant 0$. It follows that either p^* is strictly positive on $\mathrm{Int}_C\, D$, or $p^*\cdot C=0$. Suppose that $p^*\cdot C=0$; then for every i, $p^*\cdot X_i=0$, by (b) of Section 2.3 and the definition of C. Hence for every consumer i, $p^*\cdot x_i^*=\min\{p^*\cdot x_i : x_i\in X_i\}$. By the same argument used to prove the proposition on p. 270 of Debreu [3] one can show that this contradicts hypothesis (c.1) of the present theorem. Hence p^* is strictly positive on $\mathrm{Int}_C\, D$, and therefore strictly negative on $(\underset{\sim}{A}Y-\mathrm{Int}_C\, D)$. By (c.2) and the fact just proved, for every consumer i there exists $x_i\in X_i$ such that $p^*\cdot(x_i-\omega_i)<0$. Since $0\in Y_j$ for every producer j, $p^*\cdot y_j^*\geqslant 0$, and hence $p^*\cdot\omega_i+\Sigma_j\theta_{ij}p^*\cdot y_j^*\geqslant p^*\cdot\omega_i>p^*\cdot x_i$. Hence the quasi-equilibrium is an equilibrium, which completes the proof of the theorem.

I now turn to the case in which each agent has a basic set of "potentially feasible" acts, but his actual feasible set consists of all those potentially feasible ones that are compatible with a given information structure (see Section 4). Let A_0 denote the set of all acts that are constant on S for each date t.

THEOREM 2: *If conditions* (a.1)–(b.3), (d.1), (d.2) *of Theorem* 1 *are satisfied for the potentially feasible economy generated by complete information,* $\mathscr{I}^1$, *and if* (c.1)* *the potentially feasible production sets* $Y_1^1, \ldots, Y_n^1$ *are each closed and convex, and their asymptotic cones are positively semi-independent;*[15] *furthermore, there is a* z *such that*

$$z=\sum_i z_i=\sum_j y_j,$$

$$z_i+\omega_i\in\mathscr{A}(\mathscr{S}_i^0)\cap \mathit{Int}\, X_i^1, \qquad \textit{every } i,$$

$$y_j\in\mathscr{A}(\mathscr{T}_j^0)\cap \mathit{Int}\, Y_j^1, \qquad \textit{every } j;$$

[11] The relative interior of a set W in R^N is the interior of W relative to the smallest linear variety containing W. A linear variety is a set of the form $\{x\}+V$, where V is any linear subspace of R^N and x is any point of R^N (not necessarily in V). Let w_0 be any point of W; then the smallest linear variety containing W is the set of all points of the form $w_0+\Sigma_{i=1}^I\alpha_i(w_i-w_0)$ where I is any positive integer, $\alpha_1, \ldots, \alpha_I$ are any real numbers, and $w_1, \ldots, w_I$ are any points in W.

[12] Int_C here denotes "interior relative to C."

[13] This proof assumes knowledge of the terminology of Debreu [3].

[14] For any set $W\subseteq A$, write $p^*\cdot w\leqslant 0$ if $p^*\cdot w\leqslant 0$ for all $w\in W$ (and similarly for $\geqslant$ and $=$).

[15] See Debreu [2, p. 22].

and (c.2)* *for each i there exist* z_i, v_i, d_i *such that* $z_i = v_i - d_i$, $z_i \in X_i^0 - \{\omega_i\}$, $z_i \in A_0$, $v_i \in \underset{\sim}{A} Y^0$, *and* $d_i = h\Sigma_{k=1}^m (x_{ik} - \omega_k)$ *for some* $h > 0$ *and some* $x_{il}, \ldots, x_{im}$ *for which* $x_{ik} \in Int\, D_k^1$ *and* $(x_{ik} - \omega_k) \in A_0$ *for each* $k = 1, \ldots, m$; *then for every admissible information structure* $\mathscr{I}$ *for the economy there is an equilibrium (where the sets* Y^0, D^1, C^1 *are the sets Y, D, C corresponding to* $\mathscr{I}^0$, $\mathscr{I}^1$ *and* $\mathscr{I}^1$, *respectively).*

Proof: For any set W, let $\mathscr{L}(W)$ denote the smallest linear variety containing W. I preface the proof with two lemmas about linear varieties and relative interiors.

It is to be understood that everything takes place in a fixed (finite dimensional) Euclidean space.

Lemma 1: *Let U be an open set and L a subspace such that* $U \cap L \neq \varnothing$; *then* $L = \mathscr{L}(U \cap L)$.

Proof: Let u be a point in $U \cap L$, and let V be the unit sphere in L. For $\varepsilon > 0$ sufficiently small, $(\{u\} + \varepsilon V) \subset U \cap L$. Hence

$$L = \{u\} + L = \mathscr{L}(\{u\} + \varepsilon V) \subset \mathscr{L}(U \cap L) \subset L\,,$$

which proves Lemma 1.

Lemma 2: *Let* $W_1, \ldots, W_K$ *be sets with nonempty interiors; for each* $k = 1, \ldots, K$ *let* L_k *be a subspace that intersects* $Int(W_k)$; *and let* $L \equiv \Sigma_{k=1}^K L_K$ *and* $W^* \equiv \Sigma_k (W_k \cap L_k)$; *then*

$$\sum_k (Int_{L_k}[W_k \cap L_k]) \subset Int_L\,(W^*)\,, \tag{5.1}$$

$$\mathscr{L} \sum_k [W_k \cap L_k] = L\,. \tag{5.2}$$

Proof: For every k let w_k be a point of $\mathrm{Int}_{L_k}[W_k \cap L_k]$, and let $w = \Sigma_k w_k$. There exists an $\varepsilon > 0$ such that for every k the set U_k defined by

$$U_k \equiv \{u_k : u_k \in L_k \cdot \|u_k - w_k\| < \varepsilon\}$$

is contained in $W_k \cap L_k$. To demonstrate that $w \in \mathrm{Int}_L(W^*)$, I shall show that for some $\sigma > 0$ the set U defined by

$$U \equiv \{u : u \in L \cdot \|u - w\| < \sigma\} \tag{5.3}$$

is contained in W^*.

There exist $P_1, \ldots, P_K$ such that for each k, P_k is a linear transformation from L into L_k, $\Sigma_{j=1}^k P_j$ is a projection onto $\Sigma_{j=1}^k L_j$. For each k, $P_k' P_k$ is nonnegative semidefinite (P' denotes the adjoint of P), and its largest characteristic root, say r_k, is nonnegative. Let $r^2 \equiv \max(r_1, \ldots, r_K)$. For any $v \in L$, $v = \Sigma_{k=1}^K P_k v$, $\|P_k v\| \leqslant r\|v\|$. Hence $\|v\| < (\varepsilon/r)$ implies that for every k, $\|P_k v\| < \varepsilon$. Let U be defined as in (5.3) with $\sigma=(\varepsilon/r)$; then for any $u\in U$, $u-w=\Sigma_k P_k(u-w)$, $\|P_k(u-w)\|<\varepsilon$, $P_k(u-w)\in L_k$. Let $u_k\equiv w_k+P_k(u-w)$; then $u_k\in L_k$, $\|u_k-w_k\|<\varepsilon$, $\Sigma_k u_k=w+\Sigma_k P_k(u-w)=u$. Hence $u\in\Sigma_k U_k$. Therefore

$$U\subset\sum_k U_k\subset\sum_k(W_k\cap L_k)=W^*\,.$$

To prove (5.2), it follows from Lemma 1 that

$$L=\mathscr{L}(U)\subset\mathscr{L}(\sum_k[W_k\cap L_k])\subset\sum_k L_k=L\,.$$

I turn now to the proof of the theorem. Consider a fixed admissible information structure $\mathscr{I}$, and the corresponding economy with consumption sets $X_i\equiv X_i(\mathscr{I})$, preferences $\precsim_i$, resources ω_i, and production sets $Y_j\equiv Y_j(\mathscr{I})$. It is straightforward to verify that (a.1)–(b.3), (d.1), and (d.2) of Theorem 1 are satisfied, and also that $Y\equiv\Sigma_j Y_j$ is convex. Furthermore, every Y_j is closed, and the asymptotic cones $\underset{\sim}{A}Y_1,\ldots,\underset{\sim}{A}Y_n$ are positively semi-independent; hence Y is closed (see Debreu [**2**, p. 23]).

To verify the rest of (c.1) of Theorem 1, I first show that, in (c.1)* of the present theorem, $z=\Sigma_j y_j$ is in the relative interior of Y. Let $L_j\equiv\mathscr{A}(\mathscr{T}_j)$, $L\equiv\Sigma_j L_j$, and note that $y_j\in L_j$, since $L_j\supset\mathscr{A}(\mathscr{T}_j^0)$. Hence, for every j, $y_j\in\operatorname{Int}_{L_j}Y_j$. Since $Y_j=Y_j^1\cap L_j$, it follows from Lemma 2 that $z\in\operatorname{Int}_L Y$, which equals the relative interior of Y. Similarly, one can verify that z is in the relative interior of $\Sigma_i(X_i-\omega_i)$.

I turn now to the verification of (c.2) of Theorem 1. It follows from (c.2)* of the present theorem that for every i and k, $x_{ik}\in\mathscr{A}(\mathscr{S}_k)$, $x_{ik}\in\operatorname{Int}W_k$, where $W\equiv\{x_k:x_k\in Y_k^1\cdot x_k>_k X_k(\mathscr{I})\}$, since $\hat{X}_k(\mathscr{I})\subset\hat{X}_k^1$. Note that $D_k(\mathscr{I})=W_k\cap\mathscr{A}(\mathscr{S}_k)$; hence $x_{ik}\in\operatorname{Int}_{\mathscr{A}(\mathscr{S}k)}D_k(\mathscr{I})$, $x_{ik}-\omega_k\in\operatorname{Int}_{\mathscr{A}(\mathscr{S}k)}[D_k(\mathscr{I})-\{\omega_k\}]$. Hence by Lemma 2

$$\sum_{k=1}^{m}(x_{ik}-\omega_k)\in\operatorname{Int}_C\sum_{k=1}^{m}[D_k(\mathscr{I})-\{\omega_k\}],$$

where $C\equiv C(\mathscr{I})=\Sigma_{i=1}^m\mathscr{A}(\mathscr{S}_i)$. Hence $d_i\in\operatorname{Int}_C D(\mathscr{I})$. Also $v_i\in\underset{\sim}{A}Y$, since $Y^0\subset Y$. Therefore $z_i\in\underset{\sim}{A}Y-\operatorname{Int}_C D(\mathscr{I})$. Finally, $z_i\in X_i-\{\omega_i\}$, since $X_i^0\subset X_i$. This completes the verification of (c.2), and therefore the proof of Theorem 2.

6. OPTIMUM

The concepts of *optimum*[16] and of *equilibrium relative to a price system* (see Debreu [**2**, Ch. 6]) can be applied directly to the present model of an economy under uncertainty. It should perhaps be emphasized that "optimum" here must be interpreted as "optimum relative to a given structure of information in the economy." In particular, in the context of the end of Section 4, in which an economy

[16] Sometimes called Pareto optimum.

is defined in terms of potentially feasible acts constrained by a given structure of information, a refinement of information structure results in an enlargement of the set of actually feasible acts, and in principle a new set of optima.

Debreu [**2**, Ch. 6, Sections 3 and 4] gives conditions under which an equilibrium relative to a price system is an optimum, and under which the converse is true. The reader is referred to this source for the details. I might mention that again convexity of preferences, and therefore in this context, risk aversion, plays a role.

7. AN EXAMPLE

An example may help the reader to understand the formal description of the theory. Furthermore, this example will illustrate the constraints on trade that may result from differences in information among agents. To keep the example simple, time (i.e., dating of commodities and information) is left out.

Consider an economy with two consumers, one producer, and two "commodities." To aid the imagination, the two commodities may be thought of as "labor" and "food." The producer can transform any nonnegative number of units of labor into an equal number of units of food (the units of measurement are fixed). The resources of the economy consist entirely of labor, held by the two consumers; however, there is uncertainty about the actual quantities of these resources. The uncertainty is described in terms of three states of nature, as in Table I. Thus, in states 1 and 2 consumer 1 will have at his disposal one unit of labor, whereas in state 3 he will have two units, etc.

TABLE I

RESOURCES

States	Labor Resources of:	
of Nature	Consumer 1	Consumer 2
1	1	1
2	1	2
3	2	2

To complete the description of the uncertainty, we must say what each agent knows about the state of nature when he makes his economic decisions. Assume that the producer knows nothing beyond the facts in Table I, whereas, each consumer knows (in addition) the quantity of labor that he himself has at his disposal. More precisely, one may say that (i) all three agents know Table I; (ii) if the true state of nature is 1 or 2, then consumer 1 knows only that it is one of these two (but not which one), whereas, if the true state is 3, then he knows that it is 3; (iii) if the true state is 1, then consumer 2 knows it, whereas, if the true state is 2 or 3, then he knows only that it is one of these two; (iv) the producer does not know which of the three is the true state.

A decision of a consumer is a trade, and any trade results in a net consumption vector for him. A decision of a producer is a production plan, which results in a net production vector. Since consumption and production may depend upon which state of nature is realized, I shall distinguish six commodities, two for each state, as in Table II. Using this notation, the resource vectors, ω_1 and ω_2, of consumers 1 and 2, respectively, are

$$(7.1)\qquad \begin{aligned}\omega_1 &= (1, 0, 1, 0, 2, 0)\,,\\ \omega_2 &= (1, 0, 2, 0, 2, 0)\,.\end{aligned}$$

Let $x_i=(x_i^1, \ldots, x_i^6)$ denote a (net) consumption vector for consumer i $(i=1, 2)$. Consumption of labor may be interpreted as leisure, and equals the difference between resources and what is traded. To describe the constraints on the decisions of consumer 1 that are imposed by the structure of his information (see (ii) above), I assume

$$(7.2)\qquad x_1^1 = x_1^3, \quad x_1^2 = x_1^4\,.$$

Similarly, the information constraints for consumer 2 are (see (iii) above)

$$(7.3)\qquad x_2^3 = x_2^5, \quad x_2^4 = x_2^6\,.$$

If $y=(y^1, \ldots, y^6)$ denotes a (net) production vector (here outputs are positive and

TABLE II

LIST OF COMMODITIES

Commodity	Interpretation
1	labor in state 1
2	food in state 1
3	labor in state 2
4	food in state 2
5	labor in state 3
6	food in state 3

inputs are negative), the producer's information constraints are (see (iv) above)

$$(7.4)\qquad y^1 = y^3 = y^5, \quad y^2 = y^4 = y^6\,.$$

To further specify the set of feasible consumption vectors, suppose, for the purposes of this example, that whatever the state of nature, (1) each consumer must consume at least 0.1 units of food, (2) consumption of labor is nonnegative, and (3) quantity of labor sold is nonnegative. These conditions are described by the constraints

$$
(7.5)\quad
\begin{aligned}
&x_i^2, x_i^4, x_i^6 \geqslant 0.1, \qquad i=1,2;\\
&x_i^1, x_i^3, x_i^5 \geqslant 0;\\
&\quad x_1^1, x_1^3 \leqslant 1; \quad x_1^5 \leqslant 2;\\
&\qquad x_2^1 \leqslant 1; \quad x_2^3, x_2^5 \leqslant 2.
\end{aligned}
$$

The constraints on the producer's decisions are further specified by

$$(7.6)\qquad y^1 = -y^2, \quad y^3 = -y^4, \quad y^5 = -y^6; \quad y^2, y^4, y^6 \geqslant 0.$$

The constraints (7.2) and (7.5) define consumer 1's *consumption set*, X_1. Similarly, (7.3) and (7.5) define X_2. Constraints (7.4) and (7.6) define the *production set*, Y.

Suppose that there is a "market" for every commodity, i.e., for labor and food in each of the states. Let p^i denote the price of commodity i ($i=1, \ldots, 6$). Suppose further that the two consumers own between them all the shares of the production enterprise, in equal numbers. The profit of a production vector y is

$$(7.7)\qquad p \cdot y \equiv \sum_{k=1}^{6} p^k y^k.$$

The wealth w_i of consumer i is the value of his resources plus his share of the profits of production:

$$(7.8)\qquad w_i \equiv p \cdot \omega_i + \tfrac{1}{2} p \cdot y.$$

Finally, assume that the preferences of consumer i are represented by the function

$$(7.9)\qquad U(x_i) = 3(x_i^2 + x_i^4 + x_i^6) + (x_i^1 + x_i^3 + x_i^5).$$

For simplicity, I have assumed that the two consumers have identical preferences.

If, given a price vector p, the producer chooses a production vector y to maximize profit $p \cdot y$, and given p and w_i, each consumer i chooses a consumption vector in X_i to maximize $U(x_i)$, subject to the wealth constraint $p \cdot x_i \leqslant w_i$, then it is easily verified that an equilibrium of this economy is

$$
(7.10)\quad
\begin{aligned}
\hat{p} &= (7, 3, 1, 3, 1, 3),\\
\hat{y} &= (-2, 2, -2, 2, -2, 2),\\
\hat{x}_1 &= (0, 1, 0, 1, 1, 1),\\
\hat{x}_2 &= (0, 1, 1, 1, 1, 1).
\end{aligned}
$$

Note that for this equilibrium, profit from production is 0, and the wealths are

$$
(7.11)\quad
\begin{aligned}
w_1 &= (7+1+2) + \tfrac{1}{2}(0) = 10,\\
w_2 &= (7+2+2) + \tfrac{1}{2}(0) = 11.
\end{aligned}
$$

A few remarks on the interpretation of this example are in order. First, although markets for all six commodities have been assumed, the clearing of these markets, together with the constraints (7.1)–(7.4) imposed by the structure of information, imply that only contracts for delivery independent of the state of nature are in fact possible. The market clearing condition is

(7.12) $$(x_1-\omega_1)+(x_2-\omega_2)=y\,.$$

Define $\xi_i \equiv x_i-\omega_i$; then (7.12) can be rewritten as

(7.13) $$\xi_1+\xi_2=y.$$

It is easy, if slightly tedious, to verify that (7.1)–(7.4) and (7.13) imply

(7.14) $$\begin{aligned}\xi_1^1=\xi_1^3=\xi_1^5,\quad \xi_1^2=\xi_1^4=\xi_1^6\,,\\ \xi_2^1=\xi_2^3=\xi_2^5,\quad \xi_2^2=\xi_2^4=\xi_2^6\,.\end{aligned}$$

But ξ_i^k is the net amount of commodity k bought by consumer i (selling is buying a negative amount), so that an examination of (7.14) reveals that consumer 1 must sell the same quantity of labor in each state of nature, and buy the same quantity of food in each state. The same statement applies to consumer 2. The producer, by the structure of his information (constraint (7.4)), must make the same trade in each state.

A corollary of the fact that, in equilibrium, only contracts that are constant over states ("sure" contracts) will be observed (for this example), is the fact that essentially only two prices, instead of six, will be operative. To see this, note that a contract to (say) buy F units of food and sell L units of labor, in each state, has a net cost of $(p^2+p^4+p^6)F-(p^1+p^3+p^5)L$. Hence the two relevant prices for sure contracts are $(p^2+p^4+p^6)$, the price of sure delivery of food, and $(p^1+p^3+p^5)$, the price of sure delivery of labor.

The restriction to sure contracts in this example is an extreme illustration of the general phenomenon that clearing markets together with differences in information among economic agents will lead to a reduction in the number of markets.

8. INFORMATIONAL CONSTRAINTS ON TRADE

For any consumer i, and any consumption act x_i, define his *trade act* z_i by $z_i=\omega_i-x_i$. Thus $z_{itc}(s)$ is the quantity of commodity c at date t in state s that consumer i sells (if $z_{itc}(s)\geqslant 0$) or buys (if $z_{itc}(s)\leqslant 0$). Define the trade act of a producer to be identical to his production act. For the purpose of this section, I shall ignore the distinction between consumers and producers, and simply consider that there is a set K of $(m+n)$ economic agents, that agent k has an information structure $\mathscr{S}_k$, and that he must choose a trade act $z_k \in Z_k$, where Z_k, the set of feasible trades for k, is a subset of $\mathscr{A}(\mathscr{S}_k)$.

If the $(m+n)$-tuple (z_k) of trades satisfies

(8.1) $$\sum_{k\in K} z_k=0\,,$$

then (z_k) clears the market.

Let $\underset{\sim}{z}=(z_1, \ldots, z_{m+n})$ be an $(m+n)$-tuple of trades, and $I \subset K$ a subset of agents; the *net trade* of I is

$$(8.2) \qquad \zeta(\underset{\sim}{z}, I) \equiv \sum_{k \in I} z_k .$$

If $\underset{\sim}{z}$ clears the market then for every subset I of K

$$(8.3) \qquad \zeta(\underset{\sim}{z}, I) = -\zeta(\underset{\sim}{z}, \sim I),$$

(where $(\sim I)$ denotes the complement of I in K). Now note that, for every $I \subset K$,

$$(8.4) \qquad \zeta(\underset{\sim}{z}, I) \in \sum_{k \in I} \mathscr{A}(\mathscr{S}_k) ;$$

hence (8.3) implies that for every market clearing $\underset{\sim}{z}$ and every subset $I \subset K$ the net trade of I satisfies

$$(8.5) \qquad \zeta(\underset{\sim}{z}, I) \in \Big[\sum_{k \in I} \mathscr{A}(\mathscr{S}_k)\Big] \cap \Big[\sum_{k \notin I} \mathscr{A}(\mathscr{S}_k)\Big] .$$

Condition (8.5) is a formal expression of the fact that *the net trade between any group of agents and the group of all other agents in the economy can at most depend upon information that is common to both groups of agents.*

Since no agent can have a trade act that depends on information not available to him, there need be no markets for contracts that depend upon information that is not available to someone in the economy. Formally, for each k,

$$(8.6) \qquad z_k \in \sum_{k} \mathscr{A}(\mathscr{S}_k) .$$

In particular, prices for delivery at date t will not depend upon events that will occur, if at all, on some date later than t (see Debreu [**2**, Ch. 7, Sections 2, 3]).

However, the set of effective markets implied by (8.5) will typically be even smaller than that implied by (8.6) alone. This phenomenon shows up in the example of Section 7.

9. CHOICE OF INFORMATION

There is no problem in incorporating the choice of information into the present formal framework. There is a problem, however, in determining under what economically meaningful conditions the resulting model satisfies the "classical" conditions for the existence and optimality of competitive equilibrium. My general impression is that it is not typically realistic to suppose that these conditions are satisfied.

For a given act α, let $\mathscr{S}(\alpha)$ denote the least fine information structure with which α is compatible; I shall say that $\mathscr{S}(\alpha)$ is the information structure *required by* α. Thus an act α such that $\alpha_t(s)=\alpha_t(s')$ for all dates t and all states s and s' in S requires the minimal information structure ("no information"), in which $\mathscr{S}_t=\{S\}$ for all t

(see Section 3). On the other hand, an act α such that $\alpha_t(s) \neq \alpha_t(s')$ for all dates t and all *distinct* states s and s' in S $(s \neq s')$, requires complete information. Indeed, one may simply characterize $\mathscr{S}(\alpha)$ as follows: the elements of the partition $\mathscr{S}_t$ are inverse images $\alpha_t^{-1}(v)$ of points v in R^C.

The acquisition and use of information typically requires the use of resources. This may be reflected in the description of the set of feasible acts. Thus, in the example of Section 7, suppose that for the producer to obtain and use complete information about the state of nature requires the input of one unit of labor. To express this, I adjoin to his set of feasible acts the set Y'' of all $y = (y^1, \ldots, y^6)$ such that

$$y^1 = -1 - y^2,\ y^3 = -1 - y^4,\ y^5 = -1 - y^6;\ y^2, y^4, y^6 \geqslant 0\,. \tag{9.1}$$

Recall that in Section 7 it was assumed that the following production acts were also feasible: the set Y' of all y such that

$$y^1 = -y^2,\ y^3 = -y^4,\ y^5 = -y^6;\quad y^2, y^4, y^6 \geqslant 0\ ; \tag{9.2a}$$

$$y^1 = y^3 = y^5,\ y^2 = y^4 = y^6 \tag{9.2b}$$

(see equations (7.6) and (7.4)). Recall that (9.2b) expresses the constraint of "no information"; in the present context (9.2a) expresses the "potentially feasible" production possibilities, but without taking account of the "cost of information."

We may now suppose that the total production possibility set for the producer is

$$Y = Y' \cup Y''\,, \tag{9.3}$$

the union of the possibilities with and without information. From a formal descriptive point of view, this is satisfactory, but it is easy to verify that, whereas Y' and Y'' are each convex, Y is not. For example, $y' = (-1, 1, -1, 1, -1, 1) \in Y'$, $y'' = (-2, 1, -3, 2, -4, 3) \in Y''$, but $(\frac{1}{2}y' + \frac{1}{2}y'')$ is neither in Y' nor in Y''. In this example, the cost of information is a "set-up cost" (a well-known destroyer of convexity!). Notice that the set Y'' includes acts that do not require any information about the state of nature, even though the cost of obtaining that information has, in some sense, been incurred (e.g., the act $(-2, 1, -2, 1, -2, 1)$).

An important class of cases in which convexity may be reasonable is generated by situations in which future information depends in some way upon current action, and all actions can be "scaled down" to any desired size. For example, the model of dynamic production in Radner [6] can be extended in a straightforward way to the case of uncertainty, following the usual model of dynamic programming, in a manner that preserves convexity.

10. NETWORK INFORMATION

Thus far it has been assumed that each agent's set of available acts is constrained by a fixed information structure, or by a family of alternative fixed information structures, in the sense of Section 3. In any case, the only joint constraint has been the one that total supply equal total demand; apart from that constraint each agent could choose his act independently of the choices of other agents. In other words, there have been no *external effects* among the agents' acts. To make this quite precise, recall that if for each i consumer i chooses the act x_i from his consumption set X_i, then the total consumption for the economy is

$$(10.1) \qquad x = \sum_i x_i .$$

In (10.1), x is also, in a sense, an act, i.e., it is T-tuple of functions from the set S of states of nature to the commodity space. On the other hand, any act x that can be represented in the form (10.1), with x_i in X_i for each i, is a possible total consumption for the economy. In other words, the total consumption set, say X, for the economy is the (vector) sum of the individual consumption sets. Similarly, the total production set, say Y, for the economy is the sum of the individual production sets Y_j. Finally, a set of consumption acts x_i and production acts y_j is attainable if

$$(10.2) \qquad x - y = \omega ,$$

where $\omega = \Sigma_i \omega_i$ (total resources). The net excess demand for the economy, $(x-y)$, is also an act; the set of excess demands for the economy, not taking account of the constraint (10.2), is the set

$$(10.3) \qquad \sum_i X_i - \sum_j Y_j .$$

The representation (10.3) of the set of excess demands for the economy expresses the fact that there are no external effects among the acts of the several economic agents.

In Sections 3 and 4 the assumption of fixed information structure, represented by a partition of the set of states of nature, was interpreted as representing information about the environment. The constraint corresponding to such information was superimposed on a set of "potentially feasible" acts, i.e., a set of acts that would be feasible with complete information about the environment. Such constraints, together with the assumption that there be no external effects among the sets of potentially feasible acts, resulted in the absence of external effects among the sets of acts that were feasible under the given structure of information.

By contrast, I shall argue that if agents receive information about each other's decisions, then even if there are no external effects among the sets of potentially feasible acts, the sets of acts constrained by information will typically exhibit external effects. To give a precise idea of the nature of these externalities I shall describe a formal model of the kind of information structure I have in mind.[17] Since the model represents, in part, a communication network among the decision makers, this will be called *network information*.

[17] This model is based on Marschak and Radner [**4**, Chapter VIII].

Suppose that at each date each agent may receive messages from, and send messages to, other agents in the economy. For the purposes of the present discussion it is not necessary to distinguish between consumers and producers; the $(m+n)$ agents in the economy will simply be numbered from 1 to K. A message sent by agent h to agent k on date t is assumed to be received by k on date $(t+1)$. Let B_{hkt} denote the set of possible alternative messages b_{hkt} that h can send to k on date t. Direct observation of the environment will be similarly represented; let $B_{0k,t-1}$ be the set of possible alternative observations of the environment on date t. Such an observation may be interpreted as a "message from Nature to k;" hence the notation. Decisions about inputs and outputs can also be represented as "messages;" thus for every k and t let B_{k0t} be R^C, the commodity space. Finally, the process of remembering may be represented as the sending of messages to oneself; thus for every k and t, let B_{kkt} denote the set of alternative complete descriptions of what k is capable of remembering from date t to date $t+1$.

The task of each agent at each date is to transform incoming messages into outgoing messages. In particular, this includes decisions about inputs and outputs. For agent k, the set of alternative incoming messages, taking account of all sources including Nature and memory, is the Cartesian product

$$(10.4)\qquad \tilde{B}_{kt} = \mathop{\times}_{h=0}^{K} B_{hk,t-1}\ ;$$

the set of alternative outgoing messages is likewise the Cartesian product

$$(10.5)\qquad B_{kt} = \mathop{\times}_{h=0}^{K} B_{kht}\ .$$

For each k and t, agent k will have available to him some set $\mathscr{B}_{kt}$ of functions β_{kt} from $\tilde{B}_{kt}$ to B_{kt}. One may call such a T-tuple, $\beta_k \equiv (\beta_{k1}, \ldots, \beta_{kT})$, a *strategy*, thus extending the concept of strategy introduced in Section 3. The set of strategies for k will be denoted by $\mathscr{B}_k$.

Notice that the choice of a strategy by an agent is not typically sufficient to determine his act; rather it takes a determination of strategies by all of the agents to jointly determine their acts, at least in principle. There is, however, a recursive feature in the determination of acts. The component α_{kt} of the act of agent k at date t is determined by the components β_{hr} of the strategies of other agents for $r=1, \ldots, t-1$, and by the components β_{kr} of k's strategy for $r=1, \ldots, t$.

Corresponding to this recursive determination of acts is a recursive determination of information structure at each date, in the sense of partitions. Given the components β_{hr} of all strategies for $r=1, \ldots, t-1$, the joint message received by any agent k is a well defined function of the state of nature. This determines a partition, say $\mathscr{S}_{kt}$, of the set S of states, and any strategy component β_{kt} in $\mathscr{B}_{kt}$ determines a component act α_{kt} that is compatible with $\mathscr{S}_{kt}$.

Let $\mathscr{A}$ denote the set of all K-tuples of acts (one for each agent) generated by all K-tuples of strategies $(\beta_1, \ldots, \beta_K)$ such that for each k, β_k is in $\mathscr{B}_k$. For each agent k, let $\mathscr{A}_k$ denote the set of all acts α_k such that α_k is the kth component of a K-tuple in $\mathscr{A}$. It is clear from the above remarks that in general $\mathscr{A}$ is not the Cartesian product of the sets $\mathscr{A}_k$, and hence the set of excess demands for the economy cannot in general be represented in the form (10.3). It is in this sense that network information introduces external effects among the sets of acts of the various agents.

Since the choice of a strategy by an agent does not, in general, determine an act independently of the choice of strategies by others, the agent will be uncertain as to the actual act that follows from a given strategy choice. In particular, he will be uncertain about the value of a given strategy for given prices. It should be emphasized that his uncertainty is not just about what his inputs and outputs will be at various dates, but about what these inputs and outputs will be for a given state of nature. This uncertainty derives from his uncertainty about the strategies of other agents. This feature takes us outside the framework of the standard theory of competitive equilibrium, and I shall not attempt to give a rigorous analysis in the present paper.

11. MARKET INFORMATION AND DEFERRED MARKETS

Return now to the model of Sections 2–6, with fixed information structure. Recall that, under appropriate conditions, an equilibrium relative to a price system is an optimum (with respect to the given information structure), and every optimum is an equilibrium for some distribution of resources (see Section 6). To achieve an equilibrium relative to a price system, those prices have to be communicated or somehow made available to the agents in the economy. Hence the competitive equilibrium achieves an optimum relative to a given structure of information by making available to the agents some additional information, namely an equilibrium price system.

(Thus far, nothing has been said about how equilibrium prices are to be determined. Presumably, this takes place through some process of interaction among economic agents, possibly including agents whose sole function is to aid in the process of price formation. In other words, the process of price formation itself might be described in terms of the model of network information presented in the previous section, with the attendant difficulties alluded to there.)

Once the equilibrium prices have been announced, and acts have been chosen, it is assumed that no further market transactions take place; indeed, there should be no incentive for such further transactions, since the equilibrium is an optimum. But this optimum is relative to a given structure of information; hence to the extent that new market transactions provide new information, there might well be an incentive to enter into them.

Consider the possibility of setting up a new market at the last date, T. Suppose that the given structure of information is such that it does not provide each agent with complete information about the history of the environment up to that date. Nevertheless, since at that date everyone would know his own resources and stocks, and only trade decisions would be required, a market equilibrium would lead to an optimum for the last date, relative to the situation of the economy at the beginning of that period.

Let q denote the price vector for that equilibrium (assuming for the sake of simplicity that it is unique). There is no reason to suppose that q is proportional to p_T, the component of the *ex ante* equilibrium price system. In a sense, p_T is a vector of prices for futures contracts, whereas q is a vector of "spot" prices. As a matter of fact, there is every reason to believe that q would typically be different from p_T. Note that q depends on the evolution of the economy, and therefore the state of nature, up through date $T-1$, both through direct observations of the environment made by the agents, and through the decisions made, which determine the stocks at the beginning of date T. Hence, for given acts of the economic agents (at least specified through date $T-1$), q is a function defined on the set of states of nature. Therefore the announcement of q at the beginning of date T would typically provide each agent with information beyond that contemplated in his original structure of information, to the extent that he could guess the strategies (or acts) of the other agents.

What we have here is an example of network information, with the resulting externalities (see Section 10). The introduction of the spot markets brings with it the need for economic agents to be concerned not only with uncertainty about the environment, but also with uncertainty about other agents' strategies. In particular, producers can no longer assign a definite value to a strategy on the basis of futures contract prices alone. This would typically result in a demand for "liquidity," which was not present in the fixed information structure case. The need for money does not arise except in response to an "imperfection." Unfortunately, the very imperfection that gives rise to the demand for liquidity and money in this case prevents individual agents from determining their optimal demands for these things. In the next section, under the discussion of computation, this phenomenon will appear again.

12. COMPUTATION

Computation plays a role in the behavior of an economic agent in at least two ways. First, the implementation of a given strategy may require computation. Second, the choice of a preferred (or profit-maximizing) strategy from a given set typically requires computation.

The computational costs of implementing a given strategy may be described formally in the same way as was suggested for taking account of the cost of information (Section 9), and with the same attendant difficulties. Indeed, it may be difficult in many cases to meaningfully separate informational and computational costs incurred in the implementation of a given strategy.

Costs incurred in the choice of a strategy present a special problem, which threatens to involve the model builder in an "infinite regression." To focus on this problem, consider a choice by a given economic agent between two information structures. Suppose that the second structure is considerably finer than the first, and that the associated optimization problem is more complicated, requiring more resources for its solution. Until the two optimization problems are solved, or at least some computation is done, the agent cannot decide whether the finer information structure is worth having. In deciding whether or not to perform these computations he is reduced to forming "preferences" or "beliefs" about the outcome of purely logical operations, a phenomenon that has not yet been successfully incorporated into a theory of rational behavior (see Savage [**7**, p. 7, footnote]).

Brushing aside this difficulty, we may suppose that the costs of choice have been separated from the costs of implementation, and that the decision maker has a given capacity for computation associated with choice. He may remain within that capacity by using certain "rules of thumb." Or he may choose to ignore some information, or to ignore the fact that he will have some particular information in the future. To formalize the second device, we may say that in the formulation of his optimization problem he restricts himself to an information structure that is less fine than the one that is actually available to him. In effect, he restricts himself to a smaller set of acts than is actually feasible.

I would like to explore a little this last formulation. In the one-period case it leads immediately to the concept of an equilibrium (or optimum) relative to a given "structure of information and computation." Indeed, the restriction on computation has been reduced to one on information, and no new theory is needed.

In the several-period case, however, a new problem arises. If the capacity for "choice computation" imposes a limit per period, then further choices are possible after the initial period, i.e., after the initial choice of strategy. Thus if in period 1 the decision maker chose a strategy ignoring the fact that he would receive one of two alternative signals (e.g., "rain" or "shine") in period 2, then in period 2, after having actually received one of these signals, he may wish to, and be able to, revise his strategy. I emphasize that I am discussing the revision of an entire strategy, not simply the implementation of a given strategy.

In the model of Sections 2–8 a strategy is embodied in a contract to receive and deliver various commodities on various dates under various circumstances. Revising a strategy requires making a further contract for additional receipts and deliveries (these new decisions may to a certain extent have the effect of cancelling or revising parts of the old contract, as when a loan is refinanced). Such new contracting will take place under new prices. Furthermore, new markets may be opened up, since finer information structures will be taken account of than were in the first period. Note also that in our previous model payment was made only at the beginning of the history of the economic system, when all contracts were made, whereas in the present model the making of new contracts in each period imposes the need for payments in each period. Finally, there will be uncertainty about the new prices and payments, and about which new markets will open up. This uncertainty will involve more than uncertainty about the environment, but also uncertainty about the outcomes of computations by the agents in the economy, and hence extend, through uncertainty about future equilibria, to uncertainty about other aspects of economic behavior. In this respect the situation is similar to that of Section 11.

A host of additional economic phenomena and considerations will be brought into play, which were not present in the original model of uncertainty: deferred payment, trading by consumers in shares of the productive enterprises, liquidity, to name a few. For example, if a new, additional, contract by a consumer has a negative value, then it is possible only if he has not previously exhausted his wealth budget. This suggests the desirability of reserving unspent a part of his wealth budget at any date, i.e., of retaining some liquidity. Unfortunately, the consumer is not in a position to compute his optimal amount of liquidity at any time, since this would require the results of computations that are to be performed only in the future![18]

13. CONCLUSION

This exploration of competitive equilibrium under uncertainty has indicated that if economic decision makers are uncertain about the environment, and if their information is about the environment, then even if they have different information, a once-and-for-all futures market in conditional contracts can achieve an optimum allocation of resources, relative to the given structure of information. In this "Arrow-Debreu world" there is no money and no demand for liquidity. On the other hand, the introduction of information about the behavior of other decision makers introduces externalities among the sets of acts available to them. A particular case of this results from the introduction of deferred, or "spot," markets. The presence of such markets enlarges the set of acts jointly available to the individual decision makers in the economy, but also introduces the above-mentioned externalities. A demand for liquidity is generated, but individual decision makers cannot, in principle, calculate their optimal kind and degree of liquidity without knowing something about the decision rules of other individuals.

The demand for liquidity also arises from computational limitations, and with such limitations would be present even in a world of certainty about the environment, if that world were sufficiently complicated. Of course, uncertainty about the environment vastly complicates a decision problem, and so indirectly contributes to the demand for liquidity.

[18] Of course "liquidity" can also be obtained by holding, or contracting for future delivery of, commodities for which there is sure to be a market. This only complicates the consumer's decision problem.

This exploration suggests that a general equilibrium theory incorporating the most important aspects of money and liquidity cannot be based on a "classical" approach with thoroughgoing optimizing, and therefore that there may be little hope of extending the classical theorems of welfare economics to the more general case. Such an extension, however, does appear possible if one is satisfied with concepts of equilibrium and optimum that are defined in terms of long-run statistical averages; but this represents a program for future research.

University of California, Berkeley

REFERENCES

[1] Arrow, K. J.: Le Rôle des Valeurs Boursières pour la Répartition la Meilleure des Risques, *Econométrie*, Paris (1953), Centre National de la Recherche Scientifique, 41–48 (or see the translation, "The Role of Securities in the Optimal Allocation of Risk Bearing," *Review of Economic Studies*, Vol. 31, 1964, 91–96.

[2] Debreu, G.: *Theory of Value*, New York (1959), Wiley.

[3] ———: New Concepts and Techniques for Equilibrium Analysis, *International Economic Review*, Vol. 3, 1962, 257–273.

[4] Marschak, J., and R. Radner: *Economic Theory of Teams* (in preparation).

[5] Radner, R.: "The Linear Team: An Example of Linear Programming under Uncertainty," *Proceedings of the Second Symposium in Linear Programming*, Washington, D.C. (1955), National Bureau of Standards, pp. 381–396.

[6] ———: Dynamic Programming of Economic Growth, in *Activity Analysis in the Theory of Growth and Planning* (Bacharach and Malinvaud, eds.) London (1967), Macmillan.

[7] Savage, L. J.: *Foundations of Statistics*, New York (1954), Wiley.

Comment

Radner's paper has two rather distinct aims. In Sections 2-7 he shows how the model of the previous chapter may be extended to deal with some of the problems raised by the possibility that different traders may have and act on different information. In Sections 8-12 he indicates that the model cannot accommodate other natural consequences of differential information. The two problems he sees as causing the most difficulty for the Arrow-Debreu model are (1) the need to set realistic limits on the computational abilities of actors and (2) the externalities that must occur if actors learn from each other's behavior. Recent research has analyzed a special case of the last problem – the possibility that actors could extract information from market clearing prices. While the notion that prices should convey information is a reasonable one, and the assertion that that information should be correct is the basic tenet of economists who believe in rational expectations, it has proved difficult to incorporate these ideas into standard economic models. The snag is that prices in such models both convey information and clear markets. It is quite possible that small changes in prices will lead to large changes in information. As a consequence, demand functions may be discontinuous and the model may have no equilibrium. We present here a simple example of this (for which we are indebted to Martin Hellwig).

Table I lists the endowments of the two agents in a simple, two-state, two-good, exchange economy. Suppose the agents have identical utility functions such as $U(x, y) = \log x + \log y$. Then if states were known before trading took place there would be a unique equilibrium price ratio in each state.[1] The aggregate excess demand function of this economy is obviously the same in each state and so is the equilibrium price ratio, which we shall call P. Now suppose that the rules under which this economy is organized are altered and that only

Table I

	Agent 1	Agent 2
State 1	$(x, y + z)$	(x, y)
State 2	(x, y)	$(x, y + z)$

[1]Uniqueness will not hold for all utility functions, but it will for some, including $U(x, y) = \log x + \log y$.

agent 1 is informed of his endowment before trading takes place. Agent 2 always has a pretrade endowment of y units of good two; after trading he may or may not receive an extra z units of good two, depending on which state occurs.

Define a rational expectations equilibrium as a pair of price ratios P_1 and P_2 such that P_i clears the market in state i with agent 2 inferring what it is possible to infer from the prices P_i. In particular, if $P_1 \neq P_2$, then agent 2 will know which state has occurred and will condition his demand on this information. If $P_1 = P_2$, then prices reveal no information and agent 2's demand is the same in both states.

This model does not have a rational expectations equilibrium. Suppose $P_1 \neq P_2$. Since the equilibrium price will reveal to agent 2 which state has occurred, his demand functions will thus be the same as if he were informed exactly of his endowment. Thus in each state of the economy each agent will behave as if he were fully informed of the economy's state. However, as we saw above, in this event the same equilibrium price will clear the market in each state so that $P_1 = P_2$, which contradicts the supposition that $P_1 \neq P_2$.

The case $P_1 = P_2$ is also inconsistent. Let $D_s^i(P)$ be the excess demand for good 1 by agent i in state s. Then, for most utility functions [including $U(x, y) = \log x + \log y$]

$$D_1^1(P) \neq D_2^1(P) \qquad \text{for all} \quad P \tag{1}$$

If price does not inform player 2 of his endowment,

$$D_1^2(P) = D_2^2(P) = D^2(P) \qquad \text{for all} \quad P \tag{2}$$

If $P_1 = P_2 = P^*$ is an equilibrium price, then

$$D_1^1(P^*) + D^2(P^*) = D_2^1(P^*) + D^2(P^*) = 0$$

which contradicts (1) and (2). We conclude that there is no rational expectations equilibrium.

This example is delicate; perturbing the data slightly would allow a rational expectations equilibrium (with $P_1 \neq P_2$) to exist. One might hope that existence of rational expectations equilibria was in some sense a generic property of models of this sort. This turns out to be the case when (in an appropriate mathematical sense) the number of values that prices can assume is much larger than the number of different states that the economy can be in, and not necessarily otherwise. See Radner (1982) for a good comprehensive survey including discussion of this point.

References

R. Radner, Equilibrium under uncertainty. In K. Arrow and M. Intriligator (eds.), "Handbook of Mathematical Economics," Vol. II, Amsterdam: North-Holland Publishing Co., 1982.

13

P. Diamond, The role of a stock market in a general equilibrium model with technological uncertainty, *American Economic Review* 57 (1967), 759–773 (appendix omitted)

This paper takes a different tack from the preceding one in that it takes the absence of many markets as given rather than deriving their absence from an underlying structure (like differences in information, or in a separate literature, transaction costs). Given the structure of markets that do exist, the paper examines the nature and optimality properties of equilibrium.

THE ROLE OF A STOCK MARKET IN A GENERAL EQUILIBRIUM MODEL WITH TECHNOLOGICAL UNCERTAINTY

By PETER A. DIAMOND*

Moving from the certainty model of general equilibrium to one with uncertainty, the constructors of the model[1] with contingent commodity markets have given considerable insight into the problems of uncertainty for an economy. However, the construction of perfect insurance markets, where all risks are insurable, does not lend itself well to understanding the economy's imperfect solution of these problems. The model presented here is an example of an imperfect solution where a stock market permits the sharing of risks, but only incompletely. This will permit examination of the handling of risks by such an economy, as well as the shortcomings of this handling. An important element in any model involving uncertainty is the source of probabilities used in decision making and the ultimate location of risk-bearing. In the contingent commodity model, firms bear no risks in the sense that no probability distributions are needed to calculate firm decision rules or profits accruing to firm owners, and all risks are borne by consumers. With a stock market, however, where shareholders receive residual profits after the completion of production under technological uncertainty, firm owners do bear risks and need to use their subjective probabilities in determining their portfolio structures. Paralleling the contingent commodity model, however, firms planning production to maximize stock market value employ no probabilities in their calculations, relying instead on determinate, concurrent market phenomena, the prices inherent in the stock market.

By means of a one-period one-commodity model it is shown that firm behavior based on this rule, combined with trading in the stock market to maximize expected utility, results in a competitive economy's achieving a constrained Pareto optimum. The constraint does not arise from an inability of individual firms to use the pooling advantages implied by the law of large numbers, for with stock market value maximization by firms and portfolio diversification by wealth owners, all of the economy's

* The author is associate professor of economics at M.I.T. He wishes to thank Bernard Saffran for many helpful comments on this paper and the Social Science Research Council, the Guggenheim Foundation, and the National Science Foundation for financial assistance during the time he worked on this paper. During part of this time he was an Overseas Fellow at Churchill College, Cambridge. Errors and opinions belong solely to the author.

[1] The contingent commodity model of an exchange economy is presented in Arrow [1]. The model with production is in Debreu [4].

averaging possibilities are brought to bear on each production decision. Rather, the constraint, that consumption patterns across the states of nature be linear combinations of firm output patterns, arises from an inability to distinguish finely among the states of nature in the economy's trading.

The highly restrictive one-period one-good model is not employed simply for heuristic purposes, for an increase to two periods or goods in a seemingly natural way (the stock market reopening at the start of the second period or commodities traded after the completion of production) introduces a different element from technological uncertainty-price uncertainty. In the presence of only technological uncertainty, current trading on the stock market does not affect future probabilities of the states of nature. Nor does it convey information about those probabilities. Thus, in this model, individuals have subjective probabilities at the start of trading which are not altered. However, with price uncertainty current trading does affect future prices and does convey information about the tastes of other consumers which is relevant for subjective probabilities of future prices. It then becomes necessary to consider the extraction of this information, the alteration of subjective probabilities, and the change of market demands in the process of trading. These problems do not arise in the simple model considered. Thus this model is static in the important sense that all trading occurs at one time. (Both the certainty and contingent commodity uncertainty general equilibrium models are static in this sense, as is any perfect foresight model.) The model is static also in the sense that no one learns anything which affects his decisions. (Prices are reacted to, but this is not taken to convey new information which, for example, might lead to a change in subjective probabilities.)

Following a description of the technology is an examination of a centrally planned economy with restricted planning abilities, which therefore achieves a constrained Pareto optimum. In this way the conditions for the constrained optimum are obtained. It is then shown that a competitive equilibrium satisfies these conditions. The validity, in this model, of the Modigliani-Miller propositions is then examined, as well as the treatment of uncertainty for government investment. The appendix contains a brief description of the contingent commodity model in order to present the analogy between production decisions in the two models.

I. *States of Nature*

To introduce technological uncertainty, it is assumed that production functions of the individual firms can be written as functions of the input and a random variable reflecting the state of nature.[2] Thus the

[2] In addition to the assumption of a single input and a single output, it is assumed that the

output of the jth firm, if state θ occurs, is a function of the input level to the jth firm[3] (which is independent of θ) and the state of nature. Algebraically,[4]

$$y_j(\theta) = f^j(\theta, k_j). \tag{1}$$

Thus, for example, the output of corn if θ inches of rain fall depends on the number of inches of rain and the input of seed. The pattern of output of the jth firm across the states of nature, $y_j(\theta)$, can be thought of as a joint product resulting from the input level k_j. In the special case where the production function is decomposable,

$$y_j(\theta) = f_j(\theta)g_j(k_j), \tag{2}$$

the output pattern (suitably normalized) can be considered a composite commodity since its individual elements are produced in fixed proportions. In this case, a change in input level alters the scale of output but not the pattern of output across the states of nature. It is assumed that the set of firms is fixed for the analysis. This eliminates not only searching for new investment opportunities but also the creation of insurance firms (although existing insurance firms can be fitted into the model [see below, section 5]).

Each consumer is assumed to have his own subjective probability density over the states of nature, $h_i(\theta)$, and a utility function of consumption,[5] $U_i(c_i)$, and to be interested in maximizing expected utility,[6]

$$V_i = \int U_i(c_i(\theta))h_i(\theta)d\theta. \tag{3}$$

It is assumed that after its occurrence the state θ which has occurred is known by all. In an insurance setting, this rules out some of the prob-

---

states of nature can be described by a single, continuous random variable. While the assumption of knowledge of the relationship of the random variable to output is restrictive, the ability to parametrize the states of nature on a single variable is not important.

[3] Additional inputs contracted for before the state of nature is known add no complication. However, inputs hired after θ is known (e.g., labor to harvest the crop) involve trading more than once, implying price uncertainty, and thus do not fit within this model. Inputs employed after the state of nature is known but hired on a contingent basis before it is known would simply represent the addition of particular contingent commodity markets to the existing stock market. This creates no complication.

[4] It is assumed that f^j is twice continuously differentiable for all j, with $f_k^j>0$, $f^j_{kk}<0$.

[5] It is assumed that U_i is twice continuously differentiable for all i, with $U_i'>0$, $U_i''<0$.

[6] All integrals are assumed to exist. Writing expected utility in this form (additivity vis-à-vis consumption in the different states of nature with the same utility function, except for a scalar) is highly restrictive, ignoring, for example, the impact of rain on the utility derived from an umbrella. Dropping this assumption alters no results in the text, but does alter the descriptive elements in the appendix.

lems arising from moral hazards. (For a discussion of the informational aspects of insurance, which are lacking in the model, see Arrow [2].)

II. *Centrally Planned Economy*

Before examining a centrally planned economy, it is necessary to consider the expression of its objectives. A natural extension of the certainty concept is to define Pareto optimality in terms of the expected utilities, V_i. This implies that the planner uses different probabilities in calculating the expected utilities of different individuals, since, in general, the h_i vary among individuals.[7,8]

If a central planner with control over all economic variables, k_j and $c_i(\theta)$, seeks a Pareto optimum, he will produce an allocation which could be achieved by a competitive economy with a complete set of contingent commodity markets (discussed in the Appendix). The cost elements which limit the set of markets in a competitive economy might also limit the degree of control exercised by a planner. So we shall consider a planner with somewhat limited powers, chosen in a manner so that a competitive economy with a stock market can achieve the same allocation. Thus, by examining the restrictions on a planner which result in the same allocation, we can gain some insight into the limitations inherent in a stock market.

We shall continue to assume that the planner has full control over allocation of the input, but we shall lessen his control over the distribution of output at the completion of production. We shall assume that all distribution instructions are given before production occurs and that they take one of the following two simple forms. Firms are instructed to deliver to given individuals given fractions of their output independent of the state of nature. Let α_{ij} be the fraction of its output the jth firm delivers to the ith individual.[9] Individuals are instructed to

[7] This is the concept employed by Arrow [1] and Debreu [4].

[8] The social welfare function which fits with this definition of Pareto optimum, in the sense that a Pareto optimum is a necessary condition for maximizing the welfare function, is a function of the levels of expected utility. Algebraically we have $W(V_1, V_2, \cdots, V_m)$.

An alternative approach to extending the certainty concept of social welfare is to calculate expected social welfare (using a probability distribution chosen in some fashion) where welfare is a function of achieved utilities. This would be written as $\int W(U_1(c_1(\theta)), U_2(c_2(\theta)), \cdots, U_m(c_m(\theta)))h(\theta)d\theta$. In general this approach is not consistent with the definition of Pareto optimality given above. (While this approach does not require knowledge of h_i it still requires knowledge of U_i).

Each of these simplifications is well constructed for some of the aspects of social welfare. The latter can take account of the costs, e.g., through envy, in the spread of achieved utilities. The former, however, allows for a concept of justice in terms of expected utilities relative to θ. For this reason the former concept is preferred, and the definition of Pareto optimality given above, which yields optimality results similar to those under certainty, will be employed in calculating efficiency conditions.

[9] The constraint $\alpha_{ij} \geqq 0$ are assumed not to be binding in the maximization below (i.e., everyone receives something from each firm). It is assumed that there are no delivery costs. Further. the constraint $c_i(\theta) \geqq 0$, which implies a constraint on α_i is also assumed not to be binding.

deliver to other individuals fixed quantities of output independent of the state of nature. Let α_i be the net quantity the ith individual receives in this fashion. The planner then controls k_j, α_{ij}, and α_i.

These restrictions imply that consumption of the ith individual in terms of the control parameters can be written

$$c_i(\theta) = \alpha_i + \sum_{j=1}^{n} \alpha_{ij} f^j(\theta, k_j). \tag{4}$$

This, then, is the linearity constraint, that consumption patterns be a linear combination of output patterns, i.e., that consumption be the same linear combination of firm outputs in all states of nature. Using equation (4) for all individuals but the first, the constraint that total consumption equal total output can be expressed by writing the consumption of the first consumer as

$$c_1(\theta) = -\sum_{i=2}^{m} \alpha_i + \sum_{j=1}^{n} \left(1 - \sum_{i=2}^{m} \alpha_{ij}\right) f^j(\theta, k_j). \tag{5}$$

Thus the net flows between individuals add to zero and the fractions of each firm's output received add to one.

With these constraints on consumption patterns and the constraint on available input supply,

$$\sum_{j=1}^{n} k_j = k, \tag{6}$$

we can express the conditions for a Pareto optimum by maximizing expected utility of the first individual

$$\int U_1(c_1(\theta)) h_1(\theta) d\theta$$

subject to constraints on the expected utility levels of the other m−1 consumers

$$\int U_i(c_i(\theta)) h_i(\theta) d\theta = \overline{V}_i. \tag{7}$$

Substituting for $c_i(\theta)$ from equations (4) and (5) and forming the Lagrangian expression,

$$\begin{aligned} &\int U_1\left(-\sum_{i=2}^{m} \alpha_i + \sum_{j=1}^{n}\left(1 - \sum_{i=2}^{m} \alpha_{ij}\right) f^j(\theta, k_j)\right) h_1(\theta) d\theta \\ &+ \sum_{i=2}^{m} \lambda_i \left(\int U_i\left(\alpha_i + \sum_{j=1}^{n} \alpha_{ij} f^j(\theta, k_j)\right) h_i(\theta) d\theta - \overline{V}_i \right) + \mu\left(k - \sum_{j=2}^{n} k_j\right), \end{aligned} \tag{8}$$

we can calculate the first order conditions. Differentiation with respect to α_i and α_{ij} gives

$$(9)\quad \begin{aligned} &-\int U_1' h_1 d\theta + \lambda_i \int U_i' h_i d\theta = 0, && i = 2, 3, \cdots, m, \\ &-\int U_1' f^j(\theta, k_j) h_1 d\theta + \lambda_1 \int U_i' f^j(\theta, k_j) h_i d\theta = 0 && i = 2, 3, \cdots, m, \; j = 1, 2, \cdots, n. \end{aligned}$$

Eliminating λ_i from the equations we have $(m-1)n$ equations

$$(10)\quad \frac{\int U_i' f^j(\theta, k_j) h_i d\theta}{\int U_i' h_i d\theta} = \frac{\int U_1' f^j(\theta, k_j) h_1 d\theta}{\int U_1' h_1 d\theta}, \qquad i = 2, 3, \cdots, m, \quad j = 1, 2, \cdots, n.$$

Recalling the interpretation of the output pattern of a firm over states of nature as a joint product, equation (10) expresses the equality among consumers of the marginal rates of substitution for these joint products, where the marginal rate of substitution is expressed in terms of expected marginal utility.

Differentiation of (8) with respect to k_j gives

$$(11)\quad \int U_1' \left(1 - \sum_{i=2}^{m} \alpha_{ij}\right) f_k^j h_1 d\theta + \sum_{i=2}^{m} \lambda_i \alpha_{ij} \int U_i' f_k^j h_i d\theta = \mu, \qquad j = 1, 2, \cdots, n,$$

where f_k^j is the marginal product of the input (and varies with θ). Eliminating λ_i from the equations (11) we obtain

$$(12)\quad \frac{\int U_1' f_k^j h_1 d\theta}{\int U_1' h_1 d\theta} + \sum_{i=2}^{m} \alpha_{ij} \left[\frac{\int U_i' f_k^j h_i d\theta}{\int U_i' h_i d\theta} - \frac{\int U_1' f_k^j h_1 d\theta}{\int U_1' h_1 d\theta} \right] = \frac{\mu}{\int U_1' h_1 d\theta},$$

where the right-hand side is independent of θ, since θ appears solely as a variable of integration.

In the special case of a decomposable production function, equation (2), we have

$$f_k^j(\theta, k_j) = f_j(\theta) g_j'(k_j).$$

Thus the equality of marginal rates of substitution, equation (10), implies that all the terms on the left-hand side, except the first, vanish. Eliminating μ we have the allocation rule

$$\frac{g_j'}{g_1'} = \frac{\int U_1' f_1 h_1 d\theta}{\int U_1' f_j h_1 d\theta}, \qquad j = 2, 3, \cdots, n. \tag{13}$$

With the interpretation of output patterns as composite commodities, this expresses an equality between the marginal rate of transformation and the marginal rate of substitution.

III. *Stock Market Equilibrium*

Let us now consider a competitive economy with the same technology as above. The initial conditions are the ownership of the supplies of input and the shares of stock of the firms. Let w_i be the supply of input and w_{ij} the fraction of the jth firm owned by the ith consumer. Simultaneously trading occurs to reach an equilibrium in the factor market, the stock market, and a bond market, not yet introduced. At the completion of trading, each firm produces with the factors hired under whatever state of nature occurs. Factors are then paid their wages (the wage contract, although fulfilled after production, is set in real terms independent of the state of nature). Let r be the payment per unit for the factor. The remaining profits, which if state θ has occurred, are

$$\pi_j(\theta) = f^j(\theta, k_j) - rk_j, \tag{14}$$

are then distributed to the owners in proportion to their ownership of stock.

Denoting the value of the ith individual's equilibrium holdings of the stock of the jth firm by s_{ij},[10] the total stock market value of the jth firm, M_j, can be written

$$M_j = \sum_{i=1}^{m} s_{ij}. \tag{15}$$

The fraction of the firm owned by the ith consumer is then s_{ij}/M_j and the consumption goods he receives from the jth firm are

$$s_{ij} M_j^{-1} \pi_j(\theta). \tag{16}$$

Thus, s_{ij}/M_j is the equilibrium fraction of the firm owned, while w_{ij} was the initial fraction. With this framework, stockholders need to know

[10] It is assumed that the constraint $s_{ij} \geqq 0$ is not binding (i.e., everyone owns stock in each firm). This constraint, and the corresponding one for the planned economy can be dropped without altering the basic optimality results, although the analysis becomes more complicated. However, the Modigliani-Miller results may be affected by binding constraints on financial behavior.

the relationship of θ to profits although only enterpreneurs need to know the relationship between inputs and output which determines this relationship. In a certainty model firm owners know the level of profits, again without needing to know the combination of inputs and outputs resulting in the profit. This increase in information required for the result, while a natural extension is a significant increase.

In addition to the stock market let us assume there is a bond market where individuals trade promises to pay fixed amounts of consumption, independent of the state of nature, at the completion of the production process. It is assumed that all bond commitments and commitments to the factors of production, are met (bankruptcy never occurs). For convenience let us define one unit of bond as a promise to pay r units of consumption where r is the factor wage. Then, an individual receives fixed payments for both the input he owns and the bonds he holds. Let b_i be the sum of these two elements. We can now write the expression for consumption of the ith individual as

$$c_i(\theta) = rb_i + \sum_{j=1}^{n} s_{ij}\overset{-1}{M_j}\pi_j(\theta). \tag{17}$$

By trading on the stock and bond markets, the consumer seeks to select b_i and s_{ij} to maximize expected utility,

$$\int U_i\left(rb_i + \sum_{j-1}^{n} s_{ij}\overset{-1}{M_j}\pi_j(\theta)\right)h_i(\theta)d\theta \tag{18}$$

within his budget constraint,

$$b_i + \sum_{j=1}^{n} s_{ij} = w_i + \sum_{j=1}^{n} w_{ij}M_j, \tag{19}$$

that the value of bonds purchased, $b_i - w_i$, plus stocks purchased equal the value of his initial stock holdings (the bond is employed as numeraire, making the number of bonds equal their value). The consumer acts as a competitive trader in that he views r, M_j, and $\pi_j(\theta)$ as parameters.

Substituting from the budget constraint for b_i in the expression for expected utility, we have an unconstrained maximization with respect to s_{ij} which has the first order conditions

$$\int U_i'(-r + \overset{-1}{M_j}\pi_j(\theta))h_i(\theta)d\theta = 0, \qquad j = 1, 2, \cdots, n. \tag{20}$$

Rearranging terms, we can express this as an equality between relative prices (recalling that the bond is numeraire, with its price equal to one) and the marginal rate of substitution of the joint product of consumption across the states of nature obtained by buying the stock of the jth firm for the joint product obtained by buying a bond.

$$M_j = \frac{\int U_i' \pi_j(\theta) h_i(\theta) d\theta}{\int U_i' r h_i(\theta) d\theta}. \tag{21}$$

Substituting the definition of profits, equation (14), and rearranging terms we obtain a similar expression for the output pattern of a firm to that we had for its profit pattern.

$$M_j + k_j = \frac{\int U_i' y_j(\theta) h_i(\theta) d\theta}{\int U_i' r h_i(\theta) d\theta}. \tag{22}$$

The step between equations (21) and (22) is analogous to the Modigliani-Miller theorem (see [6]) that the total market value of a firm is independent of its debt-equity structure.[11] The interpretation of this step is that the market value of output, $M_j + k_j$, equals the market value of profits, M_j, plus the value of factor payments, k_j. Recalling the normalization of bonds in terms of factor payments we can view the factor payment obligation as an ordinary element of debt. If we consider two firms, of varying efficiency, so that they have the same output stream $y_{j_1}(\theta) = y_{j_2}(\theta)$ but different input levels, $k_{j_1} \neq k_{j_2}$, we can see from equation (22) that their output value must be the same, although stock market profit value will differ by the difference in present value of their future factor payments. Equivalently we could consider two firms with the same inputs and outputs, differing in that one was in debt. Then the value of debt plus market value for one would equal the market value of the other. Further we can see that a single firm could sell equities to purchase debt (e.g., to pay factors in the future) without altering the real equilibrium position since equilibrium is preserved if each stockholder preserves his fraction of the firm owned and goes into debt to finance his increased shareholdings. This result is a consequence of competitive equilibrium with price takers facing the same prices. The fact that the firm and all its stockholders can lend and borrow on exactly the same terms preserves this condition.

[11] Note that this result is independent of the fact that subjective probabilities differ among individuals. This is in contrast to Lintner [5].

IV. *Production Decisions*

Let us consider, to begin, a firm that has a decomposable production function (as in equation (2)). The fact that the market value of profits equals the market value of output less that of input payments simplifies the calculation for the price-taking firm of the market value corresponding to any level of production. If, for example, the firm is considering doubling its input, this would be calculated as doubling the value of input payments (since the firm is a price taker). The output pattern remains unchanged by the assumption of a decomposable production function, the firm's output becoming $f_j(\theta)g_j(2k_j)$ instead of $f_j(\theta)g_j(k_j)$. Acting as a price taker the firm calculates that its output value will increase in proportion to output, to

$$\frac{g_j(2k_j)}{g_j(k_j)}(M_j + k_j)$$

and thus that its stock market value would become

$$\frac{g_j(2k_j)}{g_j(k_j)}(M_j + k_j) - 2k_j.$$

In general, at an input level of $\hat{k}_j$ with a market value of $\hat{M}_j$, the firm would calculate market value at an alternative input level as

$$M_j = \frac{g_j(k_j)}{g_j(\hat{k}_j)}(\hat{M}_j + \hat{k}_j) - k_j, \tag{23}$$

and would plan to carry production to the point where the derivative of M_j with respect to k_j equalled zero. In equilibrium, this derivative is calculated at the equilibrium input level ($\hat{k}_j = k_j$). Thus the equilibrium condition for production is

$$\frac{g_j'(k_j)}{g_j(k_j)}(M_j + k_j) = 1. \tag{24}$$

Substituting from equation (22) for $(M_j + k_j)$ in this equation we have

$$\frac{g_j' \int U_i' f_j(\theta) h_i(\theta) d\theta}{\int U_i' r h_i(\theta) d\theta} = 1. \tag{25}$$

Comparing these equations, (22) and (25), with the allocation rules in the planned economy, equations (10) and (13), we see that they are equivalent and subject to the same interpretations given above. Thus in the case of decomposable production functions the competitive equilibrium is a constrained Pareto optimum.

In this special case of decomposable production functions, we can consider the output pattern of each firm, suitably normalized, as a commodity. Both production and utility functions can be expressed in terms of these commodities, making this model equivalent to a general equilibrium model under certainty. It is, then, not surprising that we can obtain the standard optimality implications of a competitive equilibrium, with optimality holding relative to these composite commodities. The restriction to these commodities is, of course, the linearity constraint resulting in a constrained rather than full optimum.

Dropping the decomposability assumption, it remains true that the price-taking firm wants to carry production to the point where the derivative of output value (in the stock market) with respect to input level equals one. In the decomposable case, the marginal output pattern and the total output pattern are identical (i.e., for some α, which is a function of k,

$$f_k^j(\theta, k) = \alpha f^j(\theta, k)$$

for all θ) and the firm can obtain the appropriate prices for its marginal calculations from its own stock value. In the absence of decomposability, this price might be found in the value of some other firm (or combination of firms) if the marginal pattern of the first firm coincided with the total pattern of the second at the equilibrium input levels. Thus if at the equilibrium values k_{j_1} and k_{j_2}

$$f_k^{j_1}(\theta, k_{j_1}) = \alpha f^{j_2}(\theta, k_{j_2}) \tag{26}$$

for all θ, the equilibrium condition for firm j_1 is

$$\alpha(M_{j_2} + k_{j_2}) = 1. \tag{27}$$

Note that exactly the same patterns of output are required for this calculation. Two firms with the same expected return and the same variance (using someone's subjective probability) will not, in general, carry production to the same point.

It would be surprising if firms were capable of carrying out this calculation exactly. However, we might expect them to approximate it reasonably well if the major risks are decomposable into particular types which are fairly common. For example, a firm may find its marginal risks simply related to the weather and a random variable independent of anything else in the economy (and, in some extension to price uncertainty, also to the business cycle, which is not, of course, a technological uncertainty). I have not found a rule for competitive production in the general case when the firm is unable to price its marginal output stream from the average profit streams valued in the market.[12]

V. *Implications*

It is interesting to contrast the allocation in the planned economy with that arising from the simple policy of dividing up output equally at the completion of production. By dividing up claims equally before production, and permitting trade in these claims, consumers are able to raise their expected utility levels, as they view them, by means of trade among persons of differing risk aversion or different subjective probabilities. Secondly, we note that even if the planner uses his own subjective probabilities, the presence of technological uncertainty which varies among investment opportunities requires knowledge of consumer risk aversion for production decisions.[13] This is analogous to the certainty model where decisions about possibilities involving different goods require information about tastes for these goods. Levels of risk aversion can be learned from market information only if consumers are offered risky alternatives. A stock market is one method of acquiring this information. In the absence of contingent commodity markets, perhaps socialist economies should have stock markets (possibly with stock on a leasehold not freehold basis, consumers owning claims to output with ownership of the firm reverting to the state at set time intervals).

[12] J. A. Mirrlees has raised the issue of exact achievement of the constrained optimum by nonmarket mechanisms. One such mechanism is a stockholders meeting, run in a particular way. Let the firm ask stockholders how much they are just willing to see the firm pay for the marginal unit of input. Each stockholder will answer by calculating the change in expected utility from a change in input as a function of the wage paid the input, ρ, and then equate this with zero. The expression is

$$\int U_i' s_{ij} M_j^{-1} (f_k^j(\theta, k_j) - \rho) h_i(\theta) d\theta = 0$$

or, solving for ρ, the wage equals

$$\frac{\int U_i' f_k^j h_i(\theta) d\theta}{U_i' h_i(\theta) d\theta} .$$

If production is carried to the point where the wage equals the average of these answers, with the fractions of the firm owned serving as weights in the averaging, the optimal allocation rule, equation (12), is achieved.

[13] Note that a stock market affects the allocation of all inputs into a risky production process (not just capital) since varying output patterns arising from varying input combinations have different stock market valuations. For example, substituting labor for fertilizer will, in general, alter the pattern of output across the states of nature.

Now let us turn to the Modigliani-Miller propositions (see [6]) that firms with the same output patterns have the same expected return on total capital (i.e., the value of debt plus equity, or in this case the present value of contracted factor payments plus stock market value). In turn this rate is the appropriate expected return for the margin of investment. The first proposition holds in general (following from expected utility maximization) while the second requires the decomposability assumption (and follows, then, from market value maximization by the firm). Both conclusions hold for any probability function. The condition of identical ouput patterns is that as functions of θ

$$y_1(\theta) = \alpha y_2(\theta)$$

for some constant α. From the conditions for expected utility maximization, equation (22), we have

$$(28) \qquad (M_1 + k_1)^{-1} \int U_i' y_1(\theta) h_i(\theta) d\theta = (M_2 + k_2)^{-1} \int U_i' y_2(\theta) h_i(\theta) d\theta$$

or, upon substitution

$$(29) \qquad (M_1 + k_1)^{-1}\alpha = (M_2 + k_2)^{-1}.$$

The expected return on total capital is

$$(30) \qquad (M_j + k_j)^{-1} \int y_j(\theta) h(\theta) d\theta.$$

Substituting for both returns and output, we have the equality of expected returns. Note that the same output pattern, and not just the same variance, is required for the conclusion of equal expected returns.

Similarly, the market value maximization equation, (24), implied that the expected marginal return equals the expected average return. However, this result depends on the identical pattern of total and marginal returns and does not hold without the decomposability assumption.

By means of portfolio diversification on the part of consumers, all of the economy's averaging possibilities are brought to bear on each production decision. Thus, in the model, large firms have no pooling advantages over small firms, nor does the government have an advantage over private business.[14] Provided that the government does not go

[14] This conclusion does not depend on the assumption that fixed interest debt obligations (or equivalently wages) are met in every state of nature. Bankruptcy for limited liability corporations still leaves well defined payment patterns for both stocks and bonds. Provided both of these are traded competitively (preserving the assumption that an internal equilibrium exists or alternatively that individuals can sell short) the basic conclusions of the model are preserved. It is true that large firms, with diversified investments, will tend to go bankrupt in fewer states of nature and so will pay a lower nominal rate for fixed interest debt. But this does not alter

outside the linearity constraints of the model, government investors should imitate private business, evaluating individual projects separately, not pooling, and looking to the stock market for the appropriate return criteria. Given market value maximization, average stock market returns reflect marginal returns to investment. Neither, in general, reflects average returns to a firm's real assets.

While some examples of government investment may fall neatly into the pattern of the model (for example, pure public goods provided equally to everyone), many of them will not. Presumably some government activity may be devoted precisely to circumventing the linearity constraint where the constraint imposes a large cost on the economy. (An analysis explaining the particular set of trade opportunities available may well relate a limit on the cost of this constraint to the costs of establishing further markets.) Also, parallel to government activity in a certainty model, some actions may be taken to correct divergences from the competitive model which interfere with the optimality properties of competitive equilibrium. Where government investment is not necessarily linked to either of these aspects it seems reasonable to expect optimal behavior to be similar to that for investment falling within the pattern of the model. For example, optimal investment with nonlinear distribution rules, unless these rules are chosen to correct limitations from linearity in the private economy, may on average involve expected returns approximating those on investments with linear distribution rules.[15]

The model assumed a given set of firms, chosen historically to reflect investment opportunities. Relaxing this assumption to permit the addition of new firms allows the introduction of a competitive insurance market.[16] This, however, raises even more seriously the problem of the informational aspect of the model and the empirical distinction among states of nature. Nevertheless, in the context of the model, by defining a pattern of output across the states of nature, trading can occur in stocks without the necessity of production behind them. This trading is neces-

---

the conclusion that large firms and small firms should pursue identical investment opportunities to the same margin. Various market imperfections would naturally alter this conclusion. Taxes, transaction costs in debt issuance, and difficulty for financial investors in obtaining information about the nature of real investment opportunities, $y_j(\theta)$, are obvious candidates for this disruption.

[15] The fact that benefits from government investment may not be tradable may decrease their social value.

[16] Another opportunity for an increase in efficiency is by the creation of two firms dividing the profits of an existing firm nonlinearly between them. This increases the number of possible patterns available to consumers. Mutual funds, however, offer no new opportunities in a perfect knowledge, no transaction cost model.

sarily buying and short selling, where selling is a promise to pay the appropriate dividend level. For example, a pattern involving payment in case of a flood in a given area, but not otherwise, is a stock which will be bought by residents of the area and sold by nonresidents. Thus, competitive insurance markets could be introduced. In the absence of all transaction costs, this could be carried to the point where it would become possible to purchase, by some combination of stocks, a unit of output in any state of nature, i.e., the set of output patterns would span the states of nature. At this point the stock market model becomes equivalent to the contingent commodity model discussed in the Appendix and the economy achieves a full Pareto optimum.

References

1. K. J. Arrow, "The Role of Securities in the Optimal Allocation of Risk-Bearing," *Rev. Econ. Stud.*, April 1964, *31*, 91–96.
2. ———, "Uncertainty and the Welfare Economics of Medical Care," *Am. Econ. Rev.*, Dec. 1963, *53*, 941–73.
3. ———, "Liquidity Preference," Lecture VI in "Lecture Notes for Economics 285, The Economics of Uncertainty," unpublished.
4. G. Debreu, *Theory of Value*. New York 1959.
5. J. Lintner, "Dividends, Earnings, Leverage, Stock Prices and the Supply of Capital to Corporations," *Rev. Econ. Stat.*, Aug. 1962, *44*, 243–69.
6. F. Modigliani and M. H. Miller, "The Cost of Capital, Corporation Finance and the Theory of Investment," *Am. Econ. Rev.*, June 1958, *48*, 261–97.
7. J. W. Pratt, "Risk Aversion in the Small and in the Large," *Econometrica*, Jan.–April 1964, *32*, 122–36.

Comment

There is now a sizable literature on the efficiency of equilibrium with missing markets. This comment is a brief guide and introduction to this subject. Briefly, the last selection shows that when there is multiplicative uncertainty, one can define composite commodities (being the output patterns of firms and of a bond) and have equivalence between this stock market model and the conventional general equilibrium model, defined in terms of composite commodities. It follows from the basic welfare theorems of economic theory that there is an equivalence between competitive equilibria on stock markets and those Pareto optima that can be achieved when there is a restriction on allocation corresponding to having all allocation rules defined in terms of these composite commodities. This result does not generalize when one allows additional trading, either with three periods or two goods in the second period. Hart (1975) has produced examples of equilibria where each person exactly predicts the prices that will occur when markets reopen and yet the equilibrium is not a constrained Pareto optimum. He provides examples of economies with several such equilibria that are Pareto comparable, i.e., everyone is better off in one of the equilibria than in the other. Even more surprisingly, he produces an example of an economy with incomplete markets where the addition of a market (leaving the set of markets still incomplete) makes everyone worse off. That inefficiency is generic (in endowments) with missing markets is shown by Geanakoplos *et al.* (1987). [For another discussion of efficiency with different sets of markets, see Green and Sheshinski (1975).]

In two interesting papers, Grossman (1977) and Grossman and Hart (1979), the welfare theorem stated above is reinterpreted in a way that does generalize to the case of many commodities. The reinterpretation is to compare the set of competitive equilibria to a set of allocations that can be achieved by a team of planners where there are restrictions on the ability of planners to coordinate different parts of the overall plan. These restrictions parallel the limitations inherent in an incomplete set of markets. This approach relates the ability of planners to do better than the market to their ability to do things that the market is not doing (or to the usual sources of market inefficiency such as noncompetitive behavior or technological externalities).

A second line of inquiry that has been fruitful and is continuing is the further analysis of firm behavior with incomplete markets. We briefly describe three lines of inquiry. Jensen and Long (1972) and Stiglitz (1972a) have used the mean-variance model to examine the constrained optimality of competitive equilibrium. They find that the equilibrium where firms maximize stock market value, taking as given the prices of mean return and variance of aggregate return, is not optimal. As LeRoy (1976) has pointed out, taking these prices as given is not equivalent to taking the prices of composite commodities as given. [Analogously, in the conventional model, taking the price of output as given is not equivalent to perceiving an equilibrium price in terms of aggregate supply and recognizing that aggregate supply depends on one's own supply, $p = p(X + x)$, where X is the supply of others' and x of one's own supply. Taking the price as given is equivalent to perceiving a demand curve and viewing aggregate supply $X + x$ as given.] Of course, the logical issue of what behavior is equivalent to competitive behavior in the conventional model is totally separate from the empirical question of how firms act. [For another discussion, see Merton and Subrahmanyam (1974).]

When firms exploit perceived market power in the stock market, the situation is different from that in an output market, for the firms are exploiting their market power over the very people who own the firm. Thus it is natural to turn to descriptions of firm behavior that look to the owners of firms rather than to prices in the market to determine the rules followed by firms. This approach has been taken by Ekern and Wilson (1974), Leland (1973, 1974), and Radner (1974). They consider as a necessary condition for an allocation to be an equilibrium that there be no change in firm production that all stockholders would prefer, given their equilibrium portfolios. Analyzing the case where available output patterns span the relevant space for firm decisions, and assuming that firm decisions do not alter the state-distributions of returns available in the economy, they conclude that any such equilibrium is Pareto optimal. This optimality follows from the unanimity of approval or disapproval of any project by the shareholders of a firm. Under these circumstances, owners of firms want firms to behave as price-taking competitors and to refrain from exercising market power over firm value. Long (1972) has taken this approach to determining firm behavior.

This analysis assumes that all decisions are simultaneous. In practice they are not; trade goes on continuously and firms make and revise plans continuously. When one distinguishes the sets of owners of firms at different dates, it becomes reasonable for one set to try to exploit perceived market power in choosing the plans of firms. Grossman and Stiglitz (1980) make this argument. [Grossman and Hart (1979) also consider revisions of the plans of firms as shares of stock change hands over time.]

These papers have assumed that all potential decisions could be evaluated in the market. (Unanimity is explored in the presence of spanning.) When markets do (or may) contain an incomplete set of composite commodities for valuing firm decisions, the problem becomes more complicated. Drèze (1974) has examined equilibrium where firms look to owners for evaluation of outcomes and have choices about techniques of production. Then, the equilibrium that occurs need not be a constrained Pareto optimum, even when the set of securities spans the set of states of nature in equilibrium. He does show that any constrained optimum can be obtained as an equilibrium where firms look to their owners for evaluation of alternative plans.

Stglitz (1972b) has analyzed the more complicated case where firms may go bankrupt.

References

J. Drèze, Investment under private ownership: Optimality, equilibrium and stability, *in* "Allocation under Uncertainty: Equilibrium and Optimality" (J. Drèze, ed.), Chapter 9. New York: Macmillan, 1974.

S. Ekern and R. Wilson, On the theory of the firm in an economy with incomplete markets, *Bell J. Econ. Manage. Sci.* 5 (1974), 171-183.

J. Geanakoplos, M. Magill, M. Quinzii, and J. Drèze, "Generic inefficiency of stock market equilibrium when markets are incomplete," MRG Working Paper 8735, Department of Economics, University of Southern California, 1987.

J. Green and E. Sheshinski, Competitive inefficiences in the presence of constrained transactions, *J. Econ. Theory* **10** (1975), 343–357.

S. Grossman, A characterization of the optimality of equilibrium in complete markets, *J. Econ. Theory* **15** (1977), 1–15.

S. Grossman and O. Hart, A theory of competitive equilibrium in stock market economies, *Econometrica* **47** (1979), 293–330.

S. Grossman and J. Stiglitz, On stockholder unanimity in making production and financial decisions, *Quart. J. Econ.* **94** (1980), 543–566.

O. Hart, On the optimality of equilibrium when the market structure is incomplete, *J. Econ. Theory* **11** (1975), 418–443.

M. C. Jensen and J. B. Long, Corporate investment under uncertainty and Pareto optimality in the capital markets, *Bell J. Econ. Manage. Sci.* **3** (1972), 151-174.

H. Leland, Production theory and the stock market, *Bell J. Econ. Manage. Sci.* **5** (1974), 125-144.

H. Leland, Capital asset markets, production, and optimality: A synthesis, Tech. Rep. 115, Institute for Mathematical Studies in the Social Sciences, Stanford University, 1973.

S. F. LeRoy, Stock market optimality: Comment, *Quart. J. Econ.* **90** (1976), 150-155.

J. B. Long, Wealth, welfare, and the price of risk, *J. Finance* **27** (1972), 419–433.

R. C. Merton and M. G. Subrahmanyam, The optimality of a competitive stock market, *Bell J. Econ. Manage. Sci.* **5** (1974), 145–170.

R. Radner, A note on unanimity of stockholders preferences among alternative production plans: A reformulation of the Ekern–Wilson model, *Bell J. Econ. Manage. Sci.* **5** (1974), 181–184.

J. E. Stiglitz, On the optimality of the stock market allocation of investment, *Quart. J. Econ.* **86** (1972a), 25–60).

J. E. Stiglitz, Some aspects of the pure theory of corporate finance: Bankruptcies and take-overs, *Bell J. Econ. Manage. Sci.* **3** (1972b), 458–82.

14
Exercise on uniform pricing

Incomplete markets caused the complications in the previous chapter. In the markets that existed commodities were well defined. Different problems arise when the definition of a commodity is unclear. Suppose several items, different in the eyes of consumers, are sold as if they were the same item. The classic example (and the subject of the next reading) is that of used cars. Similarly, firms may find that it costs different amounts to sell the "same" commodity to different buyers. In the insurance context different individuals may have different probabilities of collecting on the policy. Where free delivery is provided within a given geographic area, there will be differences in costs of delivery. Costs often differ by time of day (as in telephone and electricity supply) where prices do not differ as finely (costs vary continously but there are only two or three pricing periods). In a retail store setting, some customers use more staff time than others. The class of problems that arise when commodities are distinguished on one side of the market but are treated as identical by the other side, we will refer to as *adverse selection* problems. This is the subject of the next three readings. We begin with an exercise analyzing what happens if the same price must be charged to some set of customers. We shall ask the reader to derive the equilibrium price, assuming that all firms receive the same cross section of customers, to derive the price that maximizes a social welfare function, and to compare these two. This will be done for particular demand curves. The next reading explores the importance of this problem when the demand curves come from differential knowledge about the particular commodities. [A similar problem arises where different individuals give different externalities per unit of commodity purchased and the tax-setting authorities are constrained to uniform taxation. This problem is analyzed in Diamond (1973), Green and Sheshinski (1976), and Balcer (1980).] The issue of how finely prices should discriminate is more complicated than the issue of optimal pricing given the degree of discrimination; only the latter problem is analyzed here.[1]

Assume that utility of consumer h is

$$U^h(\alpha_h) + \mu_h$$

[1]This exercise is based on a paper presented by Diamond at the First Berlin Symposium on Planning, August 1973, and on the discussion of that paper by Michael Keren.

where α_h is consumption of the good being examined, μ_h is income available for other consumption, and U^h is strictly concave and twice continuously differentiable. Assume that the aggregate costs of production of the commodity are

$$C = \Sigma c_h \alpha_h$$

so that the price to consumer h would be set at c_h if separate prices were quoted to different consumers. Assume that a uniform price p is quoted and that consumer h has income m_h.

1 Set up the consumer's problem of utility maximization subject to a budget constraint and a nonnegativity constraint on α_h (but ignoring any nonnegativity constraint on μ_h).

2 Show that demand by consumer h is a function of price but not income, and that demand decreases with price when the quantity demanded is positive.

3 Show that maximization of the sum of utilities involves setting the price of this good at a level that maximizes $\Sigma U^h(\alpha_h(p)) - \Sigma c_h \alpha_h(p)$, where $\alpha_h(p)$ is the demand function of consumer h.

4 Show that the optimal price satisfies

$$p^* = \frac{\Sigma c_h (d\alpha_h/dp)}{\Sigma(d\alpha_h/dp)}$$

[*Hint*: Make use of the consumer's first-order condition.]

5 Determine the profits from supplying this good at the socially optimal price. Let us define a new variable Δ by

$$\Delta = \left[\frac{\Sigma c_h (d\alpha_h/dp)}{\Sigma(d\alpha_h/dp)} - \Sigma c_h\right] - \left[\frac{\Sigma c_h \alpha_h}{\Sigma \alpha_h} - \Sigma c_h\right]$$

Thus, Δ is positive when the covariance of (relative) quantities demanded and costs of production is less than the covariance of (relative) price derivatives of demand and costs of production.

6 Show that profits are positive at the socially optimal price when Δ is positive. (That is, show that when high-cost demanders demand relatively small quantities but have relatively large price derivatives of demand, profits are positive.)

7 Let η_h be the elasticity of individual demand,

$$\eta_h = \frac{p}{\alpha_h}\frac{d\alpha_h}{dp}$$

Let η be the elasticity of aggregate demand,

$$\eta = \frac{p}{\Sigma \alpha_h} \Sigma \frac{d\alpha_h}{dp} = \frac{\Sigma \alpha_h \eta_h}{\Sigma \alpha_h}$$

Show that with optimal pricing, profits equal $\Sigma c_h \alpha_h [\eta_h/\eta - 1]$.

8 Assume that $d\alpha_h/dp$ is constant over the relevant range. Show that if this industry is run by a profit-maximizing monopolist (who sets a uniform price), the price he sets is above the socially optimal price.

9 If the price in this industry is set by competitive firms that have identical costs (i.e., the average of c_h is the same for all firms) and there is free entry, show that the price may be too high or too low. Relate the determination of the equilibrium price (relative to the socially optimal price) to the pattern of individual demand elasticities and costs of meeting individual demand.

10 Consider extending the model to two commodities that are supplied by the social planner.

References

Y. Balcer, Taxation of externalities: direct versus indirect, *J. Public Econ.* **13** (1980), 1–9.

P. Diamond, Consumption externalities and imperfect corrective pricing, *Bell J. Econ.* **4** (1973), 526–538.

J. Green and E. Sheshinski, Direct versus indirect remedies for externalities, *J. Political Econ.* 84 (1976), 797–808.

15

G. Akerlof, The market for lemons: Qualitative uncertainty and the market mechanism, *Quarterly Journal of Economics* **84** (1970), 488–500

This paper shows that a market can have no trade when demanders know the average quality of cars being sold and potential sellers know the quality of the particular cars they are considering selling. The author discusses institutions that partially circumvent such market breakdowns. The assumptions of this paper exemplify the situation analyzed in the preceding exercise.

THE MARKET FOR "LEMONS": QUALITY UNCERTAINTY AND THE MARKET MECHANISM *

GEORGE A. AKERLOF

I. INTRODUCTION

This paper relates quality and uncertainty. The existence of goods of many grades poses interesting and important problems for the theory of markets. On the one hand, the interaction of quality differences and uncertainty may explain important institutions of the labor market. On the other hand, this paper presents a struggling attempt to give structure to the statement: "Business in underdeveloped countries is difficult"; in particular, a structure is given for determining the economic costs of dishonesty. Additional applications of the theory include comments on the structure of money markets, on the notion of "insurability," on the liquidity of durables, and on brand-name goods.

There are many markets in which buyers use some market statistic to judge the quality of prospective purchases. In this case there is incentive for sellers to market poor quality merchandise, since the returns for good quality accrue mainly to the entire group whose statistic is affected rather than to the individual seller. As a result there tends to be a reduction in the average quality of goods and also in the size of the market. It should also be perceived that in these markets social and private returns differ, and therefore, in some cases, governmental intervention may increase the welfare of all parties. Or private institutions may arise to take advantage of the potential increases in welfare which can accrue to all parties. By nature, however, these institutions are nonatomistic, and therefore concentrations of power — with ill consequences of their own — can develop.

* The author would especially like to thank Thomas Rothenberg for invaluable comments and inspiration. In addition he is indebted to Roy Radner, Albert Fishlow, Bernard Saffran, William D. Nordhaus, Giorgio La Malfa, Charles C. Holt, John Letiche, and the referee for help and suggestions. He would also like to thank the Indian Statistical Institute and the Ford Foundation for financial support.

Quarterly Journal of Economics **84**, 488–500.

The automobile market is used as a finger exercise to illustrate and develop these thoughts. It should be emphasized that this market is chosen for its concreteness and ease in understanding rather than for its importance or realism.

II. The Model with Automobiles as an Example

A. The Automobiles Market

The example of used cars captures the essence of the problem. From time to time one hears either mention of or surprise at the large price difference between new cars and those which have just left the showroom. The usual lunch table justification for this phenomenon is the pure joy of owning a "new" car. We offer a different explanation. Suppose (for the sake of clarity rather than reality) that there are just four kinds of cars. There are new cars and used cars. There are good cars and bad cars (which in America are known as "lemons"). A new car may be a good car or a lemon, and of course the same is true of used cars.

The individuals in this market buy a new automobile without knowing whether the car they buy will be good or a lemon. But they do know that with probability q it is a good car and with probability $(1-q)$ it is a lemon; by assumption, q is the proportion of good cars produced and $(1-q)$ is the proportion of lemons.

After owning a specific car, however, for a length of time, the car owner can form a good idea of the quality of this machine; i.e., the owner assigns a new probability to the event that his car is a lemon. This estimate is more accurate than the original estimate. An asymmetry in available information has developed: for the sellers now have more knowledge about the quality of a car than the buyers. But good cars and bad cars must still sell at the same price — since it is impossible for a buyer to tell the difference between a good car and a bad car. It is apparent that a used car cannot have the same valuation as a new car — if it did have the same valuation, it would clearly be advantageous to trade a lemon at the price of new car, and buy another new car, at a higher probability q of being good and a lower probability of being bad. Thus the owner of a good machine must be locked in. Not only is it true that he cannot receive the true value of his car, but he cannot even obtain the expected value of a new car.

Gresham's law has made a modified reappearance. For most cars traded will be the "lemons," and good cars may not be traded at all. The "bad" cars tend to drive out the good (in much the same way that bad money drives out the good). But the analogy with Gresham's law is not quite complete: bad cars drive out the good because they sell at the same price as good cars; similarly, bad money drives out good because the exchange rate is even. But the bad cars sell at the same price as good cars since it is impossible for a buyer to tell the difference between a good and a bad car; only the seller knows. In Gresham's law, however, presumably both buyer and seller can tell the difference between good and bad money. So the analogy is instructive, but not complete.

B. Asymmetrical Information

It has been seen that the good cars may be driven out of the market by the lemons. But in a more continuous case with different grades of goods, even worse pathologies can exist. For it is quite possible to have the bad driving out the not-so-bad driving out the medium driving out the not-so-good driving out the good in such a sequence of events that no market exists at all.

One can assume that the demand for used automobiles depends most strongly upon two variables — the price of the automobile p and the average quality of used cars traded, μ, or $Q^d = D(p, \mu)$. Both the supply of used cars and also the average quality μ will depend upon the price, or $\mu = \mu\ (p)$ and $S = S(p)$. And in equilibrium the supply must equal the demand for the given average quality, or $S(p) = D(p, \mu(p))$. As the price falls, normally the quality will also fall. And it is quite possible that no goods will be traded at any price level.

Such an example can be derived from utility theory. Assume that there are just two groups of traders: groups one and two. Give group one a utility function

$$U_1 = M + \sum_{i=1}^{n} x_i$$

where M is the consumption of goods other than automobiles, x_i is the quality of the ith automobile, and n is the number of automobiles.

Similarly, let

$$U_2 = M + \sum_{i=1}^{n} 3/2 x_i$$

where M, x_i, and n are defined as before.

Three comments should be made about these utility functions: (1) without linear utility (say with logarithmic utility) one gets needlessly mired in algebraic complication. (2) The use of linear utility allows a focus on the effects of asymmetry of information; with a concave utility function we would have to deal jointly with the usual risk-variance effects of uncertainty and the special effects we wish to discuss here. (3) U_1 and U_2 have the odd characteristic that the addition of a second car, or indeed a kth car, adds the same amount of utility as the first. Again realism is sacrificed to avoid a diversion from the proper focus.

To continue, it is assumed (1) that both type one traders and type two traders are von Neumann-Morgenstern maximizers of expected utility; (2) that group one has N cars with uniformly distributed quality x, $0 \leqq x \leqq 2$, and group two has no cars; (3) that the price of "other goods" M is unity.

Denote the income (including that derived from the sale of automobiles) of all type one traders as Y_1 and the income of all type two traders as Y_2. The demand for used cars will be the sum of the demands by both groups. When one ignores indivisibilities, the demand for automobiles by type one traders will be

$$D_1 = Y_1/p \qquad \mu/p > 1$$

$$D_1 = 0 \qquad \mu/p < 1.$$

And the supply of cars offered by type one traders is

$$(1) \qquad S_2 = pN/2 \qquad p \leqq 2$$

with average quality

$$(2) \qquad \mu = p/2.$$

(To derive (1) and (2), the uniform distribution of automobile quality is used.)

Similarly the demand of type two traders is

$$D_2 = Y_2/p \qquad 3\mu/2 > p$$

$$D_2 = 0 \qquad 3\mu/2 < p$$

and

$$S_2 = 0.$$

Thus total demand $D(p, \mu)$ is

$$D(p, \mu) = (Y_2 + Y_1)/p \qquad \text{if } p < \mu$$

$$D(p, \mu) = Y_2/p \qquad \text{if } \mu < p < 3\mu/2$$

$$D(p, \mu) = 0 \qquad \text{if } p > 3\mu/2.$$

However, with price p, average quality is $p/2$ and therefore at no price will any trade take place at all: in spite of the fact that *at any given price* between 0 and 3 there are traders of type one who are willing to sell their automobiles at a price which traders of type two are willing to pay.

C. Symmetric Information

The foregoing is contrasted with the case of symmetric information. Suppose that the quality of all cars is uniformly distributed, $0 \leqq x \leqq 2$. Then the demand curves and supply curves can be written as follows:

Supply

$S(p) = N \qquad p > 1$

$S(p) = 0 \qquad p < 1.$

And the demand curves are

$D(p) = (Y_2 + Y_1)/p \qquad p < 1$

$D(p) = (Y_2/p) \qquad 1 < p < 3/2$

$D(p) = 0 \qquad p > 3/2.$

In equilibrium

(3) $\quad p = 1 \qquad$ if $Y_2 < N$

(4) $\quad p = Y_2/N \qquad$ if $2Y_2/3 < N < Y_2$

(5) $\quad p = 3/2 \qquad$ if $N < 2Y_2/3.$

If $N < Y_2$ there is a gain in utility over the case of asymmetrical information of $N/2$. (If $N > Y_2$, in which case the income of type two traders is insufficient to buy all N automobiles, there is a gain in utility of $Y_2/2$ units.)

Finally, it should be mentioned that in this example, if traders of groups one and two have the same probabilistic estimates about the quality of individual automobiles — though these estimates may vary from automobile to automobile — (3), (4), and (5) will still describe equilibrium with one slight change: p will then represent the expected price of one quality unit.

III. Examples and Applications

A. Insurance

It is a well-known fact that people over 65 have great difficulty in buying medical insurance. The natural question arises: why doesn't the price rise to match the risk?

Our answer is that as the price level rises the people who insure themselves will be those who are increasingly certain that they will need the insurance; for error in medical check-ups, doctors' sympathy with older patients, and so on make it much easier for the applicant to assess the risks involved than the insurance company. The result is that the average medical condition of insurance applicants deteriorates as the price level rises — with the result that no insurance sales may take place at any price.[1] This is strictly analogous to our automobiles case, where the average quality of used cars supplied fell with a corresponding fall in the price level. This agrees with the explanation in insurance textbooks:

> Generally speaking policies are not available at ages materially greater than sixty-five. . . . The term premiums are too high for any but the most pessimistic (which is to say the least healthy) insureds to find attractive. Thus there is a severe problem of adverse selection at these ages.[2]

The statistics do not contradict this conclusion. While demands for health insurance rise with age, a 1956 national sample survey of 2,809 families with 8,898 persons shows that hospital insurance coverage drops from 63 per cent of those aged 45 to 54, to 31 per cent for those over 65. And surprisingly, this survey also finds average medical expenses for males aged 55 to 64 of $88, while males over 65 pay an average of $77.[3] While noninsured expenditure rises from $66 to $80 in these age groups, insured expenditure declines from $105 to $70. The conclusion is tempting that insurance companies are particularly wary of giving medical insurance to older people.

The principle of "adverse selection" is potentially present in all lines of insurance. The following statement appears in an insurance textbook written at the Wharton School:

> There is potential adverse selection in the fact that healthy term insurance policy holders may decide to terminate their coverage when they become older and premiums mount. This action could leave an insurer with an undue proportion of below average risks and claims might be higher than anticipated. Adverse selection "appears (or at least is possible) whenever the individual or group insured has freedom to buy or not to buy, to choose the amount or plan of insurance, and to persist or to discontinue as a policy holder."[4]

Group insurance, which is the most common form of medical insurance in the United States, picks out the healthy, for generally

1. Arrow's fine article, "Uncertainty and Medical Care" (*American Economic Review*, Vol. 53, 1963), does not make this point explicitly. He emphasizes "moral hazard" rather than "adverse selection." In its strict sense, the presence of "moral hazard" is equally disadvantageous for both governmental and private programs; in its broader sense, which includes "adverse selection," "moral hazard" gives a decided advantage to government insurance programs.

2. O. D. Dickerson, *Health Insurance* (Homewood, Ill.: Irwin, 1959), p. 333.

3. O. W. Anderson (with J. J. Feldman), *Family Medical Costs and Insurance* (New York: McGraw-Hill, 1956).

4. H. S. Denenberg, R. D. Eilers, G. W. Hoffman, C. A. Kline, J. J. Melone, and H. W. Snider, *Risk and Insurance* (Englewood Cliffs, N. J.: Prentice Hall, 1964), p. 446.

adequate health is a precondition for employment. At the same time this means that medical insurance is least available to those who need it most, for the insurance companies do their own "adverse selection."

This adds one major argument in favor of medicare.[5] On a cost benefit basis medicare may pay off: for it is quite possible that every individual in the market would be willing to pay the expected cost of his medicare and buy insurance, yet no insurance company can afford to sell him a policy — for at any price it will attract too many "lemons." The welfare economics of medicare, in this view, is *exactly* analogous to the usual classroom argument for public expenditure on roads.

B. The Employment of Minorities

The Lemons Principle also casts light on the employment of minorities. Employers may refuse to hire members of minority groups for certain types of jobs. This decision may not reflect irrationality or prejudice — but profit maximization. For race may serve as a good *statistic* for the applicant's social background, quality of schooling, and general job capabilities.

Good quality schooling could serve as a substitute for this statistic; by grading students the schooling system can give a better indicator of quality than other more superficial characteristics. As T. W. Schultz writes, "The educational establishment *discovers* and cultivates potential talent. The capabilities of children and mature students can never be known until *found* and cultivated."[6] (Italics added.) An untrained worker may have valuable natural talents, but these talents must be certified by "the educational establishment" before a company can afford to use them. The certifying establishment, however, must be credible; the unreliability of slum schools decreases the economic possibilities of their students.

This lack may be particularly disadvantageous to members of

5. The following quote, again taken from an insurance textbook, shows how far the medical insurance market is from perfect competition:

> ". . . insurance companies must screen their applicants. Naturally it is true that many people will voluntarily seek adequate insurance on their own initiative. But in such lines as accident and health insurance, companies are likely to give a second look to persons who voluntarily seek insurance without being approached by an agent." (F. J. Angell, *Insurance, Principles and Practices*, New York: The Ronald Press, 1957, pp. 8–9.)

This shows that insurance is *not* a commodity for sale on the open market.

6. T. W. Schultz, *The Economic Value of Education* (New York: Columbia University Press, 1964), p. 42.

already disadvantaged minority groups. For an employer may make a rational decision not to hire any members of these groups in responsible positions — because it is difficult to distinguish those with good job qualifications from those with bad qualifications. This type of decision is clearly what George Stigler had in mind when he wrote, "in a regime of ignorance Enrico Fermi would have been a gardener, Von Neumann a checkout clerk at a drugstore." [7]

As a result, however, the rewards for work in slum schools tend to accrue to the group as a whole — in raising its average quality — rather than to the individual. Only insofar as information in addition to race is used is there any incentive for training.

An additional worry is that the Office of Economic Opportunity is going to use cost-benefit analysis to evaluate its programs. For many benefits may be external. The benefit from training minority groups may arise as much from raising the average quality of the group as from raising the quality of the individual trainee; and, likewise, the returns may be distributed over the whole group rather than to the individual.

C. The Costs of Dishonesty

The Lemons model can be used to make some comments on the costs of dishonesty. Consider a market in which goods are sold honestly or dishonestly; quality may be represented, or it may be misrepresented. The purchaser's problem, of course, is to identify quality. The presence of people in the market who are willing to offer inferior goods tends to drive the market out of existence — as in the case of our automobile "lemons." It is this possibility that represents the major costs of dishonesty — for dishonest dealings tend to drive honest dealings out of the market. There may be potential buyers of good quality products and there may be potential sellers of such products in the appropriate price range; however, the presence of people who wish to pawn bad wares as good wares tends to drive out the legitimate business. The cost of dishonesty, therefore, lies not only in the amount by which the purchaser is cheated; the cost also must include the loss incurred from driving legitimate business out of existence.

Dishonesty in business is a serious problem in underdeveloped countries. Our model gives a possible structure to this statement and delineates the nature of the "external" economies involved. In particular, in the model economy described, dishonesty, or the

7. G. J. Stigler, "Information and the Labor Market," *Journal of Political Economy*, Vol. 70 (Oct. 1962), Supplement, p. 104.

misrepresentation of the quality of automobiles, costs 1/2 unit of utility per automobile; furthermore, it reduces the size of the used car market from N to 0. We can, consequently, directly evaluate the costs of dishonesty — at least in theory.

There is considerable evidence that quality variation is greater in underdeveloped than in developed areas. For instance, the need for quality control of exports and State Trading Corporations can be taken as one indicator. In India, for example, under the Export Quality Control and Inspection Act of 1963, "about 85 per cent of Indian exports are covered under one or the other type of quality control."[8] Indian housewives must carefully glean the rice of the local bazaar to sort out stones of the same color and shape which have been intentionally added to the rice. Any comparison of the heterogeneity of quality in the street market and the canned qualities of the American supermarket suggests that quality variation is a greater problem in the East than in the West.

In one traditional pattern of development the merchants of the pre-industrial generation turn into the first entrepreneurs of the next. The best-documented case is Japan,[9] but this also may have been the pattern for Britain and America.[1] In *our* picture the important skill of the merchant is identifying the quality of merchandise; those who can identify used cars in our example and can guarantee the quality may profit by as much as the difference between type two traders' buying price and type one traders' selling price. These people are the merchants. In production these skills are equally necessary — both to be able to identify the quality of inputs and to certify the quality of outputs. And this is one (added) reason why the merchants may logically become the first entrepreneurs.

The problem, of course, is that entrepreneurship may be a scarce resource; no development text leaves entrepreneurship unemphasized. Some treat it as central.[2] Given, then, that entrepreneurship is scarce, there are two ways in which product variations impede development. First, the pay-off to trade is great for would-be entrepreneurs, and hence they are diverted from production; second, the amount of entrepreneurial time per unit output is greater, the greater are the quality variations.

8. *The Times of India*, Nov. 10, 1967, p. 1.

9. See M. J. Levy, Jr., "Contrasting Factors in the Modernization of China and Japan," in *Economic Growth: Brazil, India, Japan*, ed. S. Kuznets, *et. al.* (Durham, N. C.: Duke University Press, 1955).

1. C. P. Kindleberger, *Economic Development* (New York: McGraw-Hill, 1958), p. 86.

2. For example, see W. Arthur Lewis, *The Theory of Economic Growth* (Homewood, Ill.: Irwin, 1955), p. 196.

D. Credit Markets in Underdeveloped Countries

(1) Credit markets in underdeveloped countries often strongly reflect the operation of the Lemons Principle. In India a major fraction of industrial enterprise is controlled by managing agencies (according to a recent survey, these "managing agencies" controlled 65.7 per cent of the net worth of public limited companies and 66 per cent of total assets).[3] Here is a historian's account of the function and genesis of the "managing agency system":

> The management of the South Asian commercial scene remained the function of merchant houses, and a type of organization peculiar to South Asia known as the Managing Agency. When a new venture was promoted (such as a manufacturing plant, a plantation, or a trading venture), the promoters would approach an established managing agency. The promoters might be Indian or British, and they might have technical or financial resources or merely a concession. In any case they would turn to the agency because of its reputation, which would encourage confidence in the venture and stimulate investment.[4]

In turn, a second major feature of the Indian industrial scene has been the dominance of these managing agencies by caste (or, more accurately, communal) groups. Thus firms can usually be classified according to communal origin.[5] In this environment, in which outside investors are likely to be bilked of their holdings, either (1) firms establish a reputation for "honest" dealing, which confers upon them a monopoly rent insofar as their services are

3. *Report of the Committee on the Distribution of Income and Levels of Living*, Part I, Government of India, Planning Commission, Feb. 1964, p. 44.

4. H. Tinker, *South Asia: A Short History* (New York: Praeger, 1966), p. 134.

5. The existence of the following table (and also the small per cent of firms under mixed control) indicates the communalization of the control of firms. *Source*: M. M. Mehta, *Structure of Indian Industries* (Bombay: Popular Book Depot, 1955), p. 314.

DISTRIBUTION OF INDUSTRIAL CONTROL BY COMMUNITY

	1911	1931 (number of firms)	1951
British	281	416	382
Parsis	15	25	19
Gujratis	3	11	17
Jews	5	9	3
Muslims	—	10	3
Bengalis	8	5	20
Marwaris	—	6	96
Mixed control	28	28	79
Total	341	510	619

Also, for the cotton industry see H. Fukuzawa, "Cotton Mill Industry," in V. B. Singh, editor, *Economic History of India, 1857–1956* (Bombay: Allied Publishers, 1965).

limited in supply, or (2) the sources of finance are limited to local communal groups which can use communal — and possibly familial — ties to encourage honest dealing *within* the community. It is, in Indian economic history, extraordinarily difficult to discern whether the savings of rich landlords failed to be invested in the industrial sector (1) because of a fear to invest in ventures controlled by other communities, (2) because of inflated propensities to consume, or (3) because of low rates of return.[6] At the very least, however, it is clear that the British-owned managing agencies tended to have an equity holding whose communal origin was more heterogeneous than the Indian-controlled agency houses, and would usually include both Indian and British investors.

(2) A second example of the workings of the Lemons Principle concerns the extortionate rates which the local moneylender charges his clients. In India these high rates of interest have been the leading factor in landlessness; the so-called "Cooperative Movement" was meant to counteract this growing landlessness by setting up banks to compete with the local moneylenders.[7] While the large banks in the central cities have prime interest rates of 6, 8, and 10 per cent, the local moneylender charges 15, 25, and even 50 per cent. The answer to this seeming paradox is that credit is

6. For the mixed record of industrial profits, see D. H. Buchanan, *The Development of Capitalist Enterprise in India* (New York: Kelley, 1966, reprinted).

7. The leading authority on this is Sir Malcolm Darling. See his *Punjabi Peasant in Prosperity and Debt*. The following table may also prove instructive:

	Commonest rates for —		
	Secured loans (per cent)	Unsecured loans (per cent)	Grain loans (per cent)
Punjab	6 to 12	12 to 24 (18 ¾ commonest)	25
United Provinces	9 to 12	24 to 37 ½	25 (50 in Oudh)
Bihar		18 ¾	50
Orissa	12 to 18 ¾	25	25
Bengal	8 to 12	9 to 18 for "respectable clients" 18 ¾ to 37 ½ (the latter common to agriculturalists)	
Central Provinces	6 to 12	15 for proprietors 24 for occupancy tenants 37 ½ for ryots with no right of transfer	25
Bombay	9 to 12	12 to 25 (18 commonest)	
Sind		36	
Madras	12	15 to 18 (in insecure tracts 24 not uncommon)	20 to 50

Source: Punjabi Peasant in Prosperity and Debt, 3rd ed. (Oxford University Press, 1932), p. 190.

granted only where the granter has (1) easy means of enforcing his contract or (2) personal knowledge of the character of the borrower. The middleman who tries to arbitrage between the rates of the moneylender and the central bank is apt to attract all the "lemons" and thereby make a loss.

This interpretation can be seen in Sir Malcolm Darling's interpretation of the village moneylender's power:

> It is only fair to remember that in the Indian village the money-lender is often the one thrifty person amongst a generally thriftless people; and that his methods of business, though demoralizing under modern conditions, suit the happy-go-lucky ways of the peasant. He is always accessible, even at night; dispenses with troublesome formalities, asks no inconvenient questions, advances promptly, and if interest is paid, does not press for repayment of principal. He keeps in close personal touch with his clients, and in many villages shares their occasions of weal or woe. *With his intimate knowledge of those around him he is able, without serious risk, to finance those who would otherwise get no loan at all.* [Italics added.] [8]

Or look at Barbara Ward's account:

> A small shopkeeper in a Hong Kong fishing village told me: "I give credit to anyone who anchors regularly in our bay; but if it is someone I don't know well, then I think twice about it unless I can find out all about him." [9]

Or, a profitable sideline of cotton ginning in Iran is the loaning of money for the next season, since the ginning companies often have a line of credit from Teheran banks at the market rate of interest. But in the first years of operation large losses are expected from unpaid debts — due to poor knowledge of the local scene.[1]

IV. Counteracting Institutions

Numerous institutions arise to counteract the effects of quality uncertainty. One obvious institution is guarantees. Most consumer durables carry guarantees to ensure the buyer of some normal expected quality. One natural result of our model is that the risk is borne by the seller rather than by the buyer.

A second example of an institution which counteracts the effects of quality uncertainty is the brand-name good. Brand names

8. Darling, *op. cit.*, p. 204.

9. B. Ward, "Cash or Credit Crops," *Economic Development and Cultural Change*, Vol. 8 (Jan. 1960), reprinted in *Peasant Society: A Reader*, ed. G. Foster *et al.* (Boston: Little Brown and Company, 1967). Quote on p. 142. In the same volume, see also G. W. Skinner, "Marketing and Social Structure in Rural China," and S. W. Mintz, "Pratik: Haitian Personal Economic Relations."

1. Personal conversation with mill manager, April 1968.

not only indicate quality but also give the consumer a means of retaliation if the quality does not meet expectations. For the consumer will then curtail future purchases. Often too, new products are associated with old brand names. This ensures the prospective consumer of the quality of the product.

Chains — such as hotel chains or restaurant chains — are similar to brand names. One observation consistent with our approach is the chain restaurant. These restaurants, at least in the United States, most often appear on interurban highways. The customers are seldom local. The reason is that these well-known chains offer a better hamburger than the *average* local restaurant; at the same time, the local customer, who knows his area, can usually choose a place he prefers.

Licensing practices also reduce quality uncertainty. For instance, there is the licensing of doctors, lawyers, and barbers. Most skilled labor carries some certification indicating the attainment of certain levels of proficiency. The high school diploma, the baccalaureate degree, the Ph.D., even the Nobel Prize, to some degree, serve this function of certification. And education and labor markets themselves have their own "brand names."

V. Conclusion

We have been discussing economic models in which "trust" is important. Informal unwritten guarantees are preconditions for trade and production. Where these guarantees are indefinite, business will suffer — as indicated by our generalized Gresham's law. This aspect of uncertainty has been explored by game theorists, as in the Prisoner's Dilemma, but usually it has not been incorporated in the more traditional Arrow-Debreu approach to uncertainty.[2] But the difficulty of distinguishing good quality from bad is inherent in the business world; this may indeed explain many economic institutions and may in fact be one of the more important aspects of uncertainty.

University of California, Berkeley
Indian Statistical Institute — Planning Unit, New Delhi

2. R. Radner, "Équilibre de Marchés à Terme et au Comptant en Cas d'Incertitude," in *Cahiers d'Econometrie*, Vol. 12 (Nov. 1967), Centre National de la Recherche Scientifique, Paris.

Comment

Consider finding social policy to mitigate the inefficiencies described in the paper. If the government puts all cars on the market, then equilibrium is efficient,[1] but not Pareto superior to the inefficient equilibrium with no trade, even if the government gives the price of a purchased automobile to each of the former owners. The problem is that some of the owners would rather have kept their cars than sold them at the price paid for an average used car. For the government to try to make everyone better off by redistributing, it would have to redistribute income in a lump sum fashion, giving more money to individuals who had owned better cars. But if the government has the information to do that, it is not clear why the market cannot use the same information in selling cars. Interestingly, Wilson (1980) finds that in some circumstances the government can make Pareto improvements.

Wilson uses a generalization of the Akerlof model, which permits both buyers and sellers to vary in their evaluation of the gain from owning a car. This means that the allocation of particular cars to particular owners has efficiency implications. (In Akerlof's model gains came from moving cars from their owners to any buyer.) Using the price mechanism buyers signal their willingness to buy by bidding on an average car (although the allocation will not be fully optimal since it would be better to have the better cars in the hands of people who are willing to pay more for higher quality). The suppliers have information on the particular value of the cars they own. Compulsory marketing of all cars would lose this information. Since supply responds to price, raising the price brings cars to the market from those people most willing to give up the cars they own. Wilson makes two observations about the equilibrium that may occur in this market. First, since the average quality of cars sold increases with price, the demand for cars might increase with price over some range. This might permit multiple equilibria. If so, the equilibrium with the highest price is Pareto superior to the equilibria with lower prices. In addition, raising the price above an equilibrium (and allocating buyers to sellers randomly) might increase everyone's expected utility if the rise in price is more important for sellers than is the fall (below one) in the probability of making a sale. The condition for this occurrence depends

[1]By efficient here is meant a maximum for the sum of utilities.

upon the relative slopes of demand and supply and the risk aversion of sellers. Paralleling the analysis in the previous exercise, one can also consider subsidizing automobile supply.

Akerlof notes the existence of many devices for avoiding market misallocations. There is another discussion of this point in Chapter 21.

Reference

C. Wilson, The nature of equilibrium in markets with adverse selection, *Bell J. Econ.* **11** (1980), 108–130.

16
Notes and exercises on the use of imperfect information[1]

In the last two chapters we considered difficulties in the market when there is no information on product quality differences. We now turn to the use made of partial information by the market, considering implications for both efficiency and income distribution. For this example, we assume that firms hire workers about whom they have partial information. We also assume that workers are paid the expected value of their output, with output depending on ability and the job in which the workers are placed. Often payment is made, at least partially, on actual output. There are a variety of reasons why payment will depend on expected output in a number of different settings.

A. The Basic Model

Suppose output Q, ability A, and job placement S, are related as follows:

$$Q(A, S) = a + bA - c(A - S)^2 \qquad b, c > 0 \tag{1}$$

Ability is a linear function of a person's characteristics denoted by a vector $X \in R^N$. That is,

$$A = \alpha' X \tag{2}$$

This specification implies that good job placement decisions are essential if maximum output is to be achieved. Characteristics may be partitioned into two groups, those which the employer can observe and use in his job placement decision and those which he may not. The partition $X = (x_1, x_2)$ conforms to this distinction, x_1 characteristics are observable, while x_2 characteristics are not. Partition $\alpha = (\alpha_1, \alpha_2)$ conformally. The distinction between observable and unobservable characteristics is not an immutable fact of life. We shall be concerned with the effect of taking a characteristic from one category and putting it into

[1]This model was developed by M. Rothschild and J. Stiglitz (1982).

another. We assume that the distribution of X in the population is normal with mean 0 and variance-covariance matrix Σ, which is also partitioned conformally.[2]

B. Job Placement

An employer who considers hiring a worker and observes his characteristics x_1 knows that his ability is the random variable

$$A(x_1) = \alpha'(X|x_1) = \alpha_1'x_1 + \alpha_2'(x_2|x_1) \tag{3}$$

If the employer is risk neutral he will try to choose $S(x_1)$ to maximize expected output. Our specification then implies

$$S(x_1) = EA(x_1) = \alpha_1'x_1 + \alpha_2'E(x_2|x_1) = \alpha_1'x_1 + \alpha_2'\Sigma_{21}\Sigma_{11}^{-1}x_1 \tag{4}$$

C. Expected Output and Wages

Expected output – and wages, if the economy is competitive – will be equal to

$$W(x_1) = a + bEA(x_1) - c\,\mathrm{Var}(A(x_1)) \tag{5}$$

This can be written

$$W(x_1) = a + bS(x_1) - c\,\mathrm{Var}(A(x_1)) \tag{6}$$

$\mathrm{Var}(A(x_1))$ is independent of the value of x_1; it is determined by the partition $X = (x_1, x_2)$ and the characteristics of Σ:

$$\mathrm{Var}A(x_1) = \alpha_2'(\Sigma_{22} - \Sigma_{21}\Sigma_{11}^{-1}\Sigma_{12})\alpha_2 \tag{7}$$

Thus wages $W(x_1)$ are entirely determined by job placement. In this model there is equal pay for equal work.

D. Exercise on Full Information

1 Calculate equilibrium wages if all characteristics are observable.
2 For x_1 and x_2 scalars, calculate the characteristics of workers who have higher wages when x_2 is not observable.
3 Show that average wages are lower if x_2 is not observable.
4 Show that a majority of workers have lower wages if x_2 is not observable.

[2]This is a convenient normalization. The coefficient a absorbs nonzero means.

E. Exercise on Differential Variances

Assume there are two groups in the population denoted by A and B. For each group output and ability are as described in Eqs. (1) and (2). However, while x is normally distributed with zero mean in each group, the variance-covariance matrix for B is $\lambda\Sigma$, while for A it is simply Σ, where $\lambda > 1$ is a known parameter.

If x_1 is observed it is efficient in each group to set

$$S(x_1) = E(A(X)|x_1)$$

For group A this is $\alpha_1' x_1 + \alpha_2' \Sigma_{21} \Sigma_{11}^{-1} x_1$. For group B it is the same since $\alpha_1' x_1 + \alpha_2' \lambda \Sigma_{21} (\lambda \Sigma_{11})^{-1} x_1 = \alpha_1' x_1 + \alpha_2' \Sigma_{21} \Sigma_{11}^{-1} x_1$. Thus individuals with the same characteristics hold the same jobs, independent of the group to which they belong.

1 Calculate expected output (as a function of x_1) for a member of A.
2 Calculate expected output (as a function of x_1) for a member of B. If wages equal expected output is there equal pay for equal work?
3 If employers were unable to distinguish between members of A and members of B (but continued to observe x_1), what would happen to job assignments, total output, wages of members of A, and wages of members of B?
4 What differences in assumptions are the basis for the different results in this section as opposed to Section D?

For an empirical study that examines the effects of restrictions on the use of information by insurance companies see Joskow (1973).

References

P. Joskow, Cartels, competition and regulation in the property-liability industry, *Bell J. Econ.* 4 (1973), 375–427.

M. Rothschild and J. Stiglitz, A model of employment outcomes illustrating the effect of the structure of information on the level and distribution of income, *Econ. Letters* **10** (1982), 231–236.

17

M. Rothschild and J. Stiglitz, Equilibrium in competitive insurance markets: An essay on the economics of imperfect information, *Quarterly Journal of Economics* **90** (1976), 629–650

The next two readings examine two devices that can occur in markets as attempts to distinguish between commodities (or individuals) that are not obviously (and costlessly) distinguishable. In this chapter we consider the situation where firms offer particular packages (rather than permitting all the purchases a consumer would like at a given price). In examining the choice made by individuals, firms may design their packages so that they attract particular individuals (e.g., those with low probability of collecting on the insurance policy). Such an approach uses the market to induce individuals to self-select, i.e., to distinguish themselves in the market. Two other examples of equilibrium with self-selection appear in the same symposium on the economics of information in the *Quarterly Journal of Economics* as this reading. In one, Akerlof (1976) examines an equilibrium where different firms select assembly lines which differ in the difficulty of work. In another paper, Salop and Salop (1976) examine the provision of different present and future wage packages, which lead workers with different probabilities of quitting to select different jobs. Also in the symposium Jaffee and Russell (1976) examine market response to the presence of honest and dishonest borrowers.

In a comment on this reading we describe the similar (and simultaneous) work of Wilson (1977).

References

G. Akerlof, The economics of caste and of the rat race and other woeful tales, *Quart. J. Econ.* **90** (1976), 599–618.

D. M. Jaffee and T. Russell, Imperfect information, uncertainty and credit rationing, *Quart. J. Econ.* **90** (1976), 651–666.

J. Salop and S. Salop, Self selection and turnover in the labor market, *Quart. J. Econ.* **90** (1976), 619–628.

C. Wilson, A model of insurance markets with incomplete information, *J. Econ. Theory* **16** (1977), 167–207.

EQUILIBRIUM IN COMPETITIVE INSURANCE MARKETS: AN ESSAY ON THE ECONOMICS OF IMPERFECT INFORMATION*

MICHAEL ROTHSCHILD AND JOSEPH STIGLITZ

INTRODUCTION

Economic theorists traditionally banish discussions of information to footnotes. Serious consideration of costs of communication, imperfect knowledge, and the like would, it is believed, complicate without informing. This paper, which analyzes competitive markets in which the characteristics of the commodities exchanged are not fully known to at least one of the parties to the transaction, suggests that this comforting myth is false. Some of the most important conclusions of economic theory are not robust to considerations of imperfect information.

We are able to show that not only may a competitive equilibrium not exist, but when equilibria do exist, they may have strange properties. In the insurance market, upon which we focus much of our discussion, sales offers, at least those that survive the competitive process, do not specify a price at which customers can buy all the insurance they want, but instead consist of both a price and a quantity—a particular amount of insurance that the individual can buy at that price. Furthermore, if individuals were willing or able to reveal their information, everybody could be made better off. By their very being, high-risk individuals cause an externality: the low-risk individuals are worse off than they would be in the absence of the high-risk individuals. However, the high-risk individuals are no better off than they would be in the absence of the low-risk individuals.

These points are made in the next section by analysis of a simple model of a competitive insurance market. We believe that the lessons gleaned from our highly stylized model are of general interest, and attempt to establish this by showing in Section II that our model is robust and by hinting (space constraints prevent more) in the conclusion that our analysis applies to many other situations.

* This work was supported by National Science Foundation Grants SOC 74-22182 at the Institute for Mathematical Studies in the Social Sciences, Stanford University and SOC 73-05510 at Princeton University. The authors are indebted to Steve Salop, Frank Hahn, and Charles Wilson for helpful comments, and to the participants in the seminars at the several universities at which these ideas were presented.

Quarterly Journal of Economics **90**, 629–650. Copyright © 1976 by John Wiley & Sons, Inc. Reprinted by permission of John Wiley & Sons, Inc.

I. The Basic Model

Most of our argument can be made by analysis of a very simple example. Consider an individual who will have an income of size W if he is lucky enough to avoid accident. In the event an accident occurs, his income will be only $W - d$. The individual can insure himself against this accident by paying to an insurance company a premium α_1, in return for which he will be paid $\hat{\alpha}_2$ if an accident occurs. Without insurance his income in the two states, "accident," "no accident," was $(W, W - d)$; with insurance it is now $(W - \alpha_1, W - d + \alpha_2)$, where $\alpha_2 = \hat{\alpha}_2 - \alpha_1$. The vector $\alpha = (\alpha_1, \alpha_2)$ completely describes the insurance contract.[1]

I.1 Demand for Insurance Contracts

On an insurance market, insurance contracts (the α's) are traded. To describe how the market works, it is necessary to describe the supply and demand functions of the participants in the market. There are only two kinds of participants, individuals who buy insurance and companies that sell it. Determining individual demand for insurance contracts is straightforward. An individual purchases an insurance contract so as to alter his pattern of income across states of nature. Let W_1 denote his income if there is no accident and W_2 his income if an accident occurs; the expected utility theorem states that under relatively mild assumptions his preferences for income in these two states of nature are described by a function of the form,

$$(1) \qquad \hat{V}(p, W_1, W_2) = (1 - p)U(W_1) + pU(W_2),$$

where $U(\ )$ represents the utility of money income[2] and p the probability of an accident. Individual demands may be derived from (1). A contract α is worth $V(p, \alpha) = \hat{V}(p, W - \alpha_1, W - d + \alpha_2)$. From

1. Actual insurance contracts are more complicated because a single contract will offer coverage against many potential losses. A formal generalization of the scheme above to cover this case is straightforward. Suppose that an individual will, in the absence of insurance, have an income of W_i if state i occurs. An insurance contract is simply an n-tuple $(\alpha_1, \ldots, \alpha_n)$ whose i-th coordinate describes the net payment of the individual to the insurance company if state i occurs. We confine our discussion to the simple case mentioned in the text, although it could be trivially extended to this more complicated case.

Many insurance contracts are not as complicated as the n-tuples described above—Blue Cross schedules listing maximum payments for specific illnesses and operations are an isolated example—but are instead resolvable into a fixed premium and a payment schedule that is in general a simple function of the size of the loss such as $F(L) = \text{Max}\,[0, c(L\text{-}D)]$, where $c \times 100\%$ is the co-insurance rate and D is the deductible. With such a contract when a loss occurs, determining its size is often a serious problem. In other words, finding out exactly what state of the world has occurred is not always easy. We ignore these problems. A large literature analyzes optimal insurance contracts. See, for example, Arrow (1971) and Borch (1968).

2. We assume that preferences are not state-dependent.

all the contracts the individual is offered, he chooses the one that maximizes $V(p, \alpha)$. Since he always has the option of buying no insurance, an individual will purchase a contract α only if $V(p, \alpha) \geq V(p, 0) = \hat{V}(p, W, W - d)$. We assume that persons are identical in all respects save their probability of having an accident and that they are risk-averse ($U'' < 0$); thus $V(p, \alpha)$ is quasi-concave.

I.2 Supply of Insurance Contracts

It is less straightforward to describe how insurance companies decide which contracts they should offer for sale and to which people. The return from an insurance contract is a random variable. We assume that companies are risk-neutral, that they are concerned only with expected profits, so that contract α when sold to an individual who has a probability of incurring an accident of p, is worth

$$\pi(p, \alpha) = (1 - p)\alpha_1 - p\alpha_2 = \alpha_1 - p(\alpha_1 + \alpha_2). \tag{2}$$

Even if firms are not expected profit maximizers, on a well-organized competitive market they are likely to behave as if they maximized (2).[3]

Insurance companies have financial resources such that they are willing and able to sell any number of contracts that they think will make an expected profit.[4] The market is competitive in that there is free entry. Together these assumptions guarantee that any contract that is demanded and that is expected to be profitable will be supplied.

3. Since the theory of the firm behavior under uncertainty is one of the more unsettled areas of economic theory, we cannot look to it for the sort of support of any assumption we might make, which the large body of literature devoted to the expected utility theorem provides for equation (1) above. Nonetheless, two arguments (and the absence of a remotely as attractive distinguishable alternative) justify (2): the first is the rather vaguely supported but widely held proposition that companies owned by stockholders who themselves hold diversified portfolios ought to maximize their expected profits; management that does not follow this policy will be displaced. The second supposes that insurance companies are held by a large number of small shareholders each of whom receives a small share of the firm's profits. If the risks insured against are independent or otherwise diversifiable, then the law of large numbers guarantees that each shareholder's return will be approximately constant and any individual insurance contract contributes to his profits only through its expected value. In this case stockholders' interests will be well served if, and only if, management maximizes expected profits.

A variant of the second argument is obtained by considering the case in which shareholders and policyholders are the same people, or in more familiar terms, when the insurance company is a mutual company. In this case the insurance company is just a mechanism for risk pooling. Under conditions where diversification is possible, each contract's contribution to the company's dividend (or loss) is proportional to its expected value.

4. The same kinds of arguments used to justify (2)—in particular the appeal to the law of large numbers—can be used to justify this assumption. Weaker conditions than independence will suffice. See Revesz (1960), p. 190, for a theorem that states roughly that, if insurance contracts can be arranged in space so that even though con-

I.3 Information about Accident Probabilities

We have not so far discussed how customers and companies come to know or estimate the parameter p, which plays such a crucial role in the valuation formulae (1) and (2). We make the bald assumption that individuals know their accident probabilities, while companies do not. Since insurance purchasers are identical in all respects save their propensity to have accidents, the force of this assumption is that companies cannot discriminate among their potential customers on the basis of their characteristics. This assumption is defended and modified in subsection II.1.

A firm may use its customers' market behavior to make inferences about their accident probabilities. Other things equal, those with high accident probabilities will demand more insurance than those who are less accident-prone. Although possibly accurate, this is not a profitable way of finding out about customer characteristics. Insurance companies want to know their customers' characteristics in order to decide on what terms they should offer to let them buy insurance. Information that accrues after purchase may be used only to lock the barn after the horse has been stolen.

It is often possible to force customers to make market choices in such a way that they both reveal their characteristics and make the choices the firm would have wanted them to make had their characteristics been publicly known. In their contribution to this symposium, Salop and Salop call a market device with these characteristics a *self-selection mechanism.* Analysis of the functioning of self-selection mechanisms on competitive markets is a major focus of this paper.

I.4 Definition of Equilibrium

We assume that customers can buy only one insurance contract. This is an objectionable assumption. It implies, in effect, that the seller of insurance specifies both the prices and quantities of insurance purchased. In most competitive markets, sellers determine only price and have no control over the amount their customers buy. Nonetheless, we believe that what we call price and quantity competition is more appropriate for our model of the insurance market than tradi-

tracts that are close to one another are not independent, those that are far apart are approximately independent, then the average return from all contracts is equal to its expected value with probability one. Thus, an insurance company that holds a large number of health policies should be risk-neutral, even though the fact that propinquity carries illness implies that not all insured risks are independent. Some risks that cannot be diversified; i.e., the risk of nuclear war (or of a flood or a plague) cannot be spread by appeal to the law of large numbers. Our model applies to diversifiable risks. This class of risks is considerably larger than the independent ones.

tional price competition. We defend this proposition at length in subsection II.2 below.

Equilibrium in a competitive insurance market is a set of contracts such that, when customers choose contracts to maximize expected utility, (i) no contract in the equilibrium set makes negative expected profits; and (ii) there is no contract outside the equilibrium set that, if offered, will make a nonnegative profit. This notion of equilibrium is of the Cournot-Nash type; each firm assumes that the contracts its competitors offer are independent of its own actions.

I.5 Equilibrium with Identical Customers

Only when customers have different accident probabilities, will insurance companies have imperfect information. We examine this case below. To illustrate our, mainly graphical, procedure, we first analyze the equilibrium of a competitive insurance market with identical customers.[5]

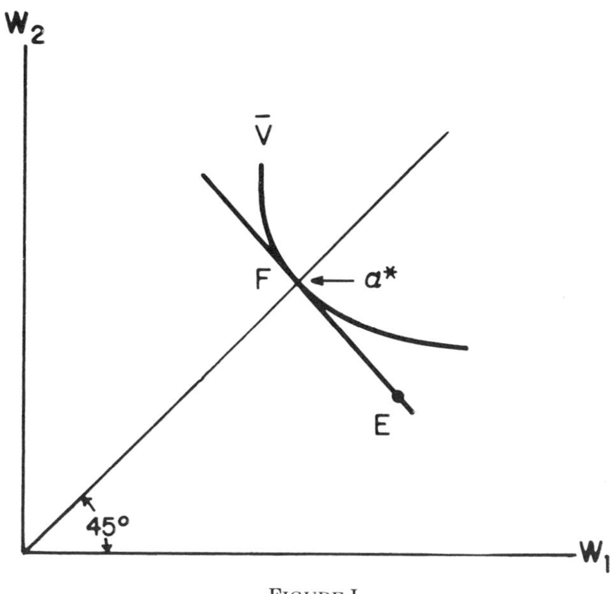

FIGURE I

In Figure I the horizontal and vertical axes represent income in

5. The analysis is identical if individuals have different p's, but companies know the accident probabilities of their customers. The market splits into several submarkets—one for each different p represented. Each submarket has the equilibrium described here.

the states: no accident, accident, respectively. The point E with coordinates $(\hat{W}_1, \hat{W}_2)$ is the typical customer's uninsured state. Indifference curves are level sets of the function of equation (1). Purchasing the insurance policy $\alpha = (\alpha_1, \alpha_2)$ moves the individual from E to the point $(\hat{W}_1 - \alpha_1, \hat{W}_2 + \alpha_2)$.

Free entry and perfect competition will ensure that policies bought in competitive equilibrium make zero expected profits, so that if α is purchased,

$$\alpha_1(1 - p) - \alpha_2 p = 0. \tag{3}$$

The set of all policies that break even is given analytically by (3) and diagrammatically by the line EF in Figure I, which is sometimes referred to as the fair-odds line. The equilibrium policy α^*maximizes the individual's (expected) utility and just breaks even. Purchasing α^* locates the customer at the tangency of the indifference curve with the fair-odds line. α^* satisfies the two conditions of equilibrium: (i) it breaks even; (ii) selling any contract preferred to it will bring insurance companies expected losses.

Since customers are risk-averse, the point α^* is located at the intersection of the 45°-line (representing equal income in both states of nature) and the fair-odds line. In equilibrium each customer buys complete insurance at actuarial odds. To see this, observe that the slope of the fair-odds line is equal to the ratio of the probability of not having an accident to the probability of having an accident ($(1 - p)/p$), while the slope of the indifference curve (the marginal rate of substitution between income in the state no accident to income in the state accident) is $[U'(W_1)\,(1 - p)]/[U'(W_2)p]$, which, when income in the two states is equal, is $(1 - p)/p$, independent of U.

I.6 Imperfect Information: Equilibrium with Two Classes of Customers

Suppose that the market consists of two kinds of customers: low-risk individuals with accident probability p^L, and high-risk individuals with accident probability $p^H > p^L$. The fraction of high-risk customers is λ, so the average accident probability is $\bar{p} = \lambda p^H + (1 - \lambda)p^L$. This market can have only two kinds of equilibria: *pooling equilibria* in which both groups buy the same contract, and *separating equilibria* in which different types purchase different contracts.

A simple argument establishes that *there cannot be a pooling equilibrium.* The point E in Figure II is again the initial endowment of all customers. Suppose that α is a pooling equilibrium and consider $\pi(\bar{p}, \alpha)$. If $\pi(\bar{p}, \alpha) < 0$, then firms offering α lose money, contradicting

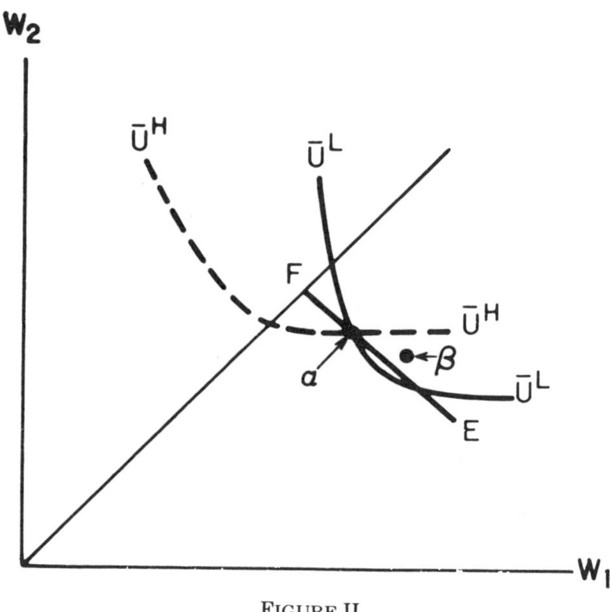

FIGURE II

the definition of equilibrium. If $\pi(\bar{p}, \alpha) > 0$, then there is a contract that offers slightly more consumption in each state of nature, which still will make a profit when all individuals buy it. All will prefer this contract to α, so α cannot be an equilibrium. Thus, $\pi(\bar{p}, \alpha) = 0$, and α lies on the market odds line EF (with slope $(1 - \bar{p})/\bar{p}$).

It follows from (1) that at α the slope of the high-risk indifference curve through α, $\bar{U}^H$, is $(p^L/1 - p^L)\,(1 - p^H/p^H)$ times the slope of $\bar{U}^L$, the low-risk indifference curve through α. In this figure $\bar{U}^H$ is a broken line, and $\bar{U}^L$ a solid line. The curves intersect at α; thus there is a contract, β in Figure II, near α, which low-risk types prefer to α. The high risk prefer α to β. Since β is near α, it makes a profit when the less risky buy it, ($\pi(p^L, \beta) \simeq \pi(p^L, \alpha) > \pi(\bar{p}, \alpha) = 0$). The existence of β contradicts the second part of the definition of equilibrium; α cannot be an equilibrium.

If there is an equilibrium, each type must purchase a separate contract. Arguments, which are, we hope, by now familiar, demonstrate that each contract in the equilibrium set makes zero profits. In Figure III the low-risk contract lies on line EL (with slope $(1 - p^L)/p^L$), and the high-risk contract on line EH (with slope $(1 - p^H)/p^H$). As was shown in the previous subsection, the contract on EH most preferred by high-risk customers gives complete insurance.

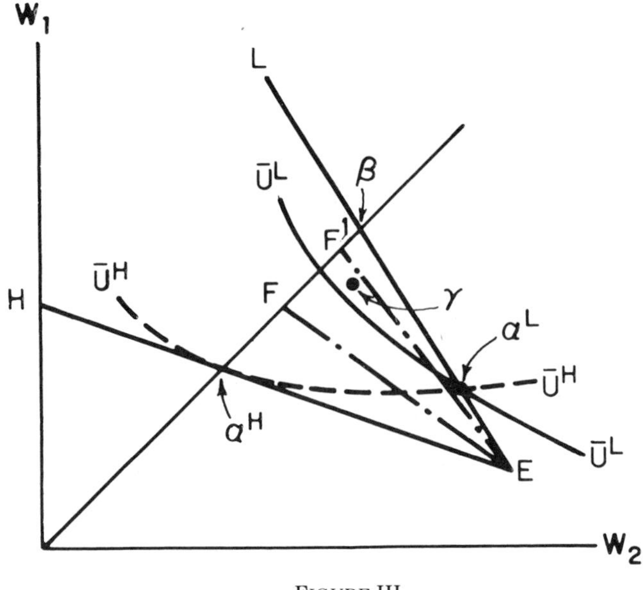

FIGURE III

This is α^H in Figure III; it must be part of any equilibrium. Low-risk customers would, of all contracts on EL, most prefer contract β which, like α^H, provides complete insurance. However, β offers more consumption in each state than α^H, and high-risk types will prefer it to α^H. If β and α^H are marketed, both high- and low-risk types will purchase β. The nature of imperfect information in this model is that insurance companies are unable to distinguish among their customers. All who demand β must be sold β. Profits will be negative; (α^H, β) is not an equilibrium set of contracts.

An equilibrium contract for low-risk types must not be more attractive to high-risk types than α^H; it must lie on the southeast side of U^H, the high-risk indifference curve through α^H. We leave it to the reader to demonstrate that of all such contracts, the one that low-risk types most prefer is α^L, the contract at the intersection of EL and U^H in Figure III. This establishes that *the set* $(\alpha^{\mathrm{H}}, \alpha^{\mathrm{L}})$ *is the only possible equilibrium for a market with low- and high-risk customers.*[6] However, $(\alpha^{\mathrm{H}}, \alpha^{\mathrm{L}})$ may not be an equilibrium. Consider the contract γ in Figure III. It lies above U^L, the low-risk indifference curve through α^L and also above U^H. If γ is offered, both low- and high-risk types

6. This largely heuristic argument can be made completely rigorous. See Wilson (1976).

will purchase it in preference to either α^H *or* α^L. If it makes a profit when both groups buy it, γ will upset the potential equilibrium of (α^H, α^L). γ's profitability depends on the composition of the market. If there are sufficiently many high-risk people that *EF* represents market odds, then γ will lose money. If market odds are given by *EF′* (as they will be if there are relatively few high-risk insurance customers), then γ will make a profit. Since (α^H, α^L) is the only possible equilibrium, in this case the competitive insurance market will have no equilibrium.

This establishes that *a competitive insurance market may have no equilibrium.*

We have not found a simple intuitive explanation for this nonexistence; but the following observations, prompted by Frank Hahn's note (1974), may be suggestive. The information that is revealed by an individual's choice of an insurance contract depends on all the other insurance policies offered; there is thus a fundamental informational externality that each company, when deciding on which contract it will offer, fails to take into account. Given any set of contracts that breaks even, a firm may enter the market using the informational structure implicit in the availability of that set of contracts to make a profit; at the same time it forces the original contracts to make a loss. But as in any Nash equilibrium, the firm fails to take account of the consequences of its actions, and in particular, the fact that when those policies are no longer offered, the informational structure will have changed and it can no longer make a profit.

We can characterize the conditions under which an equilibrium does not exist. An equilibrium will not exist if the costs to the low-risk individual of pooling are low (because there are relatively few of the high-risk individuals who have to be subsidized, or because the subsidy per individual is low, i.e., when the probabilities of the two groups are not too different), or if their costs of separating are high. The costs of separating arise from the individual's inability to obtain complete insurance. Thus, the costs of separating are related to the individuals' attitudes toward risk. Certain polar cases make these propositions clear. If $p^L = 0$, it never pays the low-risk individuals to pool, and by continuity, for sufficiently small p^L it does not pay to pool. Similarly, if individuals are risk-neutral, it never pays to pool; if they are infinitely risk averse with utility functions

$$\bar{V}(p, W_1, W_2) = \text{Min}\,(W_1, W_2), \tag{1'}$$

it always pays to pool.

I.7 Welfare Economics of Equilibrium

One of the interesting properties of the equilibrium is that the presence of the high-risk individuals exerts a negative externality on the low-risk individuals. The externality is completely dissipative; there are losses to the low-risk individuals, but the high-risk individuals are no better off than they would be in isolation.

If only the high-risk individuals would admit to their having high accident probabilities, all individuals would be made better off without anyone being worse off.

The separating equilibrium we have described may not be Pareto optimal even relative to the information that is available. As we show in subsection II.3 below, there may exist a pair of policies that break even together and that make both groups better off.

II. ROBUSTNESS

The analysis of Section I had three principal conclusions: First, competition on markets with imperfect information is more complex than in standard models. Perfect competitors may limit the quantities their customers can buy, not from any desire to exploit monopoly power, but simply in order to improve their information. Second, equilibrium may not exist. Finally, competitive equilibria are not Pareto optimal. It is natural to ask whether these conclusions (particularly the first, which was an assumption rather than a result of the analysis) can be laid to the special and possibly strained assumptions of our model. We think not. Our conclusions (or ones very like) must follow from a serious attempt to comprehend the workings of competition with imperfect and asymmetric information. We have analyzed the effect of changing our model in many ways. The results were always essentially the same.

Our attempts to establish robustness took two tacks. First, we showed that our results did not depend on the simple technical specifications of the model. This was tedious, and we have excised most of the details from the present version. The reader interested in analysis of the effects (distinctly minor) of changing our assumptions that individuals are alike in all respects save their accident probabilities, that there are only two kinds of customers, and that the insurance market lasts but a single period, is referred to earlier versions of this paper.[7] An assessment of the importance of the as-

7. See Rothschild and Stiglitz (1975). One curious result of these investigations should be mentioned. In other areas of economic theory where existence of equilibrium has been a problem, smoothing things by introducing a continuum of individuals of

sumption that individuals know their accident probabilities, while insurance companies do not (which raises more interesting issues), is given in subsection II.1 below.

Another approach to the question of robustness is the subject of the next three subsections. In them we question the behavioral assumptions and the equilibrium concepts used in Section I.

II.1 Information Assumptions

Suppose that there are two groups of customers and that not all individuals within each group have the same accident probability. The average accident probability of one group is greater than that of the other; individuals within each group know the mean accident probability for members of their group, but do not know their own accident probabilities. As before, the insurance company cannot tell directly the accident probability of any particular individual, or even the group to which he belongs. For example, suppose that some persons occasionally drink too much, while the others almost never drink. Insurance firms cannot discover who drinks and who does not. Individuals know that drinking affects accident probabilities, but it affects different people differently. Each individual does not know how it will affect him.

In such a situation the expected utility theorem states that individuals make (and behave according to) estimates of their accident probabilities; if these estimates are unbiased in the sense that the average accident probability of those who estimate their accident probability to be p actually is p, then the analysis goes through as before.

Unbiasedness seems a reasonable assumption (what is a more attractive alternative?). However, not even this low level of correctness of beliefs is required for our conclusions. Suppose, for example, that individuals differ both with respect to their accident probabilities and to their risk aversion, but they all assume that their own accident probabilities are $\bar{p}$. If low-risk individuals are less risk-averse on average, then there will not exist a pooling equilibrium; there may exist no equilibrium at all; and if there does exist an equilibrium, it will entail partial insurance for both groups. Figure IV shows that there

different types can insure existence. Not so here. If there is a continuous distribution of accident probabilities (but customers are otherwise identical), then equilibrium never exists. There is an intuitive explanation for this striking result. We argued above that, if accident probabilities were close together, then equilibrium would not exist. When there is a continuum of probabilities, there always are individuals with close probabilities with whom it pays to "pool." For a proof of this result, which is not elementary, see Riley (1976).

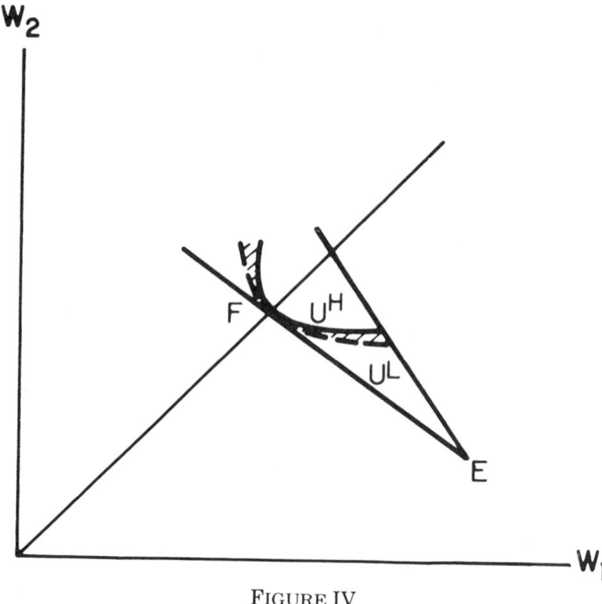

FIGURE IV

will not exist a pooling equilibrium. If there were a pooling equilibrium, it would clearly be with complete insurance at the market odds, since both groups' indifference curves have the slope of the market odds line there. If the low-risk individuals are less risk-averse, then the two indifference curves are tangent at F, but elsewhere the high-risk individuals' indifference curve lies above the low-risk individuals' indifference curve. Thus, any policy in the shaded area between the two curves will be purchased by the low-risk individuals in preference to the pooling contract at F.

Other such cases can be analyzed, but we trust that the general principle is clear. Our pathological conclusions do not require that people have particularly good information about their accident probabilities. They will occur under a wide variety of circumstances, including the appealing case of unbiasedness. Neither insurance firms nor their customers have to be perfectly informed about the differences in risk properties that exist among individuals: What is required is that individuals with different risk properties differ in some characteristic that can be linked with the purchase of insurance and that, somehow, insurance firms discover this link.

II.2 Price Competition Versus Quantity Competition

One can imagine our model of the insurance market operating in two distinct modes. The first, price competition, is familiar to all students of competitive markets. Associated with any insurance contract α is a number $q(\alpha) = \alpha_1/\alpha_2$, which, since it is the cost per unit coverage, is called the price of insurance. Under price competition, insurance firms establish a price of insurance and allow their customers to buy as much or as little insurance as they want at that price. Thus, if contract α is available from a company, so are the contracts 2α and $(1/2)\alpha$; the former pays twice as much benefits (and costs twice as much in premiums) as α; the latter is half as expensive and provides half as much coverage.

Opposed to price competition is what we call price and quantity competition. In this regime companies may offer a number of different contracts, say $\alpha^1, \alpha^2, \ldots, \alpha^n$. Individuals may buy at most one contract. They are not allowed to buy arbitrary multiples of contracts offered, but must instead settle for one of the contracts explicitly put up for sale. A particular contract specifies both a price and a quantity of insurance. Under price and quantity competition it is conceivable that insurance contracts with different prices of insurance will exist in equilibrium; people who want more insurance may be willing to pay a higher price for it (accept less favorable odds) than those who make do with shallower coverage. Under price competition customers will buy insurance only at the lowest price quoted in the market.

The argument of Section I depends heavily on our assumption that price and quantity competition, and not simply price competition, characterizes the competitive insurance market. This assumption is defended here. The argument is basically quite simple. Price competition is a special case of price and quantity competition. Nothing in the definition of price and quantity competition prevents firms from offering for sale a set of contracts with the same price of insurance. Since the argument above characterized all equilibria under price and quantity competition, it also characterized all equilibria when some firms set prices and others set prices and quantities. Thus, it must be that price competition cannot compete with price and quantity competition.[8]

This argument hinges on one crucial assumption: regardless of the form of competition, customers purchase but a single insurance contract or equivalently that the total amount of insurance purchased

8. We leave to the reader a detailed proof. A sketch follows. Suppose that there are two groups in the population. If the price of insurance is q, high- and low-risk customers will buy $\alpha^H(q)$ and $\alpha^L(q)$, respectively. It is easy to figure out what total insurance company profits, $P(q)$, are. The equilibrium price q^* is the smallest q such that $P(q) = 0$. Since $P(q)$ is continuous in q and it is easy to find q such that $P(q) > 0$ and $P(q) < 0$, such a q^* exists. To show that price competition will not survive, it is only necessary to show that $(\alpha^H(q^*), \alpha^L(q^*))$ is not an equilibrium set of contracts as defined in subsection I.4 above.

by any one customer is known to all companies that sell to him. We think that this is an accurate description of procedures on at least some insurance markets. Many insurance policies specify either that they are not in force if there is another policy or that they insure against only the first, say, $1,000 of losses suffered. That is, instead of being a simple bet for or against the occurrence of a particular event, an insurance policy is a commitment on the part of the company to restore at least partially the losses brought about by the occurrence of that event. The person who buys two $1,000 accident insurance policies does not have $2,000 worth of protection. If an accident occurs, all he gets from his second policy is the privilege of watching his companies squabble over the division of the $1,000 payment. There is no point in buying more than one policy.

Why should insurance markets operate in this way? One simple and obvious explanation is moral hazard. Because the insured can often bring about, or at least make more likely, the event being insured against, insurance companies want to limit the amount of insurance their customers buy. Companies want to see that their customers do not purchase so much insurance that they have an interest in an accident occurring. Thus, companies will want to monitor the purchases of their customers. Issuing contracts of the sort described above is the obvious way to do so.

A subtler explanation for this practice is provided by our argument that price and quantity competition can dominate price competition. If the market is in equilibrium under price competition, a firm can offer a contract, specifying price and quantity, that will attract the low-risk customers away from the companies offering contracts specifying price alone. Left with only high-risk customers, these firms will lose money. This competitive gambit will successfully upset the price competition equilibria if the entering firm can be assured that those who buy its contracts hold no other insurance. Offering insurance that pays off only for losses not otherwise insured is a way to guarantee this.

It is sometimes suggested that the term "competitive" can be applied only to markets where there is a single price of a commodity and each firm is a price taker. This seems an unnecessarily restrictive use of the term competitive. The basic idea underlying competitive markets involves free entry and noncollusive behavior among the participants in the market. In some economic environments price taking without quantity restrictions is a natural result of such markets. In the situations described in this paper, this is not so.

II.3 Restrictions on Firm Behavior and Optimal Subsidies

An important simplification of the analysis of Section I was the assumption that each insurance company issued but a single contract. We once thought this constraint would not affect the nature of equilibrium. We argued that in equilibrium firms must make nonnegative profits. Suppose that a firm offers two contracts, one of which makes an expected profit of say, $\$S$, per contract sold, the other an expected loss of $\$L$ per contract. The firm can make nonnegative expected profits if the ratio of the profitable to the unprofitable contracts sold is at least μ, where $\mu = L/S$. However, the firm can clearly make more profits if it sells only the contracts on which it makes a profit. It and its competitors have no reason to offer the losing contracts, and in competitive equilibrium, they will not be offered. Since only contracts that make nonnegative profits will be offered, it does not matter, given our assumptions about entry, that firms are assumed to issue only a single contract. If there is a contract that could make a profit, a firm will offer it.

This argument is not correct. The possibility of offering more than one contract is important to firms, and to the nature and existence of equilibrium. Firms that offer several contracts are not dependent on the policies offered by other firms for the information generated by the choices of individuals. By offering a menu of policies, insurance firms may be able to obtain information about the accident probabilities of particular individuals. Furthermore, although there may not be an equilibrium in which the profits from one contract subsidize the losses of another contract, it does not follow that such a pair of contracts cannot break what would otherwise be an equilibrium.

Such a case is illustrated in Figure V. *EF* is again the market odds line. A separating equilibrium exists $(\bar{\alpha}^H, \bar{\alpha}^L)$. Suppose that a firm offered the two contracts, $\alpha^{H\prime}$ and $\alpha^{L\prime}$; $\alpha^{H\prime}$ makes a loss, $\alpha^{L\prime}$ makes a profit. High-risk types prefer $\alpha^{H\prime}$ to $\bar{\alpha}^H$, and low-risk types prefer $\alpha^{L\prime}$ to $\bar{\alpha}^L$. These two contracts, if offered by a single firm together, do not make losses. The profits from $\alpha^{L\prime}$ subsidize the losses of $\alpha^{H\prime}$. Thus, $(\alpha^{H\prime}, \alpha^{L\prime})$ upsets the equilibrium $(\bar{\alpha}^H, \bar{\alpha}^L)$.

This example points up another possible inefficiency of separating equilibria. Consider the problem of choosing two contracts (α^H, α^L) such that α^L maximizes the utility of the low-risk individual subject to the constraints that (a) the high-risk individual prefers α^H to α^L and (b) the pair of contracts α^H and α^L break even when bought by high- and low-risk types, respectively, in the ratio λ to $(1 - \lambda)$. This

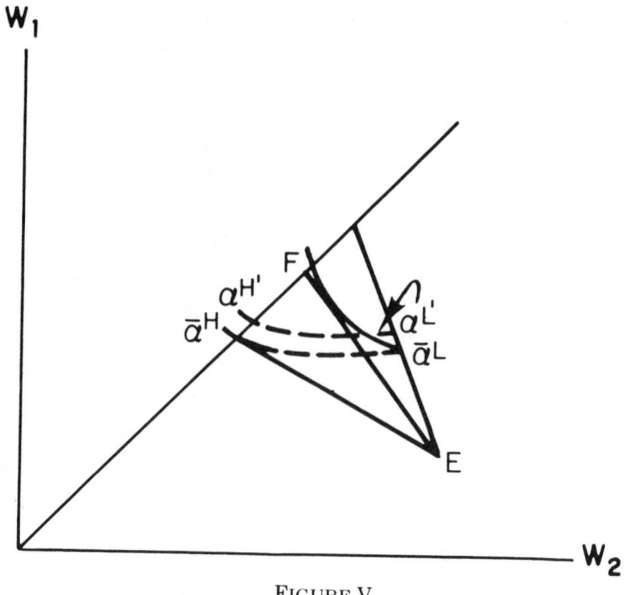

FIGURE V

is a kind of optimal subsidy problem. If the separating equilibrium, when it exists, does not solve this problem, it is inefficient. Figure V shows that the separating equilibrium can be inefficient in this sense. We now show that if there are enough high-risk people, then the separating equilibrium can be efficient.

The optimal subsidy problem always has a solution $(\alpha^{H*}, \alpha^{L*})$. The optimal high-risk contract α^{H*} will always entail complete insurance so that $V(p^H, \alpha^{H*}) = U(W - p^H d + a)$, where a is the per capita subsidy of the high risk by the low risk. This subsidy decreases income for each low-risk person by γa (where $\gamma = \lambda/(1 - \lambda)$) in each state. Net of this charge α^{L*} breaks even when low-risk individuals buy it. Thus, $\alpha^{L*} = (\alpha_1 + \gamma a, \alpha_2 - \gamma a)$, where $\alpha_1 = \alpha_2 p^L/(1 - p^L)$.

To find the optimal contract, one solves the following problem: Choose a and α_2 to maximize

$$U(X)\,(1 - p^L) + U(Z)p^L,$$

subject to

$$U(Y) \geq U(X)\,(1 - p^H) + U(Z)p^H$$

$$a \geq 0,$$

where

$$X = W_0 - \gamma a - \alpha_2 p^L/(1 - p^L),$$
$$Y = W_0 - p^H d + a,$$

and

$$Z = W_0 - d - \gamma a + \alpha_2.$$

The solution to this problem can be analyzed by standard Kuhn-Tucker techniques. If the constraint $a \geq 0$ is binding at the optimum, then the solution involves no subsidy to the high-risk persons; (α^{H*}, α^{L*}) is the separating equilibrium. It is straightforward but tedious to show that a sufficient condition for this is that

$$\frac{(p^H - p^L)\,\gamma}{p^L(1 - p)^L)} > \frac{U'(Y)[U'(Z) - U'(X)]}{U'(X)U'(Z)} \tag{4}$$

where X, Y, and Z are determined by the optimal a^*, α_2^*. The right-hand side of (4) is always less than

$$\frac{U'(W_0 - d)[U'(W_0 - d) - U'(W_0)]}{U'(W_0)^2}$$

so that there exist values of γ (and thus of λ) large enough to satisfy (4).

II.4 Alternative Equilibrium Concepts

There are a number of other concepts of equilibrium that we might have employed. These concepts differ with respect to assumptions concerning the behavior of the firms in the market. In our model the firm assumes that its actions do not affect the market—the set of policies offered by other firms was independent of its own offering.

In this subsection we consider several other equilibrium concepts, implying either less or more rationality in the market. We could, for instance, call any set of policies that just break even given the set of individuals who purchase them an *informationally consistent equilibrium*. This assumes that the forces for the creation of new contracts are relatively weak (in the absence of profits). Thus, in Figure III, α^H and any contract along the line EL below α^L is a set of informationally consistent separating equilibrium contracts; any single contract along the line EF is an informationally consistent pooling equilibrium contract. This is the notion of equilibrium that Spence (1973) has employed in most of his work. The longer the lags in the system, the greater the difficulty of competing by offering different contracts, the more stable is an informationally consistent equilibrium. Thus, while this seems to us a reasonable equilibrium concept for the models of educational signaling on which Spence focused, it is less compelling when applied to insurance or credit markets (see Jaffee and Russell's contribution to this symposium).

A *local* equilibrium is a set of contracts such that there do not exist any contracts in the vicinity of the equilibrium contracts that will be chosen and make a positive profit. If we rule out the subsidies of the last subsection, then the set of separating contracts, which maximizes the welfare of low-risk individuals, is a local equilibrium.

The notion that firms experiment with contracts similar to those already on the market motivates the idea of a local equilibrium. Even if firms have little knowledge about the shape of utility functions, and about the proportions of population in different accident probabilities, one would expect that competition would lead to small perturbations around the equilibrium. A stable equilibrium requires that such perturbations not lead to firms making large profits, as would be the case with some perturbations around a pooling point.

These two concepts of equilibrium imply that firms act less rationally than we assumed they did in Section I. It is possible that firms exhibit a greater degree of rationality; that is, firms ought not to take the set of contracts offered by other firms as given, but ought to assume that other firms will act as they do, or at least will respond in some way to the new contract offered by the firm. Hence, in those cases where in our definition there was no equilibrium, because for any set of contracts there is a contract that will break even and be chosen by a subset of the population, given that the contracts offered by the other firms remain unchanged, those contracts that break the equilibrium may not break even if the other firms also change their contracts. The peculiar provision of many insurance contracts, that the effective premium is not determined until the *end* of the period (when the individual obtains what is called a dividend), is perhaps a reflection of the uncertainty associated with who will purchase the policy, which in turn is associated with the uncertainty about what contracts other insurance firms will offer.

Wilson (1976) introduced and analyzed one such nonmyopic equilibrium concept. A Wilson equilibrium is a set of contracts such that, when customers choose among them so as to maximize profits, (a) all contracts make nonnegative profits and (b) there does not exist a new contract (or set of contracts), which, if offered, makes positive profits even when all contracts that lose money as a result of this entry are withdrawn. In the simple model of Section I, such equilibria always exist. Comparing this definition with the one of subsection I.4 above makes it clear that, when it exists, our separating equilibrium is also a Wilson equilibrium. When this does not exist, the Wilson equilibrium is the pooling contract that maximizes the utility of the low-risk customers. This is β in Figure VI. β dominates the separating pair (α^L, α^H). Consider a contract like γ, which the low risk prefer to β. Under our definition of equilibrium it upsets β. Under Wilson's it does not. When the low risk desert β for γ, it loses money and is withdrawn. Then the high risk also buy γ. When both groups buy γ, it loses money. Thus, γ does not successfully compete against β.

Although this equilibrium concept is appealing, it is not without its difficulties. It seems a peculiar halfway house; firms respond to competitive entry by dropping policies, but not by adding new policies. Furthermore, although counterexamples are very complicated to construct, it appears that a Wilson equilibrium may not exist if groups differ in their attitudes towards risk. Finally, in the absence of collusion or regulation, in a competitive insurance market, it is hard to see how or why any single firm should take into account the consequences of its offering a new policy. On balance, it seems to us that nonmyopic equilibrium concepts are more appropriate for models of monopoly (or oligopoly) than for models of competition.

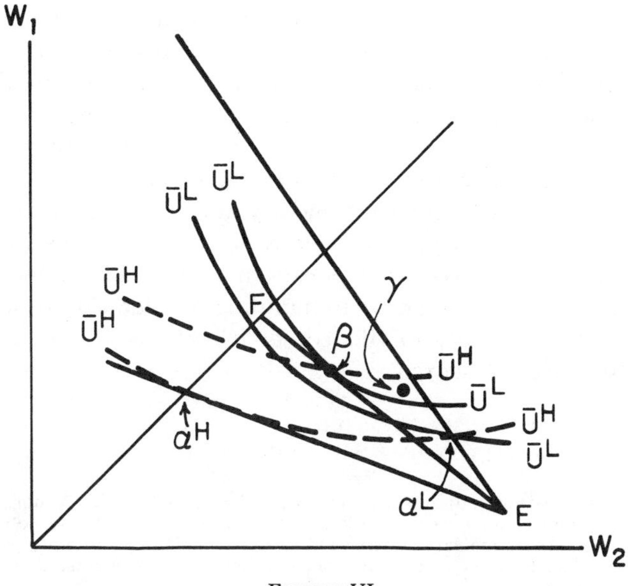

FIGURE VI

III. Conclusion

We began this research with the hope of showing that even a small amount of imperfect information could have a significant effect on competitive markets. Our results were more striking than we had hoped: the single price equilibrium of conventional competitive analysis was shown to be no longer viable; market equilibrium, when it existed, consisted of contracts which specified both prices and quantities; the high-risk (low ability, etc.) individuals exerted a dissipative externality on the low-risk (high ability) individuals; the structure of the equilibrium as well as its existence depended on a number of assumptions that, with perfect information, were inconsequential; and finally, and in some ways most disturbing, under quite plausible conditions equilibrium did not exist.

Our analysis, and our conclusions, extend beyond the simple insurance market described above. The models of educational screening and signaling studied by, among others, Arrow (1973), Riley (1975), Spence (1973, 1974), and Stiglitz (1971, 1972, 1974a, 1975b), are obvious examples. The other papers in this symposium describe models that can be profitably studied using our techniques and our concepts. Models in which communities choose the level of public goods and individuals choose among communities on the basis of the menu of public goods and taxes that the different communities offer, provide a less obvious but, we think, important case.[9]

Do these theoretical speculations tell us anything about the real world? In the absence of empirical work it is hard to say. The market on which we focused most of our analysis, that for insurance, is probably not competitive; whether our model may partially explain this fact is almost impossible to say. But there are other markets, particularly financial and labor markets, which appear to be competitive and in which imperfect and asymmetric information play an important role. We suspect that many of the peculiar institutions of these labor markets arise as responses to the difficulties that they, or any competitive market, have in handling problems of information. Establishing (or refuting) this conjecture seems to provide a rich agenda for future research.

University of Wisconsin, Madison
Stanford University and All Souls College, Oxford

9. See F. Westhoff's dissertation (1974), and Stiglitz (1974b). A more complete discussion of these is in our earlier working paper referred to in footnote 7 above. Salop and Salop (1972) demonstrated, in an early draft of their symposium paper, that contingent loan plans for repayment of tuition, and their possible defects, can be analyzed along these lines.

References

Arrow, K. J., *Essays in the Theory of Risk Bearing* (Chicago: Markham, 1971).

——, "Higher Education as a Filter," *Journal of Public Economics, II* (July 1973), 193–216.

Borch, K., *The Economics of Uncertainty* (Princeton, N.J.: Princeton University Press, 1968).

Hahn, F. H., "Notes on R-S Models of Insurance Markets," mimeo, Cambridge University, 1974.

Riley, J., "Competitive Signaling," *Journal of Economic Theory,* X (April 1975), 174–86.

——, "Informational Equilibrium," mimeo, Rand Corporation, 1976.

Revesz, P., *Laws of Large Numbers* (New York: Academic Press, 1960).

Rothschild, M., and J. E. Stiglitz, "Equilibrium in Competitive Insurance Markets," Technical Report No. 170, IMSSS Stanford University, 1975.

Spence, M., "Job Market Signaling," this *Journal,* LXXXVII (Aug. 1973), 355–79.

——, *Market Signaling* (Cambridge: Harvard University Press, 1974).

Stiglitz, J. E., "Perfect and Imperfect Capital Markets," paper presented to Econometric Society Meeting, New Orleans, 1971.

——, "Education as a Screening Device and the Distribution of Income," mimeo, Yale University, 1972.

——, "Demand for Education in Public and Private School Systems," *Journal of Public Economics,* III (Nov. 1974a), 349–86.

——, "Pure Theory of Local Public Goods," in M. Feldstein ed. IEA Conference Volume (Turin, 1974b.).

——, "The Theory of Screening, Education, and Distribution of Income," *American Economic Review,* LXV (June 1975), 283–300.

Westhoff, Frank H., "The Theory of Local Public Goods," Ph.D. thesis, Yale University, 1974.

Wilson, Charles A., "Equilibrium in a Class of Self-Selection Models," Ph.D. thesis, University of Rochester, 1976.

Comment

Working independently, Wilson (1977) has examined this model. His analysis contains two features not in this article. First, as discussed in Section II.4, Wilson considers an alternative definition of equilibrium. He drops the assumption that firms will introduce any new policy that would make money, provided all other policies remain in the market. Instead, he assumes that firms only introduce new policies that will make money even when some policies are withdrawn by other firms, so that all policies continuing to exist at least break even. With this definition an equilibrium always exists in the model used in this chapter. It may be a pooling equilibrium or a separating equilibrium. Second, Wilson analyzes government actions to make Pareto improvements in such a market. If there is a pooling equilibrium, the government can make everyone better off by compelling the purchase of the equilibrium insurance policy. The utility improvement occurs because new policies are then offered leading to a new separating equilibrium. If the original equilibrium is a separating equilibrium Wilson shows that the government may be able to improve the welfare of each person by compelling purchase of some policy (which breaks even for the population as a whole), allowing the market then to offer a different separating equilibrium. The presence of this possibility depends on the shape of the particular indifference curves. Of course, with more than two types of consumers such simple government policies may not be available. Nevertheless, it is interesting to see how adverse selection problems open the possibility for gains from additional public action.

Miyazaki (1977) has analyzed equilibria where firms are aware of the potential gains from cross subsidization of policies. (This contrasts to the assumption above that each policy breaks even.) Using the Wilson definition of equilibrium, he shows that the private market can achieve equilibria not available if each policy breaks even. Any such equilibrium is a Pareto optimum.

References

H. Miyazaki, The rat race and internal labor markets. *Bell J. Econ.* 8 (1977), 394–418.

C. Wilson, A model of insurance markets with incomplete information, *J. Econ. Theory* **16** (1977), 167–207.

18
M. Spence, Job market signaling, *Quarterly Journal of Economics* 87 (1973), 355–374

In the previous reading, firms select insurance policies that induce individuals of different risk classes to select different elements in the set of policies in the market. We have three conclusions about such markets. One is that we will not do as well in the market as would be possible with direct information on individual characteristics. Another is that government action that requires no additional information may be Pareto improving and will generally be able to increase a social welfare function. (The latter conclusion follows from applying the logic of the exercise in Chapter 14 to this problem.) Third, we may have difficulty in having an equilibrium (as opposed to some pattern of disequilibria) in the market, depending on the perceptions of competing firms.

We now turn to analysis of the circumstance where actions taken outside the market generate information that can be used by the market, and individuals are aware that they are providing this information. Suppose, for example, that the costs of obtaining education are negatively correlated with ability; a person's decision of how much education to obtain may, at the same time, reveal something about his productivity that would not otherwise be available to firms considering his employment. Firms, however, can affect individual choice of education by paying different wages to individuals with different amounts of education who are otherwise indistinguishable. The logic of this situation is identical to that described in the previous reading. The fact that education is provided by a different industry does not alter the types of analysis one might do. (Of course, there are differences in detail; the expected utility function of the insurance problem is replaced by the income net of education costs of the employment problem.) However, selection of a different problem may make reasonable different rules describing the wage or price setting behavior of individual firms.

The reading contains an example with two types of workers, similar to the example above of two risk classes. Following this reading, we shall have the reader develop the equilibrium with a continuum of skill classes. We shall then discuss additional references that bring out the implications of different behavioral assumptions.

JOB MARKET SIGNALING *

MICHAEL SPENCE

1. INTRODUCTION

The term "market signaling" is not exactly a part of the well-defined, technical vocabulary of the economist. As a part of the preamble, therefore, I feel I owe the reader a word of explanation about the title. I find it difficult, however, to give a coherent and comprehensive explanation of the meaning of the term abstracted from the contents of the essay. In fact, it is part of my purpose to outline a model in which signaling is implicitly defined and to explain why one can, and perhaps should, be interested in it. One might accurately characterize my problem as a signaling one, and that of the reader, who is faced with an investment decision under uncertainty, as that of interpreting signals.

How the reader interprets my report of the content of this essay will depend upon his expectation concerning my stay in the market. If one believes I will be in the essay market repeatedly, then both the reader and I will contemplate the possibility that I might invest in my future ability to communicate by accurately reporting the content of this essay now. On the other hand, if I am to be in the market only once, or relatively infrequently, then the above-mentioned possibility deserves a low probability. This essay is about markets in which signaling takes place and in which the primary signalers are relatively numerous and in the market sufficiently infrequently that they are not expected to (and therefore do not) invest in acquiring signaling reputations.

* The essay is based on the author's doctoral dissertation ("Market Signalling: The Informational Structure of Job Markets and Related Phenomena," Ph.D. thesis, Harvard University, 1972), forthcoming as a book entitled *Market Signaling: Information Transfer in Hiring and Related Screening Processes* in the Harvard Economic Studies Series, Harvard University Press. The aim here is to present the outline of the signaling model and some of its conclusions. Generalizations of the numerical examples used for expositional purposes here are found in *ibid.* and elsewhere.

I owe many people thanks for help in the course of the current study, too many to mention all. However, I should acknowledge explicitly the magnitude of my debts to Kenneth Arrow and Thomas Schelling for persistently directing my attention to new and interesting problems.

I shall argue that the paradigm case of the market with this type of informational structure is the job market and will therefore focus upon it. By the end I hope it will be clear (although space limitations will not permit an extended argument) that a considerable variety of market and quasi-market phenomena like admissions procedures, promotion in organizations, loans and consumer credit, can be usefully viewed through the conceptual lens applied to the job market.

If the incentives for veracity in reporting anything by means of a conventional signaling code are weak, then one must look for other means by which information transfers take place. My aim is to outline a conceptual apparatus within which the signaling power of education, job experience, race, sex, and a host of other observable, personal characteristics can be determined. The question, put crudely, is what in the interactive structure of a market accounts for the informational content, if any, of these potential signals. I have placed primary emphasis upon (i) the definition and properties of signaling equilibria, (ii) the interaction of potential signals, and (iii) the allocative efficiency of the market.

2. Hiring as Investment under Uncertainty

In most job markets the employer is not sure of the productive capabilities of an individual at the time he hires him.[1] Nor will this information necessarily become available to the employer immediately after hiring. The job may take time to learn. Often specific training is required. And there may be a contract period within which no recontracting is allowed. The fact that it takes time to learn an individual's productive capabilities means that hiring is an investment decision. The fact that these capabilities are not known beforehand makes the decision one under uncertainty.

To hire someone, then, is frequently to purchase a lottery.[2] In what follows, I shall assume the employer pays the certain monetary equivalent of the lottery to the individual as wage.[3] If he is

1. There are, of course, other informational gaps in the job market. Just as employers have less than perfect information about applicants, so also will applicants be imperfectly informed about the qualities of jobs and work environments. And in a different vein neither potential employees nor employers know all of the people in the market. The resulting activities are job search and recruiting. For the purpose of this essay I concentrate upon employer uncertainty and the signaling game that results.

2. The term "lottery" is used in the technical sense, imparted to it by decision theory.

3. The certain monetary equivalent of a lottery is the amount the individual would take, with certainty, in lieu of the lottery. It is generally thought to be less than the actuarial value of the lottery.

risk-neutral, the wage is taken to be the individual's marginal contribution to the hiring organization.

Primary interest attaches to how the employer perceives the lottery, for it is these perceptions that determine the wages he offers to pay. We have stipulated that the employer cannot directly observe the marginal product prior to hiring. What he does observe is a plethora of personal data in the form of observable characteristics and attributes of the individual, and it is these that must ultimately determine his assessment of the lottery he is buying. (The image that the individual presents includes education, previous work, race, sex, criminal and service records, and a host of other data.) This essay is about the endogenous market process whereby the employer requires (and the individual transmits) information about the potential employee, which ultimately determines the implicit lottery involved in hiring, the offered wages, and in the end the allocation of jobs to people and people to jobs in the market.

At this point, it is useful to introduce a distinction, the import of which will be clear shortly. Of those observable, personal attributes that collectively constitute the image the job applicant presents, some are immutably fixed, while others are alterable. For example, education is something that the individual can invest in at some cost in terms of time and money. On the other hand, race and sex are not generally thought to be alterable. I shall refer to observable, unalterable attributes as *indices*, reserving the term *signals* for those observable characteristics attached to the individual that are subject to manipulation by him.[4] Some attributes, like age, do change, but not at the discretion of the individual. In my terms, these are indices.

Sometime after hiring an individual, the employer will learn the individual's productive capabilities. On the basis of previous experience in the market, the employer will have conditional probability assessments over productive capacity given various combinations of signals and indices. At any point of time when confronted with an individual applicant with certain observable attributes, the employer's subjective assessment of the lottery with which he is confronted is defined by these conditional probability distributions over productivity given the new data.

From one point of view, then, signals and indices are to be re-

4. The terminological distinction is borrowed from Robert Jervis (*The Logic of Images in International Relations* (Princeton, N.J.: Princeton University Press, 1970)). My use of the terms follows that of Jervis sufficiently closely to warrant their transplantation.

garded as parameters in shifting conditional probability distributions that define an employer's beliefs.[5]

3. Applicant Signaling

For simplicity I shall speak as if the employer were risk-neutral. For each set of signals and indices that the employer confronts, he will have an expected marginal product for an individual who has these observable attributes. This is taken to be the offered wage to applicants with those characteristics. Potential employees therefore confront an offered wage schedule whose arguments are signals and indices.

There is not much that the applicant can do about indices. Signals, on the other hand, are alterable and therefore potentially subject to manipulation by the job applicant. Of course, there may be costs of making these adjustments. Education, for example, is costly. We refer to these costs as *signaling costs*. Notice that the individual, in acquiring an education, need not think of himself as signaling. He will invest in education if there is sufficient return as defined by the offered wage schedule.[6] Individuals, then, are assumed to select signals (for the most part, I shall talk in terms of education) so as to maximize the difference between offered wages and signaling costs. Signaling costs play a key role in this type of signaling situation, for they functionally replace the less direct costs and benefits associated with a reputation for signaling reliability acquired by those who are more prominent in their markets than job seekers are in theirs.

A Critical Assumption

It is not difficult to see that a signal will not effectively distinguish one applicant from another, unless the costs of signaling are negatively correlated with productive capability. For if this condition fails to hold, given the offered wage schedule, everyone will invest in the signal in exactly the same way, so that they cannot be distinguished on the basis of the signal. In what follows, we shall make the assumption that signaling costs are negatively correlated with productivity. It is, however, most appropriately viewed as a

5. The shifting of the distributions occurs when new market data are received and conditional probabilities are revised or updated. Hiring in the market is to be regarded as sampling, and revising conditional probabilities as passing from prior to posterior. The whole process is a learning one.

6. There may be other returns to education. It may be a consumption good or serve as a signal of things other than work potential (status for example). These returns should be added to the offered wage schedule.

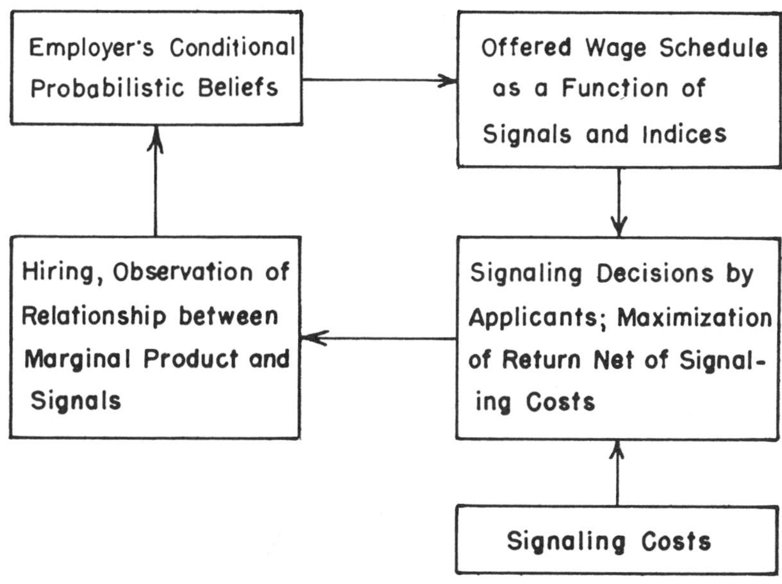

FIGURE I

Informational Feedback in the Job Market

prerequisite for an observable, alterable characteristic to be a persistently informative signal in the market. This means, among other things, that a characteristic may be a signal with respect to some types of jobs but not with respect to others.[7]

Signaling costs are to be interpreted broadly to include psychic and other costs, as well as the direct monetary ones. One element of cost, for example, is time.

4. Information Feedback and the Definition of Equilibrium

At this point it is perhaps clear that there is informational feedback to the employer over time. As new market information comes in to the employer through hiring and subsequent observation of productive capabilities as they relate to signals, the employer's conditional probabilistic beliefs are adjusted, and a new round starts. The wage schedule facing the new entrants in the market generally differs from that facing the previous group. The elements in the feedback loop are shown in Figure I.

It is desirable to find a way to study this feedback loop in the

7. The reason is that signaling costs can be negatively correlated with one type of productive capability but not with another.

market over time. To avoid studying a system in a continual state of flux, it is useful to look for nontransitory configuration of the feedback system. The system will be stationary if the employer starts out with conditional probabilistic beliefs that after one round are not disconfirmed by the incoming data they generated. We shall refer to such beliefs as self-confirming. The sense in which they are self-confirming is defined by the feedback loop in Figure I.

A Signaling Equilibrium

As successive waves of new applicants come into the market, we can imagine repeated cycles around the loop. Employers' conditional probabilistic beliefs are modified, offered wage schedules are adjusted, applicant behavior with respect to signal choice changes, and after hiring, new data become available to the employer. Each cycle, then, generates the next one. In thinking about it, one can interrupt the cycle at any point. An equilibrium is a set of components in the cycle that regenerate themselves. Thus, we can think of employer beliefs being self-confirming, or offered wage schedules regenerating themselves, or applicant behavior reproducing itself on the next round.[8]

I find it most useful to think in terms of the self-confirming aspect of the employer beliefs because of the continuity provided by the employer's persistent presence in the market.[9] Thus, in these terms an equilibrium can be thought of as a set of employer beliefs that generate offered wage schedules, applicant signaling decisions, hiring, and ultimately new market data over time that are consistent with the initial beliefs.

A further word about the definition of equilibrium is in order. Given an offered wage schedule, one can think of the market as generating, via individual optimizing decisions, an empirical distribution of productive capabilites given observable attributes or signals (and indices). On the other hand, the employer has subjectively held conditional probabilistic beliefs with respect to productivity, given signals. In an equilibrium the subjective distribution and the one implicit in the market mechanism are identical,

8. In pursuing the properties of signaling equilibria, we select as the object for regeneration whatever is analytically convenient, but usually employer beliefs or offered wage schedules.

9. The mathematically oriented will realize that what is at issue here is a fixed point property. A mapping from the space of conditional distributions over productivity given signals into itself is defined by the market response mechanism. An equilibrium can be thought of as a fixed point of this mapping. A mathematical treatment of this subject is contained in Spence, *op. cit.*

over the range of signals that the employer actually observes.[1] Any other subjective beliefs will eventually be disconfirmed in the market because of the employer's persistent presence there.

Indices continue to be relevant. But since they are not a matter of individual choice, they do not figure prominently in the feedback system just described. I shall return to them later.

5. Properties of Informational Equilibria: an Example

I propose to discuss the existence and properties of market signaling equilibria via a specific numerical example.[2] For the time being, indices play no part. The properties of signaling equilibria that we shall encounter in the example are general.[3]

Let us suppose that there are just two productively distinct groups in a population facing one employer. Individuals in Group I have a productivity of 1, while those in Group II have a productivity of 2.[4] Group I is a proportion q_1 of the population; Group II is a proportion of $1-q_1$. There is, in addition, a potential signal, say education, which is available at a cost. We shall assume that education is measured by an index y of level and achievement and is subject to individual choice. Education costs are both monetary and psychic. It is assumed that the cost to a member of Group I of y units of education is y, while the cost to a member of Group II is $y/2$.

We summarize the underlying data of our numerical example in Table I.

TABLE I

Data of the Model

Group	Marginal product	Proportion of population	Cost of education level y
I	1	q_1	y
II	2	$1-q_1$	$y/2$

1. In a multi-market model one faces the possibility that certain types of potential applicants will rationally select themselves out of certain job markets, and hence certain signal configurations may never appear in these markets. When this happens, the beliefs of the employers in the relevant market are not disconfirmed in a degenerate way. No data are forthcoming. This raises the possibility of persistent informationally based discrimination against certain groups. The subject is pursued in detail in *ibid.*

2. Obviously, an example does not prove generality. On the other hand, if the reader will take reasonable generality on faith, the example does illustrate some essential properties of signaling equilibria.

3. See Spence, *op. cit.*

4. For productivity the reader may read "what the individual is worth to the employer." There is no need to rely on marginal productivity here.

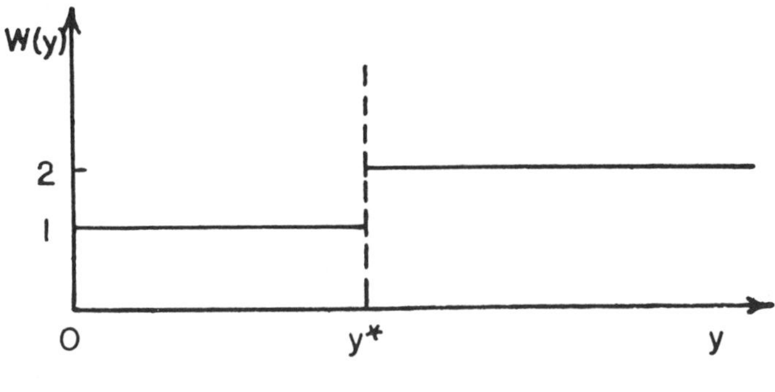

FIGURE II

Offered Wages as a Function of Level of Education

To find an equilibrium in the market, we guess at a set of self-confirming conditional probabilistic beliefs for the employer and then determine whether they are in fact confirmed by the feedback mechanisms described above. Suppose that the employer believes that there is some level of education, say y^* such that if $y<y^*$, then productivity is one with probability one, and that if $y \geqslant y^*$, then productivity will be two with probability one. If these are his conditional beliefs, then his offered wage schedule, $W(y)$, will be as shown in Figure II.

Given the offered wage schedule, members of each group will select optimal levels for education. Consider the person who will set $y<y^*$. If he does this, we know he will set $y=0$ because education is costly, and until he reaches y^*, there are no benefits to increasing y, given the employer's hypothesized beliefs. Similarly, any individual who sets $y \geqslant y^*$ will in fact set $y=y^*$, since further increases would merely incur costs with no corresponding benefits. Everyone will therefore either set $y=0$ or set $y=y^*$. Given the employer's initial beliefs and the fact just deduced, if the employer's beliefs are to be confirmed, then members of Group I must set $y=0$, while members of Group II set $y=y^*$. Diagrams of the options facing the two groups are shown in Figure III.

Superimposed upon the wage schedule are the cost schedules for the two groups. Each group selects y to maximize the difference between the offered wages and the costs of education. Given the level of y^* in the diagram, it is easy to see that Group I selects $y=0$, and Group II sets $y=y^*$. Thus, in this case the employer's beliefs are confirmed, and we have a signaling equilibrium. We can state the

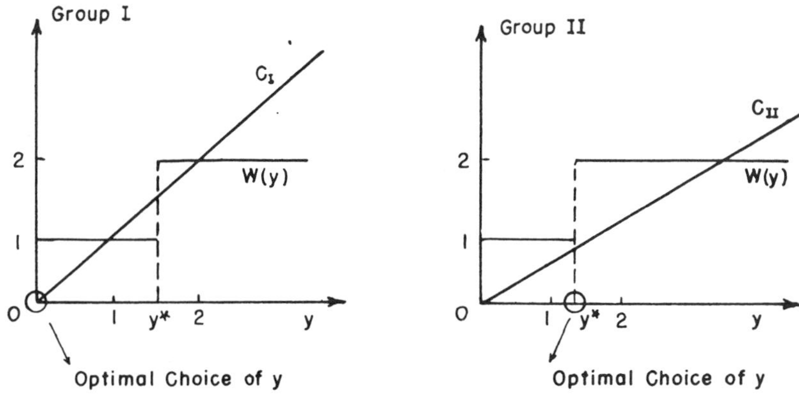

FIGURE III

Optimizing Choice of Education for Both Groups

conditions on behavior by the two groups, in order that the employer's beliefs be confirmed, in algebraic terms. Group I sets $y=0$ if

$$1>2-y^*.$$

Group II will set $y=y^*$ as required, provided that

$$2-y^*/2>1.$$

Putting these two conditions together, we find that the employer's initial beliefs are confirmed by market experience, provided that the parameter y^* satisfies the inequality,

$$1<y^*<2.$$

It is worth pausing at this point to remark upon some striking features of this type of equilibrium. One is that within the class of employer expectations used above, there is an infinite number of possible equilibrium values for y^*. This means that there is an infinite number of equilibria. In any one of the equilibria the employer is able to make perfect point predictions concerning the productivity of any individual, having observed his level of education. The reader will realize that this property is special and depends, at least in part, upon the assumption that education costs are perfectly negatively correlated with productivity. However, even in this case, there are equilibria in which the employer is uncertain, as we shall shortly see.

The equilibria are not equivalent from the point of view of welfare. Increases in the level of y^* hurt Group II, while, at the same time, members of Group I are unaffected. Group I is worse off than it was with no signaling at all. For if no signaling takes place, each person is paid his unconditional expected marginal product, which is just

$$q_1+2(1-q_1)=2-q_1.$$

Group II may also be worse off than it was with no signaling. Assume that the proportion of people in Group I is 0.5. Since $y^*>1$ and the net return to the member of Group II is $2-y^*/2$, in equilibrium his net return must be below 1.5, the no-signaling wage. Thus, everyone would prefer a situation in which there is no signaling.

No one is acting irrationally as an individual. Coalitions might profitably form and upset the signaling equilibrium.[5] The initial proportions of people in the two groups q_1 and $1-q_1$ have no effect upon the equilibrium. This conclusion depends upon this assumption that the marginal product of a person in a given group does not change with numbers hired.

Given the signaling equilibrium, the education level y^*, which defines the equilibrium, is an entrance requirement or prerequisite for the high-salary job — or so it would appear from the outside. From the point of view of the individual, it is a prerequisite that has its source in a signaling game. Looked at from the outside, education might appear to be productive. It is productive for the individual, but, in this example, it does not increase his real marginal product at all.[6]

A sophisticated objection to the assertion that private and social returns differ might be that, in the context of our example, the social return is not really zero. We have an information problem in the society and the problem of allocating the right people to the right jobs. Education, in its capacity as a signal in the model, is helping us to do this properly. The objection is well founded. To decide how efficient or inefficient this system is, one must consider the realistic alternatives to market sorting procedures in the society.[7] But notice that even within the confines of the market model, there are more or less efficient ways of getting the sorting accomplished. Increases in y^* improve the quality of the sorting not one bit. They simply use up real or psychic resources. This is

5. Coalitions to change the patterns of signaling are discussed in Spence, *op. cit.*

6. I am ignoring external benefits to education here. The assertion is simply that in the example education does not contribute to productivity. One might still claim that the social product is not zero. The signal cost function does, in principle, capture education as a consumption good, an effect that simply reduces the cost of education.

7. This question is pursued in Spence, *op. cit.*

just another way of saying that there are Pareto inferior signaling equilibria in the market.

It is not always the case that all groups lose due to the existence of signaling. For example, if, in the signaling equilibrium, $y^* < 2q_1$, then Group II would be better off when education is functioning effectively as a signal than it would be otherwise. Thus, in our example if $q_1 > \frac{1}{2}$ so that Group II is a minority; then there exists a signaling equilibrium in which the members of Group II improve their position over the no-signaling case. Recall that the wage in the no-signaling case was a uniform $2 - q_1$ over all groups.

We may generalize this bit of analysis slightly. Suppose that the signaling cost schedule for Group I was given by $a_1 y$ and that for Group II by $a_2 y$.[8] Then with a small amount of calculation, we can show that there is a signaling equilibrium in which Group II is better off than with no signaling,[9] provided that

$$q_1 > a_2/a_1.$$

How small a "minority" Group II has to be to have the possibility of benefiting from signaling depends upon the ratio of the marginal signaling costs of the two groups.[1]

Before leaving our education signaling model, it is worth noting that there are other equilibria in the system with quite different properties. Suppose that the employer's expectations are of the following form:

If $y < y^*$: Group I with probability q_1,
Group II with probability $1 - q_1$;
if $y \geqslant y^*$: Group II with probability 1.

As before, the only levels of y that could conceivably be selected are

8. It is assumed that $a_2 < a_1$.

9. Notice that the statement is that there exists a signaling equilibrium in which Group II is better off. It turns out that there always exists a signaling equilibrium in which Group II is worse off as well.

1. The calculation is straightforward. Given these signaling costs groups will make the requisite choice to confirm the employer's beliefs provided that

$$1 > 2 - a_1 y^*$$

and

$$2 - a_2 y^* > 1.$$

These translate easily into the following condition on y^*:

$$\frac{1}{a_2} < y^* < \frac{1}{a_1}.$$

Now, if Group II is to be better off for some signaling equilibrium, then

$$2 - \frac{a_2}{a_1} > 2 - q_1,$$

or

$$q_1 > \frac{a_2}{a_1}.$$

This is what we set out to show.

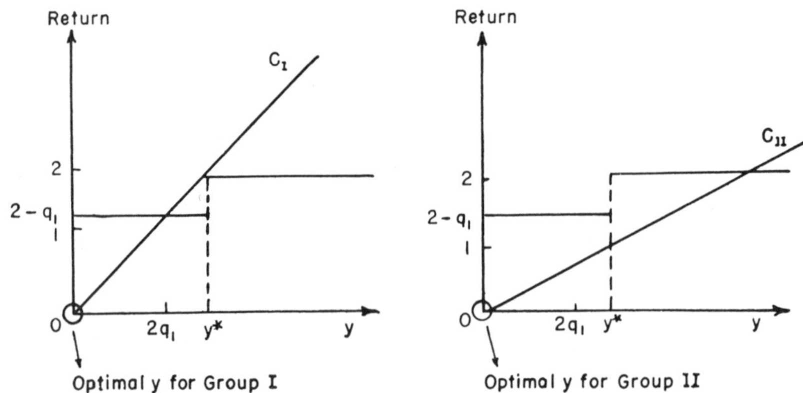

FIGURE IV

Optimal Signaling Decisions for the Two Groups

$y=0$ and $y=y^*$. The wage for $y=0$ is $2-q_1$, while the wage for $y=y^*$ is simply 2. From Figure IV it is easy to see that both groups rationally set $y=0$, provided that $y^*>2q_1$. If they both do this, then the employer's beliefs are confirmed, and we have an equilibrium.

It should be noted that the employer's beliefs about the relationship between productivity and education for $y \geqslant y^*$ are confirmed in a somewhat degenerate, but perfectly acceptable, sense. There are no data relating to these levels of education and hence, by logic, no disconfirming data. This is an example of a phenomenon of much wider potential importance. The employer's beliefs may drive certain groups from the market and into another labor market. We cannot capture this situation in a simple one-employer, one-market model. But when it happens, there is no experience forthcoming to the employer to cause him to alter his beliefs.[2]

Education conveys no information in this type of equilibrium. In fact, we have reproduced the wages and information state of the employer in the no-signaling model, as a signaling equilibrium.

Just as there exists a signaling equilibrium in which everyone sets $y=0$, there is also an equilibrium in which everyone sets $y=y^*$ for some positive y^*. The requisite employer beliefs are as follows:

If $y<y^*$: Group I with probability 1;
if $y \geqslant y^*$: Group I with probability q_1,
Group II with probability $1-q_1$.

2. This is discussed in detail in Spence, *op. cit.*

Following our familiar mode of analysis, one finds that these beliefs are self-confirming in the market, provided that

$$y^* < 1 - q_1.$$

Again, the education level conveys no useful information, but in this instance individuals are rationally investing in education. If they as individuals did not invest, they would incur lower wages, and the loss would exceed the gain from not making the educational investment. The implication of this version of the signaling equilibrium is that there can be stable prerequisites for jobs that convey no information by virtue of their existence and hence serve no function.

It is interesting to note that this last possibility does not depend upon costs being correlated with productivity at all. Suppose that the signaling costs *for both groups* were given by the one schedule y. And suppose further that employer beliefs were as described above. Then everyone will rationally select $y = y^*$, provided that

$$y^* < 1 - q_1.$$

The outcome is the same. But the interesting thing is that, because of the absence of any correlation between educational costs and productivity, education could *never* be an effective signal, in the sense of conveying useful information, in an equilibrium in this market.

We have dwelt enough upon the specifics of this model to have observed some of the effects the signaling game may have upon the allocational functioning of the market. The numerical example is not important. The potential effects and patterns of signaling are.

An alterable characteristic like education, which is a potential signal, becomes an actual signal if the signaling costs are negatively correlated with the individual's unknown productivity. Actually, the negative correlation is a necessary but not sufficient condition for signaling to take place. To see this in the context of our model, assume that the only values y can have are one and three. That is to say, one can only get units of education in lumps. If this is true, then there is no feasible value of y^* that will make it worthwhile for Group II to acquire an education. Three units is too much, and one unit will not distinguish Group II from Group I. Therefore, effective signaling depends not only upon the negative correlation of costs and productivities, but also upon there being a "sufficient" number of signals within the appropriate cost range.[3]

3. In *ibid.* it is argued that many potential signals in credit and loan

An equilibrium is defined in the context of a feedback loop, in which employer expectations lead to offered wages to various levels of education, which in turn lead to investment in education by individuals. After hiring, the discovery of the actual relationships between education and productivity in the sample leads to revised expectations or beliefs. Here the cycle starts again. An equilibrium is best thought of as a set of beliefs that are confirmed or at least not contradicted by the new data at the end of the loop just described. Such beliefs will tend to persist over time as new entrants into the market flow through.

Multiple equilibria are a distinct possibility. Some may be Pareto inferior to others. Private and social returns to education diverge. Sometimes everyone loses as a result of the existence of signaling. In other situations some gain, while others lose. Systematic overinvestment in education is a distinct possibility because of the element of arbitrariness in the equilibrium configuration of the market. In the context of atomistic behavior (which we have assumed thus far) everyone is reacting rationally to the market situation. Information is passed to the employer through the educational signal. In some of our examples it was perfect information. In other cases this is not so. There will be random variation in signaling costs that prevent the employer from distinguishing perfectly among individuals of varying productive capabilities.

In our examples, education was measured by a scalar quantity. With no basic adjustment in the conceptual apparatus, we can think of education as a multidimensional quantity: years of education, institution attended, grades, recommendations and so on. Similarly, it is not necessary to think in terms of two groups of people. There may be many groups, or even a continuum of people: some suited to certain kinds of work, others suited to other kinds. Nor need education be strictly unproductive. However, if it is too productive relative to the costs, everyone will invest heavily in education, and education may cease to have a signaling function.

6. The Informational Impact of Indices

In the educational signaling model we avoided considering any observable characteristics other than education. In that model education was a signal. Here we consider what role, if any, is played

markets effectively become indices because the "signaling" costs swamp the gains, so that characteristics that could be manipulated in fact are not. House ownership is an example of a potential signal that, in the context of the loan market, fails on this criterion and hence becomes an index.

by indices. For concreteness I shall use sex as the example. But just as education can stand for any set of observable, alterable characteristics in the first model, sex can stand for observable, unalterable ones here. The reader may wish to think in terms of race, nationality, size, or in terms of criminal or police records and service records. The latter is potentially public information about a person's history and is, of course, unalterable when viewed retrospectively from the present.[4]

Let us assume that there are two groups, men and women. I shall refer to these groups as W and M. Within each group the distribution of productive capabilities and the incidence of signaling costs are the same. Thus, within M the proportion of people with productivity one and signaling (education) costs of y is q_1. The remainder have productivity two and signaling costs $y/2$. The same is true for group W. Here m is the proportion of men in the overall population of job applicants.

TABLE IV

DATA OF THE MODEL

Race	Productivity	Education costs	Proportion within group	Proportion of total population
W	1	y	q_1	$q_1(1-m)$
W	2	$y/2$	$1-q_1$	$(1-q_1)(1-m)$
M	1	y	q_1	$q_1 m$
M	2	$y/2$	$1-q_1$	$(1-q_1)m$

Given the assumptions the central question is, "how could sex have an informational impact on the market?" The next few paragraphs are devoted to arguing that indices do have a potential impact and to explaining why this is true. We begin by noting that, under the assumptions, the conditional probability that a person drawn at random from the population has a productivity of two, given that he is a man (or she is a woman), is the same as the unconditional probability that his productivity is two. Sex and productivity are uncorrelated in the population. Therefore, *by itself*, sex could never tell the employer anything about productivity.

We are forced to the conclusion that if sex is to have any informational impact, it must be through its interaction with the educational signaling mechanism. But here again we run up against an initially puzzling symmetry. Under the assumptions, men and women of equal productivity have the same signaling (education)

4. It is, or ought to be, the subject of policy decisions as well.

costs. It is a general maxim in economics that people with the same preferences and opportunity sets will make similar decisions and end up in similar situations. We may assume that people maximize their income net of signaling costs so that their preferences are the same. And since signaling costs are the same, it would appear that their opportunity sets are the same. Hence, again we appear to be driven to the conclusion that sex can have no informational impact. But the conclusion is wrong, for an interesting reason.

The opportunity sets of men and women of comparable productivity are *not* necessarily the same. To see this, let us step back to the simple educational signaling model. There are externalities in that model. One person's signaling strategy or decision affects the market data obtained by the employer, which in turn affect the employer's conditional probabilities. These determine the offered wages to various levels of education and hence of rates of return on education for the next group in the job market. The same mechanism applies here, with a notable modification. If employers' distributions are conditional on sex as well as education, then the external impacts of a man's signaling decision are felt only by other men. The same holds for women.

If at some point in time men and women are not investing in education in the same ways, then the returns to education for men and women will be different in the next round. In short, their opportunity sets differ. In what follows, we demonstrate rigorously that this sort of situation can persist in an equilibrium. The important point, however, is that there are externalities implicit in the fact that an individual is treated as the average member of the group of people who look the same and that, as a result, and in spite of an apparent sameness the opportunity sets facing two or more groups that are visibly distinguishable may in fact be different.

The employer now has two potential signals to consider: education and sex. At the start he does not know whether either education or sex will be correlated with productivity. Uninformative potential signals or indices are discarded in the course of reaching an equilibrium. As before we must guess at an equilibrium form for the employer's expectations and then verify that these beliefs can be self-confirming via the market informational feedback mechanisms. We will try beliefs on the following form.

If W and $y < y^*_W$, productivity $=1$ with probability 1.
If W and $y \geqslant y^*_W$, productivity $=2$ with probability 1.
If M and $y < y^*_M$, productivity $=1$ with probability 1.
If M and $y \geqslant y^*_M$, productivity $=2$ with probability 1.

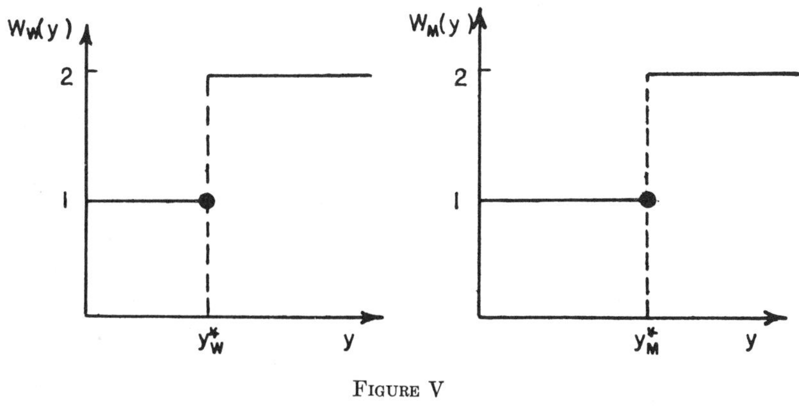

FIGURE V
Offered Wages to W and M

These lead to offered wage schedules $W_W(y)$ and $W_M(y)$ as shown in Figure V.

Because groups W and M are distinguishable to the employer, their offered wages are not connected at the level of employer expectations. Applying the reasoning used in the straightforward educational signaling model, we find that the required equilibrium conditions on y^*_W and y^*_M are

$$1 < y^*_W < 2$$

and

$$1 < y^*_M < 2.$$

No logical condition requires that y^*_W equals y^*_M in an equilibrium.

Essentially we simply have the educational signaling model iterated twice. Because sex is observable, the employer can make his conditional probability assessments depend upon sex as well as education. This has the effect of making signaling interdependencies between two groups, W and M, nonexistent. They settle into signaling equilibrium configurations in the market independently of each other. But in the first model there was not one equilibrium, there were many. Therefore, there is at least the logical possibility that men and women will settle into *different* stable signaling equilibria in the market and stay there.

As we noted earlier, the signaling equilibria are not equivalent from the point of view of social welfare. The higher that y^*_W (or y^*_M) is, the worse off is the relevant group or, more accurately, the high-productivity portion of the group. One example of an asymmetrical equilibrium would be given by $y^*_M = 1.1$ and $y^*_M = 1.9$. In this case high-productivity women have to spend more on education

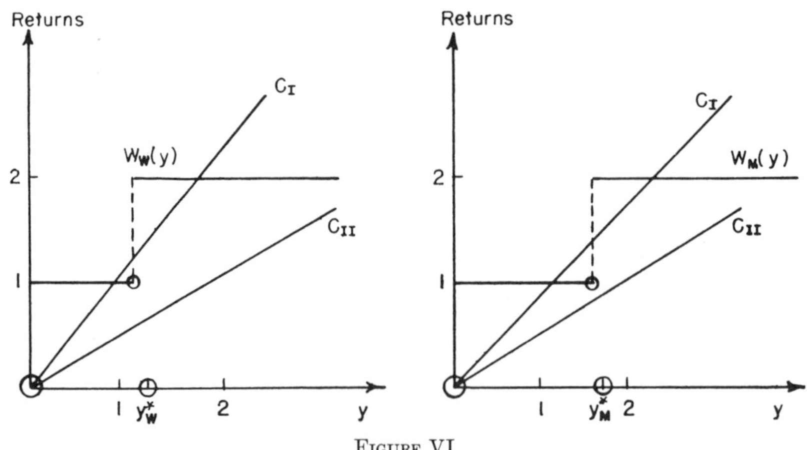

FIGURE VI
Market Equilibrium with Sex as an Index

and have less left over to consume in order to convince the employer that they are in the high-productivity group.

Notice that the proportions of high- and low-productivity people in each group do not affect the signaling equilibrium in the market. Hence, our initial assumption that the groups were identical with respect to the distribution of productive characteristics and the incidence of signaling costs was superfluous. More accurately, it was superfluous with respect to this type of equilibrium. As we saw in the educational signaling model, there are other types of equilibrium in which the proportions matter.

Since from an equilibrium point of view men and women really are independent, they might settle into different types of equilibrium. Thus, we might have men signaling $y = y^*_M = 1.1$ if they are also in the higher productivity group, while other men set $y = 0$. On the other hand, we may find that all women set $y = 0$. In this case all women would be paid $2 - q_1$, and the upper signaling cutoff point y^*_M would have to be greater than $2q_1$. Notice that all women, including lower productivity women, would be paid more than low-productivity men in this situation.[5] High-productivity women would, of course, be hurt in terms of wages received. It is conceivable, however, that returns net of signaling would be higher for women with productivity of two. In other words, it is possible that

$$2 - q_1 > w - y^*_{M/2}.$$

5. I have not assumed that employers are prejudiced. If they are, this differential could be wiped out. Perhaps more interestingly laws prohibiting wage discrimination, if enforced, would also wipe it out.

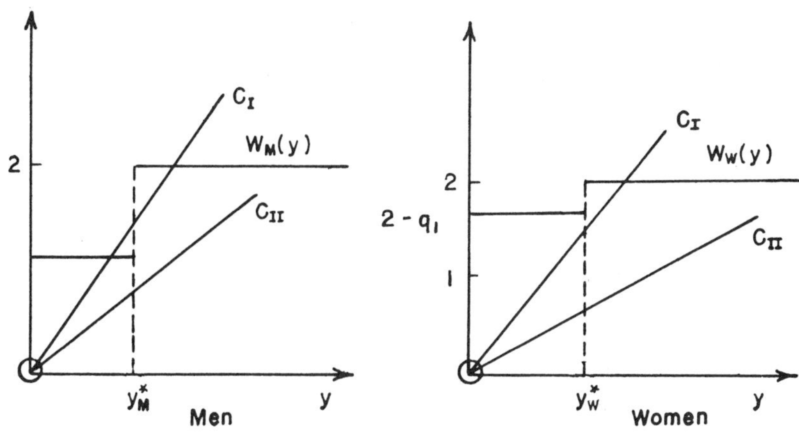

FIGURE VII

Another Equilibrium Configuration in the Market

This will occur when

$$2q_1 < y^*_M.$$

Looking at this situation from outside, one might conclude that women receive lower wages than some men because of a lack of education, which keeps their productivity down. One might then go looking outside the job market for the explanation for the lack of education. In this model the analysis just suggested would be wrong. The source of the signaling and wage differentials is in the informational structure of the market itself.[6]

Because of the independence of the two groups, M and W, at the level of signaling, we can generate many different possible equilibrium configurations by taking any of the educational signaling equilibria in our first model and assigning it to W and then taking any education equilibrium and assigning it to M. However, an exhaustive listing of the possibilities seems pointless at this stage.

We have here the possibility of arbitrary differences in the equilibrium signaling configurations of two or more distinct groups. Some of them may be at a disadvantage relative to the others. Subsets of one may be at a disadvantage to comparable subsets of the others. Since the mechanism that generates the equilibrium is a feedback loop, we might, following Myrdal and others, wish to refer to the situation of the disadvantaged group as a vicious cycle, albeit it an informationally based one. I prefer to refer to the situ-

6. Differential signaling costs over groups are an important possibility pursued in Spence, *op. cit.*

ation of the disadvantaged group as a lower level equilibrium trap, which conveys the notion of a situation that, once achieved, persists for reasons endogenous to the model. The multiple equilibria of the education model translate into arbitrary differences in the equilibrium configuration and status of two groups, as defined as observable, unalterable characteristics.

Conclusions

We have looked at the characteristics of a basic equilibrium signaling model and at one possible type of interaction of signals and indices. There remains a host of questions, which can be posed and partially answered within the conceptual framework outlined here. Among them are the following:

1. What is the effect of cooperative behavior on the signaling game?
2. What is the informational impact of randomness in signaling costs?
3. What is the effect of signaling costs that differ systematically with indices?
4. How general are the properties of the examples considered here?
5. In a multiple-market setting, does the indeterminateness of the equilibrium remain?
6. Do signaling equilibria exist in general?
7. What kinds of discriminatory mechanisms are implicit in, or interact with, the informational structure of the market, and what policies are effective or ineffective in dealing with them?

I would argue further that a range of phenomena from selective admissions procedures through promotion, loans and consumer credit, and signaling status via conspicuous consumption lends itself to analysis with the same basic conceptual apparatus. Moreover, it may be as important to explain the absence of effective signaling as its presence, and here the prerequisites for effective signaling are of some use.

On the other hand, it is well to remember that the property of relative infrequency of appearance by signalers in the market, which defines the class signaling phenomena under scrutiny here, is not characteristic of many markets, like those for consumer durables, and that, as a result, the informational structures of these latter are likely to be quite different.

Harvard University

Exercise: A signaling equilibrium with a continuum of skill classes[1]

Assume that the output S of a worker of type n who has had y years of education satisfies

$$S(n, y) = ny^a \qquad (0 < a < 1)$$

Assume that the cost C of y years of education to a worker of type n is

$$C(n, y) = y/n$$

Let $w(y)$ be the wage offered to a worker with y years of education.

1 If workers select their education levels to maximize the difference between their wage and the cost of education, what is the first-order condition for individual choice for a worker of type n?

2 If, in equilibrium, the wage offered a worker with y years of eduation equals the output of a worker who chooses that education, what relationship holds between w and y for a worker of type n who chooses y years of education?

3 Since your answers to 1 and 2 hold for all n, what equation relates dw/dy to w and y (i.e., eliminating n)?

4 Check that the solution to this equation is

$$w(y, K) = [2(y^{1+a} + K)/(1 + a)]^{1/2}$$

Thus we have an example of multiple equilibria in the labor market. Now assume that a is equal to zero for ease of calculation, i.e., that education has no productive value.

5 Determine the level of education chosen by a worker of type n in an equilibrium with parameter K.

6 If n is uniformly distributed over the range from 1 to 2, for what values of K will we have an equilibrium that does not violate the nonnegativity constraint on education?

Let K° be the largest value of K satisfying this condition.

7 Show that for any value of K that is less than K° every worker has lower income net of education costs than he would have if the parameter were K°.

8 Show that for any value of K less than K° there exists a wage w° and a level of

[1]This exercise is based on an example in Spence (1974b).

education y° such that the wage is less than the productivity of a worker of type 1 *and* the worker of type 1 prefers to get education y° and wage w° rather than the education and wage he enjoys in equilibrium. What does this imply about the stability of the equilibrium that has been described?
[*Note*: You must also consider the responses of workers of greater skill.]
9 Who would gain and who would lose if education were abolished and all workers received a wage equal to the average productivity of all workers?

Comment

This article is an introduction to Spence's more extensive analysis of market signaling (1974a,b, 1976).[1] In the reading, when no workers appear with a given level of education, employers continue to hold whatever beliefs they previously had about the productivity of workers with this education level. Of course, they have received no evidence to falsify these beliefs. However, as part 8 of the preceding exercise suggests, the set of possible equilibria is reduced if we add a restriction on the beliefs of employers about the skills of workers whom they have not employed.[2] In particular, we might consider the assumption that employers raise wages for education levels where they have no observations until a worker is just willing to appear. We shall then have an equilibrium if his marginal productivity is no greater than the wage. (This approach can also be viewed as competition by firms in the minimal education requirements for holding a higher paid job. For an equilibrium we would require the absence of any opportunity to increase profits by lowering job requirements.) This assumption eliminates the multiple equilibria discussed above. It does not alter the properties of the competitive equilibrium, however.

Alternatively, further experimentation by employers might be assumed. This leads into problems with the existence of equilibrium like those in the previous chapter.[3]

The analysis above assumed that a single wage was determined *ex ante*, in agreements between employers and employees. This is a natural approach where education is a perfect predictor of efficiency, as in the case where people of different skills choose different levels of education. However, where people of different productivities appear the same to the employer it is natural in some contexts to consider payments that are partially *ex ante* and partially *ex post*. This can occur with an ongoing employment relationship as well as with an explicitly productivity-related wage. Some analysis in this more realistic setting has been done by Stiglitz (1975b). This analysis gets into the question of moral hazard, to which we turn next.

[1]For other analyses of education and signaling, see Arrow (1973) and Stiglitz (1975a).

[2]This point has been made by Riley (1975) and by Spence (1976).

[3]Riley (1979) examines these problems and describes an alternative equilibrium concept that results in a unique separating equilibrium. His second paper also corrects an error in his initial discussion of nonexistence. For a comprehensive discussion of existence problems in a wide range of models, see Dasgupta and Maskin (1986).

For an interesting application of signaling theory to the financial structure of firms and stock market equilibrium, see Ross (1977).

References

K. Arrow, Higher education as a filter, *J. Public Econ.* 2 (1973), 193-216.

P. Dasgupta and E. Maskin, The existence of equilibrium in discontinuous economic games, I: Theory and II: Applications, *Rev. Econ. Studies* **53** (1986), 1–26 and 27–42.

J. Riley, Competitive signaling, *J. Econ. Theory* **10** (1975), 174–186.

J. Riley, Informational Equilibrium, *Econometrica* **47** (1979), 331–359.

S. Ross, The determination of financial structure: The incentive-signaling approach, *Bell J. Econ.* 8 (1977), 23-40.

M. Spence, "Market Signaling: Information Transfer in Hiring and Related Screening Processes," Cambridge, Massachusetts: Harvard Univ. Press, 1974a.

M. Spence, Competitive and optimal responses to signals: An analysis of efficiency and distribution, *J. Econ. Theory* 7 (1974b), 296-332.

M. Spence, Competition in salaries, credentials, and signaling prerequisites for jobs, *Quart. J. Econ.* **90** (1976), 51-74.

J. Stiglitz, Information and economic analysis, *in* "Current Economic Problems" (Parkin and Nobay, eds.). London: Cambridge Univ. Press, 1975a.

J. Stiglitz, Incentives, risk and information, Notes toward a theory of hierarchy, *Bell. J. Econ.* **6** (1975b), 552–579.

19

M. V. Pauly, Overinsurance and public provision of insurance: The roles of moral hazard and adverse selection, *Quarterly Journal of Economics* 88 (1974), 44–54 (part of the article is omitted)

In the previous readings we examined the situation of adverse selection, where the limitations of information availability imply that commodities or individuals that are different are treated as if they were the same. We now turn to two readings on the subject of moral hazard. For many commodities, the cost of providing the commodity depends on the behavior of the purchaser. This is obviously true of insurance where, for example, the expected cost of providing automobile insurance depends on the number of miles to be driven by the insured individual. A similar situation arises with products that come with guarantees, where the probability of a breakdown of the product within the guarantee period may depend on the way in which the product is used or the amount that it is used. If the supplier cannot observe the behavior of the purchaser, the price to be charged for the product cannot depend upon the behavior which affects costs. That is, automobile insurance does not generally depend on the number of miles to be driven. Thus the social costs of an individual's actions (additional driving) exceed the costs that he bears. Equilibrium cannot be a first best optimum. Two natural questions arise. How does the market respond in terms of the design of commodities and insurance policies? Can the government improve resource allocation by intervention in the market and if so, how? To isolate the moral hazard issue the next two readings consider an economy where all individuals are the same. In general one expects to find the moral hazard problem and the adverse selection problem occurring together.

OVERINSURANCE AND PUBLIC PROVISION OF INSURANCE: THE ROLES OF MORAL HAZARD AND ADVERSE SELECTION *

Mark V. Pauly

In this paper I shall show that in the absence of perfect information the competitive outcome in markets for insurance may be nonoptimal, not only as compared to the infeasible optimum that would have occurred if information were perfect, but also compared to optima that are feasible.

One solution to this nonoptimality turns out to be some form of public intervention, and such a solution has recently been suggested or hinted at by several economists. Specifically, Akerlof has recently suggested that compulsory public insurance might produce an improvement over the market outcome;[1] and Arrow has said that compulsory insurance might at least produce a result that is as good as the market outcome.[2]

I shall demonstrate, however, that the advantage of public provision lies in its ability to generate a particular kind of information. I shall then show that, if this information were to be made available to firms, an optimal market outcome may occur. (This outcome does not, however, correspond exactly to the usual notion of competitive equilibrium.) I conclude by examining market structures that may have arisen to deal with the problem of imperfect information in insurance.

I shall examine two cases in which the absence of information could interfere with the operation of insurance markets, or indeed, of any market in risk. One is the case of "adverse selection," in which the insurer cannot determine some characteristics of the in-

* I would like to thank R. Kihlstrom, G. Goldstein, J. Green, and the referee for helpful comments. Research support was provided in part by the Health Services Research Center of Northwestern University and the American Hospital Association.

1. George Akerlof, "The Market for 'Lemons': Qualitative Uncertainty and the Market Mechanism," this *Journal*, Vol. 74 (Aug. 1970), p. 494.

2. Kenneth Arrow, "Political and Economic Evaluation of Social Effects and Externalities," in *The Analysis of Public Output*, J. Margolis, ed. (New York: Columbia University Press, 1970), p. 11.

sured that are relevant to the determination of the probability of the future state of nature. Because the insured is assumed to know these characteristics, Arrow has called this a case of unequal distribution of information.[3] The other case is similar in that the insurer is assumed not to know or to be able to monitor the present (purchase-date) state of nature, but differs in that the insured also has the power and the incentive to change this unobservable state in response to insurance coverage. This is one kind of problem of moral hazard.[4] Both of these situations arise when the insurer can observe the outcome, but cannot observe separately the initial state and the action of nature.

It is worthwhile to mention two obvious sorts of propositions that are *not* the ones to be discussed in this paper. It is obvious that if the government had or could obtain perfect information about the purchase-date state of the world, it could in principle provide the optimal insurance, or at least achieve a result superior to that of the imperfectly informed market. In what follows, I shall assume that the government does *not* possess perfect information. It is also obvious that, if the government chose at random compulsory insurance policies that either are uniform or differ over individuals, it might select a set of policies that are Pareto optimal or represent a Pareto optimal improvement over the market outcome. But there is no reason to expect this sort of process to have, as it were, an expected insurance allocation that is obviously superior to that of the market, and so this case also will not be discussed in what follows.

I. The Competitive Allocation of Insurance Under Moral Hazard

I first wish to consider the case in which the insurance purchaser has control over actions in the present that affect the future state of nature, but in which the insurer cannot directly observe the insured's actions. As has been noted in several places, an optimal solution in this kind of "moral hazard" situation is for the insured to retain some part of his losses.[5] Thus, the optimal policy is one

3. *Ibid.*

4. Moral hazard, in several of its forms, has recently been treated by Kihlstrom and Pauly, and Spence and Zeckhauser. See Richard Kihlstrom and Mark Pauly, "The Role of Insurance in the Allocation of Risk," *American Economic Review, Papers and Proceedings*, Vol. 61 (May 1971), 371–79; and Michael Spence and Richard Zeckhauser, "Insurance, Information, and Individual Action," *American Economic Review, Papers and Proceedings*, Vol. 61 (May 1971), 380–87.

5. See Kenneth Arrow, *Aspects of the Theory of Risk-Bearing* (Helsinki: Yrjö Jahnssonin Säätiö, 1965); Mark V. Pauly, "The Economics of Moral

that achieves "the optimal trade-off between the conflicting goals of furthering risk spreading and providing appropriate incentives."[6] I now show that competitive equilibrium when moral hazard is present does not correspond to this optimal outcome. I shall then show the informational requirements for an optimal solution to be reached via a market.

Consider a simple model in which there are assumed to be two possible states of the world. In S_1 individual i suffers no loss. In S_2 he suffers a loss equal to L dollars. By varying the level of some activity, the insured can affect his probability of loss[7] $\pi(S_2)$. The activity costs one dollar per unit. The activity of z_i of individual i is assumed not to be observable by the insurer. For simplicity, it is assumed that all individuals have identical wealths and utility functions and that, given a level of z, all are subject to identically and independently distributed risks.

The level of activity z is measured by the cost of preventive activity, and it is assumed that only the cost matters. For the "prevention function" $\pi_i = \pi(z_i)$, π' is assumed to be negative, and π'' positive. Insurers offer for sale dollars to be delivered if S_2 occurs. If individual i buys X_i dollars' worth of insurance and if P_i is the total premium for that insurance and S_i^0 his initial wealth, his final wealth will be

$$W_i^1 = S_i^0 - z_i - P_i \qquad \text{if } S_1 \text{ occurs;}$$
$$W_i^2 = S_i^0 - z_i - P_i - L_i + X_i \qquad \text{if } S_2 \text{ occurs.}$$

Competitive equilibrium, under the assumption of net worth maximization by insurance firms, requires that expected profits be zero. Since π_i is the probability of state 2 for person i, this condition can be written as

$$(1) \qquad \sum_i \pi_i X_i = \sum_i P_i.$$

The total amount of insurance purchased by any individual X_i is assumed not to be observable by any firm. The firm only knows the amount it sold to the individual.

A. Utility-Maximizing z_i

We can think of a representative individual as solving the prob-

Hazard: Comment," *American Economic Review*, Vol. 58 (June 1968), 531–36; Richard Zeckhauser, "Medical Insurance: A Case Study of the Tradeoff Between Risk-Spreading and Incentives," *Journal of Economic Theory*, Vol. 2 (March 1970), 10–26.

6. Spence and Zeckhauser, *op. cit.*, p. 385.

7. It would also have been possible to set up the problem as one in which the insured affected the amount of the loss, but not the probability of the loss-producing state.

lem of how much insurance to buy in two stages. First, he determines the utility-maximizing level of z_i for every value of X_i. Then he chooses the utility-maximizing value of X_i, given its associated value of P and of utility-maximizing z_i. His expected utility is given by

$$(2) \qquad EU = (1-\pi_i(z_i))\ u(S_i^0 - z_i - P_i) + \pi(z_i)\ u(S_i^0 - z_i - P_i + X_i - L).$$

With X_i and P given, for an interior solution that value of z maximizes EU, which satisfies

$$(3) \qquad (1-\pi_i)u'(1) + \pi_i u'(2) = [u(2) - u(1)]\partial\pi_i/\partial z_i,$$

where

$$u(1) = u(S_i^0 - z_i - P_i)$$

and

$$u(2) = u(S_i^0 - z_i - P_i + X_i - L_i).$$

The left side represents the price (in terms of expected marginal utility) of additional z_i, and the right side the effect of that z_i on the individual's expected utility level.[8] Clearly if $X_i = L_i$ (full coverage) so that $u(2) = u(1)$, a corner solution is obtained, and optimal z_i will be set equal to zero.

It will also be true that z_i will be equal to zero for some values of X_i less than L_i. For at $X_i = L_i$, the left side of (3) becomes $u' > 0$, while the right side becomes zero. As X_i is reduced below L_i, although the individual is exposed to some of the loss, there must be some range of values of X_i over which the right side of (3) is still less than the left side. The amount of potential loss borne by the individual over that range is still too small to make it worthwhile to spend anything on prevention. Hence, over the range of corner solutions, a range that must exist as long as $u' > 0$, it must be the case that $\partial z_i/\partial X_i = 0$.

But *generally* it will be true that the level of preventive activity will be reduced as more insurance is bought, since the effect of increased X_i is to reduce the effect on the individual's wealth of a change in z_i. It could also happen that $\partial z_i/\partial X_i > 0$ if the effect of increased insurance coverage reduced expected marginal utility of wealth (by reducing $\pi u'(2)$ more than it increased $(1-\pi)u'(1)$ sufficiently to more than offset its effect in reducing $u(2) - u(1)$). In what follows, however, I shall assume that z_i depends on X_i, that $\partial z_i/\partial X_i \leqslant 0$, and that the strict inequality holds for some values of X_i.

8. See Isaac Ehrlich and Gary Becker, "Market Insurance, Self-Insurance, and Self-Protection," *Journal of Political Economy*, Vol. 80 (July/Aug. 1972), p. 639, for a similar derivation.

B. Moral Hazard

I specifically assume that $\left.\frac{\partial P_i}{\partial z_i}\right|_{X_i = X_i^*} = 0$. That is, no matter what the individual's level of z_i, for a given X_i he will be charged the same premium. This will be approximately true as long as there are large numbers of buyers, since the effect of each individual's variation in z_i will change $\sum_i \pi_i X_i$ and hence P_i and $\sum_i P_i$ by only an infinitesimal amount. This is the essence of moral hazard in the model — that insurance induces the individual to alter his value of z because variations in z, even though they affect his expected insurance claims for any level of coverage, do not affect the premium he pays at all.

C. Utility-Maximizing Quantity of Insurance

Given that z_i is set at the level given by equation (3) for any X_i so that $z_i = z_i(X)$, the individual determines the utility-maximizing quantity of insurance X_i to buy by maximizing EU, taking into account the dependence of z_i and P_i on X_i. The first-order condition becomes

$$
\begin{aligned}
(4) \qquad & \partial P_i \partial X_i[(1-\pi_i)u'(1)+\pi_i u'(2)] \\
& = \pi_i u'(2) - \frac{\partial z_i}{\partial X_i}[(1-\pi_i)u'(1)+\pi_i u'(2)] \\
& + \frac{\partial \pi_i}{\partial z_i}\frac{\partial z_i}{\partial X_i}[u(2)-u(1)].
\end{aligned}
$$

Given (3), two terms cancel,[9] so the final form of the expression becomes [1]

$$
(4') \qquad \frac{\partial P_i}{\partial X_i} = \frac{\pi_i u'(2)}{(1-\pi_i)u'(1)+\pi_i u'(2)}.
$$

D. Optimal Amount of Insurance

The amount of insurance the individual will buy therefore depends on $\partial P/\partial X_i$. Were it possible for the insurer to observe z_i, the premium could be made to vary with z_i and hence with π_i. Then it

9. If a corner solution occurs and the equality in (3) is not satisfied, $\partial z_i/\partial x_i = 0$, so the two terms drop out as well, and (4′) is obtained.

1. One might suppose that this is the same expression that would have been obtained by differentiating (2) partially with respect to X_i. However, the values given of $u(1)$ and $u(2)$ in (4′) are those values given by the utility-maximizing value of z, not by any value of z.

is easy to show that, if the premium were actuarially fair, the insured would set $X_i = L$ and choose that level of z_i at which $L\partial\pi/\partial z_i = 1$, i.e., the level at which the reduction in expected loss just equaled the price of z. But since z_i is unobservable, this outcome is not possible. A second-best optimum is possible if the total amount of insurance purchased by an individual can be observed. It would involve a trade-off between risks and incentives. In the general case the problem is one in the calculus of variations, in the sense that what must be chosen is a price function $P(X_i)$, which induces the individual to buy that amount of insurance that will yield the optimal pattern of insurance payments.[2] In the special case being investigated here, the optimal function $P(X_i)$ can be obtained more simply. The intuitive notion is that optimality requires setting the marginal price of insurance to an individual equal to the change in his expected claims resulting from an increment in insurance. While the actual change in his expected claims as a function of z_i cannot be observed, the change in his expected claims as his coverage changes can be seen if his total coverage is observable.

Consider an individual who purchases a given amount of insurance X^*. The premium to be charged to him that is consistent with zero expected profits for insurers is

$$P(X_i) = \pi X^*, \text{ where } \pi = \pi(X^*). \tag{5}$$

Here the subscript on the probability is dropped, since the probability is the same for all individuals who have the same amount of insurance. (Since all individuals are identical, they will purchase identical amounts of insurance given a price schedule, so that satisfaction of (5) for all values of X^* is equivalent to satisfaction of (1).) To determine the optimal schedule of marginal premiums $\partial P/\partial X$ in (4′), the expected utility of the representative individual in (2) is maximized subject to the zero-profit constraint. Substitution of πX for P_i in (2) and setting the derivative equal to zero yields the necessary optimality condition,

$$\pi + X\frac{\partial\pi}{\partial X} = \frac{\pi u'(2)}{(1-\pi)u'(1) + \pi u'(2)}. \tag{4''}$$

Hence, the optimal schedule $P(X)$ is given by setting $\partial P/\partial X$ equal to $\pi + X\dfrac{\partial\pi}{\partial X}$.

2. Spence and Zeckhauser use the calculus of variations in a more general model to determine the optimal insurance benefit function. Their model also differs somewhat from this one since they allow z to affect, not $\pi(L)$, but the actual loss L. See Spence and Zeckhauser, *op cit.*, p. 383.

II. "Competitive" Equilibrium

I shall show in this section that the optimal quantity that is described in the previous section may not be that chosen when competition between insurance firms exists. The potential non-optimality of competition arises precisely because the competitive $\partial P/\partial X$, the premium *per unit* of insurance, may well *not* be that given by equation (4″). Indeed, it will definitely not be that given by (4″) for all values of X at which $\partial z/\partial X<0$.

There are assumed to be many firms and free entry into the industry. Each *unit* X of insurance is sold at a price p, which is, as far as the purchaser is concerned, unaffected by the amount of insurance he buys. Why this should be so, even though the probability of loss in fact varies with the amount of insurance bought, is relatively easy to see. When an individual buys more insurance, his expected losses rise. But the only way he can be identified as having larger expected losses is if the insurer can determine the *total* amount of insurance he has bought. In our model the insurer knows how much insurance *he* has sold the individual, but he does not know how much the individual has bought from others. If a seller should try to adjust by increasing price with the quantity purchased from him, the insured would rationally only buy the first unit from the insurer, at the lower price, and buy the other units from other insurers. Indeed, an insurer who sells an individual additional insurance would also wish to conceal the fact from other insurers. By his doing so, the change in total premium resulting from the additional insurance will be less, and the individual will be likely both to buy more insurance and to buy it from the seller who is willing to help conceal the fact of sale.

Given the assumption that p is constant for any individual, $\partial P/\partial X$ becomes simply p, which is the same for all i. Condition (3) is satisfied with $\partial P/\partial X_i$ replaced by p. The equilibrium p, and hence the equilibrium X_i for any person i in the world of identicals, is that level of p that satisfies the zero-profit condition (1). It is easy to see that equilibrium p is given by

$$(6) \qquad p=\frac{\sum_i \pi_i X_i}{X_i}.$$

Since X_i will be the same for all i for a given p, this can be simplified to

$$(6a) \qquad p=\pi.$$

If individuals differed so that the amount of X purchased by each at a given p differed, then p would equal a weighted average of the π's applicable to each individual's purchase.

Since π is clearly less than $\pi + X\frac{\partial\pi}{\partial X}$ for any X at which $\frac{\partial\pi}{\partial X}>0$, it follows that competitive equilibrium can well be characterized by an overproduction of insurance relative to the second-best optimum and, what is perhaps more important, by an underuse of preventive activity (increase in moral hazard) even relative to that optimum. In general, there is no reason to expect competitive equilibrium to be optimal.

Note that in the optimal case the actual curve of supply prices per unit of insurance that would face the individual is an upward-sloping curve and the individual adjusts to a curve marginal to it, while in the competitive case each individual believes himself to be faced with a horizontal supply curve at p, while the aggregate supply curve is upward-sloping, reflecting the increase of π and p with increased insurance.

In the optimal case, of course, the marginal curve need not be continually upward-sloping. The value of $\partial\pi/\partial z$ is, by assumption, continuously decreasing in absolute amount with z, but, since $\partial z/\partial X$ will eventually become zero over some range of $X \geqq L$, the term $X\partial\pi/\partial z(\partial z/\partial X)$ can increase or decrease.

Indeed, it would appear that if premiums were actuarially fair and if individuals continue to purchase any insurance, they would overinsure in this "competitive" world to the extent of buying full coverage against the loss. In the competitive model, $\partial P/\partial X = p = \pi$. Substitute p for π and $\partial P/\partial X$ in (4′). Simplification yields $u'(2) = (1-p)u'(1)+pu'(2)$. This implies that $u'(1) = u'(2)$, which is possible, given risk aversion, only if $X = L$. Hence, one can conclude that a person who buys any insurance at all will buy as many dollars of coverage X as his potential loss L when $p = \pi$, even if moral hazard exists. He may, of course, decide to buy no insurance. Although reduction in the level of coverage would induce an individual to increase preventive activity that would reduce his expected loss, such a reduction would not affect his premium except by an infinitesimal amount, but would require him to pay the cost of preventive activity, so he will not voluntarily reduce coverage. Moreover, he will reduce the level of preventive activity to zero.

Even if people differed in risk aversion, they would still all buy full coverage if they purchased any coverage at all when $p = \pi$. If there was some loading, so that $p=(1+\lambda)\pi$, $\lambda>0$, and people differed in risk aversion, the premium actually charged would be a weighted average of the probabilities of loss of those who bought insurance. At this premium, people would purchase different quantities less than L.

For rational decisions the individual's premium should vary as much as possible with his expected loss.[3] But in competitive equilibrium, because price is uniform over the quantity of insurance bought, it does not vary at all with the individual's expected loss. The effect of his behavior on the premium is spread over all other insurance purchasers, because the insurer does not know which one of his customers has more insurance than the others. If a particular seller tries to vary the premium charged a buyer with purchases from that seller, each buyer will buy one unit from each seller.

At the second-best optimum described by (4″), the extent to which the marginal reduction in expected losses produced by preventive activity exceeds the cost of preventive activity is just offset by the risk-reduction benefits of additional coverage. The "competitive" outcome, on the other hand, may involve the purchase of insurance whose risk-reduction benefits are not even great enough to cover the increment in expected loss engendered by the purchase of that insurance. Each individual is induced to buy this excessive insurance because he supposes that his purchases will not appreciably affect the premium per unit. But when all individuals thus increase purchases, the market premium per unit does rise by an appreciable amount.

III. Moral Hazard and Public Provision

It is clear that, in this world of identical insurance purchasers, the optimal result would be produced by a law that required individuals to buy exactly the number of units of public insurance, say X^*, which would have been purchased had premiums varied with purchases in the way given by (4″). Many alternative quantities less than this amount would also represent Pareto optimal improvements over competitive equilibrium. Even if people differed in potential loss or risk aversion, uniform provision still might make them better off.

Note that the critical element here is that insurance purchases

3. See Kenneth Arrow, "Uncertainty and the Welfare Economics of Medical Care," *American Economic Review*, Vol. 53 (Dec. 1963), 941–73; and Mark Pauly, "The Welfare Economics of Community Rating," *Journal of Risk and Insurance*, Vol. 37 (Sept. 1970), 407–18.

are limited. If the limit could be enforced, the insurance could also be sold by competitive firms, since each firm would know, by virtue of the existence of the law, the amount of insurance bought by the individual.

It is also worth noting that if the law required the purchase of at least X^* units, but individuals could buy supplementary insurance in a private market, public provision would have no advantage over the market solution and indeed would not alter things at all. For the premium per unit at X^* would be p^*, and private firms would be willing to offer insurance at that rate. The law would convey the information that each person had bought at least X^* units, but would convey no information about *marginal* purchases.

But an alternative way of reaching optimality is available. Suppose firms were provided with information on the total amount of insurance already bought by each prospective purchaser. Either this information could be provided directly, or a law (assuming it was enforceable) could require the purchaser to provide correct information on total purchases to all firms from which he had purchased insurance. With information on the magnitude of X_i, firms could calculate premiums for incremental coverage that reflect the probability $\pi(X_i)$ associated with that level of X_i. Since all firms would know the level of X_i, all firms would charge the same premium per unit.

If we also assume that potential purchasers know the entire optimal schedule $P(X)$ (i.e., know the schedule of marginal prices), there will be a unique utility-maximizing level of X chosen by each purchaser. At this level, (4″) will be satisfied (though (4″) may, if the curve of marginal prices is not continuously upward-sloping, be satisfied for other values of X). It is, of course, possible that the utility-maximizing quantity will be $X=L$. In such a case because $\partial\pi/\partial X$ equals zero, "competitive" equilibrium and optimality will coincide. But it may well also happen that $\partial\pi/\partial X>0$, so that only the schedule $\pi+X\partial\pi/\partial X$ will lead to optimal purchases.

This discussion does suggest that information on the entire schedule of possible marginal premiums $\partial P/\partial X$ needs to be known by firms and customers for a market-like arrangement to produce optimality. It is not in general sufficient to have information only on the values of $\partial P/\partial X$ in the neighborhood of the currently prevailing premium.

If, as noted above, both public provision and competitive marketing of supplementary coverage are permitted to exist side by side, information on total purchases will be needed for optimality. Supplementary purchases raise the probability of loss and hence raise the expected loss of the purchaser within the public program as well as the loss in any private insurance. For optimality the individual would have to bear the cost of his increased use of both kinds of insurance. This means that, even if the public insurance were provided through general taxes, for optimality a premium for public insurance should be assessed on those who buy supplementary coverage.[4]

In conclusion, one should note that the failure of competitive equilibrium to be optimal occurs because a person who buys more insurance is, in effect, changing the probabilities of states of nature he faces. Thus dollars to be delivered if S_2 occurs are really different "commodities," depending on the level of insurance coverage. It is not clear whether competitive markets would necessarily be optimal if sellers had information on total purchases, since sellers might be able to price discriminate over units. But this seems unlikely, and so optimality will probably occur.[5]

[Sections IV and V of the original paper are omitted.]

4. For example, Martin Feldstein and I have recently proposed national health insurance that includes deductibles and co-insurance, the purpose of which is to limit quantitative and qualitative overuse. See Martin Feldstein, "A New Approach to National Health Insurance," *The Public Interest*, No. 23 (Spring 1971), pp. 93–105; and Mark Pauly, *An Analysis of National Health Insurance Proposals* (Washington: American Enterprise Institute, 1971). The above analysis suggests that, if individuals are permitted to buy supplementary coverage, they should be required to pay an additional premium for the public insurance. Indeed, given the average pricing policies followed by many hospitals, the premium should probably be above the cost of additional use explicitly attributable to persons with supplementary coverage.

5. Suppose sellers tried to discriminate. If they earned positive profits, new firms would enter, and price would fall. If they earned zero profits but offered the consumer an all-or-nothing arrangement, new firms could enter and make positive profits by *reducing* the quantity required to be taken.

Exercises on optimal insurance

This reading considered the efficiency problem arising when an individual can affect the probability of an unfavorable event. A similar problem arises when behavior after the random event is hard to monitor. The following two exercises make this point and give simple examples of optimal insurance policies. The first example is a model of insurance for loss of earnings (as with pensions), while the second covers medical expenditures.

A[1] If an individual works he produces L units of output and has utility function $U_1(C)$, where consumption is C. If he doesn't work he has utility function $U_2(C)$. Assume that with probability $(1 - \theta)$ he cannot work [and still has utility function $U_2(C)$]. Assume that the government deals with many identical workers so its budget constraint equates expected output and expected consumption.

1 If the government can monitor whether he can work, what rule allocating consumption between states maximizes the expected utility of a typical worker? (You may want to compare this to the competitive equilibrium assuming a full set of contingent commodity markets as in Chapter 11.) Assume that the allocation with no work and zero consumption is not optimal.

Now assume that the government cannot monitor ability to work. The government allows consumption C_1 to anyone who works and C_2 to anyone who does not. The government continues trying to maximize the expected utility of a typical worker.

2 For what combinations of C_1 and C_2 will the worker supply labor when he is able?

3 If $U_1'(C_1) = U_2'(C_2)$ implies $U_1(C_1) \geqslant U_2(C_2)$ show that the optimal policy described in (1) is still optimal.

4 If $U_1'(C_1) = U_2'(C_2)$ implies $U_1(C_1) < U_2(C_2)$ show that the optimal policy described in (1) is not feasible. What is the largest feasible value of C_2? Is this the optimal plan? Is this allocation achievable as a competitive equilibrium if individuals can buy as much insurance as they want? What if they can only buy insur-

[1]This exercise is based on Diamond and Mirrlees (1978).

ance from one company, which can restrict the amount that can be purchased?

B[2] Suppose an individual faces two states of the world. In state 1, he is sick. In state 2, he is well. Let p be the probability of state 1.

Let c^i be consumption of goods in state i, let m be the consumption of medical services in state 1. Suppose the individual preferences are given by

$$pU^1(c^1, m) + (1 - p)U^2(c^2)$$

Let the market prices of m and c be 1, with prices independent of demand.

1 If the individual can buy insurance whose payoff depends only on the state, show that an individual who purchases an actuarially fair policy, will buy insurance up to the point where

$$U_c^2 = U_c^1 = U_m^1$$

where U_c, U_m are the first derivatives of utility with respect to c and m, respectively.

2 Assume, alternatively, that insurance pays some fraction θ of medical bills, with the individual being free to select the level of consumption of medical care. Thus $1 - \theta$ is the coinsurance rate. Insurance is actuarially fair and individuals act as if the insurance premium were independent of demand for medical care.

(a) Given that state 1 has occurred, what is the marginal rate of substitution between consumption of goods and medical services when the consumer has optimized his utility? Write the medical care chosen at this optimum as $m(\theta, y)$, where y is income net of premium paid in state 1.

(b) What is the equation determining the premium $\pi(\theta)$ for an actuarially fair policy?

(c) Using the functions $m(\theta, y)$ and $\pi(\theta)$ defined above, state the level of expected utility in equilibrium as a function of θ for an individual who has purchased an actuarially fair policy.

(d) Assuming an internal solution, show that the level of θ that maximizes expected utility satisfies

$$U_c^1 m = [pU_c^1 + (1 - p)U_c^2] \frac{m + \theta\, \partial m/\partial\theta}{1 + p\theta\, \partial m/\partial y}$$

Can you give an intuitive explanation for this equation? [*Hint*: Evaluate $d\pi/d\theta$.]

[2]We are grateful to Professor C. Wilson for providing this exercise.

Comment

This paper has shown that an inability to monitor the amount of insurance purchased by an individual can lead to a competitive equilibrium that is not a Pareto optimum relative to the set of policies that do not involve observation of the care taken to avoid accidents. In addition to the policies that the author has discussed, the optimum can be achieved by a tax on insurance purchases of the correct amount equal, effectively, to the marginal externality generated when the consumer purchases an additional unit of insurance (and so takes less care, raising insurance company costs).

Shavell (1979) has considered a similar model, differing only in that the cost of avoiding accidents is in utility units rather than financial units [$c(z)$ is subtracted from EU]. He assumes that consumers only purchase insurance from a single firm, which offers a single policy on a take it or leave it basis. Shavell shows that the competitive equilibrium is then optimal (which is consistent with the same result in the model used above). In addition, he shows that the competitive solution always involves some insurance, and incomplete insurance. (Like Pauly he assumes that insurance involves no administrative costs.)

Once one generalizes the model beyond a single commodity, the competitive equilibrium can fail to be optimal even if the amount of insurance purchased is monitored by the firm.[1] It may be possible to tax or subsidize other commodities that affect the probability of an accident, and so the cost of providing insurance. For example, subsidizing fire extinguishers would improve welfare (assuming that firms do not monitor whether they have been purchased). Where auto insurance firms do not monitor the number of miles driven, taxing gasoline can also improve welfare. Even if these could be monitored at some cost by firms, general taxation might be administratively cheaper. Thus, whenever there is a marketed commodity for which the quantity purchased affects the unobserved attempts to avoid accidents, the situation is analogous to a conventional externality. By altering behavior in a way to reduce the costs of providing insurance, a welfare improvement can be achieved.[2]

[1]This has been noted by Shavell and by Diamond and Mirrlees (1978).

[2]As will be discussed below, a similar conclusion holds when the relevant externality generating behavior occurs after an accident, as with medical insurance.

References

P. Diamond and J. Mirrlees, A model of social insurance with variable retirement, *J. Public Econ.* **10** (1978), 295–336.

S. Shavell, On moral hazard and insurance, *Quart. J. Econ.* **93** (1979), 541–562.

20
B. Holmström, Moral hazard and observability, *Bell Journal of Economics* **10** (1979), 74–91

The previous reading concentrated on the efficiency properties of an equilibrium. We now consider further the design of insurance policies that maximize expected utility in the presence of moral hazard. This includes the use of imperfect information. For another treatment of the same subject, see Shavell (1979). The Shavell paper contains the additional result that the agent does not bear all of the risk if the agent is not risk neutral. For a survey of recent work in contract theory see Hart and Holmström (1987). The moral hazard problem has similarities with that of optimal taxation. For an advanced treatment of that problem see Mirrlees (1976).

References

O. Hart and B. Holmström, The theory of contracts. In T. Bewley (ed.), "Advances in Economic Theory," Cambridge: Cambridge University Press, 1987.

J. Mirrlees, Optimum tax theory: A synthesis, *J. Public Econ.* **6** (1976), 327–358.

S. Shavell, Risk sharing and incentives in the principal and agent relationship, *Bell J. Econ.* **10** (1979), 55–73.

Moral hazard and observability

Bengt Holmström
Swedish School of Economics and Business Administration

The role of imperfect information in a principal-agent relationship subject to moral hazard is considered. A necessary and sufficient condition for imperfect information to improve on contracts based on the payoff alone is derived, and a characterization of the optimal use of such information is given.

1. Introduction

■ It has long been recognized that a problem of moral hazard may arise when individuals engage in risk sharing under conditions such that their privately taken actions affect the probability distribution of the outcome.[1] This situation is common in insurance, labor contracting, and the delegation of decisionmaking responsibility, to give a few examples. In these instances Pareto-optimal risk sharing is generally precluded, because it will not induce proper incentives for taking correct actions. Instead, only a second-best solution, which trades off some of the risk-sharing benefits for provision of incentives, can be achieved.

The source of this moral hazard or incentive problem is an asymmetry of information among individuals that results because individual actions cannot be observed and hence contracted upon. A natural remedy to the problem is to invest resources into monitoring of actions and use this information in the contract. In simple situations complete monitoring may be possible, in which case a first-best solution (entailing optimal risk sharing) can be achieved by employing a forcing contract that penalizes dysfunctional behavior. Generally, however, full observation of actions is either impossible or prohibitively costly. In such situations interest centers around the use of imperfect estimators of actions in contracting. Casual observation indicates that imperfect information is extensively used in practice to alleviate moral hazard, for instance in the supervision of employees or in various forms of managerial accounting.

A natural question then arises: when can imperfect information about actions be used to improve on a contract which initially is based on the payoff alone? Secondly, how should such additional information be used optimally?

This paper is partly based on Chapter 4 of the author's unpublished dissertation, "On Incentives and Control in Organizations," submitted to Stanford University, December 1977. It was written while the author was visiting the Center for Operations Research and Econometrics, Université Catholique de Louvain, Belgium. An earlier version was presented at the European Meeting of the Econometric Society in Geneva, 1978. I am much indebted to Joel Demski, Frøystein Gjesdal, Charles Holloway, David Kreps, and Robert Wilson for many helpful discussions and to David Baron and Gerald Kramer for detailed comments on an earlier manuscript.

[1] See for instance Arrow (1970), Zeckhauser (1970), Pauly (1974), and Spence and Zeckhauser (1971).

Reprinted with permission of The Rand Corporation from *Bell Journal of Economics* **10** (1979), 74–91.

A recent interesting paper by Harris and Raviv (1976) addresses these questions in the context of a principal-agent relationship in which the agent provides a productive input (e.g., effort) that cannot be observed by the principal directly.[2] Their results relate to a very specific kind of imperfect monitoring of the agent's action. They study monitors which provide information that is independent of the state of nature and allows the principal to detect any shirking by the agent with positive probability. Such monitors are of limited interest, however, since they are essentially equivalent to observing the agent's action directly, because a first-best solution can be approximated arbitrarily closely in this case.[3] Clearly, one cannot expect imperfect monitoring to possess such strong characteristics in general.

Employing a different problem formulation from Harris and Raviv's, we are able to simplify their analysis and generalize their results substantially. Both questions posed above are given complete answers (in our particular model). It is shown that any additional information about the agent's action, however imperfect, can be used to improve the welfare of both the principal and the agent. This result, which formalizes earlier references to the value of monitoring in agency relationships (Stiglitz, 1975; Williamson, 1975), serves to explain the extensive use of imperfect information in contracting. Furthermore, we characterize optimal contracts based on such imperfect information in a way which yields considerable insight into the complex structure of actual contracts.

The formulation we use is an extension of that introduced by Mirrlees (1974, 1976). We start by presenting a slightly modified version of Mirrlees' model (Section 2), along with some improved statements about the nature of optimal contracts when the payoff alone is observed. In Section 3 a detour is made to show how these results can be applied to prove the optimality of deductibles in accident insurance when moral hazard is present. Section 4 gives the characterization of the optimal use of imperfect information and Section 5 presents the result when imperfect information is valuable. Up to this point homogeneous beliefs are assumed, but in Section 6 this assumption is relaxed to the extent that we allow the agent to be more informed at the time he chooses his action. The analysis is brief, but indicates that qualitatively the same results obtain as for the case with homogeneous beliefs. Section 7 contains a summary and points out some directions for further research.

2. Optimal sharing rules when the payoff alone is observed

■ We study a principal-agent relationship, where the agent privately takes an action $a \in A \subseteq \mathscr{R}$, A being the set of all possible actions, and a together with a random state of nature θ, determines a monetary outcome or payoff $x = x(a, \theta)$. The problem is to determine how this payoff should be shared optimally between the principal and the agent. The principal's utility function is $G(w)$, defined over wealth alone, and the agent's utility function is $H(w, a)$, defined over wealth

[2] The main results of Harris and Raviv (1976) are reported in their 1978 paper. For earlier work on principal-agent models, see Wilson (1969), Ross (1973), and Mirrlees (1976).

[3] This fact, which is not observed by Harris and Raviv (1976), can be verified by using an argument similar to the one given by Mirrlees (1974, p. 249), or by Gjesdal (1976) (cf. example in footnote 7). Obviously, it implies that monitoring, which satisfies Harris and Raviv's conditions, is valuable. This is their partial answer to the first question raised above.

and action. The model is further restricted by assuming that $H(w,a) = U(w) - V(a)$, with $V' > 0$ and $x_a \geqslant 0$.[4] The interpretation is that a is a productive input with direct disutility for the agent and this creates an inherent difference in objectives between the principal and the agent. It is convenient to think of a as effort and this term will be used interchangeably with action. Since the problem of moral hazard can be avoided when the agent is risk-neutral (Harris and Raviv, 1976), we shall assume $U'' < 0$. The principal may or may not be risk-neutral, i.e., $G'' \leqslant 0$.

In this section, we consider the case where the principal observes only the outcome x. Thus, sharing rules have to be functions of x alone. Let $s(x)$ denote the share of x that goes to the agent and $r(x) = x - s(x)$ denote the share that goes to the principal. It is assumed that both parties agree on the probability distribution of θ and that the agent chooses $\underline{a}$ before θ is known.[5] In this case (constrained) Pareto-optimal sharing rules $s(x)$ are generated by the program:

$$\max_{s(x),a} E\{G(x - s(x))\} \tag{1}$$

$$\text{subject to } E\{H(s(x),a)\} \geq \bar{H}, \tag{2}$$

$$a \in \underset{a' \epsilon A}{\operatorname{argmax}}\, E\{H(s(x),a')\}, \tag{3}$$

where the notation "argmax" denotes the set of arguments that maximize the objective function that follows.[6]

Constraint (2) guarantees the agent a minimum expected utility (attained via a market or negotiation process). Constraint (3) reflects the restriction that the principal can observe x but not $\underline{a}$. If he also could observe $\underline{a}$, a forcing contract could be used to guarantee that the agent selects a proper action even when $s(x)$ is chosen to solve (1)–(2) ignoring (3). The latter we will refer to as the *first-best solution*, which entails optimal risk sharing. It differs in general from the solution of (1) subject to (2) *and* (3), which we call a *second-best solution*.

Two approaches can be used to solve the program above. The earlier one, used by Spence and Zeckhauser (1971), Ross (1973), and Harris and Raviv (1976), recognizes explicitly the dependence of x on $\underline{a}$ and θ, so that the expectations in (1)–(3) are taken with respect to the distribution of θ. They proceed to characterize an optimal solution by replacing (3) with the first-order constraint $E\{H_1 \cdot s' \cdot x_a + H_2\} = 0$, and then apply the calculus of variations. To validate these steps one has to assume that an optimum exists and is differentiable. However, as an example by Mirrlees (1974) shows, there may commonly exist no optimal solution among the class of unbounded sharing rules, and for this reason $s(x)$ has to be restricted to a finite interval in general. As a result, the solution will become nondifferentiable and the above-mentioned approach can no longer be applied.[7]

[4] Subscripts denote partial derivatives with respect to corresponding variables.

[5] This assumption corresponds to model 1 in Harris and Raviv (1976), which is the model they use for studying imperfect information. We shall relax it in Section 6.

[6] As usual, E denotes the expectation operator. Since $E\{H(s(x),a)\}$ need not be concave in a, there may exist multiple solutions, hence the inclusion symbol.

[7] Even when an optimal solution exists among unbounded sharing rules, it may be nondifferentiable. This has been observed by Gjesdal (1976). To illustrate his ideas one can look at the follow-

A better approach to solving (1)–(3), which also gives a more intuitive characterization of an optimum, has been introduced by Mirrlees (1974, 1976). He suppresses θ and views x as a random variable with a distribution $F(x,a)$, parameterized by the agent's action. Given a distribution of θ, $F(x,a)$ is simply the distribution induced on x via the relationship $x = x(a,\theta)$.[8] It is easy to see that $x_a \geqslant 0$ implies $F_a(x,a) \leqslant 0$. It will be assumed that for every $\underline{a}$, $F_a(x,a) < 0$ for some x-values, so that a change in $\underline{a}$ has a nontrivial effect on the distribution of x. In particular, it will shift the distribution of x to the right in the sense of first-order stochastic dominance.

For the moment, assume F has a density function $f(x,a)$ with f_a and f_{aa} well defined for all (x,a).[9] Replacing (3) with a first-order constraint yields the program:

$$\max_{s(x)\in[c,d+x],a} \int G(x - s(x))f(x,a)dx \tag{4}$$

$$\text{subject to} \quad \int [U(s(x)) - V(a)]f(x,a)dx \geq \bar{H}, \tag{5}$$

$$\int U(s(x))f_a(x,a)dx = V'(a). \tag{6}$$

Note that $s(x)$ is restricted to lie in the interval $[c, d + x]$ to avoid nonexistence of a solution.[10] This restriction is natural from a pragmatic point of view as well, since the agent's wealth puts a lower bound, and the principal's wealth (augmented with x) an upper bound on $s(x)$.

Let λ be the multiplier for (5) and μ the multiplier for (6). Pointwise optimization of the Lagrangian yields the following characterization of an optimal sharing rule:

$$\frac{G'(x - s(x))}{U'(s(x))} = \lambda + \mu \cdot \frac{f_a(x,a)}{f(x,a)}, \tag{7}$$

---

ing insightful example. Let $x(a,z) = a + z$ and $z \sim \text{Unif}(0,1)$, so that $x \sim \text{Unif}(a,a + 1)$. If $(a^*,s^*(x))$ is a first-best solution it is easy to see that a contract of the form $s(x) = s^*(x)$ when $x \geqslant a^*$, $s(x) = w$ otherwise, will make the agent choose $a = a^*$ for w sufficiently low. But in that case $x \geqslant a^*$ for all outcomes of $\tilde{z}$, and the first-best solution $s(x) = s^*(x)$ is effectively realized. In other words, a nondifferentiable sharing rule, which penalizes the agent for outcomes $x < a^*$, will give both the principal and the agent the same expected utility as a first-best solution. In this example no optimal differentiable sharing rule exists for (1)–(3).

Gjesdal's analysis shows that both Spence and Zeckhauser (1971, p. 383, footnote 5) and Harris and Raviv (1976, pp. 36–37) err in giving incorrect characterizations (based on the Euler equation) for examples similar to this.

We will avoid situations like these by essentially assuming that the support of the distribution of x will not change with a, as explained below. For a more detailed comparison of the state-space approach with Mirrlees' approach, see Holmström (1977).

[8] Thus, it is always possible to go from the state space approach to Mirrlees' approach, while the reverse is not always true.

[9] In Section 3 we shall allow discrete distributions as well. The crucial assumption is that f_a exists. Note that this assumption is not satisfied by the example in footnote 7.

[10] More precisely, existence of a solution to (1)–(3) can be proved for the class of functions:

$$S_K = \{s(x) \in [c,d + x] \,|\, V_b^{b'}(s) \leq K \cdot (b' - b)\},$$

where $V_b^{b'}(s)$ is the total variation of s in the interval $[b,b']$ (Kolmogorov and Fomin, 1970), under some technical assumptions about integrability and the behavioral assumption that the agent, for almost every x for which (7) has a solution $s(x) \in [c, d + x]$; otherwise $s(x) = c$ or $d + x$, depending on whether the right-hand side $\lesseqgtr$ left-hand side throughout the interval. Furthermore, μ is given as the solution to the adjoint equation,

$$\int G(x - s(x))f_a(x,a)dx + \mu \cdot \left\{ \int U(s(x))f_{aa}(x,a)dx - V''(a) \right\} = 0, \quad (8)$$

and $\underset{\sim}{a}$ is determined by (6).[11]

From Borch's (1962) work, we know that $s(x)$ will be Pareto optimal from a risk-sharing point of view only if the right-hand side in (7) is constant. Now, $f_a/f = k$, a constant, implies $0 = \int f_a = \int f \cdot k = k$, since $\int f = 1$ for all $\underset{\sim}{a}$. Hence, $f_a \equiv 0$ would follow, which contradicts the assumption that $F_a < 0$ for some x. Consequently, perfect risk sharing could only obtain if $\mu = 0$. But, in fact, one can prove the following:[12]

Proposition 1. Assume $V' > 0$ and $F_a \leq 0$ (with strict inequality for some x-values), then $\mu > 0$, or equivalently: The principal would like to see the agent increase his effort given the second-best sharing rule.

Proof: See Appendix.

Two immediate corollaries follow:

Corollary 1. Under the assumption of Proposition 1, one has the following relationship between the second-best solution $s(x)$ and the first-best solution $s_\lambda(x)$, for a given λ:

$$\begin{cases} s(x) \geq s_\lambda(x), & \text{on} \quad X_+ = \{x \,|\, f_a(x,a) \geqslant 0\}, \\ s(x) < s_\lambda(x), & \text{on} \quad X_- = \{x \,|\, f_a(x,a) < 0\}. \end{cases} \quad (9)$$

Proof: See Appendix.

Corollary 2. Under the assumption of Proposition 1, the second-best solution is strictly inferior to a first-best solution.[13]

Proof: See Appendix.

---

in case he is indifferent, chooses his action according to the principal's preferences. By taking K large enough, the characterization in (6)–(8) will be valid for this solution, and S_K will contain all functions of practical relevance.

[11] The characterization can be proved rigorously as in Holmström (1977) using proposition 9.6.1 in Luenberger (1969). Some technical assumptions which we do not spell out are needed. More important is the fact that one has to assume that the agent's optimal choice of action is unique for the optimal $s(x)$. This assumption seems very difficult to validate except in specific problems and regrettably we have to leave the question about its validity open.

Mirrlees (1974) was the first to give a characterization of an optimum in the form above (without bounds). Earlier Spence and Zeckhauser (1971) and Ross (1973) gave alternative characterizations based on the state space formulation.

[12] This proposition generalizes Mirrlees' (1976) conclusion that $\mu > 0$ when f_a/f is increasing in x.

[13] It is worthwhile stressing the difference between Corollary 2 and the example in footnote 7. A first-best solution can be achieved in that example because f_a does not exist at the endpoints of the uniform distribution. Whenever f_a exists, Corollary 2 indicates that a first-best solution cannot be achieved. Also, note that $V' > 0$ is essential. The role played by V in the characterization is obscured by the complexity of the relationships between (6)–(8), but generally one expects that the larger V'' is, the smaller is μ and the accompanying welfare loss. At an extreme, if $V' = 0$ for $a \leq \bar{a}$ and $V' = \infty$ for $a > \bar{a}$ then the first-best outcome can be achieved since it entails $a = \bar{a}$, which the agent will choose given an optimal risk-sharing rule.

The characterization in (7) has an intuitive interpretation in terms of deviating from optimal risk sharing to provide incentives for increased effort on the part of the agent. This is accomplished by taking $s(x) \geqslant s_\lambda(x)$ when the marginal return from effort is positive to the agent, and $s(x) < s_\lambda(x)$ when it is negative (see Corollary 1). The incentive effect of deviating from optimal risk sharing is stronger the larger is $|f_a|$, and it is more costly (in terms of lost risk-sharing benefits) the greater is f. Thus $|f_a|/f$ may be interpreted as a benefit-cost ratio for deviation from optimal risk sharing, and (7) states that such deviations should be made in proportion to this ratio, with individual risk aversion taken into account.

In contrast to perfect risk sharing, the second-best solution is crucially dependent on the distribution of x and its functional relation to $\underset{\sim}{a}$. This occurs because the outcome x can be used as a signal about the action which is not directly observed. We note that f_a/f is the derivative of the maximum likelihood function $\log f$, when $\underset{\sim}{a}$ is viewed as an unknown parameter. In this sense f_a/f measures how strongly one is inclined to infer from x that the agent did not take the assumed action, and (7) says that penalties or bonuses (as expressed by deviations from first-best risk sharing) should be paid in proportion to this measure.[14]

The deviation from perfect risk sharing implies that the agent is forced to carry excess responsibility for the outcome and this points to the implicit costs involved in contracting under imperfect information (Corollary 2). Consequently, there are positive gains to observing the agent's action, since in that case a first-best solution can be achieved by using a forcing contract. This provides the basis for discussing ways to realize part of these gains by using imperfect monitoring, which is the subject of Sections 4 and 5.

To illustrate the formula in (7) and the interpretations, consider the following example: $G(w) = w$, $U(w) = 2\sqrt{w}$, $V(a) = a^2$, $x \sim \exp(1/a)$. In this example, the agent could be a machine repairman, whose effort $\underset{\sim}{a}$ will determine the expected time before the machine will break down. The monetary return x is proportional to the length of time the machine will remain operative; (here the proportionality factor has been taken $= 1$).

From (7), the optimal share is:[15]

$$s(x) = \left[\lambda + \mu \cdot \frac{(x - a)}{a^2}\right]^2, \tag{10}$$

and some simple calculations yield $\mu = a^3$, and the equation $4a^3 + 2\lambda \cdot a = 1$ for $\underset{\sim}{a}$ (using (6) and (8)). As one would expect, μ is increasing in $\underset{\sim}{a}$, since it is more costly to induce higher effort. The first-best solution is $s_\lambda(x) = \lambda^2$, $a_\lambda = 1/2\lambda$.[16]

For a numerical solution let $\lambda = \frac{1}{2}$. Then $s(x) = \frac{1}{4}(x + \frac{1}{2})^2$, $a = \frac{1}{2}$, $s_\lambda(x) = \frac{1}{4}$, $a_\lambda = 1$, as pictured below. The welfare measure for the first-best solution is $\frac{3}{4}$ and for the second-best it is $\frac{9}{16}$. (See Figure 1.) In this example,

[14] Of course, this interpretation is not quite accurate, since given $s(x)$, the principal knows from (4) what action a rational agent will take according to the model. But I think this interpretation corresponds well with reasoning in practice.

[15] This is an exceptional example in that no bounds need to be imposed on the sharing rule, and an explicit solution can thus be obtained.

[16] In this example the question of uniqueness, referred to in footnote 11, is no problem. For any fixed a, (10) gives the appropriate solution to (4)–(6), which is a relaxation of (1)–(3) when a is fixed at its optimal value. But it is easily checked that $s(x)$ in (10) makes (6) strictly concave in a, and hence the relaxed problem also solves the original one.

FIGURE 1

THE SECOND-BEST SOLUTION FOR THE REPAIRMAN EXAMPLE WITHOUT MONITORING

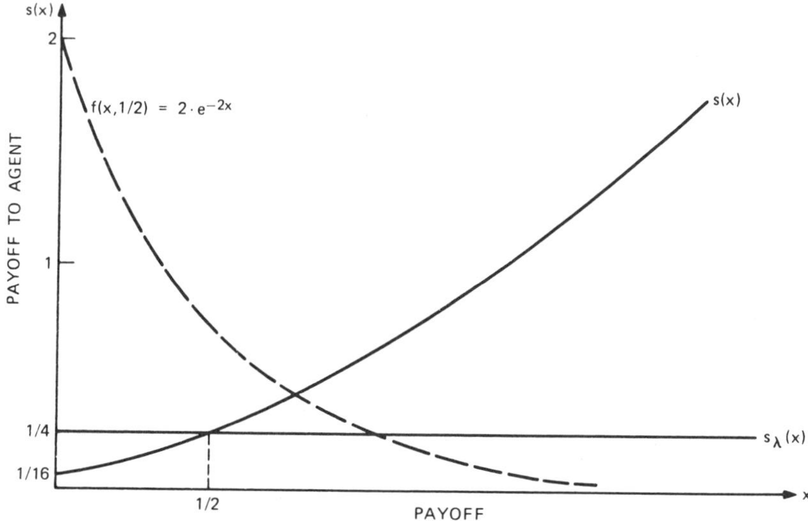

the penalties imposed on the agent for $x < ½$, which is the mean of x, are relatively small owing to the high values of $f(x, ½)$ in this region (and, of course, owing to risk aversion), and bonuses for $x > ½$ are correspondingly large. In view of risk-sharing benefits, the convexity of the second-best solution may be surprising, but this is in no way exceptional (cf. Mirrlees (1976); also in Wilson (1969), convex sharing rules may be optimal). Examples for which sharing rules are concave or linear or even two-peaked can be easily generated as well.

3. Deductibles in insurance

■ The characterization in (7) can be applied to the insurance setting to conclude that optimal accident insurance policies necessarily entail deductibles in the presence of moral hazard. To demonstrate this, the assumption that the distribution $F(x,a)$ possesses a density function will be relaxed. Since (7) is derived via point-wise optimization, a mixture of a continuous and discrete distribution can be used as well, provided the support of the discrete distribution is left unchanged by the action (cf. footnote 7). In that case simply interpret $f(x,a)$ in (7) as the probability mass rather than the value of the density function whenever x is a mass point (and correspondingly for f_a and f_{aa}, which both are assumed to exist as before).

Mixed distributions are characteristic in accident insurance. First, there is a probability that no accident occurs and this generates a mass point at $x = 0$; and conditional on an accident, there is a damage distribution over $x < 0$, which usually can be assumed continuous. If a represents a precautionary action, it is natural to assume that this mixed distribution satisfies:

$$f_a(0,a) > 0, f_a(x,a) < 0. \tag{11}$$

This assumption says that the probability of an accident decreases with $\underset{\sim}{a}$ so that each outcome $x < 0$ is less likely. For instance, driving a car more carefully will presumably decrease the probability of both small and large accidents.

Because $\mu > 0$ and the left-hand side in (7) is continuous, (11) clearly implies that the optimal sharing rule $s(x)$ is discontinuous at $x = 0$. In fact, $s(0) > s_\lambda(0) > s(x)$ for all $x < 0$, since $G'(x - s(x))/(U'(s(x))$ is increasing in $s(x)$ and nonincreasing in x (here s_λ is the solution to (7) with $\mu = 0$). If $d = \min_{x<0} \{s(0) - s(x)\} > 0$, we can write:[17]

$$s(x) = \begin{cases} k, & \text{if} \quad x = 0, \\ k - d - t(x), & \text{if} \quad x < 0, \end{cases} \tag{12}$$

where k is the agent's wealth after paying the premium, d is the deductible which is paid when an accident occurs, and $t(x) \geq 0$ is the agent's additional share in the costs of an accident. One would expect $t(x)$ to be increasing in x. This is the case if, for instance, f_a/f is increasing in x (which holds for surprisingly many standard distributions; see Holmström (1977)).

In many situations it is approximately true that the agent's action will only affect the probability of an accident and not the size of losses, given that an accident occurs. In that case one can write $f(0,a) = 1 - p(a), f(x,a) = p(a) \cdot g(x), x < 0$, where $p(a)$ is the probability of an accident ($p' < 0$) and $g(x)$ is a damage distribution independent of $\underset{\sim}{a}$. This implies $f_a(0,a)/f(0,a) = -p'(a)/(1 - p(a)) > 0$ and $f_a(x,a)/f(x,a) = p'(a)/p(a) < 0$, for $x < 0$. Hence f_a/f is independent of x for $x < 0$, which means that for $x < 0$ we have first-best risk sharing. In particular, if the insurance company is risk-neutral, only a deductible will be charged when an accident occurs.

To summarize the discussion we have:

Proposition 2. Given the assumptions in (11), optimal accident insurance policies entail a deductible. If the insured's action only affects the probability of an accident but not the size of damage and the insurance company is risk-neutral, a deductible alone is optimal.

This proposition lends additional support to the frequent use of deductibles in accident insurance. However, the reasoning is quite different from that behind the well-known proposition by Arrow (1970), which holds that pure deductibles are always optimal. Arrow does not consider moral hazard aspects, and in his case deductibles arise for instance if the firm uses loading to determine the premium (Mossin, 1968).

4. Optimal sharing rules based on additional information

■ One of the main conclusions from Section 2 is that the optimal solution under moral hazard is not first-best and, hence, that there would be gains to observing the agent's action (see Corollary 2 and the subsequent discussion). Since perfect observation of the agent's action is generally precluded, interest centers on the use of imperfect information for improvements of the contract. This issue can be studied using a straightforward extension of the model in Section 2.

---

[17] If x can be observed only at the option of the insured, (12) is not enforceable. In that case, the optimal contract is $\bar{s}(x) = \max(x, s(x))$, with $s(x)$ as in (12). This is still a contract with a deductible.

Let y be a signal (possibly vector-valued), which in addition to x, is observed by both parties and hence can be used in constructing the sharing rule. Let $F(x,y,a)$ be the joint distribution of x and y given $\underset{\sim}{a}$. As in Section 3, let $f(x,y,a)$ be either the value of the density function of the continuous part of F or the probability mass of the mass point (x,y), if such exists. As before, f_a and f_{aa} are assumed to exist. The following extension of (7) obtains for an optimal sharing rule $s(x,y)$:

$$\frac{G'(x - s(x,y))}{U'(s(x,y))} = \lambda + \mu \cdot \frac{f_a(x,y,a)}{f(x,y,a)}, \tag{13}$$

for almost every (x,y) such that (13) has a solution $s(x,y) \in [c, d + x]$; otherwise $s(x,y) = c$ or $d + x$ depending on whether the right-hand side $\gtrless$ the left-hand side throughout the interval. Here μ is the multiplier of the agent's first-order constraint and satisfies (8) and $\underset{\sim}{a}$ satisfies (6) (with obvious changes in notation).

Again $\mu > 0$ follows as in Proposition 1, and consequently the second-best solution $s(x,y)$ will be strictly worse than a first-best solution.[18] The interpretation of f_a/f in Section 2 can be repeated for (13). A new, important feature, however, is that $f_a(x,y,a)/f(x,y,a)$ may change with y. Thus, for the same value of x, but under different contingencies signalled by y, the agent should generally receive different remuneration. In particular, if for one value of y it is possible to infer less about $\underset{\sim}{a}$ via x, then the deviation from optimal risk sharing should be smaller, and *vice versa*. At an extreme, a realization of the signal y could be such that $f_a(x,y,a) \equiv 0$ for all x (which means that nothing about the action can be inferred from the payoff), and in this case the optimal risk-sharing rule should be employed. In sharecropping, for example, if a natural disaster destroys the crop, farm workers should not be held responsible for the outcome (beyond optimal risk sharing).

This is quite intuitive and corresponds well with observed practice. Equation (13) would predict that contracts are elaborate and contain a variety of provisions for unexpected events. Certainly, there is substantial empirical support for this conclusion. Contracts, at least between external parties, tend to be detailed, spelling out different responsibilities in different contingencies (e.g., strikes, accidents, natural disasters, etc.). Not doing so would be inefficient and add to the implicit costs of contracting. In the same way managers are not held responsible for events one can observe are outside their control, and implicitly at least, their performance is always judged against information about what should be achievable given, say, the current economic situation.[19]

To illustrate the point we can look at an extension of the example in Section 2. Suppose now that the machine can also break down because of a failure in a component over which the repairman has no control. Let this event have an exponential probability distribution with constant parameter $(1/k)$, and assume it is independent of the event that the components which the repairman controls will break down. The latter event still has the same probability distribution as before, namely exponential with parameter $(1/a)$.

[18] As in Section 2, this result depends crucially on the assumption that f_a exists for all (x,y,a); cf. footnote 13.

[19] Note, however, that internal labor contracts rarely contain explicit reference to monitoring information, and presumably this information is often unknown to the agent. Yet such information is and should be used. The reason the principal (i.e., the firm) will not default on such an implicit contract is its concern for reputation in the labor market.

If it is not possible to determine whether the failure occurred in a component outside the repairman's control, the optimal solution is to employ a sharing rule:

$$s(x) = \left(\lambda + \mu_1 \cdot \left[\frac{x}{a^2} - \frac{k}{a(a+k)}\right]\right)^2. \tag{14}$$

This follows from (7), since $x \sim \exp((a+k)/ak)$.

On the other hand, if one can determine which component failed, this information can be used to improve the contract. Set $y = 1$ if the failure was outside the repairman's control and $y = 0$ otherwise. Employing (13), one has:[20]

$$s(x,0) = \left(\lambda + \mu_2 \cdot \left[\frac{x}{a^2} - \frac{1}{a}\right]\right)^2,$$
$$s(x,1) = \left(\lambda + \mu_2 \cdot \frac{x}{a^2}\right)^2. \tag{15}$$

Here $\mu_1 = a^3(1 + (a/k))^2$, $\mu_2 = a^3(1 + (a/k))$ from (6). Hence, $\mu_1 > \mu_2$, indicating that it is more costly to induce a particular action a when y cannot be observed.

The interesting comparison is between $s(x,0)$ and $s(x,1)$. One can see that $s(x,0)$ is a translation of $s(x,1)$ to the right as indicated in Figure 2. Confirming our intuition, the repairman receives higher pay if it is found that the failure was outside his control than if it is found that a component that he controls failed. The optimal solution when y is not observed will lie initially between $s(x,0)$ and $s(x,1)$ and eventually go above $s(x,1)$, since $\mu_1 > \mu_2$. Notice that as $k \to \infty$, $s(x) \to s(x,0)$, since it becomes all the less likely that the failure will be caused by anything outside the repairman's control.

5. Value of information

■ Before proceeding with a discussion of the value of imperfect information, the notion of a valuable signal needs to be made precise. A signal y is said to be *valuable* if both the principal and the agent can be made strictly better off with a contract of the form $s(x,y)$ than they are with a contract of the form $s(x)$.

Equation (13) suggests that y will be valuable if and only if it is *false* that

$$\frac{f_a(x,y,a)}{f(x,y,a)} = \bar{h}(x,a), \tag{16}$$

for almost every (x,y). The reason is that when (16) holds, a contract $s(x)$ will satisfy (13), whereas if (16) is false, it must necessarily take the form $s(x,y)$. We shall prove this proposition formally below as it is the main result of the paper and no proof of (13) was given. Before doing so, let us rewrite (16) in a way which allows a surprisingly simple interpretation of this necessary

---

[20] Simple calculations show that

$$f(x,0,a) = \frac{1}{a} \cdot \exp\left\{-\frac{a+k}{ak} \cdot x\right\}$$

and

$$f(x,1,a) = \frac{1}{k} \cdot \exp\left\{-\frac{a+k}{ak} \cdot x\right\}.$$

FIGURE 2

THE SECOND-BEST SOLUTION FOR THE REPAIRMAN EXAMPLE WITH MONITORING

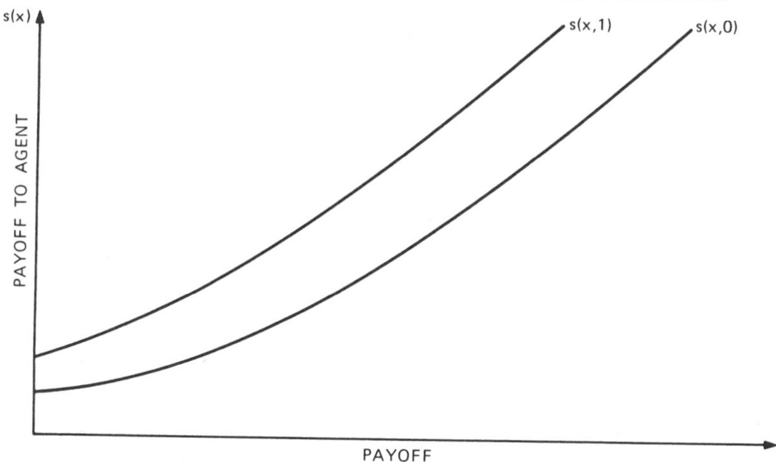

and sufficient condition. Suppose (16) holds for all $\underset{\sim}{a}$. Solving it as a differential equation in $\underset{\sim}{a}$ yields

$$f(x,y;\,a) = g(x,y)\cdot h(x,a), \qquad \text{for almost every } (x,y), \tag{17}$$

where h and g can be taken nonnegative. Conversely, (17) implies (16). Thus (16) and (17) are equivalent.[21]

Equation (17) has a natural interpretation, since it is precisely the condition for a sufficient statistic, if one views $\underset{\sim}{a}$ as a random parameter (de Groot, 1970). That is, when (17) holds, x is a sufficient statistic for the pair (x,y) with respect to $\underset{\sim}{a}$, which means that x carries all the relevant information about $\underset{\sim}{a}$, and y adds nothing to the power of inference. The signal y could only be used for risk-sharing purposes, but optimal risk sharing is independent of the distribution of the random variables when agents have homogeneous beliefs. Consequently, y should be valueless when (17) holds, which is what (13) says. On the other hand, when (17) is false, y contains some information about $\underset{\sim}{a}$ beyond that conveyed by x. In accordance with (13), y should then be used in the contract to improve welfare.

This discussion suggests the following:

Definition: A signal y is said to be *informative* about $\underset{\sim}{a}$ when (17) is false, and *noninformative* otherwise.

With this definition the main result can be stated as follows:

Proposition 3. Let $s(x)$ be an optimal sharing rule for which the agent's choice of action is unique and interior in A. Then there exists a sharing rule $s(x,y)$ which strictly Pareto dominates $s(x)$ if and only if (17) is false; or more concisely, *a signal is valuable if and only if it is informative*.

[21] This is not necessarily true if (16) only holds for a single value of a, because then we cannot integrate (16) to get (17). Such an exceptional case is of little interest, however, and in the subsequent analysis, we will only deal with distributions for which (16) is true for either all a or no a.

Proof: Suppose y is noninformative. Then, if $s(x,y)$ is an arbitrary sharing rule, a sharing rule $s(x)$ which is at least as good as $s(x,y)$ will be constructed, establishing the claim that y is of no value.

For every x, define $s(x)$ so that

$$\int U(s(x,y))g(x,y)dy = \int U(s(x))g(x,y)dy = U(s(x))\cdot \int g(x,y)dy. \quad (18)$$

Then using (17) and (18),

$$\int U(s(x,y))f(x,y;a)dxdy = \int U(s(x,y))h(x;a)g(x,y)dxdy = \int U(s(x))h(x;a)g(x,y)dxdy.$$

Consequently, $s(x)$ will result in the same action and welfare for the agent. By Jensen's inequality, (18) implies

$$\int s(x,y)g(x,y)dy \geq \int s(x)g(x,y)dy,$$

or

$$\int (x - s(x,y))g(x,y)dy \leq \int (x - s(x))g(x,y)dy.$$

This implies, using Jensen's inequality a second time, that:

$$\int G(x - s(x,y))g(x,y)dy \leq \int G(x - s(x))g(x,y)dy.$$

Since this is true for every x, and $h(x;a) \geq 0$, one obtains, by integrating,

$$\int G(x - s(x,y))f(x,y;a)dxdy \leq \int G(x - s(x))f(x,y;a)dxdy.$$

Since the agent takes the same act with $s(x)$ as with $s(x,y)$ by construction, this shows that the principal is at least as well off with $s(x)$ as with $s(x,y)$. The agent's utility is the same for both $s(x)$ and $s(x,y)$, and thus $s(x)$ is weakly Pareto superior to $s(x,y)$, which proves the first part of the proposition.

To prove the second part, let $s(x)$ be a second-best solution with the properties assumed in the proposition. Fix x for a moment. Since the agent's response is unique and interior in A, the principal's and the agent's marginal returns δE^P- and δE^A-conditional on x, from an additive variation $\delta s(x,y)$ in the sharing rule $s(x)$, are [see proposition 9.6.1 in Luenberger (1969)]:

$$\delta E^P = -G'(x - s(x)) \int \delta s(x,y)f(x,y;a)dy + \mu \cdot U'(s(x)) \int \delta s(x,y)f_a(x,y;a)dy,$$

$$\delta E^A = U'(s(x)) \int \delta s(x,y)f(x,y;a)dy. \quad (19)$$

Here μ is the solution to (8) corresponding to $s(x)$.

Suppose y is informative. From (16) it follows that there exists a set Y in the range of y, with $\int_Y f(x,y;a)dy \equiv f(x,Y;a) \neq 0$, and correspondingly for the complement Y^c, such that:

$$\frac{f_a(x,Y;a)}{f(x,Y;a)} > \frac{f_a(x,Y^c;a)}{f(x,Y^c;a)}, \tag{20}$$

Choose a variation $\delta s(x,y)$ such that $\delta s(x,Y) > 0$ and

$$\delta s(x,Y)\cdot f(x,Y;a) + \delta s(x,Y^c)f(x,Y^c;a) = 0; \tag{21}$$

($\delta s(x,Y)$ is constant for all $y \in Y$ and correspondingly for $\delta s(x,Y^c)$). From (19) and (21) it follows that:

$$\delta E^P = \mu\cdot U'(s(x))[\delta s(x,Y)\cdot f_a(x,Y;a) + \delta s(x,Y^c)\cdot f_a(x,Y^c;a)],$$

and

$$\delta E^A = 0.$$

Substituting from (21), we have:

$$\delta E^P = \mu\cdot U'(s(x))\cdot\delta s(x,Y)\cdot f(x,Y;a)\left[\frac{f_a(x,Y;a)}{f(x,Y;a)} - \frac{f_a(x,Y^c;a)}{f(x,Y^c;a)}\right] > 0,$$

since $\mu > 0$ (Proposition 1), $\delta s(x,Y) > 0$ as chosen, and the expression in brackets is positive by (20). The procedure can be repeated for a set of x-values with positive mass, since y is informative, which guarantees that one can make the principal strictly better off and the agent no worse off, for a small enough variation. Finally, utilities are continuous, so part of the principal's gain can be transferred to the agent (e.g., use the same argument as above, taking $\delta E^P = 0$), and this proves the sufficiency part of the proposition. *Q.E.D.*

Remarks:

(1) The sufficiency argument can be appropriately modified to apply to the case where the agent's utility function H is nonseparable.
(2) If, for administrative reasons, one has restricted attention *a priori* to a limited class of contracts (e.g., linear price functions or instruction-like step-functions), then informativeness may not be sufficient for improvements within this class.
(3) From the proof of the proposition one can see that if f_a/f is continuous in (x,y), then there will exist a single region Y (independent of x) such that the indicator function on Y is a valuable signal whenever y is.[22] This implies that $s(x)$ can be improved upon by a dichotomous contract of the form $(s(x,Y),s(x,Y^c))$, which does not use all the information contained in y. Since dichotomous contracts are simpler to administer, this result suggests an explanation of their frequent use.
(4) It is clear that informativeness can be directly extended to cover cases where one already observes a signal y_1 in addition to x and is interested in the value of an additional signal y_2. The necessary and sufficient condition becomes $f(x,y_1,y_2,a) \neq h(x,y_1,a)\cdot g(x,y_1,y_2)$.

The conclusion that a noninformative signal will have no value may not be surprising (even if our terminology is chosen to make this statement appear more

[22] The indicator function on Y is a function which has the signal y as an argument, and equals 1 on Y and 0 otherwise.

obvious than it is). Basically, it tells us that pure randomization does not pay. The more important part of the proposition is the result that any informative signal, regardless of how noisy it is, will have positive value (if costlessly obtained and administered into the contract). As in Harris and Raviv (1978), one might conjecture that in some situations a sufficiently noisy, yet informative, signal would add too much randomness to the contract to be acceptable by risk-averse parties. But as the proof of Proposition 3 indicates, since both parties are on the margin risk-neutral towards randomness in y, given x, the new contract can be designed so that marginally it does not increase risk, but still improves incentives for action.[23] Alternatively, equation (13) indicates that one can improve risk sharing for each y separately while at the same time retaining incentives for action. This pointwise improvement results, of course, in an overall improvement.

It is of interest to look at a few special cases of informativeness. Suppose first that y is independent of x. This could be the case if the agent is directly monitored or supervised. Then we can write

$$f(x,y,a) = h(x,a) \cdot g(y,a).$$

From this it follows that

$$\frac{f_a(x,y,a)}{f(x,y,a)} = \frac{h_a(x,a)}{h(x,a)} + \frac{g_a(y,a)}{g(y,a)}.$$

Hence y is noninformative if and only if g_a/g is constant, which readily is seen to imply $g_a \equiv 0$ (since $\int g_a = 0$). Thus, whenever g depends at all on $\underset{\sim}{a}$, it is informative and consequently valuable. Even the most casual supervision of an agent can be used to the benefit of both parties.

Second, suppose y is informative. Then we can construct another information system as follows:

$$\hat{y} = \begin{cases} y, & \text{if} \quad x \leq \bar{x}, \\ 0, & \text{if} \quad x > \bar{x}. \end{cases}$$

This signal is a conditional information system, where resources are invested to find out y only if the outcome is sufficiently bad (below $\bar{x}$). It is readily seen that $\hat{y}$ is also informative and, depending on the costs of obtaining y, the net benefits of using $\hat{y}$ may exceed those of y.[24] Conditional information systems are widely used in practice, which indicates that their cost savings are often sufficient to cover the information loss they engender.

Finally, one can construct an informative signal $\hat{y}$ from y by simply deciding randomly whether or not to find out y.[25] Again, this would save costs and is quite effective, particularly if y is a very precise signal about $\underset{\sim}{a}$.[26]

The last two examples bring attention to the fact that Proposition 3 says nothing about *how* valuable y is, which would be important whenever costs for information acquisition and administration of more complex contracts are considered. An upper bound for the value is, of course, provided by the value one

[23] This line of argument was first used in Gjesdal (1976) for the case where x and y are independent. It has also been used by Shavell (1978), who independently of us proves the sufficiency part of Proposition 3, but without employing the same notion of informativeness.

[24] Demski and Feltham (1978) discuss conditional information systems.

[25] Feltham (1977) gives an example of this kind of information system.

[26] In the limit, if $y = a$ and high penalties are allowed, we are very much in the same situation as in the example in footnote 7. An arbitrary low probability of checking y will suffice to induce the agent to take the correct action.

gets from observing $\underset{\sim}{a}$ itself. As Mirrlees' (1974) example (p. 248) indicates, this value may occasionally be negligible.

Some indications of the value of the signal can be found by studying (13). Roughly speaking, the more variation a signal causes in f_a/f, the more valuable it will be. This seems difficult to formalize, and I believe that on a general level signals can only be compared by using Blackwell's notion of fineness (see Blackwell (1951) and also remark 4 above).

6. Asymmetric information

■ In many respects the model we have analyzed is very primitive. One unrealistic feature is the assumption that the agent chooses his action having the same information as the principal, that is, before anything about θ is revealed. Commonly this will not be the case. After the sharing rule is fixed, the agent will often learn something new about the difficulty of his task or the environment in which it is to be performed. The following extension of our model applies to such cases.[27]

Let z be a signal about θ which the agent observes prior to choosing $\underset{\sim}{a}$, so that his choice becomes a function $a(z)$. As before, we suppress θ and write $f(x,y,z,a)$ for the joint density function, where y is some additional information observed by both parties. The best sharing rule $s(x,y)$ can be determined by solving the program:

$$\max_{s(x,y),a(z)} \int G(x - s(x,y))f(x,y\,|\,z,a(z))p(z)dxdydz \tag{22}$$

subject to
$$\int U(s(x,y))f(x,y\,|\,z,a(z))p(z)dxdydz - \int V(a(z))p(z)dz \geq \bar{H}, \tag{23}$$

$$a(z) \in \underset{a' \in A}{\text{argmax}} \int U(s(x,y))f(x,y\,|\,z,a')dxdy - V(a'), \forall z. \tag{24}$$

Here $f(x,y\,|\,z,a)$ is the conditional density of x and y, given z and the action a, and $p(z)$ is the marginal density of z. Letting $\mu(z)p(z)$ be the multiplier function for (24) and λ the multiplier for (23), point-wise optimization gives the characterization:

$$\frac{G'(x - s(x,y))}{U'(s(x,y))} = \lambda + \frac{\int \mu(z)\cdot f_a(x,y\,|\,z,a(z))p(z)dz}{\int f(x,y\,|\,z,a(z))p(z)dz}. \tag{25}$$

This equation closely resembles equation (13). Again the second term on the right-hand side indicates deviations from a first-best solution, and qualitatively one can draw conclusions similar to those for the earlier model. The difference is that the deviation from first-best risk sharing is determined by a weighted average of the incentive effects in the various states z, with the weight $\mu(z)p(z)$ being dependent on the probability of z and the desirability (or cost) of forcing

[27] This corresponds to Model 2 in Harris and Raviv (1976).

the action $a(z)$. It is easy to show that $\mu(z) \equiv 0$ is impossible (since $\mu(z)$ is determined by an equation similar to (8)), and hence again we have a second-best solution. However, we may have $\mu(z) > 0$ for some z, and $\mu(z) < 0$ for others, since $s'(x) > 1$ is possible (cf. our repairman example) in some x-region.

The necessary part of Proposition 3, namely that a noninformative signal is valueless, extends readily to the asymmetric case. Here noninformativeness is defined by the condition:

$$f(x,y,z;a) = g(x,y) \cdot h(x,z;a), \qquad \text{for almost every } (x,y,z). \tag{26}$$

For the sufficiency part of the proposition, an additional but insignificant qualification is needed. When (26) is false, that is, when y is informative, f_a/f will depend on y as before. Yet, when integrating as in (25), it is conceivable that the right-hand side of (25) would become independent of y, making a function $s(x)$ optimal and y valueless. However, this is extremely unlikely and will not happen generically; any small change in the problem data would take us out of such a situation. Thus, we can safely say that for all that matters, Proposition 3 is also valid in the asymmetric case.

7. Concluding remarks

■ We have studied efficient contractual agreements in a principal-agent relationship under various assumptions about what can be observed, and hence contracted upon, by both parties. When the payoff alone is observable, optimal contracts will be second-best owing to a problem of moral hazard. By creating additional information systems (as in cost accounting, for instance), or by using other available information about the agent's action or the state of nature, contracts can generally be improved. A simple necessary and sufficient condition for such imperfect information to be of value was given as well as a characterization of optimal contracts which use such information.

Principal-agent relationships are prevalent in economic organizations. The analysis presented here improves our understanding of the functioning of this basic organizational form. In view of our result that essentially any imperfect information about actions or states of nature[28] can be used to improve contracts, we have an explanation of the observed complexity of real contracts (as evidenced for instance in insurance arrangements). Additional information is of value because it allows a more accurate judgment of the performance of the agent; or viewed differently, it provides the same incentives for effort with less loss of risk-sharing benefits.

Our analysis also provides a basis for studying the design of contracts and information systems in more specific contexts. An application of this kind has recently been given by Baron and De Bondt (1978) in the context of automatic fuel adjustment clauses. Other fields of applications have been discussed in Harris and Raviv (1978) and recently Demski (1977) has used the model for a theoretical study of financial reporting.

Of course, the analysis presented here leaves unanswered many interesting questions in contracting. One important aspect of the problem, which we have

[28] Note that our analysis shows that from a theoretical point of view there is no distinction to be made between a signal which provides information about actions and one which provides information about states of nature, since these pieces of information are inherently linked via the outcome function.

not considered, is that many contracts are based on long-term relationships. When the same situation repeats itself over time, the effects of uncertainty tend to be reduced and dysfunctional behavior is more accurately revealed, thus alleviating the problem of moral hazard. Such long-term effects could be analyzed in an extension of our model. Another extension would recognize that asymmetry of information as discussed in Section 6 may warrant a renegotiation of the contract. One can view management by objectives and the New Soviet Incentive Scheme (Weitzman, 1976) as examples of this. In both cases, after observing the difficulty of his task, the agent can change the contract within certain limits to the benefit of both parties. A preliminary discussion of this kind of contracting is given in Holmström (1977), where it is seen as a special case of delegation of decisionmaking responsibility to an agent with superior information.

Appendix

■ **Proof of proposition 1.** Let $s(x)$ be a second-best sharing rule for $\lambda > 0$ and write $r(x) = x - s(x)$. If $\mu \leqslant 0$, contrary to our claim, then

$$\frac{G'(r(x))}{U'(x - r(x))} = \lambda + \mu \cdot \frac{f_a(x,a)}{f(x,a)} \leqslant \lambda = \frac{G'(r_\lambda(x))}{U'(x - r_\lambda(x))}, \tag{A1}$$

for $x \in X_+ = \{x \mid f_a(x,a) \geqslant 0\}$. Here $r_\lambda(x)$ is the first-best sharing rule (in terms of the principal's share), corresponding to λ; see Wilson (1968). Since $G'(r(x))/U'(x - r(x))$ is decreasing in $r(x)$ for fixed x, $r_\lambda(x)$ is an increasing function, and from (A1) it follows that $r(x) \geqslant r_\lambda(x)$ for $x \in X_+$.

Correspondingly, $r(x) \leqslant r_\lambda(x)$ on $X_- = \{x \mid f_a(x,a) < 0\}$. We have then,

$$\int G(r(x))f_a(x,a)dx \geqslant \int G(r_\lambda(x))f_a(x,a)dx > 0, \tag{A2}$$

where the last inequality follows, by first-order stochastic dominance, from the assumption $F_a(x,a) \leqslant 0$ (with strict inequality for some x), and the fact that $r_\lambda(x)$ is increasing.

The expression in braces in equation (8) is the second-order condition for the agent's maximization problem, and hence is <0. (It cannot be $=0$, since then (A2) and (8) would be inconsistent). Combining (8) and (A2), this implies $\mu > 0$, which contradicts our contrapositive assumption $\mu \leqslant 0$. We have arrived at a contradiction assuming $\mu \leqslant 0$ and conclude that $\mu > 0$. *Q.E.D.*

□ **Proof of corollary 1.** The proof follows from Proposition 1 and the fact that $G'(x - s(x))/U'(s(x))$ is increasing in $s(x)$ for fixed x. *Q.E.D.*

□ **Proof of corollary 2.** The solutions will differ on a set of nonzero measure, since $\mu > 0$ and f_a/f is nonconstant. *Q.E.D.*

References

ARROW, K. *Essays in the Theory of Risk-Bearing*. Amsterdam: North-Holland Publishing Company, 1970.

BARON, D. AND DE BONDT, R. "The Design of Automatic Price Adjustment Mechanisms." Onderzoeksrapport N° 7810, Departement voor Toegepaste Economische Wetenschappen, Katholieke Universiteit Leuven, Leuven, Belgium, 1978.

BLACKWELL, D. "Comparison of Experiments" in J. Neyman, ed., *Proceedings of the Second Berkeley Symposium on Mathematical Statistics and Probability*, Berkeley: University of California Press, 1951.

BORCH, K. "Equilibrium in a Reinsurance Market." *Econometrica*, Vol. 30, No. 3 (1962), pp. 424–444.

DEGROOT, M. *Optimal Statistical Decisions*. New York: McGraw-Hill Book Company, 1970.

DEMSKI, J. "A Simple Case of Indeterminate Financial Reporting." Mimeo, Graduate School of Business, Stanford University, 1977.

——— AND FELTHAM, G. "Economic Incentives in Budgetary Control Systems." *The Accounting Review*, Vol. 53, No. 2 (1978), pp. 336–359.

FELTHAM, G. "Optimal Incentive Contracts: Penalties, Costly Information and Multiple Workers." Working paper, University of British Columbia, 1977.

GJESDAL, F. "Accounting in Agencies." Mimeo, Graduate School of Business, Stanford University, 1976.

HARRIS, M. AND RAVIV, A. "Optimal Incentive Contracts with Imperfect Information." Working Paper #70-75-76, Graduate School of Industrial Administration, Carnegie-Mellon University, April 1976 (revised December 1977).

——— AND ———. "Some Results on Incentive Contracts with Applications to Education and Employment, Health Insurance, and Law Enforcement." *The American Economic Review*, Vol. 68 (1978), pp. 20–30.

HOLMSTRÖM, B. "On Incentives and Control in Organizations." Unpublished Ph.D. dissertation, Graduate School of Business, Stanford University, 1977.

KOLMOGOROV, A.N. AND FOMIN, S.V. *Introductory Real Analysis*. New York: Dover Publications, 1970.

LUENBERGER, D. *Optimization by Vector Space Methods*. New York: John Wiley & Sons, 1969.

MIRRLEES, J. "The Optimal Structure of Incentives and Authority within an Organization." *The Bell Journal of Economics*, Vol. 7, No. 1 (Spring 1976), pp. 105–131.

———. "Notes on Welfare Economics, Information, and Uncertainty" in Balch, McFadden, and Wu, eds., *Essays on Economic Behavior under Uncertainty*, Amsterdam: North Holland Publishing Co., 1974.

MOSSIN, J. "Aspects of Rational Insurance Purchasing." *Journal of Political Economy*, Vol. 76 (1968), pp. 553–568.

PAULY, M. "Overinsurance and Public Provision of Insurance: The Roles of Moral Hazard and Adverse Selection." *Quarterly Journal of Economics*, Vol. 68 (1974), pp. 44–62.

ROSS, S. "The Economic Theory of Agency: The Principal's Problem." *The American Economic Review*, Vol. 63 (1973), pp. 134–139.

SHAVELL, S. "Risk Sharing and Incentives in the Principal and Agent Relationship." *The Bell Journal of Economics*, Vol. 10, No. 1 (Spring, 1979), pp. 55–73.

SPENCE, M. AND ZECKHAUSER, R. "Insurance, Information, and Individual Action." *The American Economic Review*, Vol. 61 (1971), pp. 380–387.

STIGLITZ, J. "Incentives, Risk, and Information: Notes toward a Theory of Hierarchy." *The Bell Journal of Economics*, Vol. 6, No. 2 (Autumn 1975), pp. 552–579.

WEITZMAN, M. "The New Soviet Incentive Model." *The Bell Journal of Economics*, Vol. 7, No. 1 (Spring 1976), pp. 251–257.

WILLIAMSON, O.E. *Markets and Hierarchies: Analysis and Antitrust Implications*. New York: The Free Press, 1975.

WILSON, R. "The Theory of Syndicates." *Econometrica*, Vol. 36 (1968), pp. 119–132.

———. "The Structure of Incentives for Decentralization under Uncertainty." *La Decision*, No. 171 (1969).

ZECKHAUSER, R. "Medical Insurance: A Case Study of the Trade-off between Risk Spreading and Appropriate Incentives." *Journal of Economic Theory*, Vol. 2 (1970), pp. 10–26.

21

K. J. Arrow, Uncertainty and the welfare economics of medical care, *American Economic Review* **53** (1963), 941–969 (appendix omitted)

To see some of the complications we have been analyzing in context we now turn to two analyses of specific markets. In this article, Arrow compares the Arrow-Debreu model of allocation with a complete set of markets to the situation occurring in the market for medical care.

UNCERTAINTY AND THE WELFARE ECONOMICS OF MEDICAL CARE

By KENNETH J. ARROW*

I. *Introduction: Scope and Method*

This paper is an exploratory and tentative study of the specific differentia of medical care as the object of normative economics. It is contended here, on the basis of comparison of obvious characteristics of the medical-care industry with the norms of welfare economics, that the special economic problems of medical care can be explained as adaptations to the existence of uncertainty in the incidence of disease and in the efficacy of treatment.

It should be noted that the subject is the *medical-care industry,* not *health.* The causal factors in health are many, and the provision of medical care is only one. Particularly at low levels of income, other commodities such as nutrition, shelter, clothing, and sanitation may be much more significant. It is the complex of services that center about the physician, private and group practice, hospitals, and public health, which I propose to discuss.

The focus of discussion will be on the way the operation of the medical-care industry and the efficacy with which it satisfies the needs of society differ from a norm, if at all. The "norm" that the economist usually uses for the purposes of such comparisons is the operation of a competitive model, that is, the flows of services that would be

* The author is professor of economics at Stanford University. He wishes to express his thanks for useful comments to F. Bator, R. Dorfman, V. Fuchs, Dr. S. Gilson, R. Kessel, S. Mushkin, and C. R. Rorem. This paper was prepared under the sponsorship of the Ford Foundation as part of a series of papers on the economics of health, education, and welfare.

offered and purchased and the prices that would be paid for them if each individual in the market offered or purchased services at the going prices as if his decisions had no influence over them, and the going prices were such that the amounts of services which were available equalled the total amounts which other individuals were willing to purchase, with no imposed restrictions on supply or demand.

The interest in the competitive model stems partly from its presumed descriptive power and partly from its implications for economic efficiency. In particular, we can state the following well-known proposition (First Optimality Theorem). If a competitive equilibrium exists at all, and if all commodities relevant to costs or utilities are in fact priced in the market, then the equilibrium is necessarily *optimal* in the following precise sense (due to V. Pareto): There is no other allocation of resources to services which will make all participants in the market better off.

Both the conditions of this optimality theorem and the definition of optimality call for comment. A definition is just a definition, but when the *definiendum* is a word already in common use with highly favorable connotations, it is clear that we are really trying to be persuasive; we are implicitly recommending the achievement of optimal states.[1] It is reasonable enough to assert that a change in allocation which makes all participants better off is one that certainly should be made; this is a value judgment, not a descriptive proposition, but it is a very weak one. From this it follows that it is not desirable to put up with a nonoptimal allocation. But it does not follow that if we are at an allocation which is optimal in the Pareto sense, we should not change to any other. We cannot indeed make a change that does not hurt someone; but we can still desire to change to another allocation if the change makes enough participants better off and by so much that we feel that the injury to others is not enough to offset the benefits. Such interpersonal comparisons are, of course, value judgments. The change, however, by the previous argument ought to be an optimal state; of course there are many possible states, each of which is optimal in the sense here used.

However, a value judgment on the desirability of each possible new distribution of benefits and costs corresponding to each possible reallocation of resources is not, in general, necessary. Judgments about the distribution can be made separately, in one sense, from those about allocation if certain conditions are fulfilled. Before stating the relevant proposition, it is necessary to remark that the competitive equilibrium achieved depends in good measure on the initial distribution of purchasing power, which consists of ownership of assets and skills that

[1] This point has been stressed by I. M. D. Little [19, pp. 71-74]. For the concept of a "persuasive definition," see C. L. Stevenson [27, pp. 210-17].

command a price on the market. A transfer of assets among individuals will, in general, change the final supplies of goods and services and the prices paid for them. Thus, a transfer of purchasing power from the well to the ill will increase the demand for medical services. This will manifest itself in the short run in an increase in the price of medical services and in the long run in an increase in the amount supplied.

With this in mind, the following statement can be made (Second Optimality Theorem): If there are no increasing returns in production, and if certain other minor conditions are satisfied, then every optimal state is a competitive equilibrium corresponding to some initial distribution of purchasing power. Operationally, the significance of this proposition is that if the conditions of the two optimality theorems are satisfied, and if the allocation mechanism in the real world satisfies the conditions for a competitive model, then social policy can confine itself to steps taken to alter the distribution of purchasing power. For any given distribution of purchasing power, the market will, under the assumptions made, achieve a competitive equilibrium which is necessarily optimal; and any optimal state is a competitive equilibrium corresponding to some distribution of purchasing power, so that any desired optimal state can be achieved.

The redistribution of purchasing power among individuals most simply takes the form of money: taxes and subsidies. The implications of such a transfer for individual satisfactions are, in general, not known in advance. But we can assume that society can *ex post* judge the distribution of satisfactions and, if deemed unsatisfactory, take steps to correct it by subsequent transfers. Thus, by successive approximations, a most preferred social state can be achieved, with resource allocation being handled by the market and public policy confined to the redistribution of money income.[2]

If, on the contrary, the actual market differs significantly from the competitive model, or if the assumptions of the two optimality theorems are not fulfilled, the separation of allocative and distributional procedures becomes, in most cases, impossible.[3]

The first step then in the analysis of the medical-care market is the

[2] The separation between allocation and distribution even under the above assumptions has glossed over problems in the execution of any desired redistribution policy; in practice, it is virtually impossible to find a set of taxes and subsidies that will not have an adverse effect on the achievement of an optimal state. But this discussion would take us even further afield than we have already gone.

[3] The basic theorems of welfare economics alluded to so briefly above have been the subject of voluminous literature, but no thoroughly satisfactory statement covering both the theorems themselves and the significance of exceptions to them exists. The positive assertions of welfare economics and their relation to the theory of competitive equilibrium are admirably covered in Koopmans [18]. The best summary of the various ways in which the theorems can fail to hold is probably Bator's [6].

comparison between the actual market and the competitive model. The methodology of this comparison has been a recurrent subject of controversy in economics for over a century. Recently, M. Friedman [15] has vigorously argued that the competitive or any other model should be tested solely by its ability to predict. In the context of competition, he comes close to arguing that prices and quantities are the only relevant data. This point of view is valuable in stressing that a certain amount of lack of realism in the assumptions of a model is no argument against its value. But the price-quantity implications of the competitive model for pricing are not easy to derive without major—and, in many cases, impossible—econometric efforts.

In this paper, the institutional organization and the observable mores of the medical profession are included among the data to be used in assessing the competitiveness of the medical-care market. I shall also examine the presence or absence of the preconditions for the equivalence of competitive equilibria and optimal states. The major competitive preconditions, in the sense used here, are three: the *existence* of competitive equilibrium, the *marketability* of all goods and services relevant to costs and utilities, and *nonincreasing returns*. The first two, as we have seen, insure that competitive equilibrium is necessarily optimal; the third insures that every optimal state is the competitive equilibrium corresponding to some distribution of income.[4] The first and third conditions are interrelated; indeed, nonincreasing returns plus some additional conditions not restrictive in a modern economy imply the existence of a competitive equilibrium, i.e., imply that there will be some set of prices which will clear all markets.[5]

The concept of marketability is somewhat broader than the traditional divergence between private and social costs and benefits. The latter concept refers to cases in which the organization of the market does not require an individual to pay for costs that he imposes on others as the result of his actions or does not permit him to receive compensation for benefits he confers. In the medical field, the obvious example is the spread of communicable diseases. An individual who fails to be immunized not only risks his own health, a disutility which presumably he has weighed against the utility of avoiding the procedure, but also that of others. In an ideal price system, there would be a price which he would have to pay to anyone whose health is endangered, a price sufficiently high so that the others would feel compensated; or, alternatively, there would be a price which would be paid to him by others to induce him to undergo the immunization procedure.

[4] There are further minor conditions, for which see Koopmans [18, pp. 50-55].

[5] For a more precise statement of the existence conditions, see Koopmans [18, pp. 56-60] or Debreu [12, Ch. 5].

Either system would lead to an optimal state, though the distributional implications would be different. It is, of course, not hard to see that such price systems could not, in fact, be practical; to approximate an optimal state it would be necessary to have collective intervention in the form of subsidy or tax or compulsion.

By the absence of marketability for an action which is identifiable, technologically possible, and capable of influencing some individual's welfare, for better or for worse, is meant here the failure of the existing market to provide a means whereby the services can be both offered and demanded upon payment of a price. Nonmarketability may be due to intrinsic technological characteristics of the product which prevent a suitable price from being enforced, as in the case of communicable diseases, or it may be due to social or historical controls, such as those prohibiting an individual from selling himself into slavery. This distinction is, in fact, difficult to make precise, though it is obviously of importance for policy; for the present purposes, it will be sufficient to identify nonmarketability with the observed absence of markets.

The instance of nonmarketability with which we shall be most concerned is that of risk-bearing. The relevance of risk-bearing to medical care seems obvious; illness is to a considerable extent an unpredictable phenomenon. The ability to shift the risks of illness to others is worth a price which many are willing to pay. Because of pooling and of superior willingness and ability, others are willing to bear the risks. Nevertheless, as we shall see in greater detail, a great many risks are not covered, and indeed the markets for the services of risk-coverage are poorly developed or nonexistent. Why this should be so is explained in more detail in Section IV.C below; briefly, it is impossible to draw up insurance policies which will sufficiently distinguish among risks, particularly since observation of the results will be incapable of distinguishing between avoidable and unavoidable risks, so that incentives to avoid losses are diluted.

The optimality theorems discussed above are usually presented in the literature as referring only to conditions of certainty, but there is no difficulty in extending them to the case of risks, provided the additional services of risk-bearing are included with other commodities.[6]

However, the variety of possible risks in the world is really staggering. The relevant commodities include, in effect, bets on all possible occurrences in the world which impinge upon utilities. In fact, many of these "commodities," i.e., desired protection against many risks, are

[6] The theory, in variant forms, seems to have been first worked out by Allais [2], Arrow [5], and Baudier [7]. For further generalization, see Debreu [11] and [12, Ch. 7].

simply not available. Thus, a wide class of commodities is nonmarketable, and a basic competitive precondition is not satisfied.[7]

There is a still more subtle consequence of the introduction of risk-bearing considerations. When there is uncertainty, information or knowledge becomes a commodity. Like other commodities, it has a cost of production and a cost of transmission, and so it is naturally not spread out over the entire population but concentrated among those who can profit most from it. (These costs may be measured in time or disutility as well as money.) But the demand for information is difficult to discuss in the rational terms usually employed. The value of information is frequently not known in any meaningful sense to the buyer; if, indeed, he knew enough to measure the value of information, he would know the information itself. But information, in the form of skilled care, is precisely what is being bought from most physicians, and, indeed, from most professionals. The elusive character of information as a commodity suggests that it departs considerably from the usual marketability assumptions about commodities.[8]

That risk and uncertainty are, in fact, significant elements in medical care hardly needs argument. I will hold that virtually all the special features of this industry, in fact, stem from the prevalence of uncertainty.

The nonexistence of markets for the bearing of some risks in the first instance reduces welfare for those who wish to transfer those risks to others for a certain price, as well as for those who would find it profitable to take on the risk at such prices. But it also reduces the desire to render or consume services which have risky consequences; in technical language, these commodities are complementary to risk-bearing. Conversely, the production and consumption of commodities and services with little risk attached act as substitutes for risk-bearing and are encouraged by market failure there with respect to risk-bearing. Thus the observed commodity pattern will be affected by the nonexistence of other markets.

[7] It should also be remarked that in the presence of uncertainty, indivisibilities that are sufficiently small to create little difficulty for the existence and viability of competitive equilibrium may nevertheless give rise to a considerable range of increasing returns because of the operation of the law of large numbers. Since most objects of insurance (lives, fire hazards, etc.) have some element of indivisibility, insurance companies have to be above a certain size. But it is not clear that this effect is sufficiently great to create serious obstacles to the existence and viability of competitive equilibrium in practice.

[8] One form of production of information is research. Not only does the product have unconventional aspects as a commodity, but it is also subject to increasing returns in use, since new ideas, once developed, can be used over and over without being consumed, and to difficulties of market control, since the cost of reproduction is usually much less than that of production. Hence, it is not surprising that a free enterprise economy will tend to underinvest in research; see Nelson [21] and Arrow [4].

The failure of one or more of the competitive preconditions has as its most immediate and obvious consequence a reduction in welfare below that obtainable from existing resources and technology, in the sense of a failure to reach an optimal state in the sense of Pareto. But more can be said. I propose here the view that, when the market fails to achieve an optimal state, society will, to some extent at least, recognize the gap, and nonmarket social institutions will arise attempting to bridge it.[9] Certainly this process is not necessarily conscious; nor is it uniformly successful in approaching more closely to optimality when the entire range of consequences is considered. It has always been a favorite activity of economists to point out that actions which on their face achieve a desirable goal may have less obvious consequences, particularly over time, which more than offset the original gains.

But it is contended here that the special structural characteristics of the medical-care market are largely attempts to overcome the lack of optimality due to the nonmarketability of the bearing of suitable risks and the imperfect marketability of information. These compensatory institutional changes, with some reinforcement from usual profit motives, largely explain the observed noncompetitive behavior of the medical-care market, behavior which, in itself, interferes with optimality. The social adjustment towards optimality thus puts obstacles in its own path.

The doctrine that society will seek to achieve optimality by nonmarket means if it cannot achieve them in the market is not novel. Certainly, the government, at least in its economic activities, is usually implicitly or explicitly held to function as the agency which substitutes for the market's failure.[10] I am arguing here that in some circumstances other social institutions will step into the optimality gap, and that the medical-care industry, with its variety of special institutions, some ancient, some modern, exemplifies this tendency.

It may be useful to remark here that a good part of the preference for redistribution expressed in government taxation and expenditure policies and private charity can be reinterpreted as desire for insurance. It is noteworthy that virtually nowhere is there a system of subsidies that has as its aim simply an equalization of income. The subsidies or other governmental help go to those who are disadvantaged in life by events the incidence of which is popularly regarded as unpre-

[9] An important current situation in which normal market relations have had to be greatly modified in the presence of great risks is the production and procurement of modern weapons; see Peck and Scherer [23, pp. 581-82] (I am indebted for this reference to V. Fuchs) and [1, pp. 71-75].

[10] For an explicit statement of this view, see Baumol [8]. But I believe this position is implicit in most discussions of the functions of government.

dictable: the blind, dependent children, the medically indigent. Thus, optimality, in a context which includes risk-bearing, includes much that appears to be motivated by distributional value judgments when looked at in a narrower context.[11]

This methodological background gives rise to the following plan for this paper. Section II is a catalogue of stylized generalizations about the medical-care market which differentiate it from the usual commodity markets. In Section III the behavior of the market is compared with that of the competitive model which disregards the fact of uncertainty. In Section IV, the medical-care market is compared, both as to behavior and as to preconditions, with the ideal competitive market that takes account of uncertainty; an attempt will be made to demonstrate that the characteristics outlined in Section II can be explained either as the result of deviations from the competitive preconditions or as attempts to compensate by other institutions for these failures. The discussion is not designed to be definitive, but provocative. In particular, I have been chary about drawing policy inferences; to a considerable extent, they depend on further research, for which the present paper is intended to provide a framework.

II. *A Survey of the Special Characteristics of the Medical-Care Market*[12]

This section will list selectively some characteristics of medical care which distinguish it from the usual commodity of economics textbooks. The list is not exhaustive, and it is not claimed that the characteristics listed are individually unique to this market. But, taken together, they do establish a special place for medical care in economic analysis.

A. *The Nature of Demand*

The most obvious distinguishing characteristics of an individual's demand for medical services is that it is not steady in origin as, for example, for food or clothing, but irregular and unpredictable. Medical services, apart from preventive services, afford satisfaction only in the event of illness, a departure from the normal state of affairs. It is hard, indeed, to think of another commodity of significance in the average budget of which this is true. A portion of legal services, devoted to defense in criminal trials or to lawsuits, might fall in this category but the incidence is surely very much lower (and, of course, there

[11] Since writing the above, I find that Buchanan and Tullock [10, Ch. 13] have argued that all redistribution can be interpreted as "income insurance."

[12] For an illuminating survey to which I am much indebted, see S. Mushkin [20].

are, in fact, strong institutional similarities between the legal and medical-care markets.)[13]

In addition, the demand for medical services is associated, with a considerable probability, with an assault on personal integrity. There is some risk of death and a more considerable risk of impairment of full functioning. In particular, there is a major potential for loss or reduction of earning ability. The risks are not by themselves unique; food is also a necessity, but avoidance of deprivation of food can be guaranteed with sufficient income, where the same cannot be said of avoidance of illness. Illness is, thus, not only risky but a costly risk in itself, apart from the cost of medical care.

B. *Expected Behavior of the Physician*

It is clear from everyday observation that the behavior expected of sellers of medical care is different from that of business men in general. These expectations are relevant because medical care belongs to the category of commodities for which the product and the activity of production are identical. In all such cases, the customer cannot test the product before consuming it, and there is an element of trust in the relation.[14] But the ethically understood restrictions on the activities of a physician are much more severe than on those of, say, a barber. His behavior is supposed to be governed by a concern for the customer's welfare which would not be expected of a salesman. In Talcott Parsons's terms, there is a "collectivity-orientation," which distinguishes medicine and other professions from business, where self-interest on the part of participants is the accepted norm.[15]

A few illustrations will indicate the degree of difference between the behavior expected of physicians and that expected of the typical businessman.[16] (1) Advertising and overt price competition are virtually eliminated among physicians. (2) Advice given by physicians as to further treatment by himself or others is supposed to be completely

[13] In governmental demand, military power is an example of a service used only irregularly and unpredictably. Here too, special institutional and professional relations have emerged, though the precise social structure is different for reasons that are not hard to analyze.

[14] Even with material commodities, testing is never so adequate that all elements of implicit trust can be eliminated. Of course, over the long run, experience with the quality of product of a given seller provides a check on the possibility of trust.

[15] See [22, p. 463]. The whole of [22, Ch. 10] is a most illuminating analysis of the social role of medical practice; though Parsons' interest lies in different areas from mine, I must acknowledge here my indebtedness to his work.

[16] I am indebted to Herbert Klarman of Johns Hopkins University for some of the points discussed in this and the following paragraph.

divorced from self-interest. (3) It is at least claimed that treatment is dictated by the objective needs of the case and not limited by financial considerations.[17] While the ethical compulsion is surely not as absolute in fact as it is in theory, we can hardly suppose that it has no influence over resource allocation in this area. Charity treatment in one form or another does exist because of this tradition about human rights to adequate medical care.[18] (4) The physician is relied on as an expert in certifying to the existence of illnesses and injuries for various legal and other purposes. It is socially expected that his concern for the correct conveying of information will, when appropriate, outweigh his desire to please his customers.[19]

Departure from the profit motive is strikingly manifested by the overwhelming predominance of nonprofit over proprietary hospitals.[20] The hospital per se offers services not too different from those of a hotel, and it is certainly not obvious that the profit motive will not lead to a more efficient supply. The explanation may lie either on the supply side or on that of demand. The simplest explanation is that public and private subsidies decrease the cost to the patient in nonprofit hospitals. A second possibility is that the association of profit-making with the supply of medical services arouses suspicion and antagonism on the part of patients and referring physicians, so they do prefer nonprofit institutions. Either explanation implies a preference on the part of some group, whether donors or patients, against the profit motive in the supply of hospital services.[21]

[17] The belief that the ethics of medicine demands treatment independent of the patient's ability to pay is strongly ingrained. Such a perceptive observer as René Dubos has made the remark that the high cost of anticoagulants restricts their use and may contradict classical medical ethics, as though this were an unprecedented phenomenon. See [13, p. 419]. "A time *may come* when medical ethics will have to be considered in the harsh light of economics" (emphasis added). Of course, this expectation amounts to ignoring the scarcity of medical resources; one has only to have been poor to realize the error. We may confidently assume that price and income do have some consequences for medical expenditures.

[18] A needed piece of research is a study of the exact nature of the variations of medical care received and medical care paid for as income rises. (The relevant income concept also needs study.) For this purpose, some disaggregation is needed; differences in hospital care which are essentially matters of comfort should, in the above view, be much more responsive to income than, e.g., drugs.

[19] This role is enhanced in a socialist society, where the state itself is actively concerned with illness in relation to work; see Field [14, Ch. 9].

[20] About 3 per cent of beds were in proprietary hospitals in 1958, against 30 per cent in voluntary nonprofit, and the remainder in federal, state, and local hospitals; see [26, Chart 4-2, p. 60].

[21] C. R. Rorem has pointed out to me some further factors in this analysis. (1) Given the social intention of helping all patients without regard to immediate ability to pay, economies of scale would dictate a predominance of community-sponsored hospitals. (2)

Conformity to collectivity-oriented behavior is especially important since it is a commonplace that the physician-patient relation affects the quality of the medical care product. A pure cash nexus would be inadequate; if nothing else, the patient expects that the same physician will normally treat him on successive occasions. This expectation is strong enough to persist even in the Soviet Union, where medical care is nominally removed from the market place [14, pp. 194-96]. That purely psychic interactions between physician and patient have effects which are objectively indistinguishable in kind from the effects of medication is evidenced by the use of the placebo as a control in medical experimentation; see Shapiro [25].

C. *Product Uncertainty*

Uncertainty as to the quality of the product is perhaps more intense here than in any other important commodity. Recovery from disease is as unpredictable as is its incidence. In most commodities, the possibility of learning from one's own experience or that of others is strong because there is an adequate number of trials. In the case of severe illness, that is, in general, not true; the uncertainty due to inexperience is added to the intrinsic difficulty of prediction. Further, the amount of uncertainty, measured in terms of utility variability, is certainly much greater for medical care in severe cases than for, say, houses or automobiles, even though these are also expenditures sufficiently infrequent so that there may be considerable residual uncertainty.

Further, there is a special quality to the uncertainty; it is very different on the two sides of the transaction. Because medical knowledge is so complicated, the information possessed by the physician as to the consequences and possibilities of treatment is necessarily very much greater than that of the patient, or at least so it is believed by both parties.[22] Further, both parties are aware of this informational inequality, and their relation is colored by this knowledge.

To avoid misunderstanding, observe that the difference in information relevant here is a difference in information as to the consequence of a purchase of medical care. There is always an inequality of information as to production methods between the producer and the purchaser of any commodity, but in most cases the customer may well

Some proprietary hospitals will tend to control total costs to the patient more closely, including the fees of physicians, who will therefore tend to prefer community-sponsored hospitals.

[22] Without trying to assess the present situation, it is clear in retrospect that at some point in the past the actual differential knowledge possessed by physicians may not have been much. But from the economic point of view, it is the subjective belief of both parties, as manifested in their market behavior, that is relevant.

have as good or nearly as good an understanding of the utility of the product as the producer.

D. *Supply Conditions*

In competitive theory, the supply of a commodity is governed by the net return from its production compared with the return derivable from the use of the same resources elsewhere. There are several significant departures from this theory in the case of medical care.

Most obviously, entry to the profession is restricted by licensing. Licensing, of course, restricts supply and therefore increases the cost of medical care. It is defended as guaranteeing a minimum of quality. Restriction of entry by licensing occurs in most professions, including barbering and undertaking.

A second feature is perhaps even more remarkable. The cost of medical education today is high and, according to the usual figures, is borne only to a minor extent by the student. Thus, the private benefits to the entering student considerably exceed the costs. (It is, however, possible that research costs, not properly chargeable to education, swell the apparent difference.) This subsidy should, in principle, cause a fall in the price of medical services, which, however, is offset by rationing through limited entry to schools and through elimination of students during the medical-school career. These restrictions basically render superfluous the licensing, except in regard to graduates of foreign schools.

The special role of educational institutions in simultaneously subsidizing and rationing entry is common to all professions requiring advanced training.[23] It is a striking and insufficiently remarked phenomenon that such an important part of resource allocation should be performed by nonprofit-oriented agencies.

Since this last phenomenon goes well beyond the purely medical aspect, we will not dwell on it longer here except to note that the anomaly is most striking in the medical field. Educational costs tend to be far higher there than in any other branch of professional training. While tuition is the same, or only slightly higher, so that the subsidy is much greater, at the same time the earnings of physicians rank highest among professional groups, so there would not at first blush seem to be any necessity for special inducements to enter the profession. Even if we grant that, for reasons unexamined here, there is a social interest in subsidized professional education, it is not clear why the rate of subsidization should differ among professions. One might ex-

[23] The degree of subsidy in different branches of professional education is worthy of a major research effort.

pect that the tuition of medical students would be higher than that of other students.

The high cost of medical education in the United States is itself a reflection of the quality standards imposed by the American Medical Association since the Flexner Report, and it is, I believe, only since then that the subsidy element in medical education has become significant. Previously, many medical schools paid their way or even yielded a profit.

Another interesting feature of limitation on entry to subsidized education is the extent of individual preferences concerning the social welfare, as manifested by contributions to private universities. But whether support is public or private, the important point is that both the quality and the quantity of the supply of medical care are being strongly influenced by social nonmarket forces.[24, 25]

One striking consequence of the control of quality is the restriction on the range offered. If many qualities of a commodity are possible, it would usually happen in a competitive market that many qualities will be offered on the market, at suitably varying prices, to appeal to different tastes and incomes. Both the licensing laws and the standards of medical-school training have limited the possibilities of alternative qualities of medical care. The declining ratio of physicians to total employees in the medical-care industry shows that substitution of less trained personnel, technicians, and the like, is not prevented completely, but the central role of the highly trained physician is not affected at all.[26]

E. *Pricing Practices*

The unusual pricing practices and attitudes of the medical profession are well known: extensive price discrimination by income (with an extreme of zero prices for sufficiently indigent patients) and, formerly, a strong insistence on fee for services as against such alternatives as prepayment.

[24] Strictly speaking, there are four variables in the market for physicians: price, quality of entering students, quality of education, and quantity. The basic market forces, demand for medical services and supply of entering students, determine two relations among the four variables. Hence, if the nonmarket forces determine the last two, market forces will determine price and quality of entrants.

[25] The supply of Ph.D.'s is similarly governed, but there are other conditions in the market which are much different, especially on the demand side.

[26] Today only the Soviet Union offers an alternative lower level of medical personnel, the feldshers, who practice primarily in the rural districts (the institution dates back to the 18th century). According to Field [14, pp. 98-100, 132-33], there is clear evidence of strain in the relations between physicians and feldshers, but it is not certain that the feldshers will gradually disappear as physicians grow in numbers.

The opposition to prepayment is closely related to an even stronger opposition to closed-panel practice (contractual arrangements which bind the patient to a particular group of physicians). Again these attitudes seem to differentiate professions from business. Prepayment and closed-panel plans are virtually nonexistent in the legal profession. In ordinary business, on the other hand, there exists a wide variety of exclusive service contracts involving sharing of risks; it is assumed that competition will select those which satisfy needs best.[27]

The problems of implicit and explicit price-fixing should also be mentioned. Price competition is frowned on. Arrangements of this type are not uncommon in service industries, and they have not been subjected to antitrust action. How important this is is hard to assess. It has been pointed out many times that the apparent rigidity of so-called administered prices considerably understates the actual flexibility. Here, too, if physicians find themselves with unoccupied time, rates are likely to go down, openly or covertly; if there is insufficient time for the demand, rates will surely rise. The "ethics" of price competition may decrease the flexibility of price responses, but probably that is all.

III. *Comparisons with the Competitive Model under Certainty*

A. *Nonmarketable Commodities*

As already noted, the diffusion of communicable diseases provides an obvious example of nonmarket interactions. But from a theoretical viewpoint, the issues are well understood, and there is little point in expanding on this theme. (This should not be interpreted as minimizing the contribution of public health to welfare; there is every reason to suppose that it is considerably more important than all other aspects of medical care.)

Beyond this special area there is a more general interdependence, the concern of individuals for the health of others. The economic manifestations of this taste are to be found in individual donations to hospitals and to medical education, as well as in the widely accepted responsibilities of government in this area. The taste for improving the health of others appears to be stronger than for improving other aspects of their welfare.[28]

In interdependencies generated by concern for the welfare of others there is always a theoretical case for collective action if each participant derives satisfaction from the contributions of all.

[27] The law does impose some limits on risk-shifting in contracts, for example, its general refusal to honor exculpatory clauses.

[28] There may be an identification problem in this observation. If the failure of the market system is, or appears to be, greater in medical care than in, say, food an individual otherwise equally concerned about the two aspects of others' welfare may prefer to help in the first.

B. *Increasing Returns*

Problems associated with increasing returns play some role in allocation of resources in the medical field, particularly in areas of low density or low income. Hospitals show increasing returns up to a point; specialists and some medical equipment constitute significant indivisibilities. In many parts of the world the individual physician may be a large unit relative to demand. In such cases it can be socially desirable to subsidize the appropriate medical-care unit. The appropriate mode of analysis is much the same as for water-resource projects. Increasing returns are hardly apt to be a significant problem in general practice in large cities in the United States, and improved transportation to some extent reduces their importance elsewhere.

C. *Entry*

The most striking departure from competitive behavior is restriction on entry to the field, as discussed in II.D above. Friedman and Kuznets, in a detailed examination of the pre-World War II data, have argued that the higher income of physicians could be attributed to this restriction.[29]

There is some evidence that the demand for admission to medical school has dropped (as indicated by the number of applicants per place and the quality of those admitted), so that the number of medical-school places is not as significant a barrier to entry as in the early 1950's [28, pp. 14-15]. But it certainly has operated over the past and it is still operating to a considerable extent today. It has, of course, constituted a direct and unsubtle restriction on the supply of medical care.

There are several considerations that must be added to help evaluate the importance of entry restrictions: (1) Additional entrants would be, in general, of lower quality; hence, the addition to the supply of medical care, properly adjusted for quality, is less than purely quantitative calculations would show.[30] (2) To achieve genuinely competitive conditions, it would be necessary not only to remove numerical restrictions on entry but also to remove the subsidy in medical education. Like any other producer, the physician should bear all the costs of production,

[29] See [16, pp. 118-37]. The calculations involve many assumptions and must be regarded as tenuous; see the comments by C. Reinold Noyes in [16, pp. 407-10].

[30] It might be argued that the existence of racial discrimination in entrance has meant that some of the rejected applicants are superior to some accepted. However, there is no necessary connection between an increase in the number of entrants and a reduction in racial discrimination; so long as there is excess demand for entry, discrimination can continue unabated and new entrants will be inferior to those previously accepted.

including, in this case, education.[31] It is not so clear that this change would not keep even unrestricted entry down below the present level. (3) To some extent, the effect of making tuition carry the full cost of education will be to create too few entrants, rather than too many. Given the imperfections of the capital market, loans for this purpose to those who do not have the cash are difficult to obtain. The lender really has no security. The obvious answer is some form of insured loans, as has frequently been argued; not too much ingenuity would be needed to create a credit system for medical (and other branches of higher) education. Under these conditions the cost would still constitute a deterrent, but one to be compared with the high future incomes to be obtained.

If entry were governed by ideal competitive conditions, it may be that the quantity on balance would be increased, though this conclusion is not obvious. The average quality would probably fall, even under an ideal credit system, since subsidy plus selected entry draw some highly qualified individuals who would otherwise get into other fields. The decline in quality is not an over-all social loss, since it is accompanied by increase in quality in other fields of endeavor; indeed, if demands accurately reflected utilities, there would be a net social gain through a switch to competitive entry.[32]

There is a second aspect of entry in which the contrast with competitive behavior is, in many respects, even sharper. It is the exclusion of many imperfect substitutes for physicians. The licensing laws, though they do not effectively limit the number of physicians, do exclude all others from engaging in any one of the activities known as medical practice. As a result, costly physician time may be employed at specific tasks for which only a small fraction of their training is needed, and which could be performed by others less well trained and therefore less expensive. One might expect immunization centers, privately operated, but not necessarily requiring the services of doctors.

In the competitive model without uncertainty, consumers are presumed to be able to distinguish qualities of the commodities they buy. Under this hypothesis, licensing would be, at best, superfluous and exclude those from whom consumers would not buy anyway; but it might exclude too many.

D. *Pricing*

The pricing practices of the medical industry (see II.E above) de-

[31] One problem here is that the tax laws do not permit depreciation of professional education, so that there is a discrimination against this form of investment.

[32] To anticipate later discussion, this condition is not necessarily fulfilled. When it comes to quality choices, the market may be inaccurate.

part sharply from the competitive norm. As Kessel [17] has pointed out with great vigor, not only is price discrimination incompatible with the competitive model, but its preservation in the face of the large number of physicians is equivalent to a collective monopoly. In the past, the opposition to prepayment plans has taken distinctly coercive forms, certainly transcending market pressures, to say the least.

Kessel has argued that price discrimination is designed to maximize profits along the classic lines of discriminating monopoly and that organized medical opposition to prepayment was motivated by the desire to protect these profits. In principle, prepayment schemes are compatible with discrimination, but in practice they do not usually discriminate. I do not believe the evidence that the actual scale of discrimination is profit-maximizing is convincing. In particular, note that for any monopoly, discriminating or otherwise, the elasticity of demand in each market at the point of maximum profits is greater than one. But it is almost surely true for medical care that the price elasticity of demand for all income levels is less than one. That price discrimination by income is not completely profit-maximizing is obvious in the extreme case of charity; Kessel argues that this represents an appeasement of public opinion. But this already shows the incompleteness of the model and suggests the relevance and importance of social and ethical factors.

Certainly one important part of the opposition to prepayment was its close relation to closed-panel plans. Prepayment is a form of insurance, and naturally the individual physician did not wish to assume the risks. Pooling was intrinsically involved, and this strongly motivates, as we shall discuss further in Section IV below, control over prices and benefits. The simplest administrative form is the closed panel; physicians involved are, in effect, the insuring agent. From this point of view, Blue Cross solved the prepayment problem by universalizing the closed panel.

The case that price discrimination by income is a form of profit maximization which was zealously defended by opposition to fees for service seems far from proven. But it remains true that this price discrimination, for whatever cause, is a source of nonoptimality. Hypothetically, it means everyone would be better off if prices were made equal for all, and the rich compensated the poor for the changes in the relative positions. The importance of this welfare loss depends on the actual amount of discrimination and on the elasticities of demand for medical services by the different income groups. If the discussion is simplified by considering only two income levels, rich and poor, and if the elasticity of demand by either one is zero, then no reallocation of medical services will take place and the initial situation is optimal. The only effect of a change in price will be the redistribution of income as between the medical profession and the group with the zero elasticity of demand. With low elasticities of demand, the gain will be small. To illustrate, suppose the price of medical care to the rich is double that to the poor, the medical expenditures by the rich are 20 per cent of those by the poor, and the elasticity of demand for both classes is .5; then the net social gain due to the abolition of discrimination is slightly over 1 per cent of previous medical expenditures.[33]

The issues involved in the opposition to prepayment, the other major anomaly in medical pricing, are not meaningful in the world of certainty and will be discussed below.

IV. *Comparison with the Ideal Competitive Model under Uncertainty*

A. *Introduction*

In this section we will compare the operations of the actual medical-care market with those of an ideal system in which not only the usual commodities and services but also insurance policies against all conceivable risks are available.[34] Departures consist for the most part of

[33] It is assumed that there are two classes, rich and poor; the price of medical services to the rich is twice that to the poor, medical expenditures by the rich are 20 per cent of those by the poor, and the elasticity of demand for medical services is .5 for both classes. Let us choose our quantity and monetary units so that the quantity of medical services consumed by the poor and the price they pay are both 1. Then the rich purchase .1 units of medical services at a price of 2. Given the assumption about the elasticities of demand, the demand function of the rich is $D_R(p) = .14\ p^{-.5}$ and that of the poor is $D_P(p) = p^{-.5}$. The supply of medical services is assumed fixed and therefore must equal 1.1. If price discrimination were abolished, the equilibrium price, $\bar{p}$, must satisfy the relation,

$$D_R(\bar{p}) + D_P(\bar{p}) = 1.1,$$

and therefore $\bar{p} = 1.07$. The quantities of medical care purchased by the rich and poor, respectively, would be $D_R(\bar{p}) = .135$ and $D_P(\bar{p}) = .965$.

The inverse demand functions, the price to be paid corresponding to any given quantity are $d_R(q) = .02/q^2$, and $d_P(q) = 1/q^2$. Therefore, the consumers' surplus to the rich generated by the change is:

$$\int_{.1}^{.135} (.02/q^2)dq - \bar{p}(.135 - .1), \tag{1}$$

and similarly the loss in consumers' surplus by the poor is:

$$\int_{.965}^{1} (1/q^2)dq - \bar{p}(1 - .965) \tag{2}$$

If (2) is subtracted from (1), the second terms cancel, and the aggregate increase in consumers' surplus is .0156, or a little over 1 per cent of the initial expenditures.

[34] A striking illustration of the desire for security in medical care is provided by the expressed preferences of *émigrés* from the Soviet Union as between Soviet medical practice and German or American practice; see Field [14, Ch. 12]. Those in Germany preferred the German system to the Soviet, but those in the United States preferred (in a ratio of 3 to 1) the Soviet system. The reasons given boil down to the certainty of medical care, independent of income or health fluctuations.

insurance policies that might conceivably be written, but are in fact not. Whether these potential commodities are nonmarketable, or, merely because of some imperfection in the market, are not actually marketed, is a somewhat fine point.

To recall what has already been said in Section I, there are two kinds of risks involved in medical care: the risk of becoming ill, and the risk of total or incomplete or delayed recovery. The loss due to illness is only partially the cost of medical care. It also consists of discomfort and loss of productive time during illness, and, in more serious cases, death or prolonged deprivation of normal function. From the point of view of the welfare economics of uncertainty, both losses are risks against which individuals would like to insure. The nonexistence of suitable insurance policies for either risk implies a loss of welfare.

B. *The Theory of Ideal Insurance*

In this section, the basic principles of an optimal regime for risk-bearing will be presented. For illustration, reference will usually be made to the case of insurance against cost in medical care. The principles are equally applicable to any of the risks. There is no single source to which the reader can be easily referred, though I think the principles are at least reasonably well understood.

As a basis for the analysis, the assumption is made that each individual acts so as to maximize the expected value of a utility function. If we think of utility as attached to income, then the costs of medical care act as a random deduction from this income, and it is the expected value of the utility of income after medical costs that we are concerned with. (Income after medical costs is the ability to spend money on other objects which give satisfaction. We presuppose that illness is not a source of satisfaction in itself; to the extent that it is a source of dissatisfaction, the illness should enter into the utility function as a separate variable.) The expected-utility hypothesis, due originally to Daniel Bernoulli (1738), is plausible and is the most analytically manageable of all hypotheses that have been proposed to explain behavior under uncertainty. In any case, the results to follow probably would not be significantly affected by moving to another mode of analysis.

It is further assumed that individuals are normally risk-averters. In utility terms, this means that they have a diminishing marginal utility of income. This assumption may reasonably be taken to hold for most of the significant affairs of life for a majority of people, but the presence of gambling provides some difficulty in the full application of this view. It follows from the assumption of risk aversion that if an individual is given a choice between a probability distribution of income, with a given mean m, and the certainty of the income m, he would prefer the latter. Suppose, therefore, an agency, a large insurance company plan, or the government, stands ready to offer insurance against medical costs on an actuarially fair basis; that is, if the costs of medical care are a random variable with mean m, the company will charge a premium m, and agree to indemnify the individual for all medical costs. Under these circumstances, the individual will certainly prefer to take out a policy and will have a welfare gain thereby.

Will this be a social gain? Obviously yes, if the insurance agent is suffering no social loss. Under the assumption that medical risks on different individuals are basically independent, the pooling of them reduces the risk involved to the insurer to relatively small proportions. In the limit, the welfare loss, even assuming risk aversion on the part of the insurer, would vanish and there is a net social gain which may be of quite substantial magnitude. In fact, of course, the pooling of risks does not go to the limit; there is only a finite number of them and there may be some interdependence among the risks due to epidemics and the like. But then a premium, perhaps slightly above the actuarial level, would be sufficient to offset this welfare loss. From the point of view of the individual, since he has a strict preference for the actuarially fair policy over assuming the risks himself, he will still have a preference for an actuarially unfair policy, provided, of course, that it is not too unfair.

In addition to a residual degree of risk aversion by insurers, there are other reasons for the loading of the premium (i.e., an excess of premium over the actuarial value). Insurance involves administrative costs. Also, because of the irregularity of payments there is likely to be a cost of capital tied up. Suppose, to take a simple case, the insurance company is not willing to sell any insurance policy that a consumer wants but will charge a fixed-percentage loading above the actuarial value for its premium. Then it can be shown that the most preferred policy from the point of view of an individual is a coverage with a deductible amount; that is, the insurance policy provides 100 per cent coverage for all medical costs in excess of some fixed-dollar limit. If, however, the insurance company has some degree of risk aversion, its loading may also depend on the degree of uncertainty of the risk. In that case, the Pareto optimal policy will involve some element of coinsurance, i.e., the coverage for costs over the minimum limit will be some fraction less than 100 per cent (for proofs of these statements, see Appendix).

These results can also be applied to the hypothetical concept of insurance against failure to recover from illness. For simplicity, let us assume that the cost of failure to recover is regarded purely as a money cost, either simply productive opportunities foregone or, more generally, the money equivalent of all dissatisfactions. Suppose further that, given that a person is ill, the expected value of medical care is greater than its cost; that is, the expected money value attributable to recovery with medical help is greater than resources devoted to medical help. However, the recovery, though on the average beneficial, is uncertain; in the absence of insurance a risk-averter may well prefer not to take a chance on further impoverishment by buying medical care. A suitable insurance policy would, however, mean that he paid nothing if he doesn't benefit; since the expected value is greater than the cost, there would be a net social gain.[35]

C. *Problems of Insurance*

1. *The moral hazard.* The welfare case for insurance policies of all sorts is overwhelming. It follows that the government should undertake insurance in those cases where this market, for whatever reason, has failed to emerge. Nevertheless, there are a number of significant practical limitations on the use of insurance. It is important to understand them, though I do not believe that they alter the case for the creation of a much wider class of insurance policies than now exists.

One of the limits which has been much stressed in insurance literature is the effect of insurance on incentives. What is desired in the case of insurance is that the event against which insurance is taken be out of the control of the individual. Unfortunately, in real life this separation can never be made perfectly. The outbreak of fire in one's house or business may be largely uncontrollable by the individual, but the probability of fire is somewhat influenced by carelessness, and of course arson is a possibility, if an extreme one. Similarly, in medical policies the cost of medical care is not completely determined by the illness suffered by the individual but depends on the choice of a doctor and his willingness to use medical services. It is frequently observed that widespread medical insurance increases the demand for medical care. Coinsurance provisions have been introduced into many major medical policies to meet this contingency as well as the risk aversion of the insurance companies.

To some extent the professional relationship between physician and patient limits the normal hazard in various forms of medical insurance. By certifying to the necessity of given treatment or the lack thereof, the physician acts as a controlling agent on behalf of the insurance companies. Needless to say, it is a far from perfect check; the physicians themselves are not under any control and it may be convenient for them or pleasing to their patients to prescribe more expensive medi-

[35] It is a popular belief that the Chinese, at one time, paid their physicians when well but not when sick.

cation, private nurses, more frequent treatments, and other marginal variations of care. It is probably true that hospitalization and surgery are more under the casual inspection of others than is general practice and therefore less subject to moral hazard; this may be one reason why insurance policies in those fields have been more widespread.

2. *Alternative methods of insurance payment.* It is interesting that no less than three different methods of coverage of the costs of medical care have arisen: prepayment, indemnities according to a fixed schedule, and insurance against costs, whatever they may be. In prepayment plans, insurance in effect is paid in kind—that is, directly in medical services. The other two forms both involve cash payments to the beneficiary, but in the one case the amounts to be paid involving a medical contingency are fixed in advance, while in the other the insurance carrier pays all the costs, whatever they may be, subject, of course, to provisions like deductibles and coinsurance.

In hypothetically perfect markets these three forms of insurance would be equivalent. The indemnities stipulated would, in fact, equal the market price of the services, so that value to the insured would be the same if he were to be paid the fixed sum or the market price or were given the services free. In fact, of course, insurance against full costs and prepayment plans both offer insurance against uncertainty as to the price of medical services, in addition to uncertainty about their needs. Further, by their mode of compensation to the physician, prepayment plans are inevitably bound up with closed panels so that the freedom of choice of the physician by the patient is less than it would be under a scheme more strictly confined to the provision of insurance. These remarks are tentative, and the question of coexistence of the different schemes should be a fruitful subject for investigation.

3. *Third-party control over payments.* The moral hazard in physicians' control noted in paragraph 1 above shows itself in those insurance schemes where the physician has the greatest control, namely, major medical insurance. Here there has been a marked rise in expenditures over time. In prepayment plans, where the insurance and medical service are supplied by the same group, the incentive to keep medical costs to a minimum is strongest. In plans of the Blue Cross group, there has developed a conflict of interest between the insurance carrier and the medical-service supplier, in this case particularly the hospital.

The need for third-party control is reinforced by another aspect of the moral hazard. Insurance removes the incentive on the part of individuals, patients, and physicians to shop around for better prices for hospitalization and surgical care. The market forces, therefore, tend to be replaced by direct institutional control.

4. *Administrative costs.* The pure theory of insurance sketched in Section B above omits one very important consideration: the costs of operating an insurance company. There are several types of operating costs, but one of the most important categories includes commissions and acquisition costs, selling costs in usual economic terminology. Not only does this mean that insurance policies must be sold for considerably more than their actuarial value, but it also means there is a great differential among different types of insurance. It is very striking to observe that among health insurance policies of insurance companies in 1958, expenses of one sort or another constitute 51.6 per cent of total premium income for individual policies, and only 9.5 per cent for group policies [26, Table 14-1, p. 272]. This striking differential would seem to imply enormous economies of scale in the provision of insurance, quite apart from the coverage of the risks themselves. Obviously, this provides a very strong argument for widespread plans, including, in particular, compulsory ones.

5. *Predictability and insurance.* Clearly, from the risk-aversion point of view, insurance is more valuable, the greater the uncertainty in the risk being insured against. This is usually used as an argument for putting greater emphasis on insurance against hospitalization and surgery than other forms of medical care. The empirical assumption has been challenged by O. W. Anderson and others [3, pp. 53-54], who asserted that out-of-hospital expenses were equally as unpredictable as in-hospital costs. What was in fact shown was that the probability of costs exceeding $200 is about the same for the two categories, but this is not, of course, a correct measure of predictability, and a quick glance at the supporting evidence shows that in relation to the average cost the variability is much lower for ordinary medical expenses. Thus, for the city of Birmingham, the mean expenditure on surgery was $7, as opposed to $20 for other medical expenses, but of those who paid something for surgery the average bill was $99, as against $36 for those with some ordinary medical cost. Eighty-two per cent of those interviewed had no surgery, and only 20 per cent had no ordinary medical expenses [3, Tables A-13, A-18, and A-19 on pp. 72, 77, and 79, respectively].

The issue of predictability also has bearing on the merits of insurance against chronic illness or maternity. On a lifetime insurance basis, insurance against chronic illness makes sense, since this is both highly unpredictable and highly significant in costs. Among people who already have chronic illness, or symptoms which reliably indicate it, insurance in the strict sense is probably pointless.

6. *Pooling of unequal risks.* Hypothetically, insurance requires for its full social benefit a maximum possible discrimination of risks. Those

in groups of higher incidences of illness should pay higher premiums. In fact, however, there is a tendency to equalize, rather than to differentiate, premiums, especially in the Blue Cross and similar widespread schemes. This constitutes, in effect, a redistribution of income from those with a low propensity to illness to those with a high propensity. The equalization, of course, could not in fact be carried through if the market were genuinely competitive. Under those circumsances, insurance plans could arise which charged lower premiums to preferred risks and draw them off, leaving the plan which does not discriminate among risks with only an adverse selection of them.

As we have already seen in the case of income redistribution, some of this may be thought of as insurance with a longer time perspective. If a plan guarantees to everybody a premium that corresponds to total experience but not to experience as it might be segregated by smaller subgroups, everybody is, in effect, insured against a change in his basic state of health which would lead to a reclassification. This corresponds precisely to the use of a level premium in life insurance instead of a premium varying by age, as would be the case for term insurance.

7. *Gaps and coverage.* We may briefly note that, at any rate to date, insurances against the cost of medical care are far from universal. Certain groups—the unemployed, the institutionalized, and the aged—are almost completely uncovered. Of total expenditures, between one-fifth and one-fourth are covered by insurance. It should be noted, however, that over half of all hospital expenses and about 35 per cent of the medical payments of those with bills of $1,000 a year and over, are included [26, p. 376]. Thus, the coverage on the more variable parts of medical expenditure is somewhat better than the over-all figures would indicate, but it must be assumed that the insurance mechanism is still very far from achieving the full coverage of which it is capable.

D. *Uncertainty of Effects of Treatment*

1. There are really two major aspects of uncertainty for an individual already suffering from an illness. He is uncertain about the effectiveness of medical treatment, and his uncertainty may be quite different from that of his physician, based on the presumably quite different medical knowledges.

2. *Ideal insurance.* This will necessarily involve insurance against a failure to benefit from medical care, whether through recovery, relief of pain, or arrest of further deterioration. One form would be a system in which the payment to the physician is made in accordance with the degree of benefit. Since this would involve transferring the risks from the patient to the physician, who might certainly have an aversion to bearing them, there is room for insurance carriers to pool the risks,

either by contract with physicians or by contract with the potential patients. Under ideal insurance, medical care will always be undertaken in any case in which the expected utility, taking account of the probabilities, exceeds the expected medical cost. This prescription would lead to an economic optimum. If we think of the failure to recover mainly in terms of lost working time, then this policy would, in fact, maximize economic welfare as ordinarily measured.

3. *The concepts of trust and delegation.* In the absence of ideal insurance, there arise institutions which offer some sort of substitute guarantees. Under ideal insurance the patient would actually have no concern with the informational inequality between himself and the physician, since he would only be paying by results anyway, and his utility position would in fact be thoroughly guaranteed. In its absence he wants to have some guarantee that at least the physician is using his knowledge to the best advantage. This leads to the setting up of a relationship of trust and confidence, one which the physician has a social obligation to live up to. Since the patient does not, at least in his belief, know as much as the physician, he cannot completely enforce standards of care. In part, he replaces direct observation by generalized belief in the ability of the physician.[36] To put it another way, the social obligation for best practice is part of the commodity the physician sells, even though it is a part that is not subject to thorough inspection by the buyer.

One consequence of such trust relations is that the physician cannot act, or at least appear to act, as if he is maximizing his income at every moment of time. As a signal to the buyer of his intentions to act as thoroughly in the buyer's behalf as possible, the physician avoids the obvious stigmata of profit-maximizing. Purely arms-length bargaining behavior would be incompatible, not logically, but surely psychologically, with the trust relations. From these special relations come the various forms of ethical behavior discussed above, and so also, I suggest, the relative unimportance of profit-making in hospitals. The very word, "profit," is a signal that denies the trust relations.

Price discrimination and its extreme, free treatment for the indigent, also follow. If the obligation of the physician is understood to be first of all to the welfare of the patient, then in particular it takes precedence over financial difficulties.

As a second consequence of informational inequality between physician and patient and the lack of insurance of a suitable type, the patient must delegate to the physician much of his freedom of choice.

[36] Francis Bator points out to me that some protection can be achieved, at a price, by securing additional opinions.

He does not have the knowledge to make decisions on treatment, referral, or hospitalization. To justify this delegation, the physician finds himself somewhat limited, just as any agent would in similar circumstances. The safest course to take to avoid not being a true agent is to give the socially prescribed "best" treatment of the day. Compromise in quality, even for the purpose of saving the patient money, is to risk an imputation of failure to live up to the social bond.

The special trust relation of physicians (and allied occuptions, such as priests) extends to third parties so that the certifications of physicians as to illness and injury are accepted as especially reliable (see Section II.B above). The social value to all concerned of such presumptively reliable sources of information is obvious.

Notice the general principle here. Because there are barriers to the information flow and because there is no market in which the risks involved can be insured, coordination of purchase and sales must take place through convergent expectations, but these are greatly assisted by having clear and prominent signals, and these, in turn, force patterns of behavior which are not in themselves logical necessities for optimality.[37]

4. *Licensing and educational standards.* Delegation and trust are the social institutions designed to obviate the problem of informational inequality. The general uncertainty about the prospects of medical treatment is socially handled by rigid entry requirements. These are designed to reduce the uncertainty in the mind of the consumer as to the quality of product insofar as this is possible.[38] I think this explanation, which is perhaps the naive one, is much more tenable than any idea of a monopoly seeking to increase incomes. No doubt restriction on entry is desirable from the point of view of the existing physicians, but the public pressure needed to achieve the restriction must come from deeper causes.

The social demand for guaranteed quality can be met in more than one way, however. At least three attitudes can be taken by the state or other social institutions toward entry into an occupation or toward the production of commodities in general; examples of all three types exist. (1) The occupation can be licensed, nonqualified entrants being simply excluded. The licensing may be more complex than it is in medicine; individuals could be licensed for some, but not all, medical activities, for example. Indeed, the present all-or-none approach could

[37] The situation is very reminiscent of the crucial role of the focal point in Schelling's theory of tacit games, in which two parties have to find a common course of action without being able to communicate; see [24, esp. pp. 225 ff.].

[38] How well they achieve this end is another matter. R. Kessel points out to me that they merely guarantee training, not continued good performance as medical technology changes.

be criticized as being insufficient with regard to complicated specialist treatment, as well as excessive with regard to minor medical skills. Graded licensing may, however, be much harder to enforce. Controls could be exercised analogous to those for foods; they can be excluded as being dangerous, or they can be permitted for animals but not for humans. (2) The state or other agency can certify or label, without compulsory exclusion. The category of Certified Psychologist is now under active discussion; canned goods are graded. Certification can be done by nongovernmental agencies, as in the medical-board examinations for specialists. (3) Nothing at all may be done; consumers make their own choices.

The choice among these alternatives in any given case depends on the degree of difficulty consumers have in making the choice unaided, and on the consequences of errors of judgment. It is the general social consensus, clearly, that the *laissez-faire* solution for medicine is intolerable. The certification proposal never seems to have been discussed seriously. It is beyond the scope of this paper to discuss these proposals in detail. I wish simply to point out that they should be judged in terms of the ability to relieve the uncertainty of the patient in regard to the quality of the commodity he is purchasing, and that entry restrictions are the consequences of an apparent inability to devise a system in which the risks of gaps in medical knowledge and skill are borne primarily by the patient, not the physician.

Postscript

I wish to repeat here what has been suggested above in several places: that the failure of the market to insure against uncertainties has created many social institutions in which the usual assumptions of the market are to some extent contradicted. The medical profession is only one example, though in many respects an extreme one. All professions share some of the same properties. The economic importance of personal and especially family relationships, though declining, is by no means trivial in the most advanced economies; it is based on nonmarket relations that create guarantees of behavior which would otherwise be afflicted with excessive uncertainty. Many other examples can be given. The logic and limitations of ideal competitive behavior under uncertainty force us to recognize the incomplete description of reality supplied by the impersonal price system.

References

1. A. A. Alchian, K. J. Arrow, and W. M. Capron, *An Economic Analysis of the Market for Scientists and Engineers,* RAND RM-2190-RC. Santa Monica 1958.

2. M. Allais, "Géneralisation des théories de l'équilibre économique général et du rendement social au cas du risque," in Centre National de la Recherche Scientifique, *Econometrie,* Paris 1953, pp. 1-20.
3. O. W. Anderson and Staff of the National Opinion Research Center, *Voluntary Health Insurance in Two Cities.* Cambridge, Mass. 1957.
4. K. J. Arrow, "Economic Welfare and the Allocation of Resources for Invention," in Nat. Bur. Econ. Research, *The Role and Direction of Inventive Activity: Economic and Social Factors,* Princeton 1962, pp. 609-25.
5. ———, "Les rôle des valeurs boursières pour la répartition la meilleure des risques," in Centre National de la Recherche Scientifique, *Econometrie,* Paris 1953, pp. 41-46.
6. F. M. Bator, "The Anatomy of Market Failure," *Quart. Jour. Econ.* Aug. 1958, *72,* 351-79.
7. E. Baudier, "L'introduction du temps dans la théorie de l'équilibre général," *Les Cahiers Economiques,* Dec. 1959, 9-16.
8. W. J. Baumol, *Welfare Economics and the Theory of the State.* Cambridge, Mass. 1952.
9. K. Borch, "The Safety Loading of Reinsurance Premiums," *Skandinavisk Aktuariehdskrift,* 1960, pp. 163-84.
10. J. M. Buchanan and G. Tullock, *The Calculus of Consent.* Ann Arbor 1962.
11. G. Debreu, "Une économique de l'incertain," *Economie Appliquée,* 1960, *13,* 111-16.
12. ———, *Theory of Values.* New York 1959.
13. R. Dubos, "Medical Utopias," *Daedalus,* 1959, *88,* 410-24.
14. M. G. Field, *Doctor and Patient in Soviet Russia.* Cambridge, Mass. 1957.
15. Milton Friedman, "The Methodology of Positive Economics," in *Essays in Positive Economics,* Chicago 1953, pp. 3-43.
16. ——— and S. S. Kuznets, *Income from Independent Professional Practice.* Nat. Bur. Econ. Research, New York 1945.
17. R. A. Kessel, "Price Discrimination in Medicine," *Jour. Law and Econ.,* 1958, *1,* 20-53.
18. T. C. Koopmans, "Allocation of Resources and the Price System," in *Three Essays on the State of Economic Science,* New York 1957, pp. 1-120.
19. I. M. D. Little, *A Critique of Welfare Economics.* Oxford 1950.
20. Selma Mushkin, "Towards a Definition of Health Economics," *Public Health Reports,* 1958, *73,* 785-93.
21. R. R. Nelson, "The Simple Economics of Basic Scientific Research," *Jour. Pol. Econ.,* June 1959, *67,* 297-306.
22. T. Parsons, *The Social System.* Glencoe 1951.
23. M. J. Peck and F. M. Scherer, *The Weapons Acquisition Process: An Economic Analysis.* Div. of Research, Graduate School of Business, Harvard University, Boston 1962.

24. T. C. SCHELLING, *The Strategy of Conflict.* Cambridge, Mass. 1960.
25. A. K. SHAPIRO, "A Contribution to a History of the Placebo Effect," *Behavioral Science,* 1960, *5,* 109-35.
26. H. M. SOMERS AND A. R. SOMERS, *Doctors, Patients, and Health Insurance.* The Brookings Institution, Washington 1961.
27. C. L. STEVENSON, *Ethics and Language.* New Haven 1945.
28. U. S. DEPARTMENT OF HEALTH, EDUCATION AND WELFARE, *Physicians for a Growing America,* Public Health Service Publication No. 709, Oct. 1959.

APPENDIX

On Optimal Insurance Policies

The two propositions about the nature of optimal insurance policies asserted in Section IV.B above will be proved here.

Proposition 1. If an insurance company is willing to offer any insurance policy against loss desired by the buyer at a premium which depends only on the policy's actuarial value, then the policy chosen by a risk-averting buyer will take the form of 100 per cent coverage above a deductible minimum.

Note: The premium will, in general, exceed the actuarial value; it is only required that two policies with the same actuarial value will be offered by the company for the same premium.

Proof: Let W be the initial wealth of the individual, X his loss, a random variable, $I(X)$ the amount of insurance paid if loss X occurs, P the premium, and $Y(X)$ the wealth of the individual after paying the premium, incurring the loss, and receiving the insurance benefit.

$$Y(X) = W - P - X + I(X). \tag{1}$$

The individual values alternative policies by the expected utility of his final wealth position, $Y(X)$. Let $U(y)$ be the utility of final wealth, y; then his aim is to maximize,

$$E\{U[Y(X)]\}, \tag{2}$$

where the symbol, E, denotes mathematical expectation.

An insurance payment is necessarily nonnegative, so the insurance policy must satisfy the condition,

$$I(X) \geq 0 \quad \text{for all} \quad X. \tag{3}$$

If a policy is optimal, it must in particular be better in the sense of the criterion (2), than any other policy with the same actuarial expectation, $E[I(X)]$. Consider a policy that pays some positive amount of insurance at one level of loss, say X_1, but which permits the final wealth at some other loss level, say X_2, to be lower than that corresponding to X_1. Then, it is intuitively obvious that a risk-averter would prefer an alternative policy with the same actuarial value which would offer slightly less protection for losses in the neighborhood of X_1 and slightly higher protection for those in the neighborhood of X_2, since risk aversion implies that the marginal utility

22

S. Cheung, Transaction costs, risk aversion and the choice of contractual arrangements, *Journal of Law and Economics* 12 (1969), 23–42

We now turn to the risks of farming and the use of sharecropping as an institution to spread risks.

Reprinted for private circulation from THE JOURNAL OF LAW AND ECONOMICS, Volume XII (1), April, 1969, Copyright 1969, The University of Chicago.

TRANSACTION COSTS, RISK AVERSION, AND THE CHOICE OF CONTRACTUAL ARRANGEMENTS*

STEVEN N. S. CHEUNG
University of Chicago

Every transaction involves a contract. The transactions conducted in the market place entail outright or partial transfers of property rights among individual contracting parties. The contractual arrangements through which these transfers are negotiated are several and varied.

It is common in land tenure literature to rank the relative efficiency of various lease contracts. For example, share tenancy (or sharecropping) has long been considered inefficient, as have leases with relatively short duration. These views are based on an inquiry into the resource use implied by the existing contractual arrangements. But the inquiry has been made without explicit consideration of the pertinent property right constraint and cannot account for the frequent choice of allegedly inefficient contracts. The wrong question has been asked.

Elsewhere[1] I have derived the theory of share tenancy on the condition that transaction costs, and in particular the costs of contractual negotiation and enforcement, are zero. It shows that economic efficiency is the same under various land tenure arrangements subject to the constraint of private property rights. Although transaction costs exist in the real world, the theory enables us to understand much of the farming behavior.[2] However, the presence of a variety of contractual arrangements under the *same* constraint of competition poses the question of the choice of these arrangements. In this article, I set out an approach based on non-zero transaction costs and risk

* This article is an excerpt from my manuscript, The Theory of Share Tenancy—With Special Application to Asian Agriculture and the First Phase of Taiwan Land Reform (to be published by The University of Chicago Press). For their helpful comments I am indebted to Armen A. Alchian, R. H. Coase, Harold Demsetz, Jack Hirshleifer, D. Gale Johnson, Harry G. Johnson, John McManus, Theodore W. Schultz, and George J. Stigler. Thanks for financial support are given to the Lilly Endowment grant supporting the Study of Property Rights and Behavior at the University of California at Los Angeles, and to the Ford Foundation grant for International Studies including Agricultural Economics at the University of Chicago.

1 Steven N. S. Cheung, Private Property Rights and Sharecropping, 76 J. Pol. Econ. 1107 (1968).

2 See Steven N. S. Cheung, The Theory of Share Tenancy, chs. 3, 7 and 8.

aversion to explain the observed contractual behavior in agriculture. The observations used are largely drawn from the Chinese experience.

If a firm can increase efficiency in production by employing productive resources of more than one resource owner, a contract to combine the resources will obtain. The formation of the contract involves partial transfers of property rights in one form or another, such as leasing, hiring or mortgaging.[3] These transfers, and the associated coordination of inputs of various factors in production, are costly events.[4] There are costs of negotiating *and* of enforcing the stipulations of the contract.

Given the state of personal wealth distribution and the portfolios of assets held as private property by resource owners, some owners will seek contractual arrangements with others in combining resources for production.[5] There is a variety of arrangements under which this is done. At least two reasons may be offered for the existence of different types of contractual arrangements. First is the existence of *natural* risk, defined here as the contribution by nature or the state of the world to the variance (or standard deviation) of the product value.[6] Given a non-zero variance for the expected output yield (the total income for the contracting parties), different contractual arrangements allow different distributions of income variances among the contracting parties. Under the postulate of risk aversion, an individual will seek to avoid risk if the cost of doing so is less than the gain from the risk averted. He may avert risk either by searching for information about the future (which may not be attainable even at infinitely high cost), by choosing less risky options when investing (which options include portfolio diversification), or by choosing among arrangements with which his burden of risk can be dispersed to other individuals—such as insurance and various contractual arrangements. A second reason for the existence of different contractual arrangements lies in the different transaction costs that are associated with them. Transaction costs differ because the physical attributes of input and output differ, because institutional arrangements differ, and be-

[3] If only *outright* transfers exist for all resources, "owner" production will exist for all firms. Contracting for outright transfers does not concern us here.

[4] See R. H. Coase, The Nature of the Firm, N.S.4 Economica 386 (1937). Reprinted in Readings in Price Theory 331 (Kenneth E. Boulding & George J. Stigler, eds. 1952).

[5] Portfolio selection is a complicated subject. The two major theses that have been advanced center on anticipated changes in the general price level and on the aversion of risk. Transaction costs may imply a third.

[6] While this concept has the advantage of treating risk as a measurable quantity that can be conveniently applied to observations, it also has some theoretical difficulties. See for example, Jack Hirshleifer, Investment Decision under Uncertainty: Choice-Theoretic Approaches, 79 Q. J. Econ. 509 (1965).

cause different sets of stipulations require varying efforts in enforcement and negotiation.[7]

Let me advance the following hypothesis: the choice of contractual arrangement is made so as to maximize the gain from risk dispersion subject to the constraint of transaction costs. In the following three sections, I shall develop this hypothesis and apply it to some observations.

I. The Choice of Contracts in Agriculture

Consider the three main forms of contracts in agriculture, namely, a fixed-rent contract (rent per acre stated in cash or in crop), a share contract and a wage contract. Under private property rights, the contracting parties are free to choose among these forms. The observed patterns of contractual choices vary from place to place. For example, share contracts were more frequent than fixed rents in Taiwan and Southeast Asia before the agrarian reforms; in China fixed rents were more frequent than share rents in the 1930's; in Japan, fixed rents predominated; and in general, wage contracts (farm hands) have been infrequent, occurring in about one to five per cent of the farming households in various localities.[8] Why do the patterns of contractual choices differ? What determines the choice of contracts?

Any contract combining resources from different owners for production involves, in addition to negotiation costs, the enforcement costs of controlling inputs and distributing output, according to the terms of the contract. Contracting on a share basis appears to involve higher transaction costs as a whole (the sum of negotiation and enforcement costs) than a fixed-rent or a wage contract. The terms in a share contract, among other things, include the rental percentage, the ratio of non-land input to land, and the types of crops to be grown.[9] These are mutually decided by the landowner and the tenant. For fixed-rent and wage contracts, however, given the market prices, one party alone is sufficient to decide how much of the other party's resources he shall employ and what crops shall be grown. And since in a share contract the sharing of output is based on the *actual* yield, efforts must be made by

[7] Transaction costs may also depend on other factors, such as the number of participants and transactions, which I shall not explore here. Changes in prices and innovations will also affect the costs of transactions. See for example, Theodore W. Schultz, Transforming Traditional Agriculture 162-174 (1964).

[8] For the case in China, see J. L. Buck, Land Utilization in China 198 (1938); for Japan, see R. P. Dore, Land Reform in Japan (1959); for other parts of Asia, see sources cited in Steven N. S. Cheung, The Theory of Share Tenancy, ch. 1 nn.10 & 14.

[9] These terms are implied by the theory in Cheung, Private Property Rights and Sharecropping, *supra* note 1. Samples of share contracts obtained from China (see next section) are consistent with this statement.

the landowner to ascertain the harvest yield. Thus negotiation and enforcement are more complex for a share contract than for a fixed-rent or a wage contract.

The ranking of transaction costs of fixed-rent and wage contracts appears uncertain. The physical attributes of land are such that the cost of enforcing the contracted amount of input is lower than in the case of labor. That is, the "shirking" of labor input, which may exist in a wage contract (also in a share contract) without either enforcing the input or checking the output, is costly to prevent.[10] But while this "shirking" problem does not appear significant for land input in a fixed-rent contract, policing (or enforcing) the maintenance of soil and other assets owned by the landlord is more costly for a fixed-rent or a share contract than for a wage contract.[11]

If we accept the above reasoning, pending empirical confirmation, and if transaction cost is the only consideration, then the minimization of transaction cost implies that share contracts will never be chosen. Why, then, are share contracts chosen?

Suppose the transaction cost is zero or the same for all forms of contract. Let us employ a behavioral postulate of risk aversion, defined here to mean that an individual, given the same expected average income, prefers a lower to a higher variance. In agriculture, variables exogenous to the production function, such as weather conditions and pests, are risk factors which are difficult to forecast and which may significantly affect the variance of the value of output. Under a fixed-rent contract, the tenant bears most, if not all, of the risk; under a wage contract, the landowner bears most, if not all, of the risk. Share tenancy may then be regarded as a device for risk sharing (or risk dispersion); that is, the variance of the output yield is distributed

[10] For the tenant's incentive to use an amount of input less than that stipulated in a share contract, see Cheung, *supra* note 1. The adoption of different forms of contractual payment for *labor* alone due to "shirking" problems and enforcement costs appears to constitute an important subject which has not been explored. For example, a piece-rate contract will be preferred to a wage contract on an hourly basis if checking output costs less than enforcing input. However, with piece rates the worker is inclined to be "sloppy" and produce products of lower quality. Thus, a piece-rate contract will be less preferable if the physical attributes of the product are such that it is relatively costly to police a specified standard. Similarly, commission payments (as in the case of insurance salesmen) are preferred to other forms when the value of output depends on the intensity of work per sale; "tipping" payments (as in the case of waitresses) are preferred to other forms when the quality of services is significant—in either case, the costs of enforcing "intensity" and "quality" of work appear to be relatively high.

[11] In horticulture, for example, the usual contracts other than owner cultivation are wage or piece-rate contracts. This may imply that in horticulture, owner management involves a lower cost of policing the orchard assets than fixed-rent contracts. On the other hand, one expects wage contracts would be infrequent when the land holding is large, for high costs of labor supervision would be incurred.

among the contracting parties. Given the postulate of risk aversion, a share contract will be mutually preferred by the landowner and the tenant.[12] However, in varying degrees, risk exists in any tenancy. Why, then, are fixed-rent and wage contracts chosen at all?

I suggest that the choice of contract should be analyzed by employing both the differences in transaction costs and the postulate of risk aversion. Given the state of risk associated with a particular output, a higher transaction cost will lead to lower returns to the productive assets. On the other hand, given the transaction cost, risk aversion implies that asset values and the variances of income are negatively related.[13] While in itself the dispersion of risk under a share contract will lead to higher values for the contracted resources, the higher associated transaction cost will lead to lower asset values. Wealth maximization (or utility maximization, depending on the relevant measurement problem) implies that the contractual arrangement chosen will be the one which yields the highest values for the contracted resources.

Given the variance of output value and the rental percentage, a share contract prescribes a specific distribution of income variances for the contracting parties. The associated state of risk dispersion may not conform to the most preferable state according to the parties' preference functions. However, since some dispersion of risk is preferred to no dispersion at all, a share contract will be chosen rather than a fixed rent or a wage contract if the higher transaction cost is at least compensated for by the gain from risk dispersion. There exist, of course, still other arrangements under which the dispersion of risk can be tailored to fit each case. But as we shall discuss in the next section, the transaction cost of an arrangement for risk dispersion more flexible than a share contract may be so high as to make it undesirable.

Evidence is available to support the applicability of this kind of analysis:

(1) Since transaction cost is assertedly higher for share than for fixed rents, there would be room for some third parties to insure the amount of crop yield. That is, if a third party (an insurance company) were to insure the expected mean yield, the contracting parties would choose a fixed-rent contract and would be willing to pay the insuring party an amount no higher

[12] This result is implied in William F. Sharpe, Capital Asset Prices: A Theory of Market Equilibrium Under Conditions of Risk, 19 J. Fin. 425 (1964); Jack Hirshleifer, *supra* note 6, and Investment Decision Under Uncertainty: Applications of the State-Preference Approach, 80 Q. J. Econ. 252 (1966). "Risk-exchange" models derived from the current state-preference and mean, variability approaches, with the aid of an Edgeworth-Bowley box, suggest that risk sharing is preferred—if we ignore transaction cost.

[13] For a theoretical treatment of asset prices and risk premiums as determined in the market place, see Sharpe, *supra* note 12.

than the saving from a lower transaction cost plus a premium for the virtually certain income now obtained as compared with the variable income in a share contract. Yet we seldom find the existence of such a crop insurance without government taking an active role. The reason, perhaps, is that the cost of handling insurance transactions may be so high as to be prohibitive: the insuring agent would have to check not only the actual crop yields but also the amount of inputs. For the French metayage (sharecropping), however, Constantia Maxwell observed:

> The usual procedure for French seigneurs was, while retaining the chateau and its immediate neighborhood for their own use, to let out their lands in *gros* to middlemen or *fermiers* (to be distinguished from *fermiers exploitants*), who paid a fixed sum to the proprietor and gathered the rents from *metayage* or from *censitaires* at their own risk for a personal profit. Some of these middlemen, like the landlords, were absentees and worked the estate through sub-agents.[14]

In this case we see the *fermiers*, a third party, interposing between landlords and tenants to provide a more certain income for the former.[15] To my knowledge, no similar arrangement existed in China, though another practice prevailed (see next section). In Japan, share tenancy has been rare; and, at the same time, a compulsory crop insurance system has been enforced.[16]

(2) In China, share tenancy is reportedly more frequent in the wheat region than in the rice region. Taking the hectare yield data of wheat and rice crops in Taiwan, we find significantly higher proportional variances for wheat than for rice. This is shown in Table 1. Due to the lack of price data, only the variances of physical output are computed, although value of output would be a more appropriate measure.

14 Arthur Young, Travels in France During the Years 1787, 1788 and 1789 at 395 ed. n. (C. Maxwell, ed. 1929).

15 To interpret the existence of the *fermiers* on grounds of risk aversion alone seems inconclusive. R. H. Coase has pointed out to me that the *fermiers* resembled the "farmers" in England, who served to collect taxes and postal revenues for the Crown. Coase's explanation for the existence of the English "farmers" is as follows: a collecting agent who is allowed to take the difference between what he can collect and what he has to pay the Crown has a greater incentive to maximize receipts than if the same agent is paid a wage rate for his service. This argument, I believe, is correct, and can be expressed alternatively: transaction costs differ, among other things, because different sets of stipulations require varying efforts in enforcement and negotiation; and for collection a "farming" contract involves a lower cost of enforcement than a wage contract. The *fermier* of France may therefore be viewed as a "farming" agent as well as an "insuring" agent.

16 See Agricultural Development in Modern Japan, ch. 13 (Takekayu Ogura ed. 1963). I have been unable to discover the frequency of share contracts in Japan before the introduction of the compulsory crop insurance.

TABLE 1
Mean Yield (μ) and Proportional Variance (σ_p^2) of Wheat and Rice Hectare Yield (kg.), Taiwan, 1901–1950

Value	Crop	1901–10	1911–10	Period 1921–30	1931–40	1941–50
μ	Wheat	880	710	759	1,058	625
	Rice	1,318	1,379	1,588	1,927	1,648
σ_p^2	Wheat	0.0463	0.0118	0.0357	0.0453	0.1158
	Rice	0.0031	0.0032	0.0046	0.0062	0.0180

Source: Computed from data in Sino-American Joint Commission for Rural Reconstruction, Taiwan Agricultural Statistics 1901–1955 at 20, 24 (1956).

In Table 1,

$$\sigma_p^2 = \frac{\sum_{i=1}^{n} \left(\frac{X_i}{\mu} - 1\right)^2}{n},$$

where X_i is the hectare yield in kg., and n the number of years. The higher frequency of share contracts among wheat crops appears to be a universal phenomenon.[17]

(3) According to three independent surveys conducted in China (1930-1935), share rent is generally slightly higher than fixed (crop) rent,[18] and this premium may be regarded as a return for risk bearing to the landowner.

Let us summarize. The postulate of general risk aversion or the minimization of transaction costs, taken separately, do not explain well the observed coexistence of several forms of contracts. For this reason I use both, and the choice of contracts is determined by weighing the gains from risk dispersions and the costs of contracting associated with different contracts. Two factors appear to be important in explaining different patterns of contractual choices in different localities. First, different physical attributes of crops and types of climate often result in different variances of outputs in different

[17] See for example, J. L. Buck, *supra* note 8, at 198; and James O. Bray, Farm Tenancy and Productivity in Agriculture: The Case of the United States, 4 Food Research Institute Studies 25 (Stanford Univ. 1963).

[18] See Li Fa Yuan, Tung Chi Yueh Pao II, 5 (Legislative Yuan, Statistical Monthly, 1932); Nei Cheng Pu, Nei Cheng Kung Pao II (Dep't of Int. Affairs, Public Rep. of Inst. Affairs 1932); Shih Yeh Pu, Chung Kuo Ching Chi Nien Chien G62-83 (Dep't of Real Estates, China Econ. Yearbook, 1936). Some of these findings are reproduced in Steven N. S. Cheung, The Theory of Share Tenancy, App. B.

agricultural areas. Second, different legal arrangements, such as compulsory or subsidized crop insurance, affect the variances of incomes as well as affecting transaction costs for the contracting parties. An examination of some contractual details in the next section will suggest a third factor: different market arrangements also affect the choice of contractual forms.

II. Characteristics of Fixed and Share Contracts (China, 1925-1940)

In this and the following section we analyze in some detail the observed stipulations of fixed and share contracts. This will serve not only to clarify the hypothesis that contractual arrangements are chosen to disperse risk bearing and minimize transaction cost, but also to illustrate that the contractual stipulations in sharecropping are consistent with efficient resource use.[19] I turn to some information from China, roughly from 1925 to 1940. This choice of data is based not only on the availability of information, but also on the fact that during this period in China, some 93 per cent of the farm land was held under private ownership.[20] Let me begin by translating a few sample contracts of fixed rent.

Sample (a)—fixed (crop) rent contract with definite lease duration (Shantung Province):

> Tenant A now leases from landowner B [so many acres] of land at location C. We hereby stipulate, with the presence of referee D, that the annual rent per acre includes [so many catties] of millet, soybean and Indian corn. The payment in wheat will be one month after the wheat harvest, and autumn crops two months after the autumn harvest. In a famine year, rental payments shall be adjusted [downward] according to local customs. The duration of the lease is [so many years].[21]

Sample (b)—fixed (crop) rent contract with indefinite lease duration (Kiangsi Province):

19 The prevailing inefficiency argument against sharecropping can be briefly stated as follows. Since under sharecropping a portion of every output unit is taken as rent, it is similar to an *ad valorem* excise tax—where part of every unit produced is "taxed" by the landowner (government). The distribution of output is not the same as with fixed rent or owner cultivation—where the tiller obtains the *entire* incremental product. Sharecropping, therefore, is said to result in less intensive (and less efficient) farming because the tenant's incentive to work or invest in land is reduced. This thesis, however, ignores the terms in a share contract which the participating parties must *mutually* agree to abide by when the contract is formed.

20 See J. L. Buck, Farm Ownership and Tenancy in China (1927).

21 Kuo Min Cheng Fu, Tung Chi Chu, Chung Kuo Tsu Tien Chih Tu Chi Tung Chi Fen Hsi 52-53 (Nat'l Gov't, Statistics Dep't, Statistical Analysis of Tenancy System in China, 1942).

. . . we contractually establish an iron-sheet [firmly fixed] rent . . . . Regardless of good or bad years, not a fraction of rent can be reduced . . . . In the event that the rental payment is reduced or delayed, the landowner is free to take back the land, together with all existing crops, and [the right] to contract a new tenant for cultivation. . . . . Furthermore, the landowner shall pay the tenant 20 copper coins for the delivery of every 100 catties of grains.[22]

Sample (c)—fixed (crop) rent contract with landowner providing non-land farming inputs (Tsinghai Province):

. . . the landowner will furnish [so many catties] of seed, together with [so many pairs] of water buffalo, [so many head] of donkeys, and all essential farming equipment. The durable assets are for use purposes only, and shall not be damaged or lost [by the tenant], . . . and they must be returned to the landowner without delay at the termination of the lease. The [aforementioned] rental rate is subject to adjustment according to local customs in a famine year.[23]

The above samples of fixed (crop) rent contracts are about as representative as I could find. They are identical to cash rent contracts in all aspects except that in the latter rental payments are stated in monetary units.[24] According to observations collected by the Department of Real Estates, covering 22 provinces in China, cash rents are generally slightly lower than crop rents.[25] This differential can be explained by landowners' sharing in the product selling cost undertaken by tenants. We may also note that with inflation occurring in 1938, due to the Sino-Japanese War beginning in 1937, 13.3 per cent of cash rents were converted into crop rents and 15.3 per cent were converted into share contracts.[26] This observation, of course, is consistent with minimizing transaction cost. Under inflation, renegotiation of cash rent contracts becomes more frequent and thus more costly.

The characteristics of fixed-rent contracts are not of special interest except for one feature. The one feature which we single out to elaborate on here is the frequent inclusion of the provision for rental reduction according to "local customs" in a "famine" year [see samples (a) and (c)], a provision which is absent under an "iron-sheet" rent [see sample (b)]. Let us call this provision an *escape clause* for the tenant, the inclusion of which in a fixed-rent contract imposes a risk burden on the landowner.

22 Pe-Yu Chang & Yin-Yuen Wang, Chung Kuo Nung Tien Wen T'i 68 (Questions of Farm Tenancy in China, 1943).

23 Nat'l Gov't, *supra* note 21, at 54-55.

24 See Nat'l Gov't, *supra* note 21, at 53-54 and Chang & Wang, *supra* note 22, at 67-70.

25 Shih Yeh Pu, Chung Kuo Ching Chi Nien Chien G62-83 (Dep't of Real Estates, China Econ. Yearbook, 1936).

26 Hsing Cheng Yuan, Ti Chuan Pien Tung No. 2 (Executive Yuan, Changes in Land Rights 1942). The data were obtained from sample contracts in 14 provinces in 1938.

We may interpret "local customs" as a set of market prices for "famine" adjustments, even though the exact magnitude of the possible reduction of rent is not stated when the contract is signed. The escape clause comes into play only in a year so "bad" that the market considers it to be a "famine." Given a sufficiently large number of fixed-rent contracts which include the escape clause, competition among landowners to keep their tenants will yield certain market rates of rental reduction which each landowner will follow. Other things being equal, the increased risk burden on the landowner associated with the inclusion of the escape clause implies that a premium will be added to the "fixed" rent over the "iron-sheet."[27]

Although shifting the risk burden by including the escape clause in a fixed-rent contract is not quite the same as the risk dispersion in a share contract, we may imagine the formation of share contracts via the escape clause. Suppose "famine" is defined as occurring when the actual harvest is reduced to a certain per cent of the expected mean yield due to natural causes. The tenant under fixed rent has the option to choose between agreeing to an "iron-sheet" contract or buying an "escape" right by paying an "insurance" premium to the landowner—such that in the event of "famine," rental payment will be reduced by a certain percentage according to a market rule.

To further the argument: there could exist in the market place not just one escape clause as observed, but a wide range of similar clauses each associated with a different level of "famine," such that the tenant could obtain any or several of them by paying different premiums to the landowner. As such, the risk burden could be dispersed between the contracting parties in an infinite number of ways each with slightly different arrangements. This hypothetical world would perhaps exist if the costs of negotiating and marketing all of the different escape clauses were zero. But with increasing transaction cost associated with additional escape clauses—in particular the cost of defining different levels of "famine" in the market place and the cost of negotiating the rental reduction for each—the incremental gains of having them may be so small that no further "custom" is developed by the market. Instead, an alternative device chosen is a share contract, under which multiple "escape" provisions for the tenant will be implicit, and within which the rental payment is no longer fixed.[28]

From the above we may deduce two implications with respect to transaction cost and risk aversion. First, we have argued that the transaction cost

27 Unfortunately, I have been unable to find data that would confirm or refute this statement.

28 Note that with a share contract the landowner not only shares in the possible loss in a bad year, but also the gain of a good harvest which will reduce the risk premium by a fraction.

is higher for share rent than for fixed rent, pending empirical confirmation. Observed contractual arrangements in China suggest that the transaction cost for a wide range of escape clauses is higher than for share rent. The reason is that a wide range of escape clauses would allow a greater variety of choice for risk dispersion than a share contract, and yet only one escape clause is observed as available. Thus, the range of contractual choices is constrained by transaction cost. Second, since, as noted earlier, evidence indicates that share rent is slightly higher than fixed rent due to the added risk burden imposed on the landowner, we conjecture that the landowner's income would be higher than with a share contract if an escape clause were adopted to the effect that the tenant's income variance is reduced to zero. Imaginative as it may seem, we find such an escape clause exists in the real world, disguised under the name of a wage contract.

Available data on the frequencies of escape clause adoptions under different contracts support my suggestions. A survey conducted by the University of Nanking, covering four provinces in China in 1935, reveals that the escape clause [as in contract samples (a) and (c)] was adopted in 83 per cent of the crop (fixed) rent contracts, 63 per cent of the cash (fixed) rent contract, and not at all in share contracts.[29] The higher frequency of adoption for crop rent than cash rent is what we would expect. In the event of a generally poor harvest, the market price of agricultural yield will rise, and with cash rent the tenant's income will be compensated by the rise in price more than with crop rent; hence, the escape clause will become less preferable to the tenant.

The existence of the escape clause in the market implies, other things being equal, a more frequent choice of fixed-rent contracts than of share contracts. Outside China in Southeast Asia, before the agrarian reforms, the escape clause was unpopular. However, there existed some guaranteed minimum rents or wages associated with share contracts. These guarantees could be similarly analyzed with the suggested choice-theoretic approach if more information were available. The different market practices explain, in part, the higher frequency of share contracts in Southeast Asia than in China. Indeed, the *fermiers* of the French metayage, the escape clause associated with fixed rents in China, and the minimum guarantees associated with share rents elsewhere are market practices that serve as intermediate arrangements between pure fixed rents and pure share rents. Each of them has different risk distributions and transaction costs, thus widening the range of contractual choices. Why these intermediate arrangements differ in different markets is a question which I do not seek to answer.

[29] See the University of Nanking, Ssu Hsing Chi Tsu Tien Chi Tu 65-67, Rental Systems in Four Provinces (1936).

Turning to sample contracts of share rents in China, we find that their stipulations are more complex than those of fixed rents, due to the added stipulations on tenant inputs and crops to be grown.

Sample (d)—share contract with uniform sharing percentages for all crops (Shantung Province):

> . . . tenant A agrees to cultivate [so many mows] of land for landowner B. We hereby stipulate that tenant A provides [so many head] of water buffalo, [so many bodies] of men; and every year the tenant must cultivate wheat once, Indian corn three times, and soybean twice. Fertilizer expenses are to be shared [in certain proportions]. The yields of all crops are to be shared [in certain proportions]. The lease may terminate only after the autumn harvest . . . .[30]

Sample (e)—share contract with varying sharing percentages (Honan Province):

> [Stipulations of land size and nonland inputs] . . . . We hereby stipulate that wheat yield will be split 20-80; millet, yellow bean, sesame, green bean—all will be split 30-70; cotton and sweet potatoes split 50-50 . . . ; millet straws, and bean and sesame stalks split 30-70 . . . .[31]

Sample (f)—share contract with some products unshared (Honan Province):

> . . . Tenant A . . . voluntarily agrees to furnish [so many] men, [so many head] of water buffalo and donkeys . . . and all plowing equipment . . . . We clearly stipulate that seeds of major crops are to be provided by the landowner, and seeds of minor crops by the tenant. All crop yields will be split equally, in dry and clean form . . . . But the straws go to the [tenant's] water buffalo entirely; the droppings go to the [landowner's] soil; . . . . and all fertilizer expenses are to be borne equally by both parties. All grinding equipment and living rooms are provided [by the landowner], which the tenant shall repair for his own use. These assets must be returned to the landowner at lease cancellation.[32]

In share contracts, several things should be noted. First, the explicit stipulations of tenant inputs and crop plantations are implied by economic theory. These stipulations are unnecessary for fixed rents. Evidence indicates, however, that only the actual yields are inspected, for by comparison with adjacent farms or past experience the landowner will be able to decide whether the contracted terms have been fulfilled:

> . . . the absentee landlords send their agents, or go themselves, to the fields and

[30] Nat'l Gov't, *supra* note 21 at 54.

[31] Chang & Wang, *supra* note 22 at 63.

[32] Chang & Wang, *supra* note 22 at 63-64.

estimate the yield of the crop and the share given by the tenant is based on this estimate. Such men are very expert in approximating the true yield . . . . [The tenant] commonly cheats by skilfully hiding some of the threshed grain before division takes place and also by giving the landlord inferior crops. On the other hand, the landlord or his agent often uses a large measure. When the agent collects rent the tenant has to treat the agent very well and often has to bribe him in order to keep the land for cultivation another year.[33]

Exaggerated as this quotation might be, an intramarginal tenant with specific farming knowledge (hence, with higher yields than marginal tenants) can "hide" as much as the rent imputed to his special skill and still retain his tenancy; an agent can collect enforcement cost in "bribes" from both the landowner and the tenant as much as other competing agents allow. Nonetheless, this justifies our claim that transaction cost is higher for a share contract than for fixed rent.

A second characteristic of share contracts is that the precise and at times complex delineation of resource rights between the contracting parties suggests that the sharing of investment inputs can be adjusted together with the rental percentage so as to use resources efficiently. This is consistent with a conclusion I have reached elsewhere:[34] the landowner may either require the tenant to invest more in land and charge a lower rental percentage, or the landowner may invest in land himself and charge a higher rental percentage; the investment will be made in one way or the other if it leads to a higher rental annuity.

A third characteristic of share contracts is that the rental percentage may vary among different crops in one contract [see sample (e)]. As implied by the theory of share tenancy, the rental percentage is dependent upon the cost of tenant inputs and the relative fertility of land. Since different crops usually require different intensities of tenant inputs relative to land, the sharing percentages for different crops should be expected to differ within a single contract. However, any set of different rental percentages for different crops can also be expressed in terms of a single (weighted time average) rental percentage, uniform for all crops, to yield the same present value of the rental return. It appears that the latter option of a uniform rental percentage [see contract sample (d)] would be more convenient. However, if tenancy is subject to dismissal at any moment of time in the event of poor performance, the use of one rental percentage uniform for crops harvested at different seasons would be likely to lead to disputes or renegotiation should tenancy dismissal be in effect. We usually find a uniform rental per-

[33] J. L. Buck, Chinese Farm Economy 149-150 (1930).

[34] Cheung, *supra* note 1.

centage being used in a share lease with specified duration, and that when multiple percentages are found in a lease with indefinite duration, a uniform percentage is usually used for different crops harvested in the same season [see contract sample (e)].

We may summarize the characteristics of share contracts by quoting the observation made by two writers—who were critical of tenant farming in China:

> Under the system of share rent, the yields after each harvest are to be shared according to certain mutually stipulated percentages between the landowner and the tenant. With the exception of some land used for farmstead purposes, the tenant is required to cultivate almost all the assigned fields for the production of crops. Sometimes, the tenant is even required to furnish farming equipment . . . and other expenses. The landowner and the tenant mutually decide the area to be used for each crop . . . . Besides the above, the only affair of management over which the landowner exercises control is confined to permanent improvements of land assets. This last characteristic is identical with fixed-rent contracts.[35]

III. The Duration of Lease Contracts

An investigation conducted in China (1934), covering a total of 93 prefectures in 8 provinces, shows that the distribution of lease durations was as follows: 29 per cent of the tenant contracts were *indefinite* (that is, unspecified and usually terminable after every harvest), 25 per cent *annual* leases, 27 per cent from *3 to 10 years*, 8 per cent from *10 to 20 years*, and 11 per cent were *perpetual* leases.[36] Two things should be noted. First, a stipulated lease duration means only that tenancy may not be terminated as long as the contracted terms are fulfilled by each party. That the duration of the lease is specified does not prohibit mutual renegotiations within the lease duration. Second, as the frequency of short-term leases has been used to illustrate the turnover rate of tenancy, it should be pointed out that lease termination is not the same as tenancy dismissal. Available data reveal that the frequency of tenancy dismissal was not high.[37]

[35] Chang & Wang, *supra* note 22, at 49. For similar observations see Ching-Moh Chen, Chung Kuo Ko Hsing Te Ti Tsu (Land Rents of Various Provinces in China, 1936); Chi-Ming Chiao, Chung Kuo Nang Ch'un She Hui Ching Chi Hsueh ch. 9 (A Social and Economic Study of Farm Villages in China, 1938); and Chung Kuo Ke Hsueh Yan Ching Chi Yen Chiu So, Chung Kuo Ching Tai Nung Yeh Shih Tze Liao 1912-1927, at 89-95 (China Econ. Research Dep't, Source Materials of Recent Chinese Agricultural History, 1957).

[36] These precentages are computed from Shih Yeh Pu, Chung Kuo Ching Chi Nien Chien 101-104 (Dep't of Real Estates, China Econ. Yearbook, 1935). A similar investigation conducted in the same localities ten years earlier yielded a virtually identical distribution, *id.*

[37] According to a survey conducted by the Executive Yuan, *supra* note 26, covering 14 provinces in China (1937), 7.5% of the lease contracts were dismissed in that year.

In the literature of land tenure, two arguments have been commonly used in attacks upon the efficiency of lease durations of less than 10 years. One of these claims that short durations impose insecurity on the tenant and thus impair his incentive to farm. But insecurity, although undesirable to the tenant, may provide a stimulus to farming activity.[38] Another argument is that the short-term lease discourages investment in land. However, this is refuted by the fact that yields per acre on tenant farms are not lower than on owner farms; nor has any evidence been offered to show that, in China, productivity under tenancy varies with the duration of a leasing contract.[39]

The right to each privately owned resource is, by definition, transferable and exclusively delineated. Rights to resources invested in land and other assets are no exception. In the formation of a lease contract, the participating resource owners are free to accept or reject the contractual terms being negotiated. Again, the choice for the duration of the contract is no exception. Thus the relevant question here is not whether a "short-term" lease is inefficient; the relevant question is why different lease durations are chosen.

In a world uncomplicated by transaction costs and risks, in which the right to the income generated by private investment could be costlessly secured and transferred, and in which changes in contractual stipulations could be costlessly negotiated at any time, the duration of the lease becomes irrelevant and its explicit stipulation superfluous. With transaction costs included, I argue that the lease duration will be chosen so as to minimize these costs. To do so, it is convenient to separate the cost advantages for "long" and "short" lease durations.

1. *The Choice of Relatively Long Lease Duration*

A relatively long lease duration is chosen to reduce the cost of transferring (transacting) tenant assets attached to land. There exist differences in physical attributes of capital assets which involve different moving costs at lease dismissal. For example, a water buffalo owned by a tenant for grain

---

However, since inflation began in the same year, the cited percentage might be higher than that of preceding years. For the rise in prices due to the Sino-Japanese war, see Chang & Wang, *supra* note 22, at ch. 9.

[38] Armen A. Alchian has argued that the desire for security leads to "long-term" contracts. But his analysis is based on a property right system which is *not* private, where the private cost of acquiring security is relatively low. See his Private Property and the Relative Cost of Tenure, The Public Stake in Union Power 350-71 (Philip Bradley ed., 1959).

[39] During the period 1925-1937, surveys conducted by five organizations in China show no notable differences in acre yields or land prices that are attributable to different tenure arrangements. Among these surveys, two volumes are particularly comprehensive: Nat'l Gov't, *supra* note 21 and Land Utilization in China—Statistics—A Study of 16,786 Farms in 168 Localities and 38,256 Farm Families in Twenty-two Provinces in China, 1929-1933 (J. L. Buck ed., 1937).

grinding is easier to move at lease dismissal than an improvement in water irrigation made by him. Of course, the landowner could have invested in the water irrigation himself, or he could purchase the tenant's committed improvement outright.[40] But when assets attached to land are owned by the tenant, disputes may arise in the event of tenancy dismissal. A lease with a sufficiently long duration may become the preferred option.

However, the cost of moving the *physical* asset is not necessarily the relevant cost to consider. The tenant's property *right* to his committed investment may be transferred, either to a third party or to the landowner, at a market price. The problem is that such a price may not exist, or cannot be obtained in a short period of time, due to transaction costs. One need only point out that the depreciated value of a used asset is costly to evaluate; the landowner may choose to select his new tenant instead of allowing any party who purchases the asset to take over the lease. Also, other information problems exist in the market place. An appropriately long lease duration will thus reduce disputes and the anticipated cost of transferring the tenant's property right. This choice, however, can be made only at the expense of some cost advantage which a shorter lease duration provides.

The foregoing discussion can be supported by observations on the perpetual lease in China:

> Under perpetual leases the landowner holds ownership right to the [bottom of] land, and the tenant owns the right to the soil . . . . These two rights are separate. The occurrences of perpetual leases are confined to the following: (1) The tenant exploited [privately owned] wasteland and developed it into farm land, thus gaining a perpetual [ownership] right to the soil from the landowner. (2) Permanent improvements in land made by the tenant . . . . such as building up water-conserving devices in otherwise sandy fields . . . . (3) . . . where labor is scarce and land plentiful, the landowners attracted tenants from afar by offering the perpetual right to till [the soil] . . . . (4) The tenant had paid a lump-sum payment to obtain the perpetual right to till . . . . And (5) the peasant, when in need of money, sold the ownership right to the land bottom but retained the right to till the soil. Since ownership rights to the bottom and surface of land are separate, both the landowner and the tenant can sell their rights freely, without the consent from each other . . . .[41]

[40] Two independent surveys (China, 1921-1924 and 1935) reveal that, among tenant farms, landowners owned about 60 to 70% of the housing assets; tenants owned about 75% of the draft animals and 95% of the farming equipment. The total values of non-land assets on owner and tenant farms were roughly the same. See Nat'l Gov't, *supra* note 21, at 99-116.

[41] Chiao, *supra* note 35, at 261. For similar observations see Nat'l Gov't, *supra* note 21, at 56-58; and China Econ. Research Dep't, *supra* note 35 at 84-89.

In every case, the tenant's asset attached to land (for example, the right to the soil) is physically "permanent." With the perpetual lease and the contracted terms in effect, the landowner may not arbitrarily raise the "bottom" rent (or use other devices) to drive the tenant away. Yet such a lease duration would not be necessary if transaction costs were zero: If the "bottom" and "surface" rights were clearly delineated and costlessly enforced as private, and if these rights could be costlessly transferred, there would exist market prices for these rights at which transfers could be executed at any time.[42] Thus there would be no need for long lease durations to protect the "immobile" investments of the tenant. The same can be said for other assets attached to land.

2. *The Choice of Relatively Short Lease Duration*

The adoption of a relatively long lease duration involves forgoing some cost advantage which a shorter duration provides. When assets attached to land owned by the tenant are to be exhausted in a short period of time, or when the landowner provides all the "permanent" assets, a relatively short lease duration reduces the costs of *enforcing* the contracted terms and of *renegotiating* these terms.

When a contract is formed, the contracting parties may lack sufficient information on each other's reliability. Within a specified lease duration, the violation of the contracted terms by either party may call for increasing enforcement efforts, or for revoking the contract before its termination date through court action or other means—all to be done at some cost. The choice of a shorter lease duration, which facilitates tenancy dismissal, will reduce these costs. As noted at the beginning of this section, however, the frequency of tenancy dismissals was far less than that of short-term leases, suggesting that most terminated leases were renewed. Available data show that the frequency of lease dismissals caused by rental disputes was low.[43] I conjecture, therefore, that in China short-term leases are chosen more as a device to facilitate contractual renegotiation rather than as a device to reduce the costs of enforcing the contracted terms.

[42] I apply here the thinking in R. H. Coase, The Problem of Social Cost, 3 J. Law & Econ. 1 (1960).

[43] Legal records which cover 56 prefectures in 6 provinces (China, 1934-35) reveal a total of 124 tenancy disputes (mostly in rental payments) over a one year period. Even though the number of total tenant contracts is not available, the number of disputes brought to court appears to be so small that one suspects a substantial number of disputes were never brought to court. Over two-thirds of these recorded cases ended in tenancy dismissals, together with payment settlements. See Dep't of Real Estates, *supra* note 36, at G118-120; and *supra* note 25, at G143-144.

It is useful to distinguish two types of contractual renegotiation (revision), though at times one relates to the other. The stipulated terms in any tenure contract in essence specify two things: (a) the state of resource use, or allocation, mutually agreed upon by the contracting parties, and (b) the contracted distribution of income for the parties. To revise (a) through renegotiation for more efficient resource use may benefit *all* parties to a contract, that is, all parties may gain or lose less. However, to revise (b) one party must lose.

Consider the contractual renegotiation which entails mainly a reallocation of resources, for example, changes in relative product prices which call for shifts to different crops, or innovations which call for the adoptions of new seeds or new methods of cultivation. Renegotiations of this type are largely confined to share contracts, since under fixed rents the tenants are left to make their own decisions on resource use except improvements in land and maintenance of the landowner's assets. In principle, since all contracting parties expect to benefit from the revision, renegotiation can take place at any time and lease termination becomes unnecessary. However, different individual knowledge of the market may give rise to difference in opinions as to whether the revision is desirable. A relatively short lease duration is a convenient device which allows resource reallocation in the event of unsuccessful renegotiation.[44] This, together with the more complicated contractual enforcement required for share contracts, explains why durations for share leases are generally shorter than fixed rents.[45]

Consider further the contractual renegotiation which entails the revision of income distribution, when one party gains at the expense of the other. It applies to fixed and share contracts alike. Resource allocation may also be affected. For example, changes in relative asset prices of the contracted resources, a cash-rent contract with unanticipated inflation, or decision errors made in the initial contract—which call for a revision of the rental rates—are cases in point. Since some party must lose when revising the initial distributional terms, that is, the gainer either cannot or will not fully compensate the loser in making the revision, lease termination (hence, the choice

[44] With lease termination, for example, a share tenant who alone wants changes in production plan can request a fixed-rent contract, purchase the land outright, or seek tenancy with another landowner. Without lease termination, further negotiation may still take place if one party who wants the revision pays the reluctant party an amount to make the revision "convincing."

[45] Localities with higher frequencies of share leases (China, 1934) were associated with higher frequencies of short-term leases. See Nat'l Gov't, *supra* note 21, at 43, Tables 20 and 21; and at 59, Table 26.

of an appropriately short duration) is essential.[46] Again, this would not be necessary if transaction cost were zero (even if unanticipated events occur independently). In the absence of transaction cost, a contract would be designed to allow day to day changes in rental payments; within any lease duration, the distribution of income would not be held fixed throughout.

IV. Concluding Remarks

For generations economists and land tenure writers have sought to rank the relative efficiency of resource use under different leasing arrangements. But their inquiries were undertaken without explicit reference to the property right constraint involved. And in many cases, the characteristics of various lease contracts had not been carefully examined. Different contractual arrangements do not imply different efficiencies of resource allocation as long as property rights are exclusive and transferable. The characteristics of lease contracts presented above also confirm this statement.

In this article I have asked: Why are different contractual arrangements chosen under the same system of private property rights? To answer this question I have introduced transaction costs and risks. The attempt to formulate a choice-theoretic approach to explain the observed contractual behavior in agriculture has perhaps raised more questions than it has answered.

Among some related problems that I have avoided explicitly, the following are significant. First, with respect to risk aversion, a more general analysis would include all risky choices, and not contractual choice alone. The analysis would be less difficult if transaction costs were not involved. Second, with respect to transaction costs, a more general analysis would derive some specific and well-behaved cost function of transactions. This step is essential to the development of a model of general equilibrium including transaction costs.

Still other problems I have avoided implicitly. In particular, some level of law enforcement by legal authorities is taken for granted. We may well ask: What will happen to the choice of contracts if the government changes its enforcement efforts? To what extent will these efforts be consistent with the Pareto condition? What set of legal institutions is consistent with the operation of the market place? With these questions unanswered, the conditions defining efficiency with transaction costs are not all clear. Let me explain.

[46] Given an unexpired lease which fixes the rental rate, changing economic conditions may lead to a redistribution of income. However, the efficiency of resource allocation may not thereby be hindered.

In production, cost minimization requires not only the fulfillment of the familiar set of marginal equalities, but also the choice of the lowest-cost production method available. In transactions, one relevant consideration is the cost of alternative *contractual* arrangements, which we have discussed at some length. One might think that, as a cost constraint, efficiency will be attained when, other things equal, the set of arrangements with the lowest transaction cost is chosen. However, transaction costs also depend on alternative *legal* arrangements. For example, the varying effectiveness of law enforcement, or the varying corruptibility of courts, will affect the costs of transactions in the market place. Given the existing legal institutions, I have attempted to explain the observed contractual arrangements. But insofar as I have ignored the choice and development of the legal institutions, the Pareto condition with transaction costs is ambiguous.

I have also not explored the contractual behavior associated with different property right constraints. Various restrictions on the transfer of property rights, or various methods of attenuating the right of a resource owner to obtain income from his resource, will affect the leasing arrangements as well as resource allocation.

Comment

In this article, Cheung relates the choice of contracts in farming (rental, wage, sharecropping) to transaction costs and the magnitude of risks to be shared. This area of inquiry has since been explored by others. Higgs (1973) extends and further tests Cheung's analysis against evidence in the southern United States. In another analysis of the same subject, Rao (1971) focuses on the scope for entrepreneurship in determining the choice of contracts. He argues that where managerial decisions matter, increasing risk makes sharecropping less attractive since it makes agreement on decisions between landowner and tenant more difficult.[1] The distinction between risks related to choice and uncontrollable natural risks as well as the role of the degree of risk aversion have been discussed by Huang (1973), who examines Malayan data. Stiglitz (1974) has analyzed the theory of risk sharing under different contracts in a general equilibrium model.

This discussion raises an important issue of allocation under uncertainty. People differ in the accuracy of their (probabilistic) forecasts of the future and in their abilities to make good decisions. This aspect of resource allocation (who makes decisions) is easy to lose in analyses focusing on the sharing of risks, especially when they take subjective probabilities as given tastes, which are to be fully respected in welfare evaluations. For example, in Debreu (Reading 11) firms have no risky decisions and Pareto optimality is defined in terms of expected utilities with given preferences (i.e., subjective probabilities).

References

R. Higgs, Race, tenure, and resource allocation in southern agriculture, 1910, *J. Econ. Hist.* **33** (1973), 149–169.

Y. Huang, Risk, entrepreneurship, and tenancy, *J. Political Econ.* **81** (1973), 1241–1244.

C. H. Rao, Uncertainty, entrepreneurship and sharecropping in India, *J. Political Econ.* **79** (1971), 578–595.

J. E. Stiglitz, Incentives and risk sharing in sharecropping, *Rev. Econ. Studies* **41** (1974), 219–255.

[1]In a personal communication, Cheung expressed the view that the high level of government regulations of land use in India makes the data used by Rao inappropriate for the testing of contractual choices subject to free-market constraints.

23
Two omitted topics: Product liability and workers' compensation

The question of product quality has been addressed by economists who have considered the effects of different legal rules for law suits arising from defective products or from accidents occurring in the use of marketed commodities. (A partial list of references on product liability and on similar issues in workers' compensation appears at the end of this note.) As a reminder of the complexity of the problem of allocation, we shall consider the conditions necessary to achieve full optimality in such a complicated market setting. This will help to correct the tendency to see each of the simple models of market failure as easily correctible, losing sight of the fact that often many complications will be present simultaneously. The list ignores the institutional costs of achieving the efficient allocation as well as accidents that may affect third parties, that is, passers-by who are injured as a result of an accident arising from the interaction of a product and the purchaser–user.

Necessary conditions in each market for first best optimal allocation:

1. Each producer must design a suitably safe product and manufacture it with the appropriate attention to defects arising during production.
2. Each producer must supply the correct number of units.
3. Each consumer must use the product appropriately – with suitable care and with the correct frequency in the case of a durable good.
4. Each consumer must demand the correct number of units.
5. Demanders must be allocated among suppliers appropriately, reflecting the differences among products and among users.
6. Accident costs must not be compounded by delayed or inappropriate treatment of damage or by risk aversion not adequately insured.
7. Research and development of improved products and methods of use must be undertaken at the appropriate level.

The conventional allocation problem with homogenous commodities and certainty only faces items 2, 4, and 7. It is impossible to design a social system that can maintain all the first-order conditions in the presence of commodities involving the full range of complications. This follows from the difficulties in providing insurance and information about defects with low probability and variations across products and users. The need to employ insurance to deal with the costs mentioned in item 6 will tend to decrease the effectiveness of incentives designed for the other allocational problems. Designing reasonable laws and institutions to deal with product liability is a second-best problem. While simple models are valuable for analyzing these problems it is difficult to know just how to use them to formulate policy.

References

J. Brown, Product liability: The case of an asset with a random life, *Am. Econ. Rev.* **64** (1974), 149–161.

G. Calabresi, "Costs of Accidents." Yale University Press, New Haven, Connecticut, 1970.

P. Diamond, Insurance theoretic aspects of workers' compensation, *in* "Natural Resources, Uncertainty, and General Equilibrium Systems: Essays in Memory of Rafael Lusky" (A. Blinder and P. Friedman, eds.). Academic Press, New York, 1978.

V. Goldberg, The economics of product safety and imperfect information, *Bell J. Econ.* **5** (1974), 683–688.

K. Hamada, Liability rules and income distribution in product liability, *Am. Econ. Rev.* **66** (1976), 228–234.

R. McKean, Products Liability: Implications of some changing property rights, *Quart. J. Econ.* **84** (1970).

R. McKean *et al., Symp. Product Liability, Univ. Chicago Law Rev.* **38** (1970), 1–141.

W. Oi, The economics of product safety, *Bell J. Econ.* **4** (1973), 3–28.

W. Oi, The economics of product safety: A rejoinder, *Bell J. Econ.* **5** (1974), 689–695.

W. Oi, Workmen's compensation and industrial safety, *in* "Supplemental Studies for the National Commission on State Workmen's Compensation Laws." USGPO, Washington, D.C., 1973.

S. Shavell, "Economic analysis of accident law," Cambridge, Mass.: Harvard University Press, 1987.

M. Spence, Consumer misperceptions, product failure, and producer liability, *Rev. Econ. Studies* **44** (1977), 561–572.

24
K. J. Arrow and R. Lind, Uncertainty and the evaluation of public investments, *Amercian Economic Review* **60** (1970), 364–378

In addition to the possibility of government intervention to improve the working of private markets, the government regularly takes part in transactions and production decisions that involve uncertainty. Thus it is natural to ask how the government should treat the uncertainty associated with its decisions. This article explores one model for answering this question. In a comment following the article we discuss the applicability of the argument in the text. For an interesting analysis of central planning under uncertainty, see Weitzman (1974).

Reference

M. Weitzman, Prices vs. quantities, *Rev. Econ. Stud.* **41** (1974), 477–491.

Uncertainty and the Evaluation of Public Investment Decisions

By KENNETH J. ARROW AND ROBERT C. LIND*

The implications of uncertainty for public investment decisions remain controversial. The essence of the controversy is as follows. It is widely accepted that individuals are not indifferent to uncertainty and will not, in general, value assets with uncertain returns at their expected values. Depending upon an individual's initial asset holdings and utility function, he will value an asset at more or less than its expected value. Therefore, in private capital markets, investors do not choose investments to maximize the present value of expected returns, but to maximize the present value of returns properly adjusted for risk. The issue is whether it is appropriate to discount public investments in the same way as private investments.

There are several positions on this issue. The first is that risk should be discounted in the same way for public investments as it is for private investments. It is argued that to treat risk differently in the public sector will result in overinvestment in this sector at the expense of private investments yielding higher returns. The leading proponent of this point of view is Jack Hirshleifer.[1] He argues that in perfect capital markets, investments are discounted with respect to both time and risk and that the discount rates obtaining in these markets should be used to evaluate public investment opportunities.

A second position is that the government can better cope with uncertainty than private investors and, therefore, government investments should not be evaluated by the same criterion used in private markets. More specifically, it is argued that the government should ignore uncertainty and behave as if indifferent to risk. The government should then evaluate investment opportunities according to their present value computed by discounting the expected value of net returns, using a rate of discount equal to the private rate appropriate for investments with certain returns. In support of this position it is argued that the government invests in a greater number of diverse projects and is able to pool risks to a much greater extent than private investors.[2] Another supporting line of argument is that many of the uncertainties which arise in private capital markets are related to what may be termed moral hazards. Individuals involved in a given transaction may hedge against the possibility of fraudulent behavior on the part of their associates. Many such risks are not present in the case of public investments and, therefore, it can be argued that it is not appropriate for the government to take these risks into account when choosing among public investments.

There is, in addition, a third position on the government's response to uncertainty. This position rejects the notion that indi-

* The authors are, respectively, professor of economics at Harvard University; and assistant professor of engineering-economic systems and, by courtesy, of economics at Stanford University. R. C. Lind's work has been supported by National Science Foundation grant NSF-GK-1683.

[1] J. Hirshleifer (1965, 1966) and Hirshleifer, J. C. De Haven, and J. W. Milliman (pp. 139–50).

[2] For this point of view, see P. A. Samuelson and W. Vickrey.

vidual preferences as revealed by market behavior are of normative significance for government investment decisions, and asserts that time and risk preferences relevant for government action should be established as a matter of national policy. In this case the correct rules for action would be those established by the appropriate authorities in accordance with their concept of national policy. The rate of discount and attitude toward risk would be specified by the appropriate authorities and the procedures for evaluation would incorporate these time and risk preferences. Two alternative lines of argument lead to this position. First, if one accepts the proposition that the state is more than a collection of individuals and has an existence and interests apart from those of its individual members, then it follows that government policy need not reflect individual preferences. A second position is that markets are so imperfect that the behavior observed in these markets yields no relevant information about the time and risk preferences of individuals. It follows that some policy as to time and risk preference must be established in accordance with other evidence of social objectives. One such procedure would be to set national objectives concerning the desired rate of growth and to infer from this the appropriate rate of discount.[3] If this rate were applied to the expected returns from all alternative investments, the government would in effect be behaving as if indifferent to risk.

The approach taken in this paper closely parallels the approach taken by Hirshleifer, although the results differ from his. By using the state-preference approach to market behavior under uncertainty, Hirshleifer demonstrates that investments will not, in general, be valued at the sum of the expected returns discounted at a rate appropriate for investments with certain returns.[4] He then demonstrates that using this discount rate for public investments may lead to non-optimal results, for two reasons. First, pooling itself may not be desirable.[5] If the government has the opportunity to undertake only investments which pay off in states where the payoff is highly valued, to combine such investments with ones that pay off in other states may reduce the value of the total investment package. Hirshleifer argues that where investments can be undertaken separately they should be evaluated separately, and that returns should be discounted at rates determined in the market. Second, even if pooling were possible and desirable, Hirshleifer argues correctly that the use of a rate of discount for the public sector which is lower than rates in the private sector can lead to the displacement of private investments by public investments yielding lower expected returns.[6]

For the case where government pooling is effective and desirable, he argues that rather than evaluate public investments differently from private ones, the government should subsidize the more productive private investments. From this it follows that to treat risk differently for public as opposed to private investments would only be justified if it were impossible to transfer the advantages of government pooling to private investors. Therefore, at most, the argument for treating public risks differently than private ones in evaluating investments is an argument for the "second best."[7]

The first section of this paper addresses the problem of uncertainty, using the state-preference approach to market behavior. It demonstrates that if the returns

[3] For this point of view, see O. Eckstein and S. Marglin.

[4] Hirshleifer (1965 pp. 523–34); (1966, pp. 268–75).
[5] Hirshleifer (1966, pp. 270–75).
[6] Hirshleifer (1966, pp. 270–75).
[7] Hirshleifer (1966, p. 270).

from any particular investment are independent of other components of national income, then the present value of this investment equals the sum of expected returns discounted by a rate appropriate for investments yielding certain returns. This result holds for both private and public investments. Therefore, by adding one plausible assumption to Hirshleifer's formulation, the conclusion can be drawn that the government should behave as an expected-value decision maker and use a discount rate appropriate for investments with certain returns. This conclusion needs to be appropriately modified when one considers the case where there is a corporate income tax.

While this result is of theoretical interest, as a policy recommendation it suffers from a defect common to the conclusions drawn by Hirshleifer. The model of the economy upon which these recommendations are based presupposes the existence of perfect markets for claims contingent on states of the world. Put differently, it is assumed that there are perfect insurance markets through which individuals may individually pool risks. Given such markets, the distribution of risks among individuals will be Pareto optimal. The difficulty is that many of these markets for insurance do not exist, so even if the markets which do exist are perfect, the resulting equilibrium will be sub-optimal. In addition, given the strong evidence that the existing capital markets are not perfect, it is unlikely that the pattern of investment will be Pareto optimal. At the margin, different individuals will have different rates of time and risk preference, depending on their opportunities to borrow or to invest, including their opportunities to insure.

There are two reasons why markets for many types of insurance do not exist. The first is the existence of certain moral hazards.[8] In particular, the fact that someone has insurance may alter his behavior so that the observed outcome is adverse to the insurer. The second is that such markets would require complicated and specialized contracts which are costly. It may be that the cost of insuring in some cases is so high that individuals choose to bear risks rather than pay the transaction costs associated with insurance.

Given the absence of some markets for insurance and the resulting sub-optimal allocation of risks, the question remains: How should the government treat uncertainty in evaluating public investment decisions? The approach taken in this paper is that individual preferences are relevant for public investment decisions, and government decisions should reflect individual valuations of costs and benefits. It is demonstrated in the second section of this paper that when the risks associated with a public investment are publicly borne, the total cost of risk-bearing is insignificant and, therefore, the government should ignore uncertainty in evaluating public investments. Similarly, the choice of the rate of discount should in this case be independent of considerations of risk. This result is obtained not because the government is able to pool investments but because the government distributes the risk associated with any investment among a large number of people. It is the risk-spreading aspect of government investment that is essential to this result.

There remains the problem that private investments may be displaced by public ones yielding a lower return if this rule is followed, although given the absence of insurance markets this will represent a Hicks-Kaldor improvement over the initial situation. Again the question must be

[8] For a discussion of this problem see M. V. Pauly and Arrow (1968).

asked whether the superior position of the government with respect to risk can be made to serve private investors. This leads to a discussion of the government's role as a supplier of insurance, and of Hirshleifer's recommendation that private investment be subsidized in some cases.

Finally, the results obtained above apply to risks actually borne by the government. Many of the risks associated with public investments are borne by private individuals, and in such cases it is appropriate to discount for risk as would these individuals. This problem is discussed in the final section of the paper. In addition, a method of evaluating public investment decisions is developed that calls for different rates of discount applied to different classes of benefits and costs.

I. *Markets for Contingent Claims and Time-Risk Preference*[9]

For simplicity, consider an economy where there is one commodity and there are I individuals, S possible states of the world, and time is divided into Q periods of equal length. Further suppose that each individual acts on the basis of his subjective probability as to the states of nature; let π_{is} denote the subjective probability assigned to state s by individual i. Now suppose that each individual in the absence of trading owns claims for varying amounts of the one commodity at different points in time, given different states of the world. Let $\bar{x}_{isq}$ denote the initial claim to the commodity in period q+1 if state s occurs which is owned by individual i. Suppose further that all trading in these claims takes place at the beginning of the first period, and claims are bought and sold on dated commodity units contingent on a state of the world. All claims can be constructed from basic claims which pay one commodity unit in period q+1, given state s, and nothing in other states or at other times; there will be a corresponding price for this claim, $p_{sq}(s=1, \ldots, S; \mathrm{q}=0, \ldots, \mathrm{Q}-1)$. After the trading, the individual will own claims x_{isq}, which he will exercise when the time comes to provide for his consumption. Let $V_i(x_{i1,0}, \ldots, x_{i1,\mathrm{Q}-1}, x_{i2,0}, \ldots, x_{iS,\mathrm{Q}-1})$ be the utility of individual i if he receives claims x_{isq} $(s=1, \ldots, S; \mathrm{q}=0, \ldots, \mathrm{Q}-1)$. The standard assumptions are made that V_i is strictly quasi-concave $(i=1, \ldots, I)$.

Therefore each individual will attempt to maximize,

$$V_i(x_{i1,0}, \ldots, x_{i1,\mathrm{Q}-1}, x_{i2,0}, \ldots, x_{iS,\mathrm{Q}-1}) \tag{1}$$

subject to the constraint

$$\sum_{\mathrm{q}=0}^{\mathrm{Q}-1} \sum_{s=1}^{S} p_{s\mathrm{q}} x_{is\mathrm{q}} = \sum_{\mathrm{q}=0}^{\mathrm{Q}-1} \sum_{s=1}^{S} p_{s\mathrm{q}} \bar{x}_{is\mathrm{q}}$$

Using the von Neumann-Morgenstern theorem and an extension by Hirshleifer,[10] functions U_{is} $(s=1, \ldots, S)$ can be found such that

$$V_i(x_{i1,0}, \ldots, x_{iS,\mathrm{Q}-1}) = \sum_{s=1}^{S} \pi_{is} U_{is}(x_{is0}, x_{is1}, \ldots, x_{iS,\mathrm{Q}-1}) \tag{2}$$

In equation (2) an individual's utility, given any state of the world, is a function of his consumption at each point in time. The subscript s attached to the function U_{is} is in recognition of the fact that the value of a given stream of consumption may depend on the state of the world.

The conditions for equilibrium require that

$$\pi_{is} \frac{\partial U_{is}}{\partial x_{is\mathrm{q}}} = \lambda_i p_{s\mathrm{q}} \qquad (i = 1, \ldots, I; \; s = 1, \ldots, S; \mathrm{q} = 0, \ldots, \mathrm{Q} - 1) \tag{3}$$

[9] For a basic statement of the state-preference approach, see Arrow (1964) and G. Debreu.

[10] J. von Neumann and O. Morgenstern, and Hirshleifer (1965, pp. 534–36).

where λ_i is a Lagrangian multiplier.

From (3) it follows that

$$(4)\quad \frac{p_{sq}}{p_{rm}} = \frac{\pi_{is}\dfrac{\partial U_{is}}{\partial x_{isq}}}{\pi_{rm}\dfrac{\partial U_{ir}}{\partial \lambda_{irm}}} \qquad (i = 1, \ldots, I;$$

$$r, s = 1, \ldots, S; m, q = 0, \ldots, Q - 1)$$

Insight can be gained by analyzing the meaning of the prices in such an economy. Since trading takes place at time zero, p_{sq} represents the present value of a claim to one commodity unit at time q, given state s. Clearly,

$$\sum_{s=1}^{S} p_{s0} = 1$$

since someone holding one commodity unit at time zero has a claim on one commodity unit, given any state of the world. It follows that p_{sq} is the present value of one commodity at time q, given state s, in terms of a certain claim on one commodity unit at time zero. Therefore, the implicit rate of discount to time zero on returns at time q, given state s, is defined by $p_{sq} = 1/1+r_{sq}$.

Now suppose one considers a certain claim to one commodity unit at time q; clearly, its value is

$$p_q = \sum_{s=1}^{S} p_{sq}$$

and the rate of discount appropriate for a certain return at time q is defined by

$$(5)\quad \frac{1}{1 + r_q} = \sum_{s=1}^{S} \frac{1}{1 + r_{sq}} = \sum_{s=1}^{S} p_{sq}$$

Given these observations, we can now analyze the appropriate procedure for evaluating government investments where there are perfect markets for claims contingent on states of the world.[11] Consider an investment where the overall effect on market prices can be assumed to be negligible, and suppose the net return from this investment for a given time and state is h_{sq} $(s=1, \ldots, S; q=0, \ldots, Q-1)$. Then the investment should be undertaken if

$$(6)\quad \sum_{q=0}^{Q-1} \sum_{s=1}^{S} h_{sq} p_{sq} > 0,$$

and the sum on the left is an exact expression for the present value of the investment. Expressed differently, the investment should be adopted if

$$(7)\quad \sum_{q=0}^{Q-1} \sum_{s=1}^{S} \frac{h_{sq}}{1 + r_{sq}} > 0$$

The payoff in each time-state is discounted by the associated rate of discount. This is the essential result upon which Hirshleifer bases his policy conclusions.[12]

Now suppose that the net returns of the investment were (a) independent of the returns from previous investment, (b) independent of the individual utility functions, and (c) had an objective probability distribution, i.e., one agreed upon by everyone. More specifically, we assume that the set of all possible states of the world can be partitioned into a class of mutually exclusive and collectively exhaustive sets, E_t, indexed by the subscript t such that, for all s in any given E_t, all utility functions U_{is} are the same for any individual i $(i=1, \cdots, I)$, and such that all production conditions are the same. Put differently, for all s in E_t, U_{is} is the same for a given individual, but not necessarily for all individuals. At the same time there is another partition of the states of the world into sets, F_u, such that the return, h_{sq}, is the same for all s in F_u. Finally, we assume that the probability distribution of F_u is independent of E_t and is the same for all individuals.

Let E_{tu} be the set of all states of the world which lie in both E_t and F_u. For any given t and u, all states of the world in

[11] The following argument was sketched in Arrow (1966, pp. 28–30).

[12] Hirshleifer (1965, pp. 523–34).

E_{tu} are indistinguishable for all purposes, so we may regard it as containing a single state. Equations (3) and (5) and the intervening discussion still hold if we then replace s everywhere by tu. However, $U_{is} = U_{itu}$ actually depends only on the subscript, t, and can be written U_{it}. From the assumptions it is obvious and can be proved rigorously that the allocation x_{isq} also depends only on t, i.e., is the same for all states in E_t for any given t, so it may be written x_{itq}. Finally, let π_{it} be the probability of E_t according to individual i, and let π_u be the probability of F_u, assumed the same for all individuals. Then the assumption of statistical independence is written:

$$\pi_{itu} = \pi_{it}\pi_u \tag{8}$$

Then (3) can be written

$$\pi_{it}\pi_u \frac{\partial U_{it}}{\partial x_{itq}} = \lambda_i p_{tuq} \tag{9}$$

Since p_{tuq} and π_u are independent of i, so must be

$$\left(\pi_{it} \frac{\partial U_{it}}{\partial x_{itq}}\right) \Big/ \lambda_i;$$

on the other hand, this expression is also independent of u and so can be written μ_{tq}. Therefore,

$$p_{tuq} = \mu_{tq}\pi_u \tag{10}$$

Since the new investment has the same return for all states s in F_u, the returns can be written h_{uq}. Then the left-hand side of (6) can, with the aid of (10), be written

$$\begin{aligned} &\sum_{Q=0}^{Q-1} \sum_{s=1}^{S} h_{sq} p_{sq} \\ &= \sum_{q=0}^{Q-1} \sum_t \sum_u h_{uq} p_{tuq} \\ &= \sum_{q=0}^{Q-1} \left(\sum_t \mu_{tq}\right) \sum_u \pi_u h_{uq} \end{aligned} \tag{11}$$

But from (10)

$$\begin{aligned} p_q &= \sum_{s=1}^{S} p_{sq} = \sum_t \sum_u p_{tuq} \\ &= \left(\sum_t \mu_{tq}\right)\left(\sum_u \pi_u\right) = \sum_t \mu_{tq}, \end{aligned} \tag{12}$$

since of course the sum of the probabilities of the F_u's must be 1. From (11),

$$\sum_{q=0}^{Q-1} \sum_{s=1}^{S} h_{sq} p_{sq} = \sum_{Q=0}^{Q-1} \frac{1}{1+r_q} \sum_u \pi_u h_{uq} \tag{13}$$

Equation (13) gives the rather startling result that the present value of any investment which meets the independence and objectivity conditions, equals the expected value of returns in each time period, discounted by the factor appropriate for a certain return at that time. This is true even though individuals may have had different probabilities for the events that governed the returns on earlier investments. It is also interesting to note that each individual will behave in this manner so that there will be no discrepancy between public and private procedures for choosing among investments.

The independence assumption applied to utility functions was required because the functions U_{is} are conditional on the states of the world. This assumption appears reasonable, and in the case where U_{is} is the same for all values of s, it is automatically satisfied. Then the independence condition is simply that the net returns from an investment be independent of the returns from previous investments.

The difficulty that arises if one bases policy conclusions on these results is that some markets do not exist, and individuals do not value assets at the expected value of returns discounted by a factor appropriate for certain returns. It is tempting to argue that while individuals do not behave as expected-value decision makers because of the nonexistence of certain markets for insurance, there is no reason why the government's behavior should not be consistent with the results derived above where the allocation of resources was Pareto optimal. There are two difficulties with this line of argument. First, if we are to measure benefits and costs in terms of individuals' willingness to pay, then we must treat risk in accordance with these individual valuations. Since individuals do not have the opportunities for insuring assumed in the state-preference model, they will not value uncertainty as they would if these markets did exist. Second, the theory of the second best demonstrates that if resources are not allocated in a Pareto optimal manner, the appropriate public policies may not be those consistent with Pareto efficiency in perfect markets. Therefore, some other approach must be found for ascertaining the appropriate government policy toward risk. In particular, such an approach must be valid, given the nonexistence of certain markets for insurance and imperfections in existing markets.

II. *The Public Cost of Risk-Bearing*

The critical question is: What is the cost of uncertainty in terms of costs to individuals? If one adopts the position that costs and benefits should be computed on the basis of individual willingness to pay, consistency demands that the public costs of risk-bearing be computed in this way too. This is the approach taken here.

In the discussion that follows it is assumed that an individual's utility is dependent only upon his consumption and not upon the state of nature in which that consumption takes place. This assumption simplifies the presentation of the major theorem, but it is not essential. Again the expected utility theorem is assumed to hold. The presentation to follow analyzes the cost of risk-bearing by comparing the expected value of returns with the certainty equivalent of these returns. In this way the analysis of time and risk preference can be separated, so we need only consider one time period.

Suppose that the government were to undertake an investment with a certain outcome; then the benefits and costs are measured in terms of willingness to pay for this outcome. If, however, the outcome is uncertain, then the benefits and costs actually realized depend on which outcome in fact occurs. If an individual is risk-averse, he will value the investment with the uncertain outcome at less than the expected value of its net return (benefit minus cost) to him. Therefore, in general the expected value of net benefits overstates willingness to pay by an amount equal to the cost of risk-bearing. It is clear that the social cost of risk-bearing will depend both upon which individuals receive the benefits and pay the costs and upon how large is each individual's share of these benefits and costs.

As a first step, suppose that the government were to undertake an investment and capture all benefits and pay all costs, i.e., the beneficiaries pay to the government an amount equal to the benefits received and the government pays all costs. Individuals who incur costs and those who receive benefits are therefore left indifferent to their pre-investment state. This assumption simply transfers all benefits and costs to the government, and the outcome of the investment will affect government disbursements and receipts. Given that the general taxpayer finances government expenditures, a public investment can be considered an investment in which each individual taxpayer has a very small share.

For precision, suppose that the government undertook an investment and that returns accrue to the government as previously described. In addition, suppose that in a given year the government were to have a balanced budget (or a planned deficit or surplus) and that taxes would be reduced by the amount of the net benefits if the returns are positive, and raised if returns are negative. Therefore, when the government undertakes an investment, each taxpayer has a small share of that investment with the returns being paid through changes in the level of taxes. By undertaking an investment the government adds to each individual's disposable income a random variable which is some fraction of the random variable representing the total net returns. The expected return to all taxpayers as a group equals expected net benefits.

Each taxpayer holds a small share of an asset with a random payoff, and the value of this asset to the individual is less than its expected return, assuming risk aversion. Stated differently, there is a cost of risk-bearing that must be subtracted from the expected return in order to compute the value of the investment to the individual taxpayer. Since each taxpayer will bear some of the cost of the risk associated with the investment, these costs must be summed over all taxpayers in order to arrive at the total cost of risk-bearing associated with a particular investment. These costs must be subtracted from the value of expected net benefits in order to obtain the correct measure for net benefits. The task is to assess these costs.

Suppose, as in the previous section, that there is one commodity, and that each individual's utility in a given year is a function of his income defined in terms of this commodity and is given by $U(Y)$. Further, suppose that U is bounded, continuous, strictly increasing, and differentiable. The assumptions that U is continuous and strictly increasing imply that U has a right and left derivative at every point and this is sufficient to prove the desired results; differentiability is assumed only to simplify presentation. Further suppose that U satisfies the conditions of the expected utility theorem.

Consider, for the moment, the case where all individuals are identical in that they have the same preferences, and their disposable incomes are identically distributed random variables represented by A. Suppose that the government were to undertake an investment with returns represented by B, which are statistically independent of A. Now divide the effect of this investment into two parts: a certain part equal to expected returns and a random part, with mean zero, which incorporates risk. Let $\overline{B}=E[B]$, and define the random variable X by $X=B-\overline{B}$. Clearly, X is independent of A and $E[X]=0$. The effect of this investment is to add an amount $\overline{B}$ to government receipts along with a random component represented by X. The income of each taxpayer will be affected through taxes and it is the level of these taxes that determines the fraction of the investment he effectively holds.

Consider a specific taxpayer and denote his fraction of this investment by s, $0 \leqq s \leqq 1$. This individual's disposable income, given the public investment, is equal to $A+sB=A+s\overline{B}+sX$. The addition of sB to his disposable income is valued by the individual at its expected value less the cost of bearing the risk associated with the random component sX. If we suppose that each taxpayer has the same tax rate and that there are n taxpayers, then $s=1/n$, and the value of the investment taken over all individuals is simply $\overline{B}$ minus n times the cost of risk-bearing associated with the random variable $(1/n)X$. The central result of this section of the paper is that this total of the costs of risk-bearing goes to zero as n becomes large. Therefore, for large values of n the value of a public investment almost equals the expected value of that investment.

To demonstrate this, we introduce the function

$$W(s) = E[U(A + s\overline{B} + sX], \qquad 0 \leqq s \leqq 1 \tag{14}$$

In other words, given the random variables A and B representing his individual income before the investment and the income from the investment, respectively, his expected utility is a function of s which represents his share of B. From (14) and the assumption that U' exists, it follows that

$$W'(s) = E[U'(A + s\bar{B} + sX)(\bar{B} + X)] \tag{15}$$

Since X is independent of A, it follows that $U'(A)$ and X are independent; therefore,

$$E[U'(A)X] = E[U'(A)]E[X] = 0$$

so that

$$\begin{aligned} W'(0) &= E[U'(A)(\bar{B} + X)] \\ &= \bar{B}E[U'(A)] \end{aligned} \tag{16}$$

Equation (16) is equivalent to the statement

$$\lim_{s\to 0} \frac{E[U(A + s\bar{B} + sX) - U(A)]}{s} = \bar{B}E[U'(A)] \tag{17}$$

Now let $s = 1/n$, so that equation (17) becomes

$$\lim_{n\to\infty} nE\left[U\left(A + \frac{\bar{B} + X}{n}\right) - U(A)\right] = \bar{B}E[U'(A)] \tag{18}$$

If we assume that an individual whose preferences are represented by U is a risk-averter, then it is easily shown that there exists a unique number, $k(n) > 0$, for each value of n such that

$$E\left[U\left(A + \frac{\bar{B} + X}{n}\right)\right] = E\left[U\left(A + \frac{\bar{B}}{n} - k(n)\right)\right], \tag{19}$$

or, in other words, an individual would be indifferent between paying an amount equal to $k(n)$ and accepting the risk represented by $(1/n)X$. Therefore, $k(n)$ can be said to be the cost of risk-bearing associated with the asset B. It can easily be demonstrated that $\lim_{n\to\infty} k(n) = 0$, i.e., the cost of holding the risky asset goes to zero as the amount of this asset held by the individual goes to zero. It should be noted that the assumption of risk aversion is not essential to the argument but simply one of convenience. If U represented the utility function of a risk preferrer, then all the above statements would hold except $k(n) < 0$, i.e., an individual would be indifferent between being paid $-k(n)$ and accepting the risk $(1/n)X$ (net of the benefit $(1/n)\bar{B}$).

We wish to prove not merely that the risk-premium of the representative individual, $k(n)$, vanishes, but more strongly that the total of the risk-premiums for all individuals, $nk(n)$, approaches zero as n becomes large.

From (18) and (19) it follows that

$$\lim_{n\to\infty} nE\left[U\left(A + \frac{\bar{B}}{n} - k(n)\right) - U(A)\right] = \bar{B}E[U'(A)] \tag{20}$$

In addition, $\bar{B}/n - k(n) \to 0$, when $n \to \infty$. It follows from the definition of a derivative that

$$\lim_{n\to\infty} \frac{E\left[U\left(A + \frac{\bar{B}}{n} - k(n)\right) - U(A)\right]}{\frac{\bar{B}}{n} - k(n)} = E[U'(A)] > 0 \tag{21}$$

Dividing (20) by (21) yields

$$\lim_{n\to\infty} [\bar{B} - nk(n)] = \bar{B} \tag{22}$$

or

$$\lim_{n\to\infty} nk(n) = 0 \tag{23}$$

The argument in (21) implies that $\bar{B}/n - k(n) \neq 0$. Suppose instead the equality held for infinitely many n. Substitution into the left-hand side of (20) shows that $\bar{B}$ must equal zero, so that $k(n) = 0$ for all such n, and hence $nk(n) = 0$ on that sequence, confirming (23).

Equation (23) states that the total of

the costs of risk-bearing goes to zero as the population of taxpayers becomes large. At the same time the monetary value of the investment to each taxpayer, neglecting the cost of risk, is $(1/n)\bar{B}$, and the total, summed over all individuals, is $\bar{B}$, the expected value of net benefits. Therefore, if n is large, the expected value of net benefits closely approximates the correct measure of net benefits defined in terms of willingness to pay for an asset with an uncertain return.

In the preceding analysis, it was assumed that all taxpayers were identical in that they had the same utility function, their incomes were represented by identically distributed variables, and they were subject to the same tax rates. These assumptions greatly simplify the presentation; however, they are not essential to the argument. Different individuals may have different preferences, incomes, and tax rates; and the basic theorem still holds, provided that as n becomes larger the share of the public investment borne by any individual becomes arbitrarily smaller.

The question necessarily arises as to how large n must be to justify proceeding as if the cost of publicly-borne risk is negligible. This question can be given no precise answer; however, there are circumstances under which it appears likely that the cost of risk-bearing will be small. If the size of the share borne by each taxpayer is a negligible component of his income, the cost of risk-bearing associated with holding it will be small. It appears reasonable to assume, under these conditions, that the total cost of risk-bearing is also small. This situation will exist where the investment is small with respect to the total wealth of the taxpayers. In the case of a federally sponsored investment, n is not only large but the investment is generally a very small fraction of national income even though the investment itself may be large in some absolute sense.

The results derived here and in the previous section depend on returns from a given public investment being independent of other components of national income. The government undertakes a wide range of public investments and it appears reasonable to assume that their returns are independent. Clearly, there are some government investments which are interdependent; however, where investments are interrelated they should be evaluated as a package. Even after such groupings are established, there will be a large number of essentially independent projects. It is sometimes argued that the returns from public investments are highly correlated with other components of national income through the business cycle. However, if we assume that stabilization policies are successful, then this difficulty does not arise. It should be noted that in most benefit-cost studies it is assumed that full employment will be maintained so that market prices can be used to measure benefits and costs. Consistency requires that this assumption be retained when considering risk as well. Further, if there is some positive correlation between the returns of an investment and other components of national income, the question remains as to whether this correlation is so high as to invalidate the previous result.

The main result is more general than the specific application to public investments. It has been demonstrated that if an individual or group holds an asset which is statistically independent of other assets, and if there is one or more individuals who do not share ownership, then the existing situation is not Pareto-efficient. By selling some share of the asset to one of the individuals not originally possessing a share, the cost of risk-bearing can be reduced while the expected returns remain unchanged. The reduction in the cost of risk-bearing can then be redistributed to bring about a Pareto improvement. This result is similar to a result derived by Karl Borch. He proved that a condition for Pareto optimality in reinsurance markets requires that every individual hold a share of every independent risk.

When the government undertakes an investment it, in effect, spreads the risk among all taxpayers. Even if one were to accept that the initial distribution of risk was Pareto-efficient, the new distribution of risk will not be efficient as the government does not discriminate among the taxpayers according to their risk preferences. What has been shown is that in the limit the situation where the risk of the investment is spread over all taxpayers is such that there is only a small deviation from optimality with regard to the distribution of that particular risk. The overall distribution of risk may be sub-optimal because of market imperfections and the absence of certain insurance markets. The great advantage of the results of this section is that they are not dependent on the existence of perfect markets for contingent claims.

This leads to an example which runs counter to the policy conclusions generally offered by economists. Suppose that an individual in the private sector of the economy were to undertake a given investment and, calculated on the basis of expected returns, the investment had a rate of return of 10 per cent. Because of the absence of perfect insurance markets, the investor subtracted from the expected return in each period a risk premium and, on the basis of returns adjusted for risk, his rate of return is 5 percent. Now suppose that the government could invest the same amount of money in an investment which, on the basis of expected returns, would yield 6 percent. Since the risk would be spread over all taxpayers, the cost of risk-bearing would be negligible, and the true rate of return would be 6 percent. Further, suppose that if the public investment were adopted it would displace the private investment. The question is: Should the public investment be undertaken? On the basis of the previous analysis, the answer is yes. The private investor is indifferent between the investment with the expected return of 10 percent, and certain rate of return of 5 percent. When the public investment is undertaken, it is equivalent to an investment with a certain rate of return of 6 percent. Therefore, by undertaking the public investment, the government could more than pay the opportunity cost to the private investor of 5 percent associated with the diversion of funds from private investment.

The previous example illustrates Hirshleifer's point that the case for evaluating public investments differently from private ones is an argument for the second best. Clearly, if the advantages of the more efficient distribution of risk could be achieved in connection with the private investment alternative, this would be superior to the public investment. The question then arises as to how the government can provide insurance for private investors and thereby transfer the risks from the private sector to the public at large. The same difficulties arise as before, moral hazards and transaction costs. It may not be possible for the government to provide such insurance, and in such cases second-best solutions are in order. Note that if the government could undertake any investment, then this difficulty would not arise. Perhaps one of the strongest criticisms of a system of freely competitive markets is that the inherent difficulty in establishing certain markets for insurance brings about a sub-optimal allocation of resources. If we consider an investment, as does Hirshleifer, as an exchange of certain present income for uncertain future income, then the misallocation will take the form of under-investment.

Now consider Hirshleifer's recommendation that, in cases such as the one above, a direct subsidy be used to induce more private investment rather than increase public investment. Suppose that a particular private investment were such that the benefits would be a marginal increase in the future supply of an existing commodity, i.e., this investment would neither introduce a new commodity nor affect future prices. Therefore, benefits can be measured at each point in time by the market value of this output, and can be fully captured through the sale of the commodity. Let $\overline{V}$ be the present value of expected net returns, and let V be the present value of net returns adjusted for risk where the certainty rate is used to discount both streams. Further, suppose there were a public investment, where the risks were publicly borne, for which the present value of expected net benefits was P. Since the risk is publicly borne, from the previous discussion it follows that P is the present value of net benefits adjusted for risk. Now suppose that $\overline{V}>P>V$. According to Hirshleifer, we should undertake the private investment rather than the public one, and pay a subsidy if necessary to induce private entrepreneurs to undertake this investment. Clearly, if there is a choice between one investment or the other, given the existing distribution of risk, the public investment is superior. The implication is that if a risky investment in the private sector is displaced by a public investment with a lower expected return but with a higher return when appropriate adjustments are made for risks, this represents a Hicks-Kaldor improvement. This is simply a restatement of the previous point that the government could more than pay the opportunity cost to the private entrepreneur.

Now consider the case for a direct subsidy to increase the level of private investment. One can only argue for direct subsidy of the private investment if $V<0<\overline{V}$. The minimum subsidy required is $|V|$. Suppose the taxpayers were to pay this subsidy, which is a transfer of income from the public at large to the private investor, in order to cover the loss from the investment. The net benefits, including the cost of risk-bearing, remain negative because while the subsidy has partially offset the cost of risk-bearing to the individual investor, it has not reduced this cost. Therefore, a direct public subsidy in this case results in a less efficient allocation of resources.

We can summarize as follows: It is implied by Hirshleifer that it is better to undertake an investment with a higher expected return than one with a lower expected return. (See 1965, p. 270.) This proposition is not in general valid, as the distribution of risk-bearing is critical. This statement is true, however, when the costs of risk-bearing associated with both investments are the same. What has been shown is that when risks are publicly borne, the costs of risk-bearing are negligible; therefore, a public investment with an expected return which is less than that of a given private investment may nevertheless be superior to the private alternative. Therefore, the fact that public investments with lower expected return may replace private investment is not necessarily cause for concern. Furthermore, a program of providing direct subsidies to encourage more private investment does not alter the costs of risk-bearing and, therefore, will encourage investments which are inefficient when the costs of risk are considered. The program which produces the desired result is one to insure private investments.

One might raise the question as to whether risk-spreading is not associated with large corporations so that the same result would apply, and it is easily seen that the same reasoning does apply. This can be made more precise by assuming there were n stockholders who were identical in the sense that their utility functions were identical, their incomes were represented by identically distributed random variables, and they had the same share in the company. When the corporation undertakes an investment with a return in a given year represented by B, each stockholder's income is represented by $A+(1/n)B$. This assumes, of course, that a change in earnings was reflected in dividends, and that there were no business taxes. Clearly, this is identical to the situation previously described, and if n is large, the total cost of risk-bearing to the stockholders will be negligible. If the income or wealth of the stockholders were large with respect to the size of the investment, this result would be likely to hold. Note that whether or not the investment is a large one, with respect to the assets of the firm, is not relevant. While an investment may constitute a major part of a firm's assets if each stockholder's share in the firm is a small component of his income, the cost of risk-bearing to him will be very small. It then follows that if managers were acting in the interest of the firm's shareholders, they would essentially ignore risks and choose investments with the highest expected returns.

There are two important reasons why large corporations may behave as risk averters. First, in order to control the firm, some shareholder may hold a large block of stock which is a significant component of his wealth. If this were true, then, from his point of view, the costs of risk-bearing would not be negligible, and the firm should behave as a risk averter. Note in this case that the previous result does not hold because the cost of risk-bearing to each stockholder is not small, even though the number of stockholders is very large. Investment behavior in this case is essentially the same as the case of a single investor.

The second case is when, even though from the stockholder's point of view, risk should be ignored, it may not be in the interest of the corporate managers to neglect risk. Their careers and income are intimately related to the firm's performance. From their point of view, variations in the outcome of some corporate action impose very real costs. In this case, given a degree of autonomy, the corporate managers, in considering prospective investments, may discount for risk when it is not in the interest of the stockholders to do so.

Suppose that this were the case and also suppose that the marginal rate of time preference for each individual in the economy was 5 percent. From the point of view of the stockholders, risk can be ignored and any investment with an expected return which is greater than 5 percent should be undertaken. However, suppose that corporate managers discount for risk so that only investments with expected rates of return that exceed 10 percent are undertaken. From the point of view of the stockholders, the rate of return on these investments, taking risk into account, is over 10 percent. Given a marginal rate of time preference of 5 percent, it follows that from the point of view of the individual stockholder there is too little investment. Now suppose further that the government were considering an investment with an expected rate of return of 6 percent. Since the cost of risk-bearing is negligible, this investment should be undertaken since the marginal rate of time preference is less than 6 percent. However, in this case, if the financing were such that a private investment with a 10 percent expected rate of return is displaced by the public investment, there is a loss because in both cases the risk is distributed so as to make the total cost of risk-bearing negligible. The public investment should be undertaken, but only at the expense of consumption.

III. *The Actual Allocation of Risk*

In the idealized public investment considered in the last section, all benefits and costs accrued to the government and were distributed among the taxpayers. In this sense, all uncertainty was borne collectively. Suppose instead that some benefits and costs of sizeable magnitudes accrued directly to individuals so that these individuals incurred the attendant costs of risk-bearing. In this case it is appropriate to discount for the risk, as would these individuals. Such a situation would arise in the case of a government irrigation project where the benefits accrued to farmers as increased income. The changes in farm income would be uncertain and, therefore, should be valued at more or less than their expected value, depending on the states in which they occur. If these increases were independent of other components of farm income, and if we assume that the farmer's utility were only a function of his income and not the state in which he receives that income, then he would value the investment project at less than the expected increase in his income, provided he is risk averse. If, however, the irrigation project paid out in periods of drought so that total farm income was not only increased but also stabilized, then the farmers would value the project at more than the expected increase in their incomes.

In general, some benefits and costs will accrue to the government and the uncertainties involved will be publicly borne; other benefits and costs will accrue to individuals and the attendant uncertainties will be borne privately. In the first case the cost of risk-bearing will be negligible; in the second case these costs may be significant. Therefore, in calculating the present value of returns from a public investment a distinction must be made between private and public benefits and costs. The present value of public benefits and costs should be evaluated by estimating the expected net benefits in each period and discounting them, using a discount factor appropriate for investments with certain returns. On the other hand, private benefits and costs must be discounted with respect to both time and risk in accordance with the preferences of the individuals to whom they accrue.

From the foregoing discussion it follows that different streams of benefits and costs should be treated in different ways with respect to uncertainty. One way to do this is to discount these streams of returns at different rates of discount ranging from the certainty rate for benefits and costs accruing to the government and using higher rates that reflect discounting for risk for returns accruing directly to individuals. Such a procedure raises some difficulties of identification, but this problem does not appear to be insurmountable. In general, costs are paid by the government, which receives some revenue, and the net stream should be discounted at a rate appropriate for certain returns. Benefits accruing directly to individuals should be discounted according to individual time and risk preferences. As a practical matter, Hirshleifer's suggestion of finding the marginal rate of return on assets with similar payoffs in the private sector, and using this as the rate of discount, appears reasonable for discounting those benefits and costs which accrue privately.

One problem arises with this latter procedure which has received little attention. In considering public investments, benefits and costs are aggregated and the discussion of uncertainty is carried out in terms of these aggregates. This obscures many of the uncertainties because benefits and costs do not in general accrue to the same individuals, and the attendant uncertainties should not be netted out when considering the totals. To make this clear, consider an investment where the benefits and costs varied greatly, depending on the state of nature, but where the difference between total benefits and total costs was constant for every state. Further, suppose that the benefits and costs accrued to different groups. While the investment is certain from a social point of view, there is considerable risk from a private point of view.

In the case of perfect markets for contingent claims, each individual will discount the stream of costs and benefits accruing to him at the appropriate rate for each time and state. However, suppose that such markets do not exist. Then risk-averse individuals will value the net benefits accruing to them at less than their expected value. Therefore, if net benefits accruing to this individual are positive, this requires discounting expected returns at a higher rate than that appropriate for certain returns. On the other hand, if net benefits to an individual are negative, this requires discounting expected returns at a rate lower than the certainty rate. Raising the rate of discount only reduces the present value of net benefits when they are positive. Therefore, the distinction must be made not only between benefits and costs which accrue to the public and those which accrue directly to individuals, but also between individuals whose net benefits are negative and those whose benefits are positive. If all benefits and costs accrued privately, and different individuals received the benefits and paid the costs, the appropriate procedure would be to discount the stream of expected benefits at a rate higher than the certainty rate, and costs at a rate lower than the certainty rate. This would hold even if the social totals were certain.

Fortunately, as a practical matter this may not be of great importance as most costs are borne publicly and, therefore, should be discounted using the certainty rate. Benefits often accrue to individuals, and where there are attendant uncertainties it is appropriate to discount the expected value of these benefits at higher rates, depending on the nature of the uncertainty and time-risk preferences of the individuals who receive these benefits. It is somewhat ironic that the practical implication of this analysis is that for the typical case where costs are borne publicly and benefits accrue privately, this procedure will qualify fewer projects than the procedure of using a higher rate to discount both benefits and costs.

REFERENCES

K. J. Arrow, "The Role of Securities in the Optimal Allocation of Risk-Bearing," *Rev. Econ. Stud.*, Apr. 1964, *31*, 91–96.

———, "Discounting and Public Investment Criteria," in A. V. Kneese and S. C. Smith, eds., *Water Research*. Baltimore 1966.

———, "The Economics of Moral Hazard: Further Comment," *Amer. Econ. Rev.*, June 1968, *58*, 537–38.

K. Borch, "The Safety Loading of Reinsurance," *Skandinavisk Aktuarietid-skrift*, 1960, 163–84.

G. Debreu, *Theory of Value*. New York 1959.

O. Eckstein, "A Survey of the Theory of Public Expenditure," and "Reply," *Public Finances: Needs, Sources, and Utilization*, Nat. Bur. Econ. Res., Princeton 1961, 493–504.

J. Hirshleifer, "Investment Decision under Uncertainty: Choice-Theoretic Approaches," *Quart. J. Econ.*, Nov. 1965, *79*, 509–36.

———, "Investment Decision under Uncertainty: Applications of the State-Preference Approach," *Quart. J. Econ.*, May 1966, *80*, 252–77.

———, **J. C. De Haven, and J. W. Milliman**, *Water Supply: Economics, Technology, and Policy*, Chicago 1960.

S. Marglin, "The Social Rate of Discount and the Optimal Rate of Investment," *Quart. J. Econ.*, Feb. 1963, *77*, 95–111.

M. V. Pauly, "The Economics of Moral Hazard: Comment," *Amer. Econ. Rev.*, June 1968, *58*, 531–37.

P. A. Samuelson and W. Vickrey, "Discussion," *Amer. Econ. Rev. Proc.*, May 1964, *59*, 88–96.

J. von Neumann and O. Morgenstern, *Theory of Games and Economic Behavior*, 2d ed., New York 1964.

Comment

Arrow and Lind have considered the investment rule that the government should ignore uncertainty and behave as if indifferent to risk.[1] They discuss the limits on the range of projects that fit the model they employ. Only briefly do they mention the complications that arise, even with safe projects, with uncertainty and private market imperfections. Here we elaborate on this issue.[2]

In considering public investments, it is standard practice to select a numeraire (usually current income) and evaluate the changes induced by a public project in terms of the numeraire. Where different individuals have different marginal rates of substitution between different goods (present income relative to future, or one risky investment relative to a different risky investment), it is appropriate to convert values for different individuals into numeraire units and then aggregate, rather than to calculate aggregate income in different periods and then convert into numeraire units. However, it is now true that a change in numeraire can alter the sign of the value of a project in terms of numeraire.[3] Sometimes there are considerations (like the presence of other policy instruments) that lead to one choice of numeraire being correct for social evaluation. Otherwise, it is not clear that there will exist a good that can be used as a numeraire in this way. In addition, it may not be easy to infer individual marginal rates of substitution between present and future income from market behavior. The complication is that many assets, like bank deposits, are highly liquid, conferring a liquidity benefit as well as command over next period consumption. Other assets, like

[1]The focus of this chapter is the best use of the investment opportunities (including alternative methods of meeting public good needs) that are in the public sector. This is different from asking the question of which investment opportunities should be in the public and which in the private sectors. An attempt to answer this question would naturally analyze the relative abilities of public and private sectors to spread risks as well as the differences between public and private production under certainty. Such an analysis would have to consider issues like the patterns of risk bearing across individuals of different risk aversion for corporate and public risks; the combination in market availability of the different projects undertaken by a single firm together with the variation in future evaluation of the worth of the firm when securities are sold; and the difference in liquidity between a corporate security and future decreases in tax liability.

[2]For a discussion of investment with alternative models of private allocation see Sandmo (1972) and Mayshar (1977).

[3]This situation has been analyzed by Bradford (1970).

mortgages, involve constraints on the amounts of transactions. Thus, it is common to observe consumers simultaneously transacting in assets with different (essentially fixed) rates of return. Also there is the distinction between future real and nominal incomes, which creates a difficulty in inferring private attitudes to safe future real income.

A second issue, which also arises in evaluation of safe investment in an imperfect economy, is that the government project generally induces changes in individual behavior in the market. These changes have an impact on the social objective function when different transactors have different evaluations (relative to numeraire) of marginal units traded. The clearest example of this is trade in the presence of commodity taxation, where altered individual behavior usually implies a change in tax revenue reflecting differences between consumer and producer prices. The same situation arises with imperfect markets under uncertainty, where individuals are constrained in their abilities to transact (as, for example, with limitations on the ability to borrow).

Another complication in discussing discount rates is that the discount rate is used to compare present income with future income at different dates in the future. Thus, statements about a discount rate that are valid in an implicit or explicit two-period model (the present and one future date) may not be valid in a many-period model. For example, in a two-period model, risk aversion in the future can be equivalently handled either by an adjustment of expected income for risk and use of the discount rate for safe investments or by using the expected value of income and a higher discount rate. In a three-period model, these two general approaches have different implications for the relative valuations of risky second- and third-period incomes. Which is the better of these two approaches may depend on the type of uncertainty that is present.[4]

References

D. Bradford, Constraints on public action and rules for social decision, *Am. Econ. Rev.* **60** (1970), 642–654.

J. Mayshar, Should government subsidize risky projects? *Am. Econ. Rev.* **67** (1977), 20–28.

A. Sandmo, Discount rates for public investment under uncertainty, *Intern. Econ. Rev.* **13** (1972), 287–302.

[4]This point has been made by S. Marglin in seminar presentations.

III. Sequential Choice and Equilibrium with Limited Information

In Part II we have examined complications in equilibrium and optimality that occur with limited information about product characteristics. We now turn to analyses that have been done of the obvious fact that information about prices is not costlessly available to would-be demanders and suppliers. (Information about quality variations across suppliers may also be costly to gather.) Frequently this lack of information leads individuals to sample from the set of potential trading partners before making trades. Thus, we start this discussion with analysis of individual choice in this setting, particularly the theory of sequential choice. We then turn to some of the analyses of equilibrium in economies with limited price information.

25

M. Rothschild, Searching for the lowest price when the distribution of prices is unknown, *Journal of Political Economy* **82** (1974), 689-711

To set up the analysis of the title, this paper begins with a brief discussion of optimal search behavior when searching from a known distribution. This subject is pursued further in an exercise.

Searching for the Lowest Price When the Distribution of Prices Is Unknown

Michael Rothschild

Princeton University

Search theory, which purports to explain how individuals behave when they have imperfect or incomplete market information, has received much attention recently. Economists have derived a number of results characterizing the effects of various changes on optimal-search behavior. Almost without exception, these results depend on the untenable assumption that searchers know the probability distribution from which they are searching. This paper studies the effect of assuming instead that searchers learn about the probability distribution while they search from it. Not invariably, but in many instances, the qualitative properties of optimal-search strategies—and thus the behavior of those who follow them—are the same as in the simpler case when the distribution is assumed known.

I. Introduction

Stories about search occupy a central position in the "new microeconomics of inflation and employment." This accounts for much of the recent work by economists[1] analyzing variants of the following problem. A man is considering purchase of some good which is sold at different

A preliminary version of this paper was presented at the NBER conference on stochastic control at the University of Chicago, June 1973. I benefited from discussions with David Blackwell, Gregory Chow, Stanley Fischer, Emmett Keeler, Robert E. Lucas, Daniel McFadden, Roy Radner, and Yoram Weiss. This research was supported by the Industrial Relations Section of Princeton University, the Mathematical Social Science Board, and the National Science Foundation.

[1] See Stigler (1961, 1962), McCall (1965, 1970), Nelson (1970), Gastwirth (1971), Gronau (1971), Gould (1972), Salop (1973), Telser (1973), Whipple (1973), and Kohn and Shavell (1974).

Reprinted from *Journal of Political Economy*, Vol. 82, No. 4, July–August, 1974, stores at different prices. He can elicit price quotations from the various sellers by paying a fee.[2] What search strategy will the man follow?

Economists are interested in the rules which searchers follow, because these rules determine the demand functions that sellers in such markets face and thus, in part, the nature of the markets themselves. Although the only way to settle the question of what rules searchers follow is by observation, very little empirical work has been done on this problem.[3] Instead, researchers have proposed search rules that reasonable consumers might follow and have examined their properties. Stigler, who is largely responsible for introducing this topic into economic theory, suggested that the individual should visit n stores, obtain price quotations from each one, and then buy from the lowest-price store. The expected price paid will be

$$M_n = \int_0^\infty [1 - F(p)]^n \, dp,$$

where $F(p)$ is the distribution of prices. If such a procedure is followed, the only decision variable is n, the number of stores visited. Stigler pointed out that the familiar marginal calculations of microeconomic theory will suffice to determine n. Clearly, M_n is a decreasing function of n, while the expected gain from searching,

$$G_n = M_{n-1} - M_n = \int_0^\infty [1 - F(p)]^{n-1} F(p) \, dp,$$

also decreases with n. Therefore, n should be chosen so that

$$G_n \geq c > G_{n+1}.$$

This rule has several interesting properties:

1. If all its potential customers follow this rule, then a firm faces a well-behaved demand function; expected sales are a nonincreasing function of the price it charges.

2. Customers' search behavior is a function of the cost of search c and the distribution of prices $F(\ )$. Thus, it is possible to do comparative

[2] This fee, the cost of search, is generally interpreted as the cost of visiting a store and obtaining a price quotation. It could also include the cost of doing without the item in question while search continues, in which case the fact that search takes time would have to be formally incorporated in the model (see n. 10 below). Other rather trivial, from the formal point of view, generalizations are possible. Price and cost may be measured in utility rather than money. However, the utility function must be linear, so this is a small generalization. The same framework may be used to analyze search for jobs when wages (or the utility of jobs) are random and unknown. I shall largely ignore these matters of interpretation.

[3] A cynic might suspect that the lack of empirical work reflects a lack of interest in the real world on the part of those concerned with search rules. A glance at the authors in n. 1 above suggests that this is not the only reason. It seems to me—and my interest in such matters is admittedly casual—that the problem of determining characteristics of search rules empirically is a very difficult one.

statics so as to examine the consequences changes in $F(\ \ )$ and c. The most important results of these exercises are:

3. If costs of search increase, the amount of search decreases.

4. As prices become more dispersed, expected total costs decrease. This follows from the fact that, for all n, M_n decreases as the distribution becomes more variable.[4] Other things equal, customers prefer to draw from riskier distributions. This preference for risk or uncertainty on the part of those normally deemed risk averse can explain apparently odd or perverse phenomena. For an application to the theory of migration, see David (1973).

Interesting as these results are, they depend on people following a particular search rule—and not a particularly attractive one at that. Although fixed-sample-size rules have a certain intuitive appeal, they are not the best search procedures and are in some circumstances simply silly. A person who rigidly follows a fixed-sample-size rule will, even if he gets a price quotation less than the cost of search, keep on sampling until his quota of price quotations is fulfilled. It is thus comforting to know that the optimal-search rule has all the attractive properties of the fixed-sample-size rule. The optimal rule is sequential (after receiving each price quotation, the searcher decides whether to continue searching or to accept the quoted price) and is characterized by a reservation price; there is a price R such that the searcher will accept any price less than or equal to R while he will reject a price higher than R. Once again, familiar economic reasoning suffices to determine R. If the lowest price the cus-

[4] This is generally demonstrated by calculating $(dM_n/d\sigma^2) < 0$ for particular parametric families of distributions. However, the result is much more general. Let $F(p, t)$ be a family of distribution functions with support in $[0, B]$ indexed by t. Then, as Diamond and Stiglitz (1974) have shown, increases in t correspond to increases in risk in the sense of Rothschild and Stiglitz (1970) if

$$\int_0^B dF(p, t) = 1, \tag{i}$$

$$\int_0^Y F_t(p, t)dp \geq 0, \qquad 0 \leq Y \leq B, \tag{ii}$$

and

$$\int_0^B F_t(p, t)dp = 0. \tag{iii}$$

If $h(p)$ is any increasing function, then

$$\int_0^B h(p)F_t(p, t)dp \leq 0.$$

Note that

$$M_n(t) = \int_0^B [1 - F(p, t)]^n dp$$

and

$$\frac{dM_n(t)}{dt} = \int_0^B -n[1 - F(p, t)]^{n-1} \cdot F_t(p, t)dp \leq 0,$$

since $-n[1 - F(p, t)]$ is increasing in p.

tomer has received to date is S, then the expected gain from searching once more is

$$g(S) = \int_0^S (S - p)\, dF(p) = \int_0^S F(p)\, dp.$$

The optimal rule is to search whenever the cost of an additional search is less than the expected gain from that search so that R must satisfy

$$g(R) = c. \tag{1}$$

This reservation-price rule has the four properties listed above. That properties 1 and 2 hold is obvious. Increasing c increases the reservation price and thus lowers the intensity of search so that 3 holds. Kohn and Shavell (1974) have shown that increasing dispersion lowers the reservation price and thus total expected costs[5] so that 4 holds for this rule as well. They do this by showing that if $F(p, t)$ is, as in note 4 above, a family of price distributions which becomes more dispersed as t increases, then

$$g(S, t) = \int_0^S F(p, t)\, dp$$

is an increasing function t. Therefore, if

$$c = g(R, t) = g(R', t')$$

with $t' > t$, then $R' < R$. Thus, the reservation price decreases as price variability increases, or:

5. Increased price dispersion increases the intensity of search. This last result—which does not hold in general for fixed-sample-size rules[6]—is a kind of stability property which could be used in a complete model (one which explained price distributions endogenously) to show the existence of an equilibrium distribution of prices. It should turn out in most sensible models that increased search activity will decrease price dispersion.[7]

These results depend on the assumption that the searcher behaves as if he knows the distribution of prices. In any economic context, this is a very bad assumption. Little is known about the nature of price distributions, and it seems absurd to suppose that consumers know them with any

[5] Total expected costs to a searcher following a reservation-price rule are just equal to the reservation price. This follows from the fact that expected costs do not change as the searcher continues to sample. The logic of rule (1) might be stated as: Accept any price less than the expected costs of continuing to search; otherwise continue.

[6] If, in the notation of n. 4, $G_n(t) = M_{n-1}(t) - M_n(t)$, then it is not true that $G_n(t)$ increases with t whenever $F(p, t)$ satisfies (i), (ii), and (iii). I suspect that most increases in price dispersion which do not lead to piling up of probability mass at the extreme points of the distribution will increase $G_n(t)$, but I have not yet been able to formulate this precisely.

[7] For a discussion of the need for such a complete model, see Rothschild (1973).

degree of accuracy.[8] Since the major reason for believing that searchers follow optimal sequential rules is that they *are* optimal, it is important that their cost-minimizing properties not depend crucially on their being based on correct knowledge of the price distribution. This is unfortunately not true. Gastwirth (1971) explored the robustness of optimal-reservation-price rules. He found that modest specification errors could lead to dramatic increases in the expected number of searches and in the expected cost of buying. For example, someone who chose a reservation price on the assumption that prices were distributed uniformly on the unit interval ($F(x) = x$) when they really were distributed according to a right-triangular distribution on the same interval ($F(x) = x^2$) would on the average incur roughly twice the total costs and search five times as much as he would if he were correctly informed. If results 1–5 are to be salvaged, the problem of what the searcher should do if he does not know the price distribution must be attacked. This can be done in two ways: by exploring the properties of reasonable rules of thumb, or by characterizing optimal rules. Telser (1973) took the first approach. He calculated (using Monte Carlo techniques) the expected costs of various search rules—which had properties 1–4—against several differently shaped price distributions and compared these costs with those which would ensue if the searcher followed the naive rule of taking the first price offered him.

This paper takes the second tack. Optimal-search rules from unknown distributions are derived and characterized.[9] The results of this exercise are as follows. In Section II the problem of a man who knows prices belong to some finite set, but does not know how they are distributed, is formally described. Section III discusses an important example—the case where the prior distribution is a Dirichlet. In the next section, dynamic programming is used to derive the optimal strategy. It is possible to parameterize the problem so that the optimal-valuation functions are continuous—a fact which is exploited in Section V, where it is shown in Theorem I that if a person follows the optimal strategy, search terminates after a finite number of searches. This is used to prove that property 3 holds for search from unknown distributions, that is, that search decreases

[8] I suspect they vary a great deal. Characteristics of empirical wage distributions—which are related to (but distinct from) distributions of wage offers—are unstable over occupations and across cities (Buckley 1969).

[9] The statistical literature on optimal-search rules is extensive. Breiman (1964), DeGroot (1970, chap. 13), and Chow, Robbins, and Siegmund (1971) are surveys of increasing sophistication. Some of the results of this paper appear to be new, particularly Theorems I, II, and III. The work most closely related to that presented here is that of Yahav (1966) and DeGroot (1968). Yahav considers the general problem of searching with recall (the searcher is allowed to return to stores previously sampled) from an unknown distribution, shows that optimal rules exist under quite general circumstances, and discusses how they could be approximated. DeGroot completely solves the problem faced by a man searching (with or without recall) from a normal distribution of known variance and unknown precision.

as its cost increases. In Section VI it is shown (in Theorem II) that if prior beliefs are Dirichlet the optimal-search rule has a reservation-price property. Searchers will accept a price if and only if it is less than some particular price p_R. The reservation price is a function of the searcher's beliefs; it changes as his beliefs are revised in the light of experience. Section VII is devoted to proving, in Theorem III, an analogue of properties 4 and 5 for the Dirichlet case.

The most important results of this paper are that for the example of Section III, optimal-search rules from unknown distributions have the same qualitative properties as optimal rules from known distributions. Since it is easy to construct examples for which this is not true, it is natural to ask how general these results are. The final section considers this question. I believe them to be more general than it may appear, as they do not seem to depend on prices being confined to a finite set. However, they are still quite special, as the proofs depend on the process of revising beliefs to accommodate new information having a particular—and not terribly natural—local property. Whether similar results hold if this assumption is abandoned is an open and difficult question.

II. Preliminaries

Consider a man trying to buy a good at the lowest total expected cost. At the beginning of each period, this man pays c and receives a price quotation, which upon receiving he must decide whether to accept or to pay (at the beginning of the next period) c again and receive another price quotation. Total costs include the price actually paid as well as the costs of search.[10] I assume that the man does not have the privilege of recall, that is, that an offer once spurned cannot be taken up again. As is well known, this assumption is innocent—it has no effect on the optimal strategy—when the price distribution is assumed known. It is not innocent in the present case.

For simplicity, suppose that there are only a finite number of prices $p_1, p_2, \ldots, p_n$ and label them in ascending order so that

$$p_i < p_{i+1}. \tag{2}$$

The probability distribution of prices is a multinomial distribution. It is completely characterized by the vector Π whose ith element π_i is the probability that the ith price is chosen. Since Π is a probability distribution,

$$\Pi \in \Delta = \{(x_1, \ldots, x_n) \in R^n \mid x_i \geq 0, \sum x_i = 1\}.$$

[10] Given that the process takes place in time, perhaps it would be more logical to minimize discounted expected costs. This would introduce no serious complications. See Kohn and Shavell (1974) for a discussion of the effect of varying the discount rate on search rules.

Previous work has assumed that the searcher knows Π. Instead, I assume that he has a prior distribution $F(\ )$ over Δ. As he continues to search, he gathers more information about the distribution of prices which he assimilates by updating his prior according to Bayes's rule. All necessary information about his experience is contained in the statistics

$$N = (N_1, \ldots, N_n),$$

where N_i is the number of times price i has been observed.

It is convenient to parameterize his experience slightly differently. If $S(N) = \sum_i N_i$, then the vector whose ith element is

$$\mu_i = \frac{N_i}{S(N)} \tag{3}$$

represents the average number of times that each price has been observed, while

$$\rho = S(N)^{-1} \tag{4}$$

represents the total number of prices he has observed; therefore, (μ, ρ) also contains all the information the searcher has accumulated. This parameterization permits a distinction between the content of this information, represented by μ, and its precision, represented by ρ. With these definitions, new information is assimilated as follows. With the observation of price i, (μ, ρ) becomes

$$h_i(\mu, \rho) = \left(\frac{\mu_1}{\rho + 1}, \ldots, \frac{\mu_i + \rho}{\rho + 1}, \ldots, \frac{\mu_n}{\rho + 1}, \frac{\rho}{\rho + 1}\right). \tag{5}$$

There is a slight technical difficulty with this convention. The updating rule (5) is not consistent with the definitions (3) and (4) when $N = 0$. This problem may be finessed. Suppose $X = (x_1, \ldots, x_n)$ and $t = (t_1, \ldots, t_n)$; define

$$X^t = x_1^{t_1} x_2^{t_2} \cdots x_n^{t_n}. \tag{6}$$

A man with initial beliefs $F(\Pi)$ and no experience is no different from a man with initial beliefs $\tilde{F}(\Pi)$ and experience $N = (N_1, \ldots, N_n)$, where $\tilde{F}(\Pi)$ is a probability distribution over Δ satisfying $\tilde{F}(\Pi)\Pi^N = KF(\Pi)$ for some positive constant K or, using the definitions (3) and (4),

$$\tilde{F}(\Pi)\Pi^{(\mu/\rho)} = KF(\Pi).$$

In the sequel, we largely ignore the prior distribution $F(\ )$ and focus instead on the information

$$(\mu, \rho) \in \Gamma = \Delta \times [0, 1], \tag{7}$$

which is updated according to (5).

Corresponding to any (μ, ρ) is a vector $\lambda(\mu, \rho)$ whose ith component is given by

$$\lambda_i(\mu, \rho) = \frac{\int_\Delta \pi_i \Pi^{\mu/\rho} \, dF(\Pi)}{\int_\Delta \Pi^{\mu/\rho} \, dF(\Pi)} . \tag{8}$$

The term $\lambda(\mu, \rho)$ is a probability distribution which represents the searcher's expected beliefs in that he would take a small bet on the proposition that the next price observed would be p_i at the odds $\lambda_i(\mu, \rho)$ to $[1 - \lambda_i(\mu, \rho)]$. Since $\lambda(\mu, \rho)$ may be considered the index of a posterior distribution based on a sample size of ρ^{-1} which converges to a normal distribution with mean equal to the sample mean as sample size increases,

$$\lim_{\rho \to 0} \lambda_i(\mu, \rho) = \mu_i. \tag{9}$$

III. An Example

A simple and important example will illustrate the nature of the searcher's problem and clarify the meaning of N, (μ, ρ), and $\lambda(\mu, \rho)$. Suppose that the searcher's prior is a Dirichlet distribution. Since the Dirichlet is the conjugate prior of the multinomial distribution, the posterior distribution will also be a Dirichlet. The Dirichlet is an n parameter distribution, completely characterized by the numbers $N = (N_1, \ldots, N_n)$.[11] The properties of the Dirichlet are best illustrated by the following parable, which describes a problem exactly equivalent to that faced by the searcher.[12] Assume the N_i are integers. In an urn there are $S(N) = \sum N_i$ pieces of paper; p_1 is written on N_1 of these slips, p_2 on N_2 of them, and so on. A man draws from the urn at random. If he draws a slip with p_i on it he may either pay p_i or pay c, return the slip to the urn, place another slip with p_i on it in the urn, and draw from the urn again. That is, if he chooses to continue sampling, he faces the same problem as before except that the parameter describing the urn is

$$J_i(N) = N + e_i, \tag{10}$$

where e_i is the vector with 1 in the ith place and 0 elsewhere. The probability of getting price p_i from an urn with parameter N is just

$$\lambda_i(N) = \frac{N_i}{S(N)} .$$

[11] See, for example, DeGroot (1970, pp. 49–51) for a discussion of the properties of the Dirichlet distribution.

[12] I am indebted to David Blackwell for pointing out to me this way of looking at Dirichlet distributions.

The quantity $S(N)$ measures how fast these probabilities will change with successive drawings. If $S(N)$ is small, new drawings will alter the composition of the urn considerably; if $S(N)$ is large, they will hardly affect it. There is no reason why the N_i have to be integers. The above problem is equivalent to the searcher's problem for any positive N as long as the probability of drawing p_i from an urn with parameter N is $N_i/S(N)$ and N is updated by (10) when p_i is observed. Letting $\mu_i = N_i/S(N)$ and $\rho = S(N)^{-1}$, it is easy to check that the updating formula (10) is consistent with (5) and that $\lambda_i(\mu, \rho) = \lambda_i(N) = N_i/S(N) = \mu_i$.

It is important to realize that this story does not describe how price quotations are generated. In fact, there is a real price distribution which generates price quotations. However, the searcher does not know this distribution. His knowledge of the distribution is described by N, the composition of the urn. If price quotations are really generated by Π, then the strong law of large numbers states that the proportion of prices in the urn will, with probability 1, eventually be equal to Π.

The Dirichlet case is more general than it might appear. I have shown that if the prior is Dirichlet then it is possible to parameterize experience so that $\lambda_i(\mu, \rho) = \mu_i$. As I show below, this property characterizes the Dirichlet completely. Thus, it follows from (9) that as experience accumulates, all searchers come to behave as if their priors were Dirichlet.

Proposition 1: A searcher has a Dirichlet prior if and only if it is possible to parameterize his experience so that $\lambda_i(\mu, \rho) = \mu_i$ for all $(\mu, \rho) \in \Gamma$.

Proof: The "only if" part of the proposition has already been demonstrated. Suppose $F(\ )$ is a probability measure on Δ and that, when $\lambda_i(\mu, \rho)$ is defined by (8), $\lambda_i(\mu, \rho) = \mu_i$. There is a Dirichlet distribution $\tilde{F}(\ )$ so that, when $\tilde{\lambda}(\mu, \rho)$ is defined analogously, $\tilde{\lambda}(\mu, \rho) = \lambda(\mu, \rho)$. It follows that for all $N \geq 0$

$$\frac{\int_\Delta \Pi^{N+e_i}\, dF(\Pi)}{\int_\Delta \Pi^N\, dF(\Pi)} = \frac{\int_\Delta \Pi^{N+e_i}\, d\tilde{F}(\Pi)}{\int_\Delta \Pi^N\, d\tilde{F}(\Pi)}. \tag{11}$$

It is easy to see by induction that

$$\int_\Delta \Pi^N\, dF(\Pi) = \int_\Delta \Pi^N\, d\tilde{F}(\Pi)$$

for all nonnegative integer N. The Stone-Weierstrass theorem implies that

$$\int_\Delta u(\Pi)\, dF(\Pi) = \int_\Delta u(\Pi)\, d\tilde{F}(\Pi)$$

for all bounded continuous functions, $u(\ )$, defined on Δ. Thus, by theorem 1.3 of Billingsley (1968), $F(\ )$ and $\tilde{F}(\ )$ coincide.

IV. The Optimal Strategy

It is now possible to describe the optimal strategy of a man whose knowledge of prices is represented by the parameters (μ, ρ) which are updated according to (5). This is done in the standard way, by induction. Let

$$V_0(\mu, \rho) = \sum_i \lambda_i(\mu, \rho) p_i \tag{12a}$$

and

$$V_T(\mu, \rho) = \sum_i \lambda_i(\mu, \rho) \min \{p_i, V_{T-1}[h_i(\mu, \rho)] + c\}. \tag{12b}$$

The quantity $V_{T-1}(\mu, \rho)$ is the minimum expected cost incurred by a searcher with prior experience (μ, ρ) who is allowed to search at most T times but must accept the Tth price offer made to him. It is easy to see by induction that $V_T(\mu, \rho) \leq V_{T-1}(\mu, \rho)$ and $V_T(\mu, \rho) \geq p_1$ for all T, so that the $V_T(\mu, \rho)$ converge. Let

$$V(\mu, \rho) = \lim_{T \to \infty} V_T(\mu, \rho).$$

Then $V(\mu, \rho)$ satisfies

$$V(\mu, \rho) = \sum_i \lambda_i(\mu, \rho) \min \{p_i, V[h_i(\mu, \rho)] + c\}, \tag{13}$$

an equation which defines the optimal policy: If p_i is drawn when beliefs are (μ, ρ), accept if

$$p_i \leq V[h_i(\mu, \rho)] + c; \tag{14}$$

otherwise elicit another price offer.

Proposition 2: $V(\mu, \rho)$ is continuous.

This fact, although of little interest itself, is the basis of the proof of the next section and justifies the use of extreme examples in the sections that follow. It is important to realize that all the proofs given hold for any $(\mu, \rho) \in \Gamma$ including such strange boundary values as $(\mu = e_i, \rho = 0)$ or $(\mu = e_i, \rho = 1)$, where e_i is the vector whose ith component is 1 while all other components are equal to 0.

Proof: Since $\lambda_i(\mu, \rho)$ is continuous, so is $V_0(\mu, \rho)$. A simple induction establishes that $V_T(\mu, \rho)$ is continuous for all T. It remains to show that the V_T converge uniformly.

Let $V_T^+(\mu, \rho)$ be the expected total cost to a searcher who for T periods follows the policy of accepting the elicited price only if (14) is satisfied; if after T periods no price has been accepted, the searcher must pay p_n. The quantity $V_T^-(\mu, \rho)$ is defined similarly except that if he has not chosen after T periods he receives p_1. From their definitions it follows that

$$V_T^+(\mu, \rho) \geq V_T(\mu, \rho) \geq V(\mu, \rho) \geq V_T^-(\mu, \rho).$$

It will suffice to show that $|V_T^+(\mu, \rho) - V_T^-(\mu, \rho)|$ converges to 0 uniformly:

$$|V_T^+(\mu, \rho) - V_T^-(\mu, \rho)| \leq \beta_T(\mu, \rho) p_n,$$

where $\beta_T(\mu, \rho)$ is the probability—calculated according to the prior (μ, ρ)—that sampling will not terminate after T periods. However, from the definition of $V_T(\mu, \rho)$ it must be that

$$\beta_T(\mu, \rho) Tc \leq V_T(\mu, \rho) \leq p_n,$$

so $\beta_T(\mu, \rho) \leq p_n/Tc$ and $\beta_T(\mu, \rho)$ converges to 0 uniformly. This completes the proof.

V. Finiteness of Search

In this section it is shown that search will cease after a finite time. The idea of the proof (for which I am indebted to Robert Lucas) is a straightforward one. Regardless of his beliefs, a person will always accept p_1. If p_1 does not appear for a long time, then he will come to believe that p_2 is the lowest possible price and will of course accept it. Thus, there is a t_2 such that after t_2 trials either the person has stopped sampling or he will be willing to accept p_2. Similar arguments establish the existence of $t_3, t_4, \ldots, t_n$ with the same property. After t_n trials, the searcher has either stopped or will accept any price that occurs.

Theorem I: There is a number t such that a person following the optimal strategy will have stopped searching after t trials.

Proof: The theorem is *not* a probability statement. Let Ω be the set of all infinite sequences of the prices $p_1, \ldots, p_n$ and let ω denote an element of Ω. I shall show that there is a t such that for any ω sampling will have stopped by the time the tth price is quoted. Before I do so, some notation is necessary. For any ω, let ω_s denote its sth coordinate. Since (μ, ρ) are updated as functions of ω, we may define $(\mu, \rho)[\omega(q)]$ as the values of (μ, ρ) obtained after observation of $\omega_1, \ldots, \omega_q$.

Define the acceptance set A_i by $A_i = \{(\mu, \rho) \in \Gamma \mid p_i < V[h_i(\mu, \rho)] + c\}$. It follows from (9) that if $K_2 = \{(\mu, \rho) \in \Gamma \mid \mu_1 = \rho = 0\}$, then $K_2 \subset A_2$. Since A_2 is open and Γ compact, there is an $\varepsilon > 0$ such that if $(\mu_1, \ldots, \mu_n, \rho) \in \Gamma$ and $\mu_1 + \rho < \varepsilon$, then $(\mu_1, \ldots, \mu_n, \rho) \in A_2$. We may choose t_2 such that if

$$\omega_s \neq p_1 \qquad \text{for } s < t_2; \tag{15}$$

then $\mu_1[\omega(t_2)] + \rho[\omega(t_2)] < \varepsilon$; thus if ω satisfies (15), $(\mu, \rho)[\omega(t_2)] \in A_2$. Furthermore, if ω satisfies (15) and $\omega_{s_1} = p_2$ for $s_1 > t_2$, then sampling will have terminated by s_1, since either $\omega_s = \rho_1$ for $t_2 < s < s_1$ or $(\mu, \rho)[\omega(s_1)] \in A_2$.

Now let $K_3 = \{(\mu, \rho) \in \Gamma \mid \mu_1 = \mu_2 = \rho = 0\}$. Clearly $K_3 \subset A_3$ and, by arguments analogous to those used above, there exists a t_3 such that if ω satisfies (15) and

$$\omega_s \neq p_1, \qquad w_s \neq p_2 \qquad \text{for } t_2 \leq s < t_3,$$

then

$$(\mu, \rho)[\omega(t_3)] \in A_2 \cup A_3.$$

Continuing in this manner, we establish the existence of a t_n such that for all ω either sampling has stopped by t_n or

$$(\mu, \rho)[\omega(t_n)] \in \bigcup_{i=1}^{n} A_i.$$

Letting $t = t_n$ completes the proof.

Theorem I has three important implications. The first is substantive. The proof was based on the notion that those who fail to find low prices in their initial searches despair of ever finding them and become willing to accept high prices. In other words, persons who continue searching become less finicky as they search more. This seems an important property of search models. For example, in two very different papers, Kasper (1967) and Diamond (1971) presume such behavior and examine its consequences. They do not prove that searchers do behave this way; instead they state that economic theory (diminishing returns) implies they should. Gronau (1971), Gould (1972), and Salop (1973) provide proofs that searchers' standards fall the longer they remain in the market. Their proofs work for different reasons than the one given here. In the Gould and Gronau models, search takes time which is a scarce resource whose real value rises as more of it has been used; in effect, the cost of search increases as search goes on. In the Salop model, searchers' standards fall because searchers first explore the more attractive possibilities. If these prove unsatisfactory, they demand less of what remains.

The other consequences of Theorem I are somewhat more technical. The theorem suggests that computing optimal-search rules and the expected costs of following them is a finite problem; thus, it should be possible to compute the loss from following such ad hoc rules as those discussed by Telser (1973) instead of following optimal rules. Finally, it shows that to prove propositions about $V(\mu, \rho)$ it is sufficient to prove them for all $V_T(\mu, \rho)$. This technique is used repeatedly in the sequel. For example, it may be used to prove that property 3 holds in general.

Proposition 3: As the costs of search increase, search decreases.

Proof: Since, according to the optimal-search rule, the search continues whenever $p_i \geq V[h_i(\mu, \rho)] + c$, it will suffice to show that if $V(\mu, \rho)$ is the value of having information (μ, ρ) when costs are c and $\hat{V}(\mu, \rho)$ is the value of having the same information when costs are $\hat{c} \geq c$, then $\hat{V}(\mu, \rho) \geq V(\mu, \rho)$. Theorem I implies that this will be true if, for all T, $\hat{V}_T(\mu, \rho) \geq V_T(\mu, \rho)$. But this is clearly true if $T = 0$; that it is true for all T follows by induction from (12b), the definition of V_T.

VI. Reservation Prices

When the distribution of prices is known, optimal-search rules are characterized by a reservation price; there is a price p_R such that the searcher will accept all prices less than or equal to p_R and reject all prices greater than p_R. When the distribution of prices is unknown, acceptable prices change as information changes, so that optimal Bayesian search procedures cannot be characterized by a single reservation price. It is, however, worthwhile to ask whether or not they have a reservation price property, that is, whether for every state of information (μ, ρ) there is a $p_{R(\mu,\rho)}$ such that prices below $p_{R(\mu,\rho)}$ are accepted and those above it are rejected; if the acceptance sets of all customers in a market are characterized by reservation prices, then the demand function of each seller in that market is well behaved—if he raises prices, expected sales will not increase. Raising prices may increase sales if customers' acceptance sets are not characterized by reservation prices.

In general, optimal Bayesian search rules do not have the reservation-price property. Counterexamples are easy to construct. Suppose there are three prices, \$1.00, \$2.00, and \$3.00, and that the cost of search is \$0.01. Prior beliefs admit the possibility of only two distributions of prices. Either all prices are \$3.00 or they are distributed between \$1.00 and \$2.00 in the proportions 99 to 1. A man with these beliefs should accept a price of \$3.00 (as this is a signal that no lower prices are to be had) and reject a quote of \$2.00 (which indicates that the likelihood that a much better price will be obtained on another draw is high).

It is easy to see what makes this counterexample work. Price quotations have value as information. If my beliefs are (μ, ρ) then, the informational value of getting price i is just $V[h_i(\mu, \rho)]$. In the counterexample above, the differences in the information value of prices far exceed the differences in the prices themselves. If differences in the value of price information are less than differences in prices, then optimal-search rules have the reservation-price property.

Proposition 4: If for all $(\mu, \rho) \in \Delta$,

$$|p_i - p_k| \geq |V[h_i(\mu, \rho)] - V[h_k(\mu, \rho)]|, \tag{16}$$

then

$$V[h_i(\mu, \rho)] + c \geq p_i \geq p_k \tag{17}$$

implies

$$V[h_k(\mu, \rho)] + c \geq p_k. \tag{18}$$

Note that (17) implies (18) is precisely the reservation-price property.

Proof: Suppose that (16) holds. Then, using (17),

$$|p_i - p_k| = p_i - p_k \geq |V[h_i(\mu, \rho)] - V[h_k(\mu, \rho)]| \geq V[h_i(\mu, \rho)] - V[h_k(\mu, \rho)].$$

Thus

$$p_k - V[h_k(\mu, \rho)] + c \leq p_i - V[h_i(\mu, \rho)] + c \leq 0.$$

This is a useful criterion. It is used to prove

Theorem II: Optimal rules for searchers with Dirichlet priors have the reservation-price property.

In view of proposition 1 and equation (9), this is about the most general result that could be hoped for in this context. The proof which follows is purely formal and conveys little insight. It is not, however, hard to see why the theorem should be true. Proposition 4 implies that search rules will have the reservation price property whenever observing a price does not convey information about the relative likelihood—as measured by $\lambda(\mu, \rho)$—of observing other prices in the future. The rule for updating the Dirichlet is completely neutral in this sense. For all distinct i, j, and k, observing p_i has no effect on λ_j/λ_k.

Proof: In view of propositions 1 and 4, it will suffice to show that

$$\lambda_i(\mu, \rho) = \mu_i \tag{19}$$

implies that, for all positive integers, s,

$$|p_i - p_k| \geq |V[h_i^s(\mu, \rho)] - V[h_k^s(\mu, \rho)]|, \tag{20}$$

where

$$h_i^s(\mu, \rho) = \left(\frac{\mu_1}{1 + s\rho}, \ldots, \frac{\mu_i + s\rho}{1 + s\rho}, \ldots, \frac{\mu_n}{1 + s\rho}, \frac{\rho}{1 + s\rho}\right) \tag{21}$$

is (μ, ρ) updated according to (5) after s observations of p_i. Note that (16) is just (20) with $s = 1$. Theorem I implies that it will suffice to show, for all t,[13]

$$|p_i - p_k| \geq |V_t(h_i^s) - V_t(h_k^s)|, \tag{22}$$

which can be done by induction. Suppose, as we shall throughout the proof, that

$$p_i > p_k. \tag{23}$$

Then from (12) and (21),

$$V_0(h_i^s) = \frac{1}{1 + s\rho} \sum_j \mu_j p_j + \frac{s\rho}{1 + s} p_i.$$

[13] The arguments (μ, ρ) will be suppressed where this can be done without confusion.

Thus,

$$V_0(h_i^s) - V_0(h_k^s) = \frac{s\rho}{1 + s\rho}(p_i - p_k) \leq (p_i - p_k),$$

so that (22) holds for $t = 0$. The inductive step that if (22) holds for $t = T - 1$ then it holds for $t = T$ is proved in a series of lemmas below. The first is of independent interest. It states that if $p_i \geq p_k$, the man who has observed p_i s times expects to incur more total costs, other things equal, than the man who has observed the lower p_k s times.

Lemma 1: $p_i \geq p_k$ implies $V_T(h_i^s) \geq V_T(h_k^s)$.

Proof: I have already shown that

$$V_0(h_i^s) - V_0(h_k^s) = \frac{s\rho}{1 - s\rho}(p_i - p_k) > 0.$$

Suppose the lemma true for $t = T - 1$. Then letting

$$h_j h_i^s = h_j[h_i^s(\mu, \rho)] = h_i^s h_j,$$

$$\begin{aligned} V_T(h_i^s) - V_T(h_k^s) = {} & \frac{1}{1+\rho} \sum_j \mu_j \{\min [p_j, V_{T-1}(h_i^s h_j) + c] \\ & \qquad - \min [p_j, V_{T-1}(h_k^s h_j) + c]\} \\ & + \frac{\rho}{1+\rho} \{\min [p_i, V_{T-1}(h_i^{s+1}) + c] \\ & \qquad - \min [p_k, V_{T-1}(h_k^{s+1}) + c]\} \end{aligned} \tag{24}$$

The terms in braces which multiply $1/(1 + \rho)$ are of the form $J(A, B, C) = \min (A, B) - \min (A, C)$, where $B \geq C$ by the induction hypotheses. Thus, they are all nonnegative. Consider the term multiplying $\rho/(1 + \rho)$. It is of the form

$$J(A, B, C, D) = \min (A, B) - \min (C, D), \tag{25}$$

where $A = p_i$, $B = V_{T-1}(h_i^{s+1}) + c$, $C = p_k$, and $D = V_{T-1}(h_k^{s+1}) + c$. Thus, $A \geq C$ and $B \geq D$ by the induction hypotheses. These two inequalities imply that (25) is nonnegative. Since (24) is a weighted average of nonnegative quantities, it is nonnegative.

Lemma 2: If (22) holds for $t = T - 1$, then

$$\min [p_j, V_{T-1}(h_j h_i^s) + c] - \min [p_j, V_{T-1}(h_j h_k^s) + c] \leq p_i - p_k. \tag{26}$$

Proof: The left-hand side of (26) has the form

$$J(A, B, C) = \min (A, B) - \min (A, C),$$

where $A = p_j$, $B = V_{T-1}(h_j h_i^s) + c$, and $C = V_{T-1}(h_j h_k^s) + c$. Together (22) and lemma 1 imply

$$0 \leq B - C \leq p_i - p_k. \tag{27}$$

If $B \leq A$, then $C \leq A$ and $J = B - C$. If $B > A$, either $C \leq A$ and $J = A - C \leq B - C$ or $C > A$ and $J = A - A = 0 \leq B - C$. Thus, $J \leq (B - C) \leq p_i - p_k$.

Lemma 3: If (22) holds for $t = T - 1$,

$$\min [p_i, V_{T-1}(h_i^{s+1}) + c] - \min [p_k, V_{T-1}(h_k^{s+1}) + c] \leq p_i - p_k. \tag{28}$$

Proof: The left-hand side of (28) is of the same general form as (25), with $A = p_i$, $B = V_{T-1}(h_i^{s+1}) + c$, $C = p_k$, and $D = V_{T-1}(h_k^{s+1}) + c$. Also, by hypothesis, $A \geq C$ and lemma 1 imply $B \geq D$. We want to show that $J \leq A - C$. There are four cases to consider:

i) $A \leq B$ and $C \leq D$; so that $J = A - C$.

ii) $A \leq B$ and $C > D$. This case may be disregarded, since, if it obtains, $B - D \geq A - D > A - C$ or $V_{T-1}(h_i^{s+1}) - V_{T-1}(h_k^{s+1}) > p_i - p_k$, which contradicts the induction hypothesis (22).

iii) $A > B$ and $C > D$, so that $J = (B - D) \leq A - C$ by (22).

iv) $A > B$ and $C \leq D$, so that $J = (B - C) < A - C$, since $A > B$.

Lemma 4: If (22) holds for $t = T - 1$, it holds for $t = T$.

Proof: Use lemmas 2 and 3 to calculate

$$\begin{aligned}
|V_T(h_i^s) - V_T(h_k^s)| &= V_T(h_i^s) - V_T(h_k^s) \\
&= \frac{1}{1 + s\rho} \sum_j \mu_j \{\min [p_j, V_{T-1}(h_j h_i^s) + c] \\
&\qquad - \min [p_j, V_{T-1}(h_j h_k^s) + c]\} \\
&\quad + \frac{s\rho}{1 + s\rho} \{\min [p_i, V_{T-1}(h_i^{s+1}) + c] \\
&\qquad - \min [p_k, V_{T-1}(h_k^{s+1}) + c]\} \\
&\leq \frac{1}{1 + s\rho} \sum_j \mu_j (p_i - p_k) + \frac{s\rho}{1 + s\rho} (p_i - p_k) \\
&= (p_i - p_k) = |p_i - p_k|.
\end{aligned}$$

This completes the proof of Theorem II.

Theorem I implies that the reservation price of those searchers who remain in the market must eventually increase to p_n.[14]

[14] In previous versions of this paper, I conjectured that if the prior were Dirichlet, the reservation price would increase monotonically. I am grateful to Emmett Keeler for showing me how to construct a counterexample to this conjecture.

VII. Effects of Increasing Uncertainty

The Introduction lists some results on the effects of increased price dispersion when the price distribution is known. It is natural to ask whether these results—that increased price dispersion lowers total expected costs and increases search activity—hold when the distribution is unknown. Since the searcher's knowledge of the price distribution is defined by the parameters (μ, ρ), the question is what effect changes in μ and ρ which represent increased uncertainty have on $V(\mu, \rho)$. To answer this, it is necessary to decide what changes in (μ, ρ) correspond to increased uncertainty. There are two obvious candidates: $\lambda(\mu, \rho)$ is the expected price distribution in the sense that the searcher is just willing to bet that the next price will be p_i at odds $\lambda_i(\mu, \rho)$ to $[1 - \lambda_i(\mu, \rho)]$. However, ρ represents the precision of the searcher's knowledge of the price distribution he faces ($\rho = 0$ is subjective certainty). Thus, $\lambda(\mu, \rho)$ represents what the searcher believes while ρ represents how firmly he believes it. Increased uncertainty could correspond either to an increase in the dispersion of $\lambda(\mu, \rho)$, holding ρ constant, or to an increase in ρ, holding $\lambda(\mu, \rho)$ constant. With what I hope is a pardonable abuse of language, I shall call the first case "increasing perceived uncertainty" and the second case "increasing confidence." This terminology is justified by the fact that increasing perceived uncertainty is the natural analogue of the increases in uncertainty studied when price distributions are assumed known. Both cases are discussed below.

The effects of increased perceived uncertainty, at least for the Dirichlet case, are straightforward.

Theorem III: If the searcher's prior is a Dirichlet $[\lambda(\mu, \rho) = \mu]$, then if $\tilde{\mu}$ is riskier than μ, $V(\tilde{\mu}, \rho) \leq V(\mu, \rho)$.

Proof: Suppose $\tilde{\mu}$ is riskier than μ. It will suffice to prove the theorem if μ and $\tilde{\mu}$ differ by a single mean preserving spread (Rothschild and Stiglitz 1970), so we shall consider four prices $p_1 < p_2 < p_3 < p_4$ such that $\mu_i = \tilde{\mu}_i$ for $i \notin (1, 2, 3, 4)$ and

$$\tilde{\mu}_1 - \mu_1 = \mu_2 - \tilde{\mu}_2 = A > 0 \tag{29}$$

and

$$\mu_3 - \tilde{\mu}_3 = \tilde{\mu}_4 - \mu_4 = B > 0, \tag{30}$$

where

$$A(p_2 - p_1) + B(p_3 - p_4) = 0. \tag{31}$$

I shall prove the theorem by showing

$$V_T(\tilde{\mu}, \rho) \leq V_T(\mu, \rho) \tag{32}$$

for all T by induction. That (32) holds for $T = 0$ follows from (31) and (12). In an obvious notation, let $\tilde{h}_j = h_j(\tilde{\mu}, \rho)$.

Let R satisfy

$$V_T(\mu, \rho) = \sum_1^R \mu_j p_j + \sum_{R+1}^N \mu_j[V_{T-1}(h_j) + c].$$

Theorem II guarantees the existence of such an R. Note that

$$\begin{aligned} V_T(\tilde{\mu}, \rho) &= \sum \tilde{\mu}_j \min\,[p_j, V_{T-1}(\tilde{h}_j) + c] \\ &\leq \sum_1^R \tilde{\mu}_j p_j + \sum_{R+1}^n \tilde{\mu}[V_{T-1}(\tilde{h}_j) + c] \\ &\leq \sum_1^R \tilde{\mu}_j p_j + \sum_{R+1}^n \tilde{\mu}[V_{T-1}(h_j) + c] \end{aligned}$$

(the last inequality follows from the induction hypothesis). Let

$$H(\mu, \tilde{\mu}) = \sum_1^R (\mu_j - \tilde{\mu}_j)p_j + \sum_{R+1}^n (\mu_j - \tilde{\mu}_j)[V_{T-1}(h_j) + c]. \quad (33)$$

Then it will suffice to show that $H(\mu, \tilde{\mu}) \geq 0$.

There are five cases to consider, depending on the relationship of p_R to p_1, p_2, p_3, and p_4:

1) $p_R \geq p_4$. In this case,

$$\begin{aligned} H(\mu, \tilde{\mu}) &= (\mu_1 - \tilde{\mu}_1)p_1 + (\mu_2 - \tilde{\mu}_2)p_2 + (\mu_3 - \tilde{\mu}_3)p_3 + (\mu_4 - \tilde{\mu}_4)p_4 \\ &= A(p_2 - p_1) + B(p_3 - p_4) = 0. \end{aligned}$$

2) $p_4 > p_R > p_3$. In this case,

$$\begin{aligned} H(\mu, \tilde{\mu}) &= A(p_2 - p_1) + B\{p_3 - [V_{T-1}(h_4) + c]\} \\ &\geq A(p_2 - p_1) + B(p_3 - p_4) = 0. \end{aligned}$$

3) $p_3 > p_R > p_2$. In this case,

$$\begin{aligned} H(\mu, \tilde{\mu}) &= A(p_2 - p_1) + B[V_{T-1}(h_3) - V_{T-1}(h_4)] \\ &\geq A(p_2 - p_1) + B(p_3 - p_4) = 0. \end{aligned}$$

The second inequality follows from (22).

4) $p_2 > p_R \geq p_1$. In this case,

$$\begin{aligned} H(\mu, \tilde{\mu}) &= A[V_{T-1}(h_2) + c - p_1] + B[V_{T-1}(h_3) - V_{T-1}(h_4)] \\ &\geq A[V_{T-1}(h_2) - V_{T-1}(h_1)] + B[V_{T-1}(h_3) - V_{T-1}(h_4)]. \end{aligned} \quad (34)$$

It is shown below in lemma 5 that

$$\frac{V_{T-1}(h_2) - V_{T-1}(h_1)}{p_2 - p_1} \geq \frac{V_{T-1}(h_4) - V_{T-1}(h_3)}{p_4 - p_3}, \quad (35)$$

so that

$$A[V_{T-1}(h_2) - V_{T-1}(h_1)] \geq \frac{A(p_2 - p_1)}{p_4 - p_3}[V_{T-1}(h_4) - V_{T-1}(h_3)].$$

Combining (34) and (35), we obtain

$$H(\mu, \tilde{\mu}) \geq \frac{V_{T-1}(h_4) - V_{T-1}(h_3)}{p_4 - p_3} [A(p_2 - p_1) + B(p_4 - p_3)] = 0.$$

5) $p_1 \geq p_R$. In this case, $H(\mu, \tilde{\mu})$ is just equal to the last expression in (34), and (35) can be used to show that $H(\mu, \tilde{\mu}) \geq 0$.

To complete the proof we only need prove

Lemma 5: Inequality (35) holds for all T.

Proof: If $T = 0$, both sides of (35) are equal to $[\rho/(1 + \rho)]$. Suppose (35) holds for $t = T - 1$. Let R_k satisfy

$$V_T(h_k) = \sum_{1}^{R_k} \mu_j p_j + \sum_{R_k+1}^{n} \mu_j[V_{T-1}(h_{jk}) + c].$$

It follows from lemma 1 that $R_1 \leq R_2 \leq R_3 \leq R_4$, so that

$$V_T(h_2) - V_T(h_1) \leq \sum_{R_3+1}^{n} \mu_j[V_{T-1}(h_{2j}) - V_{T-1}(h_{1j})] \tag{36}$$

while

$$V_T(h_4) - V_T(h_3) \leq \sum_{R_3+1}^{n} u_j[V_{T-1}(h_{4j}) - V_{T-1}(h_{3j})]. \tag{37}$$

The induction hypothesis implies

$$0 \leq \sum_{R_3+1}^{n} \mu_j \left[\frac{V_{T-1}(h_{2j}) - V_{T-1}(h_{1j})}{p_2 - p_1} - \frac{V_{T-1}(h_{4j}) - V_{T-1}(h_{3j})}{p_4 - p_3}\right]$$
$$\leq \frac{V_{T-1}(h_2) - V_{T-1}(h_1)}{p_2 - p_1} - \frac{V_{T-1}(h_4) - V_{T-1}(h_3)}{p_4 - p_3}. \tag{38}$$

The last inequality follows from (36) and (37).

An immediate consequence of Theorem III is an analogue of property 4 that increased price dispersion leads to increased search.

Corollary: If the searcher's prior is Dirichlet, then increasing perceived uncertainty lowers the reservation price.

The proof, which is obvious, is omitted.

The effects of increased confidence are less clear. I suspect that if the prior is Dirichlet, then in most cases $V(\mu, \rho)$ decreases as ρ decreases. However, I have not been able to prove that this is always true or to construct an example where $V(\mu, \rho)$ increases when ρ decreases.[15]

[15] Earlier versions of this paper contained what I thought was an example of $V(\mu, \rho)$ increasing when ρ decreased. I am grateful to Mr. Richard Ressler for showing me that this example was mistaken. Ressler's senior thesis (Princeton University, 1974) contains the details of this and other calculations of the effects of various parameter changes on optimal-search strategies.

VIII. Conclusion

The most important results of this paper, Theorems II and III, state that, for what proposition 1 suggests is a quite significant example, the qualitative behavior of persons searching optimally from unknown distributions is the same as that of persons searching optimally from known distributions. Since it is easy to construct examples for which this is not true, it is natural to ask just how general these results are. This problem is best stated by focusing on a very general and abstract formulation of the problem of optimal search. Let K be a compact[16] set of the real line and let $\mathcal{M}(K)$ be the set of all probability measures on K. The quantity $\mathcal{M}(K)$ is a compact separable metric space, so that we can, in the standard way, define probability measures on $\mathcal{M}(K)$.[17] Such a probability measure, say $\mathcal{P}$, represents a searcher's a priori beliefs about the price distribution he faces (which is some probability distribution in $\mathcal{M}(K)$). If a price p is observed, then as long as the conditional distributions (on $\mathcal{M}(K)$ given p) can be calculated, Bayes's rule may be used to update his beliefs from $\mathcal{P}$ to, say, $\mathcal{P}'$. As in Sections II and IV above, the optimal Bayesian strategy can be devised. The measure $\mathcal{P}$ completely determines the optimal-search rule. The question at hand is, For what class of $\mathcal{P}$ do analogues of Theorems II and III hold?

Each $\mathcal{P}$ has two rather distinct aspects. The first is $S(\mathcal{P})$, the support of $\mathcal{P}$, which is roughly the set of price distributions which the searcher whose beliefs are described by $\mathcal{P}$ judges to be conceivable. This paper focuses on the case where $S(\mathcal{P})$ contains only multinomial distributions. The second aspect of $\mathcal{P}$ is the updating rule. Theorems II and III require that the updating rule be of a very special kind—if p_i is observed, then the (subjective) likelihood of observing p_i in the future is increased while the likelihood of observing all other prices is decreased (and by the same proportion).

Recent work of Ferguson (1973)[18] suggests that it is only the restrictions on the updating rule and not those on $S(\mathcal{P})$ that are required for Theorems II and III. Ferguson introduces a class of distributions whose support is essentially all of $\mathcal{M}(K)$; I conjecture that analogues of Theorems I, II, and III hold for these distributions. However, these probability measures imply very special updating rules. If we ignore many technicalities, Ferguson's work may be summarized as follows. Let α be a finite measure on K and let $B = (B_1, B_2, \ldots, B_n)$ be a measurable partition

[16] I continue to insist that price distributions be bounded. No meaningful generality and much complication ensues if this assumption is abandoned.

[17] See Parthasarthy (1967, pp. 39 ff.) for details.

[18] Blackwell and MacQueen (1973) show how Ferguson distributions can be understood in terms of the urn model of Section III. In terms of that model, we can phrase our question as follows: Do our results hold when the composition of the urn is altered (upon observation of price p_i) in some other way than by adding another slip with p_i written on it?

of K (that is, the B_i are measurable and $\bigcup_i B_i = K$ and $B_i \cap B_j = \phi$ if $i \neq j$). Consider the probability that the next observed price belongs to B_1, B_2, or B_n. This is a multinomial distribution described by the numbers $(P(B_1),\ldots, P(B_n)) \in \Delta$. Each such multinomial distribution belongs to $\mathscr{M}(K)$ and is thus assigned probability by $\mathscr{P}$. The distribution $\mathscr{P}_\alpha$ is a Ferguson distribution with parameter α if the distribution of $(P(B_1), P(B_2), \ldots, P(B_n))$ is Dirichlet with parameter $(\alpha(B_1), \alpha(B_2), \ldots, \alpha(B_n))$. Ferguson shows (1973, pp. 215–16) that the support of $\mathscr{P}_\alpha$ is the set of all measures $\mu \in \mathscr{M}(K)$ which are absolutely continuous with respect to α. By choosing α appropriately, $S(\mathscr{P}_\alpha)$ can be made very large.

The rule for updating $\mathscr{P}_\alpha$ is very simple. If $\mathscr{P}_\alpha$ is a Ferguson distribution with parameter α, after price p is observed, it is updated to a Ferguson distribution with parameter

$$h_p(\alpha) = \alpha + \delta_p, \tag{39}$$

where δ_p is the probability measure concentrated on the point p. This formula is an exact analogue of the rule given in equation (10) above for updating Dirichlet priors.

Proving analogues of Theorems I, II, and III for Ferguson distributions whose parameters have compact support should involve only technical problems.[19] If these could be solved, it would show that the results of this paper are quite general in the sense that they apply to searchers whose beliefs are not restricted in any way beyond boundedness. However, they are quite special in that they apply only to people who revise their beliefs in a very special way. Formula (39) implies that information is strictly local or, to put the matter more colloquially, that a miss is as good as a mile. My future beliefs about the likelihood of observing p are affected in exactly the same way by observing $p + 10^{-10}$ as by observing $p + 10^{10}$. I would like to know whether the conclusions of Theorems II and III hold when information is not so completely local. At present there seems no way to answer this question with generality. I know of no class of $\mathscr{P} \in \mathscr{M}(K)$ which has both large support and tractable updating rules other than the Ferguson distributions.

It is possible to examine the property of $\mathscr{P}$'s with rather restricted support by examining parametric families of distributions with tractable updating rules. For example, it is a simple consequence of DeGroot's (1968) work that optimal-search rules from normal distributions with unknown means and known variance have the reservation-price property when the prior distribution is also normal.

Perhaps the strongest possible result along the lines of Theorem II[20] that could be hoped for is the following

[19] It should be possible to push through proofs very similar to those in the text once a topology is found in which proposition 2 holds.

[20] I am not certain how propositions about the effects of increasing dispersion are best stated in this context.

Conjecture: Optimal-search rules from exponential families of distributions have the reservation-price property if the unknown parameters have conjugate prior distributions.

Establishing this would significantly expand the applicability of the results of this paper. Still, I think enough has been done to establish that economists can without great loss assume that the qualitative properties of demand functions which arise from optimal search from unknown distributions are the same as those which arise from optimal search from known distributions.

References

Billingsley, P. *Convergence of Probability Measures.* New York: Wiley, 1968.

Blackwell, D., and MacQueen, J. B. "Ferguson Distributions via Polya Urn Schemes." *Ann. Statis.* 1 (1973): 353–55.

Breiman, L. "Stopping-Rule Problems." In *Applied Combinatorial Mathematics,* edited by E. F. Beckenbach. Berkeley: Univ. California Press, 1964.

Buckley, J. E. "Wage Dispersion in Metropolitan Areas." *Monthly Labor Rev.* 92, no. 9 (September 1969): 24–29.

Chow, Y. S.; Robbins, H.; and Siegmund, D. *Great Expectations: The Theory of Optimal Stopping.* Boston: Houghton Mifflin, 1971.

David, P. A. "Fortune, Risk, and the Micro-Economics of Migration." In *Nations and Households in Economic Growth: Essays in Honor of Moses Abramovitz,* edited by P. A. David and M. W. Reder. New York: Academic Press, 1973.

De Groot, M. H. "Some Problems of Optimal Stopping." *J. Roy. Statis. Soc. B.* 30 (March 1968): 108–22.

———. *Optimal Statistical Decisions.* New York: McGraw-Hill, 1970.

Diamond, P. A. "A Model of Price Adjustment." *J. Econ. Theory* 3 (June 1971): 156–68.

Diamond, P. A., and Stiglitz, J. E. *Increases in Risk and in Risk Aversion. J. Econ. Theory* (1974), in press.

Ferguson, T. S. "A Bayesian Analysis of Some Nonparametric Problems." *Ann. Statis.* 1 (1973): 209–30.

Gastwirth, J. L. "On Probabilistic Models of Consumer Search for Information." Unpublished paper, 1971.

Gould, J. P. "Information and Consumer Behavior: Theory of Optimal Sequential Searching Policies." Unpublished paper, 1972.

Gronau, R. "Information and Frictional Unemployment." *A.E.R.* 61 (June 1971): 290–301.

Kasper, H. "The Asking Price of Labor and the Duration of Unemployment." *Rev. Econ. and Statis.* 49 (May 1967): 165–73.

Kohn, M. G., and Shavell, S. "Optimal Adaptive Search." *J. Econ. Theory* (1974), in press.

McCall, J. J. "The Economics of Information and Optimal Stopping Rules." *J. Bus.* 38 (July 1965): 300–317.

———. "Economics of Information and Job Search." *Q.J.E.* 84 (February 1970): 113–26.

Nelson, P. "Information and Consumer Behavior." *J.P.E.* 78 (March/April 1970): 311–29.

Parthasarthy, K. R. *Probability Measures on Metric Spaces.* New York: Academic Press, 1967.

Rothschild, M. "Models of Market Organization with Imperfect Information." *J.P.E.* 81 (November/December 1973): 1283–1308.

Rothschild, M., and Stiglitz, J. E. "Increasing Risk. I. A Definition." *J. Econ. Theory* 2 (September 1970): 225–43.

Salop, S. "Systematic Job Search and Unemployment." *Rev. Econ. Studies* 40 (April 1973): 191–202.

Stigler, G. J. "The Economics of Information." *J.P.E.* 69 (June 1961): 213–25.

———. "Information in the Labor Market." *J.P.E.* 70, no. 5, suppl. (October 1962): 94–105.

Telser, L. G. "Searching for the Lowest Price." *A.E.R. Proc.* 63 (1973): 41–49.

Whipple, D. "A Generalized Theory of Job Search." *J.P.E.* 81 (September/October 1973): 1170–88.

Yahav, J. "On Optimal Stopping." *Ann Math. Statis.* 37 (1966): 30–35.

Exercises on search rules

In these exercises you are asked to develop the properties of optimal search rules discussed in Section I of this reading. Since the most common use of search theory is to explain labor market behavior we have asked you to consider the problem of a worker searching for a job rather than a customer looking for a bargain. Suppose there is a probability distribution of wage offers and that the searcher can elicit exactly one wage offer per period. The wage distribution $G(w)$ is bounded and continuous so that there is a density function $g(w)$ such that $\int_0^B g(w)\, dw = 1$. We assume that the searcher knows the wage distribution and that it is the same every period. If the searcher accepts a wage offer of w he receives that wage for the rest of his infinite life. While searching the worker receives S per period, which can be negative. S reflects such things as the cost of search (transport costs), unemployment compensation, or welfare payments. S may be 0, reflecting the fact that an important cost of search is simply foregone earnings. We assume that S is less than the expected wage.

The searcher evaluates alternative strategies in terms of their expected discounted income.

A. Fixed Sample Size Rules

We analyze first the case of fixed sample size rules. The searcher fixes a number n, takes n observations on wages (during periods $0, 1, \ldots, n - 1$), and then in period n goes to work at the highest wage observed while searching.

1 If the sample size is one the probability of getting a wage less than w is just $Q_1(w) = G(w)$. Show that with a sample size of n, the probability that the highest wage offer is less than w is

$$Q_n(w) = G(w)^n \tag{1}$$

Show that the expected wage accepted after n searches is $N(n) = B - \int_0^B G(w)^n\, dw$. Show that $N(n)$ is an increasing function of n. This implies that those who search more get better jobs.

2 (a) Find $Q_n(w)$ for the special case where $G(w)$ is the uniform distribution on

$[0, B]$; show that the kth moment of the maximum wage about the origin is $[n/(n + k)]B^k$.

(b) $Q_n(w)$ is the distribution of wages accepted by persons in the population who chose a sample of size n. It should thus correspond to the distribution of wages of these job holders. If a statistician were to collect data on the distribution of wages, most probably he would sample from $Q_n(w)$ and not from $G(w)$, which is very hard to observe. This fact accounts, in part, for the difficulty of doing empirical work on search models. For the case described in (a), show that the mean of the distribution $Q_n(w)$ is greater than that of $G(w)$, while the variance of $G(w)$ exceeds that of $Q_n(w)$ (when $n > 1$).

3 (a) Returning to the general case, show that the expected discounted income of a worker who searches for the n periods $0, 1, 2, \ldots, n - 1$, and begins work at the best job offered is given by $Y(n)$, where

$$Y(n) = \frac{S}{1 - \beta} + \frac{\beta^n}{1 - \beta}[N(n) - S], \qquad n = 1, 2, \ldots \tag{2}$$

where $\beta < 1$ is the discount factor (i.e., β equals $1/1 + r$, where r is the interest rate).

(b) For $n > 1$, let $\Delta(n) = Y(n) - Y(n - 1)$, the gain from searching the nth time. Show that for $n > 0$, $\Delta(n)$ is decreasing in n.

(c) Show that n^*, the optimal number of searches, is the greatest integer less than or equal to $\tilde{n}$, the solution to

$$(1 - \beta)^{-1} \int_0^B G(w)^{n-1}[1 - \beta G(w)]\, dw = (B - S) \tag{3}$$

(d) Use (3) to show that increasing S (decreasing the cost of search) increases (or at least does not decrease) n^*.

(e) Show that n^* is a monotone increasing function of β so that as the discount rate increases searching declines.

B. Optimal Sequential Search

Consider now the worker who follows a sequential search strategy. Each period he searches, earning an income of S, and receives a single job offer at wage w. Wage offers are distributed according to the density $g(w)$; again we assume $\int_0^B g(w)\, dw = 1$. He may either accept the wage he is offered, in which case he receives it for every period in the future, or he may search again. If he accepts wage w after searching k times, then his discounted income will be

$$\frac{S}{1 - \beta} + \frac{\beta^k}{1 - \beta}[w - S]$$

It is well known[1] that the optimal search rule (the one that maximizes expected discounted income) is a reservation wage rule. That is, the worker should choose a wage level R and accept any wage offer above it and reject any below it.

1 Show that the expected discounted income of a searcher who follows such a rule and happens to search exactly k times is

$$\frac{S}{1-\beta} + \frac{\beta^k}{1-\beta}[\phi(R) - S] \tag{4}$$

where

$$\phi(R) = \int_R^B wg(w)\,dw/[1 - G(R)]$$

2 Let $H(w)$ be equal to $1 - G(w)$.

(a) Show that the probability that the searcher who has reservation wage R searches exactly k times is

$$G(R)^{k-1}H(R) \tag{5}$$

(b) Use (4) and (5) to show that the expected total discounted income of a worker with a reservation wage of R is

$$\frac{S}{1-\beta} + \frac{\beta}{1-\beta}H(R)\frac{\phi(R) - S}{1 - \beta G(R)} \tag{6}$$

(c) Clearly R must be chosen to maximize

$$H(R)\frac{\phi(R) - S}{1 - \beta G(R)}$$

Show that the optimal R satisfies

$$\frac{\beta}{1-\beta}\int_R^B(w - R)g(w)\,dw = R - S \tag{7}$$

Give an economic interpretation of (7). [Recall that $\beta/(1 - \beta) = \Sigma_{i=1}^{\infty}\beta^i$.] Can you use a dynamic programming approach to derive the same rule?

(d) For comparative statics purposes, it is more convenient to write (7) in the form

$$\beta\int_R^B(w - R)g(w)\,dw - R(1 - \beta) = -S(1 - \beta) \tag{8}$$

Prove the following propositions:

(1) Increasing the cost of search (decreasing S) decreases the reservation wage.

(2) Increasing the discount rate (decreasing β) decreases the reservation wage.

[1]There are many proofs of this fact. See, e.g., Lippman and McCall (1976a).

(3) A the distribution becomes riskier (in the sense of Chapter 6), the reservation wage increases.
[*Hint*: What is the expected value of the convex function $\psi_R(w) = \text{Max}[0, w - R]$?

C. Search with a Finite Life or Why Search May Appear to Be Unproductive[2]

We now abandon the assumption that the searcher has an infinite life and analyze the situation of a searcher who can work but T periods. In each period in which he searches, he receives a job offer [drawn from the probability density $g(w)$]. If the worker accepts the first job offered him, he gets that wage for the rest of his working life. If he rejects the job, he may search again next period; if he accepts that job, he works at it for $T - 1$ periods, otherwise he searches again. We assume here that jobs are offered on a take it or leave it basis; offers once spurned cannot be accepted later. For simplicity, we assume that there is no discounting and that the only costs of search are foregone earnings.

We ask you to show that the best search strategy involves following a reservation wage rule and that the reservation wage declines as the searcher ages; that is, there is a decreasing sequence of numbers R_t such that the optimal strategy for a man who is still searching and has but t periods to live is to accept all wage offers above R_t and reject those below R_t. A suggested way of proving this is outlined in questions 1-4 below, but we urge you to try to formulate and solve this problem for yourself.

If you can, go on to question 5, where you are asked to develop the somewhat paradoxical implications of this result.

1 Let V_t be the expected lifetime wages of a worker with t periods remaining in his working life who does not yet have a job and who follows an optimal strategy. A worker who has but 1 period left will take any job offered so that

$$V_1 = \mathbf{E}w = \int_0^B wg(w)\,dw$$

where $\mathbf{E}$ is the expectations operator. Show that $V_2 = \mathbf{E}\max[2w, V_1]$ and more generally that

$$V_t = \mathbf{E}\max[tw, V_{t-1}]$$

2 Show that the optimal rule is a reservation wage rule and that that reservation wage R_t satisfies

$$R_t = V_{t-1}/t$$

[2]The analysis here follows that of Gronau (1971).

3 Show that for $t > 1$, $V_t \geqslant [t/(t-1)]V_{t-1}$.
[*Hint*: Consider a searcher who has t periods left but who follows the policy of accepting only those wages a person who has but $t - 1$ periods left would accept. Let $\hat{V}_t$ be the expected value of following such a policy. Clearly $V_t \geqslant \hat{V}_t$. Now consider *any* sequence of $t - 1$ wages $(w_{t-1}, w_{t-2}, \ldots, w_1)$. A person following the policy worth $\hat{V}_t$ will accept the same wage as the person with but $t - 1$ periods left who follows the optimal policy. Suppose they both accept w_s, where, of course, $s \leqslant t - 1$. One's wages will be sw_s, the other's $(s-1)w_s$. Conclude that $V_t \geqslant V_{t-1}\, t(t-1)^{-1}$.]
4 Use 2 and 3 to show that $R_t \geqslant R_{t-1}$.
5 The implication of this result is that individuals who remain in the market lower their reservation wages as time goes on. It is sometimes argued, at least in the oral tradition, that if search is productive like any other economic activity, then those who have searched longest should get the best jobs, at least on the average. (We saw, in A.1, that this was true for those who followed fixed sample size rules.) This model yields exactly opposite conclusions. Suppose all workers initially have T periods to search. Let M_s be the average wage of those who accepted the sth job offered them (and thus searched s periods). Show that $M_1 \geqslant M_2 \geqslant \cdots \geqslant M_T$.
6 Do you think the conclusion of this exercise is robust? That is, can you think of other reasons why optimal search rules should have the declining reservation wage property?

This exercise has examined search given a stationary distribution. For analysis with different distributions as search proceeds, see Lippman and McCall (1976b), Salop (1973), and Weitzman (1979).

References

S. A. Lippman and J. McCall, The economics of job search: A survey, *Econ. Inquiry* **14** (1976a), 155–189, 347–368.
S. A. Lippman and J. McCall, Job search in a dynamic economy, *J. Econ. Theory* **12** (1976b), 365–390.
R. Gronau, Information and frictional unemployment, *Am. Econ. Rev.* **61** (1971), 290–301.
S. Salop, Systematic job search and unemployment, *Rev. Econ. Stud.* **40** (1973), 191–201.
M. Weitzman, Optimal search for the best alternative, *Econometrica* **47** (1979), 641–654.

26
Central planning, monopoly, duopoly

We have now seen models of individual behavior where the consumer has to search to locate a supplier (or one with a good price). The remainder of this section explores market equilibrium when consumers face such information constraints.[1] These articles cover situations with many suppliers, which we will refer to as competitive. To introduce this discussion, we consider the normative question of how a central planner might set prices in such a market. We also discuss how price dispersion can persist in markets with a small number of firms.

There are two different cases to discuss. We can assume that consumers know the distribution of prices in the market, or, more realistically, that consumers have subjective beliefs about the market, which are altered as a consequence of their experiences in shopping. Consider the first (and simpler) case. Assume that a central planner controls the prices at all potential outlets. (We ignore the question of the number of selling places to be provided.) To preserve the character of the analysis (i.e., its difference from conventional analysis) assume that the marginal costs of supply differ across outlets. This is reasonable where costs of delivery of the commodity to the retail outlet and rental costs of the space needed to service consumers vary with location. When the planner follows marginal cost pricing, the equilibrium is optimal relative to the class of solutions where the consumers do not know the location of suppliers with particular costs or prices (assuming that consumers follow optimal search strategies). The explanation of this result is that the individual choice problem is precisely the social choice problem. Individual and social optimization are equivalent when the prices individuals face are social costs.

In contrast, marginal cost pricing is not generally optimal when consumers do not know the distribution.[2] There are two separate reasons for this possibility. First, consumers could have arbitrary subjective beliefs about prices before beginning to search. There is then no simple relationship between the maximization of expected utility given arbitrary beliefs about prices and the maximization of expected utility given the true probabilities of making purchases at different

[1]For a survey of both individual behavior and empirical findings in labor markets with search see Lippman and McCall, cited in the previous chapter.

[2]This discussion is based on Diamond (1978).

prices (or costs of supply). Second, even when consumers have the correct prior beliefs (where that is well defined) they are not behaving optimally when they revise their beliefs as they search. The revision of beliefs tends to make consumers less willing to search because finding a high price makes them believe high prices are more likely. (This argument can be made precise for the Dirichlet case discussed in the previous reading, assuming that there are only two possible prices in the market.) Thus, a central planner attempting to set prices to minimize the costs of providing the good plus the search costs of customers does not necessarily use marginal cost pricing. Instead, he generally can alter prices to induce consumer behavior that is closer to optimal.

In practice there are many other aspects of products about which consumers are ill informed. These include the location of particular suppliers, the existence of the particular good, general characteristics of the particular good, and product quality differences.[3] There are a variety of information sources that can be used to make consumers better informed.[4] The analysis of information flows is then an important element in understanding markets under uncertainty, but one that has received little analysis.

To have an economic environment where search was relevant for a consumer, we assumed that the marginal costs of supply differed across locations for a given commodity. In considering private rather than publicly controlled markets, there has been considerable analysis of the question of whether there would be a distribution of prices in the market if all characteristics of the market were symmetric across locations. In an interesting analysis, Salop (1977) has considered whether a monopolist might not deliberately introduce price dispersion as an attempt to price discriminate in the market. Introducing price dispersion, and so costs of search, reduces demand for the product and so tends to hurt the monopolist. Nevertheless, the introduction of price dispersion can increase profits for the monopolist in some circumstances. The key element is that the monopolist, if he could discriminate, would like to charge high prices to individuals who have high search costs (and thus do not seek out the low-price outlets), while charging lower prices to consumers who have low search costs (and thus do seek out the low-price outlets). For some distributions of search costs across consumers, price dispersion is profitable.

In game theory, a stochastic (or mixed) strategy often dominates all possible determinate (or pure) strategies for an individual. If this were true in a market, then we would again have a reason for price dispersion. Shilony (1977) has considered the case of a duopoly where consumers know the distribution of prices but do not know which of the physically separate duopolists is charging what

[3]In considering flood and earthquake insurance, Kunreuther *et al.* (cited in Chapter 2) found many consumers who did not know that the product existed, what its characteristics were, or how to get it.

[4]For an interesting discussion of advertising as information see Nelson (1974).

price at any given time. He shows for this game that duopolists should follow stochastic strategies.

These theoretical explanations of price diversity may or may not convince the reader. However, it should not be concluded that price dispersion is of interest only to the abstract theorist. As the empirical work of Jung (1960), Marvel (1976), Maynes (1976, 1977), and Pratt *et al.* (1979) amply demonstrates, large and persistent price variations are alive and well.

We turn now to competitive markets, considering both the possibility of price distributions despite symmetry in the structure and the optimality properties of equilibrium whatever the source of price dispersion.

References

P. Diamond, Welfare analysis of imperfect information equilibria, *Bell J. Econ.* **9** (1978), 82–105.

A. F. Jung, Price variations among automobile dealers in metropolitan Chicago, *J. Business* 83 (1960), 31–42.

H. P. Marvel, The economics of information and retail gasoline price behavior: An empirical analysis, *J. Political Econ.* 84 (1976), 1033–1060.

E. S. Maynes, "Decision Making for Consumers." Macmillan, New York, 1976.

E. S. Maynes, Informational imperfection in local consumer markets," unpublished, 1977.

P. Nelson, Advertising as information, *J. Political Econ.* 82 (1974), 729–754.

J. Pratt, D. Wise, and R. Zeckhauser, Price differences in almost competitive markets, *Quart. J. Econ.* **93** (1979) 189–211.

S. Salop, The noisy monopolist: Imperfect information, price dispersion and price discrimination, *Rev. Econ. Stud.* 44 (1977), 393–406.

Y. Shilony, Mixed pricing in oligopoly, *J. Econ. Theory* **14** (1977), 373–388.

27

M. Rothschild, Models of market organization with imperfect information: A survey, *Journal of Political Economy* **81** (1973), 1283–1308

After this survey of models of markets with many suppliers, we shall consider some analyses that have been done since completion of this article.

For more recent surveys of results on the issues raised here, see Diamond (1987) and Mortensen (1986).

References

P. Diamond, Search theory. In J. Eatwell, M. Milgate, and P. Newman (eds.) "The New Palgrave: A Dictionary of Economics," London: MacMillan Press, 1987.

D. Mortensen, Job search and labor market analysis. In O. Ashenfelter and R. Layard (eds.), "Handbook of Labor Economics," Vol. II, Amsterdam: North-Holland Press, 1986.

Models of Market Organization with Imperfect Information: A Survey

Michael Rothschild

Princeton University

This paper surveys recent theoretical work characterizing markets whose participants act on the basis of sketchy and incomplete information. Its focus is market equilibrium. Models of what is usually called disequilibrium behavior do not make sense and cannot serve as reliable guides to further theorizing or to policy unless they are consistent and coherent. No single equilibrium concept is valid for all situations. The different models analyzed have a variety of different equilibria; some are characterized by a single price, some by a distribution of prices. An attempt is made to identify the features responsible for the different equilibria.

I

This paper is a survey of recent theoretical work characterizing markets whose participants act on the basis of sketchy and incomplete information. That such situations are common anyone can establish by recalling virtually any transaction he has ever participated in. But whether they are important is a harder question. I have a colleague whose position on this matter runs roughly as follows: "The friction caused by disequilibrium and lack of information accounts for variations in the numbers we observe at the fifth or sixth decimal place. Your stories are interesting but have no conceivable bearing on any question of practical economic interest." I think this an incorrect argument—or at least one based on incorrect information.

My ideas on the topics discussed here developed in the course of discussions with Kenneth Arrow, Peter Diamond, Joseph Stiglitz, and Menahem Yaari. Yoram Ben-Porath, Peter Doeringer, Stanley Fischer, Franklin Fisher, Melvyn Fuss, Robert Gordon, Jerry Green, Zvi Griliches, Ed Kane, Ed Leamer, and Lester Telser made detailed comments on preliminary drafts. I am grateful to all these individuals and to the National Science Foundation, which provided more material support.

There are at least three reasons for being interested in models of the sort I will survey here. The first is simply that the most pressing macroeconomic policy questions of the day concern the behavior of markets out of equilibrium. Involuntary unemployment does not occur in a world in which all participants are aware of the consequences of all their actions and all markets clear instantaneously and costlessly. Inflation is not a problem, and unanticipated inflation not even a possibility, in an Arrow-Debreu world where all trades take place in the beginning of time and the rest of history is merely a run-through of the script written on that First Market Day. It is hard to explain why individuals hold money—and thus how monetary policy works—unless it is assumed that transactions are costly and opportunities to buy and sell less than perfectly predictable. Whenever any particular opportunity is seized or rejected, the decision is based on imperfect information.

One need not go so far as Leijonhufvud (1968), who argues that the Keynesian multiplier effect should be understood as a consequence of the way in which a system of imperfectly linked markets reacts to disequilibrium in one of them, nor need one concur with the authors of the *Microeconomic Foundations of Employment and Inflation Theory* (Phelps et al. 1970)—who on occasion seem to argue that the only unemployment is voluntary frictional unemployment—to believe that it is possible that a better understanding of the way in which imperfect markets worked would improve macroeconomic theory and possibly even macroeconomic policy.

Of as much practical import are the microeconomic consequences of imperfect information. Akerlof (1970) has pointed out that a host of diverse and important market phenomena—ranging from the inability of many people to buy insurance to the seemingly inefficient organization of credit markets in underdeveloped countries—are best understood as responses to imperfect and asymmetric information. As Arrow (1972) has observed, discrimination in employment cannot be easily accommodated in a model where markets are perfect. In a perfectly competitive world, employers who develop a taste for discrimination will be undersold by less discriminating entrepreneurs. Arrow shows that, while perfect competition will not support discrimination, markets with imperfect information will. It is reasonable to hope that better policies for dealing with these social ills will come from a better understanding of the operation of the flawed markets which permit them to exist.

The third reason for being interested in models of the behavior of imperfectly informed individuals is more intellectual than practical, but it does go to the heart of the most important theoretical problems with which we grapple. Economists have devoted much effort to proving the existence and characterizing the nature of competitive equilibrium. Those who engage in such labors pay close attention to the behavior of individual economic agents. Consumers' environments are studied and their motivations examined and axiomatized. Firms receive the same scrutiny when the technology is specified and rules for profit maximization derived. The reason why such care is taken to motivate the actions of each and every person or firm in the model is not hard to find. The most important result of economic theory is the suggestion that, to quote Frank Hahn (1970), "the pursuit of private interest produces not chaos but coherence." An argument which came to this a priori surprising conclusion would hardly convince if it did not contain a close examination of the "pursuit of private interest."

In the address from which the above quote is taken, Hahn noted that, although our models show quite satisfactorily that an economy composed of profit-maximizing firms and utility-maximizing consumers can *have* an equilibrium, the question of just *how* it gets there has not received a satisfactory answer. This is not, of course, because we have no models of the adjustment to equilibrium but because the models we have are not convincing. Models of adjustment to equilibrium are weakest where proofs of existence are strongest—in their treatment of individual behavior. Until 1961, adjustment models were *tâtonnement* models: no trading took place while anonymous market forces (or omniscient auctioneers) set (and changed) prices. Then Negishi (1961) showed the stability of a process which allowed trade to take place out of equilibrium. However, neither he, nor Hahn, nor Uzawa (1962) (who also studied non-*tâtonnement* adjustment processes) began to explain who changed prices and why. In all these models,[1] market prices are postulated to change in proportion to excess demand. Whose behavior is being described is not clear. Recent work by Fisher (1972) and Gepts (1971) has improved this situation somewhat. Each has built a model of a stable non-*tâtonnement* adjustment process which places the responsibility for changing prices with individual economic agents. In each model, price setters follow rules which eventually lead to the establishment of competitive equilibrium. Neither author seems to have given any thought to explaining why they should behave as they do. It is clear that in each case the specification of price setters' behavior was chosen because it was not grossly implausible and allowed the author to push through a stability proof modeled on those in the literature.[2]

A satisfactory model of adjustment to equilibrium will have at least three parts: a discussion of the rules which market participants follow when the market is out of equilibrium; a description of how a market

[1] See Arrow and Hahn (1971, chap. 13) for a survey of non-*tâtonnement* adjustment processes.

[2] Each author took a standard non-*tâtonnement* model of adjustment and adapted it so that responsibility for setting and changing prices was clearly located with an individual. Gepts (1971) presents an individualized version of the Edgeworth process and Fisher (1972) a similar variant of the Hahn process.

system in which individuals follow these rules operates; and, of course, a convergence theorem. Most adjustment models have sacrificed the first requirement to the second and third. The work discussed here should provide ideas and encouragement to those who seek to redress this balance.

That models of the adjustment to equilibrium should not convincingly motivate the behavior of their participants is not surprising. It is only since Stigler's (1961) work on "The Economics of Information" that economists have worried about how individuals should and do behave when imperfectly informed of the consequences of their actions. By now we have assembled a fairly respectable collection of rules of behavior for disequilibrium situations. Recently, work has been done on the problem of how markets in which individuals so behave function *as markets*. It is my purpose here to survey this work.

The organizing theme of this survey is market equilibrium. This may seem surprising, since many of the economic phenomena described are what most economists would call disequilibrium. However, as I shall argue in the next section, models of disequilibrium behavior do not make sense and cannot serve as reliable guides to further theorizing or to policy unless they meet certain standards of consistency and coherence. Unfortunately, although it is clear that some sort of equilibrium concept is required, it is by no means clear which is the most appropriate. In Section III models which converge to the competitive equilibrium price are discussed. A common feature of these models is the unaggressive or nonsensical behavior of the firms in them. Either they follow optimizing rules based on incorrect assessments of their situation or they do not try to optimize at all. Models in which firms behave as aggressive and intelligent profit maximizers are the subject of Section IV. Surprisingly, it turns out that such competitive behavior, even when there are many firms, leads to noncompetitive results. The equilibrium price in these models is above the competitive price. In Section V, I discuss models in which the equilibrium is not a single price but a distribution of prices. A market may fail to converge to a single price if it is subject to continual random shocks or if the participants in the market have difficulty collecting information about their environments. Analysis of these models shows that what sort of equilibrium a market has depends on what its participants know and do. The next section discusses a stylized labor market in which the converse is true. In that model an essentially arbitrary equilibrium of self-fulfilling expectations determines people's beliefs about the value of education. The paper concludes with a brief summary and some suggestions for future research.

This survey is designed to be both provocative and expository. I have drastically simplified complex arguments and issues to make points both accessible and dramatic. I apologize to any author who feels the very essence of his work has been distorted by the Procrustean bed of this essay's logical development.

II

The need for an equilibrium concept can be seen most easily from an examination of Stigler's fundamental article "The Economics of Information" (1961), which, directly or indirectly, inspired most of the work here surveyed. In that article Stigler developed a theory of how consumers ought to behave in a market in which there is a variety of unknown prices. Obviously the consumer should buy at the lowest price he knows of. If, however, he only knows the distribution of prices at all stores and not the particular price at each store, he must search for low prices. We can conceive of his search as drawing from a random distribution; if there is a cost to finding out the price from a store, the consumer will want to limit his search activity. Stigler argued that consumers would visit a fixed number, n, of stores and then buy from the store with the lowest price. The expected price the consumer pays is the expected value of the minimum of n observations from a sample with probability distribution $F(x)$. This is

$$m_n = \int_0^\infty [1 - F(x)]^n \, dx.$$

Clearly this decreases as n increases. The expected gain from searching once more is

$$g_n = m_n - m_{n+1} = \int_0^\infty [1 - F(x)]^n F(x) \, dx,$$

also a decreasing function of n. If the cost of search is c, it is clear that one should plan on searching n times where n has the property that the gain from searching the $(n + 1)$th time is less than c or that

$$g_n \geq c > g_{n+1}.$$

Stigler then proceeds to advance and loosely test a number of hypotheses as to what causes dispersion of prices and what causes intensity of search. Stigler's theory has been expanded and criticized in a number of respects. Several authors (e.g., McCall 1965, 1970; Nelson 1970) have pointed out that the decision rule Stigler suggested is not optimal and that the best procedure is a sequential one. This can be demonstrated as follows: If the present minimum price is s, then the expected decrease in the minimum price from another search is obviously

$$\int_0^s (s - x) \, dF(x) = \int_0^s F(x) \, dx = g(s).$$

Clearly, it pays to search again when $c < g(s)$ and it does not pay to search when $c \geq g(s)$. The optimal sequential decision rule is then to continue searching if the lowest price observed up to that point is greater than R where R is the solution to $g(R) = c$. McCall (1965, 1970), Nelson (1970), and Gastwirth (1971) have all shown how this equation may be modified if there are increasing costs to search, or if the probability distribution of stores changes over time (as it will if search is conceived of as sampling without replacement), or if the good in question is heterogeneous. In all these cases, the optimal search rule is of the form: buy if the price quoted is less than R, otherwise keep on searching.

Gastwirth has also explored the robustness of optimal sequential decision rules. Suppose the buyer's estimate of the distribution of prices is wrong, that prices are really distributed according to the rule $G(\cdot)$ rather than $F(\cdot)$. What then will be the consequences of using the wrong decision rule? By working out some plausible examples Gastwirth found that modest specification errors could, if sequential decision rules were followed, lead to dramatic increases in the expected number of searches (in some cases they increased more than fivefold). This suggests that consumers unsure of the exact distribution of prices would be wiser to use Stigler's naïve fixed-sample-size rules than the optimal sequential rules. However, as Gastwirth points out, there is a class of rules which are both robust and preserve the reservation price property. These are fixed-sample-size reservation price rules. They are of the form: keep searching until either n observations have been taken or the lowest observation after the kth observation is less than R_k. An obvious lower bound for R_k is c_{k+1}, the cost of making $(k + 1)$th observation.

A much more telling criticism of Stigler's theory is the observation that it is the theory of only one side of a market. It is a partial partial-equilibrium theory. Although it explains how customers should react to variability in price, it does not explain where this variability comes from or what, if anything, preserves it. Since the behavior of price setters is unexplained, it cannot be affected by consumer behavior. For this reason, Stigler's own analyses are not free from paradox.

Stigler argues that if store prices are distributed uniformly on the unit interval (0, 1) and if customers follow the strategy of searching at n stores and buying from the store with the lowest price, then the expected number of customers who will buy from a store charging price p is equal to

$$D(p) = K(1 - p)^{n-1},$$

where K is a positive constant. The function $D(p)$, from the store's point of view, is no different from an ordinary demand function.[3] If stores knew the consumer rules which generate the function $D(p)$, they would choose p to maximize profits which are equal to

$$D(p)p - C[D(p)],$$

[3] Professor Stigler has pointed out to me that this statement is possibly misleading. The formula for $D(p)$ is correct only if prices at other stores really are distributed uniformly. To derive its "demand function," a store must assume that other store prices are fixed and independent of its own actions.

where $C(\cdot)$ is the store's cost function. If all stores have identical costs, they will choose the same p and the uniform distribution which was supposed to generate the demand function will shrink to a point.[4]

Stigler asserts that there should be less variability (as measured by the coefficient of variation) in markets for expensive goods than in those for cheap goods. I do not question his conclusion. He offers evidence to support it, but the argument he uses to explain it is, at best, incomplete. He reasons that customers will invest more effort in finding a low-price car than in finding a good buy on screwdrivers. Thus the market for automobiles will support less variation than that for screwdrivers. The argument depends on customer search behavior somehow influencing sellers' behavior. But Stigler has no model of how this happens, and as we saw above, the most obvious way of doing this leads his model to collapse. There is a further problem with his argument. If consumer search reduces price variability, if it is successful it is not needed. That is, if I know that everyone else will reduce the variability in price by doing a lot of comparative shopping, there is no need for me to do any comparative shopping myself. But if others reason as I do, no one will do any comparative shopping and the market will support more variability. Clearly, the way out of this box is to build a model of a complete set of markets in which an equilibrium distribution of prices results from the interplay of market forces. Two attempts to do this will be discussed in Section V below.

The criticism I have made of Stigler is quite general and can, I think, be fairly made of many of the recent microeconomic theories of Phillips curves. Although the models of Mortensen (1970*a*, 1970*b*), Phelps (1970), and Lucas and Rapping (1970) do attempt to explain the behavior of both sides of the labor market, they do not explain the variety of wage offers which is supposed to motivate the behavior of job seekers in the market. This makes me very skeptical of propositions about the causes and effects of altering wage variability (real and perceived) which flow from these models.

III

In this section I shall discuss models of adjustment processes in individual markets which converge to a competitive price. Fisher (1970) has built a model of a single market in which all firms have identical cost curves which exhibit increasing marginal costs. In each period, firms set output

[4] Of course, if stores have different cost functions they will choose different prices. But there is no reason to expect the price distribution which emerges after optimization to be the same as the one on which optimization was based. This method of closing the model will, almost always, lead to inconsistencies of this sort.

as if they were competitors facing infinitely elastic demand at an estimated market price. Each firm bases its estimate of market price on its experience in the previous period. If excess demand is positive, it will raise its estimate of the market price and increase its output; negative excess demand leads to a lower estimate of market price and decreased output.

Since firms have different market experiences, there may be some price variability. Consumers respond to this by searching for low-price stores. Rather than specify their behavior in detail, Fisher simply postulates that the search process is rational in that low-price stores have at least as many customers as high-price stores.

All customers have identical demand functions, and the amount a customer buys at a store depends only on the price at that store and not on the customer's search history. Thus, there is an aggregate demand function $D(p)$ as well as an aggregate supply function $S(p)$. By assumption, $S(p)$ is increasing and $D(p)$ is decreasing.

Assume there is a p^* such that $S(p^*) = D(p^*)$. If all stores charge the same price, all will experience excess supply or excess demand unless the common price is p^*. (The assumption that search is rational implies that when all stores charge the same price all will have the same number of customers.) Thus, p^* is an equilibrium price. If the market ever gets there, it will stay there. Fisher shows that prices at all stores converge to this equilibrium.

The argument goes roughly as follows: let $p_{\min}$ be the lowest price charged on the market. Then, if the market is not in equilibrium, either the minimum price is less than the equilibrium price,

$$p_{\min} < p^*, \tag{1}$$

or the minimum price is equal to or exceeds the equilibrium price,

$$p_{\min} \geq p^*. \tag{2}$$

It is a consequence of the assumption of rational search that the lowest-price store always has more than its fair share of customers. Thus, if (1) holds, the lowest-price stores experience excess demand and raise their prices. Fisher is able to show that rational search implies that if (2) obtains, stores charging the highest price get less than their proportionate share of buy orders. All such stores face negative excess demand, and all lower their prices. Thus, if the minimum price is less than the equilibrium price, it is raised, and if it is more, the maximum price is lowered. These observations plus some assumptions about velocity and continuity are sufficient to ensure that the price at all stores converges to p^*.

This result is not surprising. The model can converge only to the competitive price as long as each firm sets its output by picking a point on its supply curve. The difficulty is that the behavior rule which firms are supposed to follow—forecast equilibrium price and then produce output to the point where marginal cost equals predicted market price—is not a reasonable rule for the environments this model is supposed to describe. Unless convergence to equilibrium is terribly speedy, firms will notice that their forecasts of market prices are often incorrect. The consequences of this failure to predict correctly are lost sales when price is underpredicted (and the firm experiences excess demand) and unsold stocks[5] when it is overestimated. Fisher's suggestion that the firm will pick its quantity without considering this possible loss is unreasonable. There is a large literature on the effect of demand uncertainty on the firm summarized in Baron (1970), McCall (1971), and Leland (1972). Although the different models studied lead to an embarrassing diversity of conclusions, they agree on the basic proposition that uncertainty does affect firm decisions and thus short-run industry equilibrium.

That firms in Fisher's model can hardly fail to notice that they have market power raises a more serious problem. Firms will observe that customers walk into their stores, ask the price, and walk out without buying. Although several explanations of this phenomenon may be possible, surely the most compelling is that the customers who inquire but do not buy would have bought had they faced a lower price. When a firm observes that it is able to sell some but not all of the product it wishes and reasons that some customers would have been willing to buy had the price been lower, it is hard for it to avoid drawing the conclusion that it faces a demand curve—at least in the short run. What the firm's optimal rule should be in such a circumstance—or even what a reasonable rule is—is a difficult problem. However, it does not seem reasonable that the firm should go on pretending it is a helpless actor in a perfectly competitive market.

This analysis of Fisher's model leads to interesting, important, and difficult questions. It is a formidable task to design decision rules appropriate for dynamic, uncertain, and at least momentarily imperfectly competitive situations. To show that a model with actors following such rules converges to some sort of equilibrium is still harder. Even when this has been done, the question nags of what sort of equilibrium such a model *should* have. Will the temporary monopoly power be dissipated or will it remain? We can put this question slightly differently. More than a decade ago Arrow (1958) observed that markets out of equilibrium are imperfect

[5] It is most consistent with the spirit of the model to assume that the good in question is perishable, so that the firm which produces more than it sells loses the cost of this production. Presumably, the same results would hold if there were a possibility of, and a cost to, holding inventories.

markets. By what mechanism, if any, is market power eroded as equilibrium is approached?[6]

Sidney Winter (1971*a*, 1971*b*) has given a partial answer to these questions in two provocative papers. His answer is roughly that, if firms satisfice (rather than optimize), competitive equilibrium will result; market power not consciously sought and vigorously protected will fade away. Winter's models emphasize that it is the competitive process and not competitive behavior per se that is responsible for the benefits of competition.

The model of Winter's most relevant to this paper is a markup model (1971*b*).[7] In each period firms set two parameters: their capacity and their price—considered as a markup on the constant average variable cost at which output can be produced. In each period customers search (probabilistically) for firms.[8] The result of this search is, in each period, a demand for the firm's products. This determines the firm's sales and thus both its utilization rate and its gross profit per unit of installed capacity. Winter assumes that firms in the industry establish desired ranges for both the profit ratio and capacity utilization. (Too little capacity is excess supply; too much is excess demand. Too little profits suggest that something should be done to improve the rate of return. Extraordinary profits may suggest expansion.) If the market activity results in satisfactory values for these variables, firms will not change their markup or their capacity. If they are unsatisfactory, they may change them by, for example, increasing the markup and cutting capacity in the face of a small demand. Firms do not optimize. Instead, they respond to "unsatisfactory" results by changing their markup and size in random (but somewhat restricted) ways.

[6] An interesting paper of Phelps and Winter (1970) presumes, but does not supply, an answer to this question. They study a market in which a firm may in the short run charge more than the market price without losing all its customers instantaneously. They assume that a firm will, if it finds itself with a price above the market price, want to adjust its price to the market price and study the optimal adjustment path. They do establish conditions which guarantee that it is optimal for each individual firm to adjust its price to the equilibrium price (given that all other firms are already there) rather than run down its goodwill by keeping its price above the equilibrium price. They do not devote much attention to the question of how equilibrium is established for the market as a whole. They do not answer the question of how the other firms got to equilibrium, nor is their discussion of what determines the industry equilibrium price anything but casual. However, their results seem to imply that equilibrium once attained is stable in the sense that, once the market arrives there, it is not in any firm's interest to deviate from the equilibrium price. A similar, but simpler, model of my own which examines this problem is discussed in the next section.

[7] Winter's other earlier paper (1971*a*) applies the same technique to the question of choice of technique. Winter's papers significantly expand the class of models available to economic theorists.

[8] Winter puts weak restrictions on the consumer search process. They are rather similar to Fisher's rationality-of-search assumptions.

An important part of Winter's model is the possibility of entry. Firms not in the market may decide to enter if it appears that a satisfactory profit can be made. If their price is lower than the price of firms already in the market, they may succeed in getting customers and thus in making a successful entry.

Winter analyzes a finite (all relevant variables—prices, capacity, and demand—are allowed to take on only a finite number of values) version of the model set out above and shows that it generates a finite Markov process whose persistent states are (under certain regularity conditions) characterized by all firms (actually in the market) making satisfactory profits and observing desirable levels of capacity utilization. In these absorbing states, all firms have the same markup factor (which is, of course, set low enough that no firm out of the market desires to enter). The markup rate which discourages entry most plausibly corresponds (at a desirable utilization rate) to the profit rate which could be earned in other industries. Thus, Winter's result states that the market behavior of satisficing entrepreneurs converges to the competitive equilibrium with probability 1.

What distinguishes this model from the standard textbook story of exit and entry is that firms are not presumed to optimize anything. A firm reacts to unsatisfactory market experience by choosing a new market strategy at random. To do so requires no information (or at least no accurate information) about its cost and demand functions. Similarly, a strong competitive spirit is not required. (In Winter's model, firms may react to "unsatisfactory" performance by standing pat.) All that seems to be required for convergence to the competitive equilibrium is the possibility that some poor fool may stumble, quite inadvertently, into a competitive posture. Whether this result can hold if price setters are less lackadaisical is not clear.[9] The models of the next section will suggest it cannot, or at least it cannot if store owners are aware of and try to take advantage of their customers' ignorance.

IV

In this section I discuss two models of markets in which firms are aware of the difficulties their customers have in obtaining information and exploiting the market power it gives them. These models differ in two

[9] Another difficulty with Winter's model should be mentioned. Stability of equilibrium depends crucially on no one upsetting the applecart. It is hardly consonant with the spirit of the model to assume that firms contemplating entry are so well informed and so rational that they will never launch an enterprise when there is no chance for success. Yet Winter's result depends crucially on this assumption. If entry can occur at any time, the model will have a stochastic equilibrium similar to that of the model of Green and Majumdar (1972), which is outlined in Section V below.

respects. The first, due to Peter Diamond (1971), does not allow for any competition among firms. It does, however, contain a demonstration of convergence to equilibrium. In the second model, my own, firms do compete with each other. However, in this model, equilibrium is merely characterized and no convergence results are available.

Diamond's model of price adjustment is similar to Fisher's in that consumers search for bargains on a market where prices are known imperfectly. It differs from Fisher's model in two important respects. First, customer search is not rational. Second, firms do not behave as they would in a perfect market. Instead, they act as rational profit maximizers with a complete knowledge of the environment in which they behave. The details of the model follow.

Customers search and they visit but one store each period. At each store they visit, they decide whether to buy or not to buy depending on the price they observe. If they buy, they buy according to the demand function $D(p)$.

Search is not rational in that the store at which each customer shops is chosen at random. In this model there is no customer loyalty; stores have no incentives to acquire (or to avoid) price reputations. It is assumed that there are enough customers that the law of large numbers guarantees that during a single period each store hosts the same number and type of customers.[10] An immediate consequence of this assumption is that firms face the same demand function and solve the same optimization problem.[11] Thus, in each period there is but one price, p_t, quoted in the market.

Customers are not so homogeneous. Although all customers have the same demand function, they differ as to their reservation prices. Reservation prices of customers depend on (*a*) their type, indexed h, and (*b*) the length of time they have been in the market (since it is assumed that customers, if they have not been able to buy at their reservation price, stay in the market and try again). Thus, $q_t^{h\tau}$ is the reservation price of a consumer of type h at time t who entered the market at time τ.

Reservation prices of consumers who have been in the market but failed to buy are assumed to rise over time (that is, $q_{t+1}^{h\tau} > q_t^{h\tau}$) due to increasing costs of search and changed expectations.

The dynamics of the reservation prices of consumers who enter the market for the first time, the q_t^{ht}s, are more complex. Suppose it were known that the price which would prevail from time $t + 1$ onward was p. Then, because of search costs, any customer in the market at time t would be willing to buy at a price slightly higher than p. The price at which he would be willing to buy depends on his type h and is denoted $q^{*h}(p)$. For

[10] This assumption is not strictly necessary; identical conclusions follow if the number of customers is small but stores are concerned with expected rather than actual profits.

[11] Assuming, as Diamond does, that firms have identical cost functions.

all h and p it is assumed that $q^{*h}(p) > p + \varepsilon$ for some $\varepsilon > 0$. Diamond's assumption is that customers of type h entering the market at time $t + 1$ adjust their reservation prices from q_t^{ht} toward $q^{*h}(p_t)$. That is,

$$q_{t+1}^{ht+1} - q^{*h}(p_t) < q_t^{ht} - q^{*h}(p_t).$$

The justification for this is, roughly, that the q_t^{ht} must be based in part on a forecast of future prices and that the observation of p_t alters the forecast toward p_t—as will happen, for instance, when future expected prices are weighted averages of past observed prices—and thus the reservation price, q_{t+1}^{ht+1}, toward $q^{*h}(p_t)$. From these observations, it is easy to see that if p_t is constant at p for a long time, then $q_t^{ht} = q^{*h}(p) > p + \varepsilon$ for all h.

It is now straightforward to write down the demand functions each firm faces. If n is the number of stores in the market and if $N^t(p)$ is the number of customers in the market at time t with reservation price less than or equal to p, then $(1/n)N^t(p)$ is the number of such customers who will shop at each store in period t. The demand function of each store is thus $(1/n)N^t(p)D(p)$, and if it has costs of c its short-run profits will be

$$f_t(p) = (1/n)N^t(p)D(p)(p - c).$$

Diamond assumes that firms know their demand curves and, since they have no good will, act to maximize short-run profits, $f_t(p)$.[12] An immediate consequence is that the only stable equilibrium price is p^*, the monopoly price which maximizes $D(p)(p - c)$. To see this, suppose p_t were constant at $\bar{p}$ for a long time. It would then be possible to raise p above $\bar{p}$ without, in the short run, losing any customers. That is, there is an $\varepsilon > 0$ such that

$$N(\bar{p} - \varepsilon) = N(\bar{p}) = N(\bar{p} + \varepsilon),$$

and the equilibrium price therefore must have the property that

$$(\bar{p} - c - \varepsilon)D(\bar{p} - \varepsilon) < (\bar{p} - c)D(\bar{p}) > (\bar{p} - c + \varepsilon)D(\bar{p} + \varepsilon).$$

If we assume, as Diamond does, that $D(p)(p - c)$ has a unique local and global maximum p^*, then $\bar{p} = p^*$ is the only equilibrium. Diamond shows that, given a few more assumptions, p_t converges to p^* in finite time. I will not discuss the details of this argument.

The result follows quite naturally from the assumptions of the model. It is not by itself terribly surprising, but it does stand in somewhat awesome contrast to Fisher's (and Winter's) demonstration of convergence to the competitive price in a similar market. Fisher's and Diamond's models differ in two important respects: Fisher's consumers search rationally and Diamond's do not; Diamond's firms try to take advantage of their customer's ignorance while Fisher's do not. A natural question to ask is:

[12] It might be optimal for firms to set prices high so as to raise their customers' next-period reservation prices. Diamond ignores this possibility.

What happens if the other possibilities are examined? In particular, what sort of equilibrium will occur in a market where rational consumers are imperfectly informed of the prices of knowledgeable, profit-maximizing firms? Work has been done on this problem by Selten (1965, 1968, 1970), Phelps and Winter (1970), and myself (Rothschild 1970). I would like to discuss my own model for the simple reason that I find it somewhat easier to understand than those which preceded it.

The market consists of n identical stores. At period t the price at the jth stores is $p_j(t)$. Each customer has the same time invariant[13] demand function $D(p)$. It costs a constant amount, c, to produce a unit of output. Thus, a store which charges a price of p makes a profit of

$$f(p) = D(p)(p - c)$$

from each of its customers. Let $x_j(t)$ be the fraction[14] of consumers who bought at store j in period t. The vector of allocations of consumers is written $X(t) = [x_1(t), \ldots, x_n(t)]$. I assume that $\sum x_j(t) = 1$ or that each customer buys from one store in each period.

The most important feature of the model is its description of the dynamics of customer flow.[15] I argue that consumers move from store to store according to the following rules:

$$x_i(t) = \sum_j b_{ij}[P(t)]x_j(t - 1),$$

or, in matrix form,

$$X(t) = B[P(t)]X(t - 1).$$

We may interpret b_{ij} as the probability that a customer of j's last period will end up as a customer of i this period. Since we are assuming a large number of consumers, b_{ij} is the fraction of j's last-period customers who are i's customers this period. Two aspects of this specification are important. First, customer movement from store to store is a random process depending on the outcome of search activities. Second, this random process is a function both of prices at the various stores in the market and of the store at which the customer purchased last time. Customers who were at different stores in the previous period follow different search procedures.

This specification is quite general. It clearly can cover much of what could be meant by rational search. If, for example, b_{ij} is a decreasing function of p_i and an increasing function of p_j, then consumers can be said

[13] The good traded on this market is a nondurable, like milk.

[14] Technical considerations make it convenient to assume that there are as many consumers—each very small—as there are points in the unit interval. Thus, $x_j(t)$ may assume any value between 0 and 1.

[15] Telser (1962) developed a similar model and used it to analyze brand loyalty.

to respond rationally to price changes. I found it necessary to impose only one serious restriction on the transition matrix B—that it be strictly positive. This strong assumption means that whatever the price differential between two stores, there is some positive probability that a customer of one will become a customer of the other. The justification for this specification is that it is a convenient way to model the flow of consumers through the market. It is reasonable to assume that in each period some consumers die or move away and are replaced (as they must be if the consumer population is to remain constant) by new consumers. These new entrants have no previous market experience and may, I assume, in their first period in the market end up at any store with some finite probability. Technically there is no difference between the move of a customer from store j to store i and the death of a customer of store j occurring at the same time as a new customer shops at store i.

What price could possibly be an equilibrium price in this market if stores both understand the structure of the model and compete with one another? A satisfactory answer requires a good, reasonable theory of oligopoly. Since none exists, I had to make do with the traditional concept of a Nash equilibrium for a noncooperative game.[16] I asked if there were a single price p^* which has the property that if all stores but one were to charge it forever, the remaining store would maximize its profits by also charging p^*. It turns out to be possible to show that p^* exists and to examine its properties for fairly general examples. I have shown that p^* is less than the monopoly price p_m and greater than the competitive price $p_c(=c)$. It is also possible to construct examples in which n, the number of stores in the market, is a parameter. As n increases, p^* decreases, but it will in many plausible cases remain bounded above the competitive price as the number of stores become infinite.[17] This model thus provides support for the notion that if there is some consumer ignorance, stores which try to exploit it will succeed even if they compete with one another. Phrased somewhat loosely, this result shows that perfect competition will not protect the imperfect consumer.

There are a number of difficulties with this model. Perhaps the most serious is that all that has been shown is that equilibrium exists. Since the equilibrium concept used has so little to recommend it, a proof of convergence would be very desirable. Another difficulty is that informational requirements of the model seem quite unreasonable. It is hard to imagine

[16] Some interesting work is being done on this problem (see Friedman [1971*a*, 1971*b*] and Marschak and Selten [1971]). The most attractive generalization of the Cournot or Nash equilibrium concept is Sobel's theory of stochastic games (1971, in press). For an application to oligopoly, see Kirman and Sobel (1972).

[17] If there are decreasing costs, as there would be if there were a fixed cost to operating a store, then the equilibrium price and the number of stores are determined by a zero-profit condition. This is an example of Chamberlin's large-group equilibrium.

that stores would ever come to know exactly how the transition matrix B depends on the prices of all stores. We examine in the next section a model in which stores both behave rationally and have a reasonable amount of information. Unfortunately, in that model all awareness of direct competition among stores disappears. It would be interesting to have a model which incorporated elements of oligopolistic competition and reasonable specifications of what stores actually know.

V

The conclusions, if not the workings, of the models so far surveyed are as familiar to economists as they are distant from the real world. The equilibrium of all the imaginary markets we have examined is a single unchanging price. Variety and volatility of prices, the commonplaces of our experience which led Stigler to formulate his original model, disappear from the scene once equilibrium has been established. This is unfortunate, since these phenomena do not seem to be disappearing from the world. If our theories are going to apply to situations in which distributions of prices persist, we are going to have to develop broader equilibrium concepts. There seem to be basically two ways to do this. The first is to argue that, since the world is continually changing and the markets in it are subject to continuous random shocks, equilibrium can only be some sort of statistical regularity. Green and Majumdar (1972) have taken this approach and established the existence of stochastic equilibria in markets buffeted by exogenous disturbances. The second approach involves finding endogenous reasons for perpetual price variability. Menahem Yaari and I have tried to do this. We examined a market in which customers and stores are not aware of the exact nature of their economic environment and never find it profitable to become perfectly informed. Persistent ignorance supports a distribution of prices.

Green and Majumdar (1972) consider an exchange economy[18] in which the amount each individual demands is a function both of prices and of a random variable. One justification for this specification is that tastes vary randomly (as in the models analyzed by Hildenbrand [1971]); but of course, it fits a wide variety of other situations in which the economy is subject to random shocks of all sorts. Adding up individual demand functions, we obtain an aggregate random excess demand function, $D(P, x)$.[19] The random variable X has a distribution function $F(\cdot)$ which summarizes the random shocks to which the economy is subject.

The second building block of the model is a function which adjusts prices in response to excess demand. History in this model unfolds in the

[18] The model and the equilibrium concept fit more general situations (see below).

[19] D and P vectors; x is a particular value of the random variable X.

following way: An arbitrary initial price vector, P_1, is chosen. Nature chooses a value, x, of the random variable according to the distribution $F(\cdot)$, so that in the first period excess demand is $D(P_1, x_1)$. The adjustment mechanism operates to produce $P_2 = A[D(P_1, x_1), P_1]$. Nature chooses another value of X (equal to x_2), and the excess demand function and adjustment function together produce $P_3 = A(D[P_2, x_2), P_2]$, and so on. After the first period, each period's price, P_t, is a random variable with a distribution function $G_t(\cdot)$. Green and Majumdar show that (under quite strong regularity conditions) the distribution functions $G_t(\cdot)$ converge (weakly) to a single equilibrium distribution $G(\cdot)$ independent of the initial price P_1. This most interesting and impressive result[20] makes it possible to speak of equilibrium in economies which receive random (but regular) disturbances.

The major difficulty with this analysis lies in the crucial role played by the adjustment function. This paper began with a discussion of the inadequacies of general equilibrium models of adjustment processes which describe the behavior of no market participants. The Green-Majumdar model is in that tradition. Fortunately, they have shown that their concepts may be applied to analysis of individual markets in which the responsibility for price setting is clearly located with actual market participants. Determining whether their result holds for such a market is then simply a matter of determining whether the adjustment process in that market satisfies the regularity conditions needed to make the convergence proof go through. They have established that there is a class of rules which, if price setters follow them, will lead to stochastic equilibrium. They do not indicate why price setters should want to behave this way, and I suspect that this will be hard to do. To ensure convergence to a stationary equilibrium, sellers must change their prices according to a rule which, *if the economy were not subject to random shock*, would lead to convergence to an equilibrium. Whether such rules can be shown to be optimal, or even reasonable, when the economy *is* subject to random shock is an open, and very difficult, question.

Price variability arises in the model of Rothschild and Yaari for quite different reasons.[21] Consider the problem faced by a store trying to price a particular item in its inventory. If it knows the demand function of its customers, it will at worst have to solve a technically rather messy optimization problem. If the store does not know how its potential customers will react to the different prices it might charge (a long-winded

[20] The simplicity with which a surprising theorem can be stated is often a good index of the difficulty of establishing it. This is a case in point. It is also an illustration of the payoff to be gleaned from an investment in advanced mathematical techniques.

[21] The actual model analyzed is somewhat complex. It and the results presented here are described in the Appendix and in Rothschild (1971). Mirman and Porter (1971) have developed a similar model.

way of saying it does not know its demand function), its problem is much more difficult. That these difficulties are in general ignored by economic theory does not render them any more tractable. One obvious way of determining its demand function is simply to charge various prices and observe the result. How efficient this process is likely to be depends on how the market in question operates. If it is the perfect market of our textbooks, then the firm's only problem is to discover what the market price is. Since it will have no customers if its price is above the market price, and all customers if its price is below the market price, discovering the market price should pose no great difficulties. However, if the market is one in which consumers get price quotes for purely informational purposes and continually search for bargains, a store will find the empirical determination of its demand function a much more arduous task.

In such a market the result of charging a particular price is a random variable which, although it gives the store information as to what its demand function is, does not settle the issue. Unless the demand function is known to be of a particularly simple parametric sort, the information to be expected from charging different prices is likely to vary in quality and scope. This means that the answer to the question "What price should I charge to most increase my knowledge of my demand function?" is likely to be different from the answer to the question "What price should I charge to maximize expected profits, given what I know now?" Yaari and I analyzed a model in which stores face this dilemma. Our conclusions will surprise no one who is aware of the contempt with which businessmen and intellectuals regard one another. It does not pay for firms to be curious; optimal strategy does not entail knowing their demand function with certainty. Therefore, following the optimal strategy carries with it, of course, the possibility of making a mistake. We were able to show that a firm which follows this strategy will, in the course of its history, with positive probability charge the wrong price infinitely often and the correct price only a finite number of times. If there are many firms, then some of them will charge some prices and some others. In other words, price variability will persist.[22]

When matched with a fairly general model of customer behavior, this model of firm behavior produces an example of a market in which a distribution of prices persists in equilibrium for essentially endogenous reasons. There are two important problems with this model. The first is

[22] One might ask whether stores that are charging incorrect prices cannot simply observe that other stores charging other prices are making more profits and thus change to the most profitable price. The answer to this objection is that stores are not privy to the results of other stores' experiences. They may observe that other stores are charging different prices, but they will not, in general, find out how well those other stores are doing. The only conclusion I can draw from your doing something different from me is that you and I have had different experiences. Who is to say whose experience is a better guide to the true state of the market?

that the model of customer behavior does not at present—and perhaps cannot—encompass any but the most rudimentary aspects of brand loyalty. A somewhat related deficiency is that in this model stores do not conceive of competing with one another and in fact are not aware of one another's existence in any nontrivial way.

VI

The theme of the last three sections might be stated as follows: What equilibrium is in a particular market depends on what individuals in that market know. That the converse is true—that is, that what people know (or believe) is a function of the equilibria of the markets in which they participate—is an observation which surely must precede Marx. This section reports on some modern developments of this theme which emerge from Spence's (1972) examination of what he calls informational equilibria in labor markets. Spence's ideas are best communicated by example. Imagine a world in which there are equal numbers of two kinds of workers. Those of type A have a real annual marginal product of 1, while the marginal product of B workers is 2. The working life of each laborer is 1 year. Workers are hired for a year at a time; wages are agreed upon before work begins. If the employer could tell by observation whether a worker was of type A or type B, then he would know whether to offer him a wage of 1 or 2 (the market for labor is assumed perfectly competitive; workers are paid their marginal products). If there is no way of knowing to what class a worker belongs before the wage bargain is struck, then the employer will pay him his expected marginal product, 1.5.

Suppose that the employer cannot differentiate between workers. A worker's type is determined by an intrinsically unobservable characteristic which we shall call ability. Although an individual worker knows his own ability, an employer would be ill-advised to accept a prospective employee's description of his quality. Employees have no incentive to tell the truth; they would all assert that they were of type B if asked. If no more information is available to employers than job seekers' self-evaluations, then the market will have an equilibrium in which all employees get paid 1.5.

Suppose that employees can invest in certification. In particular, suppose there is a good that workers may purchase which has the property that it is cheaper for B workers to buy than A workers. Let us call this good education. Assume that B workers can complete a given number of credits at less expense than A workers. The reason for this might be that education is more expensive to the less able because they must buy extra tutoring if they are to complete courses satisfactorily. We shall suppose for simplicity that for an A worker to acquire a given amount, E, of education costs aE

while the cost of the same amount of education for a B worker is bE, where $a > b$.

Since education, unlike ability, is observable, employers might decide that it was correlated with ability. They might adopt policies of paying people according to the amount of education they had acquired. Suppose they adopted the simple policy of paying workers 2 if they had $\bar{E}$ units of education or more and 1 if they had less education than $\bar{E}$. What would workers do if they were aware of this hiring rule? Clearly, workers of type A would buy $\bar{E}$ units of education if its cost $a\bar{E}$ were less than the wage gains to be had from being more educated, or if $a\bar{E} < 1$. Similarly, B workers will purchase the requisite amount of education if $bE < 1$. Therefore, if $\bar{E}$ is any number such that $b < 1/\bar{E} < a$, all type B workers will fulfill the educational requirements for higher-paying jobs and no type A workers will choose to go to school. Employers will find that their expectations about the benefits of education are fulfilled; more educated workers really are more productive. Workers will find their investments in education worthwhile. The market is in equilibrium.

Three characteristics of this equilibrium are noteworthy. First, it is essentially arbitrary. Any educational requirement satisfying $a < 1/\bar{E} < b$ will generate a sequence of self-fulfilling expectations and action. The equilibrium determines what people think they know about the benefits of education.

Other interesting aspects of the equilibrium flow from the fact that education does not, by assumption, raise workers' marginal productivity. It only allows workers to be differentiated. In this model education has no social return although it does have a large private return. Attempts to infer the former from the latter will result in error.

Finally, most equilibria are not, from a social point of view, desirable. Individual investments in education decrease rather than increase net income. From a narrow point of view an equilibrium which encourages any positive investment in education is not Pareto optimal. Even if it is felt that educational screening is desirable because individuals, for reasons of justice rather than efficiency, ought to be paid according to their ability, nothing guarantees that the educational requirements will be set so that this discrimination is accomplished at least cost. Any educational requirement, $\bar{E}$, which exceeds b^{-1} is inefficient.

Education is an example of what Spence calls a signal. It is something which people can acquire to make them appear desirable. A little reflection will convince that signaling phenomena are pervasive. Spence has examined a number of much more complicated examples of signaling and informational equilibria. The conclusions of this simple example seem to be quite robust. Multiple equilibria occur everywhere. Private and social returns to investment in characteristics which are signals diverge (even when signals have real social returns). Equilibria are not optimal.

VII

This paper began with visions of the promised land of rigorous realistic theory relevant both for practical policy and for the most revered intellectual traditions of the profession. Those who have read through the preceding catalog of models and results will be only too conscious that much remains to be done before we leave the desert of illogical and irrelevant theory. Still, I think we have come a fair distance and that what remains to be done seems both clear and feasible.

By now it should be clear that it is possible to build logically consistent models of markets which depart in one way or another from the classical standards of perfection. In some ways it is almost too easy. The number and variety of different models make it hard to draw any firm conclusions about the consequences of different types of market failure, and it is, after all, conclusions of this sort which will make the game worth the candle. Results are likely to come from two kinds of work: systematic taxonomy and analysis of the restraints imposed by equilibrium. I have made some attempt at both in this paper. I argued that models of markets whose participants have imperfect information do not make sense unless the behavior of all sides of the market are modeled and the resulting activity is in some sense an equilibrium, and then went on to classify models according to the type of equilibrium they exhibit. Further progress in these directions is possible. If we are to find out what causes what, a classification of models by their conclusions is of only limited use. Although a general catalog of the different sorts of failures of information and their consequences seems premature, systematic classification in clearly defined areas where the principles of taxonomy are clear should lead to interesting results. For example, Diamond (1972) has suggested that the effects of different ways of structuring rules for product liability depend crucially on what it is assumed buyers know about sellers and sellers know about buyers.

Similarly, the concepts of equilibrium which I used were both catholic and weak. Sharper concepts should yield stronger results. An example of what can be done is Stiglitz's (1972) extension of the models of educational certification and labor force allocation described in the preceding section. He asked the natural question, which of the variety of possible systems of educational requirements for jobs and fees for education are viable given that the educational system must pay its own way either economically or politically?

A return to some of the traditional preoccupations of economic theory will probably lead to a richer understanding of the nature and consequences of market imperfections. Efficiency and welfare, the central concern of most microeconomic theory, have played only a minor role in the models of the preceding sections. The aim of most theorists has been descriptive; although some models lead naturally to remarks about welfare, these seem more casual than central. Now that we have some idea of the different ways that imperfect markets operate, we can hope to develop standards of efficiency and equity and to begin to ask what sorts of institutional arrangements seem to operate most effectively in the face of imperfect information.

Appendix

In this Appendix I set forth in somewhat more detail the model and results of Rothschild and Yaari discussed in Section V. A more complete exposition is in Rothschild (1971). In Part A store behavior is described. In Part B what consumers do is specified and the resulting equilibrium described.

A. Consider a store which is trying to price a particular item in its inventory. Potential customers arrive at a constant rate—which we may take to be 1 per period by an appropriate choice of units—unaffected by the price the store is charging.[23] Customers are ignorant of the price of the item in question. They enter the store, ask what the price is, and then either buy or leave the store. From the point of view of the store, each potential customer is a binomial random variable which will buy 1 unit with probability $\Pi(p)$ and not buy with probability $1 - \Pi(p)$. The probability $\Pi(p)$ is a function of the price quoted to the customer. If this function were known, the store would in each period simply choose p to maximize expected profits, $\Pi(p)(p - c)$, where c is the constant cost of the item to the store owner. However, if the store does not know the function $\Pi(p)$, which in this model is all that not knowing the demand function of its customers could mean, then what it should do is not so straightforward.

We can simplify the store owner's problem considerably by assuming that prices must be chosen from a finite set, indexed by i. If the store charges price p_i, then the true probability of a sale is Π_i. Again, if the store knew the parameters Π_i, it would simply choose i to maximize $\Pi_i q_i$, where $q_i = p_i - c$, the profit from making a sale at price p_i, but since the store does not, by assumption, know the values of the Π_i, its problem is more complex. However, the store can, if it chooses to, learn the value of any particular parameter Π_i, for Π_i is simply the probability of success in a single binomial trial. If the trials are repeated infinitely often, an observer will, according to the strong law of large numbers, be able to estimate Π_i exactly (that is, with probability 1). The store could come to learn all the probabilities Π_i simply by choosing a strategy which involved charging each of the prices an infinite number of times—as, for instance, by playing them in turn. We were able to show that such asymptotically perfect information strategies

[23] The assumption that price has no influence on customer flow is an obviously limiting assumption and is in general not correct. Still, it is not an unreasonable assumption for some markets and some stores. Consider, for example, markets where repeat business cannot be expected either because customers buy the item in question so rarely that their trips to the store are separated by long periods of time, during which the price policies of particular stores are largely forgotten, or because customers are transients unlikely to return to the store under any circumstances. Examples are cosmetic counters in airports and refrigerator dealers. Another class of enterprises to which our model might apply is the store that sells many items. Although customer flow does depend on its overall price reputation, the pricing of a particular item will—within a range of possible prices—not affect this. Examples are supermarkets or department stores.

are not optimal; as a consequence, different store owners can continue to hold different beliefs about the nature of market demand. Persistent price variability results.

The problem faced by the store owner is one of a class of problems studied by statisticians and probabilists under the general heading "two-armed-bandit" problems. Consider a gambler condemned to, or bent on, putting a quarter into one of several (by convention the number is usually two) slot machines (one-armed bandits) from now on until the end of time. The *i*th machine gives a payoff of q_i with probability Π_i and nothing with probability $1 - \Pi_i$. He wants to choose a strategy which will maximize his expected discounted earnings or (to put the problem more realistically) minimize his expected discounted losses. If he knew how the two machines were set, he would achieve his goal simply by selecting the most favorable machine. However, it is assumed that, although he may have prior beliefs, the man does not know which machine offers the most favorable odds. The gambler's dilemma is formally identical to that of the store owner trying to decide what price to charge. (Prices are slot machines, payoffs are profits from sales, etc.) Looking at the model this way allows us to take advantage of the insights of those who have studied two-armed-bandit problems, in particular Bellman (1956). In the language of the two-armed-bandit problem, our result states that if the discount rate is positive, the optimal policy may lead the person who follows it to play an objectively less favorable slot machine infinitely often while the most favorable machine is played but a finite number of times.

Although the proof of this proposition is somewhat lengthy and will not be given here, a simple heuristic argument shows why it should be true. Consider the two-armed-bandit problem when the probability of a payoff on one of the machines, say the second one, is known with certainty. The state of the player's information is described by his estimate of the probability of a payoff on the first machine. His choice of machine at any point in time is entirely determined by this estimate. When the first machine is played, the gambler receives, in addition to a random payoff, information which allows him to revise his estimate of the probability of a success on a first machine. When he plays the second machine, he receives only a payoff (if he is lucky) or nothing (if he is not). The outcome cannot affect his estimate of the probability of success on the second machine, since it is assumed that this is known with subjective certainty. It also cannot affect his estimate of the probability of a payoff on the first machine. Thus, if the state of the player's information were such that optimal strategy dictated that the second machine be played, it is unchanged after the second machine has been played and will lead it to be played again. If the machine whose payoff probability is known is ever played, it will be played forever. Thus, the optimal policy is in the form of a stopping rule. It is an answer to the question, When is information on the unknown arm so disappointing that play on it should be suspended? This question has an answer. There is a finite sequence of results on the unknown arm so discouraging that the rational gambler will abandon experimentation and play the known arm only. Even if the unknown arm is objectively better than the known arm, the gambler may observe such a sequence and thus play the unknown, but superior, device a finite number of times and the known but inferior device an infinite number of times.

B. Consider a consumer in a market for a good which can have only one of J possible prices. In this market, prices at particular stores are unknown; low prices can only be discovered by undertaking a random search. We may describe a consumer's state in any period by a $(J + 2)$-tuple. Its first J entries describe the consumer's market history—the number of times the consumer has observed each price. The next entry is the consumer's age. The last is a parameter registering the strength of the consumer's demand.[24] (For example, if the market is for refrigerators, this parameter might indicate the quality of the appliance he presently owns.) We assume, without specifying the rule, that consumers in a particular state will elect particular market strategies—to shop or not to shop, what reservation price to set, how many stores to visit, and the like. How consumers choose their strategies is unimportant; their choices may be optimal, merely not obviously stupid, or plainly dumb. All we care is that they, and thus the market behavior that stores observe, be uniquely determined by their state. The distribution of customers among states determines the distribution of reservation prices that stores observe in that period.

The consumer's states change from period to period in the obvious way. If he shops, his market experience is updated; the parameter indicating his demand changes randomly (as, for instance, if his present refrigerator deteriorates further or is replaced by a new one bought last period). Finally he gets older. We assume that as he reaches a certain age[25] he dies and is replaced by a young consumer with no market experience. The transitions from state to state are probabilistic and depend basically on the true distribution of prices in the market and the market strategies chosen. We have described a finite-state Markov process. Assuming a large number of customers and identifying probabilities with frequencies, we have shown the existence of a steady-state distribution of reservation prices dependent on the true distribution of prices.

Section A of this Appendix shows how a distribution of store prices dependent on a distribution of reservation prices could be developed. Putting the two together produces a model of a market with an equilibrium distribution of prices. It is not hard to find reasonable assumptions which guarantee that this equilibrium distribution is nondegenerate—that is, that price variability is preserved in equilibrium.

References

Akerlof, George A. "The Market for 'Lemons': Qualitative Uncertainty and the Market Mechanism." *Q.J.E.* 84 (August 1970): 488–500.

Arrow, K. J. "Toward a Theory of Price Adjustment." In *The Allocation of Economic Resources*, edited by P. A. Baran, T. Scitovsky, and E. S. Shaw. Stanford, Calif.: Stanford Univ. Press, 1958.

———. "Some Models of Racial Discrimination in the Labor Market." In *Racial Discrimination in American Life*, edited by A. Pascal. Lexington, Mass.: Heath-Lexington, 1972.

Arrow, K. J., and Hahn, F. *General Competitive Analysis*. San Francisco: Holden-Day, 1971.

Baron, David P. "Price Uncertainty, Utility, and Industry Equilibrium in Pure Competition." *Internat. Econ. Rev.* 11 (October 1970): 463–80.

Bellman, R. "A Problem in the Sequential Design of Experiments." *Sankhya* 16 (May 1956): 221–29.

Diamond, Peter A. "A Model of Price Adjustment." *J. Econ. Theory* 3 (June 1971): 156–68.

[24] For convenience, we assume that this parameter can take on only a finite number of values.

[25] No difficulty ensues if age at death is random.

———. Personal communication, 1972.

Fisher, F. M. "Quasi-competitive Price Adjustment by Individual Firms: A Preliminary Paper." *J. Econ. Theory* 2 (June 1970): 195–206.

———. "On Price Adjustment without an Auctioneer." *Rev. Econ. Studies* 29 (January 1972): 1–15.

Friedman, James. "A Non-cooperative Equilibrium for Supergames." *Rev. Econ. Studies* 38 (January 1971): 1-12. (*a*).

———. "A Non-cooperative View of Oligopoly." *Internat. Econ. Rev.* 12 (February 1971): 106–22. (*b*).

Gastwirth, Joseph L. "On Probabilistic Models of Consumer Search for Information." Unpublished paper, 1971.

Gepts, S. "Individual Selling Prices in an Exchange Economy." CORE Discussion Paper no. 7107, Catholic Univ., Louvain, 1971.

Green, Jerry R., and Majumdar, Mukul. "The Nature and Existence of Stochastic Equilibria." Unpublished paper, 1972.

Hahn, F. "Some Adjustment Problems." *Econometrica* 38 (January 1970): 1–17.

Hildenbrand, Werner. "Random Preference and Equilibrium Analysis." *J. Econ. Theory* 3 (December 1971): 414–29.

Kirman, Alan, and Sobel, Mathew J. "Dynamic Oligopoly with Inventories." Unpublished paper, 1972.

Leijonhufvud, A. *On Keynesian Economics and the Economics of Keynes*. New York: Oxford Univ. Press, 1968.

Leland, Hayne. "The Theory of the Firm Facing Uncertain Demand." *A.E.R.* 72 (June 1972): 278–91.

Lucas, R. E., and Rapping, L. A. "Real Wages, Employment and Inflation." In *Microeconomic Foundations of Inflation and Employment Theory*, by E. S. Phelps et al. New York: Norton, 1970.

McCall, J. J. "The Economics of Information and Optimal Stopping Rules." *J. Bus.* 38 (July 1965): 300–317.

———. "Economics of Information and Job Search." *Q.J.E.* 84 (February 1970): 113–26.

———. "Probabilistic Microeconomics." *Bell J. Econ. and Management Sci.* 2 (Fall 1971): 403–33.

Marschak, Thomas, and Selten, Reinhard. "General Equilibrium with a Monopolistic Sector: A Non-cooperative Approach." Technical Report no. 4, Collaborative Res. Econ. Systems and Org., Center Res. Management Sci., Univ. California, Berkeley, 1971.

Mirman, Leonard J., and Porter, William R. "A Microeconomic Model of the Labor Market under Uncertainty." Unpublished paper, 1971.

Mortensen, D. T. "A Theory of Wage and Employment Dynamics." In *Microeconomic Foundations of Inflation and Employment Theory*, by E. S. Phelps et al. New York: Norton, 1970. (*a*).

———. "Job Search, the Duration of Unemployment and the Phillips Curve." *A.E.R.* 60 (December 1970): 847–62. (*b*).

Negishi, T. "On the Formation of Prices." *Internat. Econ. Rev.* 2 (January 1961): 122–26.

Nelson, Phillip. "Information and Consumer Behavior." *J.P.E.* 78 (March/April 1970): 311–29.

Phelps, E. S. "Money Wage Dynamics and Labor Market Equilibrium." In *Microeconomic Foundations of Inflation and Employment Theory*, by E. S. Phelps et al. New York: Norton, 1970.

Phelps, E. S., and Winter, S. G., Jr. "Optimal Price Policy under Atomistic

Competition." In *Microeconomic Foundations of Inflation and Employment Theory*, by E. S. Phelps et al. New York: Norton, 1970.

Rothschild, M. "Prices Information and Market Structure." Unpublished paper, 1970.

———. "A Two-armed Bandit Theory of Market Pricing." Working Paper no. 10, Math. Soc. Sci. Board Workshop, Univ. California, Berkeley, 1971.

Selten, Reinhard. "Spieltheoretische Behandlung eines Oligopolmodells mit Nachfragetrageheit." *Zeitschrift Gesamte Staatswissenschaft* 121 (April 1965): 301–24.

———. "An Oligopoly Model with Demand Inertia." Working Paper no. 250, Center Res. Management Sci., Univ. California, Berkeley, 1968.

———. *Preispolitik der Mehrproduktenunternehmung in der statischen Theorie*. New York: Springer-Verlag, 1970.

Sobel, Matthew, J. "Non-cooperative Stochastic Games." *Ann. Math. Statis.* 42 (December 1971): 1930–35.

———. "Continuous Stochastic Games." *J. Appl. Probability* (in press).

Spence, M. "Market Signalling." Discussion Paper no. 4, Public Policy Program, Kennedy School of Government, Harvard Univ., 1972.

Stigler, G. "The Economics of Information." *J.P.E.* 69 (June 1961): 213–25.

Stiglitz, J. E. "Education as a Screening Device and the Distribution of Income." Unpublished paper, 1972.

Telser, L. "The Demand for Branded Goods as Estimated from Consumer Panel Data." *Rev. Econ. and Statis.* 44 (August 1962): 300–324.

Uzawa, H. "On the Stability of Edgeworth's Barter Process." *Internat. Econ. Rev.* 2 (May 1962): 218–32.

Winter, S., Jr. "Satisficing, Selection, and the Innovating Remnant." *Q.J.E.* 85 (May 1971): 237–61. (*a*).

———. "An SSIR Model of Markup Pricing." Unpublished paper, 1971. (*b*).

Comment

The two-armed bandit model discussed in the appendix to this paper has since been published.

Three of the authors whose work is discussed at length in the article have since published books on this subject.

Considerable additional work has been done on this topic since this survey; here we cite two studies. Axell (1977) has considered the possibility of a distribution of prices in a model very similar to that of Diamond discussed in the text. He finds necessary and sufficient conditions for the existence of an equilibrium with a price distribution. There are two conditions involved. One is that the distribution of individual search costs not be bounded away from zero. The second is an inequality constraint on that distribution, which requires a large part of the population to have very low search costs.

In a sequential model, Smallwood and Conlisk (1979) have considered consumers who switch to other products when they have purchased one that is defective. For different switching rules by consumers they examine the asymptotic distribution of purchasers across products in the market.

References

B. Axell, Search market equilibrium, *Scandinavian J. Econ.* **79** (1977), 20–40.

P. Diamond, "A Search-Equilibrium Approach to the Micro Foundations of Macroeconomics," Cambridge: MIT Press, 1984.

F. Fisher, "Disequilibrium Foundations of Equilibrium Economics," Cambridge: Cambridge University Press, 1983.

R. Nelson and S. G. Winter, "An Evolutionary Theory of Economic Change," Cambridge, Mass.: The Belknap Press of Harvard University Press, 1982.

M. Rothschild, A two-armed bandit theory of market pricing, *J. Econ. Theory* **9** (1974), 185–202.

D. E. Smallwood and J. Conlisk, Product quality in markets where consumers are imperfectly informed, *Quar. J. Econ.* **93** (1979), 1–24.

Exercise on information and prices

A. An Alternative Formulation of Salop and Stiglitz's (1977) Model of Monopolistically Competitive Price Dispersion.

Salop and Stiglitz have considered a model of a market where consumers purchase a single unit of some commodity. A consumer knows the distribution of prices in the market. He has three alternatives: to purchase at a randomly selected store, to pay a fixed charge for information permitting him to purchase at the lowest price store, or to forego purchase of the commodity. All consumers are willing to purchase as long as the cost of purchase does not exceed a uniform maximum u. They assumed that consumers fall into two classes with differing costs of obtaining information for low-price purchases. We shall consider a continuum of costs of information acquisition indexed by c. In addition, we shall modify their assumption on firm perceptions.

Let us consider an equilibrium where some consumers purchase complete information and some do not. If there is free entry, firms will enter offering lower prices unless the price offered to those consumers who have complete information equals the minimum value of the average cost curve (which is assumed to be identical for all firms). Thus, some firms will charge the competitive price p^*, and no firm charging a higher price will have any customers who have bought complete information. (We assume $p^* + c < u$ for some consumers.[1])

Consider a firm selling exclusively to consumers who have not purchased complete information. Such a firm is not the lowest-price firm. If the firm ignores its effect on the number of consumers who purchase information, the firm perceives higher profits at the price u than at any lower price. Since consumers compare the average price with the lowest price in the market in deciding whether to purchase information, this is a reasonable assumption if there are a large number of firms. Thus, in equilibrium there are two prices charged: p^*, the competitive price, and u, the monopoly price. Assume that a fraction of the stores b charge the lower price.

A consumer who purchases information pays c for the information and p^* for the commodity. A consumer who does not purchase information expects to pay $bp^* + (1 - b)u$ for the commodity. If consumers are risk neutral, all consum-

[1]We assume that firms are aware they can induce search by being the lowest-price firm.

ers with costs below c^*, which equates these two values, will purchase complete information. Solving for c^*, we have

$$c^* = (1 - b)(u - p^*) \tag{1}$$

Assume that $F(c)$ is the fraction of consumers with costs less than or equal to c. Then, $F(c^*) + b[1 - F(c^*)]$ of the consumers purchase at the low-price stores as a result of planning or good luck. $(1 - b)[1 - F(c^*)]$ of the consumers purchase at high price stores. Given free entry, there will be just enough stores (charging each price) so that each store will service precisely the number of customers so that it breaks even at the price it is charging.[2] Let us denote by q the ratio of the number of customers handled by a low-price store relative to the number handled by a high-price store in zero profit equilibrium.[3] Assuming U-shaped average costs, q is larger than 1.[4] The ratio of purchases at low-price stores to purchases at high-price stores must equal the ratio of sales at the two prices. Thus, we have a second equilibrium condition

$$\frac{F(c^*) + b[1 - F(c^*)]}{(1 - b)[1 - F(c^*)]} = \frac{bq}{1 - b} \tag{2}$$

Combining the two equations, eliminating alternatively c^* and b, we can give the equilibrium values in terms of the parameters p^*, u, q, and $F(c)$:

$$F[(1 - b)(u - p^*)][1 + b(q - 1)] = b(q - 1) \tag{3}$$
$$(u - p^*)F(c^*) = (u - p^* - c^*)[1 - F(c^*)](q - 1) \tag{4}$$

As long as there is positive weight on values of c below $u - p^*$ there will be a solution to these equations. Given the two equations, it is easy to calculate comparative static derivatives. First, consider looking across markets that differ in just one parameter. Then, the fraction of low-priced stores is increased by a rise in the monopoly price, a fall in the competitive price, a fall in the ratio of sales per store at low and high prices, or a fall in the costs of search. The fraction of the population purchasing complete information is increased by a rise in the monopoly price, a fall in the competitive price, a rise in the ratio of sales per store at the two prices, or a decrease in the cost of purchasing information.

To do comparative statics in a single market, we must recognize that an increase in u will increase q if the average cost curve is unchanged. A parallel upward shift in the average cost curve (and so a rise in p^*) will lower q, if u is unchanged. We can conclude that a rise in u, q adjusting, will increase the fraction

[2]If x_p is the quantity sold by a firm charging price p, then the firm breaks even if the average cost evaluated at the quantity x_p is equal to p.

[3]Thus, q is equal to the ratio of x_{p^*} to x_u, where the average cost at x_{p^*} equals p^* and that at x_u equals u.

[4]The other solution to the equations (with $q < 1$) is not economically interesting since firms could increase profits by refusing to sell to some customers.

of consumers purchasing information. Also, a parallel upward shift in the cost curve, q adjusting, will decrease the fraction purchasing information. The other two derivatives are ambiguous in sign.

Since the decision to purchase information increases the fraction of low-price stores, there is an externality from this decision to consumers who do not purchase information. Thus, the total cost of purchase by all consumers (including information costs) could be decreased by a subsidy on the cost of information (financed by lump sum taxation).

Exercise Prove the propositions in the last three paragraphs.

B. Consumer Differences and Prices in a Search Model

Diamond (1987) has extended his earlier work discussed in this chapter to a model with two classes of consumers with different reservation utilities for the consumer good. For some parameters, in equilibrium there are two different prices. Some stores set their price equal to the lower reservation utility of consumers. Other stores set their price equal to the reservation price of consumers with the higher reservation utility. The numbers of stores of the two types are such that profits are the same whichever of these two pricing policies is followed. This exercise leads you to the equations for equilibrium. You might want to derive these equations without these hints.

Time is measured continuously. For each consumer there is a Poisson process with arrival rate a. The event that arrives is the opportunity to visit one store, chosen at random. Consumers know the distribution of prices and, on observing the price, decide whether to buy one unit of the good. Denote the utilities of consumption by u_i, with $u_1 < u_2$. If price p is paid at time t, utility is $e^{-rt}(u_i - p)$. There are no search costs. There is a continuous unit flow of new consumers into the market. The ratio of those with utilities u_2 to those with utility u_1 is g. For each consumer, there is a second Poisson process with arrival rate b, which terminates search.

Exercise

1. Show that no store sets a price below u_1.

2. Show that if any store charges a price above u_1, all stores charge the same price, which equals the reservation price of the u_2 consumers.

Thus, there can be one-price or two-price equilibria. Assume the latter, with prices $p_1 = u_1$ and p_2, and denote the fraction of low-price stores by f. Assume constant marginal costs c of providing this good.

3. Derive the stocks of consumers of each type when u_1 consumers buy in low-price stores and u_2 consumers in all stores.

4. Derive the equal profit condition for the two pricing strategies.
5. Derive the reservation price of u_2 consumers.
Your answers to (4) and (5) give two equations in two unknowns, f and p_2, which represent an equilibrium provided $0 \leq f \leq 1$.

C. Cost Differences and Prices in a Search Model

Reinganum (1979) has considered the model where all consumers are alike and search sequentially, but firms differ in their (constant) marginal costs of supplying the good. Some firms price at their monopoly prices. If the spread of costs is large enough, other firms price at the reservation price of consumers.

Exercise

Assume no discounting and a constant cost per search. Assume that consumer demand when purchasing has constant elasticity, with a value less than -1. Derive the equation for the reservation price of consumers as a function of the distribution of costs of firms.

D. The Provision of Information by a Monopolist[5]

In the previous section we assumed that consumers had the alternatives of selecting a store at random or purchasing information. We now rule out both of those possibilities. Instead, we assume that the only way a consumer can locate a store is if he is provided with information. In addition, the price is quoted at the same time. In this section we shall examine the quantity of information provided by a monopolist. In the next reading we shall examine the quantity of information that would be provided if the industry were competitive.

Assume that all consumers are alike, with differentiable demand curves $x(p)$. Assume that p^* maximizes profit per customer, $x(p)(p - c)$, where c is the constant marginal cost of providing the product. Assume that it costs b per advertisement by the monopolist and that customers will purchase if and only if they receive advertisements. If n ads are purchased, it is assumed that $F(n)$ customers are reached, with F increasing and concave.

1 Derive the equation describing the number of ads purchased by the monopolist.

[5]This section is based on material developed by A. Dixit in response to a paper by Y. Kotowitz and F. Mathewson. We thank Professor Dixit for allowing us to include it here. For a further discussion of advertising and price setting with imperfect information, see Diamond *op. cit.* For a discussion of advertising that also changes demand curves when consumers purchase, see Dixit and Norman (1978). They conclude that monopolists advertise too much.

The consumer's surplus from being able to purchase at price p is $S(p)$. Following conventional consumer surplus analysis, we assume that $S'(p) = -x(p)$. Assume that the government is interested in maximizing the sum of consumers' surplus and profit.

2 If the price is set at p^*, show that the government would prefer more advertising than is undertaken by the monopolist.

3 If $x(p) = 1$ for $p \leqslant u$ and 0 otherwise, show that the monopolist does the level of advertising that the government would select.

4 Referring to a continuous $x(p)$, what price would the government set if it controlled both prices and the quantity of advertising (and could cover losses in a nondistorting way)?

5 If the government could control the price but could not control the quantity of advertising, would the government select marginal cost pricing, i.e., $p = c$? What is the equation for the price the government would set?

References

P. Diamond, Consumer differences and prices in a search model, *Quart. J. Econ.* **102** (1987), 429–436.

A. Dixit and V. Norman, Advertising and welfare, *Bell J. Econ.* **9** (1978), 1–17.

J. Reinganum, A simple model of equilibrium price dispersion, *J. Political Econ.* **87** (1979), 851–858.

S. Salop and J. Stiglitz, Bargains and ripoffs: A model of monopolistically competitive price dispersion, *Rev. Econ. Stud.* **44** (1977), 493–510.

28

G. Butters, Equilibrium distributions of sales and advertising prices, *Review of Economic Studies* (appendix omitted) Vol. XLIV(3), (1977), 465–491.

We now turn to a competitive market that is similar to the monopoly considered in the previous exercise. The author selects a specific function for the pattern of consumers reached by advertising and analyzes the case where demand is discontinuous at the price u. The reader might want to reconsider the welfare questions raised above in this competitive setting.

Reprinted from THE REVIEW OF ECONOMIC STUDIES, Vol. XLIV (3), October, 1977, GERARD R. BUTTERS, pp. 465-491.

Equilibrium Distributions of Sales and Advertising Prices

GERARD R. BUTTERS
Princeton University

1. INTRODUCTION

Stimulated primarily by Stigler [6], many economists have devoted considerable effort towards the goal of developing and formalizing the analysis of markets which operate with imperfect information. The best-known survey of this work is that of Rothschild [5].[1] He points out that the great bulk of the current work on the economics of information is of the nature of " partial partial equilibrium " analysis; the second " partial " refers to the fact that only one market is considered at a time, while the first refers to the fact that only one side of this market is analysed. For example, Stigler considers the problem of optimal consumer search when the distribution of prices is given and known. To generalize the usual Marshallian partial equilibrium analysis, we must also consider the problem of sellers' behaviour and the joint determination of the price distribution.

Once the problem is formulated in this fashion, many important questions arise. What is an appropriate concept of equilibrium? Under what conditions will equilibrium consist of a non-trivial distribution of prices, as opposed to the classical unique price? What parameters determine the level of prices and the degree of price dispersion? What kind of externalities may arise when consumers search? Can any welfare judgments be made? These questions have all been inadequately treated in the literature.

One difficulty in developing the analysis is that once the problem of information is introduced, one must face the fact that there are many types of markets, varying according to the structures of information flow, the degree of centralization, the homogeneity of the good traded, the types of services provided jointly with the good, the number of actual or potential buyers and sellers, the volatility of parameters affecting supply and demand, the time span of the market, and the geographical location of the market. The interaction of these factors and others is involved in determining price dispersions, and it is not obvious which factors and interactions should be singled out as the building blocks of a model. As a start, it is natural to take one particular market structure as given, and to derive an equilibrium for that market. This approach is certainly not the whole story, however, because the market structure itself is endogenous to a fuller model.

This paper works within the context of a given market structure, without questioning seriously why that particular structure exists. Specifically, I assume that there are many buyers and sellers of a homogeneous good, and that sellers set the price. One can picture a competitive retail market. Section 2 develops a model in which sellers have constant average cost curves, buyers are transient and buy one unit each in a single purchase, and the only possible information flow is through advertising. Section 3 introduces the possibility of consumers' search. Section 4 discusses the market's efficiency in transmitting information. Section 5 summarizes further extensions of the model. Section 6 raises several objections to the models and discusses possibilities for further research.

Before getting involved in details, a few explanatory remarks may be helpful. There is a certain difficulty in modelling equilibrium price distributions which all models must face up to. Suppose that there exists an equilibrium price distribution, that it is known by all buyers and sellers, that sellers are profit maximizers, and that consumers all have a cost of search greater than some common positive lower bound, say c. Then under quite reasonable assumptions about consumer preferences, it can be proved by contradiction that there can be at most one price, the monopoly price.[2] The argument is simplest under the assumption that each consumer buys at most one unit of the good and that each has the same limit price m (which is thus the monopoly price).[3] Suppose then, that the lowest price were below the monopoly price and consider a seller at that price. He could raise his price by ε less than c and he would lose no customers. Even in the case of repeated purchases, he could raise his price by ε so small that the total increase in future expenditure by a consumer would be less than c. Since he could thus increase his revenue without affecting his cost, he was not profit maximizing in the first place; and we have reached the desired contradiction.

One can avoid the unpleasant result of the previous paragraph only by altering its assumptions. Eliminating any one of the assumptions opens up the possibility of developing a viable model. We may assume that some sellers do not know the price distribution: they may then believe that raising prices would lose customers. We may assume that consumers do not know the price distribution; in particular, if consumers buying at the lowest price believe that even lower prices are available, even the smallest price rise may induce them to search elsewhere. We may drop the assumption of rationality and then sellers may have a desire to subsidize customers, or customers may search elsewhere in anger about a price rise. Finally, we may assume that some consumers have zero search costs or some other source of free information.

My model takes the last escape route. I assume that sellers may advertise, and that the advertisements are received and processed free of charge by consumers. In all variants of the model it turns out that there exists at least one Nash equilibrium, i.e. a situation in which no agent can improve his payoff by changing his behaviour while the behaviour of other agents is held constant. Advertisements are allocated randomly among consumers, who simply choose the advertisements that offer the lowest prices to them. High-priced sellers advertise more intensively than low-priced sellers, partly because they must advertise more to get the same number of customers, and partly because the high prices generate the revenue sufficient to pay for the extra advertising. Details follow in the next section.

2. BASIC MODEL

Assume the following:

(i) A single homogeneous good is being traded for money.

(ii) There are many buyers and sellers.

(iii) Sellers can send advertising messages informing buyers of their price and location. Sellers are not constrained to advertise the same price to all customers.[4]

(iv) Time is divided into discrete periods. At the beginning of each period a new set of buyers enters the market. During the period they may receive advertisements. By the end of the period they must buy exactly one unit of the good or forfeit their opportunity to buy.

(v) All consumers have the same limit price, m, namely the maximum price they are willing to pay for the good.

(vi) A parameter b represents the expected cost to each seller of reaching a single buyer with a single advertisement. (Henceforth the term " advertisement " will be abbreviated to " ad ".) We may assume that a single ad costs b and always reaches a single buyer, or, more generally, that an advertising expenditure of b causes a random number of buyers, with mean one, to receive the message. It will simplify the exposition without affecting the results of this section if we make the former assumption, that the number of messages sent is strictly determined by the advertising expenditure. It follows that there can be no economies of scale in advertising.

(vii) Ads are allocated randomly among buyers, with each buyer having an equal chance of receiving each message. Furthermore, the assignment of each ad to a buyer is independent of the assignment of all other ads, including those sent out by the same seller.[5] The possibility that a single seller could send exactly one ad to each buyer is thus ruled out.

(viii) Buyers receive ads free of charge and cannot affect their probability of receiving them. They have no other means of receiving information about sellers.[6] Specifically, they cannot search for sellers or obtain information from other buyers. Thus, if they receive no ads, they cannot buy the product. Those individuals who would have made a purchase, but cannot because they do not receive an ad, may be termed " potential buyers ". Those who do receive ads and make a purchase may be called " actual buyers ". The term " buyers " will be used to include both categories.

(ix) At the end of each period each actual buyer sends an order to the seller who offered him the lowest price. If there are several such sellers he chooses any one with equal probability. The cost of sending orders is zero.[7]

(x) Upon receiving an order the seller fulfils it at the price he advertised to that particular buyer. All sellers have the same constant cost of production, p_0 per unit. We may assume that the seller produces to order at no extra cost or that his inventory costs are zero.

(xi) All sellers know the consumers' limit price and the distribution of prices advertised by other sellers. They do not know which ads, if any, are received by any specific buyer.

(xii) Each seller chooses his advertising policy so as to maximize his expected profits, taking as given the behaviour of other sellers.

To summarize, the market operates as follows: first, a set of buyers enters; second, sellers mail out their ads; third, those buyers who receive ads make orders; and fourth, these orders are fulfilled by sellers. Buyers' behaviour is thus passive; they simply order at the lowest price of which they are aware. Each seller, on the other hand, can make an active choice of his advertising policy. Such a policy consists of a choice of which price or prices to advertise, and how many ads to send out at each such price.[8] A given set of advertising strategies, one for each seller, determines all the variables of economic interest in the model. It determines directly the market advertising price distribution, namely the function which gives the total number of ads sent out at each price. In combination with the random process that determines the allocation of ads among potential buyers, it determines the sales price distribution, namely the function which specifies the expected number of sales at each price. (It will be more convenient in the sequel to define the sales and advertising price distributions somewhat differently, by dividing by the number of buyers.) Finally, the given set of advertising strategies determines each seller's expected profits. A set of advertising strategies is said to be a Nash equilibrium if no single seller can increase his expected profits by changing his, and only his, strategy. Corresponding to an equilibrium set of strategies, there is an equilibrium distribution of advertising prices and an equilibrium distribution of sales prices. To find the properties of these distributions is the major purpose of this section.

For each different choice of the number of buyers and sellers in the market, say M and N, respectively, there will be a different set of Nash equilibria. Unfortunately, it is simply too difficult to solve for these equilibria explicitly. Indeed, if the sellers are restricted to fixed strategies, Nash equilibria do not exist. There are at least two separate ways to deal with this problem:

(a) As previously mentioned, we can allow sellers to use mixed strategies. It can then be shown that for any numbers M and N, at least one Nash equilibrium does exist.

(b) If we wish to maintain fixed strategies, then we can introduce the concept of a Nash ε-equilibrium. This may be defined as a set of strategies such that no seller can increase his expected profits per advertising message sent by more than ε. It can be shown that for all $\varepsilon > 0$, there exists N' such that for all $N \geqq N'$ and for all M, ε-equilibria exist. Furthermore, all the propositions proved in this section can be rephrased in terms of ε-equilibria. Intuitively, ε is a proxy for minor costs of adjustment, uncertainties about other sellers' strategies, and the like, any of which will lend stability to the market.

It is possible, however, to prove that as M and N approach infinity, the equilibrium price distributions converge in distribution to a limit which can be simply described. For the rest of this section, it is this limit which is being referred to whenever the term " the equilibrium sales price distribution ", for example, is used. Since most of the interesting results are strictly valid only as limit theorems, a rigorous statement and proof of these results requires a rather lengthy and painstaking analysis. This is provided in Appendix A. The role of the remainder of this section is to provide an intuitive development of the main results which avoids the distraction of the technical details.

Let us begin by considering in more detail the random process by which the ads are allocated. Picture, if you like, the sellers dropping their ads at random into buyers' mailboxes. It is helpful to realize that this process may be described by the classical urn model of probability theory: the mailboxes correspond to the n " urns ", and the ads correspond to the r " balls ", which are assumed to be assigned independently with equal probability to each of the urns. It is a fact that as n and r both approach infinity in such a way that r/n remains fixed, the probability distribution of the number of balls in any given urn approaches the Poisson distribution with mean r/n. (For any given r and n, the probability that a given urn has x balls is given by the binomial distribution with $r = n \cdot (r/n)$ trials and probability $p = 1/n$ of success for each trial. The fact that the binomial distribution approaches the Poisson distribution as n gets large, holding r/n fixed, is a standard theorem in probability theory.) Explicitly, the probability that any given urn contains x balls approaches the expression $\exp(-r/n) \cdot (r/n)^x/x!$. If 2,000 balls are distributed in 1,000 urns, for example, it is not true that nearly all urns will have two balls, but instead the approximate percentage of urns that contain 0, 1, 2, 3, 4 and 5 balls will be $13\frac{1}{2}$, 27, 27, 18, 9 and $3\frac{1}{2}$, respectively. The specific result which is of greatest interest here is that the probability that an urn is empty is $\exp(-r/n)$. One immediate application to the current model is that the probability that a buyer does not receive any ads is exp $(-$(number of ads)$/M)$.

We are now prepared to approach a major question: will the classical result of a unique equilibrium price carry over to a market with imperfect information? What could this price be? In classical terms, ignoring the cost of information, the model of this section assumes a vertical demand curve, at the quantity M (up to price m), and a horizontal supply curve, at price p_0. Including the cost of advertising, the minimum conceivable price sellers must charge to cover costs is p_0+b. If all the sellers were to charge price $p = p_0+b$, however, not every ad at that price would be sure to generate a sale due to the possibility that several ads might go to the same buyer. Thus the advertising cost necessary to generate one expected sale would be greater than $b = p-p_0$, which is the revenue, net of production cost, associated with the sale. Expected profits would thus be negative, so there cannot be an equilibrium in which only price $p = p_0+b$ is advertised.

Another possibility is that all sellers advertise at the same price p^*, where $p^* > p_0+b$. This cannot be an equilibrium either, because it would then be profitable for one of the sellers advertising price p^* to lower his price. Any price cut, ε, no matter how small, would win away all those buyers who would otherwise have received ads at the same price from both him and from some other seller, and who thus might not have given him business. The resulting mark-up profit of $p^*-\varepsilon-p_0$ per additional customer is a quantum gain which would exceed the small revenue loss from the lower price, as long as the reduction were sufficiently small. Indeed, the same argument may be used to show the far stronger result that in equilibrium not more than one seller can be advertising at any given price. If, on the contrary, two sellers were advertising at the same price, a small price cut would again result in a quantum increase in expected profits due to the increase in expected sales, countered by only an infinitesimal decrease in revenue due to the lower price. Furthermore, with a large number of sellers, it may be shown that each seller sends a small proportion of the total number of ads, so we may approximate the distribution of advertising prices by a continuous distribution.[9]

We are thus justified in making the following definitions, each conditional on a given set of sellers' advertising strategies:

Let $A(p)$ equal the expected number of ads sent out at prices less than or equal to p divided by the number of buyers, M. (The word " expected " is used solely in the statistical sense to cover the possibility of randomized advertising strategies, not to allude to any seller's expectations regarding another seller's behaviour.) Despite the fact that this function is normalized in such a way that at the buyers' limit price, m, $A(m)$ equals the ratio of total ads to buyers, which is not likely to be one, it is convenient to call the function A the " advertising price distribution function ". $A(p)$ also measures the amount of competition in the market for an ad at price p.

Let $p_{\min}$ be the minimum price at which ads are ever sent.

Let $p_{\max}$ be the maximum price at which ads are ever sent.

Let $a(p) = A'(p)$; this will be called the "advertising price density function", again despite the non-standard normalization. In other words:

$$a(p)\Delta p = \frac{\text{the expected number of ads at prices } p^* \in (p,\ p+\Delta p)}{M}.$$

Let $S(p)$ equal the expected number of sales at prices less than or equal to p, divided by the number of buyers. Although $S(m) < 1$, this will be called the " sales price distribution function ".

Similarly, let $s(p) = S'(p)$ be called the " sales price density function ". We also have:

$$s(p)\Delta p = \frac{\text{the expected number of sales at prices } p^* \in (p,\ p+\Delta p)}{M}.$$

Let $\pi(p)$ equal the probability that a given ad at price p results in a sale. Intuitively, for reasons of symmetry, $\pi(p)$ will not depend upon which seller sent the ad.[10] It follows that $s(p) = \pi(p)\cdot a(p)$. Moreover, in the limit as M approaches infinity, $\pi(p)$ is also equal to the probability that a single additional ad sent out at price p by any seller results in a sale. This is because the probability that both the extra ad and any specific prior ad go to the same buyer approaches zero in the limit.

Let $P(p) = (p-p_0)\cdot\pi(p)-b$. This may be interpreted as the expected profit accounted for directly by an ad at price p. This may be seen in two ways. First, an ad at price p results directly in expected sales of $\pi(p)$, which generate expected mark-up profits of $(p-p_0)\cdot\pi(p)$; from that value the cost of sending the ad, b, must be subtracted. Secondly, total profits may be written as (revenue − production cost) − advertising cost, which, when summed up over sales at individual prices, equals

$$\int [(p-p_0)s(p)-b\cdot a(p)]dp = \int [(p-p_0)\pi(p)-b]\cdot a(p)dp = \int P(p)\cdot a(p)dp.$$

In the limit as the number of buyers and sellers get large, $P(p)$ may also be interpreted as the change in expected profits received by a single seller if he alters his advertising strategy by sending out one additional ad. To put it succinctly, for a single seller, $P(p)$ is the " marginal product of advertising at price p ". This is true because one seller's ads are only a small fraction of the total number of ads, so there is little chance that an extra ad of his will go to the same buyer as one of his other ads; therefore the expected loss in his profits that results indirectly, through the reduction in his expected sales, from his change in

2H—44/3

strategy is negligible. Note that this is not true for the profits of sellers as a whole, because the extra ad has a significant probability of displacing an ad of one of the many other sellers.

The definitions of the functions A, S, π, P and $p_{\min}$ just given make sense for any M and N and for any given set of seller's advertising strategies. It may be shown as well that as M and N get large, any sequence of functions A, S, π, P and $p_{\min}$ corresponding to equilibrium sets of strategies converges uniformly. For clarity of notation, let these limits be denoted by asterisks: A^*, S^*, π^*, P^* and $p_{\min}{}^*$. We are now prepared to prove the main results of this section.

Proposition 2.1. *$P^*(p) = 0$ for all prices p that are advertised; thus $\pi^*(p) = b/(p-p_0)$.*

Proof. As noted earlier, for large enough M and N, $P(p)$ is a good approximation, say within ε, of the marginal product of advertising at price p. If $P(p) \geqq \varepsilon$, then some seller could improve his expected profits by sending one additional ad at price p. If $P(p) \leqq -\varepsilon$, then any seller advertising at price p would do better to reduce such advertising. Therefore, in equilibrium $|P(p)| < \varepsilon$; and in the limit, $P^*(p) = 0$. The second statement follows because

$$|P(p)| = |(p-p_0)\pi(p)-b| < \varepsilon \quad \text{implies} \quad |\pi(p)-b/(p-p_0)| < \varepsilon/(m-p_0).$$

Proposition 2.2. *In equilibrium, all prices $p \in (p^*_{\min}, m)$ are advertised.*[11] *Moreover, $p^*_{\min} = p_0+b$.*

Proof. Assume on the contrary that for the interval (p_1, p_2) within $(p_{\min}, m)$, no prices are advertised. We may pick (p_1, p_2) to be the largest such interval. Then a seller advertising price p_1 could increase his revenue per sale by p_2-p_1 with no loss in sales and no increase in costs simply by raising his price to p_2. This contradicts the assumption of equilibrium and proves the first statement.

An advertisement sent at the lowest price generates a sale with certainty. Therefore $\pi(p_{\min}) = 1$, and we may apply Proposition 2.1 to show that

$$|P(p_{\min})| = |(p_{\min}-p_0)\cdot\pi(p_{\min})-b| = |p_{\min}-(p_0+b)| < \varepsilon$$

for sufficiently large M and N. Thus $p^*_{\min} = p_0+b$.

Proposition 2.3. $\pi^*(p) = \exp(-A^*(p))$.

Proof. Recall that as M gets large, $\pi(p)$ may be approximated by the probability that an additional ad at price p generates a sale. This is the probability that the ad goes to a " susceptible buyer ", i.e. a buyer who has no other ads at prices less than or equal to p. Recall also the urn model discussed earlier; as before, let the urns represent the buyers, but now let the balls represent only the ads at prices less than or equal to p. Translated into the language of the urn model, $\pi(p)$ is the probability that a given urn is empty; we have seen that this probability may be approximated by exp (−balls/urns), which in this case gives $\pi(p) = \exp(-A(p))$. In the limit, $\pi^*(p) = \exp(-A^*(p))$.

Proposition 2.4. *The equilibrium distribution of sales and advertising prices may be fully characterized as follows:*

$$A^*(p) = \begin{Bmatrix} 0 & & p \leqq p_0+b \\ \ln((p-p_0)/b) & \text{for} & p_0+b \leqq p \leqq m \\ \ln((m-p_0)/b) & & p \geqq m \end{Bmatrix},$$

$$a^*(p) = \begin{Bmatrix} 0 & & p \leqq p_0+b \\ 1/(p-p_0) & \text{for} & p_0+b \leqq p \leqq m \\ 0 & & p \geqq m \end{Bmatrix},$$

$$s^*(p) = \begin{cases} 0 & \\ b/(p-p_0)^2 & \text{for} \\ 0 & \end{cases} \quad \begin{Bmatrix} p \leqq p_0+b \\ p_0+b \leqq p \leqq m \\ p \geqq m \end{Bmatrix},$$

$$S^*(p) = \begin{cases} 0 & \\ 1-b/(p-p_0) & \text{for} \\ 1-b/(m-p_0) & \end{cases} \quad \begin{Bmatrix} p \leqq p_0+b \\ p_0+b \leqq p \leqq m \\ p \geqq m \end{Bmatrix}.$$

Proof. Propositions 2.1 and 2.3 give $\exp(-A^*(p)) = b/(p-p_0)$. Taking the logarithm of both sides gives the expression for $A^*(p)$. Differentiating gives $a^*(p)$, multiplying by $\pi^*(p)$ gives $s^*(p)$ and integrating gives $S^*(p)$. The price ranges are given by Proposition 2.2.

The propositions up until now have dealt only with market behaviour. What can be said about the advertising strategies of individual sellers? In the limit these strategies are completely indeterminate, since advertising at any price or any combination of prices leads to zero profits. This indeterminacy is convenient because it allows us to constrain sellers' admissible strategies without affecting the validity of the propositions. In particular, the equilibrium price distributions are the same whether or not the sellers are restricted to advertising at only a single price each. However, this is not strictly true in the case of a finite number of sellers. This topic is pursued in Section 5.

To conclude the section, it only remains to calculate summary statistics for the equilibrium distributions and to perform a straightforward comparative statics exercise.

Let $d = p_{max} - p_0$.

Let $\bar{p}$ equal the mean of the sales price distribution.

Let var (p) equal the variance of the sales price distribution. By elementary calculus, it follows that:

$$S^*(m) = (d-b)/d \qquad \text{...(2.1)}$$

$$\bar{p} = p_0 + \frac{bd}{b-d} \cdot \ln\left(\frac{d}{b}\right) \qquad \text{...(2.2)}$$

$$\text{var}\,(p) = b(d-b) - \frac{b^2 d^2}{(d-b)^2} \cdot \ln^2\left(\frac{d}{b}\right) \qquad \text{...(2.3)}$$

$$A^*(m) = \ln\left(\frac{d}{b}\right). \qquad \text{...(2.4)}$$

To perform comparative statics, simply calculate the following derivatives:

$$\frac{\partial S^*(m)}{\partial b} = -\frac{1}{d} < 0, \qquad \text{...(2.1a)}$$

$$\frac{\partial \bar{p}}{\partial b} = \frac{d^2}{(d-b)^2} \ln\left(\frac{d}{b}\right) - \left(\frac{d}{d-b}\right) \in (\tfrac{1}{2}, \infty), \qquad \text{...(2.2a)}$$

and is strictly decreasing in b,

$$\frac{\partial\, \text{var}\,(p)}{\partial b} = d - 2b - \frac{2bd^2}{(d-b)^2} \cdot \ln\left(\frac{d}{b}\right) \cdot \left(1 + \frac{d}{d-b} \ln\left(\frac{d}{b}\right)\right), \qquad \text{...(2.3a)}$$

and

$$\frac{\partial A(m)}{\partial b} = -\frac{1}{b} < 0. \qquad \text{...(2.4a)}$$

These may be put into elasticity form as follows:

$$\frac{ES^*(m)}{Eb} = -\frac{b}{d-b} \in (-1, 0), \qquad \text{...(2.1b)}$$

$$\frac{E(\bar{p}-p_0)}{Eb} = \frac{d}{d-b} - \frac{1}{\ln(d/b)} \in (\tfrac{1}{2}, 1), \qquad \text{...(2.2b)}$$

and is rising with b, and

$$\frac{EA^*(m)}{Eb} = -\frac{1}{\ln(d/b)} < 0. \qquad \text{...(2.4b)}$$

Since an equal percentage change in b and d is equivalent to a change in units, we may read directly the elasticities with respect to d:

$$\frac{ES^*(m)}{Ed} = -\frac{ES^*(m)}{Eb} \in (0, 1), \qquad \text{...(2.1c)}$$

$$\frac{E(\bar{p}-p_0)}{Ed} = 1 - \frac{E(\bar{p}-p_0)}{Eb} \in (0, \tfrac{1}{2}), \qquad \text{...(2.2c)}$$

declining with b, and

$$\frac{EA^*(m)}{Ed} = -\frac{EA(m)}{Eb} > 0. \qquad \text{...(2.4c)}$$

Qualitatively:

(i) The cheaper the ads, the lower is the mean of the sales price distribution and the greater are the total sales. The variance may either increase or decrease.

(ii) The higher the limit price, the higher are the mean and the variance of the sales price distribution and the greater are the sales.

(iii) As b approaches zero, $S^*(m)$ approaches one, and the distribution converges to a spike at p_0. As b approaches d, $S^*(m)$ approaches 0.

(iv) As d approaches infinity, $S^*(m)$ approaches one, the mean and variance of both price distributions get arbitrarily large, the number of ads received by each buyer approaches infinity, and the expected value to a buyer of receiving an additional randomly selected ad thus approaches zero.

3. BUYERS' SEARCH

How is the model affected by the introduction of buyers' search? Clearly this depends on the specific way in which search is modelled. The most popular assumption in the current literature is that the nth search costs $c(n)$, a constant or increasing function of n, and that there is an equal probability of searching any given store. The story behind this assumption may be that buyers search randomly among the sellers listed in the Yellow Pages or that they " pound the streets " randomly. This approach can be incorporated into the basic model, but it leads to certain unpalatable complications.

An alternative assumption will be adopted in this section, namely that the probability of locating any given seller is proportional to his sales. This may be considered as a way to model " word-of-mouth " search, since it follows from the assumptions that each buyer searches randomly among other buyers and that the buyer contacted recommends the store which he himself patronizes or plans to patronize. It may also be considered as a plausible approach to " pounding the streets ", because a seller with large sales would be likely to have more branches or to be more conspicuous by nature of its size. Here we are skirting on an issue for an alternative model, namely the fact that sellers can alter the consumers' probability of searching at their store by suitable expenditures on location, displays, signs and advertising of location only.

What about the time dimensions of search? It is plausible to assume that the total cost of search, including both direct costs and costs of time, will be less the larger is the period within which the search is to be accomplished. It is also true that any combination of the duration of search, the cost of search and the probability of making a contact may be random. These complications will all be ignored for the present.

Getting down to specifics, let us take the model of Section 2 and modify it by replacing assumption (viii) with the following:

Assumption (viiia). All buyers have identical cost of search functions $c(n)$, which are constant or increasing in n. The duration of search is small compared with the length of the time period referred to in assumption (iv) (so that for purposes of analysis we may assume that if a consumer searches, he does so at the end of the period, after having had a full opportunity to receive ads). The probability that a search yields an offer from any particular seller is equal to his share in total sales. The probability that this offer is at a price within a particular interval (p_1, p_2) is proportional to the seller's sales at prices in this interval. (The objection may validly be raised that a seller may charge higher prices to those consumers who are searching than to those to whom he advertises, because he knows the searching buyers do not have acceptable alternatives. To avoid this problem we may either assume that each seller is constrained to sell at only a single price in any given time period (the single price may still be set by a random mechanism), or we may fall back on the other notion of search by asking one's neighbour.)

Consider now the decision of each consumer as he reaches the end of his period. He may either accept the lowest priced ad he has received (if any), or he may search. If there is an equilibrium in which some consumers search, then there will be a specific cut-off price, p_c, above which the expected value of search will be greater than its cost, so that he will accept no price above this level. Since all consumers are identical, there will be no sales whatsoever above p_c, so $p_{\max} \leqq p_c$. Furthermore, in equilibrium p_c can not be strictly greater than $p_{\max}$, because then a seller could make a profit by operating at any price between $p_{\max}$ and p_c, advertising at the same rate as sellers at price $p_{\max}$. Compared to these sellers, he would have identical costs, identical sales and higher revenue due to his higher price. Thus $p_c = p_{\max}$. It follows that consumers will search if and only if they receive no ads, and that in this case they will accept the first price they find. (I am implicitly assuming that $p_{\max} < m$. A discussion of what might happen otherwise is taken up in Appendix B.)

Consider now how the relationship between sales and ads is affected by the new assumption. Let us use ϕ to denote the proportion of consumers who receive at least one ad. Then $1-\phi$ is the proportion of buyers who search. By assumption (viiia) a proportion $1-\phi$ of each seller's sales is due to search. Thus only the proportion ϕ is due directly to advertising. Let us continue to use $\pi(p)$ to denote the ratio: $s(p)/a(p)$. Let $\hat{\pi}(p)$ equal the ratio: (sales due directly to ads at $p)/a(p)$. To rephrase the definition, $\hat{\pi}(p)$ is the probability that an ad at price p goes to a susceptible buyer. We have just shown that $\hat{\pi}(p) = \phi \cdot \pi(p)$, in contrast to the previous sections, in which $\hat{\pi}(p) = \pi(p)$.

The analysis proceeds very closely to that of the basic model. Proposition 2.1 carries over without change to give the equations

$$P(p) = (p-p_0)\cdot\pi(p)-b = 0 \quad \text{and} \quad \pi(p) = b/(p-p_0).$$

Since $\hat{\pi}(p_{\min}) = 1$, $\pi(p_{\min}) = 1/\phi$, and $P(p_{\min}) = (p_{\min}-p_0)\cdot\pi(p_{\min})-b = 0$ implies that $p_{\min} = p_0+b\phi$ in place of Proposition 2.2. Proposition 2.3 carries over without change in terms of $\hat{\pi}(p)$ to give $\hat{\pi}(p) = \exp(-A(p))$. Taking logarithms and using the new versions of Propositions 2.1, 2.2 and 2.3 we have

$$A(p) = -\ln(\hat{\pi}(p)) = -\ln(\phi\pi(p)) = -\ln\left(\frac{b\phi}{p-p_0}\right) = \ln\left(\frac{p-p_0}{b\phi}\right).$$

Differentiating gives:

$$a(p) = \begin{cases} 0 & p \leqq p_0+b\phi \\ \dfrac{1}{p-p_0} \quad \text{for} & p_0+b\phi \leqq p \leqq p_{\max} \\ 0 & p \geqq p_{\max} \end{cases} \qquad \text{...(3.1)}$$

The relationship $s(p) = \pi(p)\cdot a(p)$ is still valid, so

$$s(p) = \left\{ \begin{array}{ll} 0 & p \leqq p_0 + b\phi \\ \dfrac{b}{(p-p_0)^2}, \text{ for} & p_0 + b\phi \leqq p \leqq p_{\max} \\ 0 & p \geqq p_{\max} \end{array} \right\}. \qquad \ldots(3.2)$$

It remains to solve for ϕ, $p_{\min}$, $p_{\max}$ and d. We already have two equations,

$$p_{\min} = p_0 + b\phi \quad \text{and} \quad d = p_{\max} - p_0 \quad \text{(by definition)},$$

so two more will suffice. One is provided by the fact that all buyers actually do buy. Thus

$$\int_{p_{\min}}^{p_{\max}} s(p)dp = 1.$$

Carrying out the integration:

$$\int_{p_{\min}}^{p_{\max}} \frac{b}{(p-p_0)^2}\, dp = -\left[\frac{b}{p_{\max}-p_0} - \frac{b}{p_{\min}-p_0}\right] = \frac{1}{\phi} - \frac{b}{d} = 1,$$

and therefore $\phi = d/(b+d)$. The final equation is given by the fact that the expected gain from search at the cut-off price, $p_{\max}$, must be equal to the cost of search. The expected gain from search is the integral of the gain, $p_{\max}-p$, weighted by the density $s(p)$. Thus:

$$c = \int_{p_{\min}}^{p_{\max}} (p_{\max}-p)\frac{b}{(p-p_0)^2}\, dp. \qquad \ldots(3.3)$$

Carrying out the integration leads to the expression $c = d - b\cdot\ln(d/b\phi)$. Substituting $\phi = d/(b+d)$, we get equation (3.4), which is included in the following summary list:

$$c = d - b\cdot\ln\left(1+\frac{d}{b}\right) = b\left(\frac{\phi}{1-\phi} - \ln\left(\frac{1}{1-\phi}\right)\right) \qquad \ldots(3.4)$$

$$\phi = d/(b+d) \qquad \ldots(3.5)$$

$$p_{\min} = p_0 + b\phi = bd/(b+d) + p_0 \qquad \ldots(3.6)$$

$$p_{\max} = p_0 + d. \qquad \ldots(3.7)$$

It is now straightforward to solve for $\bar{p}$ = the mean of the sales price distribution, var (p) = the variance of the sales price distribution, $R(p) = p_{\max} - p_{\min}$ = the range of prices, and $A(p_{\max})$ = the average number of ads per buyer. These variables are all expressed in terms of d, which in turn depends solely on the parameters b and c as shown in equation (3.4). Unfortunately, equation (3.4) cannot be solved explicitly for d, so we can not eliminate the values of d in the other equations. Here are the results:

$$\bar{p} = p_{\max} - c = p_0 + d - c = p_0 + b\cdot\ln\left(\frac{1}{1-\phi}\right) \qquad \ldots(3.8)$$

$$\text{var}(p) = \frac{bd^2}{b+d} - (d-c)^2 = b^2\left(\frac{\phi^2}{1-\phi} - 2\ln\left(\frac{1}{1-\phi}\right)\right) \qquad \ldots(3.9)$$

$$R(p) = d^2/(b+d) = b\phi^2/(1+\phi) \qquad \ldots(3.10)$$

$$A(p_{\max}) = \ln\left(1+\frac{d}{b}\right) = \ln\left(\frac{1}{1-\phi}\right) = \frac{d-c}{b}. \qquad \ldots(3.11)$$

Comparative statics can be analysed by differentiating equations (3.4) to (3.11) with respect to b and c. We get the following:

$$\frac{\partial d}{\partial c}=\frac{b+d}{d}=\frac{1}{\phi}>0 \qquad \text{...(3.4a)}$$

$$\frac{\partial \phi}{\partial c}=\frac{b}{d(b+d)}=\frac{(1-\phi)^2}{b\phi}>0 \qquad \text{...(3.5a)}$$

$$\frac{\partial p_{\min}}{\partial c}=\frac{b^2}{d(b+d)}=\frac{(1-\phi)^2}{\phi}>0 \qquad \text{...(3.6a)}$$

$$\frac{\partial p_{\max}}{\partial c}=\frac{b+d}{d}=\frac{1}{\phi}>0 \qquad \text{...(3.7a)}$$

$$\frac{\partial \bar{p}}{\partial c}=\frac{b}{d}=\frac{1-\phi}{\phi}>0 \qquad \text{...(3.8a)}$$

$$\frac{\partial \operatorname{var}(p)}{\partial c}=\frac{b}{(b+d)d}[2c(b+d)-d^2];\quad 0<\frac{\partial \operatorname{var}(p)}{\partial c}<\frac{bc}{b+d} \qquad \text{...(3.9a)}$$

$$\frac{\partial R(p)}{\partial c}=\frac{2b+d}{b+d}=2-\phi>0 \qquad \text{...(3.10a)}$$

$$\frac{\partial A(p_{\max})}{\partial c}=\frac{1}{d}=\frac{1-\phi}{b\phi}>0 \qquad \text{...(3.11a)}$$

$$\frac{\partial d}{\partial b}=\frac{d^2-(b+d)c}{bd}=-\left(\frac{\phi+\ln(1-\phi)}{\phi}\right)>0 \qquad \text{...(3.4b)}$$

$$\frac{\partial \phi}{\partial b}=-\frac{c}{d(b+d)}=\frac{-c(1-\phi)^2}{b^2\phi}<0 \qquad \text{...(3.5b)}$$

$$\frac{\partial p_{\min}}{\partial b}=\frac{d^2-bc}{d(b+d)}=\phi-\frac{c(1-\phi)^2}{b\phi}>0 \text{ and is less than one} \qquad \text{...(3.6b)}$$

$$\frac{\partial p_{\max}}{\partial b}=\frac{\partial d}{\partial b}>0 \qquad \text{...(3.7b)}$$

$$\frac{\partial \bar{p}}{\partial b}=\frac{\partial p}{\partial b}>0 \qquad \text{...(3.8b)}$$

$$\frac{\partial \operatorname{var}(p)}{\partial b}=\frac{bcd^2-2[d^2-(b+d)c]^2}{bd(b+d)}=c\left\{\phi-2(1-\phi)\left[\frac{\phi+\ln(1-\phi)}{\phi}\right]^2\right\}>0 \qquad \text{...(3.9b)}$$

$$\frac{\partial R(p)}{\partial b}=\frac{d^2-2bc-cd}{b(b+d)}=(\phi-2)\ln(1-\phi)-2\phi>0 \qquad \text{...(3.10b)}$$

$$\frac{\partial A(p_{\max})}{\partial b}=-\frac{c}{bd}=-\frac{c(1-\phi)}{b^2\phi}<0. \qquad \text{...(3.11b)}$$

A few elasticities are of interest because of the inequalities that restrict their values:

$$\frac{Ed}{Ec}=\frac{c(b+d)}{d^2}=\frac{c(1-\phi)}{b\phi^2}\in(\tfrac{1}{2},1) \qquad \text{...(3.4c)}$$

$$\frac{E\phi}{Ec} = \frac{bc}{d^2} = \frac{c}{b}\frac{(1-\phi)^2}{\phi^2} \in (0, \tfrac{1}{2}) \qquad \text{...(3.5c)}$$

$$\frac{E(p_{min}-p_0)}{Ec} = \frac{bc}{d^2} = \frac{c}{b}\frac{(1-\phi)^2}{\phi^2} \in (0, \tfrac{1}{2}) \qquad \text{...(3.6c)}$$

$$\frac{E(\bar{p}-p_0)}{Ec} = \frac{bc}{d(d-c)} = -\frac{c}{b}\frac{1-\phi}{\phi\cdot\ln(1-\phi)} \in (0, \tfrac{1}{2}) \qquad \text{...(3.8c)}$$

$$\frac{EA(p_{max})}{Ec} = \frac{bc}{d(d-c)} = -\frac{c}{b}\frac{1-\phi}{\phi\ln(1-\phi)} \in (0, \tfrac{1}{2}) \qquad \text{...(3.11c)}$$

$$\frac{Ed}{Eb} = 1 - \frac{Ed}{Ec} \in (0, \tfrac{1}{2}) \qquad \text{...(3.4d)}$$

$$\frac{E\phi}{Eb} = -\frac{E\phi}{Ec} \in (-\tfrac{1}{2}, 0) \qquad \text{...(3.5d)}$$

$$\frac{E(p_{min}-p_0)}{Eb} = 1 - \frac{E(p_{min}-p_0)}{Ec} \in (\tfrac{1}{2}, 1) \qquad \text{...(3.6d)}$$

$$\frac{E(\bar{p}-p_0)}{Eb} = 1 - \frac{E(\bar{p}-p_0)}{Ec} \in (\tfrac{1}{2}, 1) \qquad \text{...(3.8d)}$$

$$\frac{EA(p_{max})}{Eb} = -\frac{EA(p_{max})}{Ec} \in (-\tfrac{1}{2}, 0). \qquad \text{...(3.11d)}$$

The main results are exactly as one would expect; as either search or advertising becomes more expensive, buyers pay for it in terms of higher prices: the minimum price, maximum price and the mean are all higher. More costly search and advertising also implies greater price dispersion as measured either by variance or range. If the cost of search rises, then buyers search less and sellers advertise more; if the cost of advertising rises, then sellers advertise less and buyers search more.

Limiting cases of the model reduce to results obtained previously. If we let c approach infinity holding b constant, then equation (3.4) implies that d approaches infinity. It follows that ϕ approaches one, p_{min} approaches p_0+b, and the other variables all approach infinity. This is precisely the solution to the basic model for the case where there is no limit price. On the other hand, if b approaches infinity while c is held constant, then ϕ approaches zero, $A(p_{max})$ tends toward zero, and all the other variables, p_{min} included, approach infinity. Thus the problem described in the introduction returns; if advertising is prohibitively expensive, then no amount of search can tie down the price distribution.

If we let b and c vary together, then we can get any number of further cases. I will consider just one more in detail. We know that the price distribution shifts upward when either b or c increases. What happens if b increases and c decreases, or vice versa, in such a way as to hold the mean price fixed? From equation (3.8) we see that $d-c = \bar{p}-p_0$ is a positive constant. In light of equation (3.4), this means that $b\cdot\ln(1+(d/b)) = \bar{p}-p_0$, and we can solve for $d = b(\exp((\bar{p}-p_0)/b)-1)$. Using l'Hopital's rule, $\lim_{b\to\infty} d = \bar{p}-p_0$. Therefore,

$$\lim_{b\to\infty} p_{max} = \bar{p}$$

and

$$\lim_{b\to\infty} p_{min} = \lim_{b\to\infty}(p_0+(bd/(b+d)) = p_0+\lim_{b\to\infty}(d/(1+(d/b))) = p_0+(\bar{p}-p_0) = \bar{p}$$

also. It follows that the distribution collapses to the arbitrarily assigned value $\bar{p}$. In the opposite direction, $\lim_{b\to 0} p_{min} = \lim_{b\to 0}(p_0+b\phi) = p_0$ and again using l'Hôpital's rule, both R and the variance of the price distribution approach infinity as b approaches zero. To summarize, by appropriate choice of b and c any desired combination of the mean and variance satisfying $\bar{p}>p_0$ and var >0 can be obtained.

In the case where b gets large and c diminishes sufficiently to hold $\bar{p}$ constant, we can push the analysis one step further. Since d approaches $\bar{p}-p_0$, b/d becomes small, so we can use a Taylor's expansion in equation (3.4) to derive an explicit expression for d in terms of b and c:

$$c = d-b\cdot\ln\left(1+\frac{d}{b}\right) \approx d-b\left(-\frac{d}{b}-\frac{d^2}{2b^2}\right) = \frac{d^2}{2b},$$

and therefore $d = \sqrt{(2bc)}$. Since we already showed that the distribution collapsed to $\bar{p} = p_0+d$, we may interpret d as the mark-up over production cost. This equation says that when advertising is expensive relative to search, the elasticities of the mark-up with respect to search and advertising costs are both equal to $\frac{1}{2}$.

To summarize so far, we have shown that *if* an equilibrium exists in which consumers search, and if $p_{max}<m$, then the equilibrium is given by equations (3.1), (3.2) and (3.4) to (3.7). It is easy to check that these equations plus $p_{max}<m$ are sufficient for an equilibrium to exist as well. Thus as long as m is great enough, in the precise sense that $m>f(b, c)$, where $f(b, c) = p_0+d$, and d is defined implicitly by equation (3.4) as a function of b and c, then there exists exactly one pair of equilibrium sales and advertising price distributions which incorporates buyers' search. We have not ruled out the possibility that for a single set of parameters p_0, b, c and m, there may exist other equilibria in which buyers do not search, in which the market shuts down entirely, or in which $p_{max} = m$. Indeed, all of these possibilities may actually occur! Since these complications only occur under unusual restrictions on the parameters, the full analysis will be postponed to Appendix B.

4. EFFICIENCY

What can be said about the efficiency of the markets described in the previous sections? Under conditions of imperfect information, will the free market still be optimal in some reasonable sense? Does advertising act to make competition more or less "perfect"? These questions need to be posed precisely, and it should be understood that I make no claims that the answers given here apply to "the real world". Still, there may be methodological interest in the analysis.

Consider first the model of Section 2. We may define a measure of the welfare gain resulting from the existence of the market as the value of the items bought minus the sum of the production and advertising costs. It is convenient to divide by the number of buyers, giving a measure, say W, of the average welfare gain per buyer. This may also be interpreted as the expected consumers' surplus per buyer, because sellers have zero expected profits. In the free market, the average gain is ξm, where ξ equals the proportion of buyers who get ads, and the average cost is $\xi p_0+bA(m)$. The resulting value for W is $\xi(m-p_0)-bA(m) = d-b-b\cdot\ln(d/b)$, as may be shown by using equations (2.1) and (2.4).

The question arises: could a different market organization result in a greater welfare gain? Suppose, for example, that a government agency took over the industry, so that total advertising could be considered as a control variable for a single decision maker. Could a different choice of total advertising per buyer, $A \neq A(m)$, increase W? By the usual urn model argument, if the ratio of ads to buyers were set at A, the proportion of buyers who would buy, ξ, would be $1-\exp(-A)$, and it follows that:

$$W = \xi(m-p_0)-bA = (1-\exp(-A))d-bA. \qquad \text{...(4.1)}$$

The optimal amount of advertising, A^*, may be found by differentiating with respect to A and setting the expression equal to zero, yielding: $dW/dA = d\cdot\exp(-A)-b = 0$ and therefore $A^* = \ln(d/b) = A(m)$, as in equation (2.4). The free market in this sense generates the optimal amount of advertising and the maximum possible welfare.

Does this result carry over when search is included? Taking the case in which every consumer buys, benefits per consumer and production cost remain constant, so to maximize welfare it suffices to minimize the costs per buyer of advertising and search. Since a proportion $1-\exp(-A)$ of the consumers are reached by ads and the remaining proportion, $\exp(-A)$, search, these costs are $C = bA+c\cdot\exp(-A)$; $(\partial C/\partial A) = b-c\cdot\exp(-A) = 0$ implies both $1-\phi = \exp(-A) = b/c$ and $A^* = \ln(c/b)$ for $c \geqq b$. In the case $c<b$ the most efficient way to transmit information is solely through search, so $A = 0$ is optimal. Minimum costs are $b\cdot\ln(c/b)+b$ in the case $c \geqq b$ and c in the case $c \leqq b$. The amount of search, say $\psi = 1-\phi$, in the free market is insufficient to provide the maximum benefits. This is clearest in the case $c \leqq b$, because $\psi<1$ and $A>0$ hold in the free market. It is true in general, since in the free market $c/b = \phi/(1-\phi)-\ln(1/(1-\phi)) = (1-\psi)/\psi-\ln(1/\psi)$ determines ψ, whereas in the optimal situation $c/b = 1/\psi_o$ determines ψ_o, where the " o " is short for " optimal ". Equating the right-hand sides and solving for ψ_o yields: $\psi_o = \psi/(1-\psi+\psi\ln\psi)$. Since $\psi<1$, $\ln\psi<0$, the denominator is less than one, and therefore $\psi_o>\psi$. To achieve an efficient operation of the market, any of the four following policies would be sufficient: a government takeover, the policy of outlawing sales above a maximum price p^* chosen such that $A(p^*) = A^* = \ln(c/b)$, the imposition of a tax x on advertising such that $A(p_{max}(b+x, c)) = A^*$, or the provision of a subsidy y on consumer search such that $A(p_{max}(b, c-y)) = A^*$. Needless to say, if these programmes involve costs themselves, the analysis here is incomplete.

How does the model of Section 3 bear on the relationship between advertising and competition? Since when b gets large, prices rise to the limit price m, it may be said that the existence of advertising is essential to competition; without advertising the market breaks down entirely. This is true despite the fact that advertising is excessive in the free market situation. Even when $c \leqq b$, when the optimal means of information flow is solely through search, forbidding advertising entirely instead of imposing a tax just sufficient to deter advertising would destroy the market.

Note that in this discussion the specific price advertised does not enter. This is because by assumption all consumers are alike, so the price information conveyed is not socially useful. The value of advertising and search lies solely in its role in enabling buyers to locate sellers so that they may buy. The question of efficiency relates only to the optimal number of buyers to inform and the optimal choice between different methods of transmitting information.

I do not know of a simple way to explain why the market is efficient in the case of advertising alone, but not when search is permitted. Roughly speaking, it may be because buyers convey positive externalities upon other buyers when they search, in the form of lowering the distribution of advertising prices.

5. FURTHER EXTENSIONS

This section states without proof the results of three further extensions of the basic model. The reader interested in obtaining further details is referred to Butters [2].

The first extension deals with a continuous time variant of Section 2. Instead of assuming that consumers buy only one unit of the good in question, let us assume that repeat purchase is possible. Buyers then purchase one unit of the good in each time period; indeed, it is convenient to go to the opposite extreme and assume that the good is infinitely divisible and that purchasing is continuous; in any amount of time t, no matter how small, an amount t of the good is bought as long as an acceptable price is available. To make this formal, let us first consider a model without the complications of consumer search. Specifically, consider the model of Section 2 with assumptions (iv), (v), (vi), (ix) and (x) replaced by the assumptions (iv a), (v a), (vi a), (ix a) and (x a) below. The purpose of assumption (x a) is to avoid the problem of how long ads are valid (for example, if a seller advertises a price today, will he sell at this price today only, next week also, or next year as well?).

(iv a) Consumers enter the market continuously at a constant rate. Each consumer's exit from the market is determined by a Poisson process with parameter r.

(v a) Consumers in the market have a limit price m above which they do not buy. At prices below m they buy a continuous stream of the good at the rate of exactly one unit per unit time.

(vi a) Advertisements are sent out continuously. The cost of one unit of advertising (equivalently, one advertising message run for one unit of time) is b. The number of buyers who receive one ad in one unit of time has a Poisson distribution with unit mean.

(ix a) Buyers always purchase at the lowest price known to them. There are no transactions costs associated with shifting one's patronage to a different seller.

(x a) Sellers do not change their price and advertising policies. They do not default on any advertising promise to sell at a given price. Advertising promises are permanent.

The following reinterpretation of the notation of Section 2 is necessary:

Let $a(p)$ be the new form of the advertising price density function:

$$a(p)\Delta p = \frac{\text{the rate of advertising at prices } p \in (p,\, p+\Delta p)}{\text{the expected number of consumers}},$$

where the rate of advertising is measured in units of advertising per unit time.

Let $A(p) = \int_{p_{\min}}^{p} a(u)du$, the advertising price distribution function.

Let $s(p)$ again be defined analogously to $a(p)$ by the equation

$$s(p)\Delta p = \frac{\text{the rate of sales at prices } p^* \in (p,\, p+\Delta p)}{\text{the expected number of buyers}}.$$

Let $\xi = \int_{p_{\min}}^{m} s(p)dp$, the ratio of the actual sales to the total sales that would be made if each buyer were purchasing.

Under the assumptions given above, it is still true that the equilibrium distributions of sales and advertising prices are unique. Their explicit forms are given by the following equations:

$$a(p) = \begin{cases} 0 & p \leqq p_0 + br \\ \dfrac{\sqrt{r}}{2\sqrt{b}\cdot\sqrt{(p-p_0)}} & \text{for } p_0+br \leqq p \leqq m \\ 0 & p \geqq m \end{cases} \qquad \text{...(5.1)}$$

$$s(p) = \begin{cases} 0 & p < p_0 + br \\ \dfrac{\sqrt{(br)}}{2(p-p_0)^{3/2}} & \text{for } p_0+br \leqq p \leqq m \\ 0 & p > m \end{cases} \qquad \text{...(5.2)}$$

It follows directly that:

$$\xi = 1 - \sqrt{(br/d)} \qquad \text{...(5.3)}$$

$$\bar{p} = p_0 + \sqrt{(brd)} \qquad \text{...(5.4)}$$

$$\text{var} = brd + (d+br)\sqrt{(brd)} \qquad \text{...(5.5)}$$

$$\bar{p}_{ad} = p_0 + \tfrac{1}{3}(d + br + \sqrt{(brd)}) \qquad \text{...(5.6)}$$

$$A(m) = \frac{1}{b}(\sqrt{(brd)} - br), \qquad \text{...(5.7)}$$

where $d = m - p_0$, $\bar{p}$ and var are the mean and variance of the sales price distribution, and $\bar{p}_{ad}$ is the mean of the advertising price distribution.

Let $\underline{z}$ be the vector of parameters (b, r, d), let E be the elasticity operator, and let $\mathbf{X}$ be the cartesian product symbol. Then the comparative statics of the model may be summarized as follows:

$$\frac{E(1-\xi)}{E\underline{z}} = (\tfrac{1}{2}, \tfrac{1}{2}, -\tfrac{1}{2}) \qquad \text{...(5.3a)}$$

$$\frac{E(\bar{p}-p_0)}{E\underline{z}} = (\tfrac{1}{2}, \tfrac{1}{2}, \tfrac{1}{2}) \qquad \text{...(5.4a)}$$

$$\frac{E\,(\text{var})}{E\underline{z}} \in \mathop{\mathbf{X}}_{i=1}^{3} (\tfrac{1}{2}, \tfrac{3}{2}) \qquad \text{...(5.5a)}$$

$$\frac{E(\bar{p}_{ad}-p_0)}{E\underline{z}} \in \mathop{\mathbf{X}}_{i=1}^{3} (\tfrac{1}{2}, 1) \qquad \text{...(5.6a)}$$

$$\frac{EA(m)}{E\underline{z}} \in (-\tfrac{1}{2}, 0)\mathbf{X}(-1, \tfrac{1}{2})\mathbf{X}(0, \tfrac{1}{2}). \qquad \text{...(5.7a)}$$

It may be noted that as r approaches zero, ξ approaches one and $\bar{p}-p_0$, var, $\bar{p}_{ad}-p_0$, and $A(m)$ all approach zero. Since r is the Poisson " death rate " of each buyer, this means that as consumers expected lifetimes, $1/r$, grow large, the price distributions approach a spike at the cost of production. Consumer transiency is necessary to maintain price dispersion.

The second development of this section is an oligopoly theory which contains the results of Section 2 as a limiting case. To be precise, let us consider the model of Section 2 with the single change that the number of sellers is a finite, possibly small number, n. In particular, it is still assumed that there is a large number (for convenience, a continuum) of buyers. In a fully rigorous analysis, one would need to proceed in the manner of Appendix A, by taking the limit as the number of buyers, M, gets large, holding n constant.

In this model, in contrast to the result of Section 2, the equilibrium advertising price distributions do not turn out to be unique. Indeed, I conjecture that there exists a continuum of equilibria which have different advertising price distributions, but identical sales price distributions. This conjecture is based on two specific equilibria which I have constructed, and which I consider to be polar cases of a continuum of additional equilibria. In one of these equilibria, each seller sends out ads at only a single price, chosen randomly. In the second equilibrium, each seller sends out ads at a continuum of prices, chosen deterministically. A unique solution can be ensured by requiring either that (i) each seller must advertise at most a single price, or (ii) each seller must choose his prices deterministically.

Let us continue the discussion by examining in more detail the second case. The ith seller's strategy then consists of a function $A_i(p)$, which, for each value of p, equals the number of ads sent by that seller at prices less than or equal to p, divided by the number of buyers. In addition, let us define $F_i(A_1, ..., A_n)$ as the expected profits of the ith seller per potential buyer when the sellers follow the advertising policies represented by the functions $A_1, ..., A_n$. A Nash equilibrium is then defined as a set of functions $A_1, ..., A_n$ such that, for all i, the function $F_i(A_1, ..., A_n)$ cannot be made larger by replacing A_i with a different function. In other words, each seller is choosing his strategy so as to maximize his expected profits given the strategies of the other sellers.

Computing this equilibrium is a straight-forward exercise in the calculus of variations. It turns out that the market advertising and sales price distributions are described by the following equations:

$$a(p) = \begin{cases} 0 & p \leqq p_{\min} \\ \dfrac{n}{(n-1)} \cdot \dfrac{1}{(p-p_0)} & \text{for} \quad p \in (p_{\min}, m) \\ 0 & p \geqq m \end{cases} \qquad \ldots(5.8)$$

$$s(p) = \begin{cases} 0 & p \leqq p_{\min} \\ \dfrac{n}{n-1} \cdot \dfrac{b \cdot d^{1/(n-1)}}{(p-p_0)^{2+1/(n-1)}} & \text{for} \quad p \in (p_{\min}, m) \\ 0 & p \geqq m \end{cases}, \qquad \ldots(5.9)$$

where $d = m-p_0$ and $p_{\min} = p_0+b\cdot(d/b)^{1/n}$. Each seller's advertising and sales functions are given by $a_i(p) = a(p)/n$ and $s_i(p) = s(p)/n$. It also follows that:

$$\bar{p} = p_0 + \frac{bdn}{d-b}\left[\left(\frac{d}{b}\right)^{1/n} - 1\right] \qquad \ldots(5.10)$$

$$A(m) = \ln \frac{d}{b} \qquad \ldots(5.11)$$

$$S(m) = 1 - \frac{b}{d}, \qquad \ldots(5.12)$$

and, for all i:

$$F_i(A_1, \ldots, A_n) = b\left\{\left[\left(\frac{d}{b}\right)^{1/n} - 1\right] - \ln\left(\frac{d}{b}\right)\right\}. \qquad \ldots(5.13)$$

It follows from equation (5.10) and (5.13) that profits are positive and that, as the number of sellers increases, both total profits and the mean sales price decrease at a decreasing rate. Note also from equations (5.11) and (5.12) that the total quantity of advertising and sales are independent of the number of sellers. Furthermore, from Section 4 we know that this amount of advertising is Pareto optimal as well. This result is an artifact of the assumption that all buyers have the same limit price; thus if sellers collectively raise prices, the effect is only a redistribution of wealth, not a change in sales. Indeed, in the extreme case of a single seller (who can easily be shown to send out the same quantity of advertising at the limit price), it should be no surprise that the market is efficient; for when all buyers are identical, the seller is in effect a perfectly discriminating monopolist.

The oligopoly analysis can easily be modified to incorporate either buyers' search or continuous purchasing. Since no new results of note arise, this analysis will be omitted. It is not so easy, however, to incorporate both buyers' search and continuous purchasing into a single model. This topic remains open for further work.

To conclude this section I will simply assert that one can also extend the model, in any of its variants, to the case of U-shaped average production cost curves. None of the results is adversely affected.

6. CONCLUSION

The contents of this paper are subject to a variety of criticisms. One immediate issue is whether or not the amount of price dispersion accounted for by the models is empirically significant. It may or may not be; I have not done any empirical work to test the models. Operationally, the theory is quite vague. " Advertising " may be interpreted more or less broadly to incorporate any selection of the usual advertising expenses, displays, promotions, packaging, rent for conspicuous location and the like. The parameters b, c and m are clearly difficult to specify. The question of how narrowly the good should be defined is left open. Nevertheless, the broad predictions of the theory seem consistent with at least some casual observation: Bayer's aspirin, a heavily advertised brand, sells at a much higher price than Swan's aspirin, Lavoris mouthwash sells at a price more than twice as high as Stop and Shop's brand, and Blue Cross and Blue Shield provide substantially more coverage per dollar than certain heavily promoted mail-order health insurance plans. It should be noted, however, that the above examples do not fit the conditions of the model precisely; the advertising for Lavoris mouthwash, for example, does not generally give price or location.

One may make particular criticisms by questioning the appropriateness of particular assumptions of the models. The assumption of a homogeneous good rules out all problems concerning quality differences, jointly provided services, locational convenience and the like. This leads to two problems: one is that much advertising consists of identifying more precisely the nature of a commodity and making claims about its quality; the second is that when quality is uncertain, price advertising is no longer a totally reliable guide to the best buy. Another questionable assumption is that of honest advertising; a model which explains the motivation for honesty would be an improvement over the present ones. The assumption that consumers cannot search for ads is perhaps unnecessarily restrictive. The assumption that all agents know the price distribution is especially difficult to accept. My defence to all these criticisms is simply that one must start somewhere, and it is generally both easier and more productive to start with simple models as opposed to complicated ones.

A somewhat different criticism is embodied in the following discussion. Suppose that there did exist significant price dispersion in a market for a homogeneous good with many buyers and sellers. Then one would expect a consumer agency, perhaps the local newspaper, to organize and make profits by researching various sellers, finding out which ones sell at the lowest price, and selling this information to potential buyers. One may object that public goods problems arise, or that the consumer agency must advertise its own existence and prices. However, the consumer agency could provide information on many different goods and only have to advertise its own existence. Countering this argument is the fact that a single store can carry many goods and establish a price reputation on its entire line.

Taking a slightly different tack, why do not prospective buyers simply look up sellers in the Yellow Pages and make a few phone calls to get price offers? This form of search, at least relative to high-priced items, is so cheap that it is hard to imagine how any significant price dispersion could persist. I believe that the gist of this argument is correct. One can appeal to differences in quality or variety which are either expensive to evaluate or over which consumers have varying preferences to explain why this search by telephone does not occur in many cases. How this can be modelled and whether or not the conclusions of this chapter carry over to such a general framework remains to be seen.

Another criticism along these lines is the fact that all the models predict that the amount of price dispersion depends solely on the parameters b, c and m (or d), and not on p_0. That means that the models predict that price variation should be no greater for expensive items than for cheap ones. If salt sells in the range of 15 to 25 cents a box, then automobiles of a specific type should sell in the range of \$3,000.15 to \$3,000.25. The remedy is to say that costs of advertising and search are greater for expensive items, but the reason why this is true depends fundamentally on the heterogeneity of the product. It is thus my conclusion that the most fruitful course for further research along these lines is to study how heterogeneity and lack of perfect information interact to determine equilibrium price distributions.

I would like to thank Lester Telser, William Brock and Robert Lucas, the members of my dissertation committee at the University of Chicago, for their aid and encouragement. Thanks also are due to Milton Harris, Charles Wilson and Michael Rothschild for additional helpful discussions.

NOTES

1. A more recent survey has been written by Lippman and McCall [4].
2. See Diamond [3] and Arrow and Rothschild [1] for more detailed discussions of similar propositions.
3. Indeed, in this formulation, the case in which all sellers offer their goods at the monopoly price is not an equilibrium either, because if consumers know they must pay m in addition to their search cost c, they will not find it worth while to search in the first place. The only equilibrium is the situation of no trade.
4. The use of coupons, discounts, bonuses and special sales are examples of indirect ways in which sellers may advertise different prices to different buyers.
5. Considering the cost of collating mailing lists or of reaching different audiences in television and newspaper advertising, this assumption has a certain plausibility.
6. This assumption is very restrictive and will be relaxed in Section 3.
7. Alternatively, we could assume that the cost is some non-zero constant; the point is that the sellers' locations are important only in an informational sense, not a spatial one.
8. Formally, an advertising policy is a function α: $R^+ \rightarrow Z^+$, where R^+ is the set of positive reals and Z^+ is the set of positive integers. For example, $\alpha(p) = 2$ means that two ads are to be sent out at price p. More generally, sellers may adopt randomized advertising strategies; that is, they may choose their advertising policy according to some random procedure. Formally, a mixed advertising strategy is a measure μ on the set of all functions α mapping R^+ to Z^+
9. In the case in which mixed strategies are admitted, see Proposition 2 of Appendix A for a formal proof of continuity. If only fixed strategies are admitted, then Nash equilibria do not exist at all, but Proposition 9 of the same appendix states the approximate continuity result which is valid for ε-equilibria.
10. This is not strictly true. For a more rigorous discussion, refer to the development of Appendix A up to the proof of Proposition 6.
11. This statement has one of two meanings. If randomized strategies are admitted, it means that the equilibrium advertising strategies assign a positive probability to advertising in any interval of prices within $(p_{\min}, m)$. If only fixed strategies are admitted, then one can say that as M and N get large, the maximum size of the interval on which no price is advertised approaches zero for the appropriately defined ε-equilibria. For details, see Appendix A.
12. The possibility that an opponent may advertise at exactly p_1 or p_2 is ignored because Proposition A2 asserts that in equilibrium it occurs with probability zero.

REFERENCES

[1] Arrow, K. J. and Rothschild, M. " Preliminary Notes on Equilibrium Price Distributions with Limited Information " (The Economics Series, Institute of Mathematical Studies in the Social Sciences, Working Paper No. 34, August 1973).

[2] Butters, G. R. " Equilibrium Price Distributions and the Economics of Information (Ph.D. Dissertaton, University of Chicago, 1975).

[3] Diamond, P. A. " A Model of Price Adjustment ", *Journal of Economic Theory*, **3** (1971), 156-168.

[4] Lippman, S. and McCall, J. J. " The Economics of Job Search: A Survey ", *Economic Inquiry*, **14** (1976), 113-126.

[5] Rothschild, M. " Models of Market Organization with Imperfect Information: A Survey ", *Journal of Political Economy*, **81** (1973), 1283-1308.

[6] Stigler, G. J. " The Economics of Information ", *Journal of Political Economy*, **69** (1961), 213-225.

Comment

The equilibrium in this article has a distribution of prices, with price setters doing the searching. Wilde (1977) has examined equilibrium with a distribution of wages, with firms setting wages and workers doing the searching. In contrast to these two articles, some of the models surveyed in Chapter 27 had a single price in equilibrium. With consumers identical, the distinction between the two types of equilibria depends upon the nature of the information technology. When information sending and gathering behavior results in consumers sometimes receiving one offer and sometimes more than one, there will be a distribution of prices. When offers arrive one at a time, there will be a single price. This difference has been examined by Burdett and Judd (1983).

References

K. Burdett and K. Judd, Equilibrium price dispersion, *Econometrica* **51** (1983), 955–69.

L. Wilde, Labor market equilibrium under nonsequential search, *J. Econ. Theory* **16** (1977), 373–93.

29

R. Lucas, Jr. and E. Prescott, Equilibrium search and unemployment, *Journal of Economic Theory* 7 (1974), 188–209

The readings surveyed in Chapter 27 had price-setting behavior by particular suppliers. It seems to us that this is a good description of many markets. An alternative approach to modeling price uncertainty is to have several different locations, with a standard competitive market at each location. This reading is a model of this sort, where randomness in demand across locations induces workers to move in response to anticipated job opportunities. Mortensen (1975) has considered a similar model, where the randomness comes from variations in the supply of labor at different locations as each worker randomly chooses among locations toward which he is indifferent. Mortensen shows that the competitive equilibrium is Pareto optimal. Hellwig (1976) has analyzed pairwise trade with random trade opportunities. In particular he examines convergence to the standard general equilibirium model as trading opportunities become increasingly frequent. For a very interesting overlapping generation model with random division of traders between two markets, see Lucas (1972).

References

M. Hellwig, A model of monetary exchange, Princeton Econometric Research Program, Memorandum 202, 1976.

R. Lucas, Expectations and the neutrality of money, *J. Econ. Theory* 4 (1972), 103–124.

D. Mortensen, Job matching under imperfect information, *in* "Government Programs and Labor Market Analysis" (O. Ashenfelter, ed.). Industrial Relations Section, Princeton Univ. 1975.

JOURNAL OF ECONOMIC THEORY 7, 188–209 (1974)

Equilibrium Search and Unemployment

ROBERT E. LUCAS, JR. AND EDWARD C. PRESCOTT

Graduate School of Industrial Administration, Carnegie–Mellon University Pittsburgh, Pennsylvania 15213

Received November 27, 1972

1. INTRODUCTION

Thirty years after the Great Depression, economists have again worked up the nerve to ask an obvious question: Why is it that workers *choose* (under some conditions) to be unemployed rather than to take employment at lower wage rates? Soon after serious attention began to be focused on this question, a variety of models were advanced to illustrate how workers might rationally prefer some other activity to work at wage rates they perceive to be temporarily below normal.[1] A particularly interesting class of models arises when the alternate activity is taken to be job search: The worker is faced with a wage offer which he views as a drawing from a probability distribution; his choices are to accept the offer or to take another drawing.[2] (To be of interest, obviously, these choices must be mutually exclusive: One must be unable to search and work at the same time.)

Most contributors to this literature on search behavior subscribe to some form of the Friedman–Phelps notion that there exists a natural rate of unemployment which either cannot or should not (or perhaps both) be lowered (on average) by monetary and fiscal policies.[3] Yet while the language used in discussing this natural rate suggests that it may have the properties of a competitive equilibrium, there exist no theoretical models in which a nonzero equilibrium unemployment rate is determined

[1] A number of these are collected in Phelps *et al.* [10]. The central ideas can be traced at least back to Hicks [5].

[2] For example, the Mortensen and Gordon–Hynes chapters of [10], McCall [8], and Stigler [13]. It is perhaps necessary to emphasize that the class of models in which active job search is the *only* alternative to work by no means exhausts the class of models in which unemployment is viewed as a "rational" choice.

[3] In addition to the above references, see Friedman [4].

and its properties studied.[4] Normatively, this means that there is no framework within which important welfare issues such as those raised by Phelps [11, chapter 4] and Tobin [14] can be formulated and analyzed. Empirically, it means (for example) that there is no theoretical account as to why average rates of unemployment vary so widely from one advanced capitalist economy to another.

Clearly, one cannot hope to deal with these questions by the study of the optimal search behavior of a single agent in the face of a *given* probability distribution of wage offers. The issues are those of market equilibrium and must be met in a theoretical context in which employment behavior and wages are *simultaneously* determined. As the reader who proceeds into the body of this paper will discover, this problem is more difficult than it sounds. Let us try to indicate why in the remainder of this introduction.

In order for wage rates for a single type of labor to differ at a point in time, labor must clearly be exchanged in spatially distinct markets. (Otherwise, wages would be bid into equality in a period much too short to be of economic interest.) The distribution of wage rates governing the worker's decision problem, referred to above, must then be related to his knowledge of the likely outcome of searching over these distinct markets. On the other hand, the distribution of wages over markets will evidently be influenced by the mobility of labor suppliers. In short, optimal labor supply behavior and the wage distribution on which it is based must be simultaneously determined within a model of *market* (as opposed to individual) behavior.

While quite analogous to the problem of using supply and demand schedules to determine price and quantity in a single market, this simultaneity problem is analytically more difficult for at least two reasons. First, since movement in space takes time, labor market search must be studied in a dynamic context. Second, the outcome of the process at each point in time will be a probability distribution rather than simply a number. The *solution* of the model will then be a *stochastic process.*

The rest of this paper is devoted to the elaboration of a complete "search model" of this general type. To preserve simplicity, the treatment will be abstract and illustrative. Discussion of the relationship of the theory to observed labor market behavior will be deferred to the conclusion of the paper and will there be brief.

[4] Lucas [7] provides an equilibrium in which employment fluctuates with aggregate demand. In this model, however, "unemployment" as an activity is not differentiated from "leisure" or other nonwork alternatives.

2. Structure of the Model

We think of an economy in which production and sale of goods occur in a large number of spatially distinct markets.[5] Product demand in each market shifts stochastically, driven by shocks which are independent over markets (so that aggregate demand is constant) but autocorrelated within a single market. Output to satisfy current period demand is produced in the current period, with labor as the only input. Each product market is competitive.

There is a constant workforce which at the beginning of a period is distributed in some way over markets. In each market, labor is allocated over firms competitively with actual money wages being market clearing. Each worker may either work at this wage rate, in which case he will remain in this market into the next period, or leave. If he leaves, he earns nothing this period but enters a "pool" of unemployed workers which are distributed in some way over markets for the next period. In this way, a new workforce distribution is determined, new demands are "drawn," and the process continues.

In this process, all agents are assumed to behave optimally in light of their objectives and the information available to them. For firms, this means simply that labor is employed to the point at which its marginal value product equals the wage rate. For workers, the decision to work or to search is taken so as to maximize the expected, discounted present value of the earnings stream. In carrying out this calculation, workers are assumed to be aware of the values of the variables affecting the market where they currently are (i.e., demand and workforce) and of the true probability distributions governing the future state of this market and the present and future states of all others. That is, expectations are taken to be *rational*.[6]

The economic interpretation of this assumption of rational expectations is that agents have operated for some time in a situation like the current one and have therefore built up experience about the probability distributions which affect them. For this to have meaning, these distributions must remain stable through time. Mathematically, this means that we will be concerned only with *stationary distributions* of demand and workforce and with behavior rules under these stationary distributions. Although sequences tending toward these stationary distributions will be utilized analytically, these seem to have no counterpart in observed behavior.

[5] See Phelps' introductory chapter in [10] for the description of the "island economy" which is the direct ancestor of the present model.

[6] In the sense of Lucas and Prescott [6] and Muth [9].

The task of the following sections may now be outlined in more detail. In the next section, we study the determination of equilibrium employment and wages in a single market, with the expected return to workers of *leaving* that market taken as a parameter. In Section 4, the stationary joint distribution of demand and workforce in this market is determined. In Section 5, we aggregate the workforce over markets to obtain the total economy-wide workforce as a function of the parametric expected return. This relationship serves as an aggregate demand function for labor; given a fixed total workforce, the *equilibrium* expected return is then determined in the usual way. Finally, Section 6 discusses a certain kind of stability possessed by this equilibrium, and concluding remarks are given in Section 7.

3. Equilibrium in a Single Market

In this section and the next, we study wage and employment determination in a single market, representing the impact of the rest of the economy on this market by certain given parameters. This impact takes three forms: first, product demand functions shift in an exogenously determined, stochastic manner; second, the outside economy offers alternative employment to workers; third, new workers arrive from the rest of the economy, augmenting the local work force. We discuss each effect in turn.

The individual market behaves as a Marshallian industry, faced with a demand function $p = D(s, Q)$, where p is price, Q is industry output, and s is a stochastic shift variable, *realized prior to trading*. Output is supplied by m identical firms, each with the production function $\varphi(n)$ depending on labor input only. The industry is competitive, so that the profit (and present value) maximizing policy for firms is to hire labor to the point at which the marginal value product of labor, $p\varphi'(n)$, equals the wage. When the product market is cleared, then, the function $R(s, n)$ defined by

$$R(s, n) = D(s, m\varphi(n))\, \varphi'(n)$$

gives the marginal value product of labor when demand is in state s and employment is n. Since R summarizes completely the demand side of the labor market, we shall discard the functions D and φ and place restrictions directly on R, as follows.

The function $R(s, n)$ is positive, differentiable, and bounded; its first derivatives satisfy

$$R_s(s, n) > 0, \qquad R_n(s, n) < 0. \tag{1}$$

For each fixed n,

$$\lim_{s \to 0} R(s, n) = 0. \tag{2}$$

642/7/2-5

For each fixed w, $0 < w \leqslant R(s, 0)$, the function $\hat{n}(s, w)$ defined by $R(s, \hat{n}(s, w)) = w$ satisfies

$$\lim_{s\to\infty} \hat{n}(s, w) = \bar{n}(w) < \infty. \tag{3}$$

The shift variable s follows a Markov process governed by

$$F(s', s) = \Pr\{s_{t+1} \leqslant s' \mid s_t = s\}.$$

For fixed s, F is a cumulative distribution function on $s' > 0$, with the continuous, strictly positive density $f(s', s)$. For fixed s', F is a strictly decreasing function of s on $s > 0$; further, if g is continuous,

$$\lim_{s\to 0} \int g(s')f(s', s)\, ds' = \lim_{s\to 0} g(s), \tag{4}$$

and if g is also positive and nondecreasing,

$$\lim_{s\to\infty} \int g(s')f(s', s)\, ds' \leqslant \lim_{s\to\infty} g(s). \tag{5}$$

The process defined by F is assumed to possess a unique stationary distribution.[7]

The demand shifts s are assumed to be independent *across* markets, and the number of markets is large.[8] Further, the total workforce of the economy is fixed. In consequence, once the workforce has settled down to a stationary distribution over markets, the expected present value of job search is a constant, say λ. In this section and the next, we treat λ as a given parameter; its equilibrium value will be determined in Section 5.

At the beginning of the period, each market has a fixed workforce, y, which serves as an upper bound on current period employment in that market. All currently employed workers remain into the next period; currently unemployed workers leave. In addition, new workers arrive in a stochastic fashion, the exact nature of which depends on the search process which is assumed. In the present paper, we shall impose a particular property on the *outcome* of this process, namely that unemployed

[7] For an example of a Markov process satisfying all these restrictions, including (4) and (5), let (ϵ_t) be a sequence of independent, normal variates, let $0 < r < 1$, and let s_t follow

$$\ln(s_{t+1}) = a + r\ln(s_t) + \epsilon_t .$$

[8] By large, we mean either a continuum of markets or a countable infinity. Economically, then, the assumption of independent demand shifts means that *aggregate* demand is taken to be constant through time.

workers are allocated over markets in such a way as to equate to the opportunity cost λ the expected return in each market receiving workers. The precise arrival rate which will guarantee this outcome will be specified below.[9]

To summarize, the *state* of a particular market is completely described by its state of demand, s, its beginning of period workforce, y, and the expected present value of search, λ. Of these three variables, only s and y vary from market to market; accordingly, we use (s, y) to index markets (referring, for example, to "market (s, y)"). Then for market (s, y), we seek equilibrium values of wages and employment, $w(s, y, \lambda)$ and $n(s, y, \lambda)$, as functions of the state of the market. An equilibrium must satisfy both the market clearing condition

$$w(s, y, \lambda) = R(s, n(s, y, \lambda)) \tag{6}$$

and the labor supply constraint

$$n(s, y, \lambda) \leqslant y. \tag{7}$$

Additional equilibrium conditions will be obtained by considering the present value maximizing work–search decision made by workers.

To study this choice, let $v(s, y, \lambda)$ be the expected present value of the wage stream for a worker who finds himself in (s, y) at the beginning of the period. In general, $v(s, y, \lambda)$ will equal the current wage plus the expected present value of the wage stream from next period on, discounted to the present by a constant factor β, $0 < \beta < 1$. Formally,

$$v(s, y, \lambda) = w(s, y, \lambda) + \beta E\{v(s', y', \lambda)\}$$

where the expectation is taken with respect to the distribution (as yet undetermined) of next period's state, (s', y') conditional on the information currently available to workers: (s, y, λ). The value of the terms on the right will vary with (s, y); it is convenient to consider three cases separately, as follows.

Case A. Some (or all) workers leave; some (or none) remain.

In this case, departing workers earn the expected return from search. Remaining workers earn no less, since they have the option to leave, and no more, since departing workers have the option to remain. Thus

$$v(s, y, \lambda) = \lambda. \tag{8a}$$

[9] In Eq. (19).

Case B1. All workers remain; no additional workers arrive next period.

In this case, current employment is the total workforce y and the current wage is, from (6), $R(s, y)$. Since the current workforce is maintained into the following period, next period's state is (s', y), with s' given probabilistically by $f(s', s)$. Thus

$$v(s, y, \lambda) = R(s, y) + \beta \int v(s', y, \lambda) f(s', s)\, ds'. \tag{8b1}$$

Case B2. All workers remain; some additional workers arrive next period.

In this case, the arriving workers, in common with *all* searchers, have an expected present value (discounted to the present) of λ. Thus, for them and for the workers remaining in (s, y), $\beta E\{v(s', y', \lambda)\}$ will have the common value λ, and

$$v(s, y, \lambda) = R(s, y) + \lambda. \qquad \text{(8b2))}$$

Evidently, these three cases divide the positive quadrant of the (s, y) plane into three mutually exclusive and exhaustive subsets.[10]

Now comparing cases B1 and B2, we observe that if no new workers are expected to arrive (case B1), it must be that expected rent in (s, y) is non-positive with a future workforce of y, or that $\beta \int v(s', y, \lambda) f(s', s)\, ds' \leqslant \lambda$. Thus, (8b1) and (8b2) may be combined as

$$v(s, y, \lambda) = R(s, y) + \min \left[\lambda, \beta \int v(s', y, \lambda) f(s', s)\, ds'\right]. \tag{8b}$$

Finally, comparing cases A and B, we observe that remaining workers in either case have rejected the option to search, so that $v(s, y, \lambda) \geqslant \lambda$. Thus, (8a) and (8b) may combine to yield a single functional equation valid for all cases:

$$v(s, y, \lambda) = \max \left\{\lambda, R(s, y) + \min \left[\lambda, \beta \int v(s', y, \lambda) f(s', s)\, ds'\right]\right\}. \tag{8}$$

The relevant facts about (8) are given in:

PROPOSITION 1. *Equation* (8) *has a unique solution* $v(s, y, \lambda)$. *The function* v *is continuous in* (s, y, λ), *nondecreasing in* s *and* λ, *nonincreasing in* y, *and satisfies*

$$| v(s, y, \lambda_1) - v(s, y, \lambda_2)| < (1/\beta) \mid \lambda_1 - \lambda_2 \mid \tag{9}$$

[10] See Fig. 3 (which we do not at this point in the argument have enough information to draw) for this partioning of the positive quadrant.

for any λ_1, λ_2. *For each* y, λ,

$$\lim_{s \to 0} v(s, y, \lambda) = \lambda, \tag{10}$$

and for s *sufficiently large,*

$$v(s, y, \lambda) \leqslant R(s, y)/(1 - \beta). \tag{11}$$

Proof. Let T_λ, an operator which maps bounded continuous functions u on (s, y) into the same space, be defined by

$$T_\lambda u(s, y) = \max \left\{ \lambda, R(s, y) + \min \left[\lambda, \beta \int u(s', y) f(s', s) \, ds' \right] \right\}.$$

The operator T_λ is monotonic: $u \geqslant v$ for all (s, y) implies $T_\lambda u \geqslant T_\lambda v$. For any constant c and function u, $T_\lambda(u + c) \leqslant T_\lambda u + \beta c$. By a slight modification of Theorem 5 of Blackwell [1], these two facts imply that T_λ is a contraction mapping. Thus, Eq. (8), $T_\lambda v = v$, has a unique, continuous solution and $\lim_{n \to \infty} T_\lambda u = v$ for any continuous u.

If $u(s, y)$ is increasing in s and decreasing in y, so is $T_\lambda u$, using (1). Hence, $v = \lim T_\lambda{}^n u$ is nondecreasing in s and nonincreasing in y.

Let $\lambda_1 > \lambda_2$. Clearly, $T_{\lambda_1} v(s, y, \lambda_2) \geqslant v(s, y, \lambda_2)$ for all (s, y). Since the operator T_{λ_1} is monotonic, we have

$$v(s, y, \lambda_1) = \lim_{n \to \infty} T_{\lambda_1}^n v(s, y, \lambda_2) \geqslant v(s, y, \lambda_2).$$

Hence v is nondecreasing in λ.

To verify (9), let $\lambda_1 > \lambda_2$ and define $u(s, y) = v(s, y, \lambda_2) + (\lambda_1 - \lambda_2)/\beta$. Then from the definitions of T_{λ_1} and $v(s, y, \lambda_2)$, we have, since $\beta < 1$,

$$T_{\lambda_1} u(s, y) = v(s, y, \lambda_2) + \lambda_1 - \lambda_2 < u(s, y).$$

Then by the monotonicity of T_{λ_1},

$$v(s, y, \lambda_1) = \lim_{n \to \infty} T_{\lambda_1}^n u(s, y) < u(s, y) = v(s, y, \lambda_2) + (\lambda_1 - \lambda_2)/\beta.$$

To prove (10), let $v_0 = 0$ and apply T_λ repeatedly, using (2) and (4) at each step.

To prove (11), let $v_0 = 0$ and apply T_λ repeatedly, using (5) at each step.

This proves Proposition 1.

With the value function v determined, we return to the determination of equilibrium employment and wages and of the equilibrium behavior of new arrivals. To determine employment, let $\tilde{n}(s, \lambda)$ be the employment that would occur in a market with demand s if the workforce constraint were not present. Thus, $\tilde{n}$ is the solution to

$$R(s, \tilde{n}(s, \lambda)) + \min \left[\lambda, \beta \int v(s', \tilde{n}(s, \lambda), \lambda) f(s', s)\, ds'\right] = \lambda.$$

Since R is positive, the solution cannot occur when the second term on the left is λ, so we may simplify to

$$R(s, \tilde{n}(s, \lambda)) + \beta \int v(s', \tilde{n}(s, \lambda), \lambda) f(s', s)\, ds' = \lambda. \tag{12}$$

Then, clearly, equilibrium employment is

$$n(s, y, \lambda) = \min[\tilde{n}(s, \lambda), y], \tag{13}$$

and equilibrium wages are found using (6). We summarize in

PROPOSITION 2. *For each fixed* (s, y, λ), *there exist unique equilibrium employment and wage functions* $n(s, y, \lambda)$ *and* $w(s, y, \lambda)$ *defined implicitly by* (6), (8), (12), *and* (13). *These functions are continuous in* (s, y, λ) *and satisfy the monotonicity properties*[11]

$$n_s \geqslant 0, \qquad n_y \geqslant 0, \qquad n_\lambda \leqslant 0, \tag{14}$$

$$w_s \geqslant 0, \qquad w_y \leqslant 0, \qquad w_\lambda \geqslant 0. \tag{15}$$

Also, for each fixed (y, λ),

$$\lim_{s \to 0} n(s, y, \lambda) = 0 \tag{16}$$

and

$$\lim_{s \to \infty} n(s, y, \lambda) = \min[\bar{n}(\lambda), y], \tag{17}$$

where $\bar{n}(\lambda)$ *is a finite bound, varying with* λ.

The *proof* of Proposition 2 is facilitated by reference to Fig. 1 which exhibits the left side of (12) as a function of n.

By (1) and Proposition 1, the curves in Fig. 1 are negatively sloped and shift to the right as s increases. As λ increases, these curves shift upward by Proposition 1 but, from (9), by an amount less than the increase in λ. Then, using (13), (14) is proved; (15) follows from (14) and (6).

[11] We use the usual notation for partial derivatives, recognizing that the monotonicity properties only imply that they exist almost everywhere.

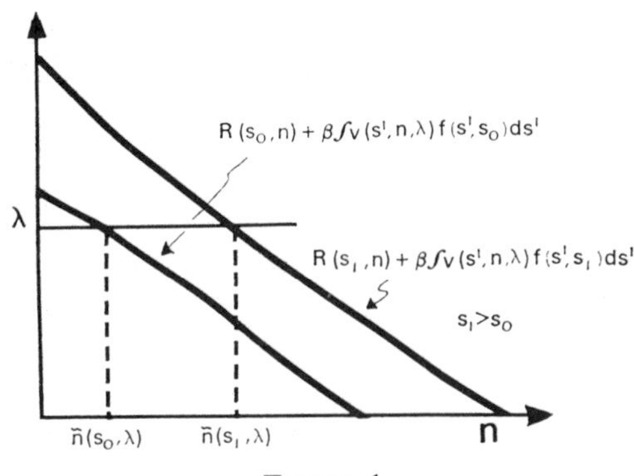

FIGURE 1

Applying (2), (4), and (10), (16) is proved.

Applying (3), (5), and (11), (17) is proved.

The results of this section may be illustrated on a conventional supply–demand diagram for labor. The demand curve is simply the marginal productivity condition (6), which shifts with the state of product demand, s. The curve SS is the relation between n and w implicit in (6) and (12): it is the locus of the wage–employment pairs which would be traced out as demand shifts if the workforce y did not constrain employment. The boldface curve is then the labor supply curve associated with the workforce y. The curve SS shifts up with increases in opportunity cost λ.

We remark that SS will not be flat, as would be the case if workers held a fixed "reservation wage" above which they accept employment and below which they do not. The reason this does not occur lies in the fact that as demand varies, wage and price changes convey information about future wage prospects as well as current earnings. Thus, as demand shifts to the left and employment declines, future prospects in (s, y) are affected

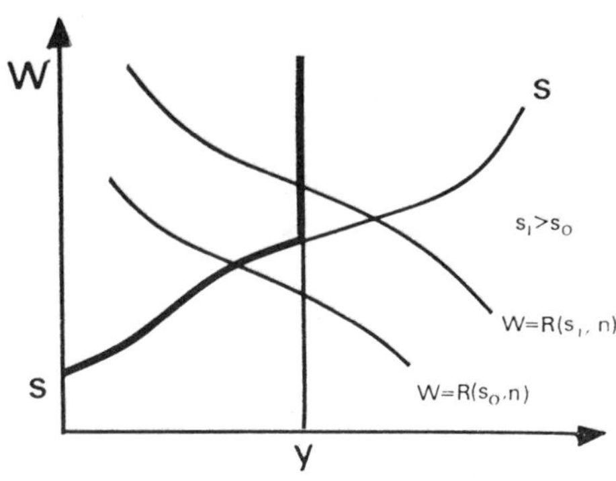

FIGURE 2

in two ways: first, lower demand this period increases the probability of a low demand next period as well; second, lower employment this period implies a lower workforce next period. These effects work in opposite directions, which is to say that on any interval, the curve SS may be either upward sloping (as drawn in Fig. 2) or downward sloping.

4. The Equilibrium Distribution of the Workforce

Implicit in the above discussion of equilibrium employment in a single market is the stochastic law relating a market's *next period* workforce to its current period demand and workforce, (s, y). In the present section, we make this law explicit, then develop its implications for the stationary joint distribution of demand and workforce.

In the preceding section, we postulated that all unemployed workers move toward markets with nonnegative expected rents. From the discussion of cases B1 and B2 above, it is clear that a market will attract new workers only if $n(s, y, \lambda) = y$ *and*

$$\beta \int v(s', y, \lambda) f(s', s)\, ds \geqslant \lambda. \tag{18}$$

If searchers were perfectly directed toward markets, each market satisfying (18) would receive exactly the arrivals a such that $y + a$ would satisfy (18) with equality. Equation (8) remains valid, however, under the somewhat weaker requirement that the search process eliminate rents on average. Specifically, let x be a positive random variable with the strictly positive density ϕ, c.d.f. Φ, and mean 1. We assume that each market (s, y) satisfying (18) receives $a(s, y, \lambda)x$ new workers, where the function $a(s, y, \lambda)$ is defined implicitly by

$$\beta \iint v(s', y + a(s, y, \lambda)\, x, \lambda) f(s', s)\, \phi(x)\, ds'\, dx = \lambda \tag{19}$$

if (s, y, λ) satisfies (18), and

$$a(s, y, \lambda) = 0 \tag{19a}$$

otherwise.[12]

[12] The arbitrariness in the search hypothesis (19) seems unavoidable, at least in the absence of a physically described process of search (e.g., the hypothesis that searchers follow a random walk over markets viewed as points in the plane). Our own attempts to formulate processes of the latter type have rapidly led to a complexity uncompensated by additional economic insight.

The hypothesis (19) seems roughly to capture the following sort of process. Unemployed workers are informed (by advertising, word of mouth, etc.) of which markets

The possible transitions from (s, y) are illustrated in Fig. 3. If (s, y) is in region I, current employment and next period's workforce is $n(s, \lambda)$, and $y - n(s, \lambda)$ workers enter the unemployed pool. Markets in region II neither contribute to nor receive from the unemployment pool, maintaining their current workforce into the next period. Markets in region III employ all their workforce and receive new workers for next period, as specified by (19).

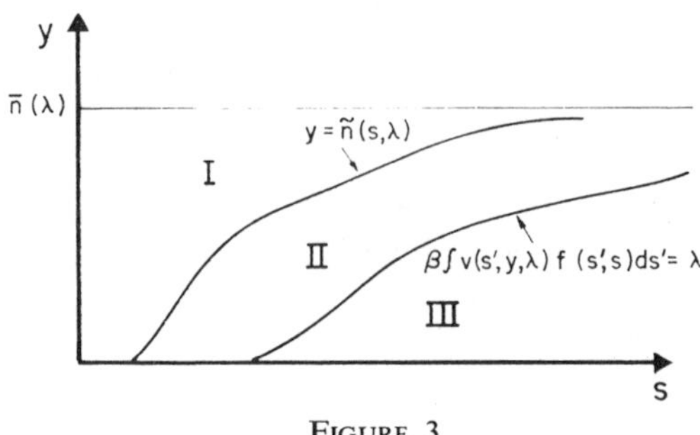

FIGURE 3

Analytically, the transitions from (s, y) are described by[13]

$$\begin{aligned}&\Pr\{s_{t+1} \leqslant s', y_{t+1} \leqslant y' \mid s_t = s, y_t = y\}\\&\quad = F(s', s) \Pr\{n(s, y, \lambda) + a(s, y, \lambda)\, x \leqslant y'\}\\&\quad = F(s', s)\, \Phi\left(\frac{y' - n(s, y, \lambda)}{a(s, y, \lambda)}\right)\end{aligned}$$

These transition probabilities define an operator P on distribution functions $\Psi(s, y)$ as follows: Suppose that at a point in time, demand and workforce are distributed according to the c.d.f. Ψ; then the demand–workforce distribution next period is

$$P\Psi(s', y') = \iint F(s', s)\, \Phi\left(\frac{y' - n(s, y, \lambda)}{a(s, y, \lambda)}\right) \Psi(ds, dy). \tag{20}$$

We wish to show that the (s, y) process has a unique stationary distribution, or to prove.

---

need workers (are in region III of Fig. 3) and in which of these demand is greatest. All workers move toward a market in this class. Since the search is not coordinated, there is a stochastic element in the relationship between the actual "shortage" and arrivals of new workers.

[13] We use the convention that when $a(s, y, \lambda) = 0$, division of a positive (negative) number by $a(s, y, \lambda)$ yields $+ (-) \infty$. A c.d.f. evaluated at $+\infty$ is 1; evaluated at $-\infty$, it is 0.

PROPOSITION 3. *With P defined by* (11), $P\Psi = \Psi$ *has a unique solution* Ψ^* *(for each fixed* λ*) and* $\lim_{n\to\infty} P^n\Psi = \Psi^*$ *for all* Ψ*. Further,* Ψ^* *possesses a continuous density* ψ^* *which is strictly positive on* $(s > 0, y \geqslant 0)$.

The proof of Proposition 3 follows the treatment of Feller [3, pp. 264–268] or Doob [2, pp. 190–221]. The essential elements are the proofs of

LEMMA 1. *For any initial distribution* Ψ*, the sequence* $\{P^n\Psi\}$ *is stochastically bounded.*

and

LEMMA 2. *For any nondegenerate rectangle* R *in* $(s > 0, y \geqslant 0)$ *and any initial distribution* Ψ*, there is some* m *such that for all* $n > m$*, the distribution* $P^n\Psi$ *assigns positive probability to* R.

The second of these two lemmas specifies that the entire set $(s > 0, y > 0)$ is the ergodic set and contains no cyclically moving subsets; the first assures that most of the probability remains concentrated on a bounded subset of $(s > 0, y \geqslant 0)$. Together, these facts imply Proposition 3.

Proof of Lemma 1

For probabilities assigned by $P^n\Psi$, we use the notation $\Pr\{(s_n, y_n) \in A\}$. For arbitrary $\epsilon > 0$ and initial distribution Ψ, we wish to find $(\bar{s}, \bar{y})$ such that

$$(P^n\Psi)(\bar{s}, \bar{y}) = \Pr\{s_n \leqslant \bar{s}, y_n \leqslant \bar{y}\} \geqslant 1 - \epsilon$$

uniformly in n. Evidently, it will be sufficient to verify this inequality for $n \geqslant m$ for some m.

We have

$$\Pr\{s_n \leqslant \bar{s}, y_n \leqslant \bar{y}\} \geqslant 1 - \Pr\{s_n \geqslant \bar{s}\} - \Pr\{y_n \geqslant \bar{y}\}.$$

Since $\{s_n\}$ has a stationary distribution, $\bar{s}$ may be chosen so that $\Pr\{s_n \geqslant \bar{s}\} \leqslant \epsilon/2$ for n sufficiently large. Let $\bar{n}(\lambda)$ be the employment bound referred to in (17), Proposition 2. Choose $\bar{y}$ so that

$$\Pr\{x \geqslant (\bar{y} - \bar{n}(\lambda))/a(\bar{s}, 0, \lambda)\} = 1 - \Phi[(\bar{y} - \bar{n}(\lambda))/a(\bar{s}, 0, \lambda)] \leqslant \epsilon/2.$$

Then since $a(s, y, \lambda)$ is increasing in s and decreasing in y,

$$\Pr\{y_n \geqslant \bar{y}\} \leqslant \Pr\{\bar{n}(\lambda) + a(\bar{s}, 0, \lambda)x \geqslant \bar{y}\} \leqslant \epsilon/2.$$

This completes the proof of Lemma 1.

Proof of Lemma 2

We shall show that if the distribution is initially concentrated on an arbitrary point (s_0, y_0), then $\Pr\{\underline{s} \leqslant s_n \leqslant \bar{s},\ \underline{y} \leqslant y_n \leqslant \bar{y}\} > 0$ for all $n \geqslant 3$, provided $\underline{s} < \bar{s}$ and $\underline{y} < \bar{y}$.

Let $\tilde{y}$ satisfy $\beta \int v(s', \tilde{y}, \lambda) f(s', \underline{s})\, ds' = \lambda$ (so that $(\underline{s}, \tilde{y})$ is on the lower curve in Fig. 3), and let $\tilde{s}$ satisfy $\tilde{y} = \tilde{n}(\tilde{s}, \lambda)$ (so that $(\tilde{s}, \tilde{y})$ is on the upper curve of Fig. 3). Then since $f(s', s)$ is strictly positive,

$$\Pr\{n(s_1, y_1) \leqslant \tilde{y},\ s_1 \leqslant \tilde{s} \mid (s_0, y_0)\} > 0$$

for any (s_0, y_0), and, therefore,

$$\Pr\{y_2 \leqslant \tilde{y},\ \underline{s} \leqslant s_2 \leqslant \bar{s}\} > 0.$$

Then since $\phi(x)$ is strictly positive,

$$\Pr\{\underline{y} \leqslant y_3 \leqslant \bar{y},\ \underline{s} \leqslant s_3 \leqslant \bar{s}\} > 0.$$

Evidently, the passage thus described may occur in any number of steps greater than three, so the proof is complete.

For each fixed λ, then, the (s, y) process has a unique stationary distribution, described by its c.d.f. $\Psi(s, y, \lambda)$ or its density $\psi(s, y, \lambda)$. In the remainder of this section, we study the behavior of mean values of functions of (s, y) taken with respect to Ψ as the parameter λ varies. The result of this examination is

PROPOSITION 4. *Let $\psi(s, y, \lambda)$ be the stationary density found in Proposition* 3, *and let $g(s, y)$ be continuous. Then if the integral*

$$h(\lambda) = \iint g(s, y)\, \psi(s, y, \lambda)\, ds\, dy$$

exists, it is a continuous function of λ.

The *proof* begins with the observation that one can always select a closed rectangle R, with the complement $\tilde{R}$ containing the (s, y) pairs with either very small or very large s-values, such that

$$\iint_{\tilde{R}} |\, g(s, y)|\ |\, \psi(s, y, \lambda_1) - \psi(s, y, \lambda_0)|\, ds\, dy \leqslant \delta$$

for any λ_0, λ_1 and $\delta > 0$. We shall be concerned, then, only with showing that the above integral taken over R tends to zero with $|\, \lambda_1 - \lambda_0\,|$. We do so with heavy reliance on Fig. 3.

As λ increases (say from λ_0 to λ_1), the curves in Fig. 3 both shift down (by Propositions 1 and 2). This implies that $\Psi(s, y, \lambda_1)$ lies everywhere (on the y-axis) to the *left* of $\Psi(s, y, \lambda_0)$. (That is, high λ values are associated with low workforce levels.) Now since the functions $\tilde{n}(s, \lambda)$ and $v(s, y, \lambda)$ are continuous, there is a maximum absolute vertical shift, $c(\lambda_0, \lambda_1)$, of the two curves on R. Further, c tends to zero with $\lambda_1 - \lambda_0$.

By the argument used to prove Proposition 3, one can find the c.d.f. $\Psi(s, y, \lambda_0, c)$ implied by a *constant* shift of c in both curves of Fig. 3. Evidently, this c.d.f. lies everywhere to the left of $\Psi(s, y, \lambda_1)$, so that the *horizontal* distance between $\Psi(s, y, \lambda_1)$ and $\Psi(s, y, \lambda_0)$ is bounded from above by the horizontal distance between $\Psi(s, y, \lambda_0, c)$ and $\Psi(s, y, \lambda_0)$. But $\Psi(s, y, \lambda_0, c) = \Psi(s, y - c, \lambda_0)$, so this latter distance is simply c, which tends to zero with $\lambda_1 - \lambda_0$.

Since Ψ possesses a continuous density, this continuity property is sufficient to guarantee the continuity of $h(\lambda)$.

5. Economy-wide Equilibrium

Propositions 1–4 describe the determination of the stationary distributions of employment, workforce, and wages in a representative market, with the expected return from search, λ, treated as a given parameter. From an economy-wide viewpoint, however, it is the size of the workforce which is fixed and the "price" λ which adjusts to clear the market.

For given λ, the system described above would behave, in the aggregate, as an occupation with a membership elastically supplied at the expected present value λ. The distribution of the workforce over locations (indexed by (s, y)) would in this case be the same as the stationary distribution of (s, y) in any one market. (This follows from our assumptions that the number of markets is large and that demand shifts are independent across markets.) Then the total workforce demanded (per market) in this occupation, at the return λ, is

$$\iint y\Psi(s, y, \lambda)\, ds\, dy. \tag{21}$$

For each fixed λ, the integral (21) converges in view of the facts that employment is bounded for each fixed λ (Eq. (17), Proposition 2), that $a(s, y, \lambda)$ is bounded, and that the random variable x has a finite mean. By Proposition 4, the expression (21) is a continuous function of λ. As observed in Section 4, increases in λ shift the distribution function $\Psi(s, y, \lambda)$ to the left (along the y-axis), so that (21) is a decreasing function of λ. As $\lambda \to 0$, $E(y; \lambda) \to \infty$ since R is a positive strictly decreasing function of n; as $\lambda \to \infty$, $E(y; \lambda) \to 0$. The demand function is thus as shown in Fig. 4.

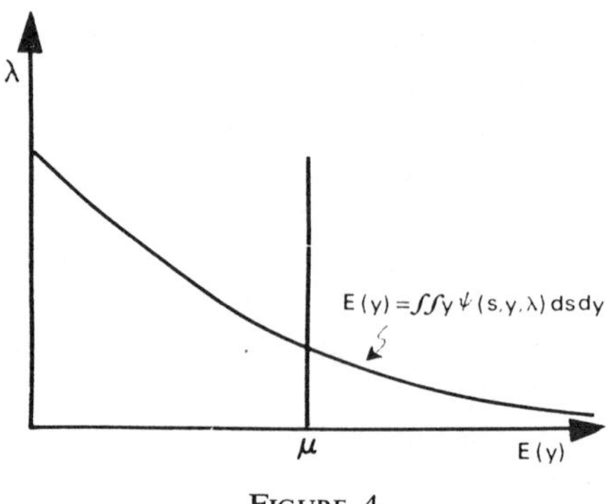

FIGURE 4

Now let μ denote the fixed workforce per market *supplied*. This vertical supply function together with the demand function just obtained gives the equilibrium λ: the solution to

$$\iint y\Psi(s, y, \lambda)\, ds\, dy = \mu. \tag{22}$$

We summarize in

PROPOSITION 5. *For all values of workforce-per-market μ, there is a unique positive equilibrium value of λ.*

Thus, Propositions 1–3 and 5 provide a full description of the equilibrium determination of wages, employment, and workforce in all markets of the economy.[14] By Proposition 3, there will always be some markets in region I of Fig. 3, where the workforce y exceeds the equilibrium

[14] Since the content of this paper consists as much in motivating and explaining a particular definition of equilibrium as in analyzing this equilibrium, we have intermingled definitions and results in a way which may be difficult for readers to disentangle. A different procedure would be to begin with the following (abbreviated)

DEFINITION. An *equilibrium* for the economy under study consists of a 5-tuple of nonnegative, continuous functions $n(s, y)$, $\tilde{n}(s, y)$, $w(s, y)$, $v(s, y)$, and $a(s, y)$, a c.d.f. $\Psi(s, y)$, and a nonnegative number λ such that (6), (8), (12), (13), (19), (20), and (22) are satisfied.

The content of Propositions 1–3 and 5, then, is that a unique equilibrium in the sense of the definition exists. Of course, these propositions also contain information useful in characterizing this equilibrium.

employment level $\tilde{n}(s, \lambda)$. This means that labor market equilibrium necessarily involves positive unemployment.

Numerical calculations of the equilibrium pictured in Fig. 4 are provided in the appendix to this paper.

6. Stability of Equilibrium

The equilibrium obtained for this model economy provides a complete description of the *time paths* of all variables involved, both at an aggregate and the individual market level. Since provision of such a description is frequently thought to be the task of "stability theory" (in the sense of, for example, Samuelson [12]), one may ask whether the latter theory has any applicability to the present model. The answer, we think, is "yes," provided one raises the stability question in its most fundamental sense of determining whether if an equilibrium approximately describes the economy at a point in time, it will continue to do so in the future.

In the present context, this approximation question is particularly pertinent, since we have provided no account as to how workers arrive at the state of perfect knowledge of the probability distributions relevant to their decision problem. Ultimately, this is a question for psychological rather than economic theory, so we do not apologize for framing it here in *ad hoc* "adaptive" terms.

The distributions F and Φ refer to variables exogenous to the markets under study; presumably, they are learned by processing observed frequencies in some sensible fashion, "Bayesian" or otherwise, which has the property that the "true" distributions become "known" after enough time has passed. The distribution $\Psi(s, y, \lambda)$, on the other hand, depends on the behavior of workers, so that as worker perceptions change, so does the "true" Ψ which is being learned. This could, in general, raise insuperable analytical difficulties, but in the present context it does not, since the *only* feature of Ψ which is relevant to worker decisions is the parameter λ. We must describe, then, how the economy operates when the λ perceived by workers differs from the equilibrium value λ^* (say) and how, under this circumstance, perceptions are revised.

For specificity, suppose $\lambda > \lambda^*$. Then the number of workers entering the pool exceeds the number which can be reassigned at an average return of λ. One could modify the reallocation mechanism in many ways, but suppose in particular that the mean of the random variable x varies so as to equate the total number of workers reallocated to the size of the pool. Then both searchers and workers who remain on the job will be disappointed (on average) in their wage expectations. Presumably, this will lead them to revise their perceived λ downward, slowly relative to the passage of trading time t. Thus, we assume

$$d\lambda/dt = g(\lambda - \lambda^*),$$

where g is a decreasing function vanishing at zero. Clearly (from Fig. 4), the equilibrium is stable. Equally clearly, this stability result can have no relevance to the dynamic response to regularly recurring shocks.[15]

7. Concluding Remarks

Although there are (by assumption) no *aggregate* dynamics in the model developed above, it should be obvious that the mechanism we have described is consistent with the now familiar account of the observed Phillips curve in terms of expectations. Thus, an unanticipated change in aggregate demand (a change in $E(s' \mid s)$) will move unemployment and wage changes in opposite directions. Of course, if aggregate demand changes were a recurrent event, as they are in reality, this fact would become incorporated into the maximum problem facing workers and would result in different equilibrium functions $w(s, y)$ and $n(s, y)$. We leave this nontrivial development for future research.

The implications one *can* draw from the model as it stands are of a comparative static nature, both positive and normative. As an example of the former, suppose a lump-sum cost is imposed on leaving one's market to search, so that the right side of (12) becomes $\lambda - c$ rather than simply λ. This will raise the curve $y = \tilde{n}(s, \lambda)$ in Fig. 3 and shift the "demand curve" in Fig. 4 downward. The result is a decrease in unemployment and a decrease in the equilibrium present value of wages, λ. (This example also shows that lower average unemployment is not, in general, associated with higher welfare for workers.) It may well be, though one could hardly demonstrate it at this level of abstraction, that differences of this sort in the actual or perceived costs of changing jobs can help to account for the observed differences in average unemployment across occupations and among countries.

We can also examine Tobin's normative concern [14, p. 8] that "the external effects [of search] are the familiar ones of congestion theory. A worker deciding to join a queue or to stay in one considers the probabilities of getting a job, but not the effects of his decision on the probabilities that others face." Now one could *add* congestion in the usual sense to the search model we have developed (say, by assuming that searching workers

[15] For reasons developed by Gordon and Hynes in [10].

travel on a congested route).[16] But it should be clear that congestion of this sort is not a necessary component of an equilibrium search model. In our scheme, the injury a searching worker imposes on his fellows is of exactly the same type as the injury a seller of any good imposes on his fellow sellers: the equilibrium expected return λ from job search serves the function of any other equilibrium price of signalling to suppliers the correct social return from an additional unit supplied.

The question of whether there exist important external effects in *actual* labor markets remains, of course, to be settled. However this may turn out, it is surely a major advance even to be discussing unemployment from the point of view of the usual (in better developed areas of economics) standard of allocative efficiency. Our intention in this paper has been to indicate the general kind of framework within which such discussions can be conducted and to begin to develop suitable analytical methods.

APPENDIX: Examples

Several examples were analyzed numerically to determine the workforce demand and unemployment rate as a function of the market parameter λ. In order to compute these solutions, it was necessary to assume a finite number of market demand states and to permit only integer values for the workforce. In addition, we assumed that x had a degenerate distribution concentrated at one.

The method of solution used the T_λ operator, defined in Section 3, to determine the value function $v(s, y, \lambda)$. The initial approximation was $v_0(s, y, \lambda) = \lambda$. The nth approximation $v_n(s, y, \lambda)$ was $T_\lambda v_{n-1}(s, y, \lambda)$. With the assumed discount factor $\beta = 0.9$, the convergence to $v(s, y, \lambda)$, the unique fixed point of T_λ, was rapid. Equation (12) was then solved to determine $\tilde{n}(s, \lambda)$, and Eqs. (19) and (19a) were used to determine $a(s, y, \lambda)$. Next period's workforce, given $x = 1$, will be

$$y' = \min[\tilde{n}(s, \lambda), y] + a(s, y, \lambda). \tag{23}$$

The workforce will be bounded, which along with the previous assumptions implies a finite number of possible market states (s, y). Thus, the stochastic process for a market is a finite-state Markov chain with some transition probability matrix, say, P. This matrix whose ijth element specifies the probability that state j will occur next period given current

[16] Phelps [11, Chapter 4, pp. 103–105] also discusses congestion problems, but in a way which makes it clear that these problems arise under nonwage rationing of jobs (i.e., under *dis*equilibrium prices) as opposed to being externalities in the usual equilibrium sense.

state i is determined by (23) and the transition probability matrix of the s-process.

Let u be a function (represented by a vector) defined on the possible market states. Using the analysis of Feller [3, pp. 264–268], the expected value of u with respect to the stationary distribution implied by P can be determined by computing

$$\lim_{n\to\infty} P^n u.$$

The limiting vector has elements all of which are equal to the expected value of u. This was the procedure we used to compute

$$\sum_{s,y} y\psi(s, y, \lambda);$$

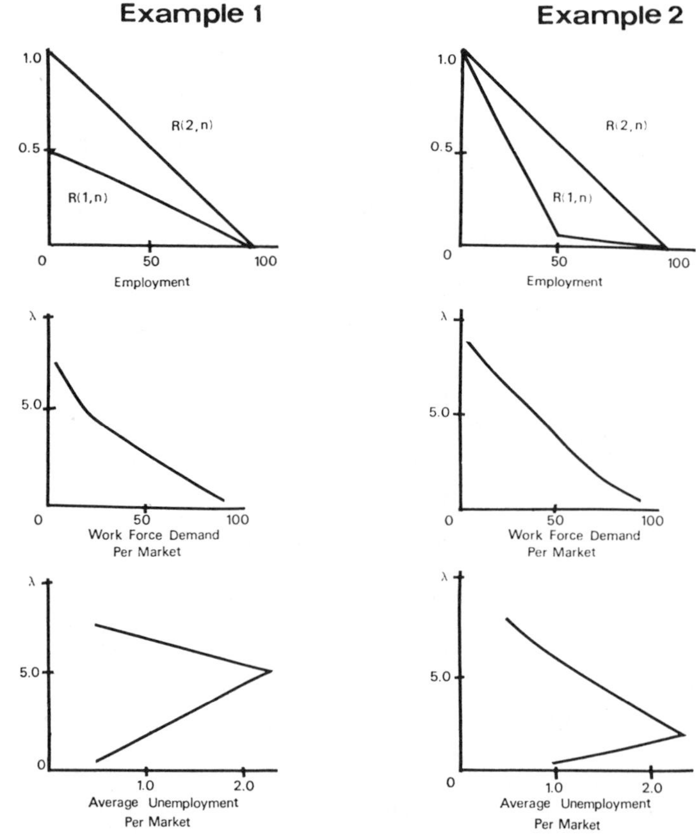

FIGURE 5

642/7/2-6

the average workforce per market, and

$$\sum_{s,y} a(s, y, \lambda)\, \psi(s, y, \lambda),$$

the average unemployment per market.[17]

Two of the examples considered had the marginal revenue schedules depicted in Fig. 5. There are but two demand states: $s = 1$ or $s = 2$. The transition probability matrix for the s process was

$$\begin{bmatrix} .9 & .1 \\ .1 & .9 \end{bmatrix},$$

so there was a strong persistence in demand. The discount factor β was 0.9.

As the theory predicts, the labor demand curve, pictured in Fig. 5, is downward sloping. On the other hand, the unemployment level, also pictured in Fig. 5, is not monotonic, having maxima. Overall, we found for low and high persistence in demand that unemployment rates were low. In the former case, there was little gained by reallocating workers, while in the latter reallocation occurred infrequently. As expected, the greater the variability of demand, holding the degree of persistence fixed, the greater the level of unemployment. This result is reasonable for more workers should be reallocated when demand conditions change.

Acknowledgment

We thank E. S. Phelps for his helpful general comments and, in particular, for pointing out an error in an earlier draft in the discussion of Fig. 2.

References

1. D. Blackwell, Discounted dynamic programming, *Ann. Math. Statist.* **36** (1965), 226–35.
2. J. L. Doob, "Stochastic Process," Wiley, New York, 1953.
3. W. Feller, "An Introduction to Probability Theory and Its Applications," Vol. ii, Wiley, New York, 1966.
4. M. Friedman, The role of monetary policy, *Amer. Econ. Rev.* **58** (1968), 1–17.
5. J. R. Hicks, "Value and Capital," Clarendon Press, Oxford, England, 1939.
6. R. E. Lucas, Jr. and E. C. Prescott, Investment under uncertainty, *Econometrica* **39** (1971), 659–81.
7. R. E. Lucas, Jr., Expectations and the neutrality of money, *J. Economic Theory* **4** (1972), 103–124.

[17] The computer program used for these calculations is available upon request.

8. J. McCall, The economics of information and optimal stopping rules, *J. Business* **38** (1965), 300–17.
9. J. F. Muth, Rational expectations and the theory of price movements, *Econometrica* **29** (1961).
10. E. S. Phelps *et al.* "Microeconomic Foundations of Employment and Inflation Theory," Norton, New York, 1969.
11. E. S. Phelps, "Inflation Policy and Unemployment," Norton, New York, 1972.
12. P. A. Samuelson, "Foundations of Economic Analysis," Harvard University Press, Cambridge, 1947.
13. G. J. Stigler, The economics of information, *J. Political Economy* **69** (1961), 213–35.
14. J. Tobin, Inflation and unemployment, *Amer. Econ. Rev.* **62** (1972), 1–18.

Comment

The brief discussion of policy in Section 7 of this paper suggests several comments. Prescott and Rios-Rull (1987) have extended Arrow–Debreu competitive equilibrium analysis to economic environments that include the one studied in this chapter. Thus, the Fundamental Welfare Theorem holds in this model.

Any discussion of policy within a given model must be tempered by the relationship of the model to economic reality. In the model, all unemployment occurs while people are in transit between different job locations. None occurs in any labor market. For example, firms do not take time to search among the different candidates for a given job to select the one most desired. Therefore, workers are not unemployed in a particular locale while waiting for a decision that may be negative. We would expect the presence of other workers to affect the likelihood of a worker getting a job for which he applies. To this extent one can make better sense of search as having external effects similar to congestion than by overcrowded travel routes. (Of course the notion of a "job" does not appear in the model.) The next chapter explores externalities in the search process, based on the endogenous determination of the time needed to find a job.

Another aspect of the model is the presence of uniform wages within any marketplace.[1] This is in contrast to the models surveyed above, where physically separate trading locations need not be very far apart.

Workers in this model are risk neutral toward both wage variation and the possibility that search (and unemployment) may become desirable. Risk-averse workers without access to perfect insurance or capital markets might show different behavior and might yield both a social advantage from unemployment compensation and an altered welfare evaluation of search unemployment for the two reasons of risk aversion itself and desired unemployment compensation. For a discussion of unemployment compensation as insurance for workers, see Baily

[1] "In order for wage rates for a single type of labor to differ at a point in time, labor must clearly be exchanged in spatially distinct markets. (Otherwise, wages would be bid into equality in a period much too short to be of economic interest.)" P. 189 in the original. (P. 518 this volume.)

(1977). For discussion of employment policies to insure workers see Azariades (1975) and Bailey (1974).

References

C. Azariades, Implicit contracts and underemployment equilibria, *J. Political Econ.* **83** (1975), 1183–1202.

M. N. Bailey, Wages and employment under uncertain demand, *Rev. Econ. Stud.* **41** (1974), 37–50.

M. N. Bailey, Unemployment insurance as insurance for workers, *Industrial and Labor Relations Rev.* **30** (1977), 495–504.

E. C. Prescott and J. V. Rios-Rull, Classical competitive analysis in a growth economy with search, working paper 329, Research Department, Federal Reserve Bank of Minneapolis, 1987.

30

P. Diamond, Wage determination and efficiency in search equilibrium, *Review of Economic Studies*, **49** (1982), 217–27.

In Chapters 25–28, prices were set by suppliers. In Chapter 29, prices were set by the Walrasian auctioneer. In this chapter, prices are set by a bargaining process between buyer and seller. In addition to exploring the implications of this method of price determination, this chapter focuses on the problem of modeling the transactions technology. The presence of externalities (and so, inefficiency) in transactions depends both on the nature of the underlying search technology and on the price determination rule (which affects incentives). There is a possibility of externalities from many different decisions, including search intensity, choice of market to enter, and job acceptance. In the comment on this chapter are references to more recent literature and a presentation of the mathematical tool used in the derivation of Equation (24).

Wage Determination and Efficiency in Search Equilibrium

PETER A. DIAMOND
Massachusetts Institute of Technology

Using a simple search technology and the Nash bargaining solution, the paper derives the steady state equilibrium negotiated wage as a function of the equilibrium unemployment and vacancy rates. For this wage, the lifetime expected present discounted value of earnings of a new worker is compared with the social marginal product of a new worker. These are not generally equal implying inefficient incentives for labour mobility.

The concept of a competitive market is a major tool in the analysis of economists. In the simplest version of a market, resource allocation responds instantly to changes in parameters, leaving no room for frictional unemployment. One response to the unreality of this implication has been to introduce spatially distinct markets, with unemployment as workers move between markets. As modeled by Lucas and Prescott (1974), workers who are not moving are not unemployed. An alternative response is contained in the sizeable fixed price equilibrium literature, where it is assumed that prices do not change to clear markets in the short run. In contrast, the conceptual starting place of this analysis is to drop the idea of a market. Rather than markets being the mechanism by which workers and jobs are brought together, it is assumed that there is a search process which stochastically brings together unemployed workers and vacant jobs pairwise. It is taken as axiomatic that the process takes time and so involves foregone output. It is assumed that a worker and a job brought together by the search process negotiate a wage, with instantaneous negotiation. Thus, the only frictions in the model are in the search process, with wages flexible.

Actual search and negotiation processes are complicated and would be difficult to model in detail. Here we make numerous simplifying assumptions to permit explicit solution of equilibrium variables and easy analysis of their efficiency properties. The focus of the analysis is the efficiency of the incentive to enter the labour market. That is, we compare the lifetime expected present discounted value of earnings of a new worker with the social marginal product of that worker. The comparison depends critically on the bargaining solution and on the nature of the search technology. Generally, equilibrium is not efficient because of search externalities. The sources of the externalities are easy to see. The presence of an additional worker makes it easier for vacancies to find workers and harder for other workers to find jobs. The wage negotiation, however, reflects the relative bargaining powers of workers and jobs. Only in special cases will the balance of bargaining powers result in a wage which reflects the balance of search externalities as well as the value of output directly produced. The analysis identifies cases where the incentive for entry is too large or too small.

This efficiency analysis complements other efficiency analyses of search intensity, job-quitting, and job-taking (Diamond (1981), Diamond and Maskin (1979, 1981), and Mortensen (1979, 1981)). These latter papers have considered markets with equal numbers of jobs and workers. This paper focuses on the implications of unequal numbers

Reprinted with permission from *Review of Economic Studies*, Vol. XLIX, 217–227, copyright 1982.

of jobs and vacancies. For earlier analysis of the effects of unemployment and vacancies see Holt (1970).

The paper divides into two parts. In the first five sections, we analyse the equilibrium negotiated wage as a function of the equilibrium unemployment and vacancy rates. With the assumptions used in this paper, the steady state wage depends on these rates but does not depend directly on the search technology which results in these equilibrium rates. The second part of the paper considers the search technology in relation to equilibrium and efficiency.

1. STEADY STATE ANALYSIS

We consider a partial equilibrium model of the labour market in steady state equilibrium. There is a fixed coefficients technology, with output of y from the combination of one worker and one job. Thus, all jobs are the same. Firms consist of a single job and workers do not organize. Unemployed workers and jobs are brought together by a stochastic process with exogenous parameters. All matches result in the start of production. In steady state equilibrium, this flow into employment is matched by an exogenous breakup of existing matches. Thus there are no economic decisions to be made (except for the trivial one to produce when able). The model focuses on wage bargains in this setting.

We begin by considering the typical worker's probability of finding a job. Denote by L the number of workers, of whom E are employed and U unemployed. We assume that there is a flow bE of workers losing their jobs, with the parameter b taken to be exogenous. With all jobs the same, there is no endogenous reason for job break up. These break ups then represent movements of jobs or workers away from each other for consumption reasons. We assume that all workers live forever. Alternatively we could have assumed a symmetric birth-death process. This would not change the expression for the equilibrium wage.

In a steady state equilibrium, we must have a flow, bE, of unemployed workers finding jobs to match the flow from breakups. If each unemployed worker has the same probability of finding a job, then each one has the flow probability bE/U of finding a job in any instant. Similarly we assume K jobs, F of which are filled and V of which are vacant. Each vacancy has the flow probability bE/V of being filled.

Since the number of filled jobs equals the number of employed workers,

$$K - V = F = E = L - U, \tag{1}$$

we have a relationship among the unemployment rate, $u = U/L$, the vacancy rate $v = V/K$, and the job-worker ratio $k = K/L$:

$$(1 - u) = (1 - v)k. \tag{2}$$

For the present, we use no other properties of the search process which brings together workers and jobs. For efficiency analysis below, we will need to consider the dependence of the equilibrium unemployment rate on the numbers of jobs and workers.

We assume that a filled job produces a constant flow of output, y, independent of the particular worker and job that have been matched. To begin, we assume no unemployment benefits, no disutility of labour, and no user cost of capital. The interest rate, r, is taken to be exogenous.

2. WAGE DETERMINATION

Next we turn to the wage bargain in this steady state setting.[1] That is, a theory of wage negotiations is added to the search and production technologies described above.[2] We assume that both firms and workers are risk neutral. This simplifies the analysis. Also, the absence of risk aversion implies that the inefficiencies found below come from search externalities given wage determination, not from the absence of insurance markets or the imperfections of the capital market. With risk neutrality workers are interested in the expected present discounted value of wages; and firms, in the expected present discounted value of profits.

Having come together, the firm and worker have a joint surplus relative to the alternatives of waiting to find another worker and another job. The bargaining problem is to divide this surplus between them. In other words, there is a wage that makes the worker indifferent between taking this job and waiting for his next job opportunity. There is a wage that makes the firm indifferent between hiring this worker and waiting for the next available worker. The bargaining problem is to agree on a wage between these two limits. By affecting the expected times to finding the next alternatives, the unemployment and vacancy rates affect these two limits to the wage bargain. We will assume that u and v do not otherwise affect the wage bargain.

Formally, we make two assumptions on the wage bargain. First, we assume that the wage bargain is independent of the way that the worker and job have come together; that is, independent of whether the worker found the job or the job found the worker, a distinction that can only sometimes be made. This is the standard economic assumption of the irrelevance of sunk costs.[3] Second, we assume that the bargaining process is symmetric in the sense that the worker and job split evenly the surplus from their coming together.[4] Splitting the surplus evenly still leaves the wage dependent on unemployment and vacancy rates, by affecting the limits of the wage bargain. The bargained wage depends upon the anticipated wage in future employment. For equilibrium, we assume that the wage is constant over wage bargains. That is, the equilibrium wage equals the wage bargained on the assumption that future wages equal the equilibrium wage.

To derive the equilibrium wage, we need to define the surplus from coming together. For this definition, we need to describe the gain from finding (or filling) a job. We denote by W_U and W_E the expected present values of lifetime wages for unemployed and employed workers respectively. We confine analysis to steady states and assume workers live forever. With the further assumptions that the probabilities of job termination and job finding are independent of worker history these wealths are constant over workers and time. With the assumptions of risk neutrality and perfect capital markets, workers care only about these present discounted values and the surplus from finding a job is $W_E - W_U$. Writing the expected present discounted values of income for filled and vacant jobs as W_F and W_V, we can express the assumed symmetry in the outcome of the negotiation process as

$$W_E - W_U = W_F - W_V. \tag{3}$$

This symmetry in dividing the surplus does not imply the irrelevance of the relative availability of alternatives. If the unemployment rate is higher than the vacancy rate, firms will have to wait less long than workers for their next best alternatives. This will affect the size of the gain from making a bargain now as a function of the wage. The assumption we make is that the availability of alternatives affects the threat point of waiting for the next best alternative but does not affect the division of the surplus in excess of the sum of the two threat points. The side with the higher threat point will get the larger share of the value of output. Only the surplus is divided evenly, not the entire value of output.

Next we need to relate the expected present discounted values in (3) to the parameters of the search environment and the wage being negotiated. Treating a worker as an asset, we have the familiar condition from asset equilibrium that the rate of return times the value of being a worker equals the flow income plus the expected capital gain, or expected change in wealth.[5] Since we are analyzing a steady state, the only source of capital gain is the change in employment status from finding or losing a job. An unemployed worker receives no cash income and has the probability bE/U of finding a job and enjoying the capital gain $W_E - W_U$. Thus we have the equation

$$rW_U = (bE/U)(W_E - W_U). \tag{4}$$

An employed worker receives a wage w and faces the exogenous probability b of suffering the capital loss $W_E - W_U$ from losing his job

$$rW_E = w - b(W_E - W_U). \tag{5}$$

Similarly the values of filled and vacant jobs satisfy

$$rW_F = y - w - b(W_F - W_V) \tag{6}$$

$$rW_V = (bE/V)(W_F - W_V). \tag{7}$$

From the four value equations (4)–(7) and the rule describing the outcome of the negotiation process, (3), we have five equations in five unknowns, the wage and the four wealths. That is, solving these equations we find the wage which gives equal splitting of the surplus, assuming that the same wage will be reached in all future wage bargains.

3. EQUILIBRIUM WAGE

Before turning to the expressions for the wage in terms of the parameters of the economy and the outcome of the search process, it is interesting to combine equations (3), (4), and (7) to note that the aggregate wealth of the unemployed equals the aggregate wealth of the pool of vacancies,

$$UW_U = VW_V. \tag{8}$$

This equality rests critically on the equal shares assumption (3).

Substituting from (4)–(7) into (3) we have

$$W_E - W_U = \frac{w}{r + b + bE/U} = \frac{y - w}{r + b + bE/V} = W_F - W_V. \tag{9}$$

The extra value of current employment over unemployment depends on the wage, the rate of interest used for discounting, the probabilistic rate of termination of this employment possibility, and the probabilistic rate of finding an alternative job if current negotiations are unsuccessful (bE/U). Similarly, the extra value from filling a job depends on profits, the rate of interest, the rate of termination of employment, and the rate of filling vacant jobs. From (9) we see that equality in the rates of finding alternatives ($U = V$), results in a wage share of one-half ($w = y - w$). As a special case, if there were no alternatives, the wage share would be one-half. As the interest rate rises, future alternatives become less and less important and the wage share tends to one-half. Similarly if the rate at which alternatives are found becomes small, their existence becomes less important. That is, if bE/U and bE/V both tend to zero, the wage share goes to one-half. When the break up rate becomes large (the arrival rate of alternatives held constant), it becomes likely that the current production opportunity will be over before either party receives an alternative offer. That also makes the alternatives less important for current negotiations and moves the wage share toward one-half.

Solving (9), we have the wage related to the equilibrium unemployment and vacancy rates.[6]

$$\frac{w}{y} = \frac{rb^{-1} + u^{-1}}{2rb^{-1} + u^{-1} + v^{-1}}. \tag{10}$$

Naturally, the wage share is lower when the unemployment rate is higher or the vacancy rate is lower, the other held constant.

4. LABOUR DISUTILITY AND UNEMPLOYMENT COMPENSATION

The discussion above assumed no disutility of labour and no use related costs of production. That is, the full output, y, was taken to be a return over and above the combined returns of an unemployed worker and a vacancy. We now add these elements. Assume that the disutility of labour, measured in financial terms, is B_U, or, alternatively, being unemployed adds B_U to utility. We must modify the objective function of workers to incorporate the disutility of work. Assume that workers want to maximize the expected present discounted value of wages less the monetary equivalent of the disutility of labour.

To make this modification, we rewrite the two value equations for workers to read

$$\begin{aligned} rW_E &= w - B_U - b(W_E - W_U) \\ rW_U &= (bE/U)(W_E - W_U). \end{aligned} \tag{11}$$

Equivalently we could consider workers to be maximizing the expected present discounted value of wages plus the monetary value of the utility of being idle. Taking this approach we would write the value equations as

$$\begin{aligned} rW_E &= w - b(W_E - W_U) \\ rW_U &= B_U + (bE/U)(W_E - W_U). \end{aligned} \tag{12}$$

The two approaches give the same gain from becoming employed,[7] $W_E - W_U$, and differ only in the level of measured wealth. We shall employ the latter formulation, (12), since it lends itself to the alternative interpretation that B_U is the unemployment compensation benefit.

Similarly we assume a user cost of capital, B_V, and rewrite the job value equations as

$$\begin{aligned} rW_F &= y - w - B_V - b(W_F - W_V) \\ rW_V &= (bE/V)(W_F - W_V). \end{aligned} \tag{13}$$

We continue to assume an even splitting of the surplus from filling a vacancy, (3). Thus we have five equations to determine the four wealths and the cash wage w. Solving these equations we obtain the generalized expression for the wage

$$\frac{w}{y} = \left(\frac{r + bu^{-1}}{2r + bu^{-1} + bv^{-1}}\right)\left(\frac{(y - B_U - B_V)}{y}\right) + \frac{B_U}{y}. \tag{14}$$

The wage equals the worker's share of the production surplus, $y - B_U - B_V$, plus compensation for the disutility of work or foregone unemployment benefits, B_U.

We are examining an economy where the surplus to worker and firm from production is $y - B_U - B_V$. As an alternative derivation of (14), let us consider an economy where B_U and B_V are zero, as above, but where the output produced, y^0, happens to equal $y - B_U - B_V$. In terms of private net productivity these two economies are equivalent and will have equilibria which reflect the same division of the surplus between workers and firms. The wage in this artificial economy will satisfy equation (10), with y^0 replacing y. For workers to be in the same net position, the money wage in the actual economy must exceed the wage in the artificial economy, w^0, by B_U. Similarly the return to the firm exceeds its return in the artificial economy $y^0 - w^0$, by B_V. From these considerations, and the wage equation (10), we can move directly to the generalized wage equation

$$\frac{w - B_U}{y - B_U - B_V} = \frac{r + bu^{-1}}{2r + bu^{-1} + bv^{-1}}. \tag{15}$$

The left-hand side of (15) is the flow gain to the worker from employment as a share in the combined flow gain to firm and worker.

We can now see the role of unemployment compensation in raising wages. The availability of unemployment compensation strengthens the bargaining position of workers. The question is how much. The answer is that the decrease in the surplus from production (coming from the need to give up unemployment compensation) is divided between workers and firms in the same proportions as the surplus is divided between them. That is

$$\frac{\partial w}{\partial B_U}=1-\frac{w^0}{y^0}=\frac{r+bv^{-1}}{2r+bu^{-1}+bv^{-1}}. \tag{16}$$

The greater the number of vacancies relative to unemployment, the smaller the impact of unemployment compensation on wages. With many vacancies per unemployed worker, workers receive a large share of the surplus from production. With our bargaining assumption, this implies that the workers bear a large share of the fall in surplus needed to finance their own additional compensation to offset the surrender of unemployment benefits.[8]

5. WEALTH

From the wealth equations, (4) and (5), we can express the wealth of an unemployed worker in terms of the wage and the parameters of the search process (where we have again assumed B_U and B_V are zero)

$$W_U=\frac{w(1-u)b}{r(ru+b)}. \tag{17}$$

This equation can be derived alternatively by considering the probability, $p(t)$, of being employed at time t, as viewed from time zero. This probability satisfies the differential equation

$$\dot{p}(t)=-bp(t)+\frac{b(1-u)}{u}(1-p(t)). \tag{18}$$

The change in the probability of employment is $-b$ if employed and $[b(1-u)/u]$ if unemployed. Since the probabilities of employment and unemployment are $p(t)$ and $(1-p(t))$, we have (18) for the change in the probability of employment. Solving (18) we have

$$p(t)=1-u+(p(0)-1+u)e^{(b/u)t}. \tag{19}$$

Since expected earnings are $w\int e^{-rt}p(t)\,dt$, we obtain (17) when $p(0)$ is zero. For $p(0)$ equal to one we have

$$W_E=\frac{w(ru+b(1-u))}{r(ru+b)}. \tag{20}$$

Combining the wealth equations, we have the average wealth of workers, $uW_U+(1-u)W_E$, equal to the discounted average wage flow $w(1-u)/r$. Substituting for w from (10) we can express W_U in terms of the unemployment and vacancy rates

$$W_U=\frac{(1-u)y}{r(2urb^{-1}+1+uv^{-1})}. \tag{21}$$

If we imbedded this market in an economy with costless labour mobility of the unemployed, W_U would be equated across markets. It is interesting therefore to compare W_U with the marginal product of labour—the present discounted value of output from the addition of a worker to a market. Thus we turn now to the details of the search technology and the effects of adding a worker to the labour pool.

6. MARGINAL PRODUCTIVITY

The addition of a worker to a market creates a change in the job–worker ratio and necessarily involves the movement of the economy out of a steady state. To analyze the output gain from the new path we need to specify the dynamics of the economy out of a steady state. Let us simply write the rate of matching of unemployed and vacancies as $f(E, L, K)$. That is, f gives the aggregate outcome of the search process. Then we have

$$\dot{E} = f(E, L, K) - bE. \tag{22}$$

With the natural assumption that $\partial f/\partial E$ is negative, this equation is stable. Setting $\dot{E}$ equal to zero we can determine the steady state equilibrium unemployment and vacancy rates.

We write the present discounted value of aggregate output as $W(E, L, K)$. That is, W measures discounted output for an economy which starts at the initial position (E, L, K) and follows the differential equation (22), L and K remaining constant.

From any initial position,

$$\begin{aligned} W(E, L, K) &= \int_0^\infty e^{-rt} E(t) y \, dt \\ \dot{E} &= f(E, L, K) - bE \\ E(0) &= E. \end{aligned} \tag{23}$$

$\partial W/\partial L$ then measures the social marginal product of an additional worker who is initially unemployed. We are interested in comparing $\partial W/\partial L$ evaluated at a steady state equilibrium with W_U, the expected income of an unemployed worker, in that steady state. At a steady state equilibrium the marginal product of labour satisfies[9]

$$\frac{\partial W}{\partial L} = \left(\frac{y}{r}\right)\left(\frac{\partial f/\partial L}{r + b - \partial f/\partial E}\right). \tag{24}$$

The first term on the right-hand side is the capitalized value of output from a permanent increase in employment. If the economy adjusted instantly to the new steady state, the second term would be the change in steady state employment, $\partial f/\partial L/(b - \partial f/\partial E)$. However, the economy does not move instantly. Rather, it follows the differential equation (22) and the second term gives the relevant change in employment for the movement between steady states. It comes from approximating f linearly, which is equivalent to approximating the employment path exponentially. We are interested in comparing (24) with the wealth equation (21). To pursue this analysis we need to specify the search technology in more detail.

7. LINEAR TECHNOLOGY[10]

We begin by considering a particularly simple technology. In the next two sections we generalize this technology in two different directions. The first assumption of the linear technology is that the matching of unemployed and vacancies depends only on the numbers of unemployed and vacancies. That is, filled jobs do not affect the ability of the unemployed and the vacancies to come together. Second, both the unemployed and the vacancies are assumed to be seeking each other, with the number of matches equal to the sum of those coming from meetings initiated by workers and those initiated by jobs. The third assumption is that any searching worker makes contact with jobs at a rate independent of the number of vacant jobs (which is assumed to be strictly positive). The same condition holds for searching vacancies.

Given these assumptions, the rate of new matches is $a_u U + a_v V$ for some positive constants a_u and a_v. That is

$$f(E, L, K) = a_v K + a_u L - (a_u + a_v)E. \tag{25}$$

With this technology, the steady state level of employment satisfies (setting (25) equal to bE)

$$E = \frac{a_v K + a_u L}{a_u + a_v + b}. \tag{26}$$

Of course this solution only holds when E is less than both K and L. Thus this solution holds when

$$b > \max\,[a_u(k^{-1} - 1),\, a_v(k-1)], \tag{27}$$

where $k = K/L$. Where there is an internal solution,[11] adding a worker increases steady state employment by $a_u/(a_u + a_v + b)$, a fraction less than one. In an internal solution, the unemployment rate satisfies

$$u = 1 - \frac{E}{L} = 1 - (a_u + a_v k)/(a_u + a_v + b). \tag{28}$$

The unemployment rate is lower the greater the job–worker ratio, the longer the expected duration of a job, and the more rapid the meeting process.

Having specified a particular search technology, we can return to comparing the marginal product of a worker with expected lifetime compensation. From (24) we have

$$\frac{\partial W}{\partial L} = \left(\frac{y}{r}\right)\left(\frac{a_u}{r + a_u + a_v + b}\right). \tag{29}$$

From (21) we can write

$$W_U = \left(\frac{y}{r}\right)\left(\frac{bE/2U}{r + b + (bE/2)(U^{-1} + V^{-1})}\right). \tag{30}$$

Substituting $a_u U + a_v V$ for bE (from the equilibrium condition) and comparing (29) and (30) we have

$$\frac{\partial W}{\partial L} \gtreqless W_U \text{ as } a_u U \gtreqless a_v V. \tag{31}$$

That is, workers receive more than their marginal products when they contribute less to the matching process than do vacancies.

To understand this result, let us consider the bargaining assumption analysed by Mortensen (1981).[12] He assumed that in a contact initiated by a worker (one of the $a_u U$ contacts) the worker receives all of the surplus from the contact. Similarly, in each of the $a_v V$ contacts initiated by vacancies, the firm receives all of the surplus from the contact. With the linear technology, the only effect of an individual on the search process arises from the contacts he initiates. With the initiator receiving all of the surplus from the contact, the present discounted value of wages is equal to the social marginal product. (Once we move away from the linear case, we will not generally have this equality since searchers affect others in more ways than just initiating contacts). The negotiation assumption we have employed treats the efforts that went into the contact as a sunk cost and irrelevant for the wage bargain. Thus workers receive one-half the surplus. This is more than they would receive in aggregate with Mortensen's assumption if workers initiate less than half of contacts; i.e. if $a_u U < a_v V$. Thus with the linear technology, expected earnings exceed the marginal product when $a_u U < a_v V$.

The results in (31) can be used to analyse the efficiency of labour mobility. For example, consider a country with equal aggregate number of jobs and workers and two separate regions. Assume jobs immobile and unemployed workers costlessly mobile, but able to engage in the search process in only one region. Thus W_U will be equated in the two regions. Assume that a_u equals a_v in both regions. If the only difference between regions is that output per worker is higher in the first region, $y_1 > y_2$, then equilibrium will require $k_1 < 1 < k_2$. These inequalities imply that the marginal product of labour in region one is larger than the lifetime wage, with the reverse holding in region two. Thus we can conclude that there are more workers in the high productivity region than is efficient.

8. AN EXAMPLE OF NON-LINEAR SEARCH

Preserving the assumption that the rate of meetings depends only on the numbers of unemployed and vacancies, let us write the rate as a general function with positive marginal products

$$f(E, L, K) = g(U, V) = g(L-E, K-E). \tag{32}$$

That is, we are assuming that $-\partial f/\partial E$ is equal to $(\partial f/\partial L + \partial f/\partial K)$.

Substituting in (24), we can write the marginal product of a worker as

$$\frac{\partial W}{\partial L} = \left(\frac{y}{r}\right)\left(\frac{\partial g/\partial U}{r + b + \partial g/\partial U + \partial g/\partial V}\right). \tag{33}$$

Substituting in (21) and using the equilibrium condition $bE = g$, we can write expected earnings as

$$W_U = \left(\frac{y}{r}\right)\left(\frac{g/U}{2r + 2b + g(1/U + 1/V)}\right). \tag{34}$$

If g displays constant returns to scale ($U\, \partial g/\partial U + V\, \partial g/\partial V = g$) the comparison of (33) and (34) gives us the generalization of (31)

$$\frac{\partial W}{\partial L} \gtreqless W_U \quad \text{as} \quad U\frac{\partial g}{\partial U} \gtreqless V\frac{\partial g}{\partial V}. \tag{35}$$

Thus the generalization preserves the property that if one factor is paid more than its marginal product, the other factor is paid less. This ceases to be true with non-constant returns to scale.

With increasing returns to scale ($U\, \partial g/\partial U + V\, \partial g/\partial V > g$) comparison of (33) and (34) gives the sufficient condition

$$U\frac{\partial g}{\partial U} \geq V\frac{\partial g}{\partial V} \quad \text{implies} \quad \frac{\partial W}{\partial L} > W_U. \tag{36}$$

Thus, as one would expect, an increasing returns function tends to have higher marginal products relative to earnings. Naturally, the converse holds with decreasing returns.

9. ANOTHER EXAMPLE OF NON-LINEAR SEARCH

It is plausible that the number of filled jobs will affect the ease with which workers can find vacancies. We can capture this idea by introducing a function of the vacancy rate, $a_u(v)$, to describe the ease of finding a vacancy. Plausibly $a_u(0)$ is zero and $a_u(v)$ increases with the vacancy rate.[13] Preserving the separation of search by workers and jobs, we write the outcome of the search process as[14]

$$\begin{aligned} f(E, L, K) &= a_u(v)U + a_v(u)V \\ &= a_u(1 - E/K)(L - E) + a_v(1 - E/L)(K - E). \end{aligned} \tag{37}$$

This form preserves the constant returns property of f. With this technology, the marginal product of a worker satisfies

$$\frac{\partial W}{\partial L}=\left(\frac{y}{r}\right)\left(\frac{a_u+(1-u)kva'_v}{r+b+a_u+a_v+uk^{-1}a'_u+vka'_v}\right). \tag{38}$$

Expected income of an unemployed worker, W_U, does not depend on the search technology *per se*, given the equilibrium unemployment and vacancy rates. Therefore W_U in this case is the same as in the linear case with parameters a_u and a_v equal to the equilibrium levels here. For this reason, we concentrate on the comparison of $\partial W/\partial L$ in (38) with the same expression in the linear case, (29), which equals (38) with a'_u and a'_v set equal to zero. Over time, an additional worker raises the unemployment rate and lowers the vacancy rate. The former makes it easier for jobs to find workers, the latter makes it harder for workers to find jobs. Thus, if a'_v is zero and a'_u positive, the latter effect dominates and the marginal product of a worker is lower in the non-linear case. If a'_u is zero and a'_v positive, the former effect dominates and the marginal product of a worker is larger in the non-linear case. (From (28), $1-u>a_u/(r+b+a_u+a_v)$, which gives the result from inspection of (38).) In the symmetric case ($k=1$, $a_u(z)=a_v(z)$) the latter effect dominates and the marginal product of a worker is larger in the non-linear case. (From (28) $(1-u/2>a_u/(r+b+a_u+a_v)$, which gives the result from inspection of (38).) In the symmetric case both firms and workers are paid less than their marginal products.

The absence of an instantaneous resource allocation mechanism (like the Walrasian auctioneer) creates a strictly positive surplus for any deal compared with the next best alternative. (In this sense there is no consumer surplus in Walrasian competitive equilibrium.) The division of this surplus between trading partners can occur in a number of different institutional settings. Here we have explored one particular setting—symmetric bargaining. With this method of determining trading prices, these prices are not generally an efficient incentive for behaviour affecting search, such as entry into a market. In addition we found that unemployment compensation affects wages even when it does not affect the rate at which workers accept jobs.

First version received November 1980; *final version accepted November* 1981 (*Eds.*).

Valuable advice from Robert Solow, Martin Weitzman, Joel Yellin, research assistance from Drew Fudenberg, and financial support from NSF gratefully acknowledged.

NOTES

1. We do not consider wages set by one side on a take-it-or-leave-it basis.
2. Mortensen (1979) has taken an alternative approach of relating market outcome to bargaining outcomes rather than specifying a single equilibrium concept.
3. Mortensen (1981) explores the alternative approach of having the wage bargain depend on the source of the match.
4. Alternative splitting rules are considered below.
5. Of course, there is no market for workers as assets. This equation can be derived alternatively by differentiating the expression for expected earnings with respect to time, $d/dt\, W_U(t)=rW_U-(bE/U)\times(W_E-W_U)=0$.
6. If workers receive $s/(1+s)$ of the surplus, $W_E-W_U=s(W_F-W_V)$, then (10) becomes $w/y=s(rb^{-1}+u^{-1})/((1+s)rb^{-1}+su^{-1}+v^{-1})$.
7. $W_E-W_U=(w-B_U)(r+b+bE/U)^{-1}$.
8. In a full equilibrium analysis, unemployment compensation would also affect the number and productivity of jobs.
9. For a derivation of (24), see Diamond (1980).
10. The linear technology has been analysed by Diamond and Maskin (1979, 1981) and by Mortensen (1979, 1981).
11. We do not analyse the corner solutions since the linear technology is not plausible with an unemployment or vacancy rate close to zero. Particularly the third assumption used in deriving the linear technology is implausible.
12. This interpretation was given to me by Mortensen.

13. For example a_u might have the form $a(1+e)v/(1+ev)$. This form would arise if job search were akin to an urn problem (sampling with replacement) with 1 ball per filled job and $1+e$ balls per vacancy.

14. Note that we no longer satisfy the condition $-\partial f/\partial E = \partial f/\partial L + \partial f/\partial K$. That is, the search outcome can no longer be written solely in terms of the numbers of unemployed and vacancies.

REFERENCES

DIAMOND, P. A. (1980), "An Alternative to Steady State Comparisons", *Economic Letters*, **5**, 7–9.

DIAMOND, P. A. (1981), "Mobility Costs, Frictional Unemployment, and Efficiency", *Journal of Political Economy*, **89**, 798–812.

DIAMOND, P. A. and MASKIN, E. (1979), "An Equilibrium Analysis of Search and Breach of Contract, I: Steady States", *Bell Journal of Economics*, **10**, 282–316.

DIAMOND, P. A. and MASKIN, E. (1981), "An Equilibrium Analysis of Search and Breach of Contract, II: A Non-Steady State Example", *Journal of Economic Theory*, **25**, 165–195.

HOLT, C. (1970), "How Can the Phillips Curve Be Moved to Reduce Both Inflation and Unemployment", in PHELPS, E. S. *et al.* (eds.) *Microeconomic Foundations of Employment and Inflation Theory.*

LUCAS, R. E., JR. and PRESCOTT, E. C. (1974), "Equilibrium Search and Unemployment", *Journal of Economic Theory*, **7**, 188–209.

MORTENSEN, D. (1979), "The Matching Process as a Noncooperative Bargaining Game" (unpublished).

MORTENSEN, D. (1981), "The Economics of Mating, Racing, and Related Games" (unpublished).

Comment

The two Mortensen papers cited in this chapter have been published. There is a sizeable literature modeling different ways that decisions affect the search environment of others and so generate externalities. Some of these are discussed in the two survey articles cited in Chapter 27. In this chapter, workers, jobs, and employment matches were identical. Much of the literature explores circumstances where workers differ from each other because of *ex ante* differences (Sattinger, 1987) or previous decisions (such as quality of match accepted or investment in job-specific human capital). Adding these possibilities adds ways in which the search environment varies with decisions, implying externalities.

The Nash bargaining solution was used to determine wages in this chapter. Implicitly, an instantaneous negotiation process was assumed. For an article that uses an explicit (potentially time consuming) bargaining process in a search setting, see Rubinstein and Wolinsky (1985).

For an application of search modeling to the housing market, see Wheaton (1988).

Efficiency analysis in the paper tracked the perturbation of the economy from a steady-state position. Since this technique is not familiar to some students we derive (24) here. Thinking of (23) as a dynamic programming problem, we can write the usual asset-value equation as

$$rW = Ey + \frac{\partial W}{\partial E}\dot{E} = Ey + \frac{\partial W}{\partial E}(f - bE). \tag{1}$$

Differentiating this equation with respect to L, we have

$$r\frac{\partial W}{\partial L} = \frac{\partial^2 W}{\partial E \partial L}(f - bE) + \frac{\partial W}{\partial E}\frac{\partial f}{\partial L}. \tag{2}$$

Differentiating (1) with respect to E, we have

$$r\frac{\partial W}{\partial E} = y + \frac{\partial^2 W}{\partial E^2}(f - bE) + \frac{\partial W}{\partial E}\left(\frac{\partial f}{\partial E} - b\right). \tag{3}$$

In a steady state, $f = bE$. This simplifies both (2) and (3). Eliminating $\partial W/\partial E$ then yields (24).

References

D. Mortensen, The matching process as a noncooperative bargaining game. In J. J. McCall (ed.) "The economics of information and uncertainty," Chicago: University of Chicago Press, 1982.

D. Mortensen, Property rights and efficiency in mating, racing, and related games, *Amer. Econ. Rev.* **72** (1982), 968–979.

A. Rubinstein, and A. Wolinsky, Equilibrium in a market with sequential bargaining, *Econometrica* **53** (1985), 1133–1150.

M. Sattinger, Efficient assignment with *ex ante* differences in workers and jobs, Department of Economics, State University of New York at Albany, 1987.

W. Wheaton, Vacancy, search, and prices in a housing matching model, Department of Economics, Massachusetts Institute of Technology, 1988.

ional expectations steady-state equilibria. The model is ve two properties: multiple steady-state equilibria and ncy of all non–corner solution equilibria. The source of ncy is a trading externality, while the source of multiple the positive feedback working through this externality. ity comes from the plausible assumption that an increase er of potential trading partners makes trade easier. The back is that easier trade, in turn, makes production more

ılts are demonstrated in a model where the trade process ic, with the production decision as the only control vari- heless, these results seem robust. Individuals control sity and advertising and have reputations for offering Once all individuals have optimized on these control ecting trading opportunities, profitability would still be the availability of more potential trading partners. That ality (and positive feedback) from increased willingness is not correctable by privately available actions given coordinating trade.

importance of this finding, consider Friedman's (1968) the natural rate of unemployment as the level occurring ns are introduced into the Walrasian equations. This s that the result of actually modeling a competitive econ- ade frictions is to find multiple natural rates of unem- his implies that one of the goals for macro policy should he economy toward the best natural rate (not necessarily after any sufficiently large macro shock.

model[1] is presented in Sections II–IV. Then, a simple is presented in Section V to illustrate the workings of the ality. Optimal policy in the dynamic model is analyzed in -VIII. An example is worked out in Section IX. A sum- ption of the model and discussion of its implications are in

Model

hly artificial model of the production and trade processes the workings of a general equilibrium search model. All are assumed to be alike. Instantaneous utility satisfies

$$U = y - c, \tag{1}$$

closest to this in structure is that of Hellwig (1976), who shows that his onverges to a Walrasian model as the rate of arrival of trade oppor- ithout limit.

31

P. Diamond, Aggregate demand management in search equilibrium, *Journal of Political Economy*, **90** (1982), 881–94.

The focus of the chapters above was on aspects of the economy that are appropriately modeled in partial equilibrium. This chapter explores the possibility of using search theory to model economy-wide macroeconomic phenomena. For a further discussion of this perspective on macroeconomics, see Diamond (1984).

References

P. Diamond, "A Search-Equilibrium Approach to the Micro Foundations of Macroeconomics," Cambridge, Mass.: MIT Press, 1984.

Aggregate Demand Manager
Equilibrium

Peter A. Diamond

Massachusetts Institute of Technology

Equilibrium is analyzed for a simple bart
risk-neutral agents where trade is coorc
matching process. It is shown that there a
rational expectations equilibria, with al
equilibria inefficient. This implies that an ec
trade friction does not have a unique natural

I. Introduction

Some economists attribute fluctuations in u
ceptions of prices and wages. Others attribu
in adjustment of prices and wages (includir
seems to be a shared view that there wou
unemployment problems if prices and wag
correctly perceived. This paper introduces
unemployment problems—the difficulty of
many-person economy. That is, once one d
ian auctioneer and introduces trade frictic
unemployment problems in an economy
flexible prices and wages.

Using a barter model with identical, risk-
trade is coordinated by a stochastic matc

Valuable discussion with Sidney Winter; helpful cc
Jerry Hausman, James Mirrlees, Richard Schmalen
Solow, and Martin Weitzman; research assistance by
Whinston; and financial support from NSF are grate

Reprinted with permission from *Journa*

examines
shown to
local ineffi
local ineffi
equilibria
The extern
in the nun
positive fe
profitable.

These re
is mechani
able. Neve
search inte
good deal
variables a
increased
is, the exte
to produc
frictions in

To see t
definition
once fricti
paper argu
omy with
ployment.
be to direc
the lowest

The bas
static mod
basic exter
Sections V
mary desc
Section X.

II. Basic

We use a h
to highligh
individual

[1] The mod
search mode
tunities rises

where y is the consumption of output and c is the cost of production (disutility of labor). The utility function is chosen to be linear as part of the simplification that leads to the conclusion that trade bargains will not vary across pairs who are trading. In addition, the absence of risk aversion permits us to ignore the absence of implicit or explicit wage insurance. Lifetime utility is the present discounted value of instantaneous utility. Since trade and production take place at discrete times, lifetime utility satisfies

$$V = \sum_{i=1}^{\infty} e^{-rt_i} U_{t_i}. \tag{2}$$

Individuals are assumed to maximize the expected value of lifetime utility, with the times of work and consumption as random variables.

Rather than modeling production as going on continuously, we assume that the arrival of production opportunities is a Poisson process. With arrival rate a, each individual learns of production opportunities. Each opportunity has y units of output and costs c ($c \geqslant \underline{c} > 0$) units to produce. We assume that y is the same for all projects but that c varies across projects with distribution G. Each opportunity is a random draw from G, with costs known before the decision on undertaking the project. Each project undertaken is completed instantly.

There are two restrictions on individual behavior. (1) Individuals cannot consume the products of their own investment but trade their own output for that produced by others. This represents the advantage of specialized production and trade over self-sufficiency. (2) Individuals cannot undertake a production project if they have unsold produced output on hand. This extreme assumption on the costs of inventory holding is also part of the simplification of the determination of trade bargains. The fact that all trades involve individuals with y units to sell implies that all units are swapped on a one-for-one basis and promptly consumed.[2] It is assumed that there is no credit so that all trade is between individuals with inventories to trade.

Thus individuals have 0 or y units for sale. The former are looking for production opportunities and are referred to as unemployed. The latter are trying to sell their output and are referred to as employed.

The basic difference between individuals in these two different states is that the latter have purchasing power while the former do not.[3] If production were modeled as time consuming, then individuals

[2] Dropping the simplifications of risk neutrality, barter, and identical inventory holdings, we would need to solve for a distribution of trade prices, which would complicate the analysis. Assuming that all trade is one-for-one, we do not basically change the model by allowing simultaneous searches for trade and production and thus inventory accumulation.

[3] This is the counterpart in search equilibrium of effective demand considerations in

would be in one of three states—unemployed, producing, or trading. Commencing production only adds to demand with a lag. In that sense, those producing are similar to those unemployed. However, it remains the case that the decision to switch from searching for production to engaging in production is the driving force in the model. A similar model can be constructed with no unemployment and varying production intensity. It seems appropriate to associate varying levels of production intensity (coming from varying levels of profitability) with varying levels of unemployment. In a more general setting, there would also be varying hours of work and varying labor intensity on the job.

The trading process is such that for each individual the arrival of potential trading partners is a Poisson process with arrival rate $b(e)$, $b' > 0$, where e is the fraction of the population employed in the trading process, that is, the fraction of the population with inventories available for trade. The presence of lags in the trading process represents primarily the time needed to sell goods. Thus the average length of time of consumer goods in inventories is assumed to increase as the rate of sales declines. For example, a trader might meet with others at a constant rate and find that, for any meeting, there is a probability that the potential trading partner has a unit to sell, that is, is employed. The probability that a potential partner is in the market is a function of the fraction of the population employed, e, with the probability increasing in e. With undirected search for trading partners the probability of finding a trading partner in any meeting would equal e. In a more complicated setting, the greater the stock of available inventories the easier it is to find the particular goods that one wants.

The economy is assumed to be sufficiently large that the expected values of potential production and trade opportunities are realized. The employment rate falls from each completed transaction, as a previously employed person becomes eligible to undertake a production opportunity, and rises whenever a production opportunity is undertaken. Assuming that all production opportunities with costs below c^* are undertaken, we have the time derivative of the employment rate satisfying

$$\dot{e} = a(1 - e)G(c^*) - eb(e). \tag{3}$$

That is, each of the $1 - e$ unemployed (per capita) has the flow probability a of learning of an opportunity and accepts the fraction

disequilibrium models (see, e.g., Clower 1965). The large difference in demand between employed and unemployed is a natural consequence of the absence of a capital market. Even with a capital market, there would remain demand differences between individuals in the two states.

$G(c^*)$ of opportunities. Each of the e employed (per capita) faces the probability b of having a successful trade meeting and being freed to seek a new opportunity.[4]

In a steady state, we have the equilibrium rate of unemployment by setting $\dot{e}$ equal to zero. Setting (3) equal to zero, we see that the steady-state employment rate rises with c^*:

$$\left.\frac{de}{dc^*}\right|_{\dot{e}=0} = \frac{a(1-e)G'(c^*)}{b(e) + eb'(e) + aG(c^*)} > 0. \tag{4}$$

We turn next to the determination of c^*.

III. Individual Choice

As modeled, the only decision to be made is which production opportunities to undertake. Assuming a steady-state equilibrium, we can describe this decision as a simple dynamic programming problem. Let us denote the expected present discounted value of lifetime utility for employed and unemployed by W_e and W_u. Then, the utility discount rate times each of these values equals the expected value of the flow of instantaneous utility plus the expected capital gain from a change in status,

$$\begin{aligned} rW_e &= b(y - W_e + W_u), \\ rW_u &= a\int_0^{c^*} (W_e - W_u - c)dG(c). \end{aligned} \tag{5}$$

With probability b, an employed person has a trade opportunity giving rise to instantaneous consumption y and a change in status to unemployed. Each unemployed person accepting a production opportunity has an instantaneous utility $-c$ and a change in status to employed.

An unemployed person accepts any opportunity that raises expected utility. Thus we have the criterion

$$c^* = W_e - W_u = \frac{by + a\int_0^{c^*} c\,dG}{r + b + aG(c^*)}, \tag{6}$$

where the second equality comes from taking the difference between the two equations in (5) and solving for $W_e - W_u$. The level of aggregate demand, measured as the number of traders seeking to

[4] We are aggregating the individually experienced process, $b(e)$, over all individuals in the process, rather than (equivalently) the rate of meetings, each of which frees two traders to seek new opportunities.

purchase, affects production decisions since the probability of a sale increases with the employment rate. Differentiating (6) we have

$$\frac{dc^*}{de} = \frac{(y - c^*)b'}{r + b + aG} > 0,$$
$$\frac{d^2c^*}{de^2} = \frac{(y - c^*)b'' - 2b'(dc^*/de) - aG'(dc^*/de)^2}{r + b + aG}. \tag{7}$$

To see that dc^*/de is positive, we note that (with positive interest) no one would undertake a project with less output than input ($y > c^*$) and $b' > 0$. With $b'' \leq 0$, d^2c^*/de^2 is also negative. Armed with (3) and (6) we can describe steady-state equilibrium.

IV. Steady-State Equilibrium

A steady state is marked by optimal production decisions (6) and a constant rate of employment, with (3) set equal to zero. In each of these equations e and c^* are positively related, which allows the possibility of multiple steady-state equilibria. Except when the shutdown of the economy ($e = 0$) is the unique equilibrium, there will be multiple equilibria. To see this, we note that c^* goes to zero as e (and so b) goes to zero. Also, $c^*(e)$ is bounded above since c^* is less than y for any finite b. Steady-state employment rates are bounded above by the employment level reached if all production opportunities are accepted ($G = 1$). As drawn in figure 1, it is assumed that there is no upper bound to the support of G. The steady-state employment rate equals zero for c^* below $\underline{c}$, the lower bound of possible production costs.

If agents expect the current unemployment rate to be permanent, then the economy is always on the optimal steady-state production decision curve, (6), with movement determined by the $\dot{e}$ equation. Then, the equilibria in figure 1 with the highest employment rate and with a rate of zero are stable. Since G does not necessarily have nice properties, there can be more equilibria than shown.

If the model were extended to allow random shocks to the aggregate economy, the presence of multiple steady-state equilibria implies that the economy can get stuck at the "wrong" steady-state equilibrium after the shock has gone away. Similarly, the presence of multiple steady-state rational expectations equilibria implies the existence of multiple rational expectations paths from some initial positions.

V. Static Model

The dynamic model used above seems useful for understanding both the workings of the externality and the design of policy. Given that

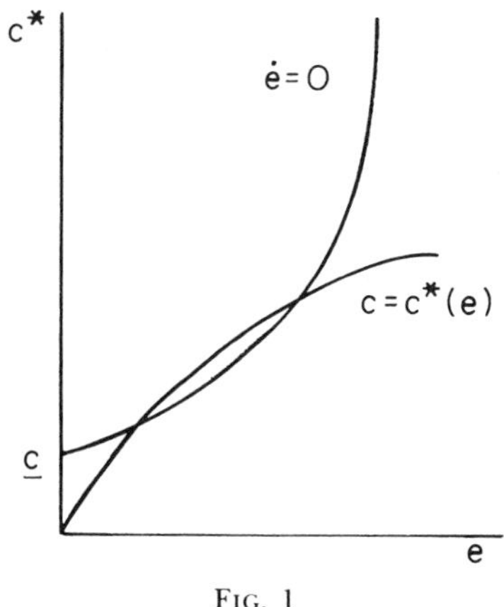

FIG. 1

model to motivate the equilibrium trade possibilities, one can describe the externality more simply in terms of a static model. Let us consider an aggregate cost function

$$c = f(y), \tag{8}$$

with $f' > 0, f'' > 0$. Let $p(y)$ be the probability of making a sale as a function of the aggregate output level. Unsold output is assumed to be wasted, so that welfare satisfies

$$U = yp(y) - c. \tag{9}$$

If individuals view p as a parameter, equilibrium occurs at a level of production satisfying

$$p(y) = f'(y). \tag{10}$$

For efficiency, the aggregate relationship between sales probability and production level must be recognized, which gives an optimality condition

$$p(y) + yp'(y) = f'(y). \tag{11}$$

By subsidizing the cost of production (financed by lump-sum taxation) the decentralized economy can be induced to produce at a point which satisfies the social optimality condition.

It is straightforward to extend this static model to include public goods. This extension will show the presence of a multiplier process and the need to consider multiplier effects in the absence of other demand management policies. Let g be the quantity of output used for public consumption and $V(g)$ the concave addition to social welfare from public consumption. We assume lump-sum tax finance, so the cost of public consumption is added to the cost of production for private consumption. The probability of a sale is assumed to increase with aggregate demand, $y + g$. Private consumption equals total sales less public consumption. Thus, social welfare can be written as

$$U = yp(y + g) - g + V(g) - c. \tag{12}$$

The equilibrium production decision with p taken to be a parameter can now be written as

$$p(y + g) = f'(y). \tag{13}$$

Implicitly differentiating (and thus assuming equilibrium y continuous in g) we have

$$\frac{dy}{dg} = -\frac{p'}{p' - f''}. \tag{14}$$

To sign this expression we need to appeal to the stability argument that the relevant equilibria have the marginal cost of production, $f'(y)$, rising more rapidly than the probability of a sale, $p(y)$. With $p' - f'' < 0$, we have $dy/dg > 0$.

Turning to the first-order condition for the optimal level of public consumption we have

$$\frac{dU}{dg} = yp' - 1 + V' + (p + yp' - f')\frac{dy}{dg} = 0. \tag{15}$$

Using the equilibrium condition, (13), we can write this as

$$V' = 1 - yp'\left(1 + \frac{dy}{dg}\right) = 1 + \frac{yp'f''}{p' - f''} < 1. \tag{16}$$

For a contrast let us consider an economy where the exogenous fraction $(1 - p)$ of output produced is lost in the distribution network. Then dy/dg would be zero and the marginal benefit of public consumption should be equated with the marginal cost of forgone consumption, which is one. Thus there is higher optimal public consumption when the profitability of production increases with increased government demand, and greater production yields a trade externality.

VI. Long-Run Stimulation Policy

To explore policy in the dynamic model we will assume that the government has sufficient policy tools to control production decisions. (In this barter economy, one cannot distinguish between aggregate demand policy and aggregate supply policy.) Below we will consider a production-cost subsidy to induce private decisions that sustain the optimal steady state. In this section we will examine a small permanent change in c^* away from a steady-state equilibrium with no intervention. In the next section we will examine the optimal path for $c^*(t)$ from an arbitrary initial position. In steady-state equilibrium, we have a flow of utility per capita satisfying

$$Q(t) = eb(e)y - a(1 - e)\int_0^{c^*} cdG, \tag{17}$$

where $eb(e)$ is the rate of sales, with consumption of y per sale, and $a(1 - e)G$ is the rate of production, with an average cost of $\int_0^{c^*} cdG/G$ per project undertaken. For social welfare we are interested in the present discounted value of Q:

$$W = \int_0^{\infty} e^{-rt} Q(t)dt. \tag{18}$$

When the economy starts at a steady-state equilibrium ($\dot{e} = 0$), the change in W (along the dynamic path of economy) resulting from a permanent change in c^* satisfies (for a derivation of [19] see Diamond [1980])

$$\begin{aligned} r\frac{\partial W}{\partial c^*} &= -a(1 - e)c^*G'(c^*) \\ &\quad + \left[y(b + eb') + a\int_0^{c^*} cdG\right]\frac{a(1 - e)G'(c^*)}{r + b + eb' + aG(c^*)}. \end{aligned} \tag{19}$$

The first term represents the increase in production costs at the steady-state employment rate, while the second represents the change in both output and production costs along the employment trajectory induced by the change in production rule. At an equilibrium without intervention (where [6] holds), we can write this as

$$\begin{aligned} r\frac{\partial W}{\partial c^*} &= -a(1 - e)c^*G' + \frac{[yeb' + c^*(r + b + aG)]a(1 - e)G'}{r + b + eb' + aG} \\ &= \frac{a(1 - e)G'eb'}{r + b + eb' + aG}(y - c^*) > 0. \end{aligned} \tag{20}$$

Thus, without intervention, there is locally too little activity in the economy.[5] This permanent increase in c^* raises expected lifetime utility for every person as well as raising aggregate welfare. The efficiency argument does not apply at the equilibrium with no economic activity ($e = 0$) since $G'(c)$ is zero for $c < \underline{c}$.

[5] In a partial equilibrium model of job matching, I have argued (Diamond 1981) that equilibrium has too rapid job filling for efficiency. I have not integrated that model with this one. If such an integration were done in a model with a single decision (by having a be a function of $1 - e$, e.g.), these would be offsetting externalities. If such an integration were done in a model with two decisions, two externalities may prove to be simultaneously present rather than offsetting.

VII. Short-Run Stabilization Policy

Continuing with the assumption that the government can control production decisions, we can examine the optimal policy for an arbitrary initial position. That is, the optimal stabilization policy satisfies

$$\max_{c^*(t)} \int_0^\infty e^{-rt}Q(t)dt,$$

$$\text{where } Q(t) = e(t)b[e(t)]y - a[1 - e(t)]\int_0^{c^*(t)} cdG, \tag{21}$$

$$\dot{e}(t) = a[1 - e(t)]G[c^*(t)] - e(t)b[e(t)],$$

$$e(0) = e_0.$$

Writing the optimal policy as $c^{**}(t)$, we get (the Euler equation)

$$\dot{c}^{**}(t) = rc^{**} - (y - c^{**})(b + eb') + a\int_0^{c^{**}} (c^{**} - c)dG. \tag{22}$$

Setting $\dot{c}^{**}(t)$ equal to zero and differentiating, we have

$$\left.\frac{dc^{**}}{de}\right|_{\dot{c}^{**}=0} = \frac{(y - c^{**})(2b' + eb'')}{r + b + eb' + aG}. \tag{23}$$

With $b'' \leq 0$, this expression is not necessarily positive, except near the origin. The phase diagram is shown in figure 2 under the assumption that the state with lowest unemployment is the optimum for any initial position.

Comparing the equation for $\dot{c}^{**} = 0$, (22), and the private choice of c^* in a steady state, (6), we see that the former is always above the latter as a function of e. That is, superimposing figures 1 and 2, we see that the $\dot{c}^{**} = 0$ curve lies above the $c = c^*(e)$ curve.

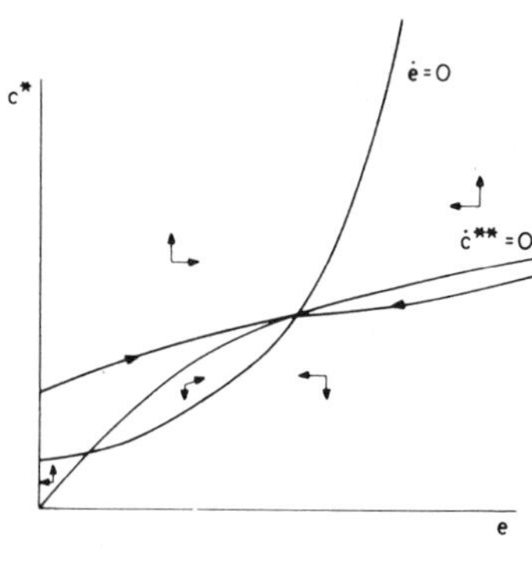

Fig. 2

VIII. Subsidizing Production

The asymptotically optimal steady state is described by setting $\dot{c}^{**}$, in (22), equal to zero (or, alternatively, by setting $\partial W/\partial c^*$, in [19], equal to zero). By subsidizing the cost of production, individuals can be induced to select this cutoff cost. In this section we derive the equation for this subsidy. We assume that the subsidy is financed by a lump-sum tax (payable in labor) that falls on the employed and unemployed equally.

With a subsidy of s per project completed, the individually optimal cutoff rule becomes

$$c^* - s = W_e - W_u = \frac{by + a\int_0^{c^*}(c - s)dG}{r + b + aG(c^*)}. \quad (24)$$

The asymptotically optimal level satisfies

$$c^{**} = \frac{by + eb'y + a\int_0^{c^{**}} cdG}{r + b + eb' + aG(c^{**})}. \quad (25)$$

Equating the expressions for c^* and c^{**} and solving, we have

$$s = \frac{eb'\left[ry + a\int_0^{c^*}(y - c)dG\right]}{(r + b)(r + b + eb' + aG)}. \quad (26)$$

This subsidy level is positive, as can be seen from (22), which implies that $y > c^*$ when $\dot{c}^{**}$ equals zero.[6]

IX. An Example

As an example, assume that $b(e) = eb$ and that all projects cost the same, $\underline{c}$. In this case there will be three steady-state equilibria provided that $\underline{c} < y/[1 + (r/b\bar{e})]$, where $\bar{e}$ is the solution to $be^2 = a(1 - e)$. For this case the curves determining equilibria and optima are shown in figure 3.

It is interesting to consider the optimal plan in more detail. Let the

[6] Laurence Weiss suggested calculating the effect of unemployment compensation, financed by a tax on output. Such a policy can be fitted into the model by giving each unemployed person a probability of receiving an output bundle just equal to the after-tax output level of a project. Such a policy moves in the wrong direction, since the incentive to production of having more potential trading partners is smaller than the disincentives coming from the sum of output taxation and unemployment subsidization.

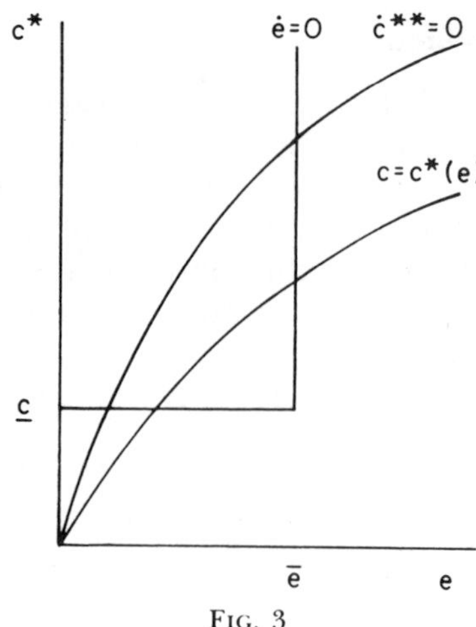

FIG. 3

rate of change of the employment rate be the control variable. Then, social welfare can be written as

$$W = \int_0^\infty e^{-rt}\{b(y - \underline{c})[e(t)]^2 + \underline{c}\dot{e}(t)\}dt, \tag{27}$$

where $\dot{e}(t)$ is constrained by

$$b[e(t)]^2 - a[1 - e(t)] \leqslant -\dot{e}(t) \leqslant b[e(t)]^2. \tag{28}$$

Since the objective is linear in $\dot{e}$, there are two possible asymptotic solutions as one or the other of the constraints on $\dot{e}(t)$ is binding. Thus, asymptotically, either no opportunities are accepted or all of them are. For initial condition e_0, let us write the levels of welfare under these plans[7] as $W_0(e_0)$ and $W_1(e_0)$. For some parameter values one or the other of these two functions is larger for all values of e_0 between zero and one. For some parameter values the functions appear as in figure 4. In this case it is optimal to take all opportunities for $e_0 > e_0'$ and optimal to take no opportunities for $e_0 < e_0'$.

X. Summary and Conclusions

It is common in theoretical economics to use a tropical island metaphor to describe the workings of a model. The island described here has many individuals, not one. When employed, they stroll along the beaches examining palm trees. Some trees have coconuts. All

[7] We are ignoring the possibility that for some parameters it might be optimal to take all opportunities for a range of employment rates above $\bar{e}$ and then switch over to taking no further opportunities.

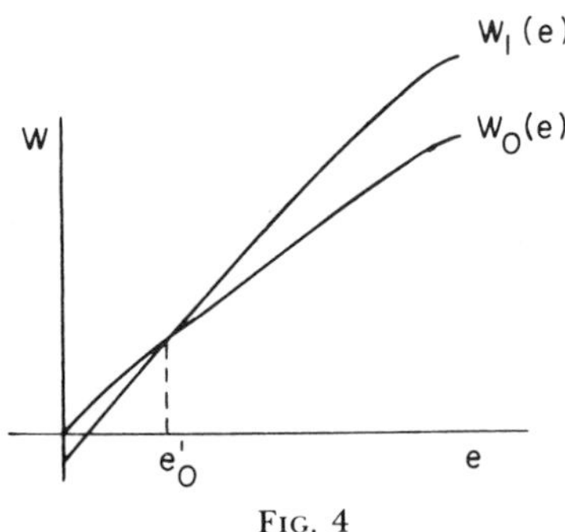

FIG. 4

bunches have the same number of nuts but differ in their height above the ground. Having spotted a bunch, the individual decides whether to climb the tree. There is a taboo against eating nuts one has picked oneself. Having climbed a tree, the worker goes searching for a trade—nuts for nuts—which will result in consumption. This represents, artificially, the realistic aspect of the small extent of consumption of one's own production in modern economies. The ease in finding a trading partner depends on the number of potential partners available. Thus the equilibrium level of production is not efficient if everyone correctly predicts the difficulty of successful trading. Of course, overoptimism can result in the efficient production level. There is no mechanism to ensure that individual by individual, or on average, forecasts of time to completed trade are correct. Errors would be particularly likely on a non-steady-state path.

When a Walrasian auctioneer organizes a competitive equilibrium, there are not unrealized mutually advantageous trading opportunities. In a complex modern economy, there will always remain unrecognized, and so unrealized, opportunities. The complexity of the many-person, many-good trades needed to realize some potential opportunities, together with costs of information, prevent the economy from achieving a full realization. The model employed here has abstracted from the many-good aspect of modern economies. However, the fact of large numbers of different goods should be kept in mind when interpreting the difficulty in completing trades as modeled here. In the presence of unrealized trading opportunities, many government policies will naturally affect the extent to which these opportunities are realized by affecting individual production and trade incentives. Policies can have two distinct goals—inducing small changes in the steady-state equilibrium position to offset externalities and inducing large changes when the economy has settled down at an inefficient long-run equilibrium.

There are several properties of this type of macro search model that seem particularly attractive. Even without lags in the ability of the government to affect private decisions, the government does not have the power to move instantaneously to a full employment position. Recognizing the costs of starting a production process, we see that there is an optimal rate of convergence to the optimally full employment steady state, which reflects the higher real costs of moving too quickly. Knowledge of private forecasts would be essential to the optimal design of tools to alter private decisions but is not necessary for recognizing a situation calling for intervention (except to the extent that the bases of private forecasts might improve the government forecast).

The model presented here is very special. One cannot draw policy conclusions directly from such a model. There are two purposes for its construction. One is to form a basis for further generalization and study. In particular, it would be interesting to introduce varying technological conditions to examine how government policy should vary with the position of the economy. The second is to provide an example to contrast with models that assume, unrealistically, the existence of a frictionless, instantaneous trade-coordination mechanism and thus the absence of the potential for corrective policies.[8] While the construction of realistic models of trade frictions (and wage rigidities) is needed for good policy analysis, the existence of this simple model indicates the feasibility of constructing consistent micro based models with a role for reactive macro policy.

References

Clower, Robert. "The Keynesian Counterrevolution: A Theoretical Appraisal." In *The Theory of Interest Rates,* edited by Frank H. Hahn and F. P. R. Brechling. London: Macmillan, 1965.

Diamond, Peter A. "An Alternative to Steady State Comparisons." *Econ. Letters* 5, no. 1 (1980): 7–9.

———. "Mobility Costs, Frictional Unemployment, and Efficiency." *J.P.E.* 89, no. 4 (August 1981): 789–812.

Friedman, Milton. "The Role of Monetary Policy." *A.E.R.* 58 (March 1968): 1–17.

Hellwig, Martin F. "A Model of Monetary Exchange." Research Memorandum no. 202, Econometric Res. Program, Princeton Univ., 1976.

Lucas, Robert E., Jr. "Expectations and the Neutrality of Money." *J. Econ. Theory* 4 (April 1972): 103–24.

Lucas, Robert E., Jr., and Prescott, Edward C. "Equilibrium Search and Unemployment." *J. Econ. Theory* 7 (February 1974): 188–209.

[8] In Lucas (1972) and Lucas and Prescott (1974) there are physically separate markets, with each market involving perfect coordination. The efficiency of movements between markets is unaffected by aggregate demand management policies. Thus these extensions of the competitive model have trade frictions but not the externalities from trading efforts modeled here.

30
J. Hirshleifer, The private and social value of information and the reward to inventive activity, *American Economic Review* **61** (1971), 561–574

The models thus far have considered only trade for the acquisition of commodities to be consumed. Information limitations made the search for a good price worthwhile. This article considers repeated trading, with individuals speculating on future price changes. This introduces an important additional element at work in some markets. For additional analysis of investment in information see the references cited in Chapter 12 and the work of Arrow (1971).

Reference

K. Arrow, "Essays in the Theory of Risk Bearing." Markham Publ. Co., Chicago, Illinois, 1971, Chapters 6 and 7.

The Private and Social Value of Information and the Reward to Inventive Activity

By Jack Hirshleifer*

A number of recent papers[1] have dealt with the economics of information in a context in which each individual is fully certain about his own endowment and productive opportunities. In those papers, the individual is imperfectly informed only about his market opportunities, i.e., about the supply-demand offers of *other* individuals. In consequence, costly patterns of search for trading partners replace the traditional assumption of costless exchange.

This paper deals with an entirely different aspect of the economics of information. We here revert to the textbook assumption that markets are perfect and costless. The individual is always fully acquainted with the supply-demand offers of all potential traders, and an equilibrium integrating all individuals' supply-demand offers is attained instantaneously. Individuals are unsure only about the size of their *own* commodity endowments and/or about the returns attainable from their *own* productive investments. They are subject to technological uncertainty rather than market uncertainty.[2]

Technological uncertainty brings immediately to mind the economics of research and invention. The traditional position has been that the excess of the social over the private value of new technological knowledge leads to underinvestment in inventive activity. The main reason is that information, viewed as a product, is only imperfectly appropriable by its discoverer.[3] But this paper will show that there is a hitherto unrecognized force operating in the opposite direction. What has been scarcely appreciated in the literature, if recognized at all, is the *distributive* aspect of access to superior information. It will be seen below how this advantage provides a motivation for the private acquisition and dissemination of technological information that is quite apart from—and may even exist in the absence of—any social usefulness of that information.[4]

I. Foreknowledge Versus Discovery

Within the category of technological (as opposed to market) information, dif-

* Professor of economics, University of California, Los Angeles. This paper is an abbreviation of a report with the same title prepared for Western Management Science Institute, UCLA (1970b). The research at WMSI was supported by the National Science Foundation and the Office of Naval Research. Valuable suggestions have been contributed by Earl Thompson, Jacob Marschak, Ross M. Starr, Benjamin Klein, and Joseph Ostroy.

[1] See S. A. Ozga, George Stigler (1961, 1962), and Armen Alchian.

[2] These two types of uncertainty have been distinguished by a number of authors: see Tjalling Koopmans (pp. 161ff), Peter Diamond, Jacob Marschak (1968b, p. 17).

[3] See Kenneth Arrow (1962, p. 619). The comment by Harold Demsetz is also of interest. On patents as a device to achieve appropriability, see Fritz Machlup.

[4] In connection with policy debates over stock market "insider trading," Henry Manne has discussed the private and social gains attached to the dissemination of corporate information. A very recent article by Eugene F. Fama and Arthur B. Laffer emphasizes the differing motivations of insiders and outsiders for the generation of such information; their analysis, though in a partial-equilibrium context, in some ways parallels the treatment here.

ferent sorts of knowledge are associated with rather different private incentives and social efficiency conditions. This paper concentrates upon a distinction between what will be called foreknowledge on the one hand, and discovery on the other. The type of information represented by foreknowledge is exemplified by ability to successfully predict tomorrow's (or next year's) weather. Here we have a stochastic situation: with particular probabilities the future weather might be hot or cold, rainy or dry, etc. But whatever does actually occur will, in due time, be evident to all; the only aspect of information that may be of advantage is prior knowledge as to what will happen. Discovery, in contrast, is correct recognition of something that possibly already exists, though hidden from view. Examples include the determination of the properties of materials, of physical laws, even of mathematical attributes (e.g., the millionth digit in the decimal expansion of "π"). The essential point is that in such cases Nature will not autonomously reveal the information; only human action can extract it. Foreknowledge information is conceptually simpler to deal with, involving as it does only the value of *priority* in time of superior knowledge; this topic will be taken up first below.

II. Elements of the Economics of Foreknowledge

The analysis of the value of priority of information necessarily involves both temporality and uncertainty. For convenience, the simplest possible paradigm of choice will be employed. Suppose that there exists but a single physical good (corn). It will be assumed, however, that a number of different types of claims may be owned or traded—claims to corn at specified dates and under specified contingencies or "states of Nature."[5] It suffices to consider a particularly simple model in which the present (time 0) is certain, and the future consists of a single date (time 1) at which just one of two alternative states (a or b) will obtain. The marketable commodities of the analysis can be denoted c_0, c_{1a}, and c_{1b}: claims to corn valid at, and only at, the subscripted dates and states.

Each individual will have a utility function governing his preferences *now* for holdings of alternative combinations of these claims. Entering into this function will be his beliefs as to the probabilities π_a and π_b of the two states. It has been shown[6] that, under certain widely accepted assumptions, it is possible to find a cardinal intertemporal function $u(c_0, c_1)$ that (a) measures desirability of alternative *certain* dated consumption sequences and (b) is such that the von Neumann-Morgenstern expected-utility rule can be employed to order preferences among *risky* sequences of time-state claims, according to the formula:

$$U = \pi_a u(c_0, c_{1a}) + \pi_b u(c_0, c_{1b}) \tag{1}$$

This utility function exemplifies the property of "state-independence," i.e., the expected utility is a sum of distinct terms each of which is associated with only one particular state of the world.[7]

The utility function to be used below

[5] The conception of state-claims as commodities stems from the pioneering work of Arrow (1953, 1964). Gerard Debreu (ch. 7) extended Arrow's model to multiple time-periods. The paradigm of choice involving time-state claims has been further developed by other authors, including Karl Borch and Hirshleifer (1965, 1966).

[6] See Jacques Drèze and Franco Modigliani; Hirshleifer (1970a, ch. 8).

[7] *State-independence* is an implication of the von Neumann-Morgenstern postulate sometimes called "irrelevance of nonaffected outcomes"—see Marschak (1968a). The key idea is that when we are dealing with *prospects* which promise to offer one consequence if state a obtains and another if state b obtains, we need not consider any relations of complementarity in preference. For there is never any question of receiving the *combined* consequences attached to the two states; the individual will necessarily receive one to the exclusion of the other.

makes the further specification that $u(c_0, c_1)$ can be written in the special form $v(c_0)+\theta v(c_1)$, where θ is a fixed time-preference parameter characteristic of the individual, and v is a cardinal preference-scaling function for income valid for him at each state and date. The essential additional property underlying this specification may be called time-independence.[8] Given both state-independence and time-independence, the utility function becomes:

$$(2) \quad \begin{aligned} U &= \pi_a(v_0 + \theta v_{1a}) + \pi_b(v_0 + \theta v_{1b}) \\ &= v_0 + \theta(\pi_a v_{1a} + \pi_b v_{1b}) \end{aligned}$$

where v_0 is condensed notation for $v(c_0)$, and v_{1a} and v_{1b} are defined analogously.

The acquisition of information will take the form of warranted revisions in the probability estimates π_a and π_b that enter into preference functions and so guide decisions. In what follows it will be essential to distinguish *private* information (available only to a single individual) from *public* information (available to everyone)—intermediate cases will generally be ignored. It will also be important to keep in mind the distinction between information that is *prior* to, and information that is *posterior* to, the individual consumption-investment decisions that must be made at t=0. Still another distinction is that between *sure* information (as to which future state will obtain) and merely *better* information—the latter would represent a sharper focusing of subjective probabilities that does not entirely eliminate uncertainty.

[8] *Time-independence*, the absence of complementarity in preference between income at time 0 and income at time 1, does not have so compelling a justification as does state-independence. For the individual will indeed be receiving a combination of consequences over time. But, in the absence of any convincing reason for anticipating positive complementarity or its reverse, the assumption of zero complementarity may be a satisfactory simplification. The assumption is widely employed in the literature of intertemporal optimization (see, e.g., Arrow (1966, p. 20)).

III. The Value of Foreknowledge: Pure Exchange

In a simplified world of pure exchange, all productive transformations among the quantities c_0, c_{1a}, and c_{1b} are ruled out—even simple storage. An individual dissatisfied with his endowment vector $Y = (y_0, y_{1a}, y_{1b})$ can modify it only by trading. Let us suppose a competitive world of "representative" individuals, characterized by identical probability beliefs and utility functions, and all holding identical endowments. Then no trading actually takes place; the price structure that emerges in market equilibrium must "sustain" the endowment pattern for every individual. Taking current corn as numeraire so that $P_0=1$, the sustaining prices must be:[9]

$$(3) \quad P_{1a} = \theta\pi_a v_{1a}'/v_0' \quad \text{and} \quad P_{1b} = \theta\pi_b v_{1b}'/v_0'$$

Wealth in c_0 units may then be determined from the definition:

$$(4) \quad W_0 = P_0 c_0 + P_{1a}c_{1a} + P_{1b}c_{1b}$$

Finally, utility attained may be calculated by appropriate substitutions in (2). This is the base situation with which the results of changes in information will be compared.

For concreteness, a numerical illustration will be employed using a logarithmic preference-scaling function v (see Table 1). Note that future state a is assumed better endowed than state b ($y_{1a}=200$, $y_{1b}=80$) as well as more probable ($\pi_a=.6$, $\pi_b=.4$). With c_0 as numeraire so that $P_0=1$, the parameters assumed lead to the solutions shown in column (4) for the sustaining prices ($P_{1a}=.3$ and $P_{1b}=.5$) and wealth ($W_0=200$). The expected utility (U

[9] The individual maximizes $U=v_0+\theta(\pi_a v_{1a}+\pi_b v_{1b})$ subject to $P_0c_0+P_{1a}c_{1a}+P_{1b}c_{1b}=P_0y_0+P_{1a}y_{1a}+P_{1b}y_{1b}$. The usual Lagrangean conditions lead to $v_0'=\lambda P_0$; $v_{1a}'=\lambda P_{1a}/\theta\pi_a$: $v_{1b}'=\lambda P_{1b}/\theta\pi_b$. With $P_0=1$, and (since all individuals have identical preferences and opportunities) $c_0=y_0$, $c_{1a}=y_{1a}$, and $c_{1b}=y_{1b}$, the results in the text are obtained.

Table 1—Data and Solution for Numerical Example

Endowments (1)	Prior Beliefs (2)	Preference Parameters (3)	Solution, Base Case (4)
$y_0 = 100$	—	$\theta = 1$	$P_0 = 1$
$y_{1a} = 200$	$\pi_a = .6$	$v = log_e c$	$P_{1a} = .3$
$y_{1b} = 80$	$\pi_b = .4$		$P_{1b} = .5$
			$W_0 = 200$

$= 9.5370$) is worked out in Table 2 (column (4)).

Now, suppose that a single individual at time 0 secures *private*, *prior*, and *sure* information that state a will obtain at time 1. Since one individual's choices would only negligibly affect the ruling prices, he could realize essentially all the market value $P_{1b}y_{1b}$ of his c_{1b} endowment (which he alone knows to be worthless) for reallocation to the purchase of more c_0 and/or c_{1a}. In the numerical example, this amount is $P_{1b}y_{1b} = .5(80) = 40$. With the parameters assumed, it can be shown[10] that he will purchase just $40/P_{1a} = 133.3$ units of c_{1a} to add to his endowed 200 units (Table 2, columns (2) and (5)). If instead he were to learn that state b will obtain, he would reallocate the entire value $P_{1a}y_{1a} = 60$ of his c_{1a} endowment to purchase $60/P_{1b} = 120$ units of c_{1b}. Table 2 also shows the expected utility given perfect information (and the consequent rearrangement of consumption) to be substantially higher than the expected utility under uncertainty. These expectations are calculated, of course, using the individual's prior probability estimates as to what the information will reveal.

We now come to the crucial contrast. What of the *social* value of the sure information just analyzed above? Suppose that by a collective payment to some knowledgeable outsider, an entire community consisting of the representative individuals above could all simultaneously be informed as to which future state will obtain—how large a payment would they be justified in making? The answer is: None at all! Such information would be absolutely valueless to the community as a whole. Information is of value only if it can affect action. But with identical endowments, preferences, and beliefs in a world of pure exchange, all individuals must still end up holding their endowment time-state distributions. The only thing that could happen, given the new public

[10] See Hirshleifer (1970b, pp. 9–11).

Table 2—Private Value of Information

	Consumptive Choices[a]			Utility[b]		
	Uncertainty[c] (1)	State a[d] to obtain (2)	State b[e] to obtain (3)	Uncertainty (4)	State a to obtain (5)	State b to obtain (6)
c_0	100	100	100	4.6052	4.6052	4.6052
c_{1a}	200	333.3	—	.6 (5.2983)	5.8091	—
c_{1b}	80	—	200	.4 (4.3821)	—	5.2983
Expected Utility Under Uncertainty:				9.5370		
Conditional Utility:					10.4143	9.9035
Expected Utility Given Perfect Information:[f]					10.2100	

[a] $P_{1a} = .3$, $P_{1b} = .5$, $W_0 = 200$
[b] Computed according to: $U = log_e c_0 + \pi_a log_e c_{1a} + \pi_b log_e c_{1b}$
[c] $\pi_a = .6$, $\pi_b = .4$
[d] $\pi_a = 1$, $\pi_b = 0$
[e] $\pi_a = 0$, $\pi_b = 1$
[f] Using prior weights $\pi_a = .6$, $\pi_b = .4$

TABLE 3—SOCIAL VALUE OF INFORMATION

	Consumptive Choices			Utility		
	Uncertainty[a] (1)	State a[b] to obtain (2)	State b[c] to obtain (3)	Uncertainty (4)	State a to obtain (5)	State b to obtain (6)
c_0	100	100	100	4.6052	4.6052	4.6052
c_{1a}	200	200	—	.6 (5.2983)	5.2983	—
c_{1b}	80	—	80	.4 (4.3821)	—	4.3821
Expected Utility Under Uncertainty:				9.5370		
Conditional Utility:					9.9035	8.9873
Expected Utility Given Perfect Information:[d]					9.5370	

[a] $\pi_a = .6$, $\pi_b = .4$; $W_0 = 200$; $P_{1a} = .3$, $P_{1b} = .5$
[b] $\pi_a = 1$, $\pi_b = 0$; $W_0 = 200$; $P_{1a} = .5$, $P_{1b} = 0$
[c] $\pi_a = 0$, $\pi_b = 1$; $W_0 = 200$; $P_{1a} = 0$, $P_{1b} = 1.25$
[d] Using prior weights $\pi_a = .6$, $\pi_b = .4$.

information, is that prices shift immediately to permit "sustaining" the endowment vector in the face of the changed beliefs entering into the utility function. In the numerical example, sure public information that state a will obtain, available *prior* to the decisions at $t=0$, will cause P_{1a} to rise to .5 (while P_{1b}, of course, falls to zero). Sure public prior information that state b will obtain raises P_{1b} to 1.25, while P_{1a} falls to zero. Table 3 confirms that in these circumstances the individual will choose the same consumptions with the same probabilities as in the original uncertainty situation.

One other very important consideration must now be taken into account. There is a possibility of still greater gain for the *privately* informed individual if he is permitted to speculate rather than merely move directly to his preferred consumptive position. Assuming private knowledge that state a was to obtain, for example, an optimally speculating individual would first convert not just his c_{1b} holdings but rather *all* of his wealth $W_0 = 200$ to c_{1a} holdings at the old price relationships. The anticipation here is that the true information will become public, P_{1a} rising to .5 and wealth to 333.3, prior to the finalizing of the consumption-investment decisions at $t=0$. Note that the individual with private information would have every incentive to publicize that information, *after* making his speculative commitment. The enormously enhanced private results achievable via speculation are detailed in Table 4.

So far, two reaction modes of the privately informed individual have been considered: consumptive adaptation, and optimal speculation. A third and even more attractive possibility is *resale of the information* itself. The potential gain then becomes enormous, since the individual is no longer constrained by his personal commodity endowment. However, it may not be easy for an informed individual to authenticate possession of valuable foreknowledge for resale purposes. After all, anyone could *claim* to have such knowledge. Feasible and optimal resale strategies, and the market value of resold information, are issues that cannot be pursued here. The crucial point remains that *the community as a whole obtains no benefit, under pure exchange, from either the acquisition or the dissemination (by resale or otherwise) of private foreknowledge.*

The contrast between the private profitability and the social uselessness of foreknowledge may seem surprising. In-

TABLE 4—PRIVATE VALUE OF INFORMATION, WITH SPECULATION

	Consumptive Choices			Utility		
	Uncer-tainty[a]	State a[b] to obtain	State b[c] to obtain	Uncertainty	State a to obtain	State b to obtain
c_0	100	166.7	250	4.6052	5.1160	5.5215
c_{1a}	200	333.3	—	.6 (5.2983)	5.8091	—
c_{1b}	80	—	200	.4 (4.3821)	—	5.2983
Expected Utility Under Uncertainty:				9.5370		
Conditional Utility:					10.9251	10.8198
Expected Utility Given Perfect Information:[d]					10.8830	

[a] $\pi_a=.6$, $\pi_b=.4$; $W_0=200$; $P_{1a}=.3$, $P_{1b}=.5$
[b] $\pi_a=1$, $\pi_b=0$; $W_0=333.3$; $P_{1a}=.5$, $P_{1b}=0$
[c] $\pi_a=0$, $\pi_b=1$; $W_0=500$; $P_{1a}=0$, $P_{1b}=1.25$
[d] Using prior weights $\pi_a=.6$, $\pi_b=.4$.

formation is widely considered to be a classic example of a "collective good," the type of commodity for which private incentives are supposed to lead to under-provision rather than over-provision on the market. Indeed, there may be something of a collective-good aspect to the *market* information alluded to earlier: information that helps improve an otherwise imperfect process of exchange. But the expenditure of real resources for the production of *technological* information is socially wasteful in pure exchange, as the expenditure of resources for an increase in the quantity of money by mining gold is wasteful, and for essentially the same reason. Just as a smaller quantity of money serves monetary functions as well as a larger, the price level adjusting correspondingly, so a larger amount of foreknowledge serves no social purpose under pure exchange that the smaller amount did not.

IV. The Value of Foreknowledge: Production and Exchange

Consider now the more realistic regime in which production and exchange both take place. Assume that endowments are just the same as before, for all individuals. But suppose that, in addition, each representative individual has a small discrete productive investment opportunity of the following form: exactly 1 unit of endowed c_0 may be sacrificed to produce additional income in either time-state $1a$ or time-state $1b$ (but not both). Suppose that the choice is between a yield of $2\frac{1}{2}$ units in state a or $2\frac{1}{2}$ units in state b. With the prices of the initial situation in the example above ($P_{1a}=.3$, $P_{1b}=.5$), every representative individual would choose the latter alternative; he would physically invest, transforming his endowment combination ($y_0=100$, $y_{1a}=200$, $y_{1b}=80$) into the attained combination ($c_0=99$, $c_0=200$, $c_{1b}=82.5$). Since the scale of the collective investment is not infinitesimal, the prices change slightly but not by enough to modify the desirability of the selection made.

Suppose now that *one single* individual is given sure, prior, and private information that state a will obtain. Here it would be socially desirable that this individual's investment sacrifice of c_0 (and everyone else's, as well) be redirected so as to produce c_{1a} instead of the useless c_{1b}. But if the information is private, the original prices must still be ruling so that the individual's incentives for production decisions remain unchanged. He will continue to invest for a c_{1b} return, despite knowing that the latter will turn out to be valueless. It is more profitable for him to commit the resources to c_{1b}, merely taking care to arrange in advance for the liquidation of the $2\frac{1}{2}$ units of c_{1b} (in addition, of course, to his endowed 80 units) at the currently ruling market prices. *Thus, as under the regime of pure exchange, private foreknowledge makes possible large private profit without leading to socially useful activity.* The individual would have just as much incentive as under pure exchange (even more, in fact) to expend real resources in generating socially useless private information.

What of the value of *public* information? If the information were made public that state *a* would obtain, P_{1a} would jump to .5 (P_{1b} falling to zero). Then the individual investments would all be shifted so as to yield c_{1a} instead of c_{1b}. This, of course, is socially efficient behavior. *Public information as to which state will obtain is indeed of social value in a regime of production and exchange.* However, it remains true that the value of private foreknowledge is enormously greater to any individual than the value to him of public foreknowledge. In the example used here, public information enables the representative individual to attain the consumption sequence ($c_0 = 99$, $c_1 = 202.5$) with probability .6, or the sequence ($c_0 = 99$, $c_1 = 82.5$) with probability .4. Private information enables him to attain with probability .6 the sequence ($c_0 = 99$, $c_1 = 337.5$)—based on converting his 82.5 units of c_{1b} at the original price ratio into 137.5 units of c_{1a} to be added to his endowed 200 units—or with probability .4 the sequence ($c_0 = 99$, $c_1 = 202.5$). Evidently, the possibilities with private information are far superior (still leaving aside the prospect of much greater gains through speculation and/or resale). Thus, the incentives for the use of resources to generate private information remain excessive.

What about speculation and resale? Having undertaken a speculative commitment, it is in the interest of the informed individual to publicize the information. Whether or not involved in speculation, the informed individual would find it advantageous wherever possible to resell the information. Under pure exchange, where foreknowledge is socially valueless, devotion of resources to dissemination is only a further social waste. In a regime of production, however, universal dissemination would improve the choice of investments. The partial dissemination that would ensue from private publicizing or through resale would also tend to shift prices and lead to some productive adaptation. Thus, *in a regime of production, the dissemination of information has social utility,* against which gain must be offset, of course, any resource cost of the dissemination process.

V. Distributive Considerations, Public Information, and Homogeneity of Beliefs

The key factor underlying all the results obtained above is the distributive significance of private foreknowledge. When private information fails to lead to improved productive alignments (as must necessarily be the case in a world of pure exchange, and also in a regime of production unless there is dissemination effected in the interests of speculation or resale), it is evident that the individual's source of gain can only be at the expense of his fellows. But even where information is disseminated and does lead to improved productive commitments, the distributive transfer gain will surely be far greater than the relatively minor productive gain the individual might reap from the redirection of his own real investment commitments.

Will *public* information have distributive implications, and if so, will this consideration provide additional private motivation for the generation of public information? The nature and direction of possible distribution effects turn upon the timing of information acquisition in comparison with the schedule of trading. Two alternative timing patterns will be considered here: 1) The information is publicly released before the opening of trading, or 2) the individuals trade to their consumptive optimum positions prior to the release of the information, with another round of trading permitted afterward.[11] Both trading and generation of information are best regarded as essentially continuous interacting processes, so that the second timing pattern seems more acceptable.[12] But the first is useful in emphasizing certain aspects of reactions to public information.

We will therefore imagine, first, a situation of pure exchange in which the true state of the world is announced in advance of any market trading whatsoever—while individuals are still at their endowment positions. Announcement that state *a* will obtain (or, more generally, release of any information tending to increase the probability π_a that individuals attach to state *a*) will, of course, enhance the position of those disproportionately endowed with state *a* claims. The rise in the price P_{1a} will enrich such individuals. It will also enhance the position of those whose tastes or beliefs previously inclined them in the direction of purchase of state *b* claims. For, such individuals would otherwise have largely wasted their income endowments in the purchase of worthless state *b* claims.

That public information has distributive implications does not, however, lead necessarily to the conclusion that private individuals will want to generate public information. Individuals disproportionately endowed with state *a* claims, for example, cannot be sure in advance that the information will not point to state *b* rather than state *a*. And indeed, it can be shown that in the circumstances assumed here, risk-averse individuals will prefer that the information not be released.[13] For, the anticipation of public information becoming available in advance of trading adds a significant *distributive risk* to the underlying *technological risk* (as to which state will obtain). A community of such individuals would actually pay something to a knowledgeable outsider not to reveal, in advance of market trading, which state will obtain! (This conclusion would have to be modified somewhat under a regime of production and exchange; the gain from redirection of productive investments achieved in consequence of the public information would have to be offset against the increased distributive risk.)

Let us turn now to the more reasonable assumption that individuals have already optimally adapted their decisions to their opportunities prior to the release of new public information. Differences of endowments would no longer have any relevance, and so there would be no net incentive for or against the acquisition of socially neutral information under pure exchange. (And there would be an appropriately small incentive for any one individual to support the acquisition of beneficial public information in a world of production.) A similar argument can be made about differences in tastes or beliefs so long as the individuals may be presumed to have

[11] If no trading were permitted once the information was revealed, individuals' consumptive baskets (here, holdings of c_0 and c_1) would in general be non-Pareto optimal. That is, differences across individuals in marginal rates of substitution between commodities would persist. Such a model has been studied by Ross Starr. The non-Pareto optimality stemming from informational differences has also been noted by Earl A. Thompson (fn. 5) and by Arrow (1969, pp. 54–56).

[12] The second timing pattern corresponds to the dictum that, at any moment of time, the market has already "discounted" (allowed for) all publicly available information.

[13] See Hirshleifer (1970b, pp. 20–22).

merely moved to their consumptive optimum positions, and not engaged in speculative behavior. But, we know that for individuals with superior information there is a strong incentive to take speculative positions. Now, differences of beliefs amount to the same thing as *each individual's thinking that he is in possession of superior information*. Such differences open up a new range of possibilities.

We saw above that it was privately rational, for a better informed individual, to expend resources for the dissemination of socially neutral information—after having adopted a speculative commitment. With inhomogeneity of beliefs every person may be better informed, in his own opinion! Thus, the generation of public information is (from his point of view) nothing other than the dissemination of information already privately available to him. He will expect to reap speculative profits from this process. But so will other individuals, with quite opposed opinions! We therefore have rather strong grounds to anticipate that in these circumstances excessive resources will be devoted to the generation of public information.

These considerations may be clarified by reference to a well-known activity for the generation of public information—horse racing. Viewed as a research activity, horse racing may be presumed to have a small positive social value: the identification of faster horses works "to improve the breed." This consideration is evidently a very minor motivating factor for the activity in comparison with the opportunity to speculate upon one's supposedly superior knowledge. Without differences of opinion, it is said, there would be no horse races. That is, the social value is insufficient to motivate the research—the activity is founded upon the contradictory expectations of speculative gain.

Suppose that it costs $100 in real resources to run a horse race, and that the social advantage of knowing which is the fastest horse is just $5. Evidently, if the race is run society is engaging in excessive research. Now imagine that the potential speculative gain, to an individual convinced that his horse is truly faster, is just $90—he could still not earn enough, himself, to cover the costs of the race. But if several individuals are so convinced, each about his own horse, they may cooperate to stage the experiment. So conflict of beliefs may enormously compound the speculative factor that, even from the point of view of a single individual, tends to promote excessive investment in information-generating activity.

VI. The Value of Discovery Information

The acquisition of technological information usually refers to the detection of properties of Nature that permit the development of new tools or the utilization of new techniques. This is the type of information categorized as discovery above, in which Nature's secret will not be autonomously revealed but must be extracted by man. The necessity for human interposition makes the analysis of the value of discovery information somewhat more complex than the analysis of foreknowledge information.

For concreteness, consider the following situation. Suppose that if an alloy with an enormously high melting point of $X°$ can be created, extremely cheap thermonuclear power will become feasible. The underlying state of the world is not the result of a probabilistic process: such an alloy may in fact be possible to create (state a) or may not (state b). While this is not a stochastic situation, it has been shown to be useful even in such circumstances to summarize our uncertainty in the form of a probability distribution.[14] Thus, just as in the case of foreknowledge,

[14] See Leonard J. Savage.

we can assume that individuals assign probabilities π_a and π_b to the two underlying states of the world. However, even if the favorable state a is the true one, Nature is not going to tell us herself. In the discovery situation, no news is bad news.

From the point of view of any individual, however, the picture may not look very different from that analyzed under the heading of foreknowledge. For any individual there is a certain probability π_A of "good news" (discovery of the alloy), due to the actions of other men if not of his own. We can think of a compound event A which consists of the joint happenings "State a is true (the required alloy is possible) *and* this fact is successfully exploited (the alloy is created) within the time-period envisaged." Evidently, $\pi_A \leq \pi_a$, the probability of good news is generally less than the probability attached to the more favorable state of Nature. And similarly, if the event B is defined in a complementary way as representing "no news" (identical with "bad news" in the circumstances considered), we have $\pi_B \geq \pi_b$. The individual's decisions—for example, whether to invest in a productive process whose profitability will be highly sensitive to the prospect of cheap thermonuclear power—will run in terms of the probabilities of good and bad news rather than the probabilities attached to the states of nature.

With this modification, the analysis is essentially similar to what has gone before. We need only consider the more general regime of production and exchange. Given private, prior, and sure information of event A, the individual in a world of perfect markets would *not* adapt his productive decisions if he were sure the information would remain private until after the close of trading. For, prices of the time-state claims c_{1A} and c_{1B} (involving the observable states A and B, of course, not the "natural" states a and b which do not directly affect markets) will not have changed. However, as before it would be in his interest to speculate and/or resell the information, in which case prices will tend to shift. The obvious way of acquiring the private information in question is, of course, by performing technological research.[15] By a now familiar argument we can show once again that the distributive advantage of private information provides an incentive for information-generating activity that may quite possibly be in excess of the social value of the information.

The conclusions reached in the analysis of foreknowledge with respect to public information again carry over to the discovery situation. Public information is socially valuable in redirecting productive decisions, and to that extent individuals will rationally combine (through government and other instruments) to generate public information (or, in some cases, it will pay even a single individual to do so). But disparities of beliefs (differences in probability estimates) may lead to agreement upon a procedure of generating public information where social costs exceed the social benefit.

VII. Implications for Patent Policy

Eli Whitney obtained one of the first American patents, in 1794, for his cotton gin. With some business associates, he spent many years and invested considerable resources in the attempt to protect his patent and prosecute infringements. These efforts were largely fruitless. It is reasonable to infer that potential inventors, both before and after Whitney, have been deterred from searching for new knowedge by the fear of a similar outcome—hence the argument for effective patent protection. On the other hand, had

[15] This is not the only way. The information might be purchased (or stolen) from some other person.

Whitney succeeded in obtaining the terms he demanded from users of his idea, the enormous expansion that actually took place in the production and consumption of cotton would have been significantly hampered.[16] This conflict between the "static" disadvantage of a patent monopoly and the "dynamic" advantage of encouraging invention is quite properly emphasized in the traditional literature.[17]

But what seems to have been overlooked is that there were other routes to profit for Whitney. The cotton gin had obvious speculative implications for the price of cotton, the value of slaves and of cotton-bearing land, the business prospects of firms engaged in cotton ware-housing and shipping, the site values of key points in the transport network that sprang up. There were also predictable implications for competitor industries (wool) and complementary ones (textiles, machinery). It seems very likely that some forethoughted individuals reaped speculative gains on these developments, though apparently Whitney did not. And yet, he was the first in the know, the possessor of an unparalleled opportunity for speculative profit. Alternatively, of course, Whitney could have attempted to keep his process secret except to those who bought the information from him.

The issues involved may be clarified by distinguishing the "technological" and "pecuniary" effects of invention. The technological effects are the improvements in production functions—interpreted in the widest sense to include the possible production of new commodities, the discovery of new resources, etc.—consequent upon the new idea. The pecuniary effects are the wealth shifts due to the price revaluations that take place upon release and/or utilization of the information. The pecuniary effects are purely redistributive.[18]

For concreteness, we can think in terms of a simple cost-reducing innovation. The technological benefit to society is, roughly, the integrated area between the old and new marginal-cost curves for the preinvention level of output plus, for any additional output, the area between the demand curve and the new marginal-cost curve. The holder of a (perpetual) patent could ideally extract, via a perfectly discriminatory fee policy, this entire technological benefit. Equivalence between the social and private benefits of innovation would thus induce the optimal amount of private inventive activity. Presumably, it is reasoning of this sort that underlies the economic case for patent protection. It is true that under a patent system there will, in general, be some shortfall in the return to the inventor, due to costs and risks in acquiring and enforcing his rights, their limited duration in time, and the infeasibility of a perfectly discriminatory fee policy. On the other side are the recognized disadvantages of patents: the social costs of the administrative-judicial process, the possible anti-competitive impact, and restriction of output due to the marginal burden of patent fees.[19] As a second best kind of judgment, some degree of patent protection has seemed a reasonable compromise among the objectives sought.

But recognition of the unique position of the innovator for forecasting and consequently capturing portions of the *pecuniary* effects—the wealth transfers due to price revaluations—may put matters in a

[16] Whitney and his partners planned to retain all the ginning in their own hands, buying the raw product and selling the ginned cotton (Dumas Malone, vol. 10, p. 159).

[17] See Machlup.

[18] For a discussion in the context of government resource-investment policy, see Roland McKean (ch. 8).

[19] A perfectly discriminatory fee system would place no marginal burden and thus would not lead to any restriction of output.

different light. The "ideal" case of the perfectly discriminating patent holder earning the entire technological benefit is no longer so ideal. For, the same inventor is in a position to reap speculative profits, too; counting these as well, he would clearly be overcompensated.

Consider now the opposite extreme. Do we have reason to believe that the potential speculative profits to the inventor, from the pecuniary effects that will follow release of the information at his unique disposal, will be so great that society need take no care to reserve for him any portion of the technological benefit of his innovation? The answer here is indeterminate. There is no logically necessary tie between the size of the technological benefit on the one hand, and the amplitude of the price shifts that create speculative opportunities on the other.[20]

Even if the prospective price revaluations are ample, however, there will be limitations to the inventor's capacity to profit from them. For, speculative profits are constrained by the magnitude of feasible speculative commitments. If the possessor of prior information acts alone, he is limited by what may be a puny wealth endowment. But if he tries to sell his information, in effect buying a share in a larger speculative pool, he will find it difficult to consummate such a transaction. The most important limitation of all has not heretofore been taken up in this paper, but must be considered in a policy discussion: imperfection of markets for time-state claims.[21] Given the inconceivably vast number of potential contingencies and the costs of establishing markets, the prospective speculator will find it costly or even impossible to purchase neutrality from "irrelevant" risks. Eli Whitney could not be *sure* that his gin would make cotton prices fall: while a considerable force would clearly be acting in that direction, a multitude of other contingencies might also have possibly affected the price of cotton. Such "uninsurable" risks gravely limit the speculation feasible with any degree of prudence.

We are left, therefore, in an agnostic position. The fundamental argument for patent protection is gravely weakened when it is recognized that the pecuniary effects of the invention are a potentially enormous source of return to the inventor, quite apart from the technological benefit that the patent system attempts to reserve for him. But we cannot show that no patent protection at all is warranted, that the profits from speculation or from resale[22] suffice for an appropriate inducement to invention. These profits may more than suffice, or they may fall substantially short; there is no necessary relation at all between the magnitudes of the technological and the pecuniary effects. Or, more precisely, between the magnitudes of that fraction of the technological effect that a patentee can capture and that fraction of the pecuniary effect that a speculator on prior information can capture.

VIII. Summary

In the model of this paper, markets are assumed to be perfect. Uncertainty attaches only to individuals' perceptions of their endowments and productive opportunities (technological uncertainty). The private and social values of two main

[20] A relatively minor shift in locomotive technology, for example, might lead railroad planners to select an entirely different route for a new line, with drastic upward and downward shifts of land values. Paul Samuelson emphasizes, p. 974, the disproportionality between the gain reaped by the first-in-time speculator and the social utility of his activity.

[21] This imperfection has been emphasized by Arrow (1962, and also 1969).

[22] Resale of information does not stand on quite the same footing as speculation. Speculation is an extra source of gain, whether or not patent has been obtained, whereas resale of information otherwise kept secret is an *alternative* to obtaining a patent.

categories of technological information were considered: 1) foreknowledge of states of the world that will in time be revealed by Nature herself (e.g., the weather), and 2) discovery of hidden properties of Nature that can only be laid bare by human action.

Private information that remains private was shown to be of no social value—in the sense of being purely redistributive, not leading to any improvement in productive arrangements. There is an incentive for individuals to expend resources in a socially wasteful way in the generation of such information. Public information, in contrast, does affect productive decisions in a socially appropriate way. Speculative profits from the price revaluations to be anticipated provide the knowledgeable individual with an incentive to disseminate (publicize) his private information. Still greater profit is possible if the information can be resold. In a world of pure exchange, there will in general be private overinvestment in information: resources committed to acquisition and to dissemination are both wasted from the social point of view. In a world of production, however, the gains from productive rearrangements due to the information must be offset against the costs of acquisition and dissemination; there may or may not be private overinvestment.

Distributive considerations enter also into the motivation for the acquisition of *public* information. To the extent that the prospect of such information imposes a distributive risk upon individuals—due, for example, to possible revaluation of endowment holdings—there will be an aversion to socially neutral and even (to some degree) to socially beneficial public information. Probably more important is a force acting in the opposed direction. With inhomogeneous beliefs, individuals with differing opinions will tend each to believe that revelation of new information will favor his own speculative commitments. Hence, a group of such individuals might willingly cooperate in making expenditures far in excess of the social value of the information to be acquired.

The standard literature on the economics of research and invention argues that there tends to be private underinvestment in inventive activity, due mainly to the imperfect appropriability of knowledge. The contention made is that, even with a patent system, the inventor can only hope to capture some fraction of the technological benefits due to his discovery. This literature overlooks the consideration that there will be, aside from the technological benefits, pecuniary effects (wealth redistributions due to price revaluations) from the release of the new information. The innovator, first in the field with the information, is able through speculation or resale of the information to capture a portion of these pecuniary effects. This fact is socially useful in motivating release of the information. Even though practical considerations limit the effective scale and consequent impact of speculation and/or resale, the gains thus achievable eliminate any a priori anticipation of underinvestment in the generation of new technological knowledge.

REFERENCES

A. Alchian, "Information Costs, Pricing, and Resource Unemployment," in E. S. Phelps et al., eds., *Microeconomic Foundations of Employment and Inflation Theory,* New York 1970.

K. J. Arrow, "Economic Welfare and the Allocation of Resources for Invention," in *The Rate and Direction of Economic Activity: Economic and Social Factors,* Universities–Nat. Bur. Econ. Res. Conference series, Princeton 1962.

———, "Le Rôle des Valeurs Boursières pour la Repartition la Meilleure des Risques," *International Colloquium on Econometrics, 1952,* Centre National de la Recherche Scientifique, Paris 1953; translated as "The Role of Securities in the Optimal Allocation of Risk-Bearing," *Rev. Econ. Stud.*, Apr. 1964, *31*, 91–96.

———, "Discounting and Public Investment Criteria" in A. V. Kneese and S. C. Smith, eds., *Water Research*, Baltimore 1966.

———, "The Organization of Economic Activity: Issues Pertinent to the Choice of Market versus Nonmarket Allocation," in U.S. Congress, Joint Economic Committee, *The Analysis and Evaluation of Public Expenditures: The* ʟ *PB System*, a compendium of papers submitted to the Subcommittee on Economy in Government, 91st Cong., 1st sess., Washington 1968, *1*, 47–64.

K. Borch, "Equilibrium in a Reinsurance Market," *Econometrica*, July 1962, *30*, 424-44.

G. Debreu, *Theory of Value: An Axiomatic Analysis of Economic Equilibrium*, New York, 1959.

H. Demsetz, "Information and Efficiency: Another Viewpoint," *J. Law Econ.*, Apr. 1969, *12*, 1–22.

P. A. Diamond, "The Role of a Stock Market in a General Equilibrium Model with Technological Uncertainty," *Amer. Econ. Rev.*, Sept. 1967, *57*, 759–76.

J. H. Drèze and F. Modigliani, "Epargne et Consommation en Avenir Aléatoire," *Cahiers du Seminaire d'Econometrie*, 1966, *9*, 7–33.

E. F. Fama and A. B. Laffer, "Information and Capital Markets," *J. Bus. Univ. Chicago*, July 1971, *44*.

J. Hirshleifer, "Investment Decision under Uncertainty: Choice-Theoretic Approaches," *Quart. J. Econ.*, Nov. 1965, *79*, 509–36.

———, "Investment Decision under Uncertainty: Applications of the State-Preference Approach," *Quart. J. Econ.*, May 1966, *80*, 252–77.

———, (1970a) *Investment, Interest, and Capital*, Englewood Cliffs 1970.

———, (1970b) "The Private and Social Value of Information and the Reward to Inventive Activity," working paper no. 158, Western Management Science Institute, UCLA, Apr. 1970.

T. Koopmans, *Three Essays on the State of Economic Science*, New York 1957.

F. Machlup, "Patents," *International Encyclopedia of the Social Sciences*, New York 1968, *11*, 461–72.

D. Malone, *Dictionary of American Biography*, New York 1964.

H. G. Manne, *Insider Trading and the Stock Market*, New York 1966.

J. Marschak, (1968a) "Decision-making: Economic Aspects," *International Encyclopedia of the Social Sciences*, New York 1968, *4*, 42–55.

———, (1968b) "Economics of Inquiring, Communicating, Deciding," *Amer. Econ. Rev. Proc.*, May 1968, *58*, 1–18.

R. N. McKean, *Efficiency in Government through Systems Analysis*, New York 1958.

S. A. Ozga, "Imperfect Markets through Lack of Knowledge," *Quart. J. Econ.*, Feb. 1960, *74*, 29–52.

P. A. Samuelson, "Intertemporal Price Equilibrium: A Prologue to the Theory of Speculation," *Welwirtschaftliches Archiv*, Dec. 1957, *79*, 181–219, reprinted in J. E. Stiglitz, ed., *The Collected Scientific Papers of Paul A. Samuelson*, Cambridge, Mass. 1966, *2*, 946–84.

L. J. Savage, *The Foundations of Statistics*, New York 1954.

R. M. Starr, "The Effect of Individual Beliefs on the Achievement of Pareto Optimal Distribution under Uncertainty," working paper no. 127, Western Management Science Institute, UCLA, Oct. 1967.

G. Stigler, "The Economics of Information," *J. Polit. Econ.*, June 1961, *69*, 213–25.

———, "Information in the Labor Market," *J. Polit. Econ.*, Oct. 1962 supp., *70*, 94–105.

E. A. Thompson, "A Pareto Optimal Group Decision Process," in G. Tullock, ed., *Papers on Non-Market Decision Making*, Charlottesville 1966.

ECONOMIC THEORY, ECONOMETRICS, AND MATHEMATICAL ECONOMICS

Edited by Karl Shell, *Cornell University*

Recent titles

Giorgio Szego, editor, *New Quantitative Techniques for Economic Analysis*

John M. Letiche, editor, *International Economic Policies and Their Theoretical Foundation: A Source Book*

Murray C. Kemp, editor, *Production Sets*

Andreu Mas-Colell, editor, *Noncooperative Approaches to the Theory of Perfect Competition*

Jean-Pascal Benassy, *The Economics of Market Disequilibrium*

Tatsuro Ichiishi, *Game Theory for Economic Analysis*

David P. Baron, *The Export-Import Bank: An Economic Analysis*

Real P. Lavergne, *The Political Economy of U.S. Tariffs: An Empirical Analysis*

Halbert White, *Asymptotic Theory for Econometricians*

Thomas G. Cowing and Daniel L. McFadden, *Macroeconomic Modeling and Policy Analysis: Studies in Residential Energy Demand*

Svend Hylleberg, *Seasonality in Regression*

Jean-Pascal Benassy, *Macroeconomics: An Introduction to the Non-Walrasian Approach*

C.W.J. Granger and Paul Newbold, *Forecasting Economic Time Series, Second Edition*

Marc Nerlove, Assaf Razin, and Efraim Sadka, *Household and Economy: Welfare Economics of Endogenous Fertility*

Jean-Michel Grandmont, editor, *Nonlinear Economic Dynamics*

Thomas Sargent, *Macroeconomic Theory, Second Edition*

Yves Balasko, *Foundations of the Theory of General Equilibrium*

Jean-Michel Grandmont, editor, *Temporary Equilibrium: Selected Readings*

Darrell Duffie, *Security Markets: Stochastic Systems*

Ross M. Starr, editor, *General Equilibrium Models of Monetary Economics: Studies in the Static Foundations of Monetary Theory*

S. C. Tsiang, *Finance Constraints and the Theory of Money: Selected Papers*

Masanao Aoki, *Optimization of Stochastic Systems: Topics in Discrete-Time Dynamics, Second Edition*

Peter Diamond and Michael Rothschild, editors, *Uncertainty in Economics: Readings and Exercises, Revised Edition*